Immeasurably More

WestBow Press books may be ordered through booksellers or by contacting:

WestBow Press
A Division of Thomas Nelson & Zondervan
1663 Liberty Drive
Bloomington, IN 47403
www.westbowpress.com
1 (866) 928-1240

ISBN: 978-1-5127-5132-1 (sc)
ISBN: 978-1-5127-5133-8 (hc)
ISBN: 978-1-5127-5131-4 (e)

Library of Congress Control Number: 2016912541

Printed in United States.

WestBow Press rev. date: 10/21/2016

CONTENTS

To the members of the Ray Stedman Ministries board of directors—Don Broesamle, Rich Carlson, Greg Sims, and Jimmy Stewart—and to the Stedman family: Laurie Stedman Higuera, Elaine Stedman, and Linda Stedman Teshima. It has been a joy to labor together and to see God do immeasurably more than we could ask or think.

God's eternal purpose is for his people to be worshipers. "Hidden in Christ with God" (Col. 3:3)—he in us and we in him—we are drawn into Christ's very life. In our inseparable intimacy with him, we grow to understand the power of the gospel: "Christ in you, the hope of glory" (Col. 1:27). We are joined with Christ in an eternal relationship, "immeasurably more than we can ask or imagine" (Eph. 3:20).

—Don Broesamle, Ray Stedman Ministries

INTRODUCTION

Ray C. Stedman (1917–92) understood the power of biblical exposition. For forty years as pastor of Peninsula Bible Church in Palo Alto, California, he committed to preaching through entire books of the Bible, or to laying open major portions of Scripture.

Unfortunately, yearly devotionals often read as if we are eating in a school cafeteria where the meals keep changing—today light fare from the gospels, tomorrow something to savor from the prophets. We may find a degree of satisfaction and yet still yearn for a more systematic, integrated feeding of our spiritual lives.

In an expository presentation of the whole counsel of God, Stedman offered the congregation balanced biblical truth by which to grow into the spiritual maturity God intends.

This treasury of daily studies faithfully captures his book-by-book exposition, fully explored in practical monthly segments. Each selection invites readers to open their Bibles and to explore the Scriptures alongside Stedman's related expository message. An introductory verse directs the focus to each day's central theme. Each selection concludes with a prayer and an application question, helping readers to weave into their lives the lessons they have learned.

Immeasurably More champions a theme that is predominant throughout Stedman's messages: the New Covenant—the believer's total dependence on the power of the indwelling Christ to live the Christian life. As we "make every effort to rest in Him" (Heb. 4:11), the Lord "is able to do immeasurably more than all we ask or imagine, according to His power that is at work within us" (Eph. 3:20).

I hope that this book will satisfy the spiritual appetites of growing believers who desire to experience immeasurably more than they can ask or imagine in their walk with Christ.

—Mark S. Mitchell

JOHN 1–12

Our Lord's Closest Friend
An introduction for the month of January

We are beginning studies in the gospel according to John. This gospel was written by the disciple of whom it was said, "Jesus loved him." John was the closest intimate of our Lord during the days of his ministry, so this constitutes an important gospel.

Three and a half years of close companionship with Jesus had a tremendous impact on John. The apostle was an old man when he wrote this gospel. As best we can tell, he wrote it from the city of Ephesus, where he settled after the destruction of the temple in Jerusalem in AD 70, in order to guide the Christian community in that great Roman center. He probably wrote toward the close of the first century. The gospels of Matthew, Mark, and Luke had already been written and widely circulated among the early Christians. All the letters of Paul had been written, as had all the letters of Peter.

This gospel was one of the last books of the New Testament to be written. Because it came so late, many have felt that John had perhaps forgotten some of the details of the things that had happened to him. He does not retrace many of the events recorded in the so-called synoptic gospels of Matthew, Mark, and Luke. John's work is different, and he told us why he wrote this gospel:

> "Jesus performed many other signs in the presence of his disciples, which are not recorded in this book. But these are written that you may believe that Jesus is the Messiah, the Son of God, and that by believing you may have life in his name" (John 20:30–31).

It is clear that John's method is selection, and his purpose is regeneration: life in the name of Jesus, exciting, compelling, fulfilling, satisfying life, what Jesus meant when he said, "I have come that you might have life and that you might have it more abundantly."

Although John allowed forty or fifty years to go by before recording the events he had witnessed, we must remember that he had been retelling this story almost every day for all those years. He was, of course, helped by the promise of Jesus that when the Spirit came, he "will teach you all things and will remind you of everything I have said to you" (John 14:26). The apostles had not only their vivid memories but also the help of the Spirit to recall what Jesus had said on specific occasions, and they meditated many long hours over those events. Perhaps that is why John could add insights and interpretations to his accounts that the others do not include. All this was burned into the apostles' memories by the constant recitation of what had happened. Through the years they never forgot what Jesus said and did. We can be certain that this is an authentic witness from an authentic disciple who recalls vividly everything that Jesus said and did in those three and a half marvelous years.

WHO IS JESUS?

A daily devotion for January 1

Read John 1:1–4.

> "He was with God in the beginning. Through him all things were made; without him nothing was made that has been made" (John 1:2–3).

John says without any doubt that Jesus is God. He declares that Jesus is the Creator of all things. This accounts for Jesus's strange and remarkable personality. He is the originator of all things. The phrase "and God said" appears eight times in the opening chapter of Genesis. God said, "Let there be light, and there was light." God said, "Let there be a firmament between the heavens and the earth and there was." God said, "Let the earth bring forth trees and vegetation," and these sprang into being. The Son of God was speaking into being what the Father had designed in that amazing mind of his.

Any scientist who studies in the natural realm is astonished when he sees the complexity of life, the marvelous symmetry of things, the microscopic components of visible matter, the molecules, the atoms, the makeup of a flower or of a star. The obvious order and design of everything are remarkable.

We have all wondered at what we have seen through the discoveries of science. All of that was in the mind of God, but it never would have been expressed until the Son said it; he spoke and these things came into being. So this amazing Man, Jesus of Nazareth, was not only a human being here on earth with us, John says, but was the One who in the beginning spoke the universe into existence. He understands it; he knows how it functions; he is able to guard it and to guide it.

Furthermore, John says, Jesus sustains it. "Without him was not anything made that was made." He is essential to the universe; he is what holds it in existence and keeps it going. I have always been fascinated by the great linear accelerator that runs out into the mountains in back of Stanford University. This great atom-smasher takes energy developed at the beginning of a great tunnel and increases its speed until it approaches the speed of light so that the energy particles smash into the target of an atom. Why does it take so much power to break loose what is in an atom so that scientists might investigate the electrons, protons, and other particles that make up that atom? Science has long asked that question but has failed to come up with an answer. A force that they cannot describe or understand holds all things together.

The apostle Paul tells us Jesus is that force. "He holds all things together" (Col. 1:17), and "He is upholding the universe by the word of his power" (Heb. 1:3). That is why we cannot forget Jesus: we are held together by his word and by his power. That is why we do not shatter into smithereens. Something holds us together, and that force is Jesus.

> *Thank you, Lord Jesus, for creating and sustaining all things. I praise you for your power, wisdom, and creativity.*

When the world and our lives seem to be falling apart, do we find sanctuary in the One who holds everything together?

BORN OF GOD

A daily devotion for January 2

Read John 1:5–13.

> "Yet to all who did receive him, to those who believed in his name, he gave the right to become children of God—children born not of natural descent, nor of human decision or a husband's will, but born of God" (John 1:12–13).

John's gospel immediately confronts us with the world's darkness and with men's blindness. They cannot see the Creator's power when it is demonstrated in their midst, and they cannot see the Messiah when he fulfills all the Old Testament prophecies. But John never calls this a failure, and we must never read it as such. God did what he set out to do—some believed and some received, as we read in verses 12 and 13.

Here is one of the strange and often-repeated paradoxes of Scripture. Somehow God allows everything to seem totally lost and all to seem a failure. You may face this situation, so you'd better be ready for it. When it seems that everything you counted on to achieve what you longed for has failed, then God starts to work. That is what he did here.

Though the Messiah was rejected and the Creator went unrecognized, in that rejection God produced a whole new creation; a new humanity came into being. John tells us this started like the old creation—with a birth. Every person enters human life by means of birth. There is no other way in except by being born. And that is true in the new creation as well. There must be a birth. There is no other way into the new kingdom except with a birth.

John then lists the ways people wrongly think they can come to God. He says first that new birth is "not of blood." That means not by inheritance or by ancestry. Being raised in a Christian family does not make you a Christian. You can attend a Christian school and spend all your life involved in Christian activities, but until you are born again you are not a Christian.

Second, the new birth is "not of the will." You cannot determine yourself to be a Christian, make yourself one, or talk yourself into being one. You cannot study Christians, act like them, join their church and sing their hymns, or even go through all the Christian externals to become a Christian.

Third, the new birth is "not of the will of man"—that is, the efforts of others. Nobody can make you a Christian, no bishop, minister, or priest. Taking part in a ceremony, reading a creed, or kneeling at a bench will not make you a Christian.

What happens in your heart makes you a Christian. This new birth is done "of God," John says—beyond any human effort, cleverness, or manipulation. It is given "to all who received him," not who merely believe in him. Many people say, "I believe in Christ. I believe that he lived, died, and rose again, and was who he said he was." But that does not make you a Christian. You become a Christian only when you receive him, yield to him, and surrender to his lordship.

If you receive Christ, a transformation occurs deep in your spirit. God does this. You cannot do it. When faith meets the Word of God, and you invite the Son of God to be Lord of your life, a new life begins in your spirit. A change of government takes place. That is the mark of a new birth. A new creation has begun and will grow into the image of Christ.

> *Creator of all things, thank you for re-creating me in the image of your Son. This is your work, Lord, and not my own. I invite you today to continue to live your life in and through me.*

Do our lives bear witness to a radical rebirth and governance?

GRACE UPON GRACE

A daily devotion for January 3

Read John 1:14–18.

> "Out of his fullness we have all received grace in place of grace already given. For the law was given through Moses; grace and truth came through Jesus Christ. No one has ever seen God, but the one and only Son, who is himself God and is in closest relationship with the Father, has made him known" (John 1:16–18).

Notice the reappearance in verse 17 of the words *grace* and *truth* and the contrast that John draws between them and the law and Moses. The law makes demands. It is hard, cold, unyielding, without mercy. The symbol of the law today is the IRS—the tax man. If we do not give up what the law requires, we are subject to penalty. "Do this and thou shalt live," says the IRS. John says that the law was given by Moses. He did not originate it, but he gave it. Moses may have disappeared, but the law remains—cold, unyielding, demanding, without mercy.

But John says, "Grace and truth came through Jesus Christ." Take away Jesus and you take away grace and truth; he is the channel of them. John's point is that law is all about demand but that grace and truth are all about supply and are designed to meet that demand.

Many people think that law and grace are contradictory, that they are opposing principles. But this is not true in the sense in which they were originally intended. Law and grace supplement one another. Law justly makes its demands, and no one can meet them, but grace and truth are given to make that possible.

Exodus 20 offers the remarkable account of the giving of the law on Mount Sinai—accompanied by smoke, thunder, earthquake, fire, fear, and trembling. But in the very next section we read the detailed plans for the building of the tabernacle—God's provision to meet the demands of the law. That tabernacle is a picture of Jesus, the meeting place where God's demands are fully met in terms of the sacrifice of blood, of a life poured out. Thus John saw in the coming of Jesus the fulfillment of that tabernacle. "The one who was after me has already been before me." So it is with us. We can say with John, "Out of his fullness [of grace and truth], we have all received grace upon grace."

God has a daily supply of grace for us. Grace is the generosity of love reaching out toward us, giving itself to us. If we come to Christ, God's promise is that every day we can take a new supply of his love. We can know that we are loved, cherished, protected, and blessed. We are strengthened, kept, and supported by his love, receiving grace upon grace, day after day, like the manna given to the Israelites in the wilderness. Because we have been loved, when we reach out in love to someone else and give as fully and freely as we have received, then we fulfill the law, for love is the fulfilling of the law.

> *Father, I thank you for the grace of our Lord Jesus. What a gift that he has come among us to reveal you to us and to bring us to you. Help me to walk in the warmth and the love of his grace today.*

God's amazing grace transforms his moral law into liberating truth. Have we grasped the rhythm of grace with truth and truth with grace?

THE SPIRIT'S WITNESS

A daily devotion for January 4

Read John 1:19–34.

> "Then John gave this testimony: 'I saw the Spirit come down from heaven as a dove and remain on him. And I myself did not know him, but the one who sent me to baptize with water told me, "The man on whom you see the Spirit come down and remain is the one who will baptize with the Holy Spirit"'" (John 1:32–33.)

If you read through the Old Testament you find in it a deep sense of unsatisfied longings. From the beginning of the Bible, people are longing for righteousness and holiness; longing to be better than they are; longing to be free from the struggle with evil inside them; wishing to take hold of the evil, self-centered tendency within themselves and to eliminate it.

Have you ever felt that way? I have sometimes wished I could have a surgical operation to remove my tendency to be sharp, critical, harsh, and caustic. When I have seen the hurt I've caused, I have wished I could stop doing those kinds of things.

That longing has been in the human heart ever since the fall of man. All through biblical times it increased as men and women cried out for deliverance, to be free at last from the power and the reign of sin. They longed for beauty of character, for reality of life, and for freedom from evil.

Scripture shows that it takes God himself to do this. The work of the Spirit is to do that very thing. John the Baptist is saying, "I deal with the externals, with what demonstrates men's change of mind as to what they want to be. That is as far as I can go. But when I baptized Jesus, I saw the Spirit coming down like a dove and lighting on his shoulder. The One who sent me to baptize had said to me, 'When you see that happening, that is the One who will not only change men outside but will change them from the inside by the baptism of the Holy Spirit.' When that happened I knew who he was. My own cousin, Jesus of Nazareth, was the One who would baptize with the Holy Spirit."

Paul emphasizes this point. "For by one Spirit have we all"—all believers in Jesus—"been baptized into one body ... and have all been made to drink of one Spirit" (1 Cor. 12:13). You cannot be a Christian without being baptized by the Holy Spirit. This is not something you feel, some experience that you can sense happening. It is a change deep within your humanity, a change that God himself does when he breaks you loose from the family of Adam and places you in the family of God. Jesus said this would happen to all who receive him. Jesus said, "'He who believes in me ... out of his heart shall flow rivers of living water.' Now this he said about the Spirit, which those who believed in him were to receive" (John 7:38–39). That is the baptism of the Holy Spirit!

John understood that his ministry was limited, that he could go only so far. He could express in some dramatic, symbolic fashion the desire for change in a heart that wanted to be right, but he could not change it. That had to be the work of Jesus. From that time on, Jesus has been the One who baptizes with the Holy Spirit. When we enter the family of God, he is the One who brings us there. Jesus is the Messiah, the fulfiller of the promises; he is the Lamb of God, the fulfiller of all the sacrifices of the Old Testament; he satisfies the longings of men for purity and freedom and is the baptizer with the Holy Spirit.

> *Lord, I thank you for the truth of this great promise. Here I am, more than two thousand years later, and yet its glory and its truth are as real to my heart as though I had stood beside the Jordan River on that day. I recognize that standing with me today is the Lord Jesus himself, the One who can fulfill my longings, take away my sins, satisfy my heart, and be King of my life.*

Baptism by the Holy Spirit occurs when we choose by faith to enter into the saving life of Jesus. Do we depend upon his power to transform us into the image of Christ?

GOD'S QUESTIONS

A daily devotion for January 5

Read John 1:35–51.

> "The next day John was there again with two of his disciples. When he saw Jesus passing by, he said, 'Look, the Lamb of God!' When the two disciples heard him say this, they followed Jesus. Turning around, Jesus saw them following and asked, 'What do you want?'" (John 1:35–38).

Two of John's disciples heard him point to Jesus, and they followed Jesus. One of those disciples was Andrew, the brother of Peter. Everyone asks, "Who was the other one?" We are not told; his name is not given. Yet this is an almost certain clue to his identity, for we discover in the gospel of John that John never mentions his own name. He always refers to himself in an indirect, oblique way, such as "the disciple whom Jesus loved" (John 21:20) or similar words. Since he does not give the name of the other disciple here, almost all scholars agree that this must be John himself. So John and Andrew are the two who heard Jesus say these words.

What they heard must have struck a responsive chord, for they immediately followed Jesus. The reason may have been curiosity, but whatever it was, they must have been drawn instantly by the question Jesus asked of them. When he saw them following him he turned and said to them, "What do you seek?" Those are the first words of Jesus in the gospel of John, and they are remarkable. According to this gospel, they are also the first words Jesus uttered in his public ministry, and they come in the form of a question.

I have always been fascinated by the questions God asks of man. These four words go right to the heart of life. In them Jesus asks the most profound question in anyone's life: "What are you looking for?" Did you ever wonder, *Why am I here? What do I really want out of life?* That is the most penetrating question you can ask yourself.

Anyone who works knows what it is to get up in the morning, eat breakfast, go to work, labor all day, come home in the evening, have dinner, read the paper, watch television, talk to the family, go to bed, and repeat that ritual day after day. Have you ever asked yourself, *Why? What do I want out of this?*

That is what Jesus is asking. He nailed those men immediately with the profundity of his question. "Whom do you seek?" would have been the natural question under the circumstances. But Jesus asked, "What do you want?" What are you looking for? What do you really seek? That is the supreme question in life!

This recalls the first question in the Bible, asked by God of Adam in the garden of Eden after the fall: "Adam, where are you?" (Gen. 3:9). That question was designed to make Adam ask himself, *Yes, where am I? How did I get here? What has happened to me?* Adam and Eve were hiding in the bushes. I do not think Adam asked himself why until God asked the question, "Where are you? What are you doing? Why are you there?" That is the most important question to answer when you are far away from God. When you answer it, you are on your way back to the God who made you.

> *Lord, what I really want and what I really need more than anything else are you and the life that only you can provide.*

Are we settling for shallow, superficial lives because we are dodging the supreme questions?

WATER TO WINE

A daily devotion for January 6

Read John 2:1–11.

> "Jesus said to the servants, 'Fill the jars with water'; so they filled them to the brim. Then he told them, 'Now draw some out and take it to the master of the banquet.' They did so" (John 2:7–8).

Notice the simplicity of this account, how easily, how quietly, and with what dignity this was done. Jesus said simply, "Fill the jars with water." And they filled them to the brim—not with decaffeinated coffee but with 120 to 180 gallons of ordinary water. Then Jesus said, "Now draw some out and take it to the steward of the feast." There was no prayer, no word of command, no hysterical shouting, no pleading with a screwed-up face, no laying-on of hands, no binding of Satan, no hocus-pocus or mumbo-jumbo—nothing. He did not even touch the water or taste it to see if a change had happened. He simply said, "Take it to the governor of the feast." What beautiful, simple dignity!

Yet this happened within the limits of a natural process. The water did not become milk, nor did it change into Coca-Cola. What happened was something that also happens in nature. Water is being changed into wine in every vineyard right now! This transformation involves a long process of growth, of gathering and crushing; it involves the activity of men and the process of fermentation. But it is a natural process. This is characteristic of the miracles of Jesus.

In his helpful book *Miracles*, C. S. Lewis has pointed out that every miracle of Jesus is simply a short-circuiting of a natural process; the Lord does instantly something that generally takes a longer time. Lewis describes Jesus's miracles as bringing into focus in understandable dimensions what God has already done or will do on such a grand scale in the natural world that it would be difficult for us to perceive.

That is what Jesus did: he overlapped the elements of time, of growth, gathering, crushing, and fermenting. He took water—an inorganic, nonliving, commonplace substance—and without a word, without a gesture, without any laying-on of hands, in utter simplicity, the water became wine, an organic liquid, a product of fermentation, belonging to the realm of life. Thus he demonstrated his marvelous ability to master the processes of nature.

Later, John writes, "This, the first of his signs, Jesus did at Cana in Galilee, and manifested his glory; and his disciples believed in him" (John 2:11). They believed that here was God's Man, ruling over all the works of God's hands, given dominion and authority over the natural world and doing with it whatever he pleased within the limits of nature itself. When the disciples saw this, they believed more deeply in him than before. They saw that here was One who could handle life. Here was One who could take a commonplace thing, simple water, and make of it wine, creating a source of joy.

Our Lord is able to take the humdrum events of any life and with his touch to fill them with flavor, fragrance, strength, and beauty—to turn them into wine. He will do this with any of us as we faithfully follow him and believe in him.

> *Jesus, please take my ordinary life and through your great power change it into something full of joy, beauty, and strength.*

Are we learning to observe and to appreciate God's awesome, transforming work even in simple and commonplace events and circumstances in our lives?

THE TEMPLE CLEANSER

A daily devotion for January 7

Read John 2:12–25.

"His disciples remembered that it is written: 'Zeal for your house will consume me'" (John 2:17.)

Can you imagine how the disciples felt while this was going on? How embarrassed they must have been by the actions of Jesus! They had not been with him very long; they did not know him very well. They had been attracted by the amazing things he said and did. They believed with all their hearts that he was the expected Messiah. They had not worked out all the theological puzzles that must have raised in their minds, but they were committed to following him. Yet the first thing he did was to humiliate them with this uncalled-for activity.

Imagine Jesus entering the temple, where this practice had been going on for decades, and without any appeal to authority, ejecting the money-changers, pouring out their money, driving out the animals, and even forcing out the people with a whip! The disciples were highly embarrassed. They also probably feared what the authorities would do in response to this flagrant challenge. They knew the self-righteous Pharisees would not let Jesus get away with this. Perhaps the disciples even felt a little anger at the Lord for being so unsocial and for being so uncooperative with the establishment. Yet, knowing who he was, they may have felt reluctant to judge him.

But as they watched Jesus do this, a verse from Psalm 69 flashed into their minds. The psalm describes the suffering of the One who is to be the Messiah, and verse 9 says, "The zeal for thy house has consumed me." It burns up, seizes hold of, and devours the Anointed One, forcing him to act. For the first time perhaps, the disciples came to a quiet realization of the divine refusal to tolerate inward impurities. They began to understand that God does not compromise with evil.

This touches on one of the great paradoxes of our Christian faith. Throughout John's gospel we see plainly how anyone can come to Christ, no matter what his background, no matter how far he has gone wrong, no matter how evil he has been. Murderers, prostitutes, swindlers, liars, perverts, drunkards, self-righteous prigs, bitter, hard-hearted cynics, religious hypocrites, proud, self-sufficient snobs—anyone who realizes there is something wrong in his life, anyone who wants to be free, can come to Jesus. He said, "Come unto me all you that are weary and heavy laden, and I will give you rest" (Matt. 11:28).

But now the disciples understood, perhaps for the first time, that if we come, Jesus will not leave us the way we are. He won't settle for clutter, compromise, extortion, and racket, or whatever may be defiling and corrupting the temple courts. He may leave us alone for a while. Many young Christians have misunderstood that. Because Jesus shows love and patience in dealing with us, we think that he will let us get by with some of the comfortable but wrongful habits we have built into our lives. But he will not. If we mistake his delay for acceptance, we are in for a surprise. If we refuse to deal with the flaws Jesus identifies in us, one day we will find him coming with flaming eyes and with a whip in his hand, and all that traffic in immorality will be driven out whether we like it or not.

Lord, cleanse my heart of all that defiles so that it may be a house of prayer that is pleasing to you.

How awesome that in Christ we are made the dwelling place of God's Holy Spirit! Are we totally cooperative with his rigorous cleansing of his holy temple?

BORN FROM ABOVE

A daily devotion for January 8

Read John 3:1–16.

> "Now there was a Pharisee, a man named Nicodemus who was a member of the Jewish ruling council. He came to Jesus at night and said, 'Rabbi, we know that you are a teacher who has come from God. For no one could perform the signs you are doing if God were not with him.' Jesus replied, 'Very truly I tell you, no one can see the kingdom of God unless they are born again'" (John 3:1–3).

Notice how Jesus cuts right across Nicodemus's inquiry with a sharp and penetrating sentence that must have felt like a sword thrust right into his heart. Observe what Jesus is saying in this startling reply to Nicodemus. A new birth is absolutely essential to enter the kingdom. John uses an interesting word here. It is the Greek word *anothen*, which means "anew," "again" or "to do something a second time." It often points to a radical new beginning that comes from above. God, not man, must bring about this second birth, which results in a new creation.

This idea appears many times in the New Testament. Paul speaks of "babes in Christ" (1 Cor. 3:1). Peter says, "As newborn babes desire the sincere milk of the word that you may grow" (1 Peter 2:2). He says we are "born again, not of corruptible seed, but of incorruptible" (1 Peter 1:23), and he speaks of being "born to a living hope" (1 Peter 1:3). Paul speaks not only of being new creatures in Christ but of a new creation, of passing from death unto life, of a radical new start. Jesus makes clear that this is the only way to enter the kingdom of God. If you do not come this way you cannot enter. There is no way you can even see the kingdom of God without this rebirth.

To be in the kingdom of God, of course, is to belong to God; it is to be a part of his reign and his domain. Paul speaks of being transferred from "the kingdom of darkness, ruled by the god of this world, into the kingdom of the Son of his love" (Col. 1:13). Thus Jesus is referring to a transfer of citizenship, a radical departure from what we once were.

Jesus senses in Nicodemus a deep hunger, an emptiness. Here is a man who is doing his level best to obey what he thinks God wants, yet he has an empty and unsatisfied heart that leads him to seek out Jesus by night, at the risk of displeasing his peers, to talk with him about the kingdom of God. Sensing this, our Lord immediately puts him on the right track, saying to him, in effect, "You are wasting your time if you think you can enter the kingdom of God the way you are. You cannot do it. You must be born again."

When John Wesley preached throughout England, Wales, and Scotland, he continually told people that they must be born again. Someone once asked Wesley why he so often preached this message. His answer was simply that it was because people must be born again! After all, that was what Jesus had said.

> *Father, thank you for the miracle of new birth, which comes only from above. It is only through your great power and love that such a thing could happen to me.*

Spiritual rebirth is generated by God, who is love. How are we responding to such infinitely costly love?

TO SAVE OR TO CONDEMN?

A daily devotion for January 9

Read John 3:16–36.

> "For God did not send his Son into the world to condemn the world, but to save the world through him" (John 3:17).

This verse is a great guideline for how we ought to talk about the gospel to people who do not know God, to those living careless, indifferent, often sinfully wretched lives. We should not come shaking a finger at them, pointing out how terrible they are and what evil things they are doing to themselves. We ought to come sensing the agony, the hurt, the inward shame, the loneliness, misery, and anguish they are experiencing. That is the way God feels, and that is the way we should feel too.

Paul puts this beautifully in writing to the Corinthians: "God was in Christ reconciling the world to himself, not counting their trespasses against them" (2 Cor. 5:19). That is why in every vignette we have of Jesus in the gospels, when he is dealing with acknowledged, blatant sinners, we never hear a word of condemnation. Witness the woman at the well in Samaria. She had five husbands and was now living with a man outside of marriage. Jesus was courteous to her. He did not attack her, blame her, or judge her. There was no condemnation.

Of course that does not mean that God is not concerned about our sins. He knows that we cannot be free until something is done about them. Everywhere in Scripture we are reminded that he came to set us free from our sins, not to leave us in them or to say they do not matter. Yet he wants us to understand that our sins do not keep us from coming to him. We can come to God, knowing he will receive us with a loving touch, a forgiving heart, and open arms.

There is a moving story about a young man who had quarreled with his father and left home. He kept in touch with his mother and wanted very badly to come home for Christmas, but he was afraid his father would not allow him. His mother wrote to him and urged him to return, but he did not feel he could until he knew his father had forgiven him. Finally, time had run out for any more letters. His mother wrote and said she would talk with the father, and if he had forgiven the young man she would tie a white rag on a tree that grew right alongside the railroad tracks near their home. He would see the tree before the train reached the station. If there was no rag, it would be better if he went on.

So the young man left for home. As the train drew near his destination, he was so nervous he said to a friend traveling with him, "I can't bear to look. Sit in my place and look out the window. I'll tell you what the tree looks like, and you tell me whether there is a rag on it or not." So his friend changed places with him and looked out the window. After a bit, the friend said, "Oh yes, I see the tree." The son asked, "Is there a white rag tied to it?" For a moment the friend said nothing. Then he turned and in a gentle voice replied, "There is a white rag tied to every limb of that tree!" That is what God is saying in John 3:16–17. He has removed the condemnation and made it possible for us to freely and openly come home to him.

Grant to me, Lord, a heart of compassion rather than condemnation. Forgive me for the times I have judged others when you were reaching out to them in love.

Refusing God's saving, sacrificial gift of love is an act of self-judgment. Are we walking in the love and the light of his forgiveness? Do we forgive others as God has forgiven us?

THIRSTY

A daily devotion for January 10

Read John 4:1–42.

> "Jesus answered, 'Everyone who drinks this water will be thirsty again, but whoever drinks the water I give them will never thirst. Indeed, the water I give them will become in them a spring of water welling up to eternal life'" (John 4:13–14).

Earlier in this chapter, Jesus is met at Jacob's well by a Samaritan woman who has come to draw water. How beautifully Jesus leaps the barriers separating him from this woman. He was a rabbi, and according to rabbinical law, rabbis were never to talk to a woman in public—not even to their wives or sisters. In fact, rabbinical law said, "It is better to burn the law than to give it to a woman." In that culture, women were regarded as unable to understand complicated subjects like theology and religion.

But notice how Jesus treats the woman. He can judge something about her from the fact that she is at this well. Although there is another well in the village, as a moral outcast she has been forced to come all the way out to this well, half a mile away. Our Lord understands this to be a sign from his Father that here is one of those sinners whom he came to call to repentance. He himself said on one occasion, "I did not come to call the righteous to repentance but sinners" (Matt. 9:13). He probably knew more about this woman's history than this introduction suggests, because later he tells her facts about herself that he evidently had learned. He had been through this small village several times and had probably heard something about her. Meeting her at the well now indicates to Jesus that God the Father wants to reach out to her.

Jesus says to her, "I am not talking about the water in the well. Drink of that water and you will thirst again." [She knows what he means. She has been coming to this well for years.] "But I will give you living water, and the one who drinks of the water I give will never thirst." He does not, of course, mean that a person could take one drink of living water and never again feel a thirst of the soul, any more than a person could take one drink of physical water and never feel thirsty again. What he means is what we Americans have discovered in our homes. How do we keep from thirsting? We have water piped in, available to us all the time, so that when we feel even a little thirsty we take a drink of it. This is what Jesus means here. The water he gives is available constantly so that when one is thirsty one can drink immediately.

Many Christians never seem to learn this truth. They never realize that there is a place where their inner thirst—their sense of restlessness, their desire for more than what they have—can be met instantly.

Jesus makes clear that this water will come from within. "The water I give them will become in them a spring of water welling up to eternal life." He means, of course, that the Spirit that he will impart is a life-giving Spirit and that as one drinks of that Spirit one experiences the quality of life that the Scriptures call eternal life.

That means far more than everlasting life. It means refreshing, invigorating, exciting life, life that has the qualities of love and joy and peace about it. When you know you lack these qualities and you then drink of the water that Jesus gives you, it can immediately slake your thirst—again and again and again. It is a beautiful picture: a well springing up to eternal life.

> *Lord, thank you that you have revealed to me the fountain within, the place of significance, the place of renewed love, of cleansing and of refreshing. Teach me to drink frequently all through the day, as many times as I need, of this refreshing fountain. Fill me so that I will not have to run after empty cisterns and follow the misleading philosophies of the world around me. Let me drink deeply of the One who has come, who has proven himself in my life to be the Savior of the world.*

Our soul's deepest thirst is for God. When his Spirit dwells within us, He is a fountain of spontaneous and continual living water. Are we drinking of him and sharing the joy with others?

FAITH'S ENCOURAGEMENT

A daily devotion for January 11

Read John 4:43–54.

> "While he was still on the way, his servants met him with the news that his boy was living. When he inquired as to the time when his son got better, they said to him, 'Yesterday, at one in the afternoon, the fever left him.' Then the father realized that this was the exact time at which Jesus had said to him, 'Your son will live.' So he and his whole household believed" (John 4:51–53).

What an exciting encounter! The servants met this man with glorious news, "Your son is living"—the same words Jesus had said to the father. Immediately the man checked the hour when his son's recovery had happened, and he realized that at the precise moment when Jesus had said to him, "Go; your son lives," the fever had suddenly left the boy and he had begun to mend. The man had a new realization, not of what Jesus could do, but of who Jesus was. He had authority over all illness. He was not limited by distance or time. He had power in areas beyond the knowledge and reach of men. When the man understood that, "he believed, and all his household with him." This is the same word for "belief" used of him before, but now it suggests a much higher level of confidence—a trust that God was at work and dealt with this matter in ways that the man could not anticipate.

The power of this story is underscored in the letter to the Hebrews, where we read, "Let us run with patience the race that is set before us, looking unto Jesus, the author and the finisher of faith" (Heb. 12:1–2). That is what Jesus has come to do—to bestow faith and to make it grow. Another translation calls Christ "the pioneer and perfecter of faith." This story tells us that we are in the hands of One who does not always answer our prayers the way we expect but who lifts us to a higher awareness of who he is, of his authority and power in the world and in life. Our faith, as a result, becomes stronger, cleaner, and truer. We can exercise it at a far higher level. Jesus is the author and perfecter of our faith. That is the meaning of the sign that he performed that day.

Tom Landry, the former coach of the Dallas Cowboys, once said that the job of a coach is to cause men to do what they don't want to do so that they can achieve what they really want. That is what Jesus does: he puts us through circumstances we do not want to experience; he makes us face things we do not like to face so that we may achieve what we have wanted with all our hearts all along. To do so requires the strengthening of faith. Faith's encouragement—that is what this incident is all about.

Heavenly Father, how this account speaks to me in my situation today! Grant that I may face that situation with fresh encouragement and trust and a renewed sense that you know what you are doing in my life and are strengthening my faith in the process.

Are we learning to view all of life's circumstances as God's opportunities to mature our faith? Do we accept his tutorials as an adventure of faith and trust, experiencing the joy of the journey?

FAITH'S ACTION

A daily devotion for January 12

Read John 5:1–17.

> "Then Jesus said to him, 'Get up! Pick up your mat and walk.' At once the man was cured; he picked up his mat and walked" (John 5:8–9).

Jesus immediately told the man to do what he had tried and failed to do for thirty-eight years. On what basis did Jesus say these words to him? Somehow the sick man sensed the answer. Perhaps he thought, *If this man tells me to rise and I cannot, it must mean that he intends to do something to make it possible.* Thus his faith was transferred from his own efforts to Jesus. *He must do it. I can't.* The man must also have reasoned along these lines: *If this man is going to help me, then I must do what he tells me to do.*

That is a critical clue many miss when they are looking for help from God. He always tells them to believe and to act on this belief. Here he issued a call to action. Jesus did not say, "Try to build up faith in your mind. Try to fasten your thoughts on this or that." He told the man to do something: "Rise! Stand up!" Obviously it was Jesus's will that this man should do what he told him to do, and the moment the man's will agreed with the Lord's will, the power was there. I don't know whether the man felt anything, but I am certain that his bones and his muscles were filled with strength and that he could stand.

Then what? The Lord did not merely say, "Rise." He said, "Take up your pallet and walk." G. Campbell Morgan states that Jesus said this "in order to make no provision for a relapse." The man might have said to himself, *I'm healed, but I had better leave my bed here; I may need it tomorrow.* If he had said that, he would have been back in his bed the next day. But he did not. Jesus said, "Take up your pallet," and the idea was to get rid of it. With those words he said something very important to people who need healing: do not make any provision to go back on what you have done.

Many people fail right here. Burn your bridges behind you. Cut off any possibility of going back. Let somebody know the new stand you have taken so that this person will help hold you to it. That is so important. Many people have been touched by God, delivered from some inner attitude or bitter spirit, but then have allowed the past to come back in and have found themselves where they were before. Our Lord knows what he is talking about: take up your pallet.

And then he told the man to walk. Do not expect to be carried—walk. Many people want to be carried after they are healed. They expect everybody to gather around them and to keep them going—a common failing. But if Jesus gives you the power to rise, he can give you the power to walk every day, to keep going. That is an important thing to see. Keep your eyes not on your friends or on yourself but on the Lord.

> *Lord Jesus, I am like so many others, lying by the pool of Bethesda, waiting to be healed, trying various ways and means, hoping somebody will help. I have not yet listened to that wonderful voice that says to me in my inner heart, Rise, take up your bed, and walk. Grant that I will do so from this moment forward.*

Do we want to be healed from whatever impediments limit our spiritual health and fulfillment? Are we settling for dysfunctional and unfruitful lives when Jesus calls us to get up and to walk in the power of his presence?

THE SECRET OF JESUS

A daily devotion for January 13

Read John 5:18–30.

"Jesus gave them this answer: 'Very truly I tell you, the Son can do nothing by himself'" (John 5:19).

That is probably the most radical statement in the Word of God, because it indicates the first step in being a channel of God's power: a recognition that any effort to use this power for one's own benefit will leave only a hollow feeling; it will never achieve anything. You may climb to the top of whatever heap you aspire to and gain the world's admiration, but if you have not learned this secret, your life will be unsatisfying to you and of no use to God. "The Son can do nothing of his own accord."

Jesus does not mean that it is impossible for him to do something apart from the Father, any more than it is impossible for us to do things apart from God. We can and we do—Jesus could have as well. Further on in this account he says that the Father has given him power to act "out of himself." Jesus could have created a whole universe over which he was God. He had the power to do so. But the crucial point is that he chose never to exercise that power for his own benefit. Never! This explains his behavior in the wilderness when he was tempted by the Devil to change stones into bread for his own satisfaction, to leap from the temple to gain the applause of people, and to gain the whole world for himself. He steadfastly refused to do so. That is the key. God gives his power to those who will not use it for their own benefit. That is one of the most important lessons in Scripture.

The release of God's power to meet human needs is a simple, yet profound truth. Our Lord lived like this all the time. It was not merely in raising men from sickbeds that he employed the power of God. He did it when he spoke to some lonely, heartsick, broken person and brought him to life and faith. This same power gave his words impact and meaning for the woman at the well who had had five husbands and was still trying to find satisfaction in living with a man without marriage. Here is the secret of power. If you say, "I have nothing in me that can accomplish this thing, but God can do this if he wants it done," the result will be a visible release of power. Jesus could say to the sick man, "Stand up," and the man was immediately on his feet.

Because Jesus was not acting of his own accord but was depending on his Father, his word to this man had power. Words are like the sails on boats. If you go out in a sailboat on a still day and raise the sail, it will hang limp and powerless. But lift that sail on a day when a strong breeze is blowing and it will fill with wind; it will begin to strain and to pull, and the boat will move rapidly through the water. That is what a word is like. Words are insignificant in themselves, but if they are in line with the working of God they are filled with power. This is what our Lord modeled for us.

There is so much I try to do on my own accord. Teach me, Lord, to recognize my helplessness, to trust in you, and to see your release of power.

Jesus's perfect unity with the Father is demonstrated in his perfect obedience and submission to his initiative. Are we compelled by his love to live in complete dependence upon his power in and through us?

BURN!

A daily devotion for January 14

Read John 5:31–47.

> "You have sent to John and he has testified to the truth. Not that I accept human testimony; but I mention it that you may be saved. John was a lamp that burned and gave light, and you chose for a time to enjoy his light" (John 5:33–35).

Jesus says something that sounds a little strange to us: "Not that the testimony which I receive is from man, but I say this that you may be saved." By this he means that though he does not need testimony from John, it may be a saving help to those who heard John. It is a strange phenomenon, frequently seen, that men and women who pay no attention to the voice of God will often listen with great interest to someone who recounts his experience with God.

I gathered with about 650 people to hear a former senator tell how God had drastically changed his life. When he was a hopeless alcoholic, wallowing in his own vomit, so despairing he was ready to take his own life, God met him and delivered him through much struggle and pain and led him to a place of prominence and power. I sat on a platform watching people hang on his every word as he described what God could do.

The Bible, of course, is the Word of God. It is the most widely distributed book ever—the perennial best-seller—having been translated into more languages than any other book. Thus it has always struck me as strange how few people ever open the Bible to see what God has said. But they will listen instead to what some man says about what God has said! That phenomenon is what Jesus is talking about here. "For your sake John has been sent. For your sake I call attention to the witness of John in order that you might be saved." This is a marvelous insight into the compassionate heart of Jesus. He is willing to use any approach as long as people will listen to what God is saying.

Jesus goes on to say a beautiful thing about John: "He was a burning and shining lamp, and you were willing to rejoice for a while in his light." John was not a light, but he was a lamp. A lamp bears the light, but it is not the light itself. If a lamp is not burning, it is not shining either. There is no light. Many people are like that. They are lamps and have the capacity to be lights, but they are not shining. John was the kind of lamp that shone brightly. He was a witness who told people where they could see and know the light.

Would you like to be a shining lamp? Let me tell you how to do it. Burn! Let the truth of God fuel your heart until it begins to burn. When you understand the amazing way God operates in this world, your heart will begin to burn, and then you will start to shine. When we sing the words to the familiar hymn, we declare that we are going to let our little light shine. This is how to do it: burn!

Lord, I want my light to shine as John's did, pointing people around me to you.

When the Light of the World who is Jesus Christ lives in us, we are called to be his light-bearers. When our hearts are aflame with his light and his love, we cannot help but burn as his witnesses.

THE TESTING OF FAITH

A daily devotion for January 15

Read John 6:1–15.

> "When Jesus looked up and saw a great crowd coming toward him, he said to Philip, 'Where shall we buy bread for these people to eat?' He asked this only to test him, for he already had in mind what he was going to do" (John 6:5–6).

Examination time had come. We are not sure why Jesus chose Philip. Perhaps he thought Philip to be most advanced in the lessons of faith. The disciples had unique personalities. Peter was loud and brassy. He had his foot in his mouth most of the time. James and John were ambitious and fiery. They lost their tempers easily. Philip was quiet and seemed to hang around in the background all the time. Yet I am sure Jesus saw in him a man of deep perception. Quiet people are often deep thinkers. Perhaps our Lord chose Philip because he was the one who would most likely understand all that lay beneath the dramatic phenomena the disciples were witnessing.

In any event Jesus said to Philip, "How are we to buy bread so that these people may eat?" He did not really expect to buy bread. In fact, Jesus knew that Philip could not possibly answer his question. There was no village or store nearby, and they had little money. His question was clearly designed to set before Philip a predicament that had no human solution.

Has that ever happened to you? Perhaps right now you are in that state. You face a predicament for which you can find no answer in the normal resources of human life. Jesus presented Philip with such a situation.

Our Lord was thinking of ministry to these people, of meeting their need. But Philip immediately thought of money. He responded to Jesus's question by saying, "Two hundred denarii would not buy enough bread for each of them to get a little." As he estimated the resources available, Philip gave up in despair; he thought there was no way this problem could be met.

God forgive us for the Philip in us all! How many times has this happened in our own experience! God commands us to feed the multitudes—not only physically, when need arises, but even more important, spiritually. I am distressed that few seem to understand that we are sent to teach the world truth that it never could find in any other way, truth that is desperately needed to handle life and make it work as God intended. In the secular realms of knowledge there are great missing elements, large blanks that the people of the world try to fill in a dozen ways, but only the church possesses the truth, the bread that can feed the hungers of life.

What do we do when we hear this command, "Feed the multitudes"? We respond like Philip. We think of committees, fundraising, and organizations. We use impressive-sounding words. We must "set our goals" and "understand the parameters of the problem." The result is that little gets done. Our Lord, however, says we should begin where we are and with what we have. I am convinced that if we would just do that, all these expensive substitutes would not be needed.

Forgive me, Lord, for trying to meet the needs around me in my own strength. Teach me to offer you what little I have and to trust that you will use it in miraculous ways.

What is our first response when faced with overwhelming predicaments? Do we calculate a purely human solution, or do we reckon on God's supply of wisdom and resources?

THE NEW RESOURCE

A daily devotion for January 16

Read John 6:16–21.

> "A strong wind was blowing and the waters grew rough. When they had rowed about three or four miles, they saw Jesus approaching the boat, walking on the water; and they were frightened. But he said to them, 'It is I; don't be afraid'" (John 6:18–20).

Our Lord said these wonderful words for our benefit. This incident involving the storm and the precarious condition of the boat was designed to teach his disciples the resources they have in their risen Lord. This is why John follows immediately by noting, "They were glad to take him into the boat." The disciples' fear was immediately relieved when they realized it was indeed Jesus who was walking on the water. They saw that he was in control of all events, so they willingly received him into the boat. Jesus immediately offered a further demonstration of his power, for they were instantly on the other side of the lake at their destination. The three or four remaining miles of the journey were suddenly accomplished, and they found themselves at the dock in Capernaum.

I am startled by the number of Christians who do not act upon this truth but succumb to the pressures and the problems of life and react just like non-Christians would. They grumble and feel put upon. They despair and lash out and strike back; they rely upon worldly schemes to deliver them from difficulties. What is more amazing is how many times I have experienced the joy of Jesus's presence, freeing me from difficult circumstances, and yet react the way others do in times of pressure and danger. But here indeed is the sign of the new covenant, the new creation: Jesus with us in the circumstances where we find ourselves—triumphant, in control, Lord of all those circumstances, the resource for life that is available to believers but that the world knows nothing about.

This leaves us with only one question: Why don't we believe this? Why are we so much like Peter, who, even while experiencing the power of God to walk above his circumstances, lost his faith and began to sink beneath the waves? You can always tell the man or woman who learns this secret, who welcomes the Lord into the boat of difficulty, who hears him say, "It is I; be not afraid."

When we accept that fact, we will find that it reveals itself in our countenances. People who have discovered this have a quiet peace in their eyes even when things are going wrong. They have a confidence that everything will work out according to God's purpose. These people do not complain. They regard their circumstances as necessary to what God wants to do in their lives—which is always for their good, for their ultimate happiness—and they accept them. They are a joy to be around. When you encourage them, you find they encourage you. That is because they have already taken Jesus into the boat. When people do that, they discover that they have already arrived at the goal toward which the rest of us are still struggling. They have found love and joy and peace.

That is why these accounts are in the Scriptures—to teach us the hidden resource of life, the place to run to when things get overwhelming and we find ourselves pressured. And this is not something reserved for the great trials of life. It is available for any time or degree of pressure. When we accept this, we discover the new creation, a resource unknown to the world.

> *Lord, may I understand afresh the inner resources that will keep me calm and confident in the midst of trouble and danger. Help me to manifest this, Lord, as a testimony to your presence.*

As our lives are rocked by worldwide turbulence, added to life's daily stresses, where do we go to find peace of heart and soul? Does the Prince of Peace have full occupancy in our lives?

WHAT ARE YOU WORKING FOR?

A daily devotion for January 17

Read John 6:22–40.

> "Do not work for food that spoils, but for food that endures to eternal life, which the Son of Man will give you. For on him God the Father has placed his seal of approval" (John 6:27).

It is clear from this passage that these people greatly misunderstood who our Lord was, what he was doing, and what he said to them. No other passage in Scripture more plainly reveals the confusion in the average person's mind about Jesus.

Notice how Jesus dealt with their confusion. First, he told them, "Do not work for the food that perishes." He was not, of course, saying, "Do not work for a living." Jesus was not advocating that. What he meant was, "Do not work merely to get food." Food is important. It is necessary for life, and you have to earn it. But do not let that be your sole reason for working. Rather, "Work for the food which endures to eternal life."

These people, like many today, clearly felt that their most important goal was to keep alive, to be healthy, strong, and economically sufficient. That was what life was all about, they thought. The majority of people all over the world today agree that this is why people work.

Jesus asks us, "What are you working for?" Are you working merely to make a living, to have a nice home, to be comfortable? Our Lord is saying that when you get all this you will find yourself wondering, *Is that all there is?* That is true of all humanity. The thing that makes human beings different from animals is that having a full belly and a comfortable place to rest does not satisfy us.

Offering an answer to this hunger, Jesus said to them, "I am the bread of life; he who comes to me shall not hunger, and he who believes in me shall never thirst" (John 6:35). Jesus recognized the universal hunger for spiritual food. You cannot go anywhere on earth today without finding people hungry for something more than a full belly and a comfortable home. There is a restlessness about us that cries for more. Jesus knew this. Everyone in this crowd wanted whatever it was he was offering. They did not understand what it was, but they wanted it. They sensed there was more to life than bread.

Jesus told the crowd plainly how to partake of the bread of life. He used two experiences everyone understood: hunger and thirst. What do you do when you are hungry? You eat, and if you eat regularly you will never hunger. What do you do when you are thirsty? You drink, and if you keep drinking you will never thirst. Jesus is saying that to eat of him is to come to him and that to come to him is to eat of him. Coming means to see him as present in your life and to expect him to do something. Eating means a sense of expectancy that he is available and that he will act. Drinking is believing, listening to what he has to say and obeying it. If you keep doing that, you will never thirst. How simple and beautiful this is! Come and believe. Keep coming. Keep believing. This is the way to lay hold of the gift of bread from heaven, true life indeed.

> *Thank you, Father, for the bread that came down from heaven, the bread of life that you have offered to me and that you give me as I believe in you.*

Is there more to life than a roof over our heads and food on the table? What is the bread of life that Jesus wants us to have?

LIFE WITH GOD

A daily devotion for January 18

Read John 6:41–59.

"Whoever eats my flesh and drinks my blood remains in me, and I in them" (John 6:56).

Those marvelous words were apparently quite offensive to these Jews. We may feel the same way if we take our Lord's words literally. Talk about eating human flesh and drinking human blood turns many people off. Evidently those listening to Jesus felt that way. You can hear the cynicism in their voices. "How can this man give us his flesh to eat? What does he think we are—cannibals?" This was most offensive to Jews because they had been taught through the centuries that God did not want flesh in which there remained any blood. The word *kosher* means "to cleanse," and it refers particularly to the preparation of meat. The Jews cannot eat any meat that has not had all the blood drained from it.

But in these words our Lord reveals the absolute necessity of receiving his life: "Truly, truly, I say to you, unless you eat the flesh of the Son of Man and drink his blood, you have no life in you." That is unequivocal, isn't it? There is no doubting what he has to say. This is essential to life. If you do not have this, you are sliding toward ultimate corruption and death. The most you can do is preserve your life for a while and hold death at arm's length. But death is inevitable unless you know the One who gives life. Then Jesus shows how that life is real: "For my flesh is food indeed, and my blood is drink indeed." It is true life that God intends for us.

This sharing of life with Jesus will, later on in this gospel, become the theme of the Upper Room Discourse. I do not think you can find any theme more exalted, more remarkable, more mysterious than this—the sharing of life between Jesus and us: "You in me, and I in you" (John 14:20). Those are simple words, but to understand what they mean is to grasp the center of truth itself. "You in me, and I in you"—this reflects our universal hunger for intimacy.

The most intimate physical act is sex, which is a way of sharing life together. Sex has been accurately described as "the urge to merge." That is what happens physically, but it also happens psychologically. Friendship is a form of sexuality, or intimacy. When you are with a friend, what do you do? You tell your friend what you have been doing and ask what he or she has been doing; you share your secrets. That is the urge to merge at the psychological level.

When we think about the greatness, the glory, and the wonder of God, what do we want? True worship is the desire to merge with God, for him to possess us and for us to possess him. That is what Jesus says happens when we eat and drink his life. When we come to him and believe in him and keep coming to him and keep believing in him, we grow into an intimate relationship with God.

Jesus has modeled this for us. "As the living Father sent me, and I live by means of the Father [the secret of his life], so he who eats me will live by means of me" (John 6:57). That is a wonderful description of the Christian life. Jesus lived by means of the Father, and we are to live by means of him in everything we do.

You in me, and I in you. That is what I want to experience more of, Lord. Help me to keep coming to you and to keep trusting in you to provide all that I need.

What does our relationship with Jesus look like? Is it the intimate relationship Jesus wants for all Christians—you in me, and I in you?

TO WHOM SHALL WE GO?

A daily devotion for January 19

Read John 6:60–71.

> "'You do not want to leave too, do you?' Jesus asked the Twelve. Simon Peter answered him, 'Lord, to whom shall we go? You have the words of eternal life. We have come to believe and to know that you are the Holy One of God'" (John 6:67–69).

Here is the mark of the true believer: he cannot quit! When Jesus asks the disciples, "Will you also go?," it is clear that he will let them leave if that is their wish. He does not hold people against their will. Responding to our Lord's words, Peter says several wonderful things.

First, he says, in effect, "Lord, we have been thinking about it. You're not easy to live with. You embarrass us. You frighten us. We don't understand you at times. We see and hear you do things that simply blow our minds. You offend people whom we think are important. We have looked at alternatives, but I want to tell you this, Lord: we have never found anyone who can do what you can do. To whom shall we go? You offer two things that hold us, two things we cannot deny. The first is your words. What you say to us has met our deepest needs, has delivered us from our sins, and has freed us from our fears. Your words, Lord, are the most remarkable we have ever heard. They explain us and they explain life. They satisfy us. Nobody speaks like you do, and nobody understands life like you do. That holds us.

"Second, Lord, we have seen your character." Notice how Peter puts it: "We have come to believe and to know." That implies a process that has continued for months or years. Peter is saying, "We have watched you, and we have come to see that there is nothing wrong in you. You are the Holy One of God, the sinless One. You fit the prophecies; you fulfill the predictions. You have drawn us and compelled us. You are the incomparable Christ. Thus there is no place to go."

I have found this conviction to be true of real Christians. Those who steadfastly continue on always feel this way about Jesus. They know their own failures, their own weaknesses. They know that despite the many times they do not understand what is happening to them, they cannot leave. This is the testimony of those who walk faithfully with Christ. I have often said that the best definition of a Christian is "someone who cannot quit." I once got a phone call from a young man, a relatively new Christian, who told me, "I can't make it. I can't continue to be a Christian. It's too hard. I blow it all the time. I'm going to hang it up." I had heard that kind of thing before, so I said to him, "That's a good idea. Why don't you do that? I think you're right. Hang it up." There was a pause on the line, and then he said, "You know I can't do that." I said, "I know it. Of course you can't. You can't quit. Who can you go to? Where can you find answers and resources such as those you have drawn on?" This is what Peter is saying to Jesus.

> *Lord, there is nowhere else to go, because only you have the words of eternal life. Help me to cling to your words, to search them out and understand them, and to obey them and believe that they alone are the words that give life.*

Do you sometimes find being a Christian too hard? Are you ready to throw in the towel and to walk away from your faith?

IS JESUS FOR REAL?

A daily devotion for January 20

Read John 7:1–24.

> "Anyone who chooses to do the will of God will find out whether my teaching comes from God or whether I speak on my own" (John 7:17).

Do you ever wonder if Jesus was what he claimed to be? Do you sometimes have trouble understanding what he is saying in these tremendous passages, especially in the gospel of John? Well, if that is the case, he tells you what to do. Practice what he says. Obey his words. Repent of your sins. Come to him. Cast yourself upon his mercy. Believe in his forgiveness, and go out in obedience and treat people as he commands you to do. Then you will know from deep inside that what he says is true, because his teaching is in line with the clear reality of God at work through you.

This is a principle that runs all through life: you learn by doing. A doctor may learn all that the medical books can teach him, but until he performs surgery or dispenses medicines to people who are sick, he never really learns. The principle holds true in any field. When you do what Jesus says, you begin to understand with a deep conviction that he knows what life is all about.

This explains a phenomenon true of certain people who become Christians—some of them early, some late in life—and who immediately practice what they have learned and grow with astonishing rapidity. They become mature, capable, well adjusted, whole persons seemingly overnight, while others who hear the teaching of the Scriptures for years hardly seem to grow at all; they are still childlike in their behavior, emotionally upset, anxious, and fear-ridden. This is because they are not doing what they hear. Those who put into practice the truth they hear grow immediately.

In Washington, D.C., years ago, I met a hard-bitten old marine general, one of those tough, self-sufficient characters who are used to giving orders. After he had retired he became a Christian and grew with astonishing rapidity. Everyone who knew him saw the change. They respected him as much as they always had, but they saw a compassion, an understanding, and a patience develop in him that were never there before. When I asked a Christian leader why this was true, he replied, "When General Silverthorn hears something from the Scripture, he obeys it immediately." That is why he grew so quickly.

Yet some people who have been exposed to the gospel for years never seem to grow. After years of sitting under the ministry of the Scriptures they still think an epistle is the wife of an apostle! I am grateful for the many people I know who put into practice what they learn. How encouraging to see how quickly they grow and become strong so that they are able to stand and to work out the problems of life.

> *Thank you, Lord, for your clear teaching about life. Forgive me for my falsehoods and for lying to myself. Keep me trusting your Word, and help me to understand what it says and to obey it.*

Do you ever ask yourself if Jesus was what he claimed to be? Do you have difficulty at times understanding his message in the Scriptures?

FOR THOSE WHO THIRST

A daily devotion for January 21

Read John 7:25–52.

> "On the last and greatest day of the festival, Jesus stood and said in a loud voice, 'Let anyone who is thirsty come to me and drink. Whoever believes in me, as Scripture has said, rivers of living water will flow from within them.' By this he meant the Spirit, whom those who believed in him were later to receive. Up to that time the Spirit had not been given, since Jesus had not yet been glorified" (John 7:37–39).

John wrote this gospel after the day of Pentecost when the Spirit was given in great power and came into the hearts of believers. When Jesus was still on earth the Spirit had not yet been given in that way. The Spirit of God is always present everywhere in the world. He was present before the day of Pentecost as well as afterward, but he was not performing the ministry of making Jesus real. So for the first time we have our Lord hinting how this will be accomplished. "I must leave. I am going back to him who sent me, but when I do so I will send the Spirit." He teaches what that means by using a beautiful symbol.

Each day during the seven days of the Feast of Tabernacles, one of the chief priests would lead a procession down through the Kidron Valley to the pool of Siloam. From the waters of the pool, he would fill a golden pitcher, carry it back to the temple, and pour it over the altar to remind the people of the days in the barren wilderness when God gave them water out of a rock. Then the people would shout and wave palm branches, rejoicing and praising God. But on the "great day," the last day, there was no such ceremony, because this day had been added to the feast. On this day Jesus seized the opportunity to cry aloud, "If anyone thirsts, let him come to me and drink." By that he means, "I am the Rock. I am the very Rock that those in the wilderness drank from." These words are confirmed by Paul in 1 Corinthians 10:4: "They all drank of the spiritual Rock which followed them, and that Rock was Christ." God is teaching us the same truth that he taught in the wilderness: Jesus is the Rock from which we can drink and satisfy the thirst of our hearts.

Notice Jesus does not limit the word *thirst.* He says simply, "If anyone thirst." People thirst for many things. Some thirst for significance and want to feel that they belong. People whom society overlooks, those who are not wealthy, handsome, or charismatic, thirst to be regarded as important. To them Jesus says, "If you thirst, come to me. You will find the significance you seek." Some seek power, the ability to accomplish things. Jesus says to them, "If that is what you want, come to me. Drink of me. Listen to my words. Enter a personal relationship with me. Draw from my wisdom, from my strength, from my presence with you. Your thirst for power will be satisfied by my power in you."

Physical thirst is the most powerful drive known to man. You can delay satisfying hunger for weeks at a time, but you cannot leave thirst unsatisfied. It becomes a driving demon that takes over your life and allows you to think of nothing else. That is what Jesus means. If you feel driven by a thirst, are restless, and long for satisfaction, then his invitation is, "Come unto me and drink, and by means of the Spirit, which I will give to those who believe in me, I will satisfy that thirst."

Thank you, Lord, that you are the One who can quench my thirst. Help me today to draw from your wisdom, your strength, and your presence with me.

When we are overwhelmed with longing we cannot satisfy, are we learning to bring our deep thirsts to Jesus, who offers his life as the fountain of living water?

BREAKING THE POWER OF SIN

A daily devotion for January 22

Read John 8:1–11.

> "'Then neither do I condemn you,' Jesus declared. 'Go now and leave your life of sin'" (John 8:11).

In this passage, a woman caught in adultery was brought by the church leaders to Jesus. I do not know if we can accurately picture what was going on when this woman appeared before him. I can see her being dragged in, red-faced, her hair in disarray. She was angry, upset, rebellious, and bitter, perhaps striking out against her accusers. But when she saw how Jesus handled this crowd of hypocritical judges, and felt that his sympathies were with her, the mercy and love in his face and his voice began to touch her. She realized how wrong she was, saw that she had sinned, and repented. When she did, Jesus forgave her.

The cross is an eternal event in the mind of God. The sins of the people who lived in Old Testament days were also forgiven through the death of Jesus on the cross. There is no other way that God can forgive sin. In anticipation of the cross, Jesus forgave the woman her sin. The proof is in the words he said, "Go, and do not sin again."

Those words should ring in our ears. If we have acknowledged our guilt, God offers his forgiveness, saying, "Go, and do not sin again." He could never have said that to this woman unless something had happened within her; the power of sin had been broken. We do not sin because we are temporarily overwhelmed by a strong passion. We sin because we have a sinful, self-centered nature; we hunger after things that are wrong, and we easily yield to sin. We cannot help ourselves at times. "Man is born unto sin," Job 5:7 says. We all are born to share that fallen nature. Unless the power of sin is broken within us, unless God does something to free us and to give us the possibility of a new life, he will never say to us, "Go, and sin no more."

But when Jesus spoke these words to this woman it was clear that she was capable of fulfilling them. He never tells us to do something that he does not also enable us to do. "Faithful is He who calls you, and He will also bring it to pass" (1 Thess. 5:24). He does not forgive us in order that we might continue in our sins. The apostle Paul wrote these wonderful words to his son in the faith, Titus: "He gave himself for us, to redeem us from all iniquity, and to purify for himself a people of his own who are zealous for good deeds" (Titus 2:14).

This beautiful story shows that God forgives our sins to free us that we might begin to live a different lifestyle by the power of his indwelling Spirit, never returning to the things we have left behind. Sometimes we are weak and need again the forgiving grace of God. But forgiveness is always designed to set us free. That is why it is given. When our Lord forgave this woman that is what he did: he set her free to be a different person than she was before.

> *You have set me free, Lord, from bondage to sin! Help me to hear these words in a new way: "Neither do I condemn you; go and do not sin again."*

Do our lifestyles reflect confidence in God's freeing forgiveness? Do we honor the incredible price paid for our sin by trusting his power to transform our lives?

THE LIGHT OF THE WORLD

A daily devotion for January 23

Read John 8:12–30.

"When Jesus spoke again to the people, he said, 'I am the light of the world. Whoever follows me will never walk in darkness, but will have the light of life'" (John 8:12).

These marvelously gracious words are a reflection on the ceremony that took place each evening in the temple courts when two giant menorahs, the many-branched candlesticks used by the Jews, were lighted, illuminating the whole temple court. Jesus refers to this when he says, "I am the light of the world [not merely Israel but the world, to anybody, anywhere]; he who follows me shall not walk in darkness, but shall have the light of life."

We must take seriously these beautiful words because Jesus means them. These are not a politician's promise that can be completely forgotten after the election. Our Lord intends to fulfill these words in any human life: "I am the light of the world; he who follows me (not just knows about me), he who walks with me, obeys me, and stays with me, will have light in his pathway."

That is a wonderful promise. There is nothing we need more in this world today than light on our path. People are walking in darkness. Later on in this gospel Jesus declares, "He that walks in darkness does not know where he is going" (John 12:35). How many people do not know where they are going, not only after they leave this life but even down the road a little? They have no idea of what is ahead; they are facing disaster and they cannot even see it coming. But the man who has light can see what is in his pathway.

Years ago, when I was driving from Dallas to Southern California, I picked up a couple of young hitchhikers. As we were driving past the entrance to the Grand Canyon, I asked them if they had ever seen the canyon. They hadn't, so we decided to spend the night there. It was late at night and pitch black when we turned off of the road. We could not see a thing, but we found what seemed to be an open space and crawled into our sleeping bags. When I awoke the sun was up. I stretched and threw out my arms, only to find that my left arm was dangling over a void! In the darkness of the dead of the night we had bedded down on the edge of a cliff that dropped into the Grand Canyon! If we had gone two steps farther, we would have fallen over the edge. I gave great thanks for the light that morning. That is what the light is for.

Jesus, you are the true light that has come into the world. Help me to walk in your light today.

Jesus's claims to be light and truth are validated by his death and resurrection. Do our words and deeds consistently reflect the reality of who he is? Are our minds being transformed by the written Word and by communion with the living Word?

TRUE FREEDOM

A daily devotion for January 24

Read John 8:31–59.

"To the Jews who had believed him, Jesus said, 'If you hold to my teaching, you are really my disciples. Then you will know the truth, and the truth will set you free'" (John 8:31–32).

What a wonderful passage! It constitutes a short course in discipleship. But it is more than that. It is a declaration that discipleship is the only true path to freedom, to being all that you were meant to be. If you want that, then Jesus says you must become his disciple. This is the only way to be all that you hope to be.

Here Jesus tells us in precise detail how to be free. It begins with belief. Jesus spoke "to the Jews who had believed in him." They had not yet trusted him, but they had believed him. They had been intellectually engaged by his arguments and his words, but they had not yet committed themselves to him. Discipleship begins with belief, even intellectual belief; they had taken the first step and were knocking at the door.

Then he sets a condition: "if you hold to my teaching" and continue in his Word. Compare what Jesus says with your experience. Does what he says agree with what you have found to be true in living life? The test of any religion is not whether it is pleasing or enjoyable. The test is whether it is true. Does it accord with life? Does it fit what is happening? Does it explain what is going on? That is the test, and that you can establish only as you continue in his Word, think long and deeply, read fully and frequently. Jesus suggests that when you do that something will happen to you: "If you continue in my Word, you will truly be my disciple." If you read his Word and continue in it, somewhere along the line a change will occur. You will find that his words have grabbed you, and you will commit yourself to him, and then you are really a disciple.

Then Jesus says, "You will know the truth." What an objective! Everybody wants to know the truth. Nobody likes to be taken in by a con artist. What, then, is the truth? I return to what underlies all of life. Truth is the genuine nature of things. Truth is seeing through all the illusions, the dreams and the wishful thinking, all the facades and the unreal images, and getting down to the heart, the core, the reality—that which really is. That is the truth.

Finally, Jesus promises that when you embrace this program, when you follow him, hear his Word, and continue in it, a wonderful thing will happen—"the truth will set you free." The truth will deliver you, permitting you to be all that you were meant to be. What does it free you from? In practical terms, it frees you from the hang-ups that keep you from being all that you were meant to be. To be hung up means that you cannot move, that you are bound and limited by something, unable to free yourself.

Hang-ups are the same for everybody, everywhere. Fear is probably the biggest one—being afraid, worried, insecure, timid, constantly threatened by anxiety. Then there is anger or hostility, the hatred, aggressiveness, and rage that keep you striking out at everybody. There is also guilt. Millions of people suffer from a terrible sense of failure, of shame about things in their past. Pride is another hang-up—a proud, aggressive, arrogant spirit that indulges in rank prejudice and bigotry; an aloofness and a withdrawal from others, with its accompanying loneliness. Do you see how practical all these things are? This is what Jesus is talking about.

His wonderful promise is that there is a way out. "Bring these hang-ups to me," he tells us. "Listen to my words. Look at life as I see it, and a wonderful thing will happen: there will be a change in you. You will be given a life that you never had before, and you will begin to be freed from your hang-ups." That is the promise of Jesus.

Lord, I want to experience the freedom you promise. Help me to continue in your Word and to learn your truth so that it can be a reality in my life.

Do we passively accept the worldly media's definition of freedom? Do we seek first the kingdom of God where we learn the truth about who we are, which sets us free?

THE PURPOSE OF DISABILITIES

A daily devotion for January 25

Read John 9:1–39.

> "As he went along, he saw a man blind from birth. His disciples asked him, 'Rabbi, who sinned, this man or his parents, that he was born blind?' 'Neither this man nor his parents sinned,' said Jesus, 'but this happened so that the works of God might be displayed in him'" (John 9:1–3).

The disciples had evidently been taught that injury and handicap are linked to sin, that human hurt is the result of human transgression. Notice that Jesus does not deny this. He recognizes such a link. However, it is not the one that many people think, as he will make clear.

This indicates that we are not living in a world where we can always expect perfection; God does not try to operate the world in such a way that everything works out beautifully. We are living in a fallen world. The Scriptures declare that we are living in a broken world, a fragmented world, a world that is not what it once was and is not what it shall be. For the present we are afflicted with hurts, injuries, and hardships.

The Scriptures confirm that everybody is affected by human evil. Many of us think we have escaped it because we were not born with evident disabilities. But in fact we all have disabilities. Everywhere humanity reflects the weakness of the fall. This is why our minds cannot operate as they should. I tried to quote a poem recently and I could not think of the first line. It fled from me. This illustrates how sin, the corruption of the fall, has attacked me, even in this simple way.

But Jesus makes clear that suffering is not always directly traceable to personal sin. Sometimes it is, but in the case of this man that is not true. Many people think it is strange that the disciples would even think that, since the man was born blind. How could his blindness be caused by his sin when he was born in this condition, before he ever had an opportunity to sin?

The disciples are probably thinking of the Jewish rabbinical teaching that it is possible for an embryo to sin. This may be what lies behind their question. But Jesus declares, "No, it is not that; nor is it the parents' sin." Why, then, was the man born blind? "That the works of God might be made manifest in him," is Jesus's response. Thus there is a positive reason for this kind of affliction. It is not a disaster but an opportunity for certain things to be manifested in such a person's life and in the lives of people who come in contact with that person, things that would otherwise never be brought out.

The disabled frequently develop peace and joy and strength that otherwise normal people do not have. They often show a tremendous strength of spirit and can take on challenges and endure difficulties that other people cannot. Fanny Crosby, that dear saint of the last century, was blind from babyhood as a result of an accident. She amazingly wrote when she was only eight years old, describing herself as a happy child, though blind. She said that she was resolved to be content since she had many blessings that others did not have and that she would not, even could not, weep or sigh because she was blind!

> *Help me, Lord, to imitate this man and to worship at your feet, to recognize that you have come into the world to give me light in my darkness, to lead me along bewildering paths, and to bring me to the place of cleansing and of opened eyes.*

Do we see our disabilities as handicaps and resent them, or are we learning the freedom and joy of viewing them as opportunities for God to use us for his good and perfect purpose?

THE GOOD SHEPHERD

A daily devotion for January 26

Read John 10:1–21.

> "I am the good shepherd. The good shepherd lays down his life for the sheep … I am the good shepherd; I know my sheep and my sheep know me—just as the Father knows me and I know the Father—and I lay down my life for the sheep" (John 10:11, 14–15).

The primary characteristic of the Good Shepherd is that he loves unto death; he is willing to die for the sheep. The disciples were astounded that Jesus loved them so much he was willing to die for them. Many of the epistles of Paul, John, James, and Peter contain awestruck references to this fact. John writes, "Unto Him who loved us and washed us from our sins in his own blood" (Rev. 1:5). Paul says, "While we were yet sinners, Christ died for us" (Rom. 5:8). Peter says, "He bore our sins in his own body on the tree" (1 Peter 2:24). The writer of the Hebrews declares, "Who through the eternal Spirit offered himself without spot unto God" (Heb. 9:14). They are amazed that this blessed One, this sinless Lord, this matchless Christ would consent to die for his own. But that is the mark of the Good Shepherd.

What a contrast with the hireling! What do all these other religious voices that we hear want from us? They want something for themselves. They regard the sheep as targets to be exploited, to be used to advance and to build themselves up. When the sheep get into trouble, when the Enemy comes, when the wolf (the Devil) strikes, they flee, leaving the sheep to fend for themselves.

Jesus declares that he is laying down his life to share it with the sheep. Notice how he puts it: "I am the good shepherd; I know my own and my own know me, as the Father knows me and I know the Father."

When I was a boy growing up I always longed to have a father. My father left home when I was ten. I cannot remember if he ever showed me any affection. He was not cruel; he just ignored me. That is probably why, as a boy, I was always sensitive to the sight of a father and a son together sharing their love for each other. God has given me four precious daughters whom I love, but in his mercy and grace he has also allowed many young men to pass through my life who have been like sons to me. It has been a rich experience to know and to share love with these fine young men and with my daughters.

That is what Jesus speaks of here, that intimacy of fellowship, that beauty of life that was evident in him as he loved the Father and the Father loved him. This, he promises, is what comes to us as a result of his sacrifice—that richness of fellowship, that beauty of life imparted by the One who was willing to lay down his life that we might have life.

> *May the God of peace, who brought from the dead Jesus, the great Shepherd of the sheep, through the blood of the eternal covenant make me perfect in every good work to do his will, accomplishing in me what is pleasing in his sight, through Jesus Christ my Lord.*

Are we so preoccupied and self-conscious about being sheep that we fail to worship the great Shepherd, who has given his life in infinite love for his sheep?

TRUE SECURITY

A daily devotion for January 27

Read John 10:22–42.

> "My sheep listen to my voice; I know them, and they follow me. I give them eternal life, and they shall never perish; no one will snatch them out of my hand" (John 10:27–29).

How can we tell if people are true Christians? Jesus says, "They follow me." That is, they obey Jesus; they do what he commands. This does not mean that they always do so instantaneously and without struggle. All of us struggle at times with what our Lord says; all of us resist at times. Sometimes the Word must be brought sharply into focus in our lives. But once we see what Jesus wants, our response as true sheep should be, "Lord, even though it hurts, even though it costs, I will do what you say. I will follow you."

Why do sheep act this way? What has made the difference? There are three factors. First, Jesus says, "I give unto them eternal life." He says this in the present indicative tense: "I keep on giving to them eternal life." What holds us to Jesus? It is the life he gives, the peace, the joy, the love that we feel, the serenity, the forgiveness, the sense of belonging and of being guarded. It is a quality of life so superior to all else that we would give up anything rather than part with it. We are drawn because he keeps giving us life, eternal life, God's kind of life.

Second, that quality of life has an element of assurance: it will never end. It offers absolute safety and security. We will never perish. Isn't that a marvelous word? We live in a world that is perishing, a world that is headed for judgment, for ultimate destruction. People all around us are committed to ways of life that will end in hell, but because Jesus has given us eternal life, we shall never perish! What a wonderful word of assurance. This is a life that survives death, that even disdains it. Everyone is headed for death, yet many are unafraid. They do not look with terrible, tragic hopelessness toward that future. They recognize that Jesus has provided a way by which they will not even know death or sense it when it happens but will be ushered immediately into glory, life, and truth.

Third, this is a life that is kept and protected by two unconquerable beings. Jesus says, "No one shall snatch them out of my hand. My Father, who has given them to me, is greater than all, and no one is able to snatch them out of the Father's hand." In Colossians, Paul puts these two things together: "Your life is hid with Christ in God" (Col. 3:3). What a wonderful view of our safety! No one, not even we ourselves, can take us out of the Father's hand (Rom. 8:38–39).

Thank you, Lord, for the assurance of eternal life and for your guarantee that life will never end. Thank you that I can trust in your promise that no one can snatch me out of your strong hand.

As sheep dependent on our Shepherd's care, are we learning to trust our Shepherd as he leads us in paths of righteousness for his name's sake?

THE GOD OF THE HERE AND NOW

A daily devotion for January 28

Read John 11:1–54.

> "'Lord,' Martha said to Jesus, 'if you had been here, my brother would not have died. But I know that even now God will give you whatever you ask.' Jesus said to her, 'Your brother will rise again.' Martha answered, 'I know he will rise again in the resurrection at the last day.' Jesus said to her, 'I am the resurrection and the life. The one who believes in me will live, even though they die; and whoever lives by believing in me will never die. Do you believe this?'" (John 11:21–26).

Martha greets Jesus with a phrase that must have been on many lips when Lazarus was sick: "Lord, if you had been here my brother would not have died." This is not a word of reproach. Martha is not saying, "Lord, why didn't you come sooner? We sent for you. If you had responded we wouldn't be in this pickle." It is clear that she realizes the message did not reach him until Lazarus was dead. There was no way he could have responded and arrived before Lazarus died. Martha's word is one of regret: "Lord, I wish you could have been here, because if you had been, my brother would not have died."

Then she adds, "But even now, whatever you ask of God, he will give it to you." Many ask at this point, "What does she expect? What is it that she wants from Jesus?" Some say that she expected him to raise Lazarus from the dead. But they miss the point, because Jesus immediately replies, "Your brother will rise again." If Martha had any idea that this would happen at once, she would have said, "How wonderful, Lord! That is exactly what I expected you to do now that you have come." But she does not say that. What she says is, "Yes, I know. He will rise again in the resurrection at the last day." No, Martha is not anticipating the immediate resurrection of her brother.

What, then, is she expecting from Jesus? What does she mean by the words, "Even now, whatever you ask of God, God will give it to you"? We have to conclude that she is looking for his comfort, for the release that God can give to a heart that is burdened and saddened, torn with grief, anticipating the loneliness and the emptiness of the days ahead. God can offer marvelous inward peace. Many have testified to that.

We can see that Martha's faith is placed right where ours often is, in what she thinks will happen, not in who Jesus is and in whom she is dealing with. So often we tell ourselves, *I know God has worked in the past, and I know that he will work again in the future, but today is not the day of miracles.* In the daily grind of life, the world seems to be so barren of miracles that we think, *Those days have gone. God can't work now. He will work again though.* This is Martha's faith—in the future, at the resurrection of the last day. Her theology is accurate, but she has forgotten that God is right there in the here and now.

That is what Jesus brings to her attention. Notice how he shifts the focus back from the program to his person by saying, "I am the resurrection and the life; he who believes in me, though he die, yet shall he live, and whoever lives and believes in me shall never die. Do you believe this?" This passage places the focus on the first word, *I.* Jesus is saying that if he is present, then anything God is capable of doing can happen! That is where our faith ought to be fastened. That is what we ought to remember.

> *Thank you, Father, for this encouraging word, this reminder of the mighty power of our Lord, who is Master of life and of death.*

Do our theological boxes limit our expectations and/or experience of God's wisdom and sovereign power? Do we live each day with joyful trust in his agenda?

EXTRAVAGANT WORSHIP

A daily devotion for January 29

Read John 11:55–12:11.

> "Then Mary took about a pint of pure nard, an expensive perfume; she poured it on Jesus' feet and wiped his feet with her hair. And the house was filled with the fragrance of the perfume" (John 12:3).

I believe John included this account so that we might understand something of what real worship is. Worship is the center of Christian life. Mary took a pound of costly ointment and poured it on Jesus. Later, Judas complained about the extravagance of using what amounted to a year's pay for a laborer to anoint the Lord's feet. This account makes clear that Mary understood the work of Jesus and the change he had made in her heart. She was also deeply appreciative not only of the restoration of her brother Lazarus but of the magnificent teaching she heard from Jesus as she sat at his feet. This accounts for her extravagance. She spared no expense; she cared nothing for the customs of the day, entering into a supper where women were usually not welcome, letting down her hair in public, an unthinkable act in that culture, and openly expressing her love for Jesus. But that's how love and worship act. They are uncaring of expense.

I don't know what young men bring to young women these days to express their love, but when I was a young man, it was a dozen American Beauty roses. I remember digging deep in my pocket for what seemed an enormous amount of money to buy a dozen such roses for a young lady. But love takes no note of things like expense.

I spent the summer one year traveling and speaking around the country while my wife had to stay at her parents' home with our two little girls. One day when I was in Buffalo, New York, I was feeling sorry for her as I thought of how she was taking care of the children and working hard while I was free to travel and to meet exciting people. I very much wanted to express my feelings of love, appreciation, and gratitude for her. As I walked down a street in the city, I saw a beautiful fur coat in a store window. The price, however, was way out of my range. I wanted to take that coat home to Elaine to show my appreciation for all she had done that summer. My quite wealthy and very sympathetic companion, when told what I wanted to do, was understanding and offered to loan me the money to buy the coat. We worked out terms whereby I could repay a few dollars a week, and I bought the coat. When I got home and gave my wife that incredible gift, which we never could have afforded, she was amazed and delighted. To this day that coat hangs in a closet in our home. I don't think she can bear to part with it, because it represents a gift of love, a delight in giving to show what is deep in the heart.

Again, that's how love and worship are—uncaring of expense. Worship is a transformed heart that expresses itself regardless of cost.

Lord, you are worthy of the most extravagant gift. Teach me to worship you with love that delights in giving.

The essence of true prayer is worship. Are our prayers characterized by adoration, by gratitude for who God is and for his unequivocal and lavish love toward us in the gift of his Son, our Lord and our Savior?

THE GRAIN OF WHEAT

A daily devotion for January 30

Read John 12:12–36.

> "Jesus replied, 'The hour has come for the Son of Man to be glorified. Very truly I tell you, unless a kernel of wheat falls to the ground and dies, it remains only a single seed. But if it dies, it produces many seeds'" (John 12:23–24).

Jesus prefaces his teaching here with words that require our focused attention: "Very truly I tell you." Whenever you see these words, pay close attention because what follows is of great importance. "Unless a grain of wheat falls into the earth and dies, it remains alone." What does he mean by that? Jesus is talking about himself. He is the grain of wheat. Unless he is willing to die, unless he goes to the cross, which he sees looming in the immediate future, his whole purpose in coming to earth will have been wasted, and he will remain alone. "But if it dies, it bears much fruit." He sees the Greek people, who were asking for him, as the firstfruits, the symbol of the great harvest on earth for which he came.

Perhaps Jesus thought something like this: *These Greeks have asked to see me. What does it mean to "see me"?* Picture a grain of wheat. Can you see that grain, so tiny and yet so obvious? Outwardly it is visible, but can you really see it? No. To see it, you must plant it in the cold, dark earth. Eventually a green sprout will appear, then the blade, then the plant, then the stem, and finally a head. At last the plant turns golden; the harvest has come. But still, have you seen everything in that grain of wheat? No, not yet. You first must plant the grains from that golden head again and again. At last, when you stand one day beside a shimmering field of wheat, rippling in the breeze, golden in the sunshine, you can say you have seen a grain of wheat. You have seen all of its possibilities; all of it has been unfolded and now is visible to the eye. That is what Jesus meant. The world would not see the full outcome of his work and of his life until he went to the cross.

If he had not died on that cross and been buried, we probably would not know any more about him than we know of any other great religious leader, like Buddha, Muhammad, or Confucius, and we might not have heard of him at all. So meager were the results of his teaching that only a relative handful of his followers stood with him to the end. But because of the cross Jesus was able to do something he could never have done otherwise: he was able to share his life with millions of people. How do we explain men like Luther, Calvin, Knox, and Zwingli who changed the Western world in their lifetimes? How do we explain the impact of men like the Wesley brothers? How do we explain the change in the hatchet man of the Nixon administration, Charles Colson, who transformed this country prison system in the name of Jesus? How do we explain Solzhenitsyn, Mother Teresa, and millions who daily evidence altered lives and changed outlooks? All this has come about because of the cross and the confirming resurrection of Christ. God is saying to us in this account that the only way to true glory is to die.

> *Lord Jesus, thank you that you were willing to die that a harvest of souls would come to fruition. Teach me to take up my cross daily that I, too, might bear fruit.*

Jesus taught and demonstrated the stunning reality that his death was necessary to our rebirth into his resurrection life. Are we willing to become the seed that surrenders to death to realize the joy and the fulfillment of reproducing his life in and through us?

THE GLORY OF THE CROSS

A daily devotion for January 31

Read John 12:27–50.

"The crowd that was there and heard it said it had thundered; others said an angel had spoken to him. Jesus said, 'This voice was for your benefit, not mine. Now is the time for judgment on this world; now the prince of this world will be driven out. And I, when I am lifted up from the earth, will draw all people to myself.' He said this to show the kind of death he was going to die" (John 12:29–33).

Jesus has no illusions about what is coming, and undoubtedly he is encouraged to hear the Father's voice confirming that he is on the right course. This voice was first heard at the baptism of Jesus and again at the transfiguration. And now, for the third time, as he faces the ordeal of the cross the voice of the Father affirms his pleasure at the faithfulness of his beloved Son, who is willing to endure what lies before him. God declares that from this ordeal will come further glory to his name.

Jesus explains by listing three things that this glory will entail. First, "Now is the judgment of this world." In the cross men will be able to see what is wrong with the philosophy of the world, what is evil in what sounds so right and necessary. Here the world's phony values are exposed. Here is revealed a standard by which all may measure the self-indulgence of the world, that destructive philosophy that cries out on every side today, "Live for yourself alone." But Jesus says that such a life must be put to death: "If anyone serves me, let him deny himself, and take up his cross daily, and follow me" (Luke 9:23). You cannot be a Christian and continue to live on the basis that your life belongs to yourself. That is the life of the world. All of that is judged in the cross.

Second, Jesus declares, "Now shall the ruler of this world be cast out." Because we are continually victims of the deceptions of Satan, we do not realize how total is his control of the human race. All men blindly follow demonic delusions that Satan sends into the world. We find ourselves manipulated by satanic values and have no idea of how helpless we are to change apart from Christ. The Devil is the prince, the ruler, of this world, the Scriptures declare. He is in control of human society. But the great word of the gospel is that when we believe in Jesus and follow him, we are freed from the power of Satan, transferred into the kingdom of the Son of God's love. For the first time we can do something permanent about the habits that destroy us, hurting us and others, wrecking our plans, and sabotaging our highest hopes and dreams. In the cross the power of the Devil over the human race was broken and the deliverance of individuals was made possible.

Finally, Jesus says, "I, when I am lifted up from the earth, will draw all men to myself." You may have heard that text interpreted to mean that if a preacher exalts Christ, everybody will be attracted to him. I wish it did mean that. As I have preached Christ, I have found that some were attracted to him, but not everybody. No, that is not what these words mean. John tells us what they mean when he adds, "He said this to show the kind of death he was going to die." These words of Jesus are clearly a reference to the cross: by means of the cross he would draw all people to himself. He means all kinds. Rich and poor, black, white, yellow, and red, children and adults, no matter what social standing or background, no matter how deeply they have fallen into sin, all kinds are drawn to the cross and can be delivered and saved. What a wonderful word of hope, and how true it has proved to be! All kinds of people have come and have found deliverance through the cross of Christ.

Lord Jesus, through the cross you judged the world, cast out Satan, and draw all kinds of people to yourself. Help me to walk in the victory you have won.

What are three essential ways in which Jesus's death on the cross brings glory to his name? As his disciples, we are compelled by his sacrificial love no longer to live for ourselves but for him. He died that we may live. Are we honoring him by steadfastly renouncing our self-indulgence?

ISAIAH

The Farseeing Prophet
An introduction for the month of February

Some of the most beautiful language in literature is found in the great prophecy of Isaiah. He was a master of language. He was also a farseeing prophet who recorded remarkable prophecies centering on the coming of God's Messiah. The fifty-third chapter of his prophecy offers such a clear picture of Christ that this book is often called "the gospel according to Isaiah." God's plan of redemption and his work of redemption are central in this prophecy. That is suggested even in the name of the prophet: Isaiah means "God saves."

The book of Isaiah could be considered a miniature Bible. There are sixty-six books in the Bible, and Isaiah has sixty-six chapters. The Bible is divided between the Old and the New Testaments, and Isaiah is divided into two halves. The Old Testament has thirty-nine books, and the first division of Isaiah has thirty-nine chapters. The New Testament has twenty-seven books, and the second half of Isaiah has twenty-seven chapters. The opening chapter of the second division of Isaiah, chapter 40, describes the ministry of John the Baptist, the forerunner of the Messiah, the voice crying in the wilderness, "Prepare ye the way of the Lord." In the New Testament, the first figure introduced is John the Baptist, crying in the wilderness, "Prepare ye the way of the Lord." The closing chapter of Isaiah deals with the creation of the new heavens and the new earth. Revelation, the last book in the New Testament, deals with the same subject. This great prophecy of Isaiah, therefore, not only captures the theme of all Scripture and its central focus on the Savior of mankind but also reflects the divisions of the Bible itself.

The opening verse of the book gives a brief introduction to the prophet and the vision of Isaiah, the son of Amoz, which he saw concerning Judah and Jerusalem in the days of Uzziah, Jotham, Ahaz, and Hezekiah, kings of Judah (Isa. 1:1). In that historical note we learn that Isaiah carried on his ministry through the reigns of four kings. (He was put to death during the reign of Hezekiah's son, Manasseh, one of the most evil kings of Judah, just before the southern kingdom was carried away to Babylon by Nebuchadnezzar.) So Isaiah lived during a time of great unrest. Israel was surrounded by enemies and crisscrossed with invading armies. In a time of danger and desolation, the prophet was sent to declare to this people the cause of their misery.

The Jews are often called the "chosen people," but they were not so named because they were superior to other peoples. The Bible is careful to point out that God chose them not because they were smarter, richer, or greater than others but because he wished to make them a sample nation, a picture of how he deals with the nations of earth.

He also chose them, of course, as the channel through which the Messiah would come. Speaking to the Samaritan woman, Jesus himself repeated the declaration of the Old Testament, "Salvation is of the Jews."

Some would ask, why bother with this ancient history of a people who lived thousands of years ago, a history that cannot possibly have any bearing on us today? To that, the apostle Paul in the New Testament says that "all these things happened to Israel as types for our edification" (1 Cor. 10:11). In the Old Testament we see ourselves portrayed. The problems it pictures are the same ones we face today.

THE HUMAN PROBLEM

A daily devotion for February 1

Read Isaiah 1:1–15.

> "Woe to the sinful nation, a people whose guilt is great, a brood of evildoers, children given to corruption! They have forsaken the Lord; they have spurned the Holy One of Israel and turned their backs on him" (Isa. 1:4).

Every breath we breathe is by the mercy of God. Everything comes from his providing hand. But man ignores and turns his back upon all that and says that only man matters. That is incredible blindness. But that is the problem Isaiah faces here. God analyzes the situation in Israel in one verse, a sevenfold indictment of the nation.

Let us take a closer look at some of God's indictments. First, he says Israel is a sinful nation. The people have been infected with a fatal virus that causes everything they do to turn out wrong. The biblical point of view is that this is the problem with the whole human race. People today find that hard to believe. But there is something terribly wrong with humanity. Man is not what he was made to be. He does not function the way he should. There is a taint, a poison, spread throughout the human world that causes even our efforts toward good to create problems. The problem, the Bible declares, is sin—that is, selfishness and self-centeredness. We are all afflicted with a tendency to take care of ourselves first, to look out for number one. That is what produces the narcissism so characteristic of our day.

Second, God says these people are weighed down because of sin. Think of the heavy burdens we shoulder because of the urge to self-centeredness within us. Think of the terrible cost of crime, child abuse, and teenage pregnancies and the staggering cost of war. All these heavy burdens load us down and leave us bent over in guilt. This message is not popular, but it is realistic.

We are proud of the technological advances of our day. But the people who invent these things labor under the same burdens that Israel faced in the days of Isaiah. We still have not learned how to keep a delinquent child from corrupting a neighborhood. We still have not learned how to save a disintegrating marriage by having those involved take an honest look at themselves and begin to work in harmony, not in estrangement. Our inability to do these things is what God is analyzing here.

These people are also the "children given to corruption," passing along their evil tendencies to the next generation. More than that, "they have forsaken the Lord." There is a strange conspiracy, prevalent in politics and education, to keep God on the fringes of life and never to mention his name or to acknowledge his presence. Any effort to insert him into public affairs meets with tremendous resistance. People have turned their backs on the living God and do not like to acknowledge that he has any part in human affairs.

Further, God declares, "They have spurned the Holy One of Israel." They have blasphemed the God of glory and have insulted his majesty. That too is evident on every side today.

The ultimate result is, "they have turned their backs on him." This means people are alienated from God and therefore from each other. History confirms that when you lose God, you lose man. You can understand man only when you understand God, for man is made in the image of God. To lose the image of God is to lose the image of man. This is the problem with the world of our day.

Father, every breath I take is by your mercy and grace. Teach me to confess my sins and to walk in obedience to you.

The fatal virus of sin has infected all of humanity, a fact highlighted in one representative nation. Does the spectacle of worldwide corruption call us to personal confession and to intercessory prayer?

HOW CAN WE CHANGE?

A daily devotion for February 2

Read Isaiah 1:16–31.

> "'Come now, let us settle the matter,' says the Lord. 'Though your sins are like scarlet, they shall be as white as snow; though they are red as crimson, they shall be like wool. If you are willing and obedient, you will eat the good things of the land; but if you resist and rebel, you will be devoured by the sword.' For the mouth of the Lord has spoken" (Isa. 1:18–20).

When we read Isaiah 1, one problem is immediately evident. God's analysis of the human race is that we are fundamentally tainted with self-centeredness so that we do not want to do good. We are concerned only with our own needs and our own lives. As a solution, God says in verse 16, "Wash yourselves; make yourselves clean; remove the evil of your doings from before my eyes; cease to do evil, learn to do good." But how can evil people do good things?

The answer is in verses 18 to 20. It could not be put any more plainly. There is no help in man himself. We cannot heal ourselves. We need more than our habits changed. We ourselves must be changed, and that change can occur only in a relationship with the living God.

This is the good news; this is the gospel, which looks forward to the coming of the Lord Jesus and to the shedding of his blood. He takes our place so that God might put our sins upon him, enabling Jesus to give us the gift of righteousness so that our hearts will be changed. Selfishness is not taken away, but it is overcome by the gift of love. An old hymn we used to sing in Sunday school says this so well.

> What can wash away my sin?
> Nothing but the blood of Jesus.
> What can make me whole again?
> Nothing but the blood of Jesus.
>
> O precious is the flow
> That makes me white as snow.
> No other fount I know,
> Nothing but the blood of Jesus.

Isaiah is true to his name: "God saves." Only God can do it. Some people attempt to clean up their lives. Every so often they get the urge to stop doing things that obviously are hurting themselves and others. Yet their efforts never seem to work. They may stop temporarily, but then another bad habit surfaces and soon they return to their old ways. They have no power to change. But the gospel, the beautiful good news, is that God has found a way to break through the human problem to change our hearts and to teach us a new way of living.

> *Thank you, Father, for this wonderfully forthright word and for the good news that we are not left in our doleful, miserable condition. Thank you that you have entered our lives by means of the Lord Jesus, by his death and resurrection, and by your indwelling are making us different.*

As we face the fact of our selfishness, do we attempt to deal with it by self-effort? Are we learning the power of the gospel to set us free?

IN LIGHT OF HIS MAJESTY

A daily devotion for February 3

Read Isaiah 6:1–5.

> "'Woe to me!' I cried. 'I am ruined! For I am a man of unclean lips, and I live among a people of unclean lips, and my eyes have seen the King, the Lord Almighty'" (Isa. 6:5).

As Isaiah observes the majesty of God, his immediate reaction is to see himself in a new light. When we see ourselves in the light of the greatness of God, we realize how far we have fallen from that wondrous image. Seeing his own pollution, Isaiah cries, "I am a man of unclean lips."

Scripture frequently uses the symbol of the lips—the tongue or the mouth—to reveal what is in the heart. Jesus said, "The things that go into a man are not what defile him." It is not what you eat, what you wear, or what you read that defiles you. It is what comes out of you, according to Jesus. "Out of the heart come murders, adulteries, fornications, jealousies, envies" (Matt. 15:19).

Notice Isaiah does not say, "Woe is me, for I am worthless!" The Scripture never teaches that man is worthless. In fact, Jesus taught quite the opposite. He said what a pity it is for a man to gain the whole world but to lose himself. That is how valuable man is. Even the world, with all its kingdoms, wealth, and glory, is not worth the life of a single individual. Isaiah declares, "I am lost. I am ruined, defiled. Woe is me." He experiences a moment of fear, a sense of failure, and cries out in despair as he sees how far he is from ever measuring up to the wholeness and the beauty of God.

When Isaiah sees the majesty of God, he feels a burning desire in his heart to be used by God, to have a part in God's glorious work. There is no greater hunger than the hunger to be used by God. But when Isaiah becomes aware of that hunger, he also becomes aware that he is not fit to be used; he feels he would mess up everything if he tried. This is not a pleasant way to feel, but it is a hopeful place at which to arrive, because pride is the source of all human evil. All the agony of life flows from our feeling that we deserve more than we are getting. We desire to be bigger, better, or more noted than others. Humility, on the other hand, is the source of all virtue. The first of the beatitudes in the Sermon on the Mount corresponds to what Isaiah declares of himself as he views the majesty of God. "Blessed are the poor in spirit [the bankrupt ones, the ones who recognize they have nothing in themselves], for theirs is the kingdom of heaven" (Matt. 5:3). God labors constantly in our lives to bring us to the awareness Isaiah experienced.

If you feel this way, thank God for it, for he never uses people without first bringing them to an awareness of their own weakness. Many find themselves unable to do what they would like. They feel powerless, unable to control their destinies. All of us face moments of truth when we see what Isaiah saw and recognize that the cause of our problems is our inner defilement. When you see yourself in this way, thank God for it, for this can be your moment of healing.

> *Thank you, Lord, for those times in my life when I have been so aware of my own weakness and sin. Help me not to lose hope but to turn to you for your promise of healing.*

Since pride is the source of all evil, and humility the source of all virtue, are we eagerly choosing the supreme value of a humble heart? Do we have a growing consciousness of God's majesty?

GO!

A daily devotion for February 4

Read Isaiah 6:8–13.

> "Then I heard the voice of the Lord saying, 'Whom shall I send? And who will go for us?' And I said, 'Here am I. Send me!' He said, 'Go and tell this people: "Be ever hearing, but never understanding; be ever seeing, but never perceiving"'" (Isa. 6:8–9).

When Isaiah hears the call of God his heart is instantly responsive. By now he believes what God said and knows that he has in fact been forgiven. He no longer feels undone and defiled. No longer does he feel unworthy or unable to serve. He is eager to go and says, "Here am I. Send me."

In seminary it was pointed out to me that when Christians hear the voice of God telling them to serve, they often say, "Here am I! Send my sister!" (This especially applies to missionary work.) Such an answer reveals that they never have felt forgiven. They have never sensed the wonder and the privilege of being used by God, the marvel of a call to serve people in need, whether a need of food and shelter, a need for knowledge, truth, or love, or a need for cleansing and forgiveness. But that is what Christians are called to do. I often think of the words of Peter Marshall, who said, "Many Christians are like men dressed in diving suits designed for many fathoms deep, marching bravely forth to pull plugs from bathtubs." Much Christian activity seems to merit that description.

But Isaiah, responding to God's call, is sent immediately to meet the need of his people. God's word is, "Go." Something great has happened to you, so go!

But do not go if you have had no vision of the majesty and the greatness of God, if you have never heard his voice speaking to your heart, if you have never cried, "Woe is me! I am undone." Unless you have felt God's cleansing and restoring grace, do not go. You will have nothing to say. You cannot help people by commiserating with them and sharing their sorrow. You must go knowing you have what they need to hear, which God will speak into their hearts just as he has spoken it into yours. If you have felt that, then you can say, as I hope you are saying, "Lord, here am I! Send me."

Father, grant me to feel the touch from your altar of the cleansing coal on my lips and in my heart that I should be like the prophet Isaiah, fit, eager, and available to go.

Every disciple of Jesus has a mandate to serve others in his name. Are we consenting to both the call and to the prerequisite cleansing that equips us to serve with dignity and humility?

A PLACE OF CLEANSING

A daily devotion for February 5

Read Isaiah 7:1–14.

> "Then the Lord said to Isaiah, 'Go out, you and your son Shear-Jashub, to meet Ahaz at the end of the aqueduct of the Upper Pool, on the road to the Launderer's Field. Say to him, "Be careful, keep calm and don't be afraid. Do not lose heart because of these two smoldering stubs of firewood—because of the fierce anger of Rezin and Aram and of the son of Remaliah"'" (Isa. 7:3–4).

We are told the precise spot on which God directed the prophet to stand when he made this announcement to the king. You probably read this thinking that God gave him only a casual direction, but it is significant. Isaiah was told to go to the "end of the aqueduct of the Upper Pool, on the road to the Launderer's Field," to stand at that spot, and to speak to King Ahaz. What is the meaning of that? At that spot and only there, the prophet was to inform King Ahaz that he had nothing to fear from the two armies threatening the city of Jerusalem. They were only "smoldering stubs" and were no threat at all. The account declared that deliverance would arrive within sixty-five years. All this came true.

Looking at this passage, we must remember the peculiar nature of Isaiah's commission. In chapter 6 he was sent with a strange message. God said to him, "Go and speak to this people, but speak in a way that they will 'hear what you say but they will not hear it,' and they will 'see what you are talking about but they will not perceive it.'" Here we are given a clue that Isaiah is to prophesy in cryptic language that carries a double meaning.

The line about the "end of the aqueduct of the Upper Pool, on the road to the Launderer's Field" is a good example of this. The word *pool* in Hebrew also means "blessing." It is obvious why a pool of water would be called a blessing. In a dry and thirsty land, any pool of water would clearly prove to be a blessing. So the word has both meanings. The word *upper* ("the Upper Pool") means more than a pool located on a higher level. It also means "the most high." So what we have as a second meaning is the phrase "the blessing of the Most High." This pool is a spring of water, located on the hillside west of the old City of David, that flowed down an aqueduct to the city. The prophet was to take his stand at the end of the spring, where it emptied into a small pool.

That was also the road by which he came there: "the road to the Launderer's Field." A road or a highway in Scripture is always an ascent. Isaiah 35 calls it "the highway of holiness," so it has to do with righteousness and moral cleansing. This meaning is underscored by the fact that the road led to the Launderer's Field. The field would be at the place of washing. We can see why a pool that was at "the end of an aqueduct" of water, coming down from an upper spring, would also be a place where people washed their clothes. That is where Isaiah was told to stand.

When these meanings are considered, we see why the prophet was sent to where these two places met. This was where the upward way of cleansing met the downward flow of the channel of the blessings of the Most High. What would that symbolize? From the New Testament, we know this could only describe the Lord Jesus. He is the end of the aqueduct, the channel of the blessing of the Most High. He is also the way of cleansing, the ascent that brought the prophet to this place. This is all a beautiful poetic description of Jesus.

Thank you, Father, for the cleansing that is available in Jesus.

When the woes of life o'ertake us, the Scriptures from start to finish offer the Lord Jesus Christ as the One through whom all blessing flows. Do we trust him as our number-one source of blessing?

THE GREAT LIGHT

A daily devotion for February 6

Read Isaiah 9:1–7.

> "For to us a child is born, to us a son is given; and the government will be upon his shoulders, and he will be called 'Wonderful Counselor, Mighty God, Everlasting Father, Prince of Peace'" (Isa. 9:6).

What a remarkable picture! It hardly needs exposition. Suddenly, after a great time of trouble, the nation will realize that its glorious King, its Messiah, has come as a little child: "to us a child is born." He who was for eternity the Son of God will be given to his people as a little baby in Bethlehem. They will recognize at last, after centuries of rejection, that this One deserves divine titles. This is Immanuel, "God with us."

The four titles Isaiah lists represent that. Did anyone ever fulfill the title of "Wonderful Counselor" more completely than Jesus? He unveils to us secrets about ourselves and counsels us about how to avoid the heartaches and the problems that otherwise would beset us, showing the way of deliverance from the taint of sin.

"Mighty God" is unquestionably a title that can only describe God. He is the mighty One, and in 10:21 the same term is unmistakably used of God.

The next title is more than simply "Everlasting Father." It is actually "Father of Eternity." This is surely a reference to the fact that Jesus alone can give eternal life; he is its father, for it originates with him. "As many as believe in him, to them gave he power to become the sons of God" (John 1:12)

No one contests the last title, "Prince of Peace." Jesus said, "My peace I give unto you" (John 14:27). The phrase "Of the increase of his government and of peace there will be no end" captures the universal character of the Messiah's reign and its extension at last to the whole created cosmos.

The key, of course, is in the words "to us a child is born, to us a son is given." Though these events, both in Isaiah and in the gospels, took place thousands of years ago, when an individual first comes into personal contact with the Lord of glory it seems to that person that he is the first recipient of this wonderful gift. We say that we "found the Lord" and that he "came to us," because the event is so real in our experience. It is to us that he came, to us that he is born. He is "God with us," strengthening and guiding us, meeting our needs, and solving our problems.

A woman once told me of her struggle with a sense of being abandoned, of being left without guidance, and of needing God's presence. And thankfully I could point her back to these marvelous promises. The Lord is with us.

> *Father, thank you for not simply sending your Son but for giving him to us. He is the most wonderful gift of all!*

Are we experiencing the life-changing reality of God with us in the presence of his Son? Do we seek first the counsel, the peace, and the power of our everlasting Father?

THE ONE COMING

A daily devotion for February 7

Read Isaiah 11:1–5.

"A shoot will come up from the stump of Jesse; from his roots a Branch will bear fruit. The Spirit of the Lord will rest on him—the Spirit of wisdom and of understanding, the Spirit of counsel and of might, the Spirit of the knowledge and fear of the Lord—and he will delight in the fear of the Lord" (Isa. 11:1–2).

This passage is a clear prediction of the Lord Jesus. In these opening verses is a hint that the Messiah will appear in history in an obscure way. That is suggested by the line "A shoot will come up from the stump of Jesse." Like a great tree that has been cut down, the ancestry of Jesus represented in David and his father Jesse has been reduced to obscurity and insignificance. But out of that lowly stump will arise a shoot, a single sprout, a man who will be filled with the Spirit of God and who will do a great work in the land, as the prophet goes on to say. When the Gospels refer to our Lord as the "son of David," they always do so in terms of his royal glory, but when they call him the "stump of Jesse," they point to his humble beginnings.

The prophet sees not only the ancestry of Jesus but recognizes him in his Spirit-filled ministry. "The Spirit of the Lord shall rest on him," he says. That Spirit consists of three pairs of characteristics. Observing these pairs more closely, you can see that they describe Jesus of Nazareth. The first pair, "the spirit of wisdom and of knowledge," speaks of his amazing insight into human affairs. Wisdom is the knowledge of the nature of things, while understanding is the awareness of the differences between them. How clearly Jesus reflected these in his ministry! One of the symbols of our age is the therapist's couch. Therapists have their patients lie on a couch and ask them questions in an effort to understand their problems. But our Lord never used a couch, for he never had to ask questions. John's gospel tells us that Jesus didn't need any man to tell him what was in man, because he knew man.

The second pair, "the spirit of counsel and of might," speaks of authority. Counsel is the ability to give good and right advice, while might is the ability to help carry it out. This is described even more fully in the words in verse three, "He shall not judge by what his eyes see, or decide by what his ears hear." What a wonderful description of Jesus as he met with people! He spoke of truth that can never be learned by human powers. He described how the angels live, what happens after death, how prayer works, how the Devil operates. These he explained with full authority. He did not have to study reference books but rather spoke so that men hearing him said, "No man ever spake like this man" (John 7:46).

The third pair, "the spirit of knowledge and the fear of the Lord," speaks of our Lord's intimate relationship to the Father. Out of that flowed the marvelous serenity of his life. He was never taken by surprise. He always seemed to be master of the occasion. This ability grew out of his full awareness of the mind of God. Jesus said on one occasion, "You do not know Him, but I know Him" (John 8:55). He came to reveal to us the mind of the Father, the graciousness, compassion, truthfulness, and faithfulness of God. All of this grew out of his "knowledge of the Lord and his fear of the Lord."

Gracious Father, I thank you for these amazing words from this ancient book. How accurately they picture One who has come to mean more than all else to me. I thank you for the confirmation of the Spirit to my heart that these words can be fulfilled in me as well.

In profoundly awesome humility Jesus came as one of us to make us one with him. Do we recognize that his power is perfected in our weakness?

A PICTURE OF HOPE

A daily devotion for February 8

Read Isaiah 11:6–9.

"The wolf will live with the lamb, the leopard will lie down with the goat, the calf and the lion and the yearling together; and a little child will lead them" (Isa. 11:6).

What a beautiful picture! Here is the time when the dreams of men will come true, when all the longings reflected in peace demonstrations and in cries for disarmament will find their fulfillment. There is a deep hunger in mankind for this kind of a world, although we do not know how to achieve it. But the One who is to come does know how. Then even the animals will lose their ferocity and will lie down one with another. How would you mothers feel if you found your child playing with a cobra? But a time is coming when that will happen, when the animals will make peace with one another, when the lion shall eat straw like the ox.

Some people ask, "Is this passage literal or is it only symbolic? Is this all metaphor?" Some commentators say this is a picture of the work of Christ in human hearts today. I believe that. I believe this is metaphor, picturing spiritual peace.

I think of our church elders in those terms. One of them is like a lion; he roars every time you cross him. Another one is like a great bear; he swallows you up as you come into contact with him. Another is like a leopard—sneaky. And here was I, a meek lamb in the midst of them! Our elders' meetings sometimes give that impression, but when we look to the Lord he comes among us as a great lion tamer. Then the lion lies down with the lamb, the bear and the leopard dwell together, and everything works out. This is what our Lord has power to do in human hearts. He can heal controversy and bring peace among men.

But I also believe this passage is literal. There will come a day when the curse will be removed from the earth. Paul sings about a day when creation shall be released from its bondage (Rom. 8:19). Then the curse will be removed, and the whole earth will break into a verdant blooming, the likes of which we have never seen; "the desert shall blossom like the rose," as Isaiah prophesies in chapter 35. The animals will lose their ferocity, and even the carnivores will return to eating grass, as in creation before the fall.

Father, I look forward to the fulfillment of these gracious words when even the animals shall lose their enmity for one another and shall lie down together and a little child shall lead them. Grant that I may discover the reality of these words in my life.

Peacemaking and peacemakers are God's business. As we anticipate its final fulfillment, are we seeking to be authentic messengers of his peace day by day?

THE ORIGIN AND NATURE OF SIN

A daily devotion for February 9

Read Isaiah 14:3–23.

> "How you have fallen from heaven, O morning star, son of Dawn! You have been cast down to the earth, you who once laid low the nations! You said in your heart, 'I will ascend to heaven, I will raise my throne on high above the stars of God ... But you are brought down to the grave, to the depths of the pit'" (Isa. 14:12–14).

These verses describe a supernatural figure who, in the invisible world of the spirit, is behind the earthly kingdom of Babylon. We are looking here at what has been called the "fall of Satan." Lucifer, the brightest and most beautiful of the angels of God, the nearest to his throne, became so entranced with his own image that he rebelled against the government of God and thus became the adversary, Satan. Here he is seen brought at last to the bottomless pit.

We are clearly looking beyond the events of earth to the spiritual world governing those events. Paul told us that we do not wrestle with flesh and blood but with wicked spirits in high places (Eph. 6:12). The great king of evil is behind all human wrong. This is why the nations rage, why we cannot achieve peace among men at the level of human counsel. We must reckon with these supernatural beings who are behind the mistaken deeds of men.

In this passage we learn the origin and the nature of sin. The root of sin is self-occupation. This is behind the narcissism of the day in which we live. The media constantly pushes people to look out for themselves, to speak of their rights, their desires, their plans, and to ask, "What's in it for me?" This is the philosophy that, like a ferment, keeps troubling the pot of international relationships, boiling over again and again in wars and conflicts.

The nature of sin is to play God in our own little world. Whether we are believers or unbelievers, sin consists of feeling that we are in control of our own destinies, that we have all it takes to handle life. We learn in 1 John 3:8 that sin is of the Devil, for the Devil sinned from the beginning. Playing God is the nature of sin. It is an extremely pleasurable experience. We love it.

A Christian businessman wrote of his own experience, "It's my pride that makes me independent of God. It's appealing to feel I am the master of my fate. I run my own life; I call my own shots; I go it alone. But that feeling is my basic dishonesty. I can't go it alone. I have to get help from other people. I can't ultimately rely on myself. I'm dependent on God for my very next breath. It's dishonest of me to pretend that I'm anything but a man, small, weak, and limited. Living independent of God is self-delusion. It's not just a matter of pride being an unfortunate little trait and of humility being an attractive little virtue. It's my inner psychological integrity that's at stake. When I am conceited I'm lying to myself about what I am. I am pretending to be God and not man. My pride is the idolatrous worship of myself, and that is the national religion of hell."

Forgive me, Father, for those areas in my life where pride still rules.

When we are knowingly complicit with Satan's "What's in it for me?" philosophy, do we consider the personal and relational consequences? What is the ferment in the pot of international relations?

WHY DO THE NATIONS RAGE?

A daily devotion for February 10

Read Isaiah 23:1–18.

> "Who planned this against Tyre, the bestower of crowns, whose merchants are princes, whose traders are renowned in the earth? The Lord Almighty planned it, to bring down her pride in all her splendor and to humble all who are renowned on the earth" (Isa. 23:8–9).

"Why do the nations rage?" That question is answered many times in the Scriptures, notably in this section of Isaiah, beginning with chapter 13 and ending in chapter 23. In these chapters the prophet is given a vision concerning the great world powers that surrounded Israel. The prophecy begins with a word concerning Babylon, then focuses on Assyria, Moab, Egypt, Edom, and other nations, and ends in chapter 23 with the burden of the city-nation of Tyre.

These messages were wholly predictive when they were uttered. They point out things that will happen from Isaiah's time onward. Looking back on history, we can see that much of this prophecy has been fulfilled. These nations are not only historic but are symbols of forces at work in every age and in every generation. What makes this passage so valuable is that through the experience of these nations we begin to understand our own struggles.

These judgments depict things that are true of us. Babylon, Tyre, Assyria, and Egypt appear throughout the Scriptures, and they always symbolize the same thing: the world in its varied attacks upon us. Egypt is ever the picture of the corruption and defilement of the world. Babylon embodies the world's deceitfulness and the great deceiver behind it, using false religion to lead us astray.

Finally, this section calls upon the colony of Tyre to behold the desolation the Lord is visiting upon this city. The prophet inquires why this is coming to pass. It is because God despises the love of luxury, the lust for creature comforts, and the pursuit of material gain that Tyre represents in the Scriptures. Jesus once said the things that men highly esteem are an abomination in the sight of God (Luke 16:15). Tyre's sin was crass materialism, storing up wealth and treasure for this life only, with little concern for the one to come. For seventy years the city was judged, following its destruction by Nebuchadnezzar the Great.

God has a solution to the world, the flesh, and behind them, the Devil. As we live in relationship with him, he provides the power to overcome these forces. In these passages Isaiah describes in a marvelous way how we too can rely on the presence of the Lord, the Holy One of Israel, in our midst and can daily triumph over these enemies of our faith.

> *Father, these words speak of the world as it really is, stripping it bare before my eyes. I have felt the attraction of the world and of the flesh. Thank you for showing me how destructive they are to me, how I cannot entertain these things, and how, with the power committed to me by the Lord Jesus and with his presence in my heart, I have the strength to say no to them and to walk in faithfulness before you.*

Through the media, we are exposed to conflict and corruption everywhere each day. Do we choose to participate in God's solutions rather than to perpetuate the problems?

LINE UPON LINE

A daily devotion for February 11

Read Isaiah 28:1–15.

> "Whom will he teach knowledge, and to whom will he explain the message? Those who are weaned from the milk, those taken from the breast? For it is precept upon precept, precept upon precept, line upon line, line upon line, here a little, there a little" (Isa. 28:9–10 RSV).

That is a beautiful description of how the Bible is written. Unlike theological books, it does not have a chapter on sin, another on heaven, another on angels. The Bible mixes all subjects together, interspersing one truth with another, offering a balanced approach to life, "precept upon precept, line upon line, here a little, there a little."

This verse sets forth the way to avoid being trapped by the seductive lure of the good life, characterized by Ephraim in verses 1 to 3. Study your Bible! Read what God says. Look at life as he sees it. See through the allurement of the television commercials. Do you sometimes catch yourself wanting more of the luxuries of life, thinking constantly of a new car, of a new house, of climbing the corporate ladder? We are besieged by appeals to accumulate the "good things of life." This is the spirit of our age. There is great danger in this. Paul said that we should not be conformed to this world but should be transformed by the renewal of our minds (Rom. 12:2). Let our thinking be changed! Let the word of truth transform our view of life so that we see life as it really is. That is the way of deliverance.

Our Lord Jesus put it beautifully in one verse in the Sermon on the Mount: "Seek ye first the kingdom of God and his righteousness, and [then] all these things will be added unto you" (Matt. 6:33). Many Christians have reversed that, giving themselves continually to efforts to get ahead, forgetting that they are to put first the things of God. But we are to forget about obtaining status symbols and accumulating wealth and to seek godliness first—concerning ourselves with being righteous men and women right where we are. God promises that he can then trust us with the things of wealth. All these things that "the Gentiles seek after," Jesus said, "can then be added safely to you" (Matt. 6:32).

Thank you, Father, for your Word. Help me to become obedient to your truth and to search after the revelation that you have given that I may be effective and powerful in my witness in this world.

Is our earthly pilgrimage being transformed by metabolizing God's Word of truth day by day, step by step? Are we finding growing contentment in God's good things?

MECHANICAL RELIGION

A daily devotion for February 12

Read Isaiah 29:1–22.

> "The Lord says: 'These people come near to me with their mouth and honor me with their lips, but their hearts are far from me. Their worship of me is based on merely human rules they have been taught'" (Isa. 29:13).

Israel's problem was what we would call "mechanical religion," meaningless, external conformity to a performance of religious tasks. This is a grave danger. When you feel yourself becoming spiritually dull, it is a warning sign that says, "Watch out! You are headed for trouble." This happens to all of us on occasion. It is healthy to ask yourself at times, *Have I lost my zest for God? Do I sing the hymns mechanically? Do the truths of Scripture appear to me dull and commonplace? Have I lost a sense of joy in my Christian experience?* That is a danger sign. That is the "woe" to which God is referring. His provision for this is found in these verses.

> "Suddenly, in an instant, the Lord Almighty will come with thunder and earthquake and great noise, with windstorm and tempest and flames of a devouring fire" (Isa. 29:5–6).

Suddenly God will send into your life some experience—a disaster perhaps—something that will get your immediate and undivided attention. That is God's attempt to awaken you to the danger of drifting away from the vitality of a spiritual walk.

I have always appreciated the story of two students at Duke University who went to a costume party each dressed as a blue devil, the school's mascot. They started out to the party, but by mistake they stumbled into a prayer meeting, setting off a great exodus through the doors and the windows. One lady became wedged in a pew and began to scream in terror. Forgetting that they were causing her agony, the two young men rushed forward to help her. As she saw them advancing, she raised her hand and said, "Stop! Don't you come any farther. I want you to know that I have been a member of this church for twenty-five years—but I've been on your side all the time!" That is what we call a moment of truth. It is a valuable experience.

At times God will send something that suddenly alerts us to the drift in our lives. This is why he has spoken so helpfully through the prophets and the apostles, warning us of the danger of spiritual drift and of living mechanically as a Christian.

> *Thank you, Lord, for your relentless pursuit of me when I fall into mechanical religion. Open my heart to the great riches awaiting me through living in vital fellowship with my living, loving Lord.*

God's love for us does not tolerate pretense and external worship. Do we gratefully acknowledge his wake-up calls as his loving pursuit of us?

THE CURE FOR FEAR

A daily devotion for February 13

Read Isaiah 36:1–37:20.

> "Say to Hezekiah king of Judah: Do not let the god you depend on deceive you when he says, 'Jerusalem will not be given into the hands of the king of Assyria.' Surely you have heard what the kings of Assyria have done to all the countries, destroying them completely. And will you be delivered?" (Isa. 37:10–11).

This communication came in the form of a letter to Hezekiah. Clearly, it was intended to keep his heart fearful and anxious. The letter told of a future threat, saying that although the king of Assyria was leaving for the moment, he would return to wreak a terrible vengeance on Judah. Had Hezekiah taken the Assyrian message in the intended way, he would have lived in constant fear.

It is important for Christians to understand that God does not want his people to live in fear. Anxieties beset us on every hand, and fear is one of the great perils of our day. We need to hear again the words of Jesus that we should not be anxious about tomorrow. Again and again our Lord told his disciples, "Fear not." Paul told us that God has not given us a spirit of fear but of power, of love, and of a sound mind. It is not within our power to remove threats to us, but we can meet them with faith. This is what Hezekiah did. He received the letter from the messengers and read it, and then he went up to the house of the Lord and placed his dilemma before God.

Have you ever gone into your bedroom, knelt beside your bed, and spread your problem before the Lord? That is the only proper response to a threat to your person or your faith. Here is the king's wonderful prayer.

> "Lord Almighty, the God of Israel, enthroned between the cherubim, you alone are God over all the kingdoms of the earth. You have made heaven and earth. Give ear, Lord, and hear; open your eyes, Lord, and see; listen to all the words Sennacherib has sent to ridicule the living God. It is true, Lord, that the Assyrian kings have laid waste all these peoples and their lands. They have thrown their gods into the fire and destroyed them, for they were not gods but only wood and stone, fashioned by human hands. Now, Lord our God, deliver us from his hand, so that all the kingdoms of the earth may know that you, Lord, are the only God" (Isa. 37:15–20).

Notice the accuracy of this prayer. Hezekiah acknowledged the facts. Assyria was a powerful force that had already swept away other kingdoms before it, but these nations depended on idols to protect them, while Hezekiah and Judah depended on the Lord of heaven and earth. Hezekiah prayed simply and plainly to him for help.

> *Lord, I come to you now and spread before you all the troubles that I face. I confess that without you I am completely helpless, but you are the God who made heaven and earth. Give ear, Lord, and hear; open your eyes, Lord, and see.*

Fear is a normal response as we walk day by day in this earth's shadow land, so are we regularly placing our fears before our sovereign King, who is ruler of everything?

THE PERILS OF PROSPERITY

A daily devotion for February 14

Read Isaiah 39.

> "Hezekiah received the envoys gladly and showed them what was in his storehouses—the silver, the gold, the spices, the fine olive oil—his entire armory and everything found among his treasures. There was nothing in his palace or in all his kingdom that Hezekiah did not show them" (Isa. 39:2).

Taken in by the flattery of Babylon, the king trusted these ambassadors despite the fact that Isaiah had spoken clearly of the threat from that quarter: what Babylon represented in spiritual terms and what Babylon's ultimate fate would be. But the king ignored Isaiah's words, as many today ignore the clear warnings of Scripture.

So Isaiah paid another visit to Hezekiah. The old prophet said to the king, "I see you have had visitors. Who were these men?" Hezekiah replied, "They are ambassadors from Babylon, the great power to the east. This superpower has recognized our tiny kingdom, and that makes me feel proud and honored." Doubtless he had shown the letter to his wife, exclaiming, "Look, dear, the king of Babylon has now taken note of us!" Asked by Isaiah what he had shown the ambassadors, Hezekiah said, "I showed them everything we've got—all our treasures, all our defenses, everything."

Isaiah predicted the result of the king's foolishness. "'Hear the word of the Lord Almighty: The time will surely come when everything in your palace, and all that your predecessors have stored up until this day, will be carried off to Babylon. Nothing will be left,' says the Lord. 'And some of your descendants, your own flesh and blood who will be born to you, will be taken away, and they will become eunuchs in the palace of the king of Babylon'" (Isa. 39:5–7.)

This teaches us that prosperity is a greater threat than adversity. When we are challenged, attacked, and insulted, we naturally run to the Lord as our defender. Ah, but when we are offered a new position with a higher salary, and to take it we must remove ourselves and our families from the influences that have shaped us morally and spiritually, or when our work eats up time we should spend seeking God's kingdom, we are being exposed to the subtle trap of Babylon. We have all known people who have fallen into this trap, losing spiritual vitality sometimes for years because they failed to heed warnings concerning the allurements of the world.

Alexander Solzhenitsyn tells of once having a close friend while he was imprisoned in the gulag. They saw eye to eye on everything. They enjoyed the same things and liked to discuss the same subjects. Solzhenitsyn thought their friendship would last a lifetime. To his astonishment, however, when his friend was offered a privileged position in the prison system, he accepted it. That was the first step in a change in his friend that ultimately saw him end up as a torturer who devised horrible and cruel torments against Soviet prisoners. Solzhenitsyn described the fear in his heart when he realized that simple decisions, made in a moment with an offer of prosperity, could wreck a life when attack and insult had been unable to shake a person's faith.

The great test of faith comes not when we receive news that offends us, insults us, or seems to threaten our lives. Rather, we ought to take offers of prosperity and blessing, spread these before the Lord, and listen to his wise words in evaluating what we are being promised.

> *Thank you, Father, for the wisdom of your Word regarding the true threats to my life. Help me to remember that I have an enemy who can blatantly attack my faith or who can come with allurements of greater prosperity, better conditions, or more honor. Grant me the wisdom to evaluate such threats.*

Do we measure our worth by worldly gain? What if we were to gain the whole world and lose our souls? Do we need a radical reassessment of our identity?

TRUE COMFORT

A daily devotion for February 15

Read Isaiah 40:1–2.

> "Comfort, comfort my people, says your God. Speak tenderly to Jerusalem, and proclaim to her that her hard service has been completed, that her sin has been paid for, that she has received from the Lord's hand double for all her sins" (Isa. 40:1–2).

If you are familiar with Handel's Messiah, you will surely hear the music of that great oratorio in your head as you read the fortieth chapter of Isaiah. Handel chose the first verses of this chapter for the opening chorus.

In a musical overture, the themes of the piece are first presented in brief form. That is what we have in the first eleven verses of chapter 40, which Isaiah uses to introduce the chapters that follow. It is noteworthy that his first emphasis is the wonderful word of forgiveness to Israel. The prophet seems to be carried forward in time to the crucifixion and the resurrection of Jesus. He is told to announce to the disobedient nation that the basis for its forgiveness has already been accomplished. He is to speak to the heart of Jerusalem (that is what the word *tenderly* means) "that her hard service has been completed, that her sin has been paid for."

That last phrase, "double for all her sins," does not mean that God has punished the nation twice what its sins required. This is a reference to a Middle Eastern custom. If a man owed a debt he could not pay, his creditor would write the amount on a paper and nail the paper to the front door of the man's house so that everyone passing would see that here was a man who had not paid his debts. But if someone paid the debt for him, the creditor would double the paper over and nail it to the door as a testimony that the debt had been fully paid. This beautiful picture is the announcement to Israel as a nation that in the death and the resurrection of her Messiah her debt has been fully paid.

Today, Jew and Gentile alike are given the same wonderful announcement concerning their sins. In a great declaration, Paul says, "God was in Christ reconciling the world to himself, not counting their trespasses against them, and entrusting to us the ministry of reconciliation" (2 Cor. 5:19 RSV). That is the gospel—the good news. You may feel burdened by your mistakes, the wrong things you have done, or the hurt you have caused. This wondrous word of forgiveness and of reconciliation is directed to you. All you need to do is to confess your sinfulness and to believe that God himself has borne your sins. Your iniquity is pardoned, and you have received from the Lord the "doubling" for all your sins.

Thank you, Father, for the comfort of your forgiveness, which is offered to me through your Son, Jesus Christ.

When godly grief leads us to repentance, the gospel of God's amazing forgiveness brings the deepest comfort. Are we then proclaiming this good news by word and deed?

RECONSTRUCTION

A daily devotion for February 16

Read Isaiah 40:3–8.

> "A voice of one calling: 'In the wilderness prepare the way for the Lord; make straight in the desert a highway for our God. Every valley shall be raised up, every mountain and hill made low; the rough ground shall become level, the rugged places a plain'" (Isa. 40:3–4).

This passage defines the ministry of John the Baptist, the forerunner of our Lord. He announced that when the Messiah came, his ministry would include not only reconciliation but reconstruction. He declared that God would travel on a highway built in the heart. Four steps would be involved in the building process: "Every valley shall be raised up, every mountain and hill made low; the rough ground shall become level, the rugged places a plain." Construction engineers know that this is exactly how highways are built even today.

In this beautiful symbolic language, the prophet is saying that this is what God undertakes when he enters our lives. When we have received his forgiveness, he begins to change us, to reconstruct our lives. Every valley shall be raised up. In the low places of life, the discouraging times, times when we feel crushed and defeated, we will receive comfort and encouragement from the Lord. Every mountain and hill will be made low. All those places where our ego manifests itself—our proud boasts, our grasping for power—these must be cut down. We will find ourselves humbled in many ways. Then the rugged places will be made a plain. In the Gospels we read that Zacchaeus paid back fourfold all the money he had stolen from people. Our deviousness will be corrected. We will steal no more; we will report our income properly.

Ah, but there is more, as we see in verses 6 to 8. There is a word of reassurance as well. What is man? "All people are like grass, and all their faithfulness is like the flowers of the field." All the great things we boast about will fade away and disappear. All man's knowledge and power will amount to nothing. "The grass withers and the flowers fall, because the breath of the Lord blows on them ... but the word of our God endures forever." What a comfort that ought to be to us! Our natural strength will never accomplish what we want; human help will fail us. "But the word of our God endures forever."

> *Lord, I see that you are at work in my life, raising up valleys, lowering mountains, and making the rugged places plain. Grant that I might stay pliable in your hands as you shape me into the person you want me to be.*

The choice for life's adventure is our way or God's highway. Whether valley, mountain, or rough ground, are we leaving the reconstruction to the chief engineer?

WHO IS LIKE OUR GOD?

A daily devotion for February 17

Read Isaiah 40:12–20.

> "Who has measured the waters in the hollow of his hand, or with the breadth of his hand marked off the heavens? Who has held the dust of the earth in a basket, or weighed the mountains on the scales and the hills in a balance?" (Isa. 40:12).

This section has some of the most majestic and superb language about God found in Scripture. God himself is asking man, "Can you do what I do? Can you hold the earth's waters in the hollow of your hand?" I stood on the beach in San Diego on a gorgeous day, watching the great combers coming in from the Pacific Ocean. As I saw those giant billows crashing on the sand, I thought of the vastness of the Pacific, extending thousands upon thousands of miles to the west. These words came to my mind: "Who has measured the waters in the hollow of his hand?" In his majesty and greatness, God controls all the forces of the earth.

Verses 13 and 14 speak of God's incredible wisdom. "Who has directed the Spirit of the Lord, or as his counselor has instructed him?" (Isa. 40:13 RSV). Who could do that? Many make the attempt. I confess there have been times when I have been confronted with a difficult problem that I analyzed and thought I had solved. Then I have come to God and told him step by step what he could do to work out the problem—only to find, to my utter astonishment, that he completely ignored my approach and did nothing about it.

I have become irritated over this. I have said to him, "Lord, even I can see how to work this out. Surely you ought to be able to understand." But as the problem remained, and a whole new situation came to light, I realized that God saw far more than I could see, that he knew of obstacles I had not recognized, complexities that touched the lives of hundreds of people. He was working out purposes that would continue not only for the moment but for one generation after another. His solution ultimately was the best one. I had to say, as the apostle Paul says, "O the depth of the riches and wisdom and knowledge of God! How unsearchable are his judgments and how inscrutable his ways!" (Rom. 11:33 RSV).

In verses 15 to 17, God compares himself with the proud nations of earth. "Behold, the nations are like a drop from a bucket, and are accounted as the dust on the scales; behold, he takes up the isles like fine dust" (Isa. 40:15 RSV). How feeble seem the boasts of men, the leaders of the nations, with their claims to glory and might, when compared with the greatness, the majesty, and the strength of God. They are nothing, God says, absolutely nothing.

> *Almighty and eternal God, I humble myself before you as the creator and sustainer of all things. Who am I that I should question your ways? I gladly submit my will to yours and trust that you will work out even the most difficult of circumstances.*

Do we consider the absurdity of questioning or propositioning the almighty and sovereign God? Do we pray with Jesus, "Thy will be done," or the futile folly of "My will be done"?

GOSPEL PARADOX

A daily devotion for February 18

Read Isaiah 44:1–5.

> "For I will pour water on the thirsty land, and streams on the dry ground; I will pour out my Spirit on your offspring, and my blessing on your descendants" (Isa. 44:3).

Chapter 44 opens with a beautiful promise, spoken by God through the prophet. Here is pictured the refreshment of spirit that God gives to those who are thirsty, those who recognize the dryness of their lives and who come to him for supply. Notice that the promise extends even to their offspring. Here is a great word for families: God will bless them as they take the role of a suppliant and bring their needs before him.

As is the case many times in Isaiah, all this is to be ultimately true of the nation of Israel. We must never steal these promises from the Jewish people. God will fulfill them one of these days. But his pledge also applies to those who, by faith in Jesus Christ, have become sons and daughters of Abraham. God's promises to pour water on the thirsty and to provide streams on the dry ground are made to us as well. This is one of the most remarkable paradoxes in the Scriptures. What man could ever devise a plan that allows us to win if we lose, to be lifted up if we are broken? But that is God's plan. He always deals realistically with us. He will not force us to be humiliated, but he wants us to face the whole picture. He is totally honest. He knows exactly who we are and what our problem is. The folly of man is that he seeks to smooth that over and to pretend to be something he is not. All this is remarkable proof that the Bible is a divine book, for no man would ever come up with a program for success that starts with an admission of failure.

A seminary professor told me how he went to a county jail one day to spend a few hours helping prisoners with their spiritual problems. As he was eating alone in the cafeteria at lunch time, he met a lawyer who would spend a whole day each week helping prisoners. But he did not use his legal expertise to counsel them. He sought instead to help by reading the Scriptures to them and by aiding them in spiritual matters. The professor said to him, "Don't you find it rather depressing, working with these losers all the time?" The man replied, "I don't look at them that way. To me, there are only two kinds of people in the world: the forgiven and the unforgiving. These men and women are locked up physically. You can find a key, open the door, and let them out, but no one yet has found the key that opens their inner life except God."

That is a beautiful expression of what Isaiah is saying. If you are locked up inside yourself, a prisoner of your pride and self-sufficiency, God can open the door and let you out. This is what he promises to do and has done for centuries.

> *Father, I thank you that my thirst can become the occasion for receiving your refreshment, which is like a stream running on dry ground. Thank you for the freedom I experience when I let go of my pride and self-sufficiency and trust you to lift me up.*

Are we polluting the heritage of our descendants by our pride and arrogance? Christ humbled himself so that he could liberate us from our illusion of self-sufficiency. Will we choose this path to wholeness?

WORTHLESS IDOLS

A daily devotion for February 19

Read Isaiah 44:6–20.

> "This is what the Lord says—Israel's King and Redeemer, the Lord Almighty: I am the first and I am the last; apart from me there is no God" (Isa. 44:6).

Critics of the Bible sometimes complain that God is constantly bragging about himself. But this is not empty boasting. He is simply declaring reality. This is God's attempt to save his creatures from the folly and danger of following false gods. Today's passage goes on to describe the stupidity of the idol worship that the Israelites were falling into. The prophet describes a blacksmith who melts metal, pours it into a mold to make an idol, and in the process becomes tired. Isaiah points out what a ridiculous thing it is that a man makes a god who has no power to help him even while he is making it. Then Isaiah describes a carpenter who carves the figure of a man out of a block of wood and uses the leftover chips of wood to build a fire to warm himself. He then bows down and worships the idol, seeking deliverance from something his own hands have made. What a ridiculous concept!

When we read a passage like this we are tempted to say, "Surely this does not apply to us. We are not idol worshipers." But we are not that far removed from this kind of practice. As I drive to church on Sunday mornings, I often notice people out in their yards worshiping a shiny metal idol. They pour expensive fluids into it, polish it, and bow down before it. Have you ever noticed the change that comes over them when they get into this idol and take off down the street? Mild, inoffensive people, who never utter a word in anger, blast out of their driveways, leaving a trail of rubber as they depart, transformed by the illusion of power. One item we worship is the automobile, which to many has become the symbol of luxury, beauty, and power.

Silicon Valley is one of the great idol-manufacturing areas of the world, shipping out computers, strange machines with flashing lights and weird symbols, to worshipers of knowledge in the far corners of the earth. Many today worship the god of sex, thinking that sex will satisfy them and fulfill their needs. But the god of sex will not deliver them. It is true we no longer have idols of wood and stone, but the ideas behind them remain the central idols of the American people.

The prophet declares of the idolater, "He feeds on ashes; a deluded mind has led him astray, and he cannot deliver himself or say, 'Is there not a lie in my right hand?'" (Isa. 44:20 RSV). The folly of worshiping any god other than the true God is that people deceive themselves. They are left dissatisfied, feeling they have been feeding on ashes. The soul, as well as the body, needs food. It looks for what satisfies. But those who look for satisfaction in drugs or sex discover that they have been feeding on ashes. They have been deceived, failing to recognize that there is a lie in their right hand.

The right hand is the symbol of what we grasp, whom we look to for help. But those who follow idols are unable to see that they will not satisfy but will leave a taste of ashes in the mouth. Many businessmen worship the god of power. They are climbing the corporate ladder to the top, seeking honor and recognition. When they have all they want, however, they will find it has turned to ashes. Many students worship knowledge. They feel confident that the wonderful things they are learning will help them control life. But it all turns to ashes. They do not recognize the lie that is in the right hand. The only hope, as this passage makes clear, is found in the God who formed us.

> *Gracious Father, you are the only true God. Forgive me for worshiping the creation rather than the Creator, and teach me to bow down before you and you alone.*

The first commandment says we are to have no other gods but God himself. Are we trying to fill the God-shaped vacuum inside us with everything and everyone but God?

TURN TO ME AND BE SAVED

A daily devotion for February 20

Read Isaiah 45:9–25.

> "Woe to those who quarrel with their Maker, those who are nothing but potsherds among the potsherds on the ground. Does the clay say to the potter, 'What are you making?' Does your work say, 'The potter has no hands?'" (Isa. 45:9).

It would be ridiculous if clay were to say to the potter, "I don't like the way you're doing this. This design does not appeal to me at all." Observe the irony of this passage: "Woe to him who says to a father, 'What are you begetting?' or to a woman, 'With what are you in travail?'" (Isa. 45:10 RSV). We are dealing with God. How incredibly arrogant of man to criticize his workings! This passage is designed to humble man in his proud confidence and to show him how dependent he is upon the God whom he dares to criticize. C. S. Lewis once pointed out that to contend with God is to contend with the One who makes it possible for us to contend in the first place, and how foolish we are to attempt that!

From this passage we learn that human folly takes two main forms: self-sufficiency—man imagining that he is God and that he can run the world—or idolatry, with man trusting in something other than the true God. Either one, according to this account and as confirmed by history, results in slavery and tragedy. This folly is behind the rise of totalitarianism in our day.

God offers an answer: "Turn to me and be saved, all the ends of the earth! For I am God, and there is no other" (Isa. 45:22–23 RSV). How hopeless it is for man to try to find his own way out of the morass he has made! In the nineteenth century, the Spirit of God used this verse to speak to the heart of a fifteen-year-old boy in England. That boy, Charles Hadden Spurgeon, took shelter in a little Methodist chapel on a cold and snowy day in 1850. As there was no preacher, the deacon read the text, "Look unto me and be ye saved, all the ends of the earth," and seeing a lonely boy sitting in the back, the deacon (who could not speak very well) addressed Spurgeon, telling him to look to God and he would be saved. Spurgeon later said that he then looked, and he was saved. He went on to become one of the great preachers of the English church.

This is the way that God offers to mankind: "Look to me." We should not look to science or to technology. These are fine in themselves, offering certain creature comforts, but they cannot deliver us. They cannot satisfy us or meet our needs. If we pursue them, they will turn to ashes. God is the only deliverer from human hurt and failure.

> *Thank you, Father, for this precious promise. How beautifully it has been fulfilled in so many lives and through all the ages. May I recognize how foolish it is to trust in anything but your presence in my life.*

When we as Christians claim Jesus is Lord, do we then surrender willingly to the process of becoming Christlike? Are we being transformed by the renewing of our minds?

WORD FOR THE DISCOURAGED

A daily devotion for February 21

Read Isaiah 49:8–26.

> "Can a mother forget the baby at her breast and have no compassion on the child she has borne? Though she may forget, I will not forget you! See, I have engraved you on the palms of my hands; your walls are ever before me" (Isa. 49:15–16).

Here Jehovah reminds Israel, "Though you may feel neglected and forgotten, I cannot cast you off. I will never forget you. Can a mother forget the baby at her breast?" Proverbially, of course, a mother's love is the strongest love of all. Many mothers continue to love their children no matter what they do. Unfortunately, mothers can forget their children. But God cannot: "See, I have engraved you on the palms of my hands." We are reminded of that scene when Jesus, after his resurrection, appeared to his frightened disciples, huddled together in the upper room, and said to them, "Behold, my hands and my feet and see that it is I" (Luke 24:39). Those wounds in his hands were marks of love; the disciples' names were engraved in his hands.

Though this passage is addressed to Israel as a nation, we Christians have a right to claim these promises for ourselves. This entire section is a great word for discouraged hearts. Do you ever feel that God has forgotten you, that he has turned his back on you? Perhaps you have made mistakes, and you think that God is going to punish you all the rest of your life. Many people feel that God has totally forgotten them.

I was speaking to a group of pastors and was encouraged to hear one of them say he had learned that he was preaching to the wrong crowd of people. He thought he was preaching to the average family: a man and a wife and their two and a half children, living in a beautiful home on an acre of ground and owning a nice car. But he discovered that he was speaking mostly to people who lived in high-rise apartments, drove sports cars, had been divorced, and had families consisting of children from current and former marriages. They were living empty lives, climbing the corporate ladder, feeling the rush and the restlessness of life, and were troubled by many inner problems and distresses. But God has a ministry to the discouraged and defeated ones. He will restore them and do a work that will leave them amazed and baffled at the wonders that he produces.

> *Thank you, Lord, that you love to reach out to the discouraged and defeated ones. Thank you that you reached out to me and that my name is engraved on your hands.*

Because we know that Jesus is God and that he assumed our sins in his body on the cross, we know that he is Immanuel, God with us in deepest compassion and love. How do we respond to such infinite love?

GOD'S SERVANT

A daily devotion for February 22

Read Isaiah 50.

> "The Sovereign Lord has given me a well-instructed tongue, to know the word that sustains the weary. He wakens me morning by morning, wakens my ear to listen like one being instructed. The Sovereign Lord has opened my ears; I have not been rebellious, I have not turned away. I offered my back to those who beat me, my cheeks to those who pulled out my beard; I did not hide my face from mocking and spitting" (Isa. 50:4–6).

Two remarkable things are described here by the servant. He says first that "morning by morning" God has taught him truth because he listened to his Father. Remember the many times in his ministry when Jesus said, "The things that I say unto you I have heard from my Father." Again and again he made that claim. He had the ear of a learner. He pored over the Scriptures and saw himself in them. He understood what his work would be and realized that he would have to endure anguish, pain, and rejection. But he says, "I was not rebellious. I was willing to go ahead. I gave my back to the smiters and my cheeks to those who pulled out my beard. I hid not my face from shame and spitting."

We do well to remember frequently the sufferings of Jesus, the sheer physical agony that he endured. Think of the Last Supper when he said his soul was "exceeding sorrowful unto death" (Mark 14:34 KJV); the shadows of Gethsemane among the olive trees; his loneliness, his prayers, his disappointment with his disciples; his bloody sweat, the traitor's kiss, the binding, the blow to the face; the spitting, the scourging, the buffeting, the mocking, the crown of thorns, the smiting; the sorrowful way and the burdensome cross he had to bear. Think of his exhaustion, his collapse, the stripping of his garments, the impaling on the cross, the jeers of his foes and the flight of his friends; the hours on the cross, the darkness, his terrible cry of anguish, "My God, my God, why hast thou forsaken me?" (Matt. 27:46, Mark 15:34 KJV). And then the end at last: "It is finished" (John 19:30). The prophet anticipated every one of these events, and all were fulfilled in Jesus.

We also do well to recall what the epistle to the Hebrews says. "We have not a high priest who cannot be touched with the feelings of our infirmities" (Heb. 4:15 KJV). Jesus has been through it all. "He was in all points tempted like as we are, yet without sin" (Heb. 4:15 KJV).

Lord Jesus, thank you for being obedient to your Father. Thank you for enduring so much so that I might be set free.

The Lord Jesus Christ voluntarily suffered far greater suffering than we will ever experience. Are we worshiping our High Priest, who continues to bear our burdens and to intercede for us?

WHERE TO LOOK?

A daily devotion for February 23

Read Isaiah 51:1–16.

> "Listen to me, you who pursue righteousness and who seek the Lord: Look to the rock from which you were cut and to the quarry from which you were hewn; look to Abraham, your father, and to Sarah, who gave you birth. When I called him he was only one man, and I blessed him and made him many" (Isa. 51:1–2).

Chapters 51 and 52 give specific steps that believers can take when they feel discouraged and forsaken by God. This marvelous section is centered around the phrase "Listen to me," which is repeated several times. These steps give great insight into God's program for the discouraged.

Notice he says that if you are discouraged, look back and see from where you have come! Israel was to look back to Abraham, back to the time before he left Ur of the Chaldees. He had nothing and was between a rock and a hard place! But God called him and gave him everything. Look at Sarah. She didn't undergo the ordeal of childbearing until she was ninety years old. Yet God multiplied her offspring to become the nation of Israel.

When you are discouraged, look back. You may not be what you want to be or even what you ought to be, but thank God you are not what you were! Remember Paul's words to the Corinthian believers. "Neither the immoral, nor idolaters, nor adulterers, nor homosexuals, nor thieves, nor the greedy, nor drunkards, nor revilers, nor robbers will inherit the kingdom of God" (1 Cor. 6:9–10 RSV). But the apostle continues, "And such were some of you. But you were washed, you were sanctified, you were justified in the name of our Lord Jesus Christ and by the Spirit of our God" (1 Cor. 6:11 RSV). Look back. Has God changed you? Has he altered your inner life and changed your heart?

Then God says, "My righteousness draws near speedily, my salvation is on the way, and my arm will bring justice to the nations. The islands will look to me and wait in hope for my arm" (Isa. 51:5). So also look ahead. A new day is coming! God is at work. We are not headed for darkness and despair. We are headed for peace, light, and glory, for power and ministry such as we could never imagine. The apostle says, "This light affliction, which is but for a moment, is working for us an exceeding weight of glory" (2 Cor. 4:17 RSV). That is what lies ahead. We must endure darkness here for a while, but it will not last forever. Once in a meeting where people were sharing their favorite Bible verses, I heard a man say, "My favorite are those verses that begin, 'And it came to pass.' When I face discouragement, I say to myself, *It didn't come to stay; it came to pass.*" That is what God is saying. The trials will not last forever. We are headed for light, for peace, and for glory.

> *Thank you, Father, you who know me so well, for encouraging me in my distress. I am not forsaken; I am not neglected. You have inscribed me on the palms of your hands, and you will not forget your promises to me.*

God's plan for his people is to give us a future with hope, and in his sovereignty he will complete that plan. Are we confidently trusting him to fulfill his certain promises?

OUR GOD REIGNS

A daily devotion for February 24

Read Isaiah 52:1–12.

> "How beautiful on the mountains are the feet of those who bring good news, who proclaim peace, who bring good tidings, who proclaim salvation, who say to Zion, 'Your God reigns!'" (Isa. 52:7).

A few years ago I was in England, preaching in churches in the London area. I spoke one night in a crowded Methodist chapel where many were singing the chorus "Our God Reigns." I was amused to see on the sheet from which the congregation was singing an error in the title of the hymn. The typist had made it "Our God Resigns"!

Many Christians act as if God has resigned. But he has not. Our God reigns! This is what we must declare. We must show it on our faces, and let it be heard in our voices. God will come and the terrible times will end. We (and Israel) will one day hear the welcome summons: "Depart, depart, go out from there! Touch no unclean thing! Come out from it and be pure, you who carry the articles of the Lord's house" (Isa. 52:11).

That is what is required of Christians today. We are not to go along with all the mistaken ways of the world, chasing illusions and seeking things that will not satisfy. Rather, we should cleanse ourselves, because we are promised, "But you will not leave in haste or go in flight; for the Lord will go before you, the God of Israel will be your rear guard" (Isa. 52:12).

We are so often like the Israelites at the Red Sea, the water before us, Pharaoh's army hard on our heels. We do not know where to turn or what to do. But then the word of the Lord comes, "Stand firm and you will see the deliverance the Lord will bring you today" (Ex. 14:13). That is the way out. We must trust in our Lord. He will open a way through the sea.

> *Thank you, Father, that I have nowhere to turn but to you and that you are faithful. I trust that you will go before me and be my rear guard.*

Does our life message confidently proclaim that our God reigns despite the difficulties we may be facing?

AN ASTONISHING IMPACT

A daily devotion for February 25

Read Isaiah 52:13–15.

> "Behold, my servant shall prosper, he shall be exalted and lifted up, and shall be very high. As many were astonished at him—his appearance was so marred, beyond human semblance, and his form beyond that of the sons of men—so shall he startle many nations" (Isa. 52:13–15 RSV).

This section, which describes the remarkable impact that the Messiah would make upon humanity, opens with a declaration that he would be successful in all that he did: "Behold, my servant shall prosper." That success would be accomplished in three specific stages: "He shall be exalted; he shall be lifted up; he shall be very high."

First, the words "He shall be exalted" point to the resurrection. Jesus was brought back from the dead, rising to a level of life that no man had ever experienced before. Lazarus had been resurrected in a sense, but he merely returned to this earthly life. Jesus, however, became the "firstborn from the dead" (Col. 1:18). He was thus exalted to a higher dimension of existence.

Second, "he shall be lifted up." After his resurrection, Jesus took his disciples to the Mount of Olives, and while he was speaking to them he ascended into the heavens where a cloud received him and transported him out of sight. So he was physically lifted up.

Third, the passage says, "He shall be very high." The Hebrew puts it rather graphically: "He shall be high, very." We cannot but recall the words of the apostle Paul: "Therefore God exalted him to the highest place and gave him the name that is above every name, that at the name of Jesus every knee should bow, in heaven and on earth and under the earth, and every tongue acknowledge that Jesus Christ is Lord, to the glory of God the Father" (Phil. 2:9–11). Thus by his resurrection, his ascension, and his kingly exaltation the Messiah has made a tremendous impact upon humanity.

Further, it says here that "many were astonished at him." This happened in two ways. First, as verse 14 implies, many were astonished at his death: "His appearance was so marred, beyond human semblance, and his form beyond that of the sons of men." This describes the face of Jesus after he had endured the terrible Roman scourging, the beatings, the blows to his face with the rod, which the soldiers mockingly called a king's scepter, and the cruel crown of thorns upon his head. This is what the prophet sees: our Lord's appearance was so marred that those who passed by were astounded at his visage.

But verse 15 describes another form of astonishment: "so shall he startle many nations." This refers to his tremendous accomplishments, not only during his ministry but through the centuries since. Many have commented on the remarkable achievements of Jesus. G. K. Chesterton, the famous English Christian novelist and literary critic, said that he'd once read of a man who dwelt in the Middle East centuries ago and that he could not from then on look at a sheep or a sparrow, a lily or a cornfield, a raven or a sunset, a vineyard or a mountain without thinking of that man. If this was not divine, Chesterton wondered, what then was it? Truly, our Lord has made an astonishing impact upon our world. He is the man who cannot be forgotten.

> *Thank you, Lord Jesus, for all you have done for me. I praise you and worship you because you continue to astonish me with your impact on my life and on many other lives throughout the world.*

The man Jesus has had an incomparable impact on world history. What are three startling fulfillments of Scripture verses describing details of his unique appearance? How do we respond to this, the greatest story ever told?

THE HEART OF THE GOSPEL

A daily devotion for February 26

Read Isaiah 53:1–6.

"We all, like sheep, have gone astray; each of us has turned to our own way; and the Lord has laid on him the iniquity of us all" (Isa. 53:6).

This, of course, is the heart of the gospel, the good news. Jesus took our place. As Peter puts it, "He himself bore our sins in his body on the cross" (1 Peter 2:24). He took our sins and paid the price for them. He had no sins of his own, and Scripture is careful to record that fact. He was not suffering for his own transgressions but for the sins of others. English Poet Dora Greenwell once introduced what we must understand about this, namely that Jesus died both for me and for a world of men, none of whom were able to give to Him the love he bestowed in that sacrifice. We could never on our own have come to Jesus to be loved like this, and so He loved us amid our worst rebellion. Jesus would not have needed to die for me if I could have loved Him first.

That is the problem, isn't it? Why do not we love him first? Why is it that we learn to love our Lord only when we have beheld his suffering—his excruciating agony on our behalf? The reason is our transgressions, as this passage declares. They have cut us off from recognizing the divine gift of love that ought to be in every human heart.

Sin is a disease that has afflicted our entire race. We cannot understand the depth of human depravity until we see the awful agony through which our Lord passed, behold the hours of darkness, and hear the terrible orphaned cry, "My God, my God, why have you forsaken me?" (Matt. 27:46). All this spells out for us what we are really like. Most of us think of ourselves as decent people, as good people. We have not done some of the terrible things that others have done. But when we see the cross of Jesus, we realize the depth of evil in our hearts and understand that sin is a disease that has infiltrated our whole lives. Man, who was created in the image of God and once wore the glory of his origin, has become bruised and marred, sick and broken, his conscience ruined, his understanding faulty, his will enfeebled. Integrity and the resolve to do right have been completely undermined in all of us. We know this to be true.

No wonder, then, that this verse comes as the best of news. Jesus was wounded for our transgressions. The bruising that he felt was the chastisement that we deserved, but it was laid upon him.

There is no way we can read this and fail to see that our Lord is the great divine substitute for the evil of the human heart. We can lay hold of this personally by the honest admission stated in verse 6: "We all, like sheep, have gone astray; each of us has turned to our own way." How true that is of us all! Who can claim anything else? I grew up in Montana, and I know something about sheep. Sheep are foolish and willful creatures. They can find a hole in a fence and get out, but they cannot find it to get back in. Someone must go and get them every time. How true it is that each of us has turned to his own way.

Years ago Frank Sinatra sang, "I did it my way." That sounds like something admirable, something everybody ought to emulate. How proud we feel that we did it "our way." But the record of Scripture shows that this is the problem, not the solution. We have a race that is in constant conflict, forever striving with one another, unable to work anything out, because we all insist on doing it "our way."

The way to lay hold of the redemption of Jesus is to admit that "we all, like sheep, have gone astray," each turning to his own way, but to remember that "the Lord has laid on him the iniquity of us all." He bore our punishment and took our place.

Thank you, Lord, for taking my punishment upon yourself. Forgive me for those times when I still seek to do things my way rather than yours.

Sin puts everyone in equal need of redemption. Jesus died for us all so that we might no longer live for ourselves but out of worship and gratitude for his atoning death. Do our lives disparage this amazing grace?

SILENT WITNESS

A daily devotion for February 27

Read Isaiah 53:7–9.

"He was oppressed and afflicted, yet he did not open his mouth; he was led like a lamb to the slaughter, and as a sheep before its shearers is silent, so he did not open his mouth" (Isa. 53:7).

Scripture emphasizes the sinlessness of Jesus. He was without sin, but he bore the sins of others. The Lord did this in silence. He had no interest in defending himself, so he never spoke in his own defense. It is striking that in the gospel accounts of the trials of Jesus he never spoke in his own behalf or tried to escape the penalty. This amazed Pilate and Caiaphas. When our Lord stood before the high priest, he was silent until the high priest put him under oath to tell who he was. When he stood before Pilate, he was silent until to remain silent was to deny his kingship. Then he spoke briefly, acknowledging who he was. When he was with the soldiers, they smote him, spat on him, and put the crown of thorns on his head, yet he said not a word. Peter says, "When they hurled insults at him, he did not retaliate" (1 Peter 2:23). When Jesus went before contemptuous, sneering Herod, he stood absolutely silent. He would not say one word to him. He was returned at last to Pilate because Herod could find no wrong in him.

It is apparent to anyone reading the gospel accounts that the trials Jesus went through were a farce. The Jewish trial before the high priest was illegal. It was held at night, contrary to the law. Pilate several times admitted that he could find no wrong in him, and yet he pronounced upon him the sentence of death. How true are these words in Isa. 53:8: "By oppression and judgment he was taken away." Remember that as the onlookers were crying out, "Crucify him, crucify him," they added these significant words: "Let his blood be upon us and upon our children." Thus they acknowledged that Jesus was indeed "stricken for the transgressions of my people."

But when at last the deed was done and our Lord cried in a loud voice, "It is finished" (John 19:30), his friends came to take him down from the cross. No enemy hands touched his body after his death, only those who loved him. As they removed his bloody body, the dear lips were silent, the wondrous voice was stilled, the light had gone from his eyes, and the great heart beat no more. But instead of throwing him on a rubbish heap, as the authorities intended, his friends "made his grave with the rich," just as Isaiah had predicted years before the event. Joseph of Arimathea, a rich man, offered to put the body of Jesus in his new tomb, which had never been used. Someone has put that rather remarkably, writing, "He who came from a virgin womb must be laid in a virgin tomb."

It is with awe and wonder, Lord, that I reflect upon all that you went through to secure the salvation of your people. Thank you, Lord.

Jesus was silent before all his accusers, since he had no sin to confess. He bore unimaginable punishment for our sin. How can we do less than confess our sins and worship the One who paid for our forgiveness?

A LOVE STORY

A daily devotion for February 28

Read Isaiah 53:10–12.

> "Because he poured out his life unto death, and was numbered with the transgressors" (Isa. 53:12).

When I first came to Peninsula Bible Church as a pastor, we had an unusual opportunity to have in our home a Japanese man who had become a Christian evangelist. He was Captain Mitsuo Fuchida, the commander of the squadron that bombed Pearl Harbor on December 7, 1941. In his broken English, he told us of that event and recalled how he felt at the time he gave the command to drop the bombs. After the war he became a hero in Japan, yet he felt his life was empty. Then he heard the amazing story of an American flier, Jacob DeShazer, one of Doolittle's bombers, who had been captured and put in prison in Japan. At first he was an intractable prisoner, but someone gave him a New Testament, and after reading it, his life was changed.

Fuchida heard about that change in DeShazer's life, and he himself began to read the New Testament. When he came to the story of the crucifixion, he told us, he was startled by the prayer that broke from the lips of Jesus as he hung upon the cross with his torturers and tormentors gathered about him: "Father, forgive them, for they know not what they are doing" (Luke 23:34). Fuchida's own heart broke. He could not understand how anyone could pray for his enemies and ask for them to be forgiven. At that moment he opened his heart to Christ. He ultimately became a Christian evangelist. For some years Fuchida traveled throughout this country, speaking especially to young people about the grace that could come into a life through One who was "numbered with the transgressors … and made intercession for them."

This is a love story. What kind of love is this that awakens within us a response of deep and abiding gratitude, a willingness to admit that we need help? Our only adequate response is found in the words of a hymn.

"Oh, love that will not let me go, I rest my weary soul in thee. I give thee back the life I owe that in thine ocean depths its flow may richer, fuller be."

I am overwhelmed by your great love,
O Lord, which will never let me go and
which is changing me into your likeness.

The realization that the perfect and sinless Jesus became sin for us should break our hearts and radically change our lives. Does his sacrificial love redefine love as both noun and verb, as both essence and expression? Are we learning to love for Jesus's sake and by the power of his presence?

WHY DOESN'T GOD DO SOMETHING?

A daily devotion for February 29

Read Isaiah 61.

> "The Spirit of the Sovereign Lord is on me, because the Lord has anointed me to proclaim good news to the poor. He has sent me to bind up the brokenhearted, to proclaim freedom for the captives and release from darkness for the prisoners, to proclaim the year of the Lord's favor and the day of vengeance of our God" (Isa. 61:1–2).

Luke's gospel records that on one occasion Jesus entered the synagogue in Nazareth, as was his custom, and asked for the scroll of the prophet Isaiah. He unrolled it until he found the place where these words were written. Then he read this passage, which said that the Spirit had come upon him and anointed him and that he was called to preach the gospel, to bind up the brokenhearted, and to proclaim liberty to captives. Jesus stopped reading in the middle of a sentence, after the words "to proclaim the year of the Lord's favor." Then he closed the scroll, handed it back to the attendant, sat down, and said, "This day is this Scripture fulfilled in your hearing."

Note carefully where Jesus stopped reading. He did not go on to read, "and the day of vengeance of our God," because when he first came he introduced "the day of God's favor," the day when God withholds his judgment.

This is the answer to the question many people ask: "Why doesn't God do something?" The answer is, because he is giving people everywhere a chance! When he finally judges, he will judge the whole world—everybody in it, without exception. The only ones who will escape the penalty of that judgment are those who have already bowed to his will. Then he will begin "the day of vengeance of our God," the phrase Jesus did not read that day in the synagogue. The comma at which he stopped reading has been called "the longest comma in history." "The year of the Lord's favor" now covers almost two thousand years, but it will be followed by "the day of vengeance of our God."

Notice the contrast between "the year of his grace" and "the day of vengeance." God does not like vengeance. He does not delight in judgment. Isaiah calls it "his strange work." But it must be done eventually, though it will be kept as brief as possible. This is what prophecy records as "the time of the end."

> *Thank you, Father, for this honest and searching book. How beautifully it describes the program of history, much of which remains unfulfilled. I see you there and begin to understand the majesty and the mercy of your being. Help me to adjust my life accordingly, to come humbly and contritely before you to obtain the mercy I so desperately need.*

What is the astounding message Jesus preached, and to whom was he preaching "the year of the Lord's favor"? Are we participating in his message of grace, peace, and release from darkness? Do we leave the judgment of evil to God's sovereign plan and timing?

PHILIPPIANS

Christ, Our Confidence and Strength
An introduction for the month of March

We begin our studies in the letter to the Philippians. I consider this the most delightful epistle of the New Testament. A wonderful note of joy and thanksgiving runs throughout this epistle, and yet this is one of the so-called prison epistles written while Paul was held captive. It was written to the saints in Philippi. If you have a Bible atlas, you will find that this was a Roman colony situated in the area called Macedonia in ancient times. It was the first place Paul preached the gospel in Europe. You will remember the thrilling account in the sixteenth chapter of Acts of Paul and Silas as they entered Macedonia in answer to the call of the people there. They ended up in a prison cell where in the dead of night they were singing praises to the Lord when an earthquake shook loose the prison walls and they were delivered. As someone has cleverly observed, the gospel first entered Europe in a sacred concert that was so successful it brought down the house. So this letter to the Philippians has a tremendously interesting background.

We probably know more about Philippi than about any church, and the apostle was writing believers there as a prisoner in Rome awaiting trial. We know the background of this letter from the closing chapter of the book of Acts. In the sixteenth verse of chapter 28, Luke writes, "When we came into Rome Paul was allowed to live by himself, with a soldier to guard him." Luke doesn't tell us this, but we know from Roman custom that the soldier was chained to the apostle. The guard was changed about three times a day, and the apostle was never allowed to be more than a chain's length away from the soldier who guarded him.

But Luke also tells us Paul lived those two years at his own expense, welcoming all who came to him, preaching the kingdom of God, and teaching about the Lord Jesus Christ quite openly and unhindered though under house arrest. Though he was fettered and guarded and watched continuously, Paul had a degree of freedom that permitted him to have his friends visit, to have his own home. In that setting he wrote this letter to the church in Philippi.

Lord, what a marvelous reminder of the peace you alone give us, not conditional or circumstantial, but wholly dependent on your presence within us. Thank you for Paul's faithfulness from a place where he could easily have quit. May I find strength and confidence in you alone, in whatever place you may lead me, as I study this letter to the Philippians. In your Son's name. Amen.

IN CHRIST

A daily devotion for March 1

Read Philippians 1:1–2.

> "Paul and Timothy, servants of Christ Jesus, to all God's holy people in Christ Jesus at Philippi" (Phil. 1:1).

The ancient practice of correspondence had one distinct advantage over our modern method. The writers signed their names at the beginning of the letters. Have you ever received a letter, perhaps two or three pages long, and had to flip through to the end to find out who sent it? The ancients were much more efficient, putting their names at the start.

The address of the letter is distinctive: "to the saints in Christ at Philippi." "In Christ" was the source of their lives. Philippi was the sphere in which they lived their faith. Both are important in this letter, for what these people would be as citizens of Philippi would be determined by who they were as Christians—"in Christ."

As you read this letter, you will see that four major propositions govern the Christian life. First, there are those who are without Christ. There was a time when we all were without Christ, strangers with no inheritance. As Paul wrote to the Ephesians, we were under the control of the god of this age, driven by forces of which we were unaware, and we accepted the same concepts and lies that brainwash people everywhere. We were without Christ.

Then, as with these Christians, there came a time when we were in Christ; we entered into his life, and his life entered into us by faith in his work and in his person. We became personally related to the living God. We didn't merely exercise faith in what he did or said. We knew him. We became part of him, a vital part of his life. "If anyone be in Christ he is a new creation. Old things have passed away. All things become new" (2 Cor. 5:17).

Then as we go along in life, the relationship grows, and we speak, work, and reach out for Christ. Our lives are increasingly lived on his behalf. He becomes the focus of every activity. Then, finally, there will be that moment when, as the old hymn says, "Face to face I shall behold him." We shall be with Christ forevermore.

These four propositions govern the Christian life. That life begins with our being "in Christ" in Philippi or wherever God may lead us.

> *Thank you, Father, for placing me in Christ. Teach me to see and to lay hold of all that you have for me in him.*

If we have truly entered into Christ's life, and he into ours, are we moving toward the goal of serving others in his name and by the power of his indwelling presence?

WHERE IS YOUR CONFIDENCE?

A daily devotion for March 2

Read Philippians 1:3–6.

> "Being confident of this, that he who began a good work in you will carry it on to completion until the day of Christ Jesus" (Phil. 1:6).

Perhaps Paul's joy in the people of Philippi was that he was seeing them not as they were but as they would be when God's work was done. He was viewing them with the eyes of faith. Paul was sure that the One who had begun a good work in them would finish it, so he could say, "Even though you rub me the wrong way once in a while, I know what you are going to be." This is the key to getting along with other Christians. Sometimes it's difficult, but when we realize what they will be we can do it. I heard of an artist who asked a friend to comment on a picture he was painting. He said, "This is my masterpiece. It is beautiful." The friend said, "I guess I don't see what you see. It just looks like dabs of different colors to me, without form." The artist said, "Oh, I forgot. I'm seeing it as it will be when it's finished. You are seeing it as it is now."

This is what Paul was doing. He was seeing these Christians as they would be, and he thanked God that this would happen. What a comforting verse! Many times when I am discouraged with myself, I utterly despair of being what I ought to be. I am so aware of the deceitfulness and subtlety of the flesh. Even when I want to be what I ought to be, I end up deceiving myself. I see the complete futility of depending on myself to get this job done. In those times, I try to remember this verse, "being confident of this, that he who began a good work in you will carry it on to completion until the day of Christ Jesus."

This means that life is not perfect yet. It has an adequate goal, and the goal will be reached. The final responsibility, however, is not in my hands but in God's. I love that! Paul places his confidence in the Lord, not in himself. If we know Christ, we are in the hands of the One who can change us. Sometimes we don't want to be what God wants us to be, but he is working the change in us despite ourselves. God knows how to bring us into the circumstances that will make us willing to be made willing. It's a great consolation to recognize in whose hands we are.

We Christians often give the impression that our main task is to keep Christianity going. Christianity didn't start that way. These early Christians gave the clear impression that it was their faith in Christ that kept them going. There are those who tell us that we can lose our Christian life, but if this is something we can lose, it must be based on a human factor; it must depend on us. But if it depends on us, we can't depend on it. I am so grateful that this rests upon the One who is capable of doing the work and who has promised to complete it. Thanks be to God, who is able to keep us from falling.

> *Lord, keep me from the folly of thinking that it is the crusade I launch or the activity I undertake or my busy-ness that accomplishes your will rather than what I am in Jesus Christ and all of your marvelous love flooding through my soul into my experience and my actions.*

Joy is the "serious business of heaven." It is a consequence of being preoccupied with the living and indwelling Christ, confident that he will complete his redeeming work in us and through us. Are we there yet? No, but God isn't finished either, so let's pay attention.

LOVE WITH KNOWLEDGE

A daily devotion for March 3

Read Philippians 1:7–11.

> "And this is my prayer: that your love may abound more and more in knowledge and depth of insight" (Phil. 1:9).

Now if you and I were writing a letter to new Christians, wanting to stir them to activity, what would we say? Would we not urge them to witness? That's likely because somehow in our day there has come the idea that all Christian life exists for but one purpose—that the believer may be a verbal witness. And if we are talking with someone about God, we are fulfilling all that is expected of us in our Christian lives.

But Paul doesn't say a word about this, because love in action is the greatest witness. He hopes that "your love may abound more and more"—that the love of Christ, which is in you and which you will surely find there if you are at all a believer, may now find expression in affection. That means a resulting activity—love in action, not promise but performance. I think they needed this message in Philippi, and I think we need it as well so that our love may abound in activity. Otherwise, it's as James says: "Faith without works is dead." If love doesn't show itself in action, then it's not real love.

Paul adds two things: "knowledge and depth of insight." Love by itself, left to flow unchecked, can sometimes be disastrous. Love acts like hate when it refuses to think. All of us have had experience with people who mean well but who never bother to get the facts and to see if they can help intelligently. These people can become a great nuisance. Paul says that love alone isn't enough. We must love with knowledge; we must learn the situation and see how we can help. We can't help without first investigating whether our assistance will do the job.

Paul also says we must love with depth of insight. By this he means that there are times to help and people to be helped but that there are times not to help and people who ought not to be helped. One weakness of present church life is that we give money freely to people and causes that shouldn't have it. We don't exercise discernment. Because of their attitude and their situation, some people can't be helped right away. I think of the Prodigal Son, who was living a sinful life in the far country. I believe his father had an inkling of where that boy was and what he was doing, but he never offered to help him. He couldn't. He let him go off to the far country because for the moment there was nothing else he could do. He couldn't help his son until the boy returned, and when he did his father's help was available to him.

Father, you are the One of whom it is said, "God is love." More and more, may your love come to define me and all my actions.

Are our lives as Christ's disciples motivated and informed by his quality of love? Do we seek wisdom and insight from the Holy Spirit in studying the Word and in prayer?

ADVERSITY MEANS ADVANCE

A daily devotion for March 4

Read Philippians 1:12–15.

> "Now I want you to know, brothers and sisters, that what has happened to me has actually served to advance the gospel" (Phil. 1:12).

Paul is in jail in Rome, writing to his friends far across the sea in Philippi. His reaction inevitably makes the world sit up and take notice. He understands that adversity means advance. This attitude is a mark of Christian maturity. The Christian who has become well enough acquainted with the God of the impossible whom he serves knows that even through apparent defeat, God still is able to work. Such a Christian has begun to grow up in the Lord. He recognizes that in God obstacles are opportunities and that nothing can imperil the gospel. That is an amazing declaration. Nothing intended to defeat ever brings defeat, God works his way despite obstacles, and all obstacles serve ultimately to spread the Christian faith.

I ran across the story of a Swiss pastor who was imprisoned by the Nazis during World War II. He said this: "I was not able to stand firm except by remembering every day that the Gestapo was the hand of God—the left hand. The worst of tyrants will only end by accomplishing Christ's will."

That is the glorious mark of Christianity that has made it an invincible force through all the centuries. Here is Paul, under arrest, chained day and night to a Roman soldier, unable to leave the house or the city of Rome. Imagine what this must have meant to the restless, surging spirit of this man. God had sent him out to preach the gospel to the ends of the earth.

Paul could easily have become discouraged. There is no doubt he was tempted many times to feel sorry for himself and to wonder why God would let such a thing happen to him when all he was trying to do was fulfill God's will. He could have chafed under these circumstances as month after month passed and there seemed to be no change. But in the letters he wrote during those days there is not one word of complaint. Instead we see a marvelously triumphant spirit and an expression of confidence. Why? When he was tempted Paul undoubtedly fell back on what he knew about his God. In the face of temptation to fret and to chafe, he believed God.

Earlier he had written to these Roman Christians with whom he was now meeting, saying, "All things work together for good to those who love God, who are the called according to His purpose." He believed that! Even though the immediate hour didn't bring relief, Paul believed God, and out of that confidence he could see that even those things that seemed to be against him were working out the Lord's purposes.

> *Father, help me to recognize that confidence doesn't come through an effort to convince myself or through a struggle to think positively but from a quiet reliance upon an unchangeable fact—that Jesus Christ lives his life within me and that he is quite competent to meet every situation. May I look to him and learn to rejoice in his victory.*

Paul's friends anxiously awaited news of him, but the focus of the apostle's letter was not on his imprisonment but on the undefeated purpose of God, who works to accomplish his will in every circumstance. Are we learning to trust God's ways and means so that others are encouraged by our confidence in him?

REJOICING IN OUR RIVALS

A daily devotion for March 5

Read Philippians 1:15–18.

"But what does it matter? The important thing is that in every way, whether from false motives or true, Christ is preached. And because of this I rejoice" (Phil. 1:18).

It's evident in this passage that certain Christians were jealous of Paul. These were not Judaizers. These were not false teachers. They were preaching a true gospel. They were genuine Christians, but they were jealous of Paul. Evidently they felt that they were there first and that he had usurped some of their positions. There is always readiness for envy. But many false doctrines had fallen before the Spirit of power and the cool logic and authority of the apostle as he ministered to them.

Now these people saw a chance to regain their popularity. They planned extensive campaigns in Rome and surrounding cities, hoping to eclipse the apostle in their activity and zeal for the gospel. They hoped that when word got back to Paul of how much they were doing he might feel the jealous pain they felt. But the prisoner couldn't care less. The magnanimous spirit he had in Christ made him rejoice that Christ was being preached. He said, "It doesn't matter whether they are doing it to make me feel bad. Christ is being preached, and in that I rejoice."

Can you take the success of others? That's one of the hardest tests of Christian maturity, isn't it? I don't think there is a clearer mark of Christian maturity than to be able to rejoice—not just to say pious words—in the success of another. Most of us react like the Christian I heard of in the mountains of West Virginia who, when asked how things had been going that year, said, "Oh, things have been terrible. We've had an awful year. Things have never been worse. Instead of having any progress in the church we've had setbacks and lost people." But then he smiled and said, "But thank God the Methodists haven't done any better." That spirit is the opposite of what Paul reveals here. Rivalry caused him to rejoice.

I confess, Lord, that I often have not rejoiced in the success of others and have seen it as a threat to my own sense of worth. Teach me, like Paul, to rejoice even in the success of my rivals.

Christian envy is an oxymoron! Are we among those who dishonor Christ by competitive envy? Or do we share the apostle Paul's joy when the good news is spread by whatever means?

TO LIVE OR DIE?

A daily devotion for March 6

Read Philippians 1:19–26.

> "For to me, to live is Christ and to die is gain. If I am to go on living in the body, this will mean fruitful labor for me. Yet what shall I choose? I do not know!" (Phil. 1:21–22).

The Christian view of death is given in four words in this passage: "with Christ, far better." That sums it up. But before we look more closely at that, it's important that we see what this man's view of life is, because these are not the words of someone who is sighing after heaven but is resigned to living on earth. This is not the declaration of someone who is fed up with living and is left hoping that heaven is close at hand. For Paul, to live is Christ, and that is exciting! Living, he says, means fruitful labor in which he can take the greatest delight. Paul does not find the prospect of continuing to live unwelcome. In fact, he says, "I hardly know which to choose," since both death and earthly life are so enticing and inviting. Christians are not so neurotically desirous of death that we no longer want to live. We sometimes give the wrong impression. We sing wonderful songs about the glory up there, but sometimes, unfortunately, we lead people to believe that all we're living for is what comes at the end.

The Christian does not live with some unutterable longing to escape, to evade life, to run from it. No! Paul is not saying that! He says, "To live is Christ." I love it! And evidently the Spirit of God tips the scale in favor of life, so he goes on to say, "Convinced of this I know that I shall remain, and continue with you all"—because these people need him and he will have the joy of coming to them again. But facing the possibility of death does not mean that he is tired of life but that death can only mean a deeper, more wonderful companionship with Christ. That is what makes life worth living. Paul says, "To die is gain," and you can say that only if you are prepared to say, "To live is Christ."

What for you is really living? What kind of circumstance must you have before you can say, "Oh, now I'm really living"? What do you substitute for Christ in these words of Paul? "To me, to live is money"? Then to die is to lose it all, isn't it? "To me, to live is fame"? To die means to have your name in a newspaper obituary and never to have it there again. "To me, to live is pleasure"? To die is to go out into an unknown. "To me, to live is health"? To die is to lose your health. You can see that the only thing that makes sense in life is to say with the apostle, "For me, to live is Christ," because then you can say, "To die is gain." The truth about the Christian faith is that heaven begins down here.

Father, thank you that you have given me a purpose for living. Teach me to be able to genuinely say, "For me, to live is Christ and to die is gain."

Do we live out our Christian expectations as escapists? Or are we choosing to be the planted seed that dies in order to experience abundant life? Are we experiencing the joy of union with the living Christ whether we live with him on earth or in heaven?

CITIZENS OF HEAVEN

A daily devotion for March 7

Read Philippians 1:27.

> "Whatever happens, conduct yourselves in a manner worthy of the gospel of Christ" (Phil. 1:27).

Paul uses an interesting word here, translated as "conduct" in the New International Version. From this word we get the words *politics* and *politician*. The Greek word is *politeuma*, which means conduct as a citizen or as a colony. This is the first indication in this letter of a unique condition in Philippi. Everyone in that city was aware that its people were citizens of Rome even though they were a thousand miles away. This was because the Roman emperor had won a great battle in Philippi, and in gratitude the residents were made citizens of Rome.

Paul builds on this idea and says to them, in effect, "You Christians in Philippi are members of another government. You cannot have the same attitude as the rest of the citizens of Philippi. You belong to a colony of heaven; therefore you must behave like citizens of heaven. You must let your conduct be worthy of the government to which you belong, the kingdom of God and the gospel of Christ."

As citizens of heaven, how are we to live? Paul mentions two essential things. First, "stand firm in one Spirit." We must never depart from complete dependence on the Spirit of God to do through us everything that must be done. The Christian life is totally different from the one we lived before coming to Christ. It is God's life through us. It is the indwelling Lord Jesus expressing himself in terms of our human personality. We must always keep that in mind. The second essential point is never to let anything but serious heresy keep us from working side by side in the gospel.

All the wiles of the Devil, all the thrust and the power of his activity, are aimed at these two things. To keep us from observing them, the Enemy tests us first on one point, and if he can't derail us there he goes to the other point. First, he tries to get us to depend upon ourselves, not on the indwelling life of Christ, and to make us therefore fearful, worried, discouraged, impatient, or upset. As Christians, we have all felt this. It is the attack of the Enemy, trying to budge us from our position in Christ, which makes for victory.

Whenever we get discouraged we are depending on ourselves. We're discouraged because we were expecting that we could do something and we failed. We've been self-confident, counting on ourselves, thinking we have all it takes to do the job. We think we don't need any help from God. We then move from dependence on God's Spirit. We get anxious, fearful, timid, and impatient. We have yielded to the attack of the Enemy and have temporarily shifted from that position of dependence.

If that doesn't work and we stand firm, the Enemy tries another strategy. He attempts to create a breach between us and those who labor with us. He tries to divide us, to create suspicion, smoldering resentments. and personality conflicts. He tries to stop us from talking with each other; he wants us to have nothing to do with one another, to look down on others, to cut them off from our fellowship and contact.

During spiritual warfare we often feel that every time we turn around we're under attack, that we never know when the Enemy will strike next, and that we must be constantly on guard. But that isn't true. We have only two things to watch: that we stand firm in one Spirit and that we strive side by side together in the gospel. That's all. If we are careful to keep our eyes open to the power of God working in these two areas, our conduct will become worthy of the gospel of Christ.

> *Thank you, Lord, that you have made me a citizen of heaven. Teach me to stand side by side with my brothers and sisters in Christ.*

As Christians we are fellow citizens of the commonwealth of heaven, and Satan, the Enemy, will use two main strategies in his attempt to divide and conquer us. How do we stand firm in one Spirit, behaving in a manner worthy of our high calling?

THE PRIVILEGE OF SUFFERING

A daily devotion for March 8

Read Philippians 1:28–30.

> "For it has been granted to you on behalf of Christ not only to believe in him, but also to suffer for him" (Phil. 1:29).

Remember: the Lord Jesus said, "He who saves his life shall lose it. But he who loses his life for my sake and the gospel's shall save it." We continue to try to hold on to our lives, to enjoy the things we want, and to insist on satisfying our desires and pleasures without realizing that inevitably this life is slipping through our fingers and we are losing it. The one who is willing to abandon it, throw it away if need be—waste it, seemingly—for the cause of Christ and the gospel has saved his life. If we are not prepared to suffer, we can forget about being Christians, for the Word warns us that those who would live in Christ Jesus shall suffer some degree of persecution. The Lord said, "In the world you shall have tribulation, but be of good cheer, I have overcome the world." Inevitably in the Christian life we must put up with misunderstanding, patronizing pity, ridicule, or scorn. Someone has rightly said that when we appear before the Lord he won't look us over for medals but for scars. They may not always be physical scars. The trials and the suffering we endure deepen our lives.

Oswald Chambers beautifully expressed this. He said that God is working to make us into fine wine but that we can never become what he wishes if we keep objecting to the fingers he uses to crush us. We could accept this if God used his own fingers to make us his specially broken bread and poured-out wine. But when he uses someone we dislike or circumstances that we do not want to allow, we push back. Chambers reminds us that we must not dispute the place of our own martyrdom. If we are ever to be made fine wine to drink, we must be crushed. Grapes cannot be drunk. They become wine only when they submit to the crusher.

So God has wisely ordained that life involve suffering. And this is not a sacrifice; it is a privilege that we are granted for Christ's sake. Paul said, "This is the same struggle you saw I had." He suffered emotionally and physically.

Paul endured criticism, difficulty, suffering, and rejection from his friends. This is necessary to our growth in grace. But there is one thing we need not ever do during conflict, and that is to be afraid. Fear is the enemy that will remove us from faith.

> *Father, I thank you for the struggles and difficulties you have placed in my life. I trust that these circumstances are under your control and that through them you are conforming me into the image of your dear Son.*

God's amazing grace provides the dual privileges of believing in him and of suffering with and for him. Shall we be fearful, or shall we surrender to his good and perfect purpose?

RECONCILABLE DIFFERENCES

A daily devotion for March 9

Read Philippians 2:1–4.

> "Therefore if you have any encouragement from being united with Christ … then make my joy complete by being like-minded" (Phil. 2:1–2).

Do you ever catch yourself picking someone apart flaw by flaw? Perhaps you salve your conscience by interjecting, "Now don't misunderstand me. I think the world of him, but," and off you go again. What's happened? Well, you're irritated and unconsciously seeking justification for not seeing this person again by pointing out all the terrible faults in him that make breaking off the relationship necessary. The trouble with this philosophy is that you act as though there are no alternatives left. You know how this works, don't you?

Paul says that is not true. You say there is no way to reconcile personality differences. He says that isn't true. You say there is no way you can work with a certain person, because your spiritual maturity is so much superior. Paul says that isn't true. He says there are resources in Christ that make this possible. I know what he is talking about, because I've been wrestling with this problem. Paul says you have forgotten something if you think that another person's faults are an excuse to break off a relationship. You've forgotten what you share in Christ. You've forgotten the power of Christ's life within you to overlook injuries, to forgive insults, and to be patient with weakness and immaturity. There is an alternative to breaking off relationships. You can forget faults. You can bear with others.

Then Paul discusses the resources that will allow you to do this. Is there any encouragement in Christ? That is, does the encouragement of Christ's presence and his indwelling mean anything to you? Does the Spirit within you, who loves you, offer you any incentive to love the unlovely? Does a participation in the Spirit of God give you and the other person something in common so that you know that God is at work from this person's end as well as yours? Do problems the one who is irritating you may be undergoing cause you to sympathize with him? Have you looked at the situation from his point of view? Have you tried to put yourself in his place and to appreciate the pressures he may be facing? Paul says if you can identify any such problems or pressures, then act on that basis—not with the caustic, critical attitude that tears someone apart. Cast off that attitude, which is one of Satan's best weapons for dividing Christians.

> *Lord, let me not go one more day with resentment against another, shunning the encouragement found in Christ and the incentive of his love in my heart. Make me mindful of participation in the Holy Spirit that there may be affection and sympathy in active friendship.*

Christian unity is one of the great privileges to be appreciated and preserved in his body. Are we exploring the alternatives to disunity in order to preserve this precious heritage?

THE MINDSET OF CHRIST

A daily devotion for March 10

Read Philippians 2:5–8.

"In your relationships with one another, have the same mindset as Christ Jesus" (Phil. 2:5).

Now we come to what I think is the most breathtaking passage in all of Scripture. This passage on the glorification of our Lord Jesus is the Mount Everest among the lofty peaks of revelation concerning the person of Christ, the amazing story of how the Son of God stepped out of eternity into time and became a man as God intended man to be. These few short verses capture some of the most amazing truths that have confronted the minds of men.

As we study this passage we may be tempted to remove it from its context and to treat it as a passage on theology. We must never forget that this passage is set against the background of two quarreling ladies in the church at Philippi. That quarrel threatened to destroy the unity of the whole church. The apostle has made it clear that the secret to maintaining unity is humility. Contentiousness always points to the presence of pride. Whether in a single life, in a family, in a church, in government, or in a nation, pride destroys, divides, sets one person against another, perpetuates conflict, and breaks up marriages and partnerships of every sort.

When people are quarreling, the path to peace is to seek humility rather than to weigh arguments one against another, because when we do that we run into values that are so subjective that it's impossible to come to a conclusion. When tempers are hot, passions are aroused, and patience is strained, how can we get people to calm down and to consider adopting a humble attitude? How do we stifle the urge to defend ourselves and to end our stubborn insistence on what we call our rights? The answer is in this marvelous passage concerning Christ.

Christians can achieve peace—not merely a truce, a cold war, or a settlement, but peace, which begins with a mutual admission of wrongdoing. All those involved must acknowledge that they have contributed to the problem and bury the past in forgiveness. The result is a deeper sense of acceptance than ever before. When we come to this point, the quarrel actually promotes unity rather than destroying it. This process will result in deeper understanding and love. That is what the apostle wanted for these two ladies in Philippi and for those in the church who were taking sides with them.

Father, may the Spirit apply these words to the practical situations of my life. May I give way and let my stubborn will accept these conditions and bring me to peace.

The humility of our Lord and Savior Jesus Christ runs totally counter to this world's system, exposing the folly of our pride. Have we grasped the transcendent beauty of humility?

THE WAY TO PEACE

A daily devotion for March 11

Read Philippians 2:9–11.

> "Therefore God exalted him to the highest place and gave him the name that is above every name" (Phil. 2:9).

In his resurrection and his ascension, our Lord Jesus was given the name that is above every other name ever given in heaven and on earth. It is the name we call "Jehovah." It is translated as "Lord" in English versions of the New Testament. Paul urges that "every tongue confess that Jesus Christ is Lord."

Paul says Christ has won that position because he unhesitatingly and unreservedly committed himself to that attitude of the heart that led him first to mortality, then to ignominy, and finally to unequaled glory.

The result is peace! Do you see how this picture is drawn for us? Here is the end of the story: every knee bowing, every tongue confessing, every voice ascribing praise to Christ above all the created universe. If you want to complete the picture, read the closing chapters of the book of Revelation and chapter 5 where you will see every tribe, tongue, people, and nation gathered before the throne singing, "Worthy is the Lamb who was slain, to receive power and wealth and wisdom and might and honor and glory and blessing."

This is the word of peace, and it results from the work of our Lord. Now all of this is wonderfully true, and I'm sure every Christian subscribes to this doctrinally. But do you subscribe to this in terms of your relationship with others? The King James Version reads, "Let this mind be in you which was also in Christ Jesus." In his first letter to the Corinthians, Paul says, "We have the mind of Christ." He doesn't say, "Seek the mind of Christ. Struggle to achieve this. Try to imitate it." He says that you have the mind of Christ if you have him. All that he is becomes available to the one who is available to him. You must stop resisting him. The inevitable result will be peace.

If you were holding the door closed and I wanted to enter the room and asked you to let me in, what would you do? Wouldn't you stop resisting, step aside, open the door, and let me in? That is what Paul is saying here: let the mind of Christ, involving the renunciation of your rights and the willingness to accept injury, break through in your life. Accept these conditions as God's will for you. This is why you have Christ in you. Accept the hurt without complaint, and without fail he will bring you through to victory and to peace. Do you believe that? You will experience the mind of Christ only to the degree you accept it. If you don't believe it, then don't say Christianity doesn't work or that having Christ makes no difference. You are simply not using what is available to you.

> *Thank you, Lord, that through your Spirit you have given me the mind of Christ. Teach me to use what is available to me in every circumstance.*

Through the miracle of his indwelling presence, Christ's disciples have access to the mind of Christ himself! Do we value this incomparable treasure, bringing our thinking under his lordship?

GOD AT WORK

A daily devotion for March 12

Read Philippians 2:12–13.

> "Continue to work out your salvation with fear and trembling, for it is God who works in you to will and to act in order to fulfill his good purpose" (Phil. 2:12–13).

You do not "work out your own salvation" by your own effort, as some have interpreted this passage to mean. The apostle is saying, "Now that I am no longer present with you, you don't need to rely on my insights and my counsel. Begin to walk without my assistance, for you have God in you, and that is all you need. So stop leaning on me, and start applying these things yourselves. This is a necessary stage in Christian growth."

When I taught my oldest daughter how to drive, she had a learner's permit that required me to be with her in the front seat of the car. As we were driving, she would sometimes give me a questioning look as a driver pulled out in the road or a situation developed ahead of us. Then I'd tell her to do this or that. She was relying on me, but the time would come when I moved out of the front seat and in faith committed her to what she had learned. From then on, she had to work out her own salvation with fear and trembling, even with me right there with her in the back seat!

Now salvation here does not mean settling your eternal destiny. A better word would be *solution.* Work out your own solution, because what Paul has in mind here is dealing with the trials and difficulties presented in ordinary life. He is saying, "Use your mind and your will to solve your problems with the confident expectation that in doing so God is also at work in you to conform everything to his will and his good pleasure." That is a marvelous statement of the Christian's experience of being led by God.

But we are not automatons, robots simply responding when the Spirit pushes buttons within us. It's true we have another life within: God's life—Christ living within us. But our lives, hearts, and wills are involved too. It is true that we will never be saved apart from Christ. But it is likewise true that he will never save us apart from ourselves. We do the living, the choosing, and the acting, but we know a secret—that all along it is he who is living, acting, and choosing through us.

That is what we see so beautifully outlined here in Paul's letter to the Philippians. Paul says that we are now to do our own choosing and living and that as we do this God is acting in us both to will and to work. I think this is the most unbelieved verse in the Bible. What we really say is something like this: "Lord, I know you want to work in me, but my stubborn will is so set on my own ways that you cannot. I desire to have you express yourself through me, but my will prevents that and you can't." Now that is unbelief. God is at work to will and to do. He knows how to do it. Now we must believe it! The will of God will properly direct the expression of our wills so that what we will, he wills—unless we know our choice is wrong, which is also the work of the Holy Spirit in us.

> *Father, thank you for this glimpse of the glorious secret of the Christian life. I realize that I am a laborer together with you, and as I am changed and begin to manifest your work within me the world will see the crookedness of my life made straight.*

"Christ in you" is a mystery that God reveals to his children. Alive in us, he harmonizes our choices with his will and his actions for his good pleasure. Through the tutelage of his Spirit, are we seeking to make choices that conform to God's good pleasure?

HOW TO SHINE

A daily devotion for March 13

Read Philippians 2:14–15.

"Do everything without grumbling or arguing" (Phil. 2:14).

That is trustful obedience. Perhaps some of you remember an old radio-show character named Lightning. He would always do what he was told, but he did so with a continuing undercurrent of mumbling comments that became quite hilarious. I am reminded of many Christians who claim to reckon on the indwelling God but at the same time grumble and complain. That reveals a basic unbelief. It shows they don't believe life's trials are sent by the Lord, and they don't believe that he is adequate to meet every situation. They are not expecting him to work. Otherwise they wouldn't be murmuring, grumbling, and disputing with one another.

What happens when a Christian behaves in unbelief? As Paul points out, the surrounding world cannot see Christ, so there is no light in the darkness. In other words, if the life your neighbors see in you is explainable only in terms of your human personality and background, what do you have to say to your neighbors that will awaken them to their need for Christ? If the situations you face cause you to react with the same murmuring, discontent, and bitterness they display, what's the difference between your quality of life and theirs? They will simply say, "My life is explained in terms of my personality. I like certain sports and certain kinds of music and entertainment, and you like religion—that's all." Unless you exhibit a quality of life that can be explained only in terms of God, you offer nothing to challenge the world. People are waiting to see God, and they will when Christians stop their mumbling and complaining and disputing.

Paul says we live amid a crooked and perverse generation, but when that quality of life explainable only in terms of God becomes visible, the light of the gospel will shine into the darkness. This is what Jesus means when he says, "Let your light shine before men that they may see your good works." Stop your mumbling and complaining and disputing about everything that happens in your life. Only the obedience of faith produces a quality of life that cannot be explained simply in terms of your human personality.

Forgive me for my grumbling, Lord. Help me to trust you in every situation and in doing so to shine brightly in a dark world.

Do we have a lifestyle of complaint that discredits our Christian witness? What is the counterpart to grumbling and argument that will release the light of Christ in this world's darkness?

POURED OUT

A daily devotion for March 14

Read Philippians 2:16–18.

"And then I will be able to boast on the day of Christ that I did not run or labor in vain" (Phil. 2:16).

Paul looks forward to the great day when time will be rolled up as the dawn and cast aside and when all the fruit of Christian labor will be made visible—with all the gold, silver, and precious stones resulting from Christ's work in us gathered up and displayed. All of the wood, hay, and stubble produced by our self-effort for him will be burned. Christ's continuing work in us enables us to hold fast to the word of life, and this will result in praise and rejoicing on that day. Regardless of the circumstances or the praise of men or whether we see immediate results, we must hold fast and refuse to give up! Paul says, "When I see the results of your faith, my heart will swell with pride because I'll know I've not helped you in vain."

Reflecting on his impending death, Paul says he will be happy "even if I am being poured like a drink offering on the sacrifice and service coming from your faith." Even if that should occur, he is saying, "if I should know that you are holding fast to the indwelling Christ, I will die with gladness in my heart. If you hear I have died that way, you too can rejoice and be glad." This is the basis for Christian rejoicing—a refreshing, fruitful life, pouring out rivers of living water for others, conditioned upon unrelenting reliance on the indwelling Lord Jesus.

We read in Hebrews 12:2 that our Lord "for the joy set before him … endured the cross, scorning its shame, and sat down at the right hand of the throne of God." The joy set before him was his glorious expectation that his healing life would enter into the lives of people who were being torn apart by sin and rebellion. He would integrate all of life, bring focus and perspective, and call men and women to the fruitfulness of the Christian life. Anticipating what his life would accomplish, and knowing he would be reunited with his Father, Jesus endured the cross. He poured out his blood as a drink offering upon our faith and is now seated victorious on the throne on high.

When we come to the Lord's Table, we celebrate this drink offering poured out for us. Jesus emptied himself that we might have in us the source of love, joy, peace, patience, kindness, goodness, faithfulness, gentleness, self-control—the fruits of his Spirit. This is the underlying principle of Christian living, the self-giving love poured out on behalf of another. How beautifully it is exemplified in the life of Paul. Such a life is possible only as we reckon on Christ's life within us to will and to do according to his good purpose.

Lord Jesus, you have poured out your life for me. Help me to endure whatever you have in store for me, knowing that your purpose is to display your life to me and thereby to those around me.

What is our highest goal in this earthly pilgrimage? What is our greatest joy? Do we need to reaffirm the privilege of a life poured out in joyful obedience to the One who alone can produce the fruit of his Spirit?

NO ONE ELSE LIKE HIM

A daily devotion for March 15

Read Philippians 2:19–24.

"I have no one else like him, who will show genuine concern for your welfare" (Phil. 2:20).

We meet two friends of the apostle Paul in this last half of chapter 2. These are men who quite unconsciously display the character of Jesus Christ, excellent examples of all Paul has been writing about.

We are introduced to Timothy in verses 19 to 24. As Paul writes about him, we see that the underlying quality that marks the man is Jesus Christ. Timothy is an exceptional man. Paul says, "I have no one like him." Wouldn't we like to have that written about us? I know there were many things at which Timothy did not excel. With his frail body, I am sure he was not much of an athlete. He could easily have been beaten at sports or possibly surpassed in learning. But there was one area where no one even came close to this man, and that was his selfless care, his demonstration of concern for the welfare of others. Here he is displaying that peculiarly Christian virtue, that distinctive mark of the presence of Christ within: selflessness! That is what the Lord Jesus said of himself: "Learn from me, for I am meek and lowly in heart."

I recently read a tremendous definition of *meekness*. I had been searching for a definition of that word for years. I don't know any word in Scripture that is more thoroughly misunderstood. Most of us think of meekness in terms of weakness. We picture some chinless Caspar Milquetoast who lets people walk all over him. But that description would never apply to our Lord. What did he mean when he said, "I am meek"? The definition I saw said, "Meekness is that quality which receives injury without resentment, and praise without pride." Timothy is demonstrating that utter unconcern for the rights and privileges of self and a deep concern for the needs of others.

I don't know quite what Paul means when he says, "For all others look after their own interests." I think, however, that this tells a bit of a story, for as Paul searched among his acquaintances in Rome for someone to go to Philippi, he must have asked a number of them to do this. Evidently all of them turned him down, though not because they couldn't do it. I'm sure Paul would not have asked them if that had been the case. They turned him down because they were interested solely in their own concerns. They all had perfectly good excuses for why they could not undertake the journey to Philippi.

Timothy was the only one who made Christ's business his business. You can imagine what an encouragement he must have been to the apostle, who was longing to send someone to the Philippians to help them with their problems but had everyone turn him down out selfish concerns. But Timothy said, "All right, Paul, I'm ready to go—any time, any place, anywhere." This was the selflessness of the man. No wonder he was a channel of power wherever he went, as he was always ready to be an instrument of God's grace.

Father, teach me to be a person who cares for the welfare of others and who is willing to demonstrate that care in selfless acts of service.

Are we self-satisfied with random acts of kindness that may cost us little? As we consider the incomparable sacrifice of our Lord on our behalf, can we do less than worship him with all we have and are?

HELPFULNESS

A daily devotion for March 16

Read Philippians 2:25–30.

"But I think it is necessary to send back to you Epaphroditus, my brother, co-worker and fellow soldier, who is also your messenger, whom you sent to take care of my needs" (Phil. 2:25).

In verses 25 to 30 we meet Epaphroditus. Here is a man of different temperament from Timothy. Epaphroditus is the one who brought the gift from Philippi and the one who bore this wonderful letter back to the Philippian church. His popularity is evident from the fact that he was chosen by the church for this difficult task. We can gather from this letter that he was probably one of those affable, courteous, well-liked men whose natural dispositions make them popular and prominent in any group.

Paul says the quality he most appreciates in Epaphroditus is helpfulness. Notice he says, "I am sending back to you ... my brother, co-worker and fellow soldier, who is also your messenger, whom you sent to take care of my needs." All of this spells out a helpful disposition. *Brother* speaks of family life, a mutual source of life in Christ. *Co-worker* reveals how they labored together in full fellowship and with a common interest. A *fellow soldier* is one who shares a loyalty to the same cause as the apostle. Epaphroditus is the *messenger* of the Philippians. The word really is *apostle.* He is an ambassador, a representative of someone else.

All these wonderful titles add up to one who is a marvelous helper, a faithful laborer with other people who shows the selfless concern that is the distinctive mark of the believer in Jesus Christ. Verse 26 says, "For he longs for all of you and is distressed because you heard he was ill." Word has gotten back to the Philippians that this man has been terribly sick, and Epaphroditus is concerned that they may be overanxious about him. He is stressed because they heard he was ill.

I can't help contrasting this man with so many today who become distressed because we have not heard they were ill. I occasionally meet people like that. Now and then I will greet someone and notice a bit of coolness. Finally the person will say, "Didn't you hear that I was sick?" I reply, "No, I didn't hear that." Then the person says, "Well, I expected I would have a visit, but no one came." I have to wonder how people expect a visit on that basis. It's interesting that people will call a doctor or a lawyer to help deal with their problems, but they expect their pastor or their Christian friends to learn of these things by osmosis. Then these people get distressed when word didn't arrive.

Well, there is no such self-pity in Epaphroditus. Evidently he has learned to count self-interest and self-seeking as the unprofitable things that they are, and he has learned to reckon on the indwelling self-giving love of Christ. His concern is not for himself because he is so desperately sick but for others lest they become overwrought in their worry for him. Even amid personal distress of a most serious nature, Epaphroditus has learned to manifest selfless concern for others. What a beautiful picture! He has learned to labor with others and to be concerned for others. You can see the character of Christ in him.

Lord, I am captured by that spirit of helpfulness. I know it doesn't come by any fervor of the flesh or by passionately losing myself in some cause of my own making, but rather by quiet dependence upon you and by a readiness in little things to be expendable for your sake.

Random acts of kindness can be self-satisfying, even self-promoting. What is the contrasting source of a life characterized by helpful, un-self-concious caring for others?

REJOICE!

A daily devotion for March 17

Read Philippians 3:1.

"Further, my brothers and sisters, rejoice in the Lord!" (Phil. 3:1).

If you wanted to sum up Christianity in four words this might be the best phrase you could use: rejoice in the Lord. This is the mark of a truly spiritual Christian. It is the distinctive sign of a victorious Christian. It is the one attitude that invariably brings peace and contentment to the heart. Therefore, it is the one thing Paul repeats over and over again: rejoice in the Lord. He knows he has said this many times before, and he will say it two more times before he ends this letter. But it is so important, Paul says, that he doesn't mind saying it as many times as necessary.

As we saw earlier in this letter, Paul points out the opposite as well. Grumbling and disputing are always signs of unbelief in the Christian life. Carry on without murmuring and questioning, he says, because these things signify someone who doesn't believe what God is telling him. Rejoicing is the mark of one who has learned to believe. Remember that definition of a Christian we have heard from time to time: one who is completely fearless, continually cheerful, and constantly in trouble. It is continual rejoicing in the midst of trouble that marks the Christian life.

It is a sad commentary on Christian unbelief that the mark the world usually associates with a Christian is not a smile but a long face. This reveals how little we believe in the God we love. The story is told of a little girl who first saw a mule in the countryside. She looked at it for quite a while and then said, "I don't know what you are, but you must be a Christian. You look just like my grandfather." Unfortunately, the mark of a Christian has become a sober, solemn mien, casting gloom on every occasion. This isn't Christianity. The mark of a true Christian is a smile of confidence whatever the circumstances. It is not a screwed-on smile that makes us appear to be something we are not, but a genuine smile, sometimes through tears, but a smile nevertheless. We can smile this way when we accept all events as ordered by the Lord. That's the secret. This attitude arises from a quiet trust in God's ability to handle whatever comes. We are living out of his adequacy.

Living out of inadequacy is what puts the frown on our faces. We are trying to face the onrushing tumult of life with inadequate resources. This strain shows in the face. But if we believe what God tells us, that we have within us One who is completely competent to deal with every situation, we never feel any strain, for whatever difficulty comes we know he is adequate to meet it in and through us. We rest on that fact, and that quiet confidence marks the Christian.

There is nothing new about this experience. It is the experience of the believer in any age. When we learn this secret we discover mysterious bridges flung over every abyss to which we come. We gain an invisible strength to meet every stress life lays on us. No matter how long we have been Christians, if we are still griping and grousing about what life gives us, we need to be taught again the first principles, the ABCs, of the gospel of Christ.

I rejoice in you, Lord. You have put a smile in my heart because I know that you are Lord and that I can trust in you even during the most challenging times of my life. I thank you for this.

While the world seeks happiness, the Christian finds joy in knowing and trusting the character of God. Are we missing out on that heritage because we fail to seek to know him through his Word?

THE MENACE OF EXTERNAL RELIGION

A daily devotion for March 18

Read Philippians 3:2.

"Watch out for those dogs, those evildoers, those mutilators of the flesh" (Phil. 3:2).

This is a warning about the menace of external religion. This seems like a rather abrupt change of subject, but there is a vital connection between this verse and the previous one. What is it that destroys rejoicing in the Lord? It's making external circumstances the crucial thing. It's turning away from the indwelling Lord to an outward event with which you are concerned and counting that as more important. This will inevitably destroy a spirit of rejoicing. So Paul warns against false teachers who were posing as Christians and were trying to center people's faith on outward things.

The terms he uses to describe these men are bold and blunt, because in matters of this importance the apostle never minces words. He calls them three things: dogs, evildoers, mutilators. The reference to dogs is not to the pampered, shampooed, manicured pets we have today. These were not cultured canines. These were the snarling, half-wild curs found on city streets. They can still be found today. *Dogs* was a term of reproach used by both Jew and Gentile. Because of what the dogs fed on, they were regarded as unclean animals. They fed on the refuse of the streets—the decayed meat and rotten vegetables that had been tossed out.

Paul is referring to a group of men who hounded him wherever he went, following his footsteps, trying to upset Christians. We usually call them Judaizers. These men taught that to be a Christian it was necessary to observe the law of Moses and the food restrictions of the Mosaic covenant and especially to be circumcised. They claimed that these things were not done away with by Christ. Unfortunately, these people are still with us. Paul says they were feeding like dogs on the garbage of carnal ordinances. They were holding up as invaluable rituals that once had worth but had become overripe and decayed and were fit to be thrown out.

These men were evildoers because of their zeal. They tirelessly sought to convert young believers to their views, to return them to the bondage of legalistic restrictions. They gloried in this activity as a mark of their claim on God's blessing. They were sure God would bless them because they were so zealous, so devoted to their work. These people are clearly still with us. They are the tireless, zealous workers who go from door to door with books under their arms, ready to convert anyone to a legalistic, Judaistic system. These are exactly the kind of people to whom Paul is referring.

Such teaching has a strong appeal because of its apparent show of devotion. I think all of us at one time or another have sensed the appeal of some ornate, solemn ritual done in a religious manner and believed it was worthy of merit before God. The earnest, sincere endeavor of a tireless worker is appealing. It is gratifying to the religious ego to perform some solemn ritual, to be constantly busy at religious work, or even to mock the flesh in some way, perhaps with distinctive garb or an identifying posture. All of this, Paul says, is the enemy of true spirituality. It destroys the spirit of rejoicing, and it makes religion a barren mockery. It puts the emphasis on the external and removes religion from the vital interior aspects of faith.

> *Forgive me, Lord, for so often choosing external religion instead of the real thing and missing out on the joy that comes from knowing you live within me and are always working out your good purposes in my life.*

Grace, God's unearned, unmerited favor, is counterintuitive to the world's system. Are we learning to serve God and others out of gratitude and worship, rejoicing that he does his work in and through us?

TRUE SPIRITUALITY

A daily devotion for March 19

Read Philippians 3:3.

"Who put no confidence in the flesh" (Phil. 3:3b).

Those who place their confidence in self-effort are at odds with true spirituality. Paul says Christians "put no confidence in the flesh." We live in a world that continually strives to get us to put our trust in the flesh. We are taught from childhood that the way to become proficient and competent and to accomplish our aims is to develop self-confidence. But this is what destroys human life. God did not intend that we find strength in ourselves. Instead, we must put our confidence in him. We are supposed to face life recognizing we are weak, ineffectual, and unable so that we rely upon the One who is totally adequate and can be our complete strength. This is the way God intended us to live. Therefore, the spirit of self-confidence is the deadliest lie ever perpetrated upon the human race.

We may have self-confidence based on God in us, but when it comes from something in ourselves, something we have learned or achieved, it is deadly. Paul says we have learned at last to put no confidence in the flesh. Even in religion there is a strong emphasis on putting confidence in the flesh, or perhaps I should say that it is especially in the religious arena where we encounter this pressure.

Recently I read from a pamphlet that purports to be a guide to developing the Christian life and is widely distributed each month throughout the nation. The writer said, "What I didn't know and had to discover the hard way is that if you don't have faith in yourself you hardly can have faith in people in the world or in God. I had to see that God created us in his image, and we must have faith in the image. If we achieve that, then we have his spirit within us and we can accomplish anything, even ridding oneself of sin."

That is the kind of perverted philosophy that is being widely purveyed today and is holding millions of people in bondage to the flesh. No wonder the spirit of the apostle flamed with indignation against this. Knowing the liberty that is in Christ Jesus, he puts the matter frankly. We must begin with faith in God and eliminate faith in self. When we have no confidence in the flesh, we discover we can have full confidence in him who can do anything through us.

We don't mind a little confidence, but we don't want to become overconfident. But Paul says any confidence at all is overconfidence. He has no confidence in himself to do anything. He has no confidence in his background, his training, his talents, or his accomplishments; no confidence in the time he spends in prayer, the number of chapters of Scripture he reads, or the number of verses he memorizes; no confidence in the power of his eloquence to persuade people or in his devotion to move them. Furthermore, Paul has no confidence in anyone who trusts in these things. The only one in whom he has confidence is Jesus Christ.

Thank you, Father, that I need not look within myself to find the source of strength and confidence. Today I put my full confidence in him who is able to do anything through me.

Jesus as man said he could do nothing of himself but depended completely upon the Father. Has Christ's resurrection life emancipated us from the unbearable burden of self-assertive control?

DANGEROUS CONFIDENCE

A daily devotion for March 20

Read Philippians 3:4–7.

"But whatever were gains to me I now consider loss for the sake of Christ" (Phil. 3:7).

What was the basis of Paul's confidence that he could achieve his mission? He could be confident in four things: his ancestry, his orthodoxy, his activity, and his morality. But it is important to see how and when Paul changed his mind about these matters. Most commentators suggest the change came in the dust of the road on the way to Damascus when he was converted in that remarkable encounter with Jesus Christ. I don't think that is true. He changed only one of these values at that time.

When Saul of Tarsus, the persecutor, blinded by the light, was led captive into Damascus, he immediately got busy, plunging into a new activity in which he took great pride. For five to ten years after his conversion, Paul was just as confident in the flesh as before his conversion. His life was therefore as barren and ineffective as when he was Saul and persecuted the church, with one exception: he was born again, and the indwelling Holy Spirit was teaching him what he needed to become an effective minister for Jesus Christ.

Eventually, Paul learned that all his background, training, and education, his ancestry, morality, and activities, added not one thing to God's purpose in him. He came to the place where he could write, "But whatever were gains to me I now consider loss for the sake of Christ."

This is the great secret of a Christian's life. You cannot have confidence in the flesh and in Christ. It's one or the other. If you believe that more education or more prayer, more effort or more zeal, more Bible study, or more anything will make you a better servant of God, you are putting confidence in the flesh. No, Christ is all you need. He can supply every need. He can cope with every lack and every situation. Believe that! Count it true! He will probably begin to lead you to study more, to pray more, to work hard, to learn more, but you will know that these are only instruments through which the power of his life can flow. When Paul stepped out of himself, he stepped into the fullness of Christ. Have you learned that?

Father, may these verses be more than mere words to me so that I will catch this glowing secret from the heart of this apostle and may indeed see that you have provided another way by which life may be lived. I rely not on my own strength or on any confidence in what I do but on who you are.

Do we assess our worth by our possessions and/or achievements? Are we caught up in a syndrome of self-effort and self-defeat? Isn't it time to cut our losses and to choose the surpassing worth of our union with Christ?

ADEQUATE LIVING

A daily devotion for March 21

Read Philippians 3:8.

> "I consider everything a loss because of the surpassing worth of knowing Christ Jesus my Lord" (Phil. 3:8).

Have you ever made this evaluation of your own life? Have you ever tried? Sit down and list your assets, the things that are important to you, the things you think you could not do without, the factors that you believe bring respect, advancement, and acceptance in the eyes of the world. What are your physical and financial assets, your background, your name, your family standing, your fame, your personality, your education, your training? Have you learned Paul's secret concerning them?

Write them down and see what it is you are counting on. Then remind yourself that as long as you depend on these you cannot lay hold of the riches of God in Christ Jesus. You cannot serve two masters. You cannot cling to both. You cannot drink from an empty cistern and at the same time from the inexhaustible rivers that flow from Christ. You must end your dependence upon these things, counting them as loss, as refuse. You must be glad to see them go, indifferent to whether they stay. Then you are set free to lay hold of all that Paul experienced in the Lord, what he calls the "surpassing worth" of Jesus Christ.

It is quite possible as Christians to have Christ living in our hearts but be unable to gain him, to experience him, to sense his life flowing through ours, at work in us. We cannot have this until we count the rest as garbage. That is what Paul is saying. We must learn to drop the rod as Moses had to learn—that staff he leaned on for support—so that God might take it, remove the snake, and return the rod, as he did with Moses. This is the experience of all those people God wants to use for himself: they learn to surrender everything else but dependence upon Christ in them. It wasn't difficult for Paul to consider all those things as loss. Once he began to sense the tremendous possibilities offered by Jesus Christ, what Christ could and would be through him, he gladly threw away the tattered rags of the reputation he once enjoyed so that he might enter into that fully adequate place in Jesus Christ.

This other method of living—clinging to our standing, a desperate worry lest we appear unprepossessing or different to others, the continual defense of our position in the eyes of men—is the reason we have such totally inadequate lives. It is why we never can discover the rich resources that are in Christ. As Jesus said, "No man can serve two masters." There is no grasping both. It's one or the other. Paul says that when he had thrown away the shreds of his reputation he immediately found that though the Lord led him through hardships, prisons, and pain, what Christ was to him and what he did through Christ were of such value that he could find no adequate words to express it.

Today, Lord, I choose to lay down the things in which I so often put my confidence and instead seek to rely totally on you and on your accomplishments.

Are we choosing to live by the power and the presence of Christ, or are we held hostage to our dependence on our own weak and inadequate resources?

KNOWING HIM

A daily devotion for March 22

Read Philippians 3:9–11.

"I want to know Christ—yes, to know the power of his resurrection and participation in his sufferings, becoming like him in his death" (Phil. 3:10).

Paul says he is quite ready to give up the usual status symbols of the Christian for the knowledge and friendship of Jesus Christ. This is not an academic subject. This is not a course in Christology or on the person of Christ. This is not knowing about Christ. This is knowing him. As has wisely been said, "Knowing about has value; knowing has vitality."

The knowledge the apostle means is not simply casual contact now and then. You don't get to know your friends that way. The friends you know best are the ones you have spent the most time with or the ones with whom you have shared deep experiences. This knowledge of Christ comes by a continual sharing of experiences, by living your life moment by moment with Jesus. It comes by gazing on the face of Jesus Christ as he appears in the pages of Scripture. It comes by allowing every circumstance to make you lean on his adequate life, by hiding nothing from his eyes, by bringing every friendship and every loyalty to his gaze for his approval or disapproval, by walking every day reckoning upon him to be with you. That's the secret of a successful ministry.

That is exactly what Paul says comes from knowing Christ. First there is the "power of the resurrection." The risen Lord dwells within us, and that power can do in us "above all that we ask or think." The power of Christ's resurrection is perfectly adequate for every possible circumstance. We may act with full assurance that he is acting with us simultaneously and that this risen power is ours!

The second thing that stems from knowledge of Christ is the "participation in his sufferings." The remarkable thing about the sufferings of Christ is that they are always for someone else. We all earnestly long for such compassion. It doesn't come by trying. It comes by knowing him, by entering into what he is to us. That makes us compassionate. This is the primary reason Christians suffer—not so much for themselves but for others. Have you ever noticed that when a Christian gets desperately sick and uses his suffering as an opportunity to manifest the grace of Christ, that Christian becomes the center of victory, hope, and blessing for everyone who visits him?

The last thing is "becoming like him in his death." What does that mean? The death of Jesus Christ was the end of the old life of sin and self-pleasing. We know that there was no sin or self-pleasing in his life, but on the cross he was made to be all that we are, sinful and self-pleasing, and then this was put to death. The cross was the end of it. That is liberty, because if we accept this as being true, we are set free from our selfish, luxury-seeking ways. We are free to be real men and real women—unbound, delivered, no longer constantly concerned about what happens to us but concerned only about what happens to Christ.

These gifts are freely offered to every believer. I must stress that they are not achieved by struggling and striving. They come as a byproduct of knowing Christ.

Thank you, Lord, for the joy of simply knowing you. I pray that I may know the power of your resurrection, participate in your sufferings, and be conformed to your death.

Do we want to know Christ merely to define our theology and to refine our doctrinal views? Are we missing the life-defining pursuit of knowing Christ intimately? How can we truly learn to know him?

THE GREAT MOTIVE

A daily devotion for March 23

Read Philippians 3:12–14.

> "Not that I have already obtained all this, or have already arrived at my goal, but I press on to take hold of that for which Christ Jesus took hold of me" (Phil. 3:12).

Paul says this is the great motive of his life. He is not citing the resurrection but is referring back to verse 10. "I have not exhausted the riches of knowing Christ," he says. "I do not yet know all the power of his resurrection and have not been perfected so that I no longer need the fellowship of his sufferings. No, but I press on to lay hold of that for which Christ Jesus has laid hold of me." The Phillips translation renders this as "grasping ever more firmly that purpose for which Christ grasps me."

This was Paul's mighty motive, to achieve all that Christ desired when he laid hold of him on the road to Damascus. Paul is saying, "I want to lay hold of him that he might use my life as an instrument to do everything he had in mind when he stopped me on the road, hoping this might fulfill the purpose of his coming and we might all be together at the resurrection of the dead." Remember what the Lord said to Ananias on the day Saul of Tarsus was struck on the road and he sent Ananias to baptize him? Ananias didn't want to go because he was afraid of this persecutor of the church, but the Lord told Ananias, "Go, for he is a chosen instrument of mine to carry my name before the Gentiles and kings and the sons of Israel; for I will show him how much he must suffer for the sake of my name." Paul says, "The thing that motivates me in everything I do is that I may fully lay hold of that and give myself to Christ so he may do everything he had in mind when he saved me."

Now this is adequate living. That's what it was in the first century. That's what it is in the present century. What does it consist of? First of all, there is a purpose for living, a reason for existing. Why do you exist? What are you here for? Have you discovered the purpose for which God has laid hold of you, the part of his work he has in mind for you? There is also the power by which to live his purpose, the power of his indwelling life. God also provides an unshakable platform of morality that can withstand any examination. That is adequate living. May God grant that we discover it.

> *Lord, I sense that Paul experienced a great deal that I have not yet discovered. Save me from the folly that says this was possible for him but not for me. Teach me to know that Christ in me can be all that he was in Paul.*

"Who am I?" "Why am I here?" We might also ask, "Who owns me?" Do we respond with Paul, "Christ Jesus has made me his own"? Do we press on to lay hold of him and of his purpose for our lives?

ANOTHER ALTERNATIVE

A daily devotion for March 24

Read Philippians 3:15–21.

> "But our citizenship is in heaven. And we eagerly await a Savior from there, the Lord Jesus Christ" (Phil. 3:20).

As members of the church of Jesus Christ, we have been sent by our Lord to form a colonial outpost from which to spread the influence of heaven. The church has often opted for one of two extremes. It has withdrawn from the world to avoid being stained by it, or it has entered the world to dominate it. Both inclinations have their basis in fear. When we withdraw, we fear contamination. When we dominate, we fear annihilation.

The Bible offers us another alternative, one that takes neither direction. We gather together to adopt and to reinforce Christ's pattern of self-sacrifice. Then we enter the world and influence it through this pattern—through the power of love rather than the love of power. This third alternative will always have some tension to it. We will often wonder if we're tending toward withdrawal or domination, and we will feel pulled in both directions. Isolation and power each have their appeal. We will have to think and pray and use all the wisdom that God gives us in order to take this third path, but it is the path we are called to follow.

When we withdraw, we lose whatever influence we might have. When we dominate, opting for the love of power rather than the power of love, we model the pattern of the culture instead of the pattern of Christ, and again we lose our influence.

Levi the tax collector was an outcast. Jews considered him a traitor for collecting taxes for the Romans. But Jesus went to Levi's house and had dinner with many other tax collectors and sinners there. The scribes and the Pharisees were appalled. Jesus was spreading the influence of heaven at a party of sinners without being influenced by them (Mark 2:13–17). We should consider attending such parties. If sinners won't come to our parties, we need to go to theirs. When Jesus entered the world of sinners, he was not contaminated by their sin. Rather, his holiness cleansed their sin (Mark 5:25–34). Jesus resides with us by his Spirit. He has made us holy (Eph. 1:4). We too can venture forth into the world as a sanctifying influence.

Jesus said, "You are the salt of the earth. But if the salt loses its saltiness, how can it be made salty again? It is no longer good for anything, except to be thrown out and trampled by men" (Matt. 5:13). Salt was used as a preservative. Jesus was telling his followers that they must influence life on earth. To say "you are the salt of the earth" is another way of saying our citizenship is in heaven. We are the salt of the earth and a colony of heaven, sent by God to influence the earth through the heavenly pattern of self-giving love.

> *Lord, teach me to choose the other alternative, not to withdraw from the world or to seek to dominate it but rather to influence the world through the power of love.*

Since our citizenship is in heaven, do we renounce our responsibility to this colonial outpost? What is the appropriate alternative to a fear-based withdrawal from the world?

STANDING WHILE RUNNING

A daily devotion for March 25

Read Philippians 4:1.

> "Therefore, my brothers and sisters, you whom I love and long for, my joy and crown, stand firm in the Lord in this way, dear friends!" (Phil. 4:1).

Paul begins this fourth chapter with what looks like a mixed metaphor. The *therefore* refers back to what he wrote in chapter 3. There he talked about running a race, seeing life as an obstacle course. He said he ran this race by pressing on toward the prize of the high calling of God in Christ Jesus. He urged others to run with him. But Paul now says, "Stand firm." He seems confused as to which he means for us, whether to run the race or to stand firm. One is a picture of extreme effort, the other of immobility and inaction. How can we follow this call to stand and yet to run?

If we take Paul literally, we will be confused. But thinking this through we see the paradox of the Christian faith marvelously presented. Life is indeed a swiftly moving obstacle course. We've all discovered that. At every turn we face new challenges and new demands, and time itself brings these things into our lives so that we are indeed running a race.

But the secret of running the race successfully, the apostle tells us, is learning how to stand still. We must take a lasting hold of the unchanging life of Jesus Christ within us. This is the theme of Paul's marvelous letter. He tells us that there is a secret to the Christian life. It is the fact that Jesus Christ lives within us. To lay hold of that life we must willingly forgo the exercise of our own lives. Thus he says, "I have learned to count all things as loss in order that I might gain Christ." The secret of running life's obstacle course is to get a solid grip on the life of Jesus Christ within. So Paul's metaphors are not mixed after all. They are quite true to life.

We have an excellent illustration of this in those delightful little cable cars that run up and down the hills of San Francisco. If you have stood and listened, you have heard the cables running beneath the streets. The cable car is incapable of moving. It has no motor, and it is impossible to be self-propelled. The only possibility of movement is to get a firm grip on the cable. You may have watched the gripman pulling back the levers to grab hold of the cable and to run up a hill. In its relationship to the cable, the car never moves. It remains steadfast, firmly grasping that one point on the cable. But the cable moves continually, and the car, gripping firmly, is able to overcome all obstacles, even the steepest hills of San Francisco.

This is a beautiful picture of what Paul is saying, for as we are running the race of life we are continually confronted with obstacles, demands, and pressures. The answer is not to try to do something but to get a firmer grip on the life of Jesus Christ, who is intent on acting in us. As we do this, we discover we have an adequacy that handles all the obstacles. He is quite able to overcome all.

Teach me to stand, Lord, in all that you are and all that you have done on my behalf. Then and only then will I learn to run the race successfully.

Has our life's race deteriorated into a self-propelled rat race? What is the sure and essential power by which we may surmount the obstacle course of life and follow God's upward call?

THE CURE FOR CONFLICT

A daily devotion for March 26

Read Philippians 4:2–5.

"I plead with Euodia and I plead with Syntyche to be of the same mind in the Lord" (Phil. 4:2).

In these few verses Paul turns a spotlight on the problem that has been dimly discernible all along in this letter. There were in the church in Philippi two lovely ladies who were quarreling with one another. They were in some kind of disagreement, and the quarrel had spread to others in church. Some were taking sides, and the dispute was beginning to threaten the unity of the church. Believers hadn't divided yet—there wasn't a church split—but they were on the verge of it.

Paul details what is needed to settle the difficulty, on the basis of his marvelous revelation in this letter of the life we have in Jesus Christ. It comes down to practical actions—two things to be done. First of all, agree in the Lord. That means finding common ground. When we quarrel with others or their personalities rub us the wrong way—they're among those irritating people who always do things differently and are hard to live with—our tendency is to say we have nothing in common with them and to go our separate ways. But the apostle says this is absolutely wrong for Christians. Separations between believers in Jesus Christ must never be permitted, for it is quite wrong to say we have nothing in common. Christians always have something in common in the Lord. Therefore they are to agree and to reconcile in the Lord.

It's impossible to know what this quarrel was about, but we don't need to know. Whatever the areas of disagreement, there are always vast areas of agreement in the Lord for believers. The apostle is urging these two ladies to meet and to talk about those areas and from that agreement to begin working on the problems dividing them. He believes that starting from that basis they will soon find the areas of disagreement shrinking until there is nothing left and they agree in the Lord.

The second activity is the theme of the letter: rejoice in the Lord. That is also necessary. To agree we must find that place where we can begin to rejoice in what is taking place. "Rejoice in the Lord, and again I say rejoice in the Lord." This is the mark of spiritual maturity. "In everything give thanks, for this is the will of God in Christ Jesus concerning you," Paul writes to the Thessalonians. We must recognize that all that comes into our lives, even those irritating disagreements with others, is sent by the Lord either to reveal something in our hearts that we haven't seen or to give us an opportunity to manifest the sweet reasonableness of the Lord Jesus.

Father, in the conflicts and disagreements in which I find myself with my brothers and sisters in Christ, teach me to agree with them in the Lord and to rejoice that through these struggles you may work out your good purpose in each of us.

Are we learning to see disagreements with other Christians as opportunities to affirm our spiritual unity in Christ and to deepen our mutual joy in being his servants?

THE CURE TO WORRY

A daily devotion for March 27

Read Philippians 4:6–7.

"Do not be anxious about anything, but in every situation, by prayer and petition, with thanksgiving, present your requests to God" (Phil. 4:6).

There is nothing more prevalent in our age than worry. This powerful force disintegrates the human personality, leaving us frustrated, puzzled, and bewildered by life. We hear the expression "sick with worry," and anyone who has experienced anxiety knows this is no empty expression. We can indeed be sick with worry. Paul's answer to this is a blunt: "Do not be anxious about anything." The entire Word of God is an exhortation to believers to stop worrying. Worry is everywhere forbidden to those who believe in Jesus Christ, and one of the most serious areas of unbelief is our failure as Christians to face the problem of worry as sin, because that is what it is. Worrying is not all right just because it's something everyone does. It is definitely labeled a sin in the Scriptures, which tell us everywhere, "Stop it!"

Well, you say, "It's fine to say, 'Don't worry,' but how do you stop? Every time I try to stop worrying I worry all the more. You can't stop it just by the exercise of will power." Again, here's the secret of running the race: "In every situation, by prayer and petition, with thanksgiving, present your requests to God."

I love the words "in every situation." That means there is nothing too insignificant to bring to him. Someone asked, "Is it all right to bring small things before the Lord? Is he concerned about the small things in our lives?" Is there anything that looks big to God? Everything is small to him, so take everything to him in prayer. Prayer is the expression of your dependence upon his promises. It isn't necessary to get on your knees or to shut yourself in a closet. That quiet "arrow prayer" of the heart can be enough with continual recognition that you need to rely upon his grace and strength in everything, constantly relating to the indwelling life of God the Son in you.

To petition means to persist in prayer. Whenever problems develop, pray to the One who is able and competent within you through his indwelling life. Thanksgiving is that forward look of faith that thanks God for the answer before you see it. Knowing his character, you know something—the right thing, the perfect thing—will be done.

God is not saying you should ask for everything you want. Instead, you're to ask for everything you need. You may often find yourself praying for things he never promises. For instance, if you are facing a trial or a catastrophe strikes in your life, the perfectly understandable human reaction is to say, "Lord, take this away." But God never said he would do that. He does not always want to take it away. Sometimes he will, sometimes not. That kind of prayer must always have appended to it what our Lord prayed in the garden of Gethsemane: "Father, if it be possible, let this cup pass from me. Nevertheless, not my will but thine be done."

But there are things for which we can immediately ask, knowing that we will receive them. God's grace, strength, insight, wisdom, patience, love, and compassion are always available. And as we make that expression of faith that is prayer, we can also give thanks that the answer has come. As always, when we make our requests known to God, the result is peace. The peace of God that passes all understanding will keep our hearts and our minds in Christ Jesus.

I confess, Lord, that I often prefer worry over prayer. Thank you for inviting me to cast all my cares upon you. I pray that I may learn to do that with a heart of continual thanksgiving.

Are we learning to confess our anxiety as sinful distrust in the character of God? Are we choosing to pray with thanksgiving, affirming our trust in God's wise and faithful care?

POSITIVE THINKING

A daily devotion for March 28

Read Philippians 4:8–9.

> "Finally, brothers and sisters, whatever is true, whatever is noble, whatever is right, whatever is pure, whatever is lovely, whatever is admirable—if anything is excellent or praiseworthy—think about such things" (Phil. 4:8).

Consider a common failure in many of our lives but one we seldom recognize. It's the problem of a pessimistic outlook, of a negative imagination. You may find your attitude soured after imagining what could happen in a situation and be so frustrated and flustered by your thoughts that you are unable to handle the problem when it actually occurs. This difficulty is the subject of many books on the power of positive thinking. There is a place for positive thinking but only after you have discovered a positive life, the life of Christ.

The story is told of a man who had a flat tire on the way home and found he had no jack in his car. He set out to borrow one but worried about how his neighbor might react to being awakened and asked to get out of bed in the middle of the night to fetch a jack. The man thought about how angry and resentful the neighbor would be and how he wouldn't want to get up and give him the jack. He probably wouldn't be able to find it in the garage anyway, the man surmised, and he'd have to dig around and maybe get a flashlight and go to an awful lot of trouble. The longer the man thought about what lay ahead the madder he got. Finally he arrived at the neighbor's house and pounded on the door. When the neighbor appeared the man said, "Well, you can keep your lousy jack if that's the way you feel about it."

Unfortunately, that story illustrates a problem that too frequently occurs in our lives because we give no heed to the apostle's exhortation, "whatever is true." That's the first reality. We must focus on things as they are, not as they might be. "Whatever is noble, whatever is right, whatever is pure, whatever is lovely—if there is any excellence, if there is anything worthy of praise, think about these things." We must make a deliberate choice to refuse to think about the negative and instead to think about the positive in any situation or about any person. Then the God of peace will be with us. If we set our minds on the positive, the God who dwells within us will express himself in terms of peace rather than of strife and confusion.

Christianity was meant for life. I am impressed by the fact that when our Lord Jesus came he didn't talk to people about religion. He talked to them about life—about their work in the kitchen or the shop, about how they lived and thought and acted, about what they said to their children and to each other, and about how they got along with their neighbors. He didn't talk to them about theological problems, about existential relations and interpersonal demands and epistemological confusion. He came to talk to them about the way they were living and to show them what life is. Jesus said that the secret to life is a person who dwells within, whose life may be manifested in terms of our personalities, and that everything is designed to drive us back to that.

> *Father, teach me that faith-filled optimism is not rooted in my own strength but in the knowledge that you are in control and that you are adequate to meet any need or challenge that I face.*

Are we prayerfully aligning our thinking with the reality of Christ alive within us and remaining confident in the good and perfect outcome of God at work in all of life's circumstances?

TO BE CONTENT

A daily devotion for March 29

Read Philippians 4:10–13.

"I have learned the secret of being content in any and every situation" (Phil. 4:12).

Paul's statement teaches us three things about contentment. The first is something we must learn. We are not born content. Our natural inclination is to strive to get more. The outlook from our youth is to keep looking for something new to temporarily titillate our senses and to satisfy our desires. We are always striving for something. The apostle is saying here that he has learned not only to experience contentment but to recognize true contentment. To learn this is to learn a new definition of the word.

I suspect that most of us would define contentment as having everything we want. I don't think that is the true definition. Contentment is not having all that we want. True contentment is wanting only what we have. This is what Paul learned. He realized that God had created man to love people and to use things. But we have reversed that truth and have learned to use people and to love things. But through the years the Spirit of God had taught Paul that circumstances are illusive. They do not minister to the deep needs of the heart whether one has want or abundance. The major value of life is the ability to love people and to use things. This was the lesson Paul had learned at last, to face life as it really is.

The second thing to notice is that Paul states clearly that poverty and wealth are both trials. This is not the usual perspective but again something that must be learned. We are naturally inclined to view poverty as a severe trial and abundance as a great blessing, and we continually pursue a state in which we have everything we want. This indicates that we don't know how to define contentment. It is not having all we want but wanting what we have. We are beset by the philosophy of the age illustrated by the Horatio Alger story in which the young man rises from the depths of poverty and through his own efforts becomes a tycoon and gains abundance. This is the American way. But Paul takes issue with this thinking. Poverty and wealth are both demanding extremes. Both are grievous weights to the human spirit. Both tend to distort and to degrade the personality. Both are trials of severe intensity and can be destructive to human life.

The third thing to notice is the secret to victory over both of these impostors: "I can do all this through him who gives me strength." This theme runs through nearly every verse of the letter, a continual harking back by the apostle to his great discovery that he had nothing in himself. All his background, his ambition, and his abilities and all that he counted as gain were useless as far as what he could do for the cause of Christ. Paul learned that he had nothing, was nothing, and could do nothing and that God's expression of life was the secret of human living. Once again the apostle writes of a life fully adequate to meet any demand placed upon it, God's indwelling life lived out in Christ. We must be confident that Jesus Christ remains sufficient for every situation and is continually available to us. This is the secret the apostle sets forth here. If we are unwilling to learn the secret, we will not enjoy true contentment.

Father, what foolish attitudes I often take toward the circumstances of my life. How quickly I murmur and complain, forgetting that you are the potter and I am the clay. Teach me to rejoice, knowing that all of my circumstances were planned to be the means by which you express the adequacy of the Lord Jesus.

Commercial ads appeal to our innate desire to claim happiness as our right. What are three factors that call this appeal into question? Are we learning the secret to true contentment?

WHY GIVE?

A daily devotion for March 30

Read Philippians 4:14–18.

> "I have received full payment and have more than enough. I am amply supplied, now that I have received from Epaphroditus the gifts you sent. They are a fragrant offering, an acceptable sacrifice, pleasing to God" (Phil. 4:18).

Here Paul expresses his thanks for the gifts these people had sent him by way of Epaphroditus, yet he is quick to point out that he is far more interested in what their giving does for them than what it does for him. The Lord Jesus said, "It is more blessed to give than to receive." This is what the apostle means when he says, "Not that I seek the gift; but I seek the fruit which increases to your credit." These are financial terms. The word *fruit* was commonly used in the business world of that day to mean "interest." Paul is saying, "I don't desire the capital. I want only the interest, which is continually increasing to your account." As these people give to Paul, they receive a blessing that is continually building up for their own enjoyment. That's what Paul is after—not that he needs the gift. He wants them to be blessed in the giving, and that is why he so gladly receives their gifts.

Then in verse 18 he writes what is nothing less than a receipt: "I have received full payment and have more than enough." Don't be misled. The apostle doesn't do this to receive an income tax deduction. This is the reason we give receipts today. But Paul provides this receipt so that these people may know that their gift has gone farther than Rome. It has also reached to heaven where it is presented as a fragrant incense, delighting the heart of God, who sees this gift given so freely to the apostle out of their poverty. In another epistle Paul speaks of the deep poverty out of which they give. God is pleased with the evidence of the work of the Holy Spirit in their lives.

Each offering in the church, and each gift a Christian gives to meet any need, ought to be a willing, generous expression of love and thanksgiving. God will be delighted that the spirit of love prompts this giving.

We are told that the Lord Jesus "sat down opposite the treasury, and watched the multitude putting money into the treasury." In a sense he always does that. He watches as we drop our check into the offering plate or a coin into the box. And he knows the intent of our hearts in this. That is why the apostle so strongly says, "God loves a cheerful giver," one who gladly pours out his offering. This delights God's heart because this is the way he gives to us in his Son.

How often, Lord, I have given with the wrong motives. Thank you for the opportunity to give out of a cheerful heart that has already received so much more.

In the ebb and flow of giving and receiving, is self-concern our primary interest? How does this affect our contentment? Is our bottom line gratitude for all of God's good and perfect gifts?

GOD'S SUPPLY

A daily devotion for March 31

Read Philippians 4:19–23.

"And my God will meet all your needs according to the riches of his glory in Christ Jesus" (Phil. 4:19).

This is a promise for givers, not for nongivers. It's what God does in return for our gifts. Unfortunately, we often remove this promise from its context and take it as a blank check that we can cash anytime we are in need. This promise has sometimes been taken to apply to everyone everywhere. It does not. Half the world goes to bed hungry every night. God does not promise to meet every human need. He will not, and he permits the world to express its innate tendencies and desires.

This is a promise in exact accord with our Lord's words in the Sermon on the Mount. He said, "Give and it will be given to you." This is a promise for givers. We give, and God will give back to us. Of course we have all received freely from him first, and recognizing that, let us give. The Lord says, "Give and it will be given to you; good measure, pressed down, shaken together, running over, will be put into your lap. For the measure you give will be the measure you get back."

That is what Paul is saying here. He says, "You have given to me out of your poverty, out of your lack, at cost to yourselves. I am grateful for that, not because of the gift, which was a delightful fragrance to God, but because God will also abundantly give back to you and supply every need out of the riches of Christ Jesus."

Notice the source of supply: "my God." And he is not just a supplier but a God known through personal experience. He is not some remote power running the earth, giving to the just and the unjust alike, but a personal Father. This is a family matter. This is a promise for the children of God, those who belong to him.

Notice also the limits of supply: "all your needs." Paul doesn't say, "All your wants." Our wants are sometimes far beyond our needs. The great theologian Dr. H. A. Ironside said he delighted in walking through Woolworth's dime stores because he always found comfort in seeing so many things he could get along without. We have many wants in our lives and relatively few needs. God has promised to supply our needs, and we must let him decide what those needs are.

Notice, finally, the method of supply. It's according to the riches of God's glory in Christ Jesus. There are many kinds of riches. There are the riches of his goodness, which are available to all people. God makes the sun to shine and the rain to fall upon the just and the unjust. Then there are the riches of his grace, which are available only to sinners who admit their need. God's grace takes over, forgives and cleanses us, and gives us purity and all we need. There are also "the riches of his glory" in Christ Jesus. These are available to saints, to those who know him. All that God has in terms of the glory and the fullness of his deity is available to any believer. The weakest saint holds in his hands all that the greatest saint ever had. He has Christ, and in having Christ he has everything!

Father, thank you for all you have given me and will give me. You have not only supplied my every need but you have given me untold riches in Christ. Help me to live as one so blessed that I can say with Paul, "My God will meet all your needs according to the riches of his glory in Christ Jesus."

Do we give to others with care and prayer? Are we giving in order to be rewarded? What should be the motivation for joyful, spontaneous, even costly giving?

April

LEVITICUS

The Way to Wholeness
An introduction for the month of April

I do not know how you feel about the book of Leviticus, but I suspect that you don't find it terribly exciting. This book is where most people bog down when they start reading through the Bible. You finish Genesis with ease, learning about Abraham, Isaac, and Jacob and the incredible events of their lives. Then you get to Exodus and dramatic episodes such as Moses' confrontation with Pharaoh in the court of Egypt, the parting of the Red Sea, and the giving of the law. Then you start Leviticus. After you have plodded through the offerings, you get into the priesthood, the ceremonies, all the diet restrictions, the specifications for the dress of the high priest, and other strange functions and feasts. About that time your interest evaporates, you run out of gas, and that is the end of your reading through the Bible. That is the experience of many.

I can understand why this happens. I know that this book is a bit difficult and appears dry. If you can penetrate the dryness barrier, however, you will find the Bible a fascinating book to read all the way through.

The purpose of the book of Leviticus is found in chapter 20 when God says to his people, "You are to be holy to me because I, the Lord, am holy, and I have set you apart from the nations to be my own" (Lev. 20:26). When we Christians read this we must understand that we are the people of God today. What God said to Israel he also says to us, for in the new relationship we have in Jesus Christ there is neither Jew nor Gentile; there is but one man, one body in Christ. The promises that appear in picture form in the Old Testament also belong to us who live this side of the cross.

Perhaps you were turned off right away by the word *holy* in this verse. I do not know what you think *holy* means. You probably recall experiences that make the word unpalatable to you. Most of us associate it with grimness. We think of holy people as looking like they have been steeped in vinegar or soaked in embalming fluid. I used to think of the word that way, and holiness was not attractive to me at all. It repelled me. But then I ran across a verse in Scripture that spoke of "the beauty of holiness" (1 Chron. 16:29). I asked myself, *What in the world is beautiful about holiness?* When I found out, I agreed that holiness is indeed a beautiful thing.

If you want to get at the meaning of this word you must go back to its original root. This word is derived from the same root from which an attractive English word comes. This is the word *wholeness*. So *holiness* means "wholeness," being complete. And if you read *wholeness* in place of *holiness* everywhere you find it in the Bible, you will be much closer to what the writers of that book meant. *Wholeness* means to have together all the parts that were intended to be there and to have them functioning as they were meant to function.

That is what God is talking about. He says to his people, "You shall be whole because I am whole." God is complete; he is perfect. There is no blemish in God; he lives in harmony with himself. He is a beautiful person. He is absolutely what a person ought to be. He is filled with joy, love, and peace. He lives in wholeness. And he looks at us in our brokenness and says to us, "You, too, shall be whole."

The word *wholeness* has the power to awaken a desire within us. We long to be whole people. Don't you want to be what God made you to be, with all the ingredients of your personality expressed in balance? To be that way is to be a beautiful person, and that is what God is after. That is what Leviticus is all about.

THE NEED TO BELONG

A daily devotion for April 1

Read Leviticus 1.

> "The Lord called to Moses and spoke to him from the tent of meeting. He said, 'Speak to the Israelites and say to them: "When anyone among you brings an offering to the Lord, bring as your offering an animal from either the herd or the flock"'" (Lev. 1:1–2).

Leviticus discusses five offerings: the burnt offering, the meal offering, the peace offering, the trespass offering, and the sin offering. All five represent aspects of the work of Jesus Christ. The first offering is the burnt offering. The most important characteristic of this offering is that it had to involve a death. In these offerings, death always points to Christ's sacrifice on our behalf. So when the Israelites offered this sacrifice they were learning the great truth that only by means of the death of an acceptable substitute can man ever satisfy his great longing to belong. You can satisfy that longing only in the recognition of Jesus Christ's death for your sake. He is the expression of the love of God. So you must give yourself to God through Christ, acknowledging that he owns you. "You are not your own; you are bought with a price" (1 Cor. 6:19–20 RSV). God does not and will not exploit you and run you like a robot or a slave. He loves you and wants to fulfill you and to set you free. But you belong to him. That is the most basic truth of all.

You can find a certain amount of satisfaction in having a family. You will be restless if you do not have one. You can find satisfaction in having a background, an identity. But you will never be wholly satisfied that way. You will find that the cry of your heart, the hunger to be possessed and to belong, can be satisfied only by God in Jesus Christ entering your life. By the death of Christ that door is open. Only through Christ's death and only through the relationship with God that his death enables can this hunger be stilled, can this basic desire to belong be met. That is what accounts for the sense of joy and relief upon becoming a Christian. Do you remember that? "Now I belong! God is my Father! I'm in a family. I'll never be alone again! God will never forsake me nor abandon me! I belong to God!"

Thank you, Father, that you have made provision for this most basic of all needs to be met in Jesus Christ, who died for me that I might have it. Teach me to rejoice in my relationship with you.

The death of Christ has provided a way to fulfill our deepest longings. He has paid an immeasurable cost to bring us joy. Are we accessing this inheritance as our first and primary resource for living?

THE NEED TO RESPOND

A daily devotion for April 2

Read Leviticus 2.

> "When anyone brings a grain offering to the Lord, their offering is to be of the finest flour. They are to pour olive oil on it, put incense on it and take it to Aaron's sons the priests" (Lev. 2:1–2).

Now we come to the grain offering. Many versions call it the meal offering. In the King James Version it is called the meat offering because *meat* was the old English word for "food" or "meal." But there is no meat in this offering. In fact, this is the only one of the offerings that is bloodless. In all the others animals had to die, but in this one no blood was shed.

It is obvious that the essence of this offering was that it was bread. It was food, the staff of life. This theme is the key to the grain offering. Throughout the Old Testament we find people making meal offerings, often in the form of three loaves of bread. And the tabernacle contained the showbread.

The reason for all this becomes apparent when we remember that in the New Testament, after the great miracle when he took loaves and fishes and fed five thousand people, Jesus stood before the people and said, "I am the bread of life. Whoever comes to me will never go hungry, and whoever believes in me will never be thirsty" (John 6:35). He was indicating that he himself is to be our food and that we are to feed upon all of his character and his life.

This gives us a clue to what the grain offering depicts. It is a description of humanity as God intended it to be. This was seen in its perfect form only in Jesus Christ—the unsullied, God-pleasing humanity of the Lord Jesus. This perfection bears relationship to us only if we as Christians are drawing from, or feeding upon, the humanity of Jesus that is given to us.

I find that many people have the idea that the gospel, the good news, is that Jesus Christ died for us on the cross so that we might go to heaven when we die. That is a portion of the gospel. Unfortunately, that is the only part we hear in many places. But that is not the whole gospel by any means. If that is all we think the good news is, we have believed only a part of the gospel. The really good news is that Jesus Christ died for us so that he might live in us. The exciting part of Christianity is that he is living in us now. If we are not linked with his humanity and with all that he is, if his perfect humanity is not available to us, we are not enjoying the fullness of the Christian life or experience, because that is what it is all about.

This is what the grain offering anticipates. Eventually it looks toward us—we who can say with Paul, "I am crucified with Christ: nevertheless I live; yet not I, but Christ liveth in me" (Gal. 2:20 KJV). His perfect humanity is available to me. The fullness of his life, the fineness of his character, the balanced quality of his humanity are all available to me. And as I draw upon this by faith, as I expect him to link himself with me and to be an indwelling part of me while I work and live, I shall find that I am privileged to present that perfect humanity back to God to be used as he wants. That is the fullness of the gospel, and that is what the grain offering is all about.

> *Thank you for the love that is always reaching out toward me and that never seems to stop. Take me this day, Lord, and be my God and live through me so that everything you are I may be.*

It is possible to miss the core truth of authentic Christian living, resorting to our own best efforts. Are we ready and willing to exchange this futility for the exciting adventure of Christ living his life through us?

THE NEED FOR PEACE

A daily devotion for April 3

Read Leviticus 3.

"If your offering is a fellowship offering, and you offer an animal from the herd, whether male or female, you are to present before the Lord an animal without defect" (Lev. 3:1).

Next we read of the fellowship offering, which is better rendered the peace offering. In the peace offering we recognize another fundamental need of the human heart. No proper life is possible without peace.

I am not referring to the peace of forgiveness. That will come in the next two offerings: the sin and the trespass offerings. This is not peace with God; it is the peace of God we are talking about here. It is peace not in the sense of hostility having ceased but in the sense of emotional stability, of an untroubled heart. That is what we need—a sense of security, of well-being, of confidence that things are under control and are going to work out. That is the kind of peace this offering represents.

Many of us have heard the story of the artists who were commissioned to paint a picture of peace. One artist depicted peace as an absolutely calm sea lying under the moonlight without a ripple on the water. But the one who won the prize pictured a turbulent mountain waterfall, a cataract with its noisily plunging waters. Half-hidden behind the waterfall, amid all the thunder and the tumult, was a bird's nest with a mother bird sitting serenely on her eggs. That was peace. That is what this offering is all about—peace in the midst of trouble, in the midst of conflict.

This kind of peace is perhaps best known and most visible by its absence. We know when we are not at peace. We all have had the sense of tension and pressure, that knot at the back of the head, those butterflies in the stomach that won't leave us. There's a restlessness so intense that we feel we can't sit down. We have got to do something, anything, to get our minds off of whatever is troubling us. No matter what we do, it remains, throbbing away, and it keeps returning. A troubled heart indicates the absence of peace.

We all are familiar with the physical difficulties that can come with this absence. It can create all kinds of disturbances in the body—ulcers, nervous twitches, indigestion, stuttering, and other maladies. Emotional breakdown and nervous collapse can follow. So it is evident that we are dealing with a fundamental need. Anyone who does not think the Bible is practical has not even begun to understand this book. It deals with human life as it really is.

Thank you, Father, for the eloquent truths taught through these Old Testament sacrifices. Give me an open and responsive heart so that I will recognize that in the dying of the Lord Jesus, and in his living again, I have all that it takes to bring me through my troubles and to find peace.

Is our peace sadly dependent upon outward circumstances? Have we discovered the secret of inner tranquility as we increasingly trust in our Father's wise, loving, and sovereign control of all things?

THE NEED TO CONFESS

A daily devotion for April 4

Read Leviticus 4.

"Then the priest is to take some of the blood with his finger and put it on the horns of the altar of burnt offering and pour out the rest of the blood at the base of the altar" (Lev. 4:30).

The five great offerings specified in the book of Leviticus clearly set forth the basic needs of our humanity, needs that God has built into every one of us, and show the only way these needs can be met. Here we come to the fourth of these offerings, the sin offering.

In other offerings, blood had to be shed and a death had to occur. All the blood of the animal was poured out at the foot of the altar. But something unusual was always done with the blood of the sin offering. The blood had to be sprinkled seven times before the Lord. Then, in the case of the offering for the anointed priest as we see here, it had to be put on the horns of the altar of incense that stood in the holy place, right in front of the veil that guarded the Holy of Holies—right before the presence of the Lord.

What was the significance of this? It is obvious that a special emphasis was placed upon the blood. It was to be put in a visible place, a place obviously connected with God. It was to be recognized openly as being on the horns of the altar before the Lord. And the individual for whom the offering was being made had to be able to see the blood there. That was the point. In other words, the one who had sinned was supposed to understand that this blood had now covered his sin, forgiven it, and before God it was acknowledged to be forgiven. And when he understood that, his conscience could be at rest.

I encounter many people who have never understood that God accepts the death of Jesus fully on their behalf. They are always troubling themselves about some terrible sin that they have committed and that they think God is not able to forgive. They do not see the blood on the horns of the altar. As a result, they torture themselves endlessly with guilt. But God is trying to make clear that there is a way to be free of guilt. And once the blood is there on the altar, it provides a way out. There is no guilt left! "He shall be forgiven," the Scripture says—not only of sinful acts but of the guilt of his nature. This offering teaches that this is the only way man can be free from the nagging guilt that alienates him from God.

Men are always trying to find their own ways to be free of guilt. Some try to forget it. Most attempt simply to avoid the whole subject. They don't want to think of their guilt. But remember how David said he felt when he tried that: "When I kept silent, my bones wasted away through my groaning all day long. For day and night your hand was heavy on me; my strength was sapped as in the heat of summer" (Ps. 32:3–4).

This is what unacknowledged guilt will do. It will dry up your life, reducing it to a shallow, superficial level of living in which you must be caught up in endless diversions to avoid thinking about your relationship with God. And forgetting will never work either.

Help me to be honest, Lord, about my guilt and not try to avoid it but to know that there is no way out unless I acknowledge it. Thank you for providing a way out of my guilt so that I no longer need to be far off from you.

Honest confession and open repentance are never risk-taking with God but rather the open door to forgiveness of all our sin. Do we seek this invaluable gift often and with joyful expectancy?

UNINTENTIONAL SIN

A daily devotion for April 5

Read Leviticus 5.

> "The Lord said to Moses: 'When anyone is unfaithful to the Lord by sinning unintentionally in regard to any of the Lord's holy things, they are to bring to the Lord as a penalty a ram from the flock, one without defect and of the proper value in silver, according to the sanctuary shekel. It is a guilt offering'" (Lev. 5:14–15).

A distinction of the sin offering was that the sin was often said to be unintentional. The offering dealt not with acts of deliberate evil, which all of us commit from time to time, but with the nature prompting those acts. This nature takes us by surprise.

Most of us, if asked, would say that we are pretty nice people. Most of us have a fairly good opinion of ourselves. We acknowledge that we have a few minor problems, peccadilloes that we could overcome with only a slight effort if we had the proper motivation.

But every now and then some event surprises us, and we act in a way we didn't expect. A situation catches us unaware and suddenly we do just what we never thought we'd do. We come to the sudden and shattering realization that evil is more deeply embedded in us than we had imagined. That is what the sin offering addressed—that kind of evil, the part of our nature that takes us by surprise because we fancy that we had gotten rid of it or did not even possess it.

In *The Brothers Karamazov*, Dostoevski offers a fable about a wicked woman who died. The devils took her to hell and threw her into the lake of fire. Her guardian angel was puzzled as to how he might help her, so he scrutinized her whole life to see if he could find at least one good thing that she had done that he might present before God. Finally he approached God and said, "Once a beggar came by when she was weeding her garden, and she pulled an onion out and gave it to him to eat." God told the angel, "All right, then go down and get that onion and hold it out to her in the lake of fire. Tell her to take hold of it, and if you can pull her out with that onion she can enter paradise." So the angel took the onion, went down to the lake of fire, and held the onion out to the woman, who grabbed hold of it. He pulled and pulled, and sure enough, she began to emerge from the lake. She was almost completely free when some other sinners grabbed her ankles so they could be pulled out with her. At first the onion held, and they too were being pulled out. But the woman became angry and cried, "This is my onion, and you're not going to go out with me!" As she kicked them loose, the onion broke and she fell back in, and she is burning there to this day.

That is a graphic illustration of the very thing this offering addresses. Even in moments of triumph there is that taint of selfishness, of that evil, in every human heart. That is what the sin offering deals with.

Father, how thoroughly you understand me! You know what can lurk in my life, hidden away, keeping me from knowing the full measure of your grace. Thank you for making provision for all my sins, even those of which I am unaware.

As we encounter the surprise, often the shock, of our sinfulness, does it increase our awe at the astounding sacrifice paid for our forgiveness? Do we respond with life-changing gratitude and worship?

THE NEED TO RESTORE

A daily devotion for April 6

Read Leviticus 6.

> "If anyone sins and is unfaithful to the Lord by deceiving a neighbor about something entrusted to them or left in their care or about something stolen, or if they cheat their neighbor ... when they sin in any of these ways and realize their guilt, they must return what they have stolen or taken by extortion ... And as a penalty they must bring to the priest, that is, to the Lord, their guilt offering, a ram from the flock, one without defect and of the proper value" (Lev. 6:2, 4, 6).

Here we will deal with the last of the five basic human needs represented by the five offerings that God taught the Israelites from the tent of meeting. The guilt offering is the final one of this series because it deals with the relationship of man with man, with how to maintain a workable relationship with our neighbor. This is the offering that teaches us how to restore harmony to broken human relationships.

One of the sins covered by the trespass offering concerns robbing or defrauding a neighbor. When this happens, the relationship is broken and must be restored. It will never heal, however, until the offense is admitted. Time will not cure this kind of hurt. You can wrong somebody today, and fifty years might go by before you see the person again. When you see that person the relationship will still be broken, the hurt will remain, and you will immediately feel the restraint on your spirit.

When I was a young Christian I was working for a contractor. It was my task to make out the checks at the end of the month, including my own. One month I needed some money and asked my boss if I could have an advance of twenty-five dollars, to which he consented. I wrote out a check, which he signed, and I cashed it. Then at the end of the month when I was making out the regular checks, I forgot that I had already drawn twenty-five dollars, so I made out my own check for the usual amount. It wasn't until after the boss had signed it and had given it to me that I remembered. I realized that he hadn't remembered either. I rationalized, saying to myself, *Well, he owes it to me anyway. I've been working very hard. So I'll just say nothing about it.* My job soon ended and I returned to school, and for a couple of years I lived with that dishonesty, but I never could forget it. So one day, I wrote my old boss a letter and I sent back the money. I told him what I had done, said that I was wrong, and asked him to forgive me. Soon I received a gracious letter from him inviting me to come back to work for him anytime. What a load this lifted from my spirit!

This trespass offering is provided for us, fulfilled in Jesus Christ, that we might heal all the broken relationships of the past. If you want to have a clear conscience before God, you may have to go back and heal broken relationships. You may have to make restitution. You may have to admit errors. But once you do, those relationships will be healed before God and will be a glory and a blessing to you for the rest of your life.

> *Father, how thoroughly you understand what can lurk in my life, hidden away, keeping me from living comfortably with others. And how wonderfully and wisely you have made provision for me in your Word so that I can live, love, and enjoy life with others without constant tension.*

The Scriptures equate defrauding our neighbor with unfaithfulness to the Lord. Are we taking care to guard the integrity of our human relationships so that God is glorified?

THE SECRET OF PEACE

A daily devotion for April 7

Read Leviticus 7.

> "The meat of their fellowship offering of thanksgiving must be eaten on the day it is offered; they must leave none of it till morning" (Lev. 7:15).

Isn't that strange? The Israelites could eat the flesh on the day they offered it if it was an offering of thanksgiving for a particular thing. If it was just a general expression of their gratitude toward God, they could save some of it for the second day. But under no circumstances were they ever to eat of the flesh of that peace offering on the third day. It had to be burned. If they tried to eat any of it, they committed an abomination unto God.

God offers a practical truth here. He is saying that there must be no separation between the peace that we feel and the source of that peace, the sacrifice that provided it. We must not separate the two. In other words, we must not depend upon the feelings of peace that are given to us. We shouldn't try to live on those. Once we are given peace as a result of trusting the work of Jesus Christ on our behalf, we can't simply say, "Ah, now I feel much better! I think I can go on now, and tomorrow I'll expect this peace to remain, and I'll reckon on that." We must not shift our dependence from the One who gives peace to the feeling it produces.

What a practical warning that is, because we all tend to do this, don't we? As soon as the load is lifted we think, *Well, everything's fine now. I'll shift back now and continue on my own.* But if we try that, within two days we are in the same mess again, with a troubled heart. No, there is only one source of peace. It comes by reckoning upon the wisdom, love, and power of a risen Lord who can work out any situation in ways that we can't anticipate or even imagine if we will put the problem into his hands. That doesn't mean we should simply forget it. We may be part of the solution. God's way of working it out may be to use us. But we don't know when he may want to do this. We must stand ready and he will let us know. But the responsibility for working out problems is no longer ours. It is God's. That is the secret of peace.

> *Thank you, Father, for truths taught through these Old Testament sacrifices. Help me to remember that peace will only come as I trust in the sacrifice that made peace with you possible.*

Peace that endures is grounded in the character and the work of Jesus Christ. What does that suggest about times when peace feels elusive and fears are overwhelming?

THE NEED FOR A PRIEST

A daily devotion for April 8

Read Leviticus 8:1–9.

> "The Lord said to Moses, 'Bring Aaron and his sons, their garments, the anointing oil, the bull for the sin offering, the two rams and the basket containing bread made without yeast, and gather the entire assembly at the entrance to the tent of meeting.' Moses did as the Lord commanded him, and the assembly gathered at the entrance to the tent of meeting" (Lev. 8:1–4).

These verses introduce us to priesthood by describing in brief the ingredients that make it possible. First comes the word of God. True priesthood never originates from man's conception of what he needs. It comes from God's word, God's thoughts. God knows us and he has designed this for us. It doesn't come from a pope, a council, a convention, a synod of bishops, or any other human committee.

The second element is Aaron and his sons. Aaron was the brother of Moses. He and his descendants were the only family in the Old Testament authorized to serve as priests. Aaron was to be the high priest. As the letter to the Hebrews makes clear, we too have a High Priest. Aaron is the picture of that Great High Priest, Jesus Christ our Lord, whose priesthood is as necessary to us as Aaron's was to the Israelites. Aaron's sons represent every believer in Jesus Christ. Everyone who knows Jesus Christ as Lord and Savior is constituted a priest to the other members of the human family. John says that Jesus has made us a kingdom of priests (Rev. 1:6).

The third ingredient of the priesthood is the garments. In the symbolism of Scripture, garments are always a revelation of the character of the individual who wears them. So as we examine the list of garments we will understand what a priest is, what he does, and how he functions.

The fourth ingredient of the priesthood is the anointing oil, which in Scripture always speaks of the Holy Spirit. This means that a priest, to be effective, must always walk in the Spirit. We will never be effective priests unless we learn the ministry of the Holy Spirit, how he works in us and imparts the life of Christ to others through us.

The next ingredient is the sacrifices. These always speak of redemption, of the need for dealing with the problem of sin and guilt. Since Aaron and his sons were but men, they too needed sacrifices.

The sixth element of the priesthood was God's command to Moses to bring all the congregation together. God insisted that all the adults and the children be there. He wanted the humblest and the greatest in Israel to be present. Moses had to assemble the whole congregation—more than a million people. That must have created quite a seating problem! Perhaps the Israelites erected grandstands. In any event they were all to be there so that God himself might teach them what priesthood meant.

> *Our Father, help us to lift our eyes unto the Great High Priest who is within us, ready to release to us all the mighty resources available to him. Help us to lay hold of these resources and to understand that you have made provision to meet all our needs.*

Every aspect of God-ordained priesthood has been fulfilled in our High Priest, the Lord Jesus Christ. When he enters as our Savior and Lord, he ministers to all our needs and invites us to serve as his representative priests. Have we entered into this amazing inheritance?

THE WORK OF A PRIEST

A daily devotion for April 9

Read Leviticus 8:10–36.

> "He then presented the other ram, the ram for the ordination, and Aaron and his sons laid their hands on its head. Moses slaughtered the ram and took some of its blood and put it on the lobe of Aaron's right ear, on the thumb of his right hand and on the big toe of his right foot" (Lev. 8:22–23).

This was the offering of ordination for the priest. What a strange ceremony! What does it signify? Blood is always a reminder to us that we have no value apart from the death of Christ on our behalf. That is all God ever accepts as being of any value during our time on earth. And here the priest is to have a bloodstained ear, a bloodstained thumb, and a bloodstained toe.

He is to hear God's Word as someone who has already been redeemed and who recognizes that he is not merely hearing some good ideas but is listening to the instruction that can release him and can relieve him of pressures and problems—all because he has already been bought by that blood. We are to hear the Word of God not as mere philosophy but as God's instruction deep within our hearts.

Then we are to serve man. That command is always symbolized by the hand, probably the most useful member of the human body. We are to serve as bloodstained people, recognizing that we have no righteousness in ourselves, that we are no better than anyone else. We offer our help not as people who have achieved perfection but as ones who, like those we help, very much need the constant cleansing of the blood of Jesus Christ.

Paul says, "Brothers and sisters, if someone is caught in a sin, you who live by the Spirit should restore that person gently. But watch yourselves, or you also may be tempted" (Gal. 6:1). Remind yourself that you may be the next one to fall. And when you fall you don't want someone pointing a finger at you and judging you severely. Rather, you want someone to come to you and say, "Brother, maybe I've never done what you've done, but I know I certainly could have. I just want you to know that I understand how you feel right now, and I want to see you cleansed as only God is able to cleanse."

Finally there is the bloodstained foot, a reminder that we need the cleansing of God's grace every day, that we never are perfect in this life, that though God has made provision for a life of service and of walking in the Spirit, we all have failed to some extent every day in laying hold of it. God has understood that and has made provision for it.

Father, thank you for this look at Aaron and his sons. Open my spiritual eyes so that I can see beyond them to Jesus Christ and his family, the great body of Christ of which I am a part.

Our high and holy calling as servant-priests requires constant cleansing by the blood Jesus shed for us. Are our ears tuned to his holy wisdom, our hands available at his direction, our feet walking to his drumbeat?

THE PRESENT GLORY

A daily devotion for April 10

Read Leviticus 9.

> "Moses and Aaron then went into the tent of meeting. When they came out, they blessed the people; and the glory of the Lord appeared to all the people" (Lev. 9:23).

What a dramatic scene! A million or more people, the whole camp of Israel, are somehow gathered at vantage points where they can observe what is happening in the open space before the door of the tabernacle. They watch Aaron and his sons kill these animals, put them on the altar, sprinkle the blood, and pour it out. When everything is completed exactly as the Lord has commanded Moses and Aaron enter the tabernacle. A hush falls over the whole assembly.

Then Moses and Aaron come out and bless the people. Suddenly the glory of the Lord appears. This radiant cloud of light, the *shekinah*, fills the whole area, and a supernatural fire proceeds from it, consuming in a flash all the rest of the offerings upon the altar. A most impressive scene! No wonder the people fall on their faces and shout. This is a shout of victory, an expression of awe and wonder at the fact that the God of glory is in their midst.

All of this is designed for our instruction (1 Cor. 10). What is the lesson? We are to be priests like these, and the objective of priesthood is to produce the glory of the Lord. That glory is manifest when the priesthood is operating properly. When all is done as God commands, everything works together to produce the glory of the Lord.

The counterpart of that glory in our lives today is the beauty of the character of Jesus. The New Testament says that the Spirit of God is at work in our hearts to produce glory unto glory. And Paul, in 2 Corinthians 4:6, says that the glory of God is found "in the face of Jesus Christ." So it is God's character, the character of Jesus, appearing in us in our daily encounters with people, that is represented by the glory of the Lord here in Leviticus.

Father, help me to stop resisting what you are doing in me so that I might be a minister and a priest of your glory to others.

Is the glory of God the chief end for which we love and serve? Have we grasped the joy of spreading the knowledge of him everywhere? Shine, Jesus, shine, to show your glorious power in our jars of clay!

STRANGE FIRE

A daily devotion for April 11

Read Leviticus 10:1–10.

> "Aaron's sons Nadab and Abihu took their censers, put fire in them and added incense; and they offered unauthorized fire before the Lord, contrary to his command. So fire came out from the presence of the Lord and consumed them, and they died before the Lord" (Lev. 10:1–2).

The same *shekinah* that had consumed the sacrifice now flashes out again to destroy these two priests. What a shock this must have been to Aaron, to his remaining two sons, and to the whole camp of Israel.

What would your reaction have been if you had witnessed this scene? Many of us reading stories like this have come away with the idea that God, especially the "God of the Old Testament," is a God of vengeful judgment. But God is acting here just as much as a God of love as he is in any other part of the Bible. His nature is love, and he never deviates from what he has revealed himself to be. So this action must be in line with his nature and with the character of his love.

Several points about this passage help us to understand the truth. The first is that the sin of these two priests was not one of ignorance but one of presumption. They knew better. They had been told emphatically that God would be offended by what they had decided to do. In Exodus 30:7–9 God had precisely said, "Be careful; do not offer the wrong kind of incense." So this was a violation of God's direct command. He never visits judgment on anybody who is struggling in ignorance to find him.

The second thing we need to note is that this sin was dealt with so severely because it distorted God's revelation of himself. In all these priestly sacrifices and rituals God is explaining something about himself so that we might learn what kind of God he is. But by their disobedience these priests were teaching wrong concepts about the being of God. That is why he judged them.

The third thing to notice about this episode is that this judgment was exemplary. God made an example of these two priests, and he never did such a thing again. This was not something that happened every time a priest violated a regulation. It happened only once—at the beginning of the priesthood. Later in the priesthood of Israel priests did many terrible things before the altar, but God never killed them for it. But it is important that this happened at least this one time, for this was an example and therefore a manifestation of God's love and concern. He was trying to stop this kind of thing from happening again, and he was giving fair warning of the consequences to anyone presumptuous enough to sin deliberately in this way.

> *Father, I feel a sense of awe when I consider that you are a holy God. I pray that this will help me to understand that my life is not a game and that the priesthood to which I am called is a serious matter.*

Are we carelessly offering a pretense of worship to God? How can we offer him worship that honors and delights him? What circumstances best produce the sweet fragrance of burning frankincense?

THE INTENT OF THE LAW

A daily devotion for April 12

Read Leviticus 10:11–20.

> "Aaron replied to Moses, 'Today they sacrificed their sin offering and their burnt offering before the Lord, but such things as this have happened to me. Would the Lord have been pleased if I had eaten the sin offering today?' When Moses heard this, he was satisfied" (Lev. 10:19–20).

Do you see the problem here? There were two kinds of sin offering, as explained in the law of the sin offering in chapter 6. In one the blood was to be carried into the inner sanctuary, into the holy place, and there it was to be sprinkled on the horns of the golden altar of fragrant incense. That was required as a picture of the depravity of man's evil. And because of that depravity no part of the animal was to be eaten but it was all to be taken outside the camp and burned.

But there was another kind of sin offering in which the blood was sprinkled on the horns of the brazen altar in the outer court. There the flesh of the animal was to be eaten by the priests as a picture of their understanding of the nature of their evil and as a token of their acceptance of God's forgiveness.

This offering was of the second kind. The blood had not been brought into the sanctuary, and so Moses said, "You should have eaten this meat! Why didn't you?" He was afraid lest the judgment of God consume the rest of the priests. But Aaron explained, "Two of my sons sinned. And even though a sin offering was made this morning, they died. Evidently there is some depth of depravity here that we don't understand and that has taken their lives. Therefore it seemed to me that the Lord would not be pleased if I ate the sin offering. So we have treated it as though the blood were sprinkled before the golden altar, and the body of this animal has been burned in its entirety."

When Moses heard that, he realized that Aaron had gone deeper than the letter of the law; he had understood the intent of it. He had understood what God was after in these sacrifices and ceremonies. And so God, mercifully, did not exercise any judgment here. Aaron had pressed beyond the letter to the deep intent of the law. Moses was content with that.

This attitude always pleases God. He is not at all interested in our ritual. That is something we need so desperately to understand. He is not impressed by the fact that we come to church every Sunday if that is all we do. He doesn't care that we stand and sing and pray and witness if our hearts are not in it. He concerned only with what happens in the heart. David understood this when he wrote, "My sacrifice, O God, is a broken spirit; a broken and contrite heart you, God, will not despise" (Ps. 51:17).

That is what God is after with us. He doesn't want any kind of religious nonsense. What he wants is a heart that is open, responsive, honest, and obedient before him. With that God is greatly pleased. That delights his heart.

> *Lord, I want to meet you, the living Word. Make my life a medium not of biblical scholarship but of fellowship with Christ.*

God is not pleased with mere outward conformity to the law but desires that we always seek to understand its intent. Are we learning what is holy and pleasing to God by the renewal of our minds?

THE NEED FOR A STANDARD

A daily devotion for April 13

Read Leviticus 11.

> "I am the Lord, who brought you up out of Egypt to be your God; therefore be holy, because I am holy" (Lev. 11:45).

In this section we face the need for a standard, a measuring stick by which we can distinguish between good and evil. That is not easy to do. Modern philosophies tell us that nothing is harmful, that only our perverted thinking makes things wrong, and that if we changed this thinking, we would see that anything and everything are right. But we don't find anything like that in Scripture. The Bible tells us that we are living in a world where truth and error are inextricably mixed and that we cannot easily tell one from the other. How do we tell the difference before it is too late, before we have to learn through sorrows?

God expressed his concern for the Israelites on a physical level—he regulated their diet. This chapter includes dietary laws distinguishing clean animals from unclean and prescribes sanitary practices as well. Many of these practices offer a commonsense basis for staying healthy. God kept his people physically whole through many of these regulations.

There was nothing wrong with many of the animals which were prohibited to the Israelites as food. Their prohibition was simply to teach a symbolic lesson, even though they may have been perfectly healthy as food. In this case it is the symbolism that we must take into account.

There was nothing wrong with many of the animals prohibited to the Israelites as food. They were forbidden only because the prohibition taught a symbolic lesson. It is this symbolism that we are interested in.

We have seen that the word *holy* essentially means "whole." To be holy is to be a complete person, to fulfill one's humanity. A whole person is one who performs the function for which he was designed. Our function is to belong to God, to be his image. It is to be the vehicle for the expression of his life. This is what he wants for us. He wants us to be whole and to fulfill our humanity.

That is what God is after. It is not the religious activities we perform or how much time we spend in Bible study that interests God. He is concerned with the expression of his character where we work, in our homes, and among family, neighbors, and friends. He desires that the character we show to others reflect love, joy, and peace, tenderheartedness and a willingness to forgive, forbearance and understanding, and the absence of grudge-holding, bitterness, hatred, and enmity. That is the character of a whole person. So God says to us, "Therefore be holy and avoid these things that I have warned you against, for they will defile you."

> *Lord, help me to take these guidelines seriously. Help me to be obedient to you and to offer my body as a living sacrifice. Though I live in a broken world, I long to be a whole person.*

Secular thinking leaves us adrift in the turbulent waters of relativity, in stark contrast with the teaching of the Bible, which aims at our wholeness. Are we being nurtured in body, soul, and spirit by feeding on God's Word?

NATURE OR NURTURE?

A daily devotion for April 14

Read Leviticus 12.

> "The Lord said to Moses, 'Say to the Israelites: "A woman who becomes pregnant and gives birth to a son will be ceremonially unclean for seven days, just as she is unclean during her monthly period. On the eighth day the boy is to be circumcised"'" (Lev. 12:1–3).

This text certainly reminds us of Mary and Joseph and the baby Jesus. In fact, that baby came into the world to deal with the problem that made this chapter necessary. God is not against childbirth or against babies. Nor is human birth an inherently unclean event. There is nothing wrong with birth or with sex. But God gave these requirements to the people so that we might remember a fundamental fact: that since the fall of Adam every human being born into this world is born into a fallen race.

There is no way by which man in his natural condition can solve the basic problems of human relationships. We are born in a tainted and twisted condition. Someone threw a monkey wrench into the human machinery at the beginning, and it doesn't operate as God intended. God impressed this upon his people with this restriction, this reminder that something connected with birth is unclean. The fact that a mother was considered unclean for a week after the birth of a male child (two weeks for a female child), and that she had to go through another thirty-three days of purification after that, forcefully reminded her and her family that the baby was born with a tainted nature. The circumcision of the male baby was an additional reminder that something needed to be removed from the life inherited from Adam.

This fact is important because it makes a difference in the way a child is trained. If you think that babies are born absolutely innocent, you will raise your child in quite a different way than if you believe the truth about them. They need guidance and training and help in handling this twisted nature. The world, of course, forgets about this principle. Many people prefer to pretend that babies are innocent and that if they are left alone and given the opportunity to express themselves, they will grow into whole, fulfilled persons. So God teaches his people right from the beginning that there is a problem that must be handled and cannot be ignored.

Thank you, Lord, for always teaching me according to reality. I am forever grateful that two thousand years ago you sent a baby into the world, born of a woman, who would bring cleansing for all my sin.

The Bible begins our tutorial for life with birth, reminding us of our fallenness and offering carefully prescribed procedures for recovery, again beginning at childbirth. How awesome that the Son of God was born of woman on our behalf!

DEALING WITH THE LEPROSY OF LIFE

A daily devotion for April 15

Read Leviticus 13.

"When anyone has a defiling skin disease, they must be brought to the priest" (Lev. 13:9).

The purpose of this chapter is to enable the detection of leprosy. When the Bible uses this word, it is not referring only to the disease that we call leprosy today, Hansen's disease. That is included in the term, but the Hebrew word translated as "leprosy" here includes other contagious and infectious skin diseases. They all were recognized to be dangerous and damaging, a serious threat not only to the individual but to the whole camp of Israel, and so they were to be detected. The process of detection was prolonged and careful inspection. The priest was to look at the symptoms, isolate the diseased person for seven days, examine him again, and shut him away for another seven days. At the end of that time the priest could determine whether the disease was leprosy or something less serious.

All of this has its counterpart in our spiritual lives. This passage is talking to us about the afflictions and diseases of the spirit, the hurtful attitudes we have, the burning resentments, the feelings of anger and upset we experience, and the grudges we carry around in our hearts toward one another. These must be detected because they can be dangerous, and the way to do this is to expose them to a priest. Remember that in the New Testament pattern all believers are priests. But we are all blind to ourselves. In my own eyes I am a genial, gracious, inoffensive person. I don't know why it is, but others don't always see me the same way. I am blind to my failings. We all have these blind spots. That is why we need each other. And so when he had a manifestation of disease, the Israelite was instructed to present himself to a priest.

In the spiritual realm, this means that the evil in question must be brought under the judgment of the Word of God in order to be cleansed. The evil must be faced and named for what it is, as God sees it. All the defenses that we have built around it to protect it must be taken down, and we must admit our wrong. Then God can cleanse us from it, and this evil will leave our life. The scars may remain, but there is no need to fear any longer; the action of the evil has been arrested. We see a beautiful picture of this in 1 John 1:9: "If we confess our sins, he is faithful and just and will forgive us our sins and purify us from all unrighteousness." What a gracious provision this is!

Are your leprous spots being judged? Are they being dealt with openly in the light of the Word of God? Are they being brought to the One who can heal leprosy with a touch? Or are they being protected, hidden to avoid examination? Your moods, your disposition, your temperamental outbursts, your displays of anger or depression—what about them?

> *Lord Jesus, how often I have injured others by my leprous condition. I know that you want me to be clean and to walk in victory. So by the faithfulness of your Spirit, please judge the leprosy in my life. Touch it and heal it as I bow before you.*

Are we open to others' observations about our attitudes and behaviors? What about our priestly service to others who may need our insight but most of all our compassion?

THE NEED FOR CLEANSING

A daily devotion for April 16

Read Leviticus 14.

"The priest is to go outside the camp and examine them. If they have been healed of their defiling skin disease, the priest shall order that two live clean birds and some cedar wood, scarlet yarn and hyssop be brought for the person to be cleansed" (Lev. 14:3–4).

Chapter 14 elaborates on the issue of handling leprosy. This passage addresses the cleansing of the leper. Notice that the leper does not go through all the ritual that follows to be healed; he does it to be cleansed. He is already healed. Only God can heal. This divine act takes place in the inner life of a believer. Cleansing allows the one who is healed to understand God's basis and purpose for the healing. God wants the inner cleansing to be reflected in the outward life of the person who is healed. That is the picture drawn here.

We can't heal our leprous hearts. If there is some wrongful attitude within us, if we burn with envy or jealousy or resentment toward one another, if we are impatient and upset and angry at heart, we seldom see these things in ourselves until God puts us into circumstances where they are made clear. Then the only thing we can do is take them to him, because we are helpless victims caught up in these dangerous attitudes. When we finally see ourselves like that, then we can say, "Lord, heal me!" And God does! With a touch of his grace he changes our attitude. We stop being defensive about it and we admit it. And then the leprosy is arrested, its action is stopped, and we are healed.

But then we need cleansing. We need to understand the basis on which that inward healing occurred so that our outward behavior can be adjusted to a new pattern. That is brought out here in the cleansing of the leper. He had to go through a prescribed ritual consisting of several steps before he could resume a normal life. The basis for healing is always blood. God never heals, never blesses, never arrests the action of evil, apart from the shedding of blood.

This blood here is a picture of the blood of the Lord Jesus. The death of Christ, which ends the old nature, the old life, is constantly pictured for us in these sacrifices. God is not in the business of putting Band-Aids on cancer. He strikes at the root of the cancer. He never deals only with symptoms. He eliminates the whole problem. That is why God is never content merely to clear up a few symptoms in our lives. He wants us to see that these problems arise out of an evil nature that must be ended by death—either of the individual or of an innocent substitute on his behalf. There is no other way. So the shedding of the blood of this bird is a beautiful picture of the Lord Jesus and his death for us.

Lord, I want to be whole, fulfilled, and healed. Deal with me so that I might understand and apply these principles. With David I pray, "May these words of my mouth and this meditation of my heart be pleasing in your sight, Lord, my Rock and my Redeemer" (Ps. 19:14).

Do we presume to heal ourselves and others of sins of the spirit? Why must we keep the focus on Jesus's atoning blood? Are we dealing honestly and compassionately with the cleansing process in addressing the outward symptoms of inner sins?

DEALING WITH THE DISCHARGES OF LIFE

A daily devotion for April 17

Read Leviticus 15.

> "When a man is cleansed from his discharge, he is to count off seven days for his ceremonial cleansing; he must wash his clothes and bathe himself with fresh water, and he will be clean. On the eighth day he must take two doves or two young pigeons and come before the Lord to the entrance to the tent of meeting and give them to the priest" (Lev. 15:13–14).

The unavoidable diseases, afflictions, and discharges mentioned in this chapter are of a much less serious nature than the leprosy dealt with in previous chapters. When the leper was cleansed he had to go through a much more rigorous ceremony that included several offerings. But here the simplest of the offerings is prescribed: two turtledoves or two young pigeons, one for a sin offering, one for a burnt offering—the cheapest and the most available of the offerings. Yet God never sets aside the requirement for the blood of an innocent substitute to be shed in the place of one who is defiled, whatever the reason. By this means he underscores the fact that human nature must be dealt with by blood. This deep and complicated problem cannot be solved by a rearrangement of surface symptoms. God is constantly underscoring that for us in these offerings.

So God has provided a way, a remedy. First, a person who is defiled shall bathe. Washing is always a picture of the action of the Word of God. The person's defiling thought, his statement, his tone of voice, his attitude of heart, he shall take to the Word and see what the Word has to say about it. Washing through the Word is the beginning of cleansing.

Then the person shall be "unclean until the evening." Uncleanness is what we call being "out of fellowship." It means to revert momentarily from rest and dependence upon the Spirit of God to a manifestation of the flesh, the old life, the old nature. This break in communion with the Spirit of God temporarily arrests the flow of the life of Christ in the believer. Although Christ never forsakes him, for the moment, the person finds no enjoyment in his life. That is what it means to be unclean, and the condition continues until evening.

The third element in the cleansing is the offering of blood. All through this book you find that God's cleansing agents are always water and blood. The blood speaks of the death of Jesus on our behalf, which frees God to love us without restraint. The water represents the Word. It cleanses our conscience. People can say, "Yes, God has forgiven me." But many do not forgive themselves. They don't allow their consciences to be cleansed. But we read in the Word of God that he has washed away our sins and has forgiven us all unrighteousness, and if we believe that Word, then our consciences are clear, and we are cleansed by the Word. Therefore there is no longer any reason for us to be beating ourselves up about sins. God has cleansed us. We are no longer dirty or defiled. We are clean. That is the effect of the water.

> *Father, I need the cleansing of your Word, the purifying of your blood. Thank you for making it available to me. I pray that I will be honest about these matters and will not let them go unattended. Help me to keep short accounts with you and to let your Holy Spirit cleanse away all the defilement of my life.*

What three steps are indicated for cleansing of the defilement of sin? What are the two essential prerequisites for exposing and addressing these issues?

THE DAY OF ATONEMENT

A daily devotion for April 18

Read Leviticus 16.

> "When Aaron has finished making atonement for the Most Holy Place, the tent of meeting and the altar, he shall bring forward the live goat. He is to lay both hands on the head of the live goat and confess over it all the wickedness and rebellion of the Israelites—all their sins—and put them on the goat's head. He shall send the goat away into the wilderness in the care of someone appointed for the task. The goat will carry all their sins on itself, to a remote place; and the man shall release it in the wilderness" (Lev. 16:20–22).

All the iniquities, all the transgressions, all the sins are placed upon the head of this goat. The goat is a picture of Jesus, who satisfies the heart of God for us and renders God free to love us without restraint by his justice. God's justice has been satisfied. He is free to forgive us at any time. Christ also bears the whole weight of our guilt, all that the Devil tries to use as a basis for his accusations against us. All this is to be sent back to him whence it comes. When our Lord died he entered the wilderness of death like this goat and returned to Satan all his accusations against believers throughout time.

This passage teaches us what we are to do with these accusations. In Ephesians 6:16, Paul calls them "the fiery darts of the wicked one." They are all those suggestions to us that we aren't accepted and loved by God, that he still has reservations about us, and that we can't openly and boldly come before his presence. These are all the haunting memories of our past shame, our feelings of unworthiness, our filthy thoughts, and the flashes of fear that come upon us. What are we to do with them? We are simply to put them right on the head of Jesus and say, "Lord, take them back to Satan. They don't belong to me. They belong to him. That is where they came from, and I am sending them back."

Do you want to worship God? Well, how do you do it? Simply by believing that he has accepted you the way you are and has already dealt with everything that is wrong—everything—and is now ready to use you without hesitation. Say to the Lord, "Here I am. I am counting on it. Thank you for it. What are you going to do through me today? What are you going to do this next moment in the relationship I am beginning with this person? How are you going to handle it?" Then your mind and heart can be at peace.

Father, thank you for this promise and for the beauty of this ceremony, which in Israel of old could occur only once a year but which for me is to be daily, over and over again. I come boldly into your presence with joy, with a heart washed from an evil conscience, and with gladness and thanksgiving, not on my merit but on the merit of another. I give thanks for this and pray that it may be my experience, not only this moment but every day of my life!

Does this incredibly awesome picture of Jesus—as the scapegoat bearing our sin and our guilt—cause us to worship with unending gratitude? Have we even begun to grasp the magnitude of this gift of pure grace?

HANDLING LIFE

A daily devotion for April 19

Read Leviticus 17.

> "This is so the Israelites will bring to the Lord the sacrifices they are now making in the open fields. They must bring them to the priest, that is, to the Lord, at the entrance to the tent of meeting and sacrifice them as fellowship offerings ... They must no longer offer any of their sacrifices to the goat idols to whom they prostitute themselves. This is to be a lasting ordinance for them and for the generations to come" (Lev. 17:5, 7).

The object of this requirement is to teach that all life belongs to God and that he alone can handle it rightly. Only God understands life. That is the basis for all proper behavior. If we don't understand this fact, we won't behave properly. We can't. We must understand that our lives belong to God. All other life around us, including animal life, must be brought before God and related to him, with the acknowledgment that life is a mystery that we cannot handle and that man is incapable of properly directing his own affairs.

This requirement is set against the pagan practice of offering animals to demons, called "goat idols" here. A goat idol is a mythological figure, half goat and half man. This practice is an objectified form of demon worship. God says that the Israelites must not try to placate the spirits, as though man could manipulate the unseen spirit world and run life according to his desires by some kind of magic. It is amazing what a grip this idea has upon people's minds! It is becoming more and more fashionable in our day, with the rise again of interest in the occult. All of this is motivated by people's desire to manipulate and to control the world of the spirits so that man thus handles life by himself. But God wants us to stop trying to do this. We cannot handle life by ourselves. To teach them that fundamental fact, God encourages people to bring him every bit of life and to offer it to him.

Both primitive cultures and civilized nations such as ours have accepted the lie that man is capable of handling life by himself. We are witnessing a revival of this ancient lie that man can control and manipulate powers greater than himself and make them work for him.

God answers all that by commanding his people to cease these practices and to recognize that he alone is sovereign in life, that he runs the world, and that he controls our lives. We live in his universe, and we cannot handle life ourselves. Therefore, we must first recognize the fundamental truth underlying all behavior: that all lives belong to God and that God is sovereign in these affairs.

> *Father, I am thankful that life belongs to you alone. Help me to cease looking to my own ways to handle and even to manipulate life.*

Do we fail to trust the power and the wisdom of our sovereign Lord to guard and to guide our lives? What is the alternative? Do we need to relinquish control of our lives and the lives of others?

THE TRUTH ABOUT SEX

A daily devotion for April 20

Read Leviticus 18.

"No one is to approach any close relative to have sexual relations. I am the Lord" (Lev. 18:8).

Next to the preservation of life, the most powerful human drive is sex. As we are beginning to understand these days, sex is like a great river which, when it flows quietly between its banks, is a blessing to us. But when it rages in full flood, inundating the landscape in permissiveness and promiscuity, it is terribly destructive and hurtful. God's Word is careful to regulate us and to help us in this area. It is amazing that God takes the risk of letting us have this fantastic power. He doesn't take sex away from us if we misuse it. He takes that risk with us, with a plea that we learn to keep it within its banks.

We can see how God underscores the purpose of these instructions. They are intended so that we might live, not die. They are not meant to restrict us, to hem us in, or to prohibit us from expressing ourselves. No, quite the contrary! They are designed so that we might enjoy life to the fullest degree, finding it whole and rich.

So God instructs us about sex, and here we learn the truth, which we will never learn by reading a secular book. Throughout the Scriptures we are taught that sex is to be a total union of a man and his wife, expressing physical, emotional, and spiritual oneness. That is what sex is all about. Therefore marriage is its only possible expression—anything else immediately becomes abortive and hurtful because the union cannot be total outside of marriage.

Sex with the wrong person is always harmful. And the most harmful of all, according to this passage, is sex with near kin. When a proper regard for the sexual limitations prescribed by God vanishes, the barrier protecting us from the unseen forces of darkness that surround us is vitiated and demonic invasion can occur easily. This is what destroys a race. A nation begins to fall apart at that point. Society comes apart at the seams. We only need to read the first chapter of Romans to see how inevitable are the decay and the decline.

Father, thank you for the revelation of your truth, which goes beyond the shallow thinking of my day and ties together things that I would think are quite disparate. Lord, help me to understand this, and enable me to be an island of righteousness in a sea of iniquity.

The Bible is our Creator's handbook for his creation, with instructions specific to our full enjoyment of life. Are we heeding his wisdom, seeking his guidance, and honoring his presence in all aspects of our lives?

WHAT NOT TO MIX TOGETHER

A daily devotion for April 21

Read Leviticus 19.

> "Keep my decrees. Do not mate different kinds of animals. Do not plant your field with two kinds of seed. Do not wear clothing woven of two kinds of material" (Lev. 19:19).

How many of us observe that last law? Almost all garments today are made of mixed stuff, of blends of natural and synthetic fibers. A literal adherence to this stricture is no longer of any significance, because it deals with substances that never were inherently wrong. Whenever God employs items symbolically and says that something connected with them is wrong, this is no longer to be taken literally but is meant to illustrate dangerous attitudes of mind and heart. The Israelites had to obey these restrictions literally, because that is how they learned what these attitudes were. But we need to understand that God is teaching in a graphic way here that certain principles are unalterably opposed to one another and that we must not try to put the two together.

As an example, a believer in Christ should not marry an unbeliever, the New Testament says. To do so is to mix two ways of life that are categorically separated, and this only creates confusion, hardship, and pressure. Therefore it is crucial that a believer not marry an unbeliever. This is how the teaching of this kind of truth applies in our times.

Similar prohibitions are found in verses 26 to 28. The Israelites were not to eat flesh with blood in it, because blood is the life of the flesh, and life belongs to God. Life can never be handled properly unless it is related to God. Everything in life must relate to him. That is the great truth illustrated here. The New Testament tells us that these restrictions on food are shadows that have passed away, but the meaning abides.

The meaning of the rest of the section is given in verse 31: "Do not turn to mediums or seek out spiritists, for you will be defiled by them." Their practices were part of the pagan ceremonies accompanying their witchcraft. They cut their hair and beards in certain ways, and cut and tattooed their bodies. These things are not wrong in themselves today unless they are connected with practices that lead to pagan worship and to control by demons. That is eternally wrong, because it exposes us to demonic powers that can influence our minds and, without our awareness, can gradually seize and possess our personalities. Therefore God warns against this.

The same standard of life is proclaimed in the Old Testament as in the New. God's character is to be revealed through his children. By his power he lives through us to do the things he desires. We can't do them by ourselves. But God stands ready to do them in us as we draw upon his grace and strength.

> *Thank you, Lord, that your Word provides me with a trustworthy guide to life. I am grateful that you never ask me to do something, or not to do something, unless it is for my own good. You are the author of life, and I pray that I can live according to your instructions by the power of your Spirit within me.*

God clearly loves purity and holiness and has taught their importance both symbolically and practically in his Word. How is God's character revealed or confirmed in honoring these truths?

POWER TO DO

A daily devotion for April 22

Read Leviticus 20.

> "I am the Lord your God, who has set you apart from the nations. You must therefore make a distinction between clean and unclean animals and between unclean and clean birds. Do not defile yourselves by any animal or bird or anything that moves along the ground—those that I have set apart as unclean for you. You are to be holy to me because I, the Lord, am holy, and I have set you apart from the nations to be my own" (Lev. 20:24–26).

Note how carefully God identifies himself with these instructions. He signs his name, as it were, after each one. He offers a practical admonition and then says, "I am the Lord your God." Here he uses his covenant name: Jehovah. Thus he is saying, "I am the living One, the eternal One, the sufficient One. I am the God who is enough." That is what Jehovah means.

What is God trying to impart to us by this format? Two things are involved. The first is authority. This underscores something important. We must discover how to distinguish between right and wrong, truth and error, on the basis of what God says—if we are in relationship with him. There is a different standard for the people of God.

This standard is practical, because God is reality. What God says and what he sees and how he looks at life mirror the way life is. If you look at it in some other way, you are being unrealistic. You are out of step with reality and are trying to live according to an illusion, a fantasy, a figment of your imagination. Such ideas and standards may be widespread. People around you may sincerely believe lies that govern their way of living. But God says, "Not for you. Not for my people. I am your God, and I am telling you the truth, the way life is, what will hurt you and what will not. So believe me, because I am the Lord your God."

But God is not only authority; he is also resource. This is the second reason he gives his name with each command. He says, "Do this or don't do that: I am the Lord your God." He means, "I am available to you. I am the strength by which you can do what I command. I never tell you to do something without making available to you the power to do it."

Have you discovered what Paul discovered and recorded for us in Romans 7—that you cannot do all the things you'd like to do and know you ought to do? This is the way Paul puts it from his experience: "I do not understand my own actions. For I do not do what I want, but I do the very thing I hate" (Rom. 7:18–20). If you feel that way, God understands. This is the most common problem of life. You lack the power to respond. You must learn that there is another source of power, that you can reckon on "the God who is there," the God who is available to you. And that is why God signs his name this way several times. "Here is something to do or not to do: I am the Lord your God—standing here, available to you, ready for you to draw upon my strength. When you start drawing on it, you can do, or not do, what I command. This is possible by the power of an available God, the God who is enough. I am Jehovah."

> *Father, help me to see that simply being moral, being fair to others, and treating them as they treat me are insufficient. Your standard for living is much higher. I am to be loving in return for evil. I can do that only by the grace that is in you, Lord Jesus. Help me to obey you in this and to expect to see your life at work in me.*

What are two essential ways in which Jehovah God is made available to his people so that we may live by his truth about life? Are we trusting his authority and the resource of his indwelling presence and power?

FREE TO SERVE

A daily devotion for April 23

Read Leviticus 21.

"They must be holy to their God and must not profane the name of their God" (Lev. 21:6).

In "the gospel according to Leviticus," we come to a section specifically addressed to priests, to Aaron the high priest and his sons. This family was set aside in Israel to do a specific work of ministry in relationship to God. All the members of Aaron's family were priests by birth. They did not become priests by choice or by desire on their part but by being born into the family of Aaron. There was no other way to become a priest. No other family was ever recognized as having valid membership in the priesthood.

But even though they were members of the family of Aaron, they could serve as priests only if they met certain qualifications. So there is a difference between merely being a priest and serving as a priest. That is important and instructive for us because this priesthood of the family of Aaron is a picture of the ministry that we have uniquely as believers in Jesus Christ. Every one of us who is born again, born into the family of our Great High Priest Jesus Christ, is by that fact a priest. But whether we can serve as priests depends upon our qualifications. Membership in the family is by birth; service in the family is by qualification.

To exercise this priesthood, a priest must be holy. Again, the word *holy*, like so many other words from the Bible, has been distorted so that we usually take it to mean something unattractive. We are likely to think that to be holy is to be long-faced, solemn, and sour, but that isn't true at all! Holiness means "wholeness." It means to be healed.

How can you help someone unless you yourself have been helped? How can you encourage someone when your own heart is discouraged and defeated? How can you help somebody to cheer up and to be joyful in the midst of pressure unless you have learned how to be glad amid your struggles? How can you deliver somebody from a loathsome moral sickness if you are a victim of the same thing? How can you help somebody who has a blemish in his spiritual life unless you have been delivered from that blemish and thus know how to say the delivering word?

You must be set free first. You must have experienced the joy of God, the life of liberty in the Spirit of God, in order to help. You may not be whole in every way, but by the redeeming work of Christ indwelling, you must be whole in that area where you are trying to help.

Lord Jesus, how often I have found renewed ministry when I have dealt with those areas that were wrong in my life! Teach me now to draw strength from you, to be holy, and to set aside my blemishes.

What are the incredible privileges and the attendant responsibilities of being born into the family of the Lord Jesus Christ, our High Priest? Are we healed, whole, and free to serve the One who heals and makes whole?

ENJOYING OUR PRIESTHOOD

A daily devotion for April 24

Read Leviticus 22.

> "Keep my commands and follow them. I am the Lord. Do not profane my holy name, for I must be acknowledged as holy by the Israelites. I am the Lord, who made you holy and who brought you out of Egypt to be your God. I am the Lord" (Lev. 22:31–33).

What tenderness and compassion we see in those verses! "I am the Lord," he says, "who brought you out of bondage, out of slavery. I set you free. And I want to heal your life and to bring you into a land of abundance and promise, of excitement and blessing and fruitfulness, with a sense of worth and of power. I want to be your God, to be available to you to teach you how to live as men were ordained to live in the beginning—in dominion over all the earth, over all the powers and principalities in the universe, and to walk as free people, healed and whole. That is why I speak to you this way. That is why at times I will not allow you to exercise ministry until you deal with the blemishes in your life. When they are healed, your ministry can begin."

When we submit to this standard, we discover that our priesthood becomes rich, fulfilling, and exciting. God enlarges our borders. We gain a sense of worth beyond anything that we ever imagined. We discover that God is not so much interested in our activities as he is in our attitudes—our being rather than our doing. With the right attitude of heart, we can please God while we are washing the dishes; we can please God and be used of him when we are spading in the yard or working in the shop. His life begins to flow through us so that we are effective in applying the death of Christ to the disease and the heartbreak of humanity around us and in encouraging, building up, feeding, and enriching by the bread of God the lives of those with whom we come in contact. There is an entire world around us waiting for our ministry, hundreds and thousands of people with whom we are in touch each day and who need to be helped and delivered.

> *Thank you, Lord, because deep in my heart I don't want to be phony. I want to be genuine. I want to be whole and to able to help others to wholeness. Thank you for that possibility, Father, and thank you for the privilege of my priesthood.*

Are we continually mindful that our actions and attitudes reflect on our High Priest, whom we are called and are privileged to serve? What is his purpose in calling us to a lifestyle distinctly different from the world's values?

THE TRUE SABBATH

A daily devotion for April 25

Read Leviticus 23:1–3.

> "There are six days when you may work, but the seventh day is a day of sabbath rest, a day of sacred assembly. You are not to do any work; wherever you live, it is a sabbath to the Lord" (Lev. 23:3).

The weekly Sabbath had begun at creation. God worked six days and then he rested on the seventh day. God did no work on the Sabbath. In giving the law on Mount Sinai, God reminded his people that the Sabbath was at the heart of all his work.

I often hear Sunday referred to as "the Sabbath." Some think that is an old-fashioned term for Sunday. But that is completely wrong. Sunday is never the Sabbath and never was! The linking of these ideas is totally unbiblical. The seventh day was Saturday. The first day was Sunday. And Saturday was to be observed as the Sabbath, as it still is in Israel today.

Some Christians feel that Christians still ought to observe the seventh day as God's appointed day of rest. They tell us that we should be worshiping on Saturday, not on Sunday. In contending that God has never diminished the importance of the Sabbath, they are absolutely right. For the Sabbath was to be a day of rest, with no labor done on that day. But this was but a shadow, a symbol, and the symbol is never all-important. The observance of a day of rest is a picture of something else that God wants, something of great significance to him.

Paul tells us that the observance of a day is one of those shadows that, for the believer, ended at the coming of Christ (Col. 2:16–17). So what is God is after? It does no good to end an observance if we don't identify what it points toward and fulfill that. In fact, the reality of the Sabbath remains. It is given to us, among many other places in Scripture, in Hebrews 4, where the apostle reminds us that Sabbath means "rest" and that this refers to the secret of life. Humans were made to operate out of rest, not out of tension, anxiety, or pressure.

What is that rest? Hebrews 4:10 tells us, "For anyone who enters God's rest also rests from their works, just as God did from his." On the seventh day of creation, God ceased all work. He who enters into rest has stopped his own work and is resting on the work of another. So if we learn the principle of operating out of dependence upon God at work in us, and if we don't try to do everything ourselves—but instead learn to rest on what God is ready to do in us, through us, and around us and expect him to do it—then we are observing the Sabbath as God intended it to be observed.

> *Father, thank you for this picture of the Sabbath as a symbol of rest, not just for one day a week but for every day. Teach me to rest in the finished work of Christ and in the enabling power of the Holy Spirit.*

High-energy performance is standard in our world where rest is considered a luxury. How does this compute in God's economy? Are we learning the true Sabbath principle of work out of rest?

NO LEAVEN

A daily devotion for April 26

Read Leviticus 23:4–44.

> "On the fifteenth day of that month the Lord's Festival of Unleavened Bread begins; for seven days you must eat bread made without yeast" (Lev. 23:6).

Linked with the Passover was the Feast of Unleavened Bread. It began on the fifteenth day and lasted seven days. This feast also looked back to Egypt, to God's command that the Israelites clear all leaven from their houses. To this day, orthodox Jews meticulously do this in preparation for the Passover season.

Leaven is yeast, an apt symbol of what tends to puff us up. Yeast makes bread swell. Something at work in us makes us puff up as well. A doctor once told me, "The strangest thing about the human anatomy is that when you pat it on the back, the head swells up."

Why is that? A principle at work in us drives us to be self-sufficient. This is clearly a universal tendency. "Mother, please. I'd rather do it myself!" We don't want help. We don't even want to tell people our problems, to let them know that we are not sufficient in ourselves. We all have this tendency within us to want to protect our images and to look as if we've got it made and don't need help. If someone makes us mad by offering aid, we say, "Get lost! Drop dead! I don't need you!" That is leaven. It can take many forms.

Jesus often spoke of leaven. He said, "Beware of the leaven of the Pharisees, which is hypocrisy" (Luke 12:1), i.e., pretending. We Christians do so much of that, don't we? We pretend we don't have problems when we do. We are pretending we're spiritual when we're not. We pretend we're joyful when we're filled with misery. We pretend we tell the truth when we don't. That is hypocrisy, leaven that comes from this detestable aversion to admitting that we need help.

Jesus spoke of the leaven of the Sadducees, which was rationalism, the denial of the supernatural, the feeling that everything can be explained by what we see, taste, touch, smell, and feel, that there is no power beyond man and that man is sufficient to himself (Matt. 16:5–12).

Our Lord spoke of the leaven of the Herodians (Mark 8:14–21), who were materialists. They lived for pleasure, for comfort and luxury, and for status and prestige and the favor of people. They had their ears to the ground to manipulate and to maneuver politically and thus to advance themselves.

Avoiding such leaven is what this feast is all about. Preceding it, through the Passover, God begins his work with the blood of the Lamb to protect us from his just wrath so that we might be freed from leaven.

Father, thank you for working in me through the death of Jesus, the Passover Lamb, to rid me of leaven.

Leaven is symbolic of attitudes that are antithetical to every aspect of a God-pleasing, fruitful discipleship. Are we open to identifying them, eager for renewal of mind and heart?

THE PATTERN OF MAN

A daily devotion for April 27

Read Leviticus 24.

"Now the son of an Israelite mother and an Egyptian father went out among the Israelites, and a fight broke out in the camp between him and an Israelite" (Lev. 24:10).

Here is a story of a young man who was half Egyptian and half Israelite. There must have been hundreds of young men and women in the camp of Israel who had that background. There was nothing inherently wrong with that. But this person is highlighted for us because his life typifies a spiritual conflict.

In the Scriptures, Israel is a picture of the Spirit at work within us, of the new life, the redeemed life, while Egypt is always a picture of the world, of the old life. Here is someone who, in type, is trying to mix the two—trying to live midway between them. He is perhaps still attempting to conduct his business affairs by the laws of Egypt, by the ways of the world, but is also trying to mix in the outlook of God. This always spells trouble.

This young man has gotten into a quarrel with somebody in the camp and in the heat of anger and passion has blurted out what was hidden deep within his thoughts. Someone has stirred him up—we don't know what the quarrel is about—and he's gotten mad. He doesn't merely get angry at the man he is quarreling with; he curses the name of God. That represents the settled conviction of his heart that it is all God's fault and that he doesn't want anything to do with God.

God pronounces judgment in this case. This is not because he has been offended by this man, not because he is vindictive and retaliates. God is not that kind of person. He is a patient, loving God who could have borne this affront for centuries, as he has our cursing and bitterness. But he prescribes immediate death to teach the truth that a man who curses God, who rejects God, has denied himself the basis of life.

Thus we know that this is what happens to us spiritually. We shouldn't point a finger at this young man, should we? How often do we do this very thing! We get angry with God and we shake our fists at him. We say, "It's your fault! Get lost, God. I don't need you anymore." And when we take that attitude, God says, our life has come to an end. Our spiritual life is stopped right there. This doesn't mean that we have lost our salvation; it means that his supply of life to us, permitting us to live day by day, is ended until we see what is wrong and his grace restores us. Then we can begin again.

Teach me, Father, how to live by the power of your Spirit within me. Help me to be single-minded in my dependence on you rather than on the flesh.

When we compromise godly principles with worldly concepts, the consequence is a form of spiritual death. Do we then blame God? Isn't it instead time to seek the grace of his forgiveness?

THE TRUE BASIS FOR SOCIAL CONCERN

A daily devotion for April 28

Read Leviticus 25.

> "Throughout the land that you hold as a possession, you must provide for the redemption of the land. If one of your fellow Israelites becomes poor and sells some of their property, their nearest relative is to come and redeem what they have sold" (Lev. 25:24–25).

This chapter offers God's instructions on how to deal with poverty. This is a problem seething beneath the surface in every land on earth. People all over the world feel a sense of injustice because they face a system that they believe does not permit them to escape poverty. They have no way of breaking the stranglehold over them and of improving their economic lot. God says, "You must do something about that. You must help your brother."

The passage goes on to outline specific circumstances. First, in verses 25 to 34 God says a person must be given the right to redeem his land. The next division, verses 39 to 46, takes up the case of slavery. No Israelite was to be a slave. Finally, in verses 47 to 55, God says there must be the right to redeem slaves, to buy a person back and to restore him to his dignity as a human being.

What a commentary this is, and what a correction of the way we usually operate. We are always rushing around and putting Band-Aids on the cancerous sores of society. But God never does that. He strikes at the root of the problem. He says, "If you will deal with it at this level, then over time it will gradually work out. In the meantime you must take care of those in need."

History is full of illustrations of this fact. William Wilberforce, speaking before the English Parliament, pleaded with great passion for an end to the African slave trade. He was motivated by Christian concern and by his conviction that slavery was not God's choice for human beings. Florence Nightingale, whose work gave birth to the Red Cross, was motivated by Christian compassion and by the recognition that God can do something to alleviate human misery. The civil rights movement of our own land was motivated by a recognition that God is concerned with human affairs and that he could and would work when people expected him to do so and gave him the opportunity. Behind most of the beneficial social movements of history have been Christian compassion and concern.

Father, help us as a people to repent, to humble ourselves and to seek your face, to cry out in prayer unto you that you may heal our land. I thank you for that promise.

Worldwide media make it impossible to ignore the issues of poverty, injustice, and inequity. Are we content to leave the root problems to the mercy of political wonks?

BLESSED PROMISES

A daily devotion for April 29

Read Leviticus 26.

> "If you follow my decrees and are careful to obey my commands, I will send you rain in its season, and the ground will yield its crops and the trees their fruit" (Lev. 26:3–4).

What a beautiful passage! What a beautiful array of promises. When God asked the Israelites to observe his commandments he wasn't referring to the Ten Commandments alone. He knew that fallen human nature, with its inbuilt tendency to self-sufficiency, would never be able to keep them. He meant not only the Ten Commandments but all the provisions for redemption accompanying them—the offerings, the sacrifices, the cleansings, the healings, and all the other conditions that point to Jesus Christ. "If you walk before me," God said, "using the provisions that I have made available to you to deal with the sin and the rebellion of your heart, these blessings will be yours."

The blessings are sixfold. There is a counterpart for each of these in the spiritual life today. God meant these materially for his people Israel, but they are also a picture of the spiritual blessings that can be ours. So this passage has direct application to us.

The first promise is fruitfulness. God said, "Your land will bring forth its fruit." Our lives will be fruitful and will be a blessing to others. Second, there will be full supply. "Your threshing shall last to the time of vintage, and the vintage to the time of sowing; and you shall eat your bread to the full." We will have all we need; every resource will be provided for us. Third, we will have security. "I will give peace in the land, and you shall lie down, and none shall make you afraid." No enemy that comes against us shall be able to overwhelm us or to take us captive. God will protect us.

The fourth blessing is increase. "I will have regard for you and make you fruitful and multiply you, and will confirm my covenant with you." Our lives will affect others. We will find our influence increasing, extending to larger dimensions. Fifth, we will have a sense of God's presence, of fellowship with the living God. "I will walk among you, and will be your God, and you shall be my people." We will have an intimate sense of communion with God. All of this is guaranteed by the character of God, the One who delivered Israel from the land of Egypt, the One who is able to offer a sixth blessing: to deliver and to dignify, to make people "walk erect" as they ought to walk and to live. That is the kind of God he is, and that is what he says he will do.

These blessings find their counterparts in our lives in terms of the spiritual fruitfulness that God will produce if we lay hold of the provision that he has made for us in Jesus Christ and if we deal honestly and openly with him. That is all God asks. He doesn't ask us to be sinless; he asks us to be honest. He asks us not to kid ourselves, not to pretend, not to erect a facade, a wall that we hide behind, not to put on a mask but to be honest and open and to avail ourselves of the resources that he has given in Jesus Christ.

> *Father, thank you for your relentless love and for all the blessings you have provided as I abide in Jesus Christ.*

The beautiful physical promises God makes have a sixfold spiritual counterpart for us in the Lord Jesus Christ, who is our life. Are we claiming them by faith in him for his glory and for our joy?

VOWS

A daily devotion for April 30

Read Leviticus 27.

> "The Lord said to Moses, 'Speak to the Israelites and say to them: "If anyone makes a special vow to dedicate a person to the Lord by giving the equivalent value, set the value of a male between the ages of twenty and sixty at fifty shekels of silver, according to the sanctuary shekel"'" (Lev. 27:1–3).

This chapter lists several categories of vows. They largely apply to the prevailing conditions of the nation Israel in its relationship with God. Yet the principles behind them have permanent application. Several items in this passage require comment.

First of all, this vow was made about persons, either the individual who made the vow or someone else—a parent, a child, a servant, or a friend—who was expected to benefit from it. We sometimes become concerned about someone and tend to pray, "Lord, if you'll just do such-and-such for this person, I'll do something for you. I'll invest to an unusual degree in your work." The Israelites were in effect saying to God, "We'll support the work of the priesthood and give above and beyond what we ordinarily would give if you'll just benefit or bless or help so-and-so."

When a promise of this nature was made, Moses was to transmit a scale of values determined by God from which no deviation was permitted. If the person in question were a certain age and sex, an amount was set, and it had to be paid if the blessing was received. God gave careful instructions to his people regarding this kind of promise.

On the spiritual level, this applies to us. If we promise God certain things in moments of danger, or if we try to bargain with him and to get him to work for us, God expects us to pay to the full exactly what we promise. But if a man recognized that he didn't have what it took, that he was too poor to pay the price, he could still offer a promise to God out of thanksgiving, and the priest, the representative of God's grace, would enter the picture and, in a sense, intercede on his behalf and establish a valuation he could meet.

This is a beautiful picture of those vows and promises we make not to bargain with God but to express to him our thanksgiving for all that he has been to us. When our hearts are melted by grace and we stand awed in his presence and say, "Lord, here I am; take me," or "Here are my children, Lord; take them and use them as you like," these are vows made on a gracious basis, and God promises to meet any attendant need. What the people of God cannot gain by the law they can have by grace and, as the New Testament puts it, "exceeding abundantly above all they could ask or think" (Eph. 3:20 KJV). That is the way God always operates in grace.

Father, I don't want to bargain with you or to make rash promises I cannot fulfill. I want to trust your love and your grace, returning to you what is rightfully yours. Keep me from robbing you, Lord Jesus, of your rightful inheritance.

God's promises to us are sure, founded on his character, while our best intentions often falter when we depend upon our own resources. Are we making life commitments by faith in his power at work in us?

ACTS 1–12

An Unfinished Story
An introduction for the month of May

The book of Acts is the action story of the New Testament and is therefore one of the most exciting books of the Bible. Its full name is "The Acts of the Apostles," but few apostles are mentioned in these pages. James, John, Peter, and Paul are the only ones who appear in any prominence. Through the centuries Christians have shortened this title and made it simply "Acts." I like that better, for this is a tale of action, revealing how God is at work through Christians.

There is intense conflict throughout the book, but a conflict met by a ringing confidence that is wonderful to see. This book is a record of power exercised in the midst of persecution; an account of life and health pouring from a living Christ into a sick society through the channel of obscure men and women very much like you and me.

We could never understand the New Testament if we did not have the book of Acts, for it fills the gap that would otherwise exist between the Gospels and the letter to the Romans, which follows. At the end of the Gospels we find a handful of Jews gathered in Jerusalem talking about a kingdom to come in Israel. In the letter to the Romans we find an apostle who is not even mentioned in the Gospels, and who was not one of the twelve, writing to a band of Christians in the capital city of Rome, talking about going to the ends of the earth. The book of Acts tells us how this happened and why this change occurred.

THE UNFINISHED BOOK

A daily devotion for May 1

Read Acts 1:1–14.

> "In my former book, Theophilus, I wrote about all that Jesus began to do and to teach until the day he was taken up to heaven, after giving instructions through the Holy Spirit to the apostles he had chosen" (Acts 1:1–2).

The first few verses of chapter 1 constitute an introduction to Acts, giving us the key to the book. Here we have revealed the essential strategy by which Jesus Christ proposes to change the world, the secret of the revolutionary character of the church when it is operating as it was intended to operate. I strongly suspect that most Christians suffer from a terrible inferiority complex when we confront the world around us. We have bought the idea of many that the church is quite irrelevant, a not-at-all-important segment of society. That view is absolutely false. The church is the most important body in the world today—far and away above every other body—because whatever happens in the world happens as a result of something that is or is not taking place in the church.

In his first statement here, Doctor Luke gives us the great strategy by which the Lord works among humanity. He says, "In my former book … I wrote about all that Jesus began to do and to teach." The gospel of Luke is the record of the incarnation of the Son of God. Jesus, the man, came to begin something, "to do and to teach," and the record of that beginning is in the Gospels. But by clear implication, this second book is about the continuation of what Jesus began to do. In a real sense, Acts does not concern the acts of Christians but the continuing acts of Jesus. It is an account of what Jesus continues to do and to teach. In the Gospels he did this in his physical body. In the book of Acts he does this through the bodies of men and women in whom his life dwells. Thus, whether in the Gospels or in Acts, incarnation is the secret strategy by which God changes the world.

When God wants to get a message across to us he does not simply send someone to announce it; his final way of driving it home is to dress the message in flesh and blood. He takes a life and aims it in a certain direction, and by the manifestation of his own life through the flesh and blood of a human being, he makes clear what he has to say. That is the strategy of the book of Acts. It is the record of incarnation—of men and women, possessed by Jesus Christ, owned by him, and thus manifesting his life. That is the secret of authentic Christianity. A Christianity that is not doing that is a false Christianity. No matter how much it may adapt the garb and language of Christianity, if it is not the activity of human beings possessed and indwelt by the life of Jesus Christ it is not authentic Christianity. That is the true power of the church, as we shall see in this book.

Acts, therefore, is an unfinished book. It is still being written. The book abruptly closes with an account of Paul in the city of Rome, living in his hired house. It ends there as though we might turn the page and begin the next adventure. This book is volume 1, and we are writing volume 21 now. It may well be the last volume in the series. I hope so.

Father, thank you for this insight into the way you do your work. Forgive me for my blindness toward this plan and for my failure to take seriously these words. But thank you for the excitement that is mine as I rediscover this power in my own age.

In our fervor to adapt to cultural changes, have we neglected the fundamental principles taught by the Lord of the church?

THE BIRTHDAY OF THE CHURCH

A daily devotion for May 2

Read Acts 1:15–2:4.

"When the day of Pentecost came, they were all together in one place" (Acts 2:1).

Here is the story of the birth of the body of Jesus Christ, the church. Notice the day on which this occurred—the day of Pentecost. The Greek word *Pentecost* means "fifty." The day was called that because it came fifty days after the Passover feast. Pentecost was a Jewish feast presented to us in the Old Testament under the title the Feast of Weeks. It is also called the Feast of the Wave Loaves because it involved two loaves of bread baked with grain from the new harvest. Pentecost came at the end of the wheat harvest in Palestine, and the Jews were to take this new wheat, the firstfruits of the harvest, and from it bake two loaves.

All of this shows how the New Testament has its roots in the Old. These two loaves were symbols of the two bodies from which the church was to be formed: the Jews and the Gentiles. Jesus said he came first to the lost sheep of the house of Israel, the Jews. But he said, "I have other sheep that are not of this sheep pen" (John 10:16). He was referring to the Gentiles. Here, on the day of Pentecost, God brought the Jews and the Gentiles together and baptized them into one.

The loaves of the Old Testament were to be baked with leaven. This is yeast and is a symbol of sin. The wave loaves were the only sacrifice in all the Old Testament that included leaven. This is God's wonderful way of telling us that the church is not made up of perfect people. It is made up of saints, but they are sinful saints. They have sin in them. It is not made up of those who have reached perfection but of those who are becoming what God wants them to be, who have a divine authority and life at work within them changing them. Thus the loaves are baked with leaven.

In that beautiful symbolism lies the heart of the church. On the day of Pentecost, right in line with this Old Testament prediction, the Holy Spirit came. He took 120 people who were gathered in one place and made one out of them. Here were 120 individuals who had been living their lives quite separately, held together only by a mutual interest in Jesus Christ. But now they were baptized by the Spirit into one body. The baptism of the Holy Spirit had nothing to do with any outward demonstration. It was not necessarily associated with tongues, fire, or wind. These were the incidentals. The essential was the making of one body. This was the birthday of the church.

Father, thank you for your Word, which clarifies, which opens our eyes to make us see things the way they are. Help me to understand your church and my part in it as a member of your body.

Do we continue to acknowledge the weakness and the sin of our independent efforts to build Christ's body, his church? Are we steadfastly relying upon his Word and the power of his presence for wisdom and strength?

ALL PEOPLE

A daily devotion for May 3

Read Acts 2:4–21.

> "In the last days, God says, I will pour out my Spirit on all people. Your sons and daughters will prophesy, your young men will see visions, your old men will dream dreams" (Acts 2:17).

Notice how alert Peter was, led by the Holy Spirit. He immediately began to speak. Seminary students are taught that there are three basic rules for public address: stand up, speak up, then shut up. Peter never got to shut up. The crowd interrupted before he reached his conclusion and gave the altar call. He never got the chance to finish his message. That is a wonderful thing to have happen. When a crowd responds as positively as this, it is an amazing thing.

This occurred because Peter stated the truth. His message was simply an explanation of reality. That is what the preaching of the gospel is. It is an explanation of what things really are. Those preaching the gospel seize the occasion to make clear what lies behind events. That is what Peter did. His message consisted of an explanation concerning the event, the phenomenon of tongues; a declaration regarding Jesus of Nazareth; and an application concerning the crowd.

First, he explained to them that this was not what they thought. The translation from Greek is, "He stood up and said to them, 'Not as you suppose are these men drunk.'" In other words, they were drunk but not from what people supposed. It was not new wine that made them drunk; it was what Joel had said would happen—the Spirit of God had come upon them. It is true that to be controlled by the Holy Spirit affects one somewhat like alcohol does. Paul implies the same thing: "Be not drunk with wine, wherein is excess; but be filled with the Holy Spirit" (Eph. 5:18 KJV).

The onlookers noted that these men and women were excited and voluble, speaking freely and easily and acting rather strangely. It was not, therefore, unreasonable to conclude that these people were drunk. But Peter said, "No, you have the wrong explanation. The reason you're wrong is because it is only nine in the morning. Everyone knows that hardly anyone drinks before eleven! So it can't be that they are drunk with wine; they are drunk with the Spirit."

Peter then quoted an amazing passage from the prophet Joel in verses 17 to 21. His explanation was simple. This, he said, was what Joel had declared would happen. The key to this passage from Joel is the phrase "all people." "I will pour out my Spirit upon all people." If you read the prophecy in Joel, you will find that before this passage, the prophet had predicted that the Lord would visit his people. He would come to them and would live in their midst. Then, after this visitation, "I will pour out my Spirit upon all people."

The contrast is between the visitation of God to Israel and the pouring out of the Spirit upon all peoples everywhere—Gentiles as well as Jews. The good news about Jesus Christ would go out to the Gentiles as well as to the Jews. Up to this point it had been confined to the Jewish nation. Peter announced that the time had come when God would pour out his Spirit upon Jews and Gentiles alike and not only on people everywhere but on all kinds of people—including young men and young women. "Your sons and daughters will prophesy, your young men will see visions." Note the emphasis upon youth. God is saying that in this age of the Spirit, leadership, effectiveness, and power will not be limited to gray hairs but that young men and young women shall also speak and lead. God will pour out his Spirit even on servants, obscure people, insignificant people, and they will prophesy. All classes will receive this gift.

Thank you, Father, for this amazing phenomenon of the Spirit and for the fact that I still live in the age of the Spirit when all that you are doing today is done by the power of the Holy Spirit. Grant that I may understand and experience this.

The Holy Spirit does not discriminate in choosing vessels for his service. Do we place limitations on his work in others or in ourselves because they or we do not fit our human categories for eligibility?

JESUS THE CHRIST

A daily devotion for May 4

Read Acts 2:22–31.

> "But God raised him from the dead, freeing him from the agony of death, because it was impossible for death to keep its hold on him" (Acts 2:24).

This passage reveals the power of God among men—the resurrection power, which man cannot duplicate. The ability to bring life out of death, to correct a hopeless situation, and to change a person who is irremediable—that is resurrection power.

I met with a high school boy who told me about his conversion and about the reaction of his father. His father was baffled by this conversion. It fit no psychological pattern he could recall. He could not explain why his son was so suddenly and drastically different. Because he could not explain the change, it angered him, and he was fighting it all the way. This is the frequent reaction of those who come into contact with the power that raised Jesus Christ from the dead.

Man is always dreaming of finding ways to beat death. It has been suggested, for instance, that if you feel you are about to die, you should have yourself deep-frozen and have your body put away in a storage vault for fifty to a hundred years. Then, when science has supposedly found a cure for the disease you are dying of, you will be thawed out and given a chance to go on living. What a miserable farce! What a far cry from resurrection! This is not what happened to Jesus Christ when he rose from the dead in all the fullness and vitality of his person.

Peter says, "We disciples are the witnesses of these things. We saw him." The remarkable thing is that not one cry of protest is heard in this crowd of people. One of the greatest proofs of the resurrection of Jesus is right here—that this man could stand up in the city where these events had taken place a little more than a month earlier and tell these people that Jesus has risen from the dead, and not one voice challenges him! These people had not seen Jesus—he appeared only to his disciples—but they knew that the body was not there. They could go out to the tomb and see that it was empty. They knew that the authorities could not produce the body of Jesus. They had heard all the wild rumors that spread through the city that Jesus was alive and that he was appearing to his disciples from time to time. No one challenges what the apostle says. Instead the people stand in mute and stricken silence as the apostle drives home with powerful blows the sword of the Spirit, convicting them of the truth of his claim.

> *Father, thank you for the truth in this mighty declaration that Jesus Christ is indeed Lord. I pray that those who do not know him as Lord may now open their lives, cry out to him as these men and women did, hear the call to repent and to believe, and thus receive the promised Spirit.*

Are we equipped by study and faith to bear witness to the reality of the Lord Jesus Christ's resurrection? Is his living presence a reality in our daily lives so that our witness is authentic?

CUT TO THE HEART

A daily devotion for May 5

Read Acts 2:32–37.

> "'Therefore let all Israel be assured of this: God has made this Jesus, whom you crucified, both Lord and Messiah.' When the people heard this, they were cut to the heart and said to Peter and the other apostles, 'Brothers, what shall we do?'" (Acts 2:36–37).

As Peter preached the gospel at Pentecost, he proclaimed the authority of the Lord Jesus based on his resurrection from the dead. Suddenly all this made perfect sense to the multitude. The full force of Peter's arguments hit home, and these people realized that they were in a precarious position. This Jesus, whom he had proven by indisputable evidence to be Lord, was the One they had crucified fifty days earlier.

Can you understand how they felt? Imagine that you went to apply for a job and that on the way you got into an automobile accident. And when the other driver got out, you beat and cursed and kicked him in anger. Then you drove off to apply for the job. When you were all cleaned up and ready, you were ushered in to see the man whom you had just beaten and cursed out on the street. Think of your reaction. That is what these people felt. No wonder they were cut to the heart and cried out, "Brothers, what shall we do?"

There is where Christianity rests its case. Jesus Christ is Lord whether men know it or not. The forces that control their lives are dependent upon him. It would be almost laughable, if it were not so sad, to hear people dismiss Jesus Christ as though he were merely one option, as though they had the choice of believing or not believing in him, whatever they felt like, and it did not make much difference one way or another.

Peter's declaration on this day was that Jesus is the inevitable man. There is no way you can avoid him. Your life depends upon him. He is Lord over all things. Eventually, you must deal with Jesus Christ whether you like it or not.

Thank you, Father, for bringing me to a place where I know the answer to the question, "What shall we do?" Thank you for opening my eyes to see that Jesus is the Messiah who conquered death.

Does the reality of Christ as the inevitable man determine issues of our identity as well as our worldview? Is he the governing authority in the way we think as well as in our behavior?

WHAT TO DO?

A daily devotion for May 6

Read Acts 2:38–41.

"Peter replied, 'Repent and be baptized, every one of you, in the name of Jesus Christ for the forgiveness of your sins. And you will receive the gift of the Holy Spirit'" (Acts 2:38).

The apostle Peter is answering the question, "What shall we do?" He acknowledges that there is something to be done. When you finally understand that Jesus is Lord and that you are out of harmony with his purposes and his life, you must take action. There are two things you need to do, Peter says, and then one thing God will do.

You first need to repent. *Repent* is a greatly misunderstood word. Most people think repentance means that you feel sorry and that you begin to weep. That has nothing to do with repentance. You may feel sorry and you may begin to weep, but that is not necessary, and these things do not mean that you have repented. To repent means to change your mind, to change your thinking. You have been thinking that your life is fine. You have been thinking that Jesus is nothing but a great teacher or a great prophet but that he is not the Son of God, the Lord of glory, the Lord of all the earth. Well, think again. Repent! "Change your mind, and get in tune with reality,," Peter is saying. "You have been kidding yourself; you have been deluded. Well, change your mind." Jesus of Nazareth is the Son of God. Repent and put him where he belongs in your life.

The second thing you need to do is be baptized. Baptism adds nothing to your repentance. It does not make you better. It does not do anything magic for you so that you are suddenly forgiven of your sins. But baptism is the outward declaration of the change of mind that you have experienced within. Baptism is an open identification with Jesus Christ. To be baptized means that you are telling everybody, "I belong to him. I follow him. I am one of his disciples." It means you have ended your old way of thinking and have begun a new life.

Finally, there is the one thing that God will do. "When you repent," says the apostle, "you will receive the Holy Spirit." God, the third person of the Trinity, will come to live in you. His work will be to make Jesus Christ real, visible, and close to you, to impart his life to your own. This is what happens when you repent. Peter does not say to these people, "When you repent you will receive the gift of the Holy Spirit and you will speak in tongues." He does not promise this, because that is not part of receiving the Holy Spirit. The Holy Spirit initially came with this symbol, but this gift is not promised to every individual. The Spirit of God enters the human heart without any demonstration or sign after a change of mind about the Lord Jesus and a willingness to receive him. On that basis, these three thousand people received the promise of the Father.

Father, thank you for bringing me to that place of repentance and faith, and thank you for the gift of the Holy Spirit, who manifests in me and through me the life of the Lord Jesus.

What are two actions God asks of us in order that the Holy Spirit can make his home in our lives? Do we celebrate these events as the means of God's grace and power in us and through us?

THE YOUNG CHURCH

A daily devotion for May 7

Read Acts 2:42–47.

"They devoted themselves to the apostles' teaching and to fellowship, to the breaking of bread and to prayer" (Acts 2:42).

The young church devoted itself to fellowship, which means holding all things in common—in other words, sharing. Here three thousand people are suddenly added to a little band of twenty. Most of them probably were strangers before this time. Many had come from other parts of the world to Jerusalem. Now they were one in Christ, and they loved each other. They began to talk to find out what others were thinking and how they were reacting, to share their problems and their needs, and to pray together about them. There was a wonderful sense of community, of commonality, of belonging to each other. This fellowship is the life intended for the body of Christ.

God has willed that his life should be manifest through a body. If the body is not operating, the life is not manifest. That means there is no power, because the life of God is always power. The reason the church has been so powerless lately is that it has been so fragmented and broken. We have estranged ourselves from each other. The apostle Paul says, "And do not grieve the Holy Spirit of God" (Eph. 4:30). Then he lists the things that grieve the Spirit. "Get rid of all bitterness, rage and anger, brawling and slander, along with every form of malice. Be kind and compassionate to one another, forgiving each other, just as in Christ God forgave you" (Eph. 4:31–32).

If that is not happening, the Spirit of God is grieved. When he is grieved, he does not act. There is no life. The church becomes dull and dead, sterile and mediocre. All this is manifest in an empty ritual without vitality. God intends that Christians should have fellowship and should share one another's lives and thoughts and problems—bearing one another's burdens and so fulfilling the law of Christ. This is not optional; it is essential. This is why, when the Holy Spirit begins to move in any congregation or in any assembly of Christians, he starts at this point. He begins to heal the brokenness of people's lives and their relationships with one another, to get them to admit to each other their malice and their anger, their frustration and their grudges, and to forgive one another. This is when life begins to flow once again through the body of the Lord Jesus Christ.

Father, open my heart to others and to you. Break down the wall of resistance that I put up against others. Let me be of one heart and one mind with others in the body, generous in giving, glad to participate in anything that advances the marvelous work going on in a world rapidly drifting into darkness, emptiness, and coldness. Thank you, Lord, for the warmth of your Spirit, for your power, and for the grace you have given your people.

What is the biblical meaning of fellowship? When the body of Christ becomes powerless, what remedy is indicated? Are we committed to building bonds among those with whom we worship and serve?

LOOK AT US!

A daily devotion for May 8

Read Acts 3:1–10.

"Peter looked straight at him, as did John. Then Peter said, 'Look at us!'" (Acts 3:4).

Here was this man waiting at the gate of the temple. The striking thing about this is that when he asked alms of Peter, the apostle said to him, "Look at us." This is important because it is right in line with the actions of Jesus whenever he wanted to heal somebody. He never touched and healed someone without first directing the person's attention to himself. Jesus always captured the attention of the people he wanted to heal, directing them to focus their gaze upon him. This created a sense of expectation and always quickened faith. That is what happened here. The man expected to receive something from Peter and John. He did not know what he was going to get, but his faith was quickened by Peter's words. This is necessary to receive anything from God. We must expect something from him.

There are people who attend church but whose lives are hardly any different than when they first came. One of the reasons is that they have never given their attention to God. They have never expected to receive anything when they come. Unfortunately, there are those, young and old alike, who turn off their minds when they get into a church service. They think of all kinds of other things, take mental trips, and play mind games. I have always thought it would be most interesting after a service to find out where everyone has been! But unfortunately, these people miss the life-changing truth of the Scriptures, and they can sit in church for years and never be changed.

Young people who have been raised in church are no different, exhibiting no evidence that God is at work. This is largely because they never have heard someone command, "Look at me," and paid attention. This is why Jesus always told the crowds to which he preached, "He who has ears, let him hear" (Matt. 11:15). Let everyone listen. This is always necessary for the working of faith.

The minute Peter had this man's attention, he did two most interesting things. First, he admitted his bankruptcy in the material realm. "Silver or gold I do not have," he said. "That's what you are looking for, but I can't help you there." He then demonstrated his amazing adequacy in the spiritual realm, saying, "In the name of Jesus Christ of Nazareth, walk." At that electric moment, as this man looked at Peter and John and heard these words, something remarkable happened. At the mention of the name of Jesus, strength came flowing into his ankles, and Peter, sensing this, took him by the right hand and lifted him up. The man rose and began to leap and shout and jump around, trying out a strength in his legs that he had never known, because he had been lame from birth.

Father, thank you for the name of Jesus. It has lost none of its power. It is still transforming men and women as it always has—and not only spiritually but sometimes physically. Thank you for those demonstrations of your power today. I know that you can change an ailing body and make it well. But you can also take a sick spirit and make it whole.

When people look at us are they drawn to the power and the presence of the Lord Jesus Christ? Do we purposefully divert their attention and their expectations from us to him?

BY FAITH IN HIS NAME

A daily devotion for May 9

Read Acts 3:11–26.

> "Repent, then, and turn to God, so that your sins may be wiped out, that times of refreshing may come from the Lord, and that he may send the Messiah, who has been appointed for you—even Jesus" (Acts 3:20–21).

The healing of the lame man provides the background for Peter's address in which he says, "Repent, then, and turn to God, so that your sins may be wiped out," and two great things will happen: "times of refreshing" will come from the face of the Father, and he will ultimately send Jesus Christ to you to restore all things. That is a remarkable statement. Looking at the ages to come, Peter says, "Here are the principles by which God is going to operate: wherever people turn back to him, God will immediately deal with the problem of guilt. He wipes out sins."

I do not know of anything more difficult to get people to believe than that. I am amazed at how many Christians have heard all their lives that God forgives their sins and blots them out and deals with the great problem of guilt that is at the root of all human ills—and yet they still do not believe it! They are still trying in some way to work out standing or merit before God or to do something that will make themselves acceptable to him. But Peter says God arouses guilt only because he has the solution for it: wiping out sins through faith in the name of Jesus. And from that, Peter says, two things will happen. First, there will come "times of refreshing," periods characterized by relative peace and prosperity, times of order and happiness and general contentment in society.

After the spiritual awakening led by the Wesleys, England was saved from the disaster of revolution that the French had just suffered. The country was turned around, and a period of relative prosperity, joy, and contentment followed. There were still many problems, but this was a time of refreshing. There have been other such times in history. But these seasons of refreshing come only when a people turns to God and seeks to have sin wiped out.

Furthermore, says Peter, turning to God will ultimately result in the return of Jesus Christ. Only when God's people return to him will he again send his Son from heaven. That confirms what I have long suspected from reading the Scriptures—that Jesus Christ will not return at a time when faith is at a low ebb. He won't come when faith is almost burned out and God's people are going through a time of barrenness in a spiritual desert. Rather, he will come back at the height of an awakening when God's people have returned to him, sins have been blotted out, and the fullness of the power of the Spirit has been released. In the midst of that, Jesus Christ will return. The world around will be barren, disconsolate, and despairing, but this will be a time of vitality in God's people.

Father, thank you for your eagerness to deliver men and women from their sins. Thank you for promising times of refreshment and for the impending return of Jesus, which will bring the fulfillment of the hopes and dreams of every heart.

When the church and the culture are dysfunctional, we can point to a widespread lack of repentance. But what if the enemy is us? Are we part of the blight or of God's bountiful blessings?

THE RADICAL RESURRECTION

A daily devotion for May 10

Read Acts 4:1–12.

> "Jesus is 'the stone you builders rejected, which has become the cornerstone.' Salvation is found in no one else, for there is no other name under heaven given to mankind by which we must be saved" (Acts 4:11–12).

This is a startling declaration! It says that only Jesus can be the cornerstone of authority in the world. There is no other name! None of the religious or political leaders of all time could possibly do this work. There is only One adequately equipped and qualified to be the foundation of human government, the basis for human authority. Look at all the religious figures from history—Buddha, Muhammad, Confucius, Mahatma Gandhi, Ramakrishna, Joseph Smith, Mary Baker Eddy, or others. The most that can be said of these men and women is that they were moral teachers. The best we can say of them is that many taught what is right.

Christians are often accused of being bigoted, of being intolerant of other faiths. In a sense that accusation is perfectly just. We are intolerant of other faiths in the final analysis. But this does not mean that Christians do not recognize that there is much truth in other religions. Great leaders of other religions have offered fine moral teachings and precepts that have helped people. But there is one thing they could not do: they could tell us what was right, but they could not enable us to do it. That is the difference between Jesus of Nazareth and any other name in this world. That is why we can never consider any other name to be equal to Jesus of Nazareth. No other has solved the problem of death. No other has broken through this ghastly terror that hangs over the human race—only Jesus of Nazareth. God has made him the cornerstone, and there is no other name by which we can be saved.

We do not need someone to tell us what to do; we know what to do. Most of us know better than we are doing! What we need is One who will change us, give us a new motivation, make us want to do what we ought to do, and give us a new heart, a new outlook, a new ability, a new capacity, a new life. This is what Jesus does.

> *Lord Jesus, thank you for being ready to save anyone who will trust and believe in you by the wonderful miracle that you have made possible—that whenever a heart in emptiness and loneliness, in pain and despair, cries out to you and asks you to enter it and dwell within, you take up residence there.*

What is the unique distinction that makes Jesus's moral authority comparable to no other? Do we, like the apostle Paul, want to know Christ and the life-changing power of his resurrection?

WHEN THE ESTABLISHMENT IS WRONG

A daily devotion for May 11

Read Acts 4:13–22.

> "But Peter and John replied, 'Which is right in God's eyes: to listen to you, or to him? You be the judges! As for us, we cannot help speaking about what we have seen and heard'" (Acts 4:19–20).

The inconsistency of the Jewish rulers led to what was basically an illegal act. They were the representatives of God to this nation, and as such they were ostensibly committed to doing his will. Yet here, despite the evidence they had received of what God wanted done, they directly opposed his will and his word and forbade these apostles to speak in the name of Jesus. The disciples, wisely and courteously, declined to obey this command. They pointed out that they had no choice, that they could not help speaking about the things they had seen and heard. The message they declared was so challenging, so transforming in its implications, both for the nation and for the world, that they could not be silent and still be true to their relationship to God. This message was so desperately needed and so powerful in its effect that they could not, out of sheer humanity, maintain silence. They thus respectfully declined to obey what these rulers commanded.

At this point the question of civil disobedience comes into view. These apostles were forbidden by the properly constituted authorities to preach in the name of Jesus. The apostles told them to their faces that they would not obey the rule. This incident has been used through the centuries to justify many activities such as racial strife, draft evasion, violent demonstrations, boycotts, and strikes. We cannot read this account without asking whether it is right for a Christian to disobey a law because of a conscientious scruple. The clear answer of this passage is yes! There are times when it is necessary and right to disobey properly constituted authority. The establishment can be wrong as well as right.

The Scriptures are clear that governments are given by God. Paul says that government authorities are the servants of God (Rom. 13:1–7). The emperor on the throne when Paul wrote those words was none other than Nero, a wicked, vile, and godless man. Yet Paul writes that the governing authorities are the servants of God and that those who resist them resist what God has ordained. He acknowledges that governments have certain powers, derived not from the people but from God—the power to tax, the power to keep law and order, the power to punish evildoing, even to the point of death. The Scriptures make perfectly clear that all this is right and ordained by God and exhorts believers to obey the authorities.

But there is a place for civil disobedience. Notice that it occurs here only because the consciences of these men rested directly on the word of God, which contradicted the human law. The issue is so clear that Peter even calls on the rulers to be the judges of what the apostles should do. He says, "Which is right in God's eyes? You are religious men. You know which is the higher authority. Who should we obey, God or man?" The matter is so plain that these authorities cannot say a word. All they can do is threaten and bluster and try to maintain control by the threat of force. They fear the people, who are convinced that this is a remarkable sign from God.

Preserve me, Father, from misguided zeal. Reveal to me the underlying turmoil in society that is the result of your Spirit at work among men and help me to line up with you and to take my stand with these men and women of old.

Are we dutifully and earnestly seeking God's wisdom in the issue of civil disobedience? Jesus calls us to be salt and light, both desperately needed in our rapidly decaying culture. Are we prayerful and obedient?

THE MYSTERY OF HISTORY

A daily devotion for May 12

Read Acts 4:23–31.

> "On their release, Peter and John went back to their own people and reported all that the chief priests and the elders had said to them. When they heard this, they raised their voices together in prayer to God. 'Sovereign Lord,' they said, 'you made the heavens and the earth and the sea, and everything in them'" (Acts 4:23–24).

After being released from the custody of the Sanhedrin, the apostles did not organize a revolutionary committee to overthrow these leaders. They did not even try to arouse a demonstration in protest. The clear evidence of this passage is that they had popular support. But the apostles did not rely for even one minute upon political or popular pressure. They cast themselves upon the unique resource of the church in any age, one on which it must rely lest it become nothing more than an instrument of distortion. They cast themselves wholly upon the sovereign power of God at work in history. The world has never seen a force better able to alter a power structure. The church has ignored it many times, and thus Christians have frittered away their efforts on useless activities that make a lot of noise but accomplish nothing.

The apostles found encouragement in two things. First, there was the sovereignty of God, with his complete control of human events. Their prayer opened by recognizing this "sovereign Lord." God holds the world in the palm of his hand and is intimately involved in every human event. They took great consolation in that, but I find many Christians have forgotten it. These disciples recognized that God had even predicted the opposition they faced. Later, they quoted Psalm 2 as evidence. They had clearly been doing what Christians ought to do under pressure. They had gone to the Scriptures. They had found in the psalm a prediction of the opposition they were facing.

The second thing the apostles saw is what we might call the mystery of history. We see it in verse 28 where they say of the Sanhedrin, "They did what your power and will had decided beforehand should happen." In other words, the God of history uses the opposition to accomplish his purposes! That is what they saw. God worked through the free will of man. These people opposed God's plan. They tried to thwart his purposes and to derail his program. But God operates in such a marvelous way that he uses even the opposition to accomplish his will. That is the story of the cross and of the resurrection of Jesus.

These Christians reckoned upon that principle. They recognized a principle at work in human affairs that is the most powerful force known to man and that the church frequently ignores at its peril.

Thank you, Father, that I can trust in your sovereign power and control even over those events that do me harm.

What are two important principles we derive from God's Word regarding our reactions to deepening moral decay and human suffering? Are we willing to act faithfully while acknowledging the mystery and the majesty of God's sovereignty?

BODY LIFE

A daily devotion for May 13

Read Acts 4:32–36.

"All the believers were one in heart and mind. No one claimed that any of their possessions was their own, but they shared everything they had" (Acts 4:32).

This is a beautiful glimpse of what life was like in the early church. After the dramatic events of the day of Pentecost, the healing of the lame man, and the great response of multitudes in Jerusalem, the church faced life in the world of that day—a world of darkness, despair, and death on every side—and met it with a flowing out of the life of Jesus Christ. This is ideal Christianity, genuine Christianity. Unfortunately, there is also a counterfeit Christianity. It arose shortly after this in the early church, and evidences of it will be seen throughout the book of Acts. Wherever the true church has gone throughout the world, counterfeit Christianity has accompanied it.

Counterfeit Christianity can be recognized externally as a kind of religious club in which people, largely of the same social status or class and bound together by a mutual interest in some religious project or program, meet to advance that cause. But that is a far cry from true Christianity, which consists of individuals who share the same divine life, who are made up of all ages, backgrounds, and classes of society, and who, when meeting, regard themselves as what they really are—brothers and sisters in one family. From that mutual background of love and fellowship they manifest the life of Jesus Christ.

That is what we have here. The key idea is community with everything in common. They were of one heart and mind. The word *heart* is used for the human spirit. It denotes the deepest part of human life. It is the unconscious level of existence, the spirit, the most essential part of our nature. Here were people who, by the Holy Spirit, had been united in one life. They were of one heart. At the deepest level of their lives they belonged to each other, and that was possible only by means of the Holy Spirit. They did not need to have met someone before to recognize that if the person was a Christian they belonged to each other, they were of the same family, and they had a vast area in common. This was true of these people.

Not only did they have this unity, but it manifested itself in the fact that everyone had a new attitude toward the material life. This was not a forced redistribution of goods. It was not an attempt to make everyone give up material things and hand them over to others. No, it was a change of attitude, with believers thinking, *Nothing that I possess is mine for my exclusive use, but everything that I possess is God's, and therefore it is available to anyone who needs it.* So here were these early Christians, one in heart and mind and body. That is the church as it ought to be.

Father, thank you for the renewed life being imparted to your body. How true it is that it flows through the interchange of those who belong to one another, made so by the life of Jesus Christ that we share, brothers and sisters together in Christ.

What can we as members of Christ's body do to facilitate community among our fellow believers? Do we realize the importance of oneness as members together under the headship of Christ, the Lord of the church?

THE PRINCE OF PRETENSE

A daily devotion for May 14

Read Acts 5:1–11.

> "At that moment she fell down at his feet and died. Then the young men came in and, finding her dead, carried her out and buried her beside her husband. Great fear seized the whole church and all who heard about these events" (Acts 5:10–11).

Why did this occur? Why was the Holy Spirit so severe? Is this what he always does with his church? Someone has said, "Thank God this doesn't happen anymore; if it did, we'd have to put a morgue in every church." This is a picture of what happens when a person indulges in pretense. The moment we pretend to be something that we are not, the second we assume a stance of spiritual impeccability that we do not possess, death enters in. We are immediately cut off from the flow of the life of Christ. This does not mean we are no longer Christians, but it means that the life of the body is no longer flowing through us. Instead of being part of a vital movement, we become dead and unresponsive cells in that body.

That is what is wrong with the church today. It is the tragic sickness of the church in any age—pretense, sham, hypocrisy—to pretend to be something we are not. The most astonishing thing is that this is unconscious hypocrisy for the most part. I seldom meet deliberate hypocrites. We are all frequently guilty of being unconscious hypocrites. We think it is somehow religious or Christian not to show what we really are.

That is what this story of Ananias and Sapphira underscores for us. The minute they pretended to be something they were not—death! When we come to church we put on a mask of adequacy, but inside we are inadequate, and we know it. We are struggling with problems in our homes, but we don't want to tell anyone about them. We can't get along with our children, but we'll never admit that to anyone. The pride that doesn't want anyone else to know what is going on between husbands and wives, and between parents and children, keeps us from sharing. We pretend that everything's wonderful. Somebody asks us how things are going at home. "Great, great! Fine! We're having a wonderful time!" The minute we tell this untruth, we die. Death sets in. Soon that death pervades the whole church. That is why dishonesty is the primary characteristic of the church today.

How do we deal with this problem within ourselves? In Scripture the way to cure a spiritual disease is always the same: repent and believe. To repent means to acknowledge that we have been doing wrong. To believe means to understand that God has already given us, in Jesus Christ, all that it takes to do what we should. Then we must start doing it! We must open up and share our burdens. We may start in a small way, and it will be difficult at first. But the sharing of lives makes power and grace flow through the body.

Father, forgive me for my own pretense, and teach me to open up with my brothers and sisters in Christ so that when people look at us they might say, "My, how these Christians love one another!"

Are we contributing to the serious issue of hypocrisy? What steps must we take to address this threat to the life of Christ in us and through us?

TRUE HEALING

A daily devotion for May 15

Read Acts 5:12–16.

> "The apostles performed many signs and wonders among the people. And all the believers used to meet together in Solomon's Colonnade. No one else dared join them, even though they were highly regarded by the people. Nevertheless, more and more men and women believed in the Lord and were added to their number" (Acts 5:12–14).

This sounds like the days of Jesus all over again, does it not? Here was a tremendous display of physical healing power at the hands of the apostles. The result was that multitudes were added to the church, increasing it far beyond the five thousand we noted before. This is obvious evidence of the power of God at work.

But many people are troubled by this account. They say, "What is wrong with the church now? Why don't we have signs and wonders and mighty events like these taking place?" Many people, feeling that such signs are the mark of power, have tried to reproduce these wonders, and the result has been a movement in our day of faith healers who travel about declaring that they are able to heal as the apostles did.

We must notice some details about this account carefully given to us by Doctor Luke. First, he says, these healings were done by the hands of the apostles. These were not done by all believers. They constitute what the apostle Paul calls "the signs of an apostle" (2 Cor. 12:12). He said to the Corinthians, "You are questioning my apostleship. You're asking if I really am an apostle, because I'm not one of the Twelve. Well, let me ask you this. Have you not seen the signs of an apostle that I have done among you?" These signs were specifically to accompany the ministry of the apostles, who were assigned the task of laying the foundations of the church, of giving the Scriptures upon which the church must rest.

Not only were the apostles to manifest the power of God in physical ways, but this physical manifestation was to be a sign of the spiritual power that God would release among the people. It is always a mistake to spotlight a physical miracle. Although they attract attention, physical miracles also confuse people so that ultimately they miss the point of what God is saying. God wants to heal the whole of man, the hurt in man's spirit most of all. That is where the problem lies.

Every person ever healed by the Lord Jesus, or by the disciples in the church's early days, died. The physical healing was a temporary thing, with no exceptions: all those cured died. But when God heals the spirit, it is an eternal event. There is an inward change that is never lost. When God heals a man from the inside out, he makes him a whole person. It does not matter what happens to the physical—any change is at best only a temporary thing. God is after a higher goal, the healing of the hurt of humanity in its spiritual sickness, its evil, its darkness, and its desperation. That is always where he desires to start. God has not stopped healing physically. But the deepest need of man is spiritual healing. That is what this passage is saying. And when spiritual healing happens, multitudes will be added to the church.

Father, thank you for your power to heal, not just in the physical realm but in the deeper realm of the heart.

Are we trivializing God's healing at the deepest level of our souls by focusing primarily on physical healing? Do we trust his power to heal and his wisdom to choose how and when?

CONFRONTATION!

A daily devotion for May 16

Read Acts 5:17–42.

> "They called the apostles in and had them flogged. Then they ordered them not to speak in the name of Jesus, and let them go. The apostles left the Sanhedrin, rejoicing because they had been counted worthy of suffering disgrace for the Name. Day after day, in the temple courts and from house to house, they never stopped teaching and proclaiming the good news that Jesus is the Messiah" (Acts 5:40–42).

I love that. They did not stop. They counted themselves fortunate to suffer dishonor for Jesus's name. Christians take so long to face up to the simple declaration of Scripture that, when they were called to be Christians, they were called to suffer. As Paul said, "For it has been granted to you on behalf of Christ not only to believe in him, but also to suffer for him" (Phil. 1:29). We are called to this. Suffering is an integral part of the Christian experience. It is not unusual or reserved for just a few; it is for all. Peter wrote, "Do not be surprised at the fiery ordeal that has come on you to test you, as though something strange were happening to you" (1 Peter 4:12). We go through problems, heartaches, disappointments, ostracism, and coolness from others, all for the sake of "the name." We shouldn't think this strange. It is that to which we are called.

In a world run by illusions, governed by deceptions, and enslaved by malicious falsehoods, what else can we expect if we stand for the truth? At times people will think we are strange. They will think we react in funny ways. We will feel some degree of coolness even among those who are, in many other ways, friendly toward us. They will think we are a little odd. But it is they who are odd; it is we who are normal. A world full of oddballs will find normal people odd. But that is the suffering to which we are called. Like these disciples, we ought to thank God for it and rejoice in it. Jesus said that, didn't he? "Blessed are you when men revile you and persecute you and say all manner of evil against you falsely for my name's sake. Rejoice, and be exceeding glad … for so persecuted they the prophets which were before you" (Matt. 5:11–12 KJV).

The church, then, is not to wring its hands and say, "Oh what a terrible thing! We're being opposed!" No! We should rejoice as these early Christians did. We should count it an honor that we have been called to suffer a little for his name's sake. We must stand up and be counted.

Father, help me to understand that we are the salt of the earth, that we are the light of the world, and that we must begin to act that way again.

When truth has fallen in the public squares are we prepared to fulfill our calling to speak for truth? Do we resist the forces of evil for Christ's sake, in his wisdom and with his truth?

HOW THE BODY FUNCTIONS

A daily devotion for May 17

Read Acts 6:1–8.

> "So the Twelve gathered all the disciples together and said, 'It would not be right for us to neglect the ministry of the word of God in order to wait on tables. Brothers and sisters, choose seven men from among you who are known to be full of the Spirit and wisdom. We will turn this responsibility over to them and will give our attention to prayer and the ministry of the word'" (Acts 6:2–4).

It would be easy to read this passage as though the apostles were saying, "We're too good to serve tables. After all, we're apostles. Let's pick out seven flunkies who can do that, while we devote ourselves to the tremendously spiritual work of prayer and preaching the word." But this would be a complete misreading, because that is not what they meant at all.

These apostles had been in the upper room with the Lord Jesus. They had seen him divest himself of his garments, gird himself with a towel, take a basin of water, and wash their dirty feet. They had heard him say, "The greatest among you should be like the youngest, and the one who rules like the one who serves" (Luke 22:26). They were not, in any sense, downgrading the ministry of serving tables. They made this decision on the basis of a difference in spiritual gifts. Here we have a clear example of the way the early church assigned duties according to the distribution of gifts by the Holy Spirit.

The glory of this church was that believers were conscious of the superintendency of the Holy Spirit—aware that the Lord Jesus himself, by means of the Spirit, was the head of the church. He was apportioning gifts, assigning ministries to individuals and sending them out, giving the orders. All through Acts we see a tremendous manifestation of the direction of the Holy Spirit.

The apostles recognized that he had given varying gifts. They understood that their gift was apostleship. They were to lay the foundation of the church, for it was given to the apostles to do that. That foundation is the Scriptures. It is on the Scriptures that the church rests. The minute the church departs from the Scriptures it loses its strength, its light and understanding, and its ability to operate. That has always been true. Whenever it has rested upon the foundation laid by the apostles, the truth as it is in Jesus, the church has had strength, power, and grace.

Therefore it was necessary that the apostles give themselves to the ministry of apostleship, which involved "prayer and the ministry of the word." As they met together in prayer, they learned and understood the mind of God. The Spirit of God reminded them of things that the Lord Jesus had taught them, and they in turn imparted this to the church. At that time, none of the New Testament was in writing. Yet all of the truths in the New Testament pages were being uttered by the apostles as they taught the people from place to place. They taught them what we now have written down for us. And all we have, of course, is the word of the apostles. The New Testament is nothing but the word of the apostles given to us.

They found it essential to devote themselves to this, but they recognized that there were other gifts of the Spirit. There were gifts of helps and gifts of wisdom, and men and women in this vast congregation had these gifts. So all the apostles were doing was charging the church with finding among its members those who had gifts that would qualify them to do this kind of work—gifts of helps and gifts of wisdom—that they might solve practical problems within the church. They were saying, "Every gift is important. We simply are sticking with the gifts that were given to us, and we want you to find among yourselves those who have other gifts."

> *Father, thank you for the gifts you have given me. I ask that you teach me to serve you accordingly.*

Do we seek to discover and to use the gifts distributed by the Holy Spirit? Do we honor each gift for its distinctive value as we use them to serve his calling? Do we exhibit the beauty of Jesus's humility in our serving?

THE TRUE HOUSE OF GOD

A daily devotion for May 18

Read Acts 6:8–7:56.

> "However, the Most High does not live in houses made by human hands. As the prophet says, 'Heaven is my throne, and the earth is my footstool. What kind of house will you build for me?, says the Lord. Or where will my resting place be? Has not my hand made all these things?'" (Acts 7:48–50).

Chapter 7 records the longest sermon in the book of Acts. It is Stephen's brilliant defense of what he believes and is a review of the history of the people of Israel. He answers the two charges against him, and he brings a charge against the people.

In verses 48 to 50 Stephen argues that God himself, through the prophet Isaiah, had predicted that the temple would not always be an adequate place to worship him. In fact, no building ever will be. God is bigger than buildings. God is the One who makes all things, who makes the material from which a building is constructed, and who makes the men who put that building together. God does not intend that he should be worshiped in a building made with hands.

Stephen makes an important point. I have always been disturbed by the widespread teaching that a building can be called the house of God. We should labor diligently to keep our teachers from saying that to our children. No building is the house of God or ever was. Even the temple, as Stephen points out here, was not rightly called the house of God. When a church building is filled with people, who are indeed the house of God (for man is the house in which God intends to dwell), there is a sense in which the building is the house of God, because God is there in his people. But when everyone leaves and the lights are turned out, the church building is no more the house of God than any other building. It is no more holy, no more sacred. It is nothing more than an empty building to be used for whatever purpose is helpful at the moment. It is not the house of God. Each of us is the house of God. That is the great truth that Stephen tries to get across to these people.

> *Father, thank you for choosing to dwell with your people and for making us the house of God. I pray that you will be completely at home in my heart.*

Is it scripturally accurate to call a building the house of God? What is the amazing truth about where Christ has chosen to live? How does this affect the way we regard his ownership of his residence?

THE FIRST MARTYR

A daily devotion for May 19

Read Acts 7:57–8:1.

> "While they were stoning him, Stephen prayed, 'Lord Jesus, receive my spirit.' Then he fell on his knees and cried out, 'Lord, do not hold this sin against them.' When he had said this, he fell asleep. And Saul approved of their killing him" (Acts 7:59–8:1).

A vivid picture, is it not? It is noteworthy how God stands by his faithful martyr here. Stephen's eyes are opened, even in the presence of the council, and he sees the Lord Jesus standing at the right hand of the Father. It is my conviction that every believer who dies sees the same thing, that when a believer steps out of time into eternity the next event awaiting him is the coming of the Lord Jesus for his own.

Stephen sees the Lord waiting to step out and to receive him in a few moments when he will be taken out of the city and stoned to death. This is the sight that greets the eyes of those who fall asleep in Jesus, as Stephen does. He prays in words that echo those of Jesus himself on the cross. Jesus had prayed, "Father, forgive them, for they know not what they do" (Luke 23:34). Stephen says, "Lord, receive my spirit, and do not hold this sin against them." When he has said this, he falls asleep.

Twice in this account we see young Saul of Tarsus. All of those who killed Stephen laid their garments at his feet. Saul kept the garments of the rest while they were doing the stoning. He had voted against Stephen in the council; he was consenting to his death. But the idea the Holy Spirit wants us to grasp from this account is a truth exemplified here and manifested through the church many times since this day: the blood of the martyrs is the seed of the church. When the church suffers this way, it always grows immensely. Out of the blood of Stephen came the preaching of Paul. The death of this first martyr brought to the church the heart and the soul of the mighty apostle to the Gentiles, Paul. This scene was etched in his memory so that he could never forget.

Jesus referred to this memory when he said to Saul, arresting him on his way to Damascus, "Saul, Saul ... It hurts you to kick against the goads" (Acts 26:14 RSV). What did he mean? This memory of Stephen was like a goad digging at Saul's conscience, bothering him constantly, and preparing his heart for that moment when the Lord Jesus, who had received Stephen's spirit, would appear and reveal himself to this young man, who would be converted and become Paul the apostle.

> *Father, this account has sobered me with the truth that this life is a battle and that it can come to blood, sweat, and tears. I pray that I may, like Stephen, be found faithful unto death, recognizing that the One whom I serve is the rightful Lord of heaven and of earth.*

Heroes of faith have left us a heritage of their stoning, flogging, torture, imprisonment, and martyrdom, perhaps never more prevalent than today. Are we prepared to submit to the suffering God may choose for us so that he may accomplish his sovereign purpose?

FROM PERSECUTION TO PROCLAMATION

A daily devotion for May 20

Read Acts 8:1–4.

> "And Saul approved of their killing him. On that day a great persecution broke out against the church in Jerusalem, and all except the apostles were scattered throughout Judea and Samaria. Godly men buried Stephen and mourned deeply for him. But Saul began to destroy the church. Going from house to house, he dragged off both men and women and put them in prison. Those who had been scattered preached the word wherever they went" (Acts 8:1–4).

In the persecution that arose over Stephen, these early Christians were forced out of Jerusalem into surrounding areas, into Judea and Samaria, and began to preach the Word, all according to God's program. He used Saul of Tarsus even before he became a Christian to accomplish this. God uses the obstacles thrown in the path of Christians to advance his cause. Young Saul, enraged over what he regarded as a heresy, tried to stamp it out with all the energy of his flesh, entering house after house, dragging off men and women, and committing them to prison. This was the rage of a tortured conscience, which tried, by zealous activity, to cover up its anxiety, emptiness, and hurt. Yet God used this as an instrument to accomplish his purpose.

God did two things with Saul's rage. He forced the church out of Jerusalem into Judea and Samaria to fulfill the divine program he had outlined, and he made the early church depend not upon the apostles but upon the gifts of the Spirit distributed to everyone—for those who were scattered abroad were not the apostles. Doctor Luke is careful to tell us that. These were ordinary, plain-vanilla Christians like us, and yet they had gifts of the Spirit. But they would never have discovered their gifts if they had not been pushed out and put to work. So God used this pressure to place them in circumstances where they developed the gifts of evangelism, of witnessing, of helps, of wisdom, of knowledge, of teaching, of prophecy, and all the other gifts of the Spirit that had been made available to them.

Sometimes I think that God will have to do this in our day before people will believe that they have spiritual gifts and will put them to work. He may have to bring persecution upon us so that we cannot depend upon a central ministry and that each of us will begin to use the gifts that God has provided.

If we are enduring hardship, it is not punishment for our sins. Jesus took our punishment fully on the cross. The pressure, the trials, and the problems that come are by no means always the result of sin in our lives. Sometimes they are, but this may be God's way of moving us, of pressuring us into new experiences, into a new understanding of his truth and of the equipment he has provided us, giving us a new opportunity to put it to work.

> *Thank you, Lord, for being completely sovereign over my life. I trust you to use me wherever you see fit.*

Jesus said, "In the world you will have tribulation; but be of good cheer, I have overcome the world!" (John 16:33). Our cheer is not with our trials but with God, who is at work, causing "all things to work together for His good" (Rom. 8:28). Will we rest in God as he works within our difficulties to make us more like his Son?

CHRIST-CENTERED OR SELF-CENTERED?

A daily devotion for May 21

Read Acts 8:5–24.

> "Now for some time a man named Simon had practiced sorcery in the city and amazed all the people of Samaria. He boasted that he was someone great, and all the people, both high and low, gave him their attention and exclaimed, 'This man is rightly called the Great Power of God'" (Acts 8:9–10).

All false faith exalts personalities, making much over men. It involves the inflation of an individual, usually by self-aggrandizement. These individuals are always egocentric, always pointing to themselves and using religious terminology to make a great deal over themselves. That is the quality of counterfeit Christianity. Genuine Christianity makes nothing of the individual. "For what we preach is not ourselves," says the apostle Paul, "but Jesus Christ as Lord and ourselves your servants, for Jesus' sake" (2 Cor. 4:5). But here we have a man who exalts himself.

A few years ago I attended a service put on by one of the famous faith healers of our day, a man who has milked millions of dollars from earnest Christians. I attended this meeting just to hear what he was saying. He began by preaching what I thought sounded like a good gospel message. He took his text from the Scripture and developed it well, and I settled back and said to myself, *I've been wrong about this man*—until he came to the conclusion! Rather than inviting the thousands who were present to come to know Jesus Christ, this is what he said: "If you want to know God, then have faith in my prayers. If you want to meet God, believe that my prayers will lead you to God. Come forward and kneel here, and I'll pray for you." The whole direction of his message was toward himself and his prayer.

That is false Christianity. It always attempts to interject a mediator between a believer and his God. But "There is one God and one mediator between God and mankind, the man Christ Jesus" (1 Tim. 2:5), no other. Counterfeit Christianity tries to insert a priesthood of one sort or another, a mediator, someone great, someone who has a special channel to God that other people don't have. When you hear that sort of thing, you know that you are hearing the same kind of false Christianity that appears here in the book of Acts.

Thank you, Father, for the exhortation of this passage—that I should be Christ-centered instead of self-centered.

Why is it sometimes easier to identify self-centeredness in others than in ourselves? Do we grasp the reality of our true identity in Christ, which sets us free to live for him?

THE DIVINE WIND

A daily devotion for May 22

Read Acts 8:25–40.

> "After they had further proclaimed the word of the Lord and testified about Jesus, Peter and John returned to Jerusalem, preaching the gospel in many Samaritan villages. Now an angel of the Lord said to Philip, 'Go south to the road—the desert road—that goes down from Jerusalem to Gaza'" (Acts 8:25–26).

An angel suddenly appeared to Philip. I've never had an angel appear to me. I do not know anyone to whom an angel has appeared. Some may ask, "Does God still work through angels today?" The answer is a resounding yes. However, the angels are not always visible. The ministry of angels, according to the Bible, goes on all the time. They are ministering spirits sent forth to serve those who are heirs of salvation (Heb. 1:14). All of us are touched by the ministry of angels, but we do not see them. There have been well-documented appearances of angels recorded in church history. I believe that as we draw nearer to the return of Jesus Christ, we may well see a return of angelic manifestation.

Here was an unexpected agency through which the Holy Spirit worked. An angel appeared to Philip and gave him an unexplained command to go south and take the road leading from Jerusalem to Gaza. He could not have picked an emptier stretch of road. It was desert road. There were no cities or villages there. The wonderful thing to me is the beautiful way in which Philip obeyed this command of the angel. He did not say, "Well, I'll have to pray about this." He did not say to himself, *I wonder if this is a call to a larger field of service.* He just went. He left the awakening that was going on in Samaria, with its demands for training and teaching. He arose and went down to a desert road.

This is a beautiful picture for us of what we might call the wind of God, the sovereign blowing of the Holy Spirit, and of the adventure that is always characteristic of someone who is being led by the Holy Spirit. Verses 25 and 26 are records of Spirit-filled activity. Peter and John were obeying the Holy Spirit when they testified, prophesied, and evangelized. But Philip was also obeying the Holy Spirit when he was sent by an angel out to a desert place. Both were part of the Spirit-filled, Spirit-led life.

That must be made clear because we tend to run to extremes. The Spirit often leads through the ordinary, the usual, and he can be effective that way. But that is not the only way. This is the lesson that God is forever teaching us. This is the creative strategy of the Holy Spirit. He has the freedom to interfere, the freedom to override a program, to change it, and to make something new. The church has suffered terribly by ruling that out, by so organizing everything that there is no room for the Spirit to move.

> *Father, thank you for directing me in ways that I cannot predict. What a note of excitement this adds for me, Lord! What a glorious sense of expectation becomes mine as I constantly wonder when you are going to break through and do the unusual again in my life.*

Is the wind beneath our wings the Holy Spirit, or are we guided by whim or another lesser motivation? Are we missing the wonder and the worship of being led by the Spirit of the living God?

BELOVED ENEMY

A daily devotion for May 23

Read Acts 9:1–19.

> "In Damascus there was a disciple named Ananias. The Lord called to him in a vision, 'Ananias!'
>
> "'Yes, Lord,' he answered.
>
> "The Lord told him, 'Go to the house of Judas on Straight Street and ask for a man from Tarsus named Saul, for he is praying. In a vision he has seen a man named Ananias come and place his hands on him to restore his sight'" (Acts 9:10–12).

Paul has been converted. Now he is a Christian. And what is the first thing he experiences as a Christian? The life of the body of Christ. That is wonderful, is it not? Two unknown, obscure Christians are sent to him. He meets them and is immediately helped by the strengthening that can come from the body, from other Christians. First there is a man called Judas. His name is all we know about him. Saul is led to his house though he has never met before. While he is there a man named Ananias is sent to minister to him.

Is there not a joyful irony about this, that the Holy Spirit has chosen two names that are tainted elsewhere in the New Testament, Judas and Ananias? These names belong to two other people: Judas, the betrayer of our Lord, and Ananias, the first Christian to manifest the deceit and the hypocrisy of an unreal life. Yet here are two people, bearing the same names, who are honored and used of God. Though it's a small thing, it seems so much like the Holy Spirit to use names like this.

These men minister to Paul. Ananias is reluctant to come. Saul had been ready to drag people off to prison and to put them to death because they were Christians, and so Ananias is understandably hesitant. But the Lord reassures him, telling him to go because Saul is praying.

That is the first mark of a Christian. He recognizes that God rules and that there is a relationship between man and God, and so he starts to pray. God says to Ananias, "You needn't be afraid of a man who prays. Go to him, because he is praying." Thus Saul of Tarsus begins to experience the joy of body life through these other Christians ministering to him.

> *Father, thank you for the amazing story of Saul of Tarsus. Thank you for the impact his life has had upon the world as a result of his encounter with you on the road to Damascus. Thank you for the wonderful picture of one like Paul being included in the body of Christ. Teach me to include others with the same spirit of love.*

Do we tend to think of nonbelievers as pariahs, enemies, adversaries? Have we forgotten our own state but for God's saving grace? Are we available to be instruments of grace to whomever God leads us?

LEARNING MEEKNESS

A daily devotion for May 24

Read Acts 9:19–31.

> "After many days had gone by, there was a conspiracy among the Jews to kill him, but Saul learned of their plan. Day and night they kept close watch on the city gates in order to kill him. But his followers took him by night and lowered him in a basket through an opening in the wall" (Acts 9:23–25).

What humiliation! Here Paul was, equipped to win the day for Jesus Christ. He was going to show the world how much he could do for this new Master whom he had found. Instead he finds himself humiliated, cast off, and rejected. His friends finally have to lower him over a wall at night. He walks away into the darkness in abject failure and defeat.

The amazing thing is that many years later, as he is writing to the Corinthians and looking back over his life, he recounts this episode. Paul says, "You ask me to boast about the most important event in my life? The greatest event in my life was when they took me at night and let me down over the wall of Damascus in a basket. That was the most meaningful experience I have had since that day when I met Christ" (2 Cor. 11:32–33).

The apostle points to this event because then and there he began to learn the truths that he records in the third chapter of Philippians, where he says, "Whatever gain I had, I learned to count as loss for the excellency of the knowledge of Christ Jesus" (Phil. 3:7–8 RSV). That is, "I had to learn that all the things that I felt were so necessary to do what God wanted were absolutely useless. I did not need them at all. That great lesson began on the night they let me down over the wall in a basket. It took me a long time to catch on. But there I began to learn that God didn't need my abilities; he needed only my availability. He just needed me as a person. He didn't need my background or my ancestry. He didn't need my knowledge of Hebrew or my knowledge of the law. In fact, he didn't have any intention of using me to reach the Jews. He was going to send me to the Gentiles."

And though he did not fully understand it then, Paul began to assume the yoke of Christ and to learn what Jesus says every one of us must learn if we are going to be useful to him.

Jesus gives us the curriculum: "I am meek and lowly in heart" (Matt. 11:29 KJV). Ambition and pride must die. We no longer live to aggrandize ourselves. We do not live to be big shots in religious or secular life. We live only to be instruments of Jesus Christ. And we must learn the truth that Jesus taught his disciples when he was here in the flesh: "Without me you can do nothing" (John 15:5). We may do a lot in the eyes of the world. What we do might be esteemed there. But in the eyes of God, without him it is nothing. If we are depending on ourselves, God evaluates all we do as worth nothing. This is what Paul learned. Through this experience his pride began to die.

Lord, I pray that I will learn the lesson and will no longer hold on to control of the program myself but will follow where you lead, trusting that your life in me is all that it takes to do everything that must be done.

Are we learning the liberty and the beauty of humility, or are we still counting on our personal resources, real or imagined, to accomplish God's work in us and through us?

THE CURE FOR DEATH

A daily devotion for May 25

Read Acts 9:32–10:23.

> "Peter sent them all out of the room; then he got down on his knees and prayed. Turning toward the dead woman, he said, 'Tabitha, get up.' She opened her eyes, and seeing Peter she sat up. He took her by the hand and helped her to her feet. Then he called for the believers, especially the widows, and presented her to them alive" (Acts 9:40–41).

This was a marvelous miracle—a restoration from the dead. Here was a woman known for her ministry of love and selflessness, and then this ministry was interrupted by death. But by the hand of God and the power of Jesus Christ, she was restored to ministry and resumed her good works. Of course she later died again. This account is intended to teach us what can happen to the human spirit. Something can interrupt the progress of a spiritual life that is beginning to blossom, to flourish and to bear fruit, to grow and to minister to others. Some circumstance, some event or experience, can change it and cause it to die. The person loses zeal, earnestness, and eagerness and becomes hard and unconcerned, bitter of spirit. He is like someone dead.

Many people are like that. Some have been dead for years and are still walking around. I am reminded of the famous comment by Dorothy Thompson, the newspaper reporter, when she heard of the death of Calvin Coolidge. She said, "How could they tell?" Many people's lives of service have been interrupted by some incident that has been like the hand of death laid upon a vibrant ministry. They have grown cold and indifferent, the picture of death.

This can go on for years. Edwin Markham, the great Christian poet, once entrusted a banker with the settlement of an estate. The banker betrayed him, and Markham lost all his money. This left him bitter, and for several years he could write no poetry. One day as he was trying to write, he sat at his desk, aimlessly scrawling circles. As he doodled, Markham was suddenly struck by the thought of how the great circle of God's love encompasses us. He was hit with inspiration and wrote these words:

> I drew a circle and shut him out;
> Heretic, rebel, a thing to flout.
> But Love and I had the wit to win:
> We drew a circle that took him in.

Markham forgave the banker and was able to resume his ministry. After that he produced some of his greatest poems. This is what Jesus Christ can do. He can heal a dead spirit, raise it to life, and restore it. He can heal the bitterness that may be in our lives, rendering us cold and indifferent to the needs of others.

> *Lord, I pray that your Spirit will keep me alive and responsive to you and that I will confess my sin and allow your life to work through me.*

"To set the mind on the flesh is death, but to set the mind on the Spirit is life and peace" (Rom. 8:6). Are we choosing life, seeking the renewal of our minds through honest confession of named sins? The alternative is spiritual death, the wages paid by sin.

FORGIVEN!

A daily devotion for May 26

Read Acts 10:23–11:18.

> "All the prophets testify about him that everyone who believes in him receives forgiveness of sins through his name" (Acts 10:43).

Peter says, "You may not appreciate this fully, but everything that Jesus did was predicted by the prophets. Long before he came, what he would be like and what he would do were written down. Every prophet bore witness to this one fact: the only way you can find forgiveness of sins is by believing in him. That is the great, final, glorious thrust of the gospel. The good news is that men have been given a way to be forgiven of their sins."

That is the basic need of every human heart. Each of us suffers from the terrible consciousness of guilt. We are guilty people, and we know it. That is what makes us so restless. That is why we often cannot stand to be alone with ourselves; we are afraid of that sense of guilt that oppresses us. So the prime need of our lives is to be forgiven, to have nothing in the past to worry about, and to have nothing that makes us uncertain of the future, especially nothing that makes us unwilling to appear before God. Through Jesus Christ sins are forgiven.

Have you reflected upon that, Christian friend? Have you recently stopped and thanked God that your sins are forgiven? Have you ever? Not just the ones you committed before you became a Christian but all your sins. All the future ones as well as those of the past are forgiven already in Jesus Christ. God therefore has no quarrel with you. He loves you and accepts you. Whatever you do, he will continue to love you and to accept you.

You cannot take that truth and use it as a license to sin, to go out and do as you like. To do so would indicate that you have never been regenerated, have never understood why God bore your sins. But if you have been born again you know that this is the greatest and most unending blessing of your life—to wake up every morning and to remember that you stand as a beloved child in God's presence. You are his, and for that reason he will be with you all day long in every circumstance.

> *Thank you, Father, for the forgiveness of my sins. Thank you for sending your Son to die for me so this could be possible. And thank you that he rose victorious over death to give me the hope of eternal life.*

The apostle Paul exults, "Your life is hidden with Christ in God" (Col. 3:3). Such is our security, our identity in Christ, that nothing can separate us from him. Are we living in the understanding of Christ's total forgiveness? Do we wake up each day to the guilt-free joy of his presence?

A GOOD MAN

A daily devotion for May 27

Read Acts 11:19–30.

> "News of this reached the church in Jerusalem, and they sent Barnabas to Antioch. When he arrived and saw what the grace of God had done, he was glad and encouraged them all to remain true to the Lord with all their hearts. He was a good man, full of the Holy Spirit and faith, and a great number of people were brought to the Lord" (Acts 11:22–24).

The gospel had broken through the Jewish barriers that had held it in and was now reaching the Gentiles. As a result of this first preaching, many Gentiles came to Christ. This news was a bit disconcerting to the disciples in Jerusalem. They did not know what to do about this movement of the Holy Spirit. As Jews, raised in the tradition that they were God's chosen people, they never thought that God would show interest in the Gentile world. They hardly knew what to make of it. When word came to them that Gentiles were becoming converts to Jesus Christ, they were utterly astounded. Were these real Christians?

To settle the issue, they sent Barnabas to Antioch. He did not come to control this new thrust by the Holy Spirit; he came to investigate it, to see what God had been doing. The disciples chose Barnabas because he was a good man, full of the Spirit, and full of faith.

"Good man" means more than that he behaved himself. This is a reference to his disposition. He was an easygoing, cheerful, open-hearted, gracious individual. He has appeared this way to us already in the pages of Acts. He defended Paul when he returned from Damascus, disillusioned and defeated. The other apostles would have nothing to do with Paul because he was still suspect. But Barnabas brought him in and championed his cause. He was that kind of man.

He was "full of the Holy Spirit." That was the supreme qualification. Being full of the Holy Spirit meant that the fruits of the Spirit were evident in his life. Barnabas was filled with love, joy, long-suffering, patience, and gentleness. He lived this way not because of his easygoing character but because he was drawing upon the power of an indwelling Holy Spirit.

Third, Barnabas was a man of faith. That means he acted upon what God said. He did not depend on his feelings. A man of faith simply believes God and expects him to act. He doesn't think about how he himself feels. Faith is not a feeling. It has nothing to do with feelings. Faith is simply a recognition that God has promised something and an expectation that since he is God, he will do it. A man of faith acts on that basis. That is the kind of man who gets something done.

Make me available to you, Lord, filled with the Holy Spirit, a person of faith, flexible and ready to move according to the steps that you outline. Make me willing to change. Save me from being unbending in my attitudes toward others.

The one who depends solely on God living through him will be like Barnabas in his relationships with others: gracious, Christlike, and overflowing with encouragement. Will we look for ways God can use us to strengthen and to bless others?

A NEW MAN AND A NEW NAME

A daily devotion for May 28

Read Acts 11:25–26.

"Then Barnabas went to Tarsus to look for Saul, and when he found him, he brought him to Antioch. So for a whole year Barnabas and Saul met with the church and taught great numbers of people. The disciples were called Christians first at Antioch" (Acts 11:25–26).

It has been as much as ten years since we have seen Saul. Ten years before he left Jerusalem with his tail between his legs and went to Tarsus, his hometown, defeated and disillusioned because he had been trying to serve God in his own eager zeal. He had not yet learned to depend upon the Holy Spirit, upon the life of Jesus within. But in those ten years he had learned a lot. He was not entirely idle, as he tells us in Galatians. He preached the Word throughout the regions of Syria and of Cilicia, the area around Tarsus.

Saul had learned one great secret. He had discovered that what he had regarded as his credentials for activity, all that he had previously reckoned upon as useful in his life—his ancestry, his orthodoxy, his morality, his zeal—were for naught. He had learned that such things would not make him an effective worker for Christ and that only his dependence upon Jesus at work in him would make a difference. As he tells us in Philippians 3:8, he learned to count as manure all this other stuff in order that he might gain Christ.

When he had learned that, the Lord sent Barnabas to Tarsus to find him. God had his address all the time, but Barnabas didn't; he had to look for him. When he found him he brought him to Antioch. There the apostle Paul began the great ministry that shook the world and has changed the course of human history time after time.

We then learn of another first: the disciples were for the first time called Christians. It is clear from this brief statement that it was not the Christians themselves but the people of Antioch who called them that. The word means "those belonging to Christ" or "Christ's men." As these Christians spoke about Jesus to people everywhere—Jesus the Christ, the Messiah—the Gentiles around them labeled them "Christ's men." At first it was a contemptuous term, a term of reproach. "Look at these crazy people! They come into our city. They don't worship our idols. They live lives entirely different from ours." But the disciples thought it was wonderful to be called Christ's men, so they adopted the name and called themselves Christians. That is why today we are called Christians.

Thank you, Lord, for the privilege of being called a Christian. May my life reflect all that you are as you live your life in me and through me.

Do we regard lightly the name Christian? Consider the words of Isaiah 43:7: "Everyone who is called by my name, whom I created for my glory, whom I formed and made." Are we honored, awed, and humbled by the power of God's life-changing presence?

TO CAUSE TO SHINE

A daily devotion for May 29

Read Acts 11:27–30.

> "During this time some prophets came down from Jerusalem to Antioch. One of them, named Agabus, stood up and through the Spirit predicted that a severe famine would spread over the entire Roman world ... The disciples, as each one was able, decided to provide help for the brothers and sisters living in Judea" (Acts 11:27–29).

Here is a ministry of one of the gifts of the Spirit—prophecy. Unfortunately, the gift of prophecy has become associated only with the ability to predict the future. But that is not prophecy's primary meaning. Primarily it means "to cause to shine." Prophecy is the ability to illuminate the Word of God and to make it shine. Peter wrote, "We have a more sure word of prophecy which shines as a light in a dark place" (2 Peter 1:19 KJV). These were men who could take the Word of God and make it shine. They illuminated the darkness in people's lives with the truth of God. Occasionally they were also able to illuminate the future, and that was what happened here.

A disciple named Agabus foretold by the Spirit that there would soon be a great famine throughout the world, and although it is not stated here, that it would be especially severe in Judea. This came true just a few months later. When these disciples heard that there was going to be a great famine, they began to prepare for it. They realized that it would be worse in Judea, so they decided to send a gift there. This account is a beautiful picture of the concern of the body. The disciples knew this was coming. They did not wait until they finally got heart-rending appeals from Judea. They anticipated the famine by the Spirit, and they had the gift ready when the disaster struck. They sent it by their favorite teachers, Barnabas and Saul, who had been instructing the church there for a year.

What wonderful lessons in the Holy Spirit believers must have had under the leadership of these two men! They understood the essential character of the church—that it is a body that shares life, one member with another. There was no sense of hierarchy here, no priesthood. There was just the body of Christians together, one group in Jerusalem and one in Antioch. One had need and the other had plenty. And so the body in Antioch sent to the body in Jerusalem what was required to meet its need as the two shared the life that is in Jesus Christ. What a wonderful picture this is of the church. The essential characteristics of a church are all here: the gifts of the Spirit, the shared life in Jesus, the proclamation of the Word, the teaching of the Scripture, the sharing of the body.

> *Lord, thank you for your Word. I pray that you will cause it to shine in me and that I will respond as these early Christians did.*

Godly, biblical leadership in Christ's body will assure the outworking of the spiritual gifts, including sensitive, compassionate attention to others' needs. Are we attentive and obedient to our personal gifting by the Spirit? Do the love and compassion of Jesus find full expression in our serving? Shine, Jesus, shine!

THE DIFFERENCE PRAYER MAKES

A daily devotion for May 30

Read Acts 12:1–19.

"So Peter was kept in prison, but the church was earnestly praying to God for him" (Acts 12:5).

As we review the events of Acts 12:1–19, a question comes to mind. Why was James killed (see verses 1–2) and Peter delivered? There is no question that God could have saved James as well. Why didn't he? The only answer that this chapter suggests is found in verse 5. Peter was kept in prison just like James. The difference was that the church made earnest prayer to God for Peter, and as a result, Peter was set free. Some might ask, "What difference did it make? Couldn't God have set Peter free anyhow? If God determined that James would die and that Peter would be set free, what difference did the prayer of the church make?"

But let us never forget what James (not this James but Jesus's brother, who wrote the epistle of James) says: "You have not because you ask not" (James 4:2). In his wisdom God has designed that his people shall participate in what he does. He is impressing upon his people here that when danger threatens the program of God or the people of God, it is a call to prayer. God will hear that prayer, answer it, and set people free when he would not otherwise have done so.

That is the great lesson of this chapter. We are not simply to accept the events of our day as though there is nothing we can do about them. Prayer becomes a mighty weapon that God's people can use to change events. Prayer is the most natural response of a heart dependent upon God. If we are counting on God to do something, we will pray about it. We will trust him; we will communicate with him. If we are not counting on him, we will not pray. If we are really counting on someone else—if we think that by our own clever maneuvering we can get out of a situation or if we are trusting other human beings to come through—we will not pray.

The basic motive for prayer is a sense of dependence. If we think that God alone can change a situation, we pray. This is what happened in the early church. When the disciples discovered that James had been put to death and that the Enemy's vicious attack could be successful, they suddenly realized that they had a part to play in God's program. They were to go to God in earnest prayer that Peter might be delivered. And God set him free in a wonderful way.

This passage highlights for us what prayer does, and that is basic for us to learn today. God works in the same way today as he did in the first century, and he will respond to our prayers in much the same way.

Father, teach me how to pray. I don't always need to know what to pray for, but I do desperately need to pray. I need to pray for others, to pray about the dangers that beset us as a nation and as a world. Help me to open my heart and to be honest before you. I know that in the mystery of prayer, a mystery that I cannot fathom, something allows your Spirit to work in ways that otherwise would never happen.

When prayer is worship, the focus is on the character and the will of God. Are we learning to worship him by praying Jesus's prayer: "Nevertheless, not my will but Thine be done"?

THE FOLLY OF PRIDE

A daily devotion for May 31

Read Acts 12:19–25.

"On the appointed day Herod, wearing his royal robes, sat on his throne and delivered a public address to the people. They shouted, 'This is the voice of a god, not of a man.' Immediately, because Herod did not give praise to God, an angel of the Lord struck him down, and he was eaten by worms and died" (Acts 12:21–23).

The Jewish historian Josephus also records the death of Herod. He describes this occasion when Herod met with the people of Tyre and Sidon in what we now call Lebanon. These people were dependent upon Judea, and especially upon Galilee, for food. So when the king came out, dressed in his royal robes, they flattered him. When he spoke to them they cried out, "This is the voice of a god, not of a man!" And this pompous, vain king believed them. It is incredible—the tragic, twisted mentality of a man like this, who could believe that he had so much power that he had become a god.

But this was not uncommon in those days, nor is it in our own times. This is exactly what happens in any man's mind when he begins to think of himself as what we call a self-made man. Sometimes men who own a lot of property will say, "Well, I worked for it. I produced it all myself. Nobody helped me." They are falling into the same tragic error as this egotistical and fatuous king who imagined that he had power in himself to operate. But Luke tells us that Herod was immediately stricken by an angel of the Lord and that he was eaten by worms and died. I do not know Luke's exact diagnosis, but some sudden catastrophe befell Herod, and as Josephus tells us, within two or three days he died.

This is God's way of demonstrating the ultimate folly of the person who thinks that he can live without God, who thinks that we are not dependent people. This is the tragedy of mankind. We can easily discern from newspapers and from television programs that as a people we imagine that we have what it takes to produce all that life requires and that we do not need anyone or anything else—especially God. The great tragedy of the American nation is that more often than not we are in effect saying, "Please, God, I'd rather do it myself!" We want to do everything ourselves. But God often strikes to remind us that our life, our breath, all that we have and are, come from him and that we are fools to think that we can exist, act, and react on our own. This episode shows how blind and how tragically twisted becomes the thinking of men who depart from a sense of dependence upon God.

Father, forgive me for the folly of my pride and of my dependence on self. Teach me that in everything I am dependent on you.

"Pride goes before destruction, and a haughty spirit before a fall" (Prov. 16:18). Do we aim to have the mind of Christ, who emptied himself, taking the form of a servant, humbled himself, and became obedient unto death on a cross? This is "Christ in you the hope of glory"!

PRAYING TO THE FATHER

An introduction for the month of June

This month I offer a series of devotions on the subject of prayer, developing this series from the Old and New Testaments. My method will remain expositional—understanding what each passage says—but it will be centered around this theme of prayer.

I do this because I feel a great lack in my own life in this regard. I want to understand more the ministry, the power, and the necessity of prayer. I sense that this lack is a problem among most Christians. Do you feel that your prayer life lacks something?

Prayer is simply conversation with God. Only two people are represented in true prayer—you and God. Hundreds of people may be present, but real prayer is always a conversation directly between a single human being and God. We will examine many kinds of prayer during these studies. We will look at intercession, thanksgiving, supplication, and various forms of petition, but fundamental to them all is simply a dialogue between an individual and God.

This is what Jesus had in mind in his great teaching on prayer in the Sermon on the Mount. He said, "When you pray." He did not say if you pray. He took it for granted that, in the Christian life, there would be prayer. Prayer, as one hymn puts it, is "the Christian's native breath." We cannot live without it. Jesus said, "When you pray, go into your closet, and shut the door, and pray to your Father who is in secret." He certainly did not mean that we are to pray only in closets. I'm sure if we tried that we would probably feel it so stuffy we could not breathe, so prayer would not continue for long. Also, we do not always have closets available. Jesus was speaking metaphorically, saying, "Shut out everything else. When you pray do not let anything else interfere. Do not think about other things or people but talk only to God."

I find it interesting to listen to people pray. Sometimes I hear amazing things. When I listen I often detect that people do not think about God so much as they think about the people listening to their prayer. I know a wonderful man who almost invariably begins by directing his prayer to God but then becomes so aware of other people listening that he starts preaching to them in prayer. This man will start out by praying, "Our heavenly Father, we thank you that we can come before you. We know that God is a prayer-hearing God and that all those who come to God in prayer shall be blessed by him." Before you know it, he is speaking not only to God but to those present about God. But that is not prayer. Prayer is a conversation, simple and direct, between one person and God.

WHY PRAY?

A daily devotion for June 1

Read Luke 18:1–8.

> "And the Lord said, 'Listen to what the unjust judge says. And will not God bring about justice for his chosen ones, who cry out to him day and night? Will he keep putting them off?'" (Luke 18:6–7).

It is sometimes taught that Jesus is here encouraging what is called "prevailing prayer," an attempt to belabor God, to give him no peace, to picket the throne of heaven until we get what we want. This is not biblical.

Some years ago an article appeared in the press concerning a man who announced that he was troubled about moral conditions in this country and had determined to fast and to pray until God sent a great awakening, a sweeping revival to correct the degeneracy of the day. He declared that he would persist even until death if necessary, expecting God to move. The papers carried the story day after day. His strength began to fail, and he grew weaker and weaker and finally was confined to his bed. Bulletins were issued each day about his condition. He was evidently a man of unusual determination, for most of us would have quit after the third day and settled for a good steak, but this man did not. He went on with his fast until he died. The funeral was widely covered, and many lauded his persistence.

Was that really prayer? No, it was not! It was an attempt to blackmail God. This man was holding his own life as a pistol to the head of God and demanding all his money! He was insisting that God move on his terms and according to his time schedule. That was not prayer.

Jesus says God is not an unrighteous God demanding that we wheedle and struggle and persuade him to move. He is not grudging. Prayer is forever the cry of a beloved child to his father, and frequently it is the cry of a lost child who does not know his way, who is lost in dark woods, with strange, frightening noises in the bushes. The child may cry out to be led to an open road or to be home safe in bed or at least to see a light in the distance so he can know his way, but his prayers are not always answered as he expects, for God is a father, and as Jesus said, he knows what we need before we pray.

Paul reminds us that we do not know what we need or what we should pray for but that God does. The Father knows, and because he is a father he knows if it is not yet time to answer in a particular way, if it is the best thing to do, or if it is even possible given the circumstance. While a specific answer may indeed be long delayed, there is no delay at all in God answering our prayer. This is what Jesus is saying, that when we cry out there is an immediate answer. God rushes to help his child. The answer is the squeeze of the Father's hand on ours, the quiet comfort of the Father's voice, the reassurance of the Father's presence even though the woods are still dark and the noises grow louder. We receive immediate reassurance that the Father is with us and that in his own time and his own way he will lead us to the house and put us safely in bed or bring us to the light again.

> *Father, these words of Jesus have made me aware of my lack of faith. I cry out to you now in my weakness and in my failure to exercise faith and say, O Father, teach me to pray. Teach me to depend continually upon you, to pour out to you every aspect of my life without reservation, and to listen to you about all things.*

How significant to us is our astounding relationship with God as our everlasting Father? Are we learning to value prayer as communication with him, or is prayer no more to us than an SOS?

TRUE PRAYER

A daily devotion for June 2

Read Luke 18:9–14.

> "But the tax collector stood at a distance. He would not even look up to heaven, but beat his breast and said, 'God, have mercy on me, a sinner.' I tell you that this man, rather than the other, went home justified before God" (Luke 18:13–14).

How this captures the true character of prayer. This man entered the temple and stood with his eyes cast down. He did not assume the posture of prayer. All he could do was beat his breast and say, "God, have mercy on me, a sinner."

What do we learn about prayer from this man? Is it not obvious that authentic prayer involves an awareness of our helpless need? This man saw himself as being on the lowest possible level, a sinner. In fact, in the original language he called himself "the sinner," the lowest kind, the worst kind. He believed that without God he could do nothing to help his position.

Is it not remarkable that this man did not try to add anything by way of merit? He did not say, "God, be merciful to me, a penitent sinner." He was penitent, but he did not mention that as a basis for God's blessing. He did not say, "God, be merciful to me, a reformed sinner. I'm going to be different from now on." He did not even say, "God, be merciful to me, an honest sinner. Here I am, Lord, willing to tell you everything. Surely you can't ignore honesty like that." In fact, he did not even say, "God, be merciful to me, a praying sinner." He cast away everything and said, "Lord, I haven't a thing to lean on but you."

How did he come to this place? In exactly the opposite way of the Pharisee whom Jesus spoke of earlier. This man did not look down on someone below him; he looked up to God. He judged upward to God. He saw no one but God and heard nothing but God's high standard: "Love the Lord thy God with all thy heart and all thy soul and all thy strength and all thy mind" (Matt. 22:37, Luke 10:37 KJV). "Lord, I'm the sinner," he said. "I'll never be any better in myself. I'm simply a sinner."

In this tax collector we also learn that true prayer is always an acknowledgment of divine adequacy. Our help must be in God. This man looked for help nowhere else. He did not say, "Lord, perhaps this Pharisee standing here can help me." No, he said, "God, be merciful to me." In the words "have mercy" is hidden the wonderful story of the coming of Jesus, the cross, and the resurrection. He used a theological word meaning "be propitiated to me," that is, "Having had your justice satisfied, Lord, now show me your love." And he believed that God's mercy was available, for Jesus said he "went home justified." He was changed; he was made whole. He laid hold of what God said and believed him.

This is where Jesus leaves us. Perhaps for the first time we can say, "Lord, be merciful to me, the sinner." Even after years of Christian life we can start again and say, "Lord, let me reckon upon your faithfulness to me. Let me count upon your willingness to be in me and to work through me to make my life all that it ought to be."

Holy Father, I ask now that I may, in this quiet moment, begin to live a life of prayer. I have no other help, but you are fully adequate. On this I rest.

Do we come before our Father as empty vessels, needing and expecting him to meet us in our weakness and inadequacy? Do we look to God alone to change us and to make us whole?

HOW JESUS PRAYED

A daily devotion for June 3

Read Luke 11:1.

> "One day Jesus was praying in a certain place. When he finished, one of his disciples said to him, 'Lord, teach us to pray, just as John taught his disciples'" (Luke 11:1).

This was a significant request because the disciples were undoubtedly already men of prayer. When they said, "Lord, teach us to pray, as John taught his disciples," they did not mean to imply that John had a superior school of ministry. They were not saying, "In that traveling seminary that John conducted he had a course on prayer, but you have not told us anything about this yet." What they meant was, "Some of us once were John's disciples and were taught by him how to pray, but Lord, we have been watching you, and we see that you are a master at prayer. Now as John once taught us how to pray, would you also impart to us the secrets of prayer? For as we have been watching you, we have seen that in some manner the marvel and the mystery of your character are linked with your prayer life, and this has made us aware how little we really know about prayer. Lord, would you teach us to pray?" What did they see in his life that wrung this cry from their hearts? What was it that impressed them as they watched Jesus pray and convinced them that his prayer life and his amazing power and wisdom were somehow related?

They saw that with Jesus, prayer was a necessity. It was more than an occasional practice for him; it was a lifelong habit. It was an attitude of mind and heart. It was an atmosphere in which he lived, the very air he breathed. Everything he did arose out of prayer. He prayed without ceasing.

It was not always formal prayer. Jesus did not kneel every time. He did not continually stand with a bowed head in an attitude of prayer. If he had done that, he would not have accomplished anything. The amazing thing is that he fulfilled his prayer life amid an incredibly busy ministry. Like many of us, Jesus was subjected to a life of increasing pressure, of continual interruption. Despite this, he was constantly in prayer. He was praying in spirit when his hands were busy healing. He gave thanks as he was breaking the bread and feeding the five thousand. Before commanding Lazarus to come forth from the tomb, he openly gave thanks to the Father. When the Greeks wanted to see Jesus, his immediate response was a prayer, "Father," he said, "glorify Thy name" (John 12:28 KJV). Jesus had a continual expectation that the Father would be working through him, and thus he was praying by his attitude all the time.

Surely this is what our Lord is teaching us and what we must learn: that every facet of life requires prayer, a sense of expectation of God at work. Is not this what that disciple felt as he watched our Lord praying? He knew that for him, prayer was merely an option. He prayed when he felt like it, when he thought it necessary, thinking that prayer was designed for emergency use only, for the big problems of life.

Do we not need to begin in the here and now? This phone call that I am about to make—I can't do it right except in prayer. It will never have the effect it ought to have except as my heart looks up to God and says, "Speak through me in this." This e-mail I am about to write—how can I do it properly without looking to you, Lord, to do it through me? This interview that I am about to conduct, this chart that I have to make for my studies, this report that I must turn in tomorrow, this room that I am sweeping, this walk I am going to take, this game I am about to play—these are the unending needs from which prayer rises.

> *Father, what can I say in this hour but to cry out as these disciples did, "Lord, teach us to pray"? Give me a conscious sense of dependence, an awareness that nothing I do will be of any value apart from you.*

Is prayer so important to us that we cry out with the disciples, "Lord, teach us to pray"? Do we see the profound implication for us in the fact that Jesus consulted his Father about everything? Are we people of prayer?

PRAYER TO THE FATHER

A daily devotion for June 4

Read Luke 11:2–4.

"He said to them, 'When you pray, say: "Father"'" (Luke 11:2).

The Lord's Prayer begins with a word of relationship, *Father*. And let's note that it is Father, not Daddy-o! There is a reverence about the word *father* that is absent in some modern expressions of fatherhood. When we come to prayer, we are not talking about God. We are not engaging in a theological dialogue. We are talking with God. We are going to converse with him directly, and so it is essential that we understand to whom we are speaking. Our Lord employs this marvelously expressive word and says true prayer must begin with a concept of God as Father.

That immediately eliminates a number of other concepts. It shows us that real prayer is never to be addressed to the chairman of the committee for welfare and relief. Sometimes our prayers take on that aspect. We come expecting a handout. We want something to be poured into our laps, something that we think we need, and in making an appeal we are simply filling out the prescribed forms.

Nor is prayer addressed to the chief of the bureau of investigation. It is never to be merely a confession of our wrongdoing, with the hope that we may cast ourselves upon the mercy of the court. Nor is it an appeal to the secretary of the treasury, some genial international banker whom we hope to interest in financing our projects. Prayer is to be made to a Father with a father's heart, a father's love, and a father's strength, and the first and truest note of prayer must be our recognition that we come to this kind of father. We must hear him and come to him in trust and simplicity and with all the frankness of a child. Otherwise it is not prayer.

Someone has pointed out that the word *father* answers all the philosophical questions about the nature of God. A father is a person. Therefore God is not a blind force behind the inscrutable machinery of the universe. A father is able to hear, and God is not an impersonal being, aloof from all our troubles. Above all, a father is predisposed by his love and his relationship to give a careful, attentive ear to what his child says. From a father, a child can surely expect a reply.

We are not only to address God as Father, simply placing the word upon our lips, but we are to believe that he is a Father, for all that God makes available to humanity must always come to us through faith, must always operate in our lives through belief. Belief invariably involves a commitment of the will, a moving of the deepest part of our nature. Therefore if we begin our prayer by addressing God as "almighty God" or "dreadful Creator" or "ground of all being," we betray our fatal ignorance or unbelief. The greatest authority on prayer says that God is a father! When I come home I do not want my children to meet me in awe and say, "Oh thou great and dreadful pastor of Peninsula Bible Church, welcome home." That would be an insult to my father heart. I want my children to greet me as a father. We are not praying until we recognize that we are coming to a patient and tender father. That is the first note in true prayer.

Thank you for inviting me to call you Father. Teach me to trust that you are patient and tender, always welcoming me into your arms.

What attitudes are implied in addressing our prayers to God as our Father? Should we think of prayer as a theological dialogue?

HIS NAME IS HOLY

A daily devotion for June 5

Read Luke 11:2–4.

"He said to them, 'When you pray, say, "Father, hallowed be your name"'" (Luke 11:2).

The second petition of the Lord's Prayer is one of surrender, "Hallowed be your name." I am quite sure this petition makes hypocrites out of most of us. For we can say "Father" with grateful sincerity, but when we pray "Hallowed be your name," we say this with the guilty knowledge that as we pray, his name is not hallowed in certain areas of our lives and that furthermore, we don't want it to be hallowed. When we say "Hallowed be your name," we are praying, "May the whole of my life be a source of delight to you, and may it be an honor to the name that I bear, which is your name. Hallowed be your name."

The trouble is that we so frequently know that great portions of our lives are not hallowed. We have reserved certain monopolies for ourselves and do not wish to surrender these privileged areas where the name of our boss or the name of our girlfriend or some other dear one means more to us than the name of God. But if we pray this with any sincerity or openness, we are saying, "Lord, I open to you every closet. I am taking every skeleton out for you to examine. Hallowed be thy name." There cannot be any contact with God, any touching of his power, any genuine experience of the glorious fragrance and wonder of God at work in human life until we truly pray, and the second requisite of true prayer is that we say "Hallowed be your name."

But we are not only aware that in each of us there are areas where God's name is not hallowed, but we know deep in our being that no matter how we may try to arrange our lives to please him, a flaw somehow makes us miss the mark. Even when we try hard we find ourselves unable to do this. But this prayer is not phrased simply as a confession or as an expression of repentance to the Father. We are not to pray as we so frequently do, "Father, help me to be good" or "Help me to be better." Throughout this prayer, not once do we find an expression of a desire for help in the sanctification of life. No, Jesus turns our attention entirely away from ourselves to the Father. The phrase "Hallowed be your name" is a cry of helpless trust through which we are saying, "Father, not only do I know that there are areas in my life where your name is not hallowed, but I also know that only you can hallow them, and I am quite willing to stand still and let you be the Holy One who will be first in my life."

The person who lets God be his Lord and surrenders to him is drawn spontaneously into a great learning process and becomes a different person. Martin Luther once said, "You do not command a stone which is lying in the sun to be warm. It will be warm all by itself." When we say, "Father, there is no area of my life that I'm not willing to let you talk to me about; there is no area that I will hide from you, my sexual life, my business life, my social life, my school life, my recreation times, my vacation periods," we are saying, "Hallowed be your name." When we pray that way, we discover that God will walk into the dark closets of our lives where the odor is sometimes too much for us to stand and clean them out, straighten them up, and make them fit for his dwelling. "If we walk in the light as he is in the light, we have fellowship one with another, and the blood of Jesus his Son cleanses us from all sin" (1 John 1:7 RSV). Walking in this light does not mean sinlessness; it means our recognition that God sees everything.

Father, teach me to say the words "Hallowed be your name" with a heart of complete surrender and faith that you are the only One who can make me holy.

What is our attitude toward the hallowed name of our Father? Do we use his name with shallow flippancy? Are we evading the implications of being his name-bearers? Do we experience prayer as a personal, awesome encounter with our awesome, holy Father?

A CRY OF HOPE

A daily devotion for June 6

Read Luke 11:2–4.

> "He said to them, 'When you pray, say: "Father, hallowed be your name, your kingdom come"'" (Luke 11:2).

The third cry of true prayer, again concerned with God, is a cry of hope, "Your kingdom come." This can be a sigh for heaven. Who among us does not get homesick for heaven once in a while, longing to be free from the boredom of life and to experience the glory we read about in the Bible? Or this can be, as it ought to be, a cry for heaven to come to earth. "Your kingdom come" can mean "May the kingdoms of this world become the kingdoms of our Lord and of his Christ." There is much in Scripture about this, and who does not weary of war and poverty, of misery and despair, and long for that day to come when God shall rule in righteousness over all the earth?

But this prayer is more than a long, wistful look into the future, whether on earth or off earth. It is a cry that God's will may be done through the blood, sweat, and tears of life right now—that is, "Your kingdom come through what I am enduring at this very moment." That is what this prayer means. Scripture reveals to us a truth that man would never know by himself but one that becomes self-evident as we look at life through the lens of the Word of God: the Lord builds his kingdom in secret. When it is least evident that he is at work he is frequently accomplishing the most. Behind the scaffolding of tragedy and despair, God is often erecting his empire of love and glory. In hardships, disappointments, heartbreak, and disasters, when we think God is silent, when we feel God has removed his hand and we no longer sense the friendship of his presence, he frequently is accomplishing the greatest things of all.

I once sat down with a young man who told me the story of his life. He had gone through a fearsome accident that had left a physical mark upon him, but a broken marriage had caused an even deeper scar. He had been raised in a church environment, and before some of his difficulties took place, his outlook was one of self-righteous judgment of others, a pious disdain for those who could not keep free from troubles. But he said, "You know, the humiliation of my divorce cut the ground right out from under my self-righteous attitude. I know that I never would have come to my present joy and understanding of God's purpose if I had not been a divorce statistic." It is through these ways that God builds his kingdom.

What a glorious mystery this is! Out of darkness God calls forth light, out of despair, hope. From death comes resurrection. You cannot have resurrection without death, hope without despair, or light without darkness. By means of defeat, the kingdom of God is born in human hearts. That is what this prayer means.

"Oh, Lord, I am but a little child. I do not understand the mysteries of life. I do not know the ways of the world of men, but Lord, I pray that through the circumstances in which I now find myself, through these troubles, these struggles, your kingdom come."

> *Father, how frequently I misunderstand life even though you have gone to such great lengths to show me its secrets. How many times, Father, have I rebelled in foolish resentment against you and your workings in my life? But I have also seen that through these hours of resentment and bitterness, you have been at work in love to bring me to an understanding of reality, to bring me back to your loving heart.*

Do we pray with joyful anticipation for Christ's triumphant reign on earth? Do we also pray for his unbridled reign in our daily walk with him?

PRAYING FOR YOUR BODY

A daily devotion for June 7

Read Luke 11:2–4.

"Give us each day our daily bread" (Luke 11:3).

Jesus begins this section of the prayer with the needs of the body. I like that! We have such distorted ideas about prayer that we often feel there is something wrong with praying about physical needs. This reflects a pagan concept of life. The Greeks regarded the body as unworthy of redemption, and they therefore mistreated it. They beat and tormented their bodies. This philosophy is widespread today, the idea that the body must be subdued by physical torment or suffering, but it is found nowhere in the New Testament.

Prayer must begin on this level. God likes bodies. He engineered and designed them. It is perfectly proper that we pray about the needs of the body. Bread here is a symbol of all the necessities of physical life. It stands for all that physical life demands—shelter, drink, clothing—anything that the body requires. The vital concern in this area is that we have available an immediate, unbroken supply. This prayer addresses the issue when it says, "Give us each day our daily bread." The only limit in this prayer is that we are never to pray for a warehouse—a full supply for a year ahead. We are to pray for one day's supply.

Do we pray daily for our physical needs? Do we pray about the supply of our food, clothing, shelter, and all the other necessities of life? Do we take time to ask God for them or at least to give thanks for them? Perhaps this has become such a familiar request in repeating the Lord's Prayer that we do not take it seriously. This may be the most flagrant and frequent area of Christian disobedience. After all, our Lord meant it when he told us to pray "Give us each day our daily bread."

Some might argue that Jesus said elsewhere, "Your Father knows that you have need of these things even before you pray" (Matt. 6:8), so we don't have to inform God of our needs. Others say it makes little difference whether or not they pray about physical things. They get the necessities of life regardless. Furthermore, some say there are many people who never bother to pray and who are eating steak and ice cream while we Christians are trying to get along on hamburgers and Jell-O. What is the point, then, of praying?

If we want to see why, we should ask ourselves what happens when we neglect this area of prayer. If we are honest, we will see that a slow and subtle change occurs in our hearts when we do not pray about material things, when we do not take time to thank God for our daily supply of the necessities and the luxuries of life. We take these things for granted, and gradually we succumb to the foolish delusion that we can provide these necessities ourselves. We become possessed with the incredible vanity that our wisdom and our abilities have made these things possible. And when we begin to think that way, pride swells within us and a blindness settles upon us, darkening our spiritual insight, and we become moody, restless, and depressed.

We need to give thanks to God, always reminding ourselves that everything we have comes from his hand and that at any moment and for any reason he may choose to cut off these benefits—that only his grace and his goodness keep the supply flowing unhindered to us. The only way that we can avoid the terrible sin of ingratitude is to pray daily for our physical needs.

Father, today I can't but echo the words the Lord Jesus taught me: give us this day our daily bread.

Do we take for granted the daily supply of our physical needs? Are we neglecting petition and gratitude? Is that negligence resulting in despair or self-congratulation?

FORGIVEN AND FORGIVING

A daily devotion for June 8

Read Luke 11:2–4.

"Forgive us our sins, for we also forgive everyone who sins against us" (Luke 11:4).

Here we see the need for a cleansed conscience, for a sense of peace, of rest with God and man. This is the arena where the emotional clutter of life takes a deadly toll. Who has not experienced troublesome mental symptoms, morbid depressions, and unreasoning fears and insecurity? Scripture and modern psychology, in its groping after truth, agree that underneath these symptoms lurk two frightening monsters: fear and guilt. If we can find a way to slay these fiery dragons, we will find peace.

When we pray, "Forgive us our sins," we are asking for the reality that God promises to every believer in Jesus Christ: "There is therefore now no condemnation to them which are in Christ Jesus" (Rom. 8:1 KJV). Nothing troubles Christians more than a sense of guilt. But in this simple prayer is a fully adequate answer, for if we have laid hold of the forgiveness of God, we know there is no longer anything between us and the Lord. Our hearts are absolutely free before him, and the result is a pervading sense of peace.

But Jesus immediately adds a limitation to this. We cannot say to God, "Forgive us our sins," unless we are willing and have said to others that they are forgiven for their sins against us. Jesus is not referring to the divine forgiveness that accompanies conversion. The Lord's Prayer is meant for Christians—for only Christians can pray it intelligently. No non-Christian ever receives forgiveness from God on the basis of claiming to forgive everyone else. It is impossible for him to forgive until he himself has received the forgiveness of God, and that forgiveness is offered because of the death of Jesus. We Christians come thanking him for what his death on the cross has already done in taking away the awful burden of our sin.

But having received that forgiveness, we will still never rest in God's forgiveness for the defilements of our Christian walk unless we are ready to extend that same forgiveness to those who offend us. This forgiveness keeps us enjoying unbroken fellowship with the Father and with the Son, which is the secret of emotional quietness and rest. Jesus is simply saying that there is no use praying "Father, forgive my sins" if we are holding a grudge against someone, are burning with resentment, or are filled with bitterness. Our souls will always be distracted. He tells us, "First be reconciled with your brother, then come and offer your gift at the altar" (Matt. 5:24 RSV). Forgive him, and then the healing forgiveness of God will flood our hearts, and we will find there is nothing that can destroy the God-given peace at the very center of our beings. If we refuse to forgive someone, we are withholding from another the grace already shown to us. It is only because we have already been forgiven the staggering debt of our own sins that we can find the grace to forgive the relatively paltry slights someone else has heaped upon us.

Father, thank you for the forgiveness you have promised through the work of Jesus on the cross, the forgiveness that frees me to forgive others.

Are we blocking the fullness and the freedom of God's forgiveness of our sins by refusing to extend to others the same grace of forgiveness that God has made available to us?

UNRECOGNIZED TEMPTATION

A daily devotion for June 9

Read Luke 11:2–4.

"And lead us not into temptation" (Luke 11:4).

This part of the Lord's Prayer deals with the realm of the spirit. In the unseen war of the spirit, our greatest needs are deliverance and protection. But an immediate problem arises here, for Scripture reveals that temptation is necessary to us, a real part of life in this fallen, flawed world. No one escapes it in the Christian life. Furthermore, though God never tempts us to sin, he does test us in difficult and discouraging circumstances, and these things become his instruments to strengthen us, to build us up and thus to give us victory. When we read this prayer, we are confronted with this question: "Are we really expected to pray that God will not do what he must do to accomplish his work within us?" After all, even Jesus, we are told, was led by the Spirit into the wilderness to be tempted by the Devil. What, then, does he mean?

I have puzzled and prayed and read about this, and I am convinced that Jesus intends this as a prayer to be kept from unrecognized temptation. When temptation is recognized as such, it can be resisted, and resistance is always a source of strength and growth for us. If I am filling out a tax form and I find that some income has come to me through unusual channels and that there is no way anyone can know this, I am confronted with a temptation to omit it. But I know this is wrong, and no one has to tell me so. When I resist that temptation, I find I am stronger the next time when a larger amount is involved.

When we recognize lust as lust and hate as hate and cowardice for what it is, that is one thing. It is a simple matter to resist obvious evil if we mean to walk with God. But temptation is not always so simple. There are times when I think I am right, and with utmost sincerity and integrity of heart I do what I believe is the right thing. But later I look back upon it and see that I was tragically wrong.

Peter is an example on this. In the upper room, with brashness, confidence, and utter naiveté, Peter told the Lord, "Even if all fall away on account of you, I never will" (Matt. 26:33). The apostle walked out of the upper room with the words of our Lord ringing in his ears. "Truly I tell you," Jesus answered, "this very night, before the rooster crows, you will disown me three times" (Matt. 26:34). In the garden, Jesus told a still-confident Peter, "Watch and pray so that you will not fall into temptation" (Matt. 26:41). But Peter did not heed that word. Instead he slept, and our Lord woke him again and asked him to pray. But Peter did not pray, and when the apostle entered the court of the high priest and stood before the fire, Satan wrung the courage out of him and hung him up like a limp dish rag to dry in the presence of a little girl. There, cursing and swearing, he found himself trapped, denying his Lord, and in the awful realization of what he had done he went out into the blackness of the night and wept bitterly.

This is what our Lord refers to in this phrase. This prayer is the recognition of our foolish weakness and of our tendency to stumble into blind folly. We desperately need to pray that we will not fall into this trap.

Lord, I confess my utter helplessness apart from you. Lead me not into unrecognized temptation.

Are we self-confident about our ability to recognize the subtleties of temptation? Do we follow our own instincts or do we honestly, consistently pray for the discernment of God's Holy Spirit?

ASK, SEEK, KNOCK

A daily devotion for June 10

Read Luke 11:5–13.

> "So I say to you: Ask and it will be given to you; seek and you will find; knock and the door will be opened to you. For everyone who asks receives; the one who seeks finds; and to the one who knocks, the door will be opened" (Luke 11:9–10).

Take careful note of what Jesus says, for he suggests that there are three levels of prayer: ask, seek, and knock. You can remember them if you note the fact that the initial letters—*a* in *ask*, *s* in *seek*, and *k* in *knock*—spell the word *ask*. There you have a little formula for prayer. Now mark these three levels. The circumstances of each are vastly different, but the answer is the same.

The simplest and easiest level, of course, is ask. Jesus is saying that God will immediately and invariably meet certain needs if only we make the request. The range of these needs is far wider than we might think. For instance, reading through the New Testament, it becomes clear that our need for Christlike attributes lies in this category. If we need love, courage, wisdom, power, or patience, they all lie in this realm. If we ask, the answer will come immediately. Is that not what James says? "If any man lack wisdom, let him ask of God who giveth to all men liberally and upbraideth not" (James 1:5 KJV). Ask for wisdom, and it shall be given, as will other virtues.

A second level of prayer is denoted by the word *seek*. We cannot understand what it means to seek without noting that our Lord injects an element of time. Seeking is not a simple act. It is a process, a series of acts. Jesus says there are areas of life that require more than asking; there must be seeking, searching. Something is lost, hidden from us, and prayer then becomes a search, a plea for insight, for understanding, for an unraveling of the mystery confronting us. Again, the answer is certain. Seek, and we will find!

The third level involves knocking. Here, time and repetition are required. A knock is not a single rap but a series of raps. It is a request for admittance, repeated if necessary, and it suggests situations in which we seek entrance or an opportunity. Someone has perhaps erected a barrier against our witness or against our friendship, and we are seeking to get past the wall of resistance and to have an opportunity to speak, to share, or to enter a life. That requires knocking. Perhaps we have an unshakable desire to begin a type of work or ministry from which we are now excluded. We long to move into that area and feel God leading us, calling us, to be this or to do that. This requires knocking. Perhaps we are pursuing knowledge or friendship or "hungering and thirsting after righteousness" (Matt. 5:6). We are looking for an opportunity, seeking entrance to an area now restricted from us. This requires knocking. We come before God and boldly and repeatedly ask, each time making an endeavor to enter, for we rest on the solid assurance that what Jesus says is true: "Knock, and it shall be opened."

> *Lord Jesus, I ask that these words may enter my heart with fresh and vital meaning—that I recognize there are things I need to ask for and take immediately from your hand, others that I need to seek, and still others for which I need to knock and wait and knock again, knowing that in every case your word is sure.*

Are we carefully noting the three levels of prayer given us by Jesus? Are we observing these as we make our requests of our Father? Do we lack these things because we are not even asking him?

PRAYING TOGETHER

A daily devotion for June 11

Read Matthew 18:18–20.

"For where two or three gather in my name, there am I with them" (Matt. 18:20).

The full expression of the power of Jesus Christ is never seen in an individual Christian but only in the church as a whole. The simplest form of the church is here described: "where two or three gather in my name." As individual Christians, we cannot fully reflect Jesus Christ. The power committed to Jesus Christ is fully manifested in this life only when two or three, or two or three hundred, or two or three thousand are gathered in his name, which is above every name in this age and in the age to come. This means we can never fully know Jesus Christ unless we know him in relation to someone else.

Paul prays that we may know what is the breadth and the length and the depth and the height and come to know with all saints the love that is in Jesus Christ (Eph. 3:17–19). This will happen only with all saints. We will never know it by ourselves. We can take the Bible and study it by ourselves; we can analyze it, saturate our minds with it, and memorize it, but until we share it with other Christians we will never grasp Jesus Christ in his fulness.

Furthermore, we can never learn how mighty and glorious he is unless we make demands upon his power and his glory and thus learn that we can never touch bottom. That is what gives meaning to the gatherings of believers today. "Where two or three gather in my name," Jesus says, "there I am with them." The power of the church does not lie in the numbers that it can gather together. How mistaken is the idea that if we can get enough people together to pray, we shall have the power to right the world's wrongs! Nothing could be further from the truth.

Nor is the power of the church in its community status. We think if we can get people who are in positions of authority or stature in a community—civic leaders, the mayor, bankers, businessmen, tycoons—into our church, then we will have enough status to wield great power in the minds and hearts of people. How foolish we are. The power of the church does not rest in its numbers, its status, or its wealth. The power of the church of Jesus Christ is stated here. "Where two or three gather in my name, there I am with them."

Out of Jesus alone flows this marvelous power to bind and to loose. He is the source of this tremendous unity by which the mind of the Spirit becomes known and God moves through Christian lives to alter the destiny of the world around us. If we wish to glory in anything, let us glory in the fact that the indwelling Jesus Christ lives and moves in our midst, that we belong to him, and that his life is expressed through us. It is through him that prayer has meaning and value.

Father, how wonderful it is to return to the simplicity of a relationship with a mighty, victorious Lord in the midst of his church. Lord, teach me to glory in this and to pray on that basis alone.

Have we falsely assumed that the power of God's response to our prayers will be measured by the numbers or the status of the people praying? Or do we take the lone ranger route, ignoring our need and the effectiveness of prayer with fellow believers?

IN MY NAME

A daily devotion for June 12

Read John 14:12–17.

> "And I will do whatever you ask in my name, so that the Father may be glorified in the Son. You may ask me for anything in my name, and I will do it" (John 14:13–14).

"Whatever … anything … I will do it." We sense immediately that this promise is too wide. If we see it as absolutely unlimited, a sort of Aladdin's lamp that we can rub and ask for anything in the world, we have missed the point of this passage. We also sense that the promise can be contradictory if taken without limit. We can see problems arising. What if a Christian athlete is praying for clear weather and a Christian farmer is praying for rain? Which one wins?

No, this promise cannot be limitless. There is a condition here. Our Lord means exactly what he says, but we must understand what he says. This is a magnificent promise of vast scope, but Jesus says it will be fulfilled only "if you ask in my name." This is the condition.

That certainly means a great deal more than a magical formula tacked on to the end of our prayers. There is nothing quite as pagan, or as silly, as adding the meaningless phrase "This we ask in Jesus's name" to our prayers without understanding the meaning of this request. We do this because it is traditionally acceptable, but we do not understand what "in his name" means. "In Christ's name" means in his authority and on the basis of his character.

All of us are familiar with the phrase "in the name of the law." Policemen do their business "in the name of the law." Suppose a policeman is called to a city slum because some murderous activity is taking place. He finds the address that has been given him, knocks at the door, and says, "Open in the name of the law." No one opens the door, so he knocks again and requests that it be opened in the name of the law. When there still is no answer, he breaks down the door and enters. But what if that policeman is drunk? He is out in a residential area, and in his drunken stupor, he stumbles up the steps of a house, knocks on the door, and says, "Open in the name of the law." Those within hear the thick voice, recognize that he is a drunk, and refuse to open. So the policeman breaks down the door, and when he does, he is arrested and taken to jail himself.

Why? The same man has carried out the same action. What is the difference? One was truly done in the name of the law, and the other was done outside the law, even though the same words were used. One was authorized activity, the other was unauthorized. That is what Jesus means. When we ask in Jesus's name we are to ask within the realm of his work and his character. If he is interested in having something done on earth, then we, as the instruments of his activity, are involved in accomplishing it. "Whatever you need," he says, "ask for it and it shall be done." Whatever! Anything! If it is a need within this limit, we can ask for it and it shall be done without fail.

Lord, search my heart and save me from talking truth but not living it, from echoing orthodoxy but refusing to submit in practical ways. Keep me from this so that I may see the fullness of the glory of these promises fulfilled in my life.

Have we been naively tacking the name of Jesus on to our prayers? Is this equivalent to using his name in vain—a manipulative gimmick? How can we truly honor the name of our Lord Jesus in our prayers?

THE HOUR HAS COME

A daily devotion for June 13

Read John 17:1–3.

"After Jesus said this, he looked toward heaven and prayed: 'Father, the hour has come'" (John 17:1).

"The hour has come." With these words Jesus was looking forward with obvious anticipation to a time of boundless opportunity lying before him. Surely these words mean a good deal more than the phrase we employ when we face the end of life, "My time has come." Dr. J. Vernon McGee once told of a man who had been studying the doctrine of predestination and had become so entranced by the idea of God's sovereign protection of the believer under every circumstance that he told McGee, "You know, I am so convinced that God is keeping me no matter what I do that I think I could step right out into the midst of the busiest traffic at noontime, and if my time had not come, I would be perfectly safe." Characteristically, McGee replied, "Well, if you go down and stand in the middle of traffic at noontime, brother, your time has come!"

To use a phrase like "My time has come" shows resignation, but this is not what Jesus meant. He was speaking of realization of the time he had been looking forward to all his life. Throughout his ministry, Jesus referred to this hour. In the beginning of John we have the story of the first miracle when Jesus turned the water into wine in Cana. His mother came to him and said, "Son, they have no wine," and he answered, "Woman, what have I to do with thee? Mine hour is not yet come" (John 2:3–4 KJV). He meant that, although he would do what his mother had suggested, this would not have the results that she anticipated, for the hour had not yet come, the time had not struck. Repeatedly he told the disciples, "My hour is not yet" (John 7:30, 8:20). He was awaiting a time when opportunity would abound, and here, as he came to the cross, he lifted his eyes to the heavens and said, "Father, the hour has come." By that he meant the time had come when all that he had lived for would begin to be fulfilled.

This was an anticipation based upon a principle that he had earlier stated: "Unless a kernel of wheat falls to the ground and dies, it remains only a single seed. But if it dies, it produces many seeds" (John 12:24). This is why his hour had not come previously, for Jesus knew that God's work is never accomplished apart from the principle of death, that all his mighty miracles and all his mighty words, all the marvelous power of his ministry among men, would be totally ineffective until he had passed through the experience of giving up all that he was. Unless this corn of wheat dies, it remains alone; it never will do anything else; it cannot! Only when it dies does it bring forth fruit.

That is why we also must pray this prayer, for we are always coming to hours like this in our own lives. We come to places where we must say, with Jesus, "Father, the hour has come—the hour when I must make a choice either to hold my life for myself and to act in self-centeredness as I have been doing all along or to fling it away and, passing into apparent death, to lay hold of the hope, the glory, and the realization that lie beyond it."

These hours are always coming to us. For us they are disappointments, setbacks, tragedies. Here is where God works his best in us, but we think of him as invading our privacy, our right to live our own lives. Yet if we see them as Jesus saw them, we will recognize that each moment like this is an hour of great possibility. If we act on the principle of giving ourselves away, we will discover an open door to a vast and an almost unimaginable realm of service and blessing and glory. That is what Jesus meant when he said, "The hour is come." It was a time of abounding opportunity.

Father, strike away the shackles of my unbelief and teach me to make the choice to die to myself in hope and faith to bring blessing and glory.

If we ask, "What would Jesus do?," we must be prepared to be the grain of wheat that dies in order to bear fruit for his glory and for our joy. Do we consider all of our circumstances opportunities to die with Christ in order to live in the power of his indwelling life?

THE COST OF DISOBEDIENCE

A daily devotion for June 14

Read John 17:4–8.

> "I have brought you glory on earth by finishing the work you gave me to do. And now, Father, glorify me in your presence with the glory I had with you before the world began" (John 17:4–5).

Jesus prayed this prayer before going to the cross, but in its scope it reaches beyond and includes the cross. Our Lord knew where he was headed, what he would be doing in the next few hours, and what he would accomplish. That work included more than the cross. It encompassed his ministry of healing and of mercy and even those thirty silent years back in Nazareth. They were all part of his life and of the work the Father had given him to do.

Our Lord included this in his prayer to indicate to us the character of his work while he was here. He was suggesting that his work was marked by a continual self-emptying, a laying aside of glory. Having reached the end, he was ready to resume the glory that was properly his, but he was thinking back over the thirty-three years of his life and recognizing that all during that time he had voluntarily surrendered his right to be worshiped, his right to the glory that belonged to both the Father and the Son. Jesus was pointing out that his work glorifying the Father was essentially a self-emptying.

We are so confused about this. We think that God is interested in our activity, that we can perform certain religious acts that will please God no matter our frame of mind in doing them. That is why we sometimes drag ourselves out to church week after week when we have little interest in attending—because we think that doing this is what God wants. How little we understand God! He doesn't desire activity. It was not merely what Jesus did that glorified the Father. It was not his ministry of mercy and of good works. Others have done similar things. But it was the fact that throughout his life Jesus had a heart ready to obey, an ear ready to hear, a will ready to be subject to the Father. He glorified God with his continual willingness to be available and to give of himself.

Many books have been written about the so-called cost of discipleship. They declare, in one way or another, that to have power with God we must pay a high price. They say that to become a victorious Christian, an effective Christian, requires a difficult and demanding discipline. I am not impressed with this type of literature. It puts the cart before the horse. I do not mean that such an approach is wrong, for the fact is that obedience to God does require saying no to a lot of things. I do not mean that living for the glory of God does not cost us pleasures and relationships that we might want to keep. But greater than the cost of discipleship is the cost of disobedience! There is where the emphasis should be placed.

How well we know that cost. What a tremendous toll our disobedience, our unwillingness to give of ourselves, takes in our lives in terms of frustrated, restless spirits; the shameful, degrading acts that we hope nobody discovers; the skeletons that rattle around in our closets; the irritated, vexatious dispositions that keep us in a nervous frenzy all the time; the weak, spineless, crowd-following ways that we often exhibit; the self-righteous, smug religiosity that we call Christianity, which is a stench in the nostrils of the world and an offense unto God and men. Is this not the terrible price that we pay for an unwillingness to yield ourselves to the lordship of Christ? We say we want to do God's will—as long as it is what we want to do. At the center of our lives self is still king, and that is the problem. Our own glory is in view. We still want what we want, and we are not willing as Jesus was to walk in glad obedience. But only this obedience glorifies the Father.

> *Father, may I be among those who are ready to fling their lives away for Jesus Christ, to be utterly careless of what happens to them in order that he may be glorified.*

Do we consciously or otherwise count on our good works to compensate for our self-serving attitudes? Is the glory of God motivating a glad obedience as he leads us in paths of righteousness for his name's sake?

CHRIST PRAYS FOR YOU

A daily devotion for June 15

Read John 17:9–19.

> "Holy Father, keep them in thy name, which thou hast given me, that they may be one, even as we are one" (John 17:11 RSV).

This is the great prayer Jesus prayed before he went to the garden of Gethsemane. Jesus was leaving the disciples by means of the garden, the betrayal, the judgment seat of Pilate, and the cross, and to them it appeared that he was abandoning them. They felt frightened, helpless, alone, and unable to understand what was taking place. They could not see that our Lord was merely introducing a higher and a better relationship to them.

Do we not feel this way? God leads us to a place of change and we are frightened by it. We wonder if we are not losing everything we held dear in the past. We scarcely realize that God is leading us to a higher, a newer, and a greater relationship. Like these disciples, we are fearful.

My concern is how to convey something of the gripping reality of these requests of Jesus, something of the intense practicality of what he is saying. I am so afraid that we will fail to realize that Jesus is actually praying for us—for what he prays for his disciples he prays for us. Notice the plea that Jesus makes for his disciples. "Holy Father," he says, "keep them" (John 17:11 RSV). Later he says, "I do not pray that thou shouldst take them out of the world, but that thou shouldst keep them from the evil one" (John 17:15 RSV). This is the theme of his prayer: that they might be protected and kept.

Why? There are so many other things that I would pray for if I were in his place. They are the usual things we request for one another. Why doesn't Jesus pray to his Father to use the disciples, to strengthen them, to teach them, or to guide them? This is what we would pray for each other. But when he comes to this place where he is leaving them and he wants to put into one brief phrase all that is in his heart for them, Jesus sums it up in those two words: keep them.

All of this simply points to the fact, highlighted for us in this prayer of Jesus, that relationship is the supreme thing. Whom we are with is far more important than what we do. Our Lord, aware of that, gathers all of these requests in these words: "Keep them, Father, keep them." Whom you fellowship with determines what you are, so his prayer is that our relationship with the Father will remain intact, for all else he desires will come from that. So he prays, "Keep them."

> *Lord, thank you for praying for me, and thank you for the knowledge that your prayer is being answered and that you will keep me to the very end.*

At the center of life's unnerving, destabilizing circumstances is Jesus's prayer for us to be kept. Do we cling to the flotsam of our own devices, or are we learning to take refuge in the certainty of his purpose and in the supreme power of his prayer for us?

THE PRAYER FOR UNITY

A daily devotion for June 16

Read John 17:20–26.

> "I in them and you in me—so that they may be brought to complete unity. Then the world will know that you sent me and have loved them even as you have loved me" (John 17:23).

Note the strategy by which God intends to accomplish his objective of reaching the world: "that they may be brought to complete unity." There are those who tell us that this prayer of Jesus concerning the church must now be answered after remaining unfulfilled for twenty-one centuries, that we must forget all the differences that have separated us into various denominations and sectarian groups through the centuries and join in one great organization or union. But let us first ask, "Is this prayer really unanswered today?" Can twenty-one centuries roll by before God the Father begins to fulfill this last request of Jesus?

No, this prayer has been answered ever since the day of Pentecost. This strategy is not of human making. The business of making all Christians one does not depend upon us but upon the Spirit of God. Paul's great chapter on the Holy Spirit in 1 Corinthians clearly establishes that in his coming the Spirit accomplished what Jesus prayed for. This is the divine strategy by which the world may be led to believe in him. All Christians are one, not in union but in unity.

Union is an outward agreement, an alliance formed by the submerging of differences for the sake of merger. But is this artificial union, this joining together in an organization, the answer to Jesus's prayer? The test consists of two questions: Does it accomplish what Jesus says will be accomplished when the church is one? Does it cause unbelievers to believe that Jesus is the authentic voice of God? There is little evidence that this is the case. My observation is that when churches or denominations join together (though there may be good in much of this), they create a vast, monolithic power structure that causes men and women of the world to fear the church as a threat to their power structures, as a rival force in world politics and world affairs.

Unity, as indicated here, is the sharing of a life. Look at verse 23 again: "I in them and you in me—so that they may be brought to complete unity." That is quite different, is it not? The divine strategy by which the Lord intends to bring the world to an awareness of Jesus Christ is to create in its midst a family and a shared life so that men and women all over the earth, becoming by new birth members of that life, enter a family circle so unmistakable and so filled with joy and warmth that unbelievers observing it will envy it and, like homeless orphans with their noses pressed up against the window, will long to join this fellowship. The remarkable thing is that when the church is like this there is no more potent evangelistic thrust.

> *Father, you are the God of love. When I look at the cross of our Lord Jesus Christ I see that love poured out for me. Lord, this is the nature of the love shed abroad in my heart by the Holy Spirit. Teach your people to love one another.*

We are members of God's redeemed family, partakers of his life and of his love. Does our family witness honor this distinctive heritage? Do they know we are Christ's ones by our united witness to his redeeming love and his amazing grace?

THE BEGINNING OF PRAYER

A daily devotion for June 17

Read Genesis 3:8–13.

> "Then the man and his wife heard the sound of the Lord God as he was walking in the garden in the cool of the day, and they hid from the Lord God among the trees of the garden. But the Lord God called to the man, 'Where are you?'" (Gen. 3:8–9).

This is the beginning of prayer. This passage suggests that this was a habitual thing in the lives of Adam and Eve. It is rather remarkable, but the first prayer is recorded only after the fall. Yet this account suggests plainly that prayer had been a continual delight and a blessing for Adam and Eve and was a part of their daily experience. God's action seems to be habitual. He enters the garden in the cool of the day to converse with the two who had come from his creative hand, and they talk.

The most surprising thing about this incident is that God takes the initiative to begin this prayer. It is the Lord who comes into the garden. It is the Lord who calls out for man. Prayer, therefore, begins with God. In many ways, that is the greatest truth about prayer that we can learn from this incident. Through the rest of Scripture that truth underlies every prayer that is uttered, so we must always read biblical accounts from that point of view.

A lot of false teaching pictures prayer as something man does to God. In the messages on prayer that I have heard, it sometimes seems that by praying at the right time man rescues God from his proclivity to judge. But people are never more compassionate than God. Compassion is born of God and shows up in human beings only when it is implanted by the Spirit of God. We cannot feel compassion, mercy, and pity without the moving of the Spirit. It is always a mistake to think that in the act of prayer we are called on to do something to God or that we are summoned to persevere in prayer to such a degree that we "pray through" and persuade a reluctant God to do or not to do something. That is not prayer. As in this first instance in the garden of Eden, prayer begins with God. It is God who calls. It is God who helps. When we feel a need or a desire to pray or to set up a disciplined habit of prayer, it is the prompting of God. He has planted that desire in us, and we are responding. We must remember that, because it is the first great truth about prayer in the Scripture.

> *Father, there are times when I hide myself as Adam and Eve did. Thank you for the voice that refuses to let me go but gently calls on me to deal with my infirmities and enables me to find the place of cleansing, forgiveness, and restoration.*

Our desire and our need to pray result from God's initiative. Does knowing this generate confidence in his willing response to our prayers? Do we dishonor his loving initiative by presuming to manipulate his response? Are we learning transparency and trust in our communication with our Father?

PRAYER'S ANCHOR

A daily devotion for June 18

Read Genesis 18:22–33.

"Then Abraham approached him and said: 'Will you sweep away the righteous with the wicked?'" (Gen. 18:23).

Abraham has been informed that the hour of judgment has arrived for Sodom. He is appalled by this, but it is important for us to see what is really troubling him. Abraham isn't trying to save these cities. That is not his true concern. He knows that God's hour of judgment has struck and that the Lord has shown great patience up to this point. He knows that it is only unrighteousness that will ultimately be judged, so he is not trying to save the cities. He expresses his concern in these words: "Will you sweep away the righteous with the wicked?" Will God treat righteous people the same way he treats wicked people? That is what is troubling him.

A cold fist of fear grips Abraham's heart. He is afraid he will find that God is not quite who he thought he was. Perhaps he understands that righteous people have a way of salting the world, preserving it from corruption and from judgment. Perhaps he is worried that if God destroys a city full of wicked people, with some righteous among them, the word will go out that righteousness is of no effect and that a wrong impression will be left. Abraham has a troubled heart and questions whether God is the kind of God he has thought him to be.

Have you ever felt that way? In your prayers or in your confrontation with life, have you suddenly seen God moving in ways you did not anticipate, allowing things to happen that you did not think he ought to allow? Have you thought, *Lord, can you really do this? 'Shall not the judge of all the earth do right?' This is not right.* We are getting very close to how Abraham felt when we experience that sudden horror that God is not going to act as we expected. The question Abraham raises here is, "Does righteousness make any difference? If God wipes out these cities filled with both wicked and righteous people, if they are all treated alike, doesn't that tell us that righteousness doesn't matter?"

In the rest of his prayer, we see how timidly Abraham responds. "Lord, just a moment. Supposing there are fifty righteous in that city. Will you then destroy it?" Immediately the response comes, "No, I'll not destroy it for fifty." Again, Abraham timidly asks, "How about forty-five?" "No," says God immediately. "If I find forty-five I won't destroy it." Then Abraham musters his courage and says, "Lord, now don't get upset, but I'm going to press this a little further. How about forty or thirty or twenty?" Finally, he goes as far as he dares, feeling his concern ebb as he says, "Lord, how about ten? If there are ten righteous, will you save them and the city?" God's immediate response once again is, "As far as you go, Abraham, I will go. If there are ten righteous, I will not destroy the city."

Each prompt answer by God eases the fear gripping Abraham's heart. Each answer is a reassurance that God will honor his promise, that he will preserve the righteous in the hour of danger. Abraham is reassured that God means what he says, that righteousness does make a difference, that God's promises are valid in this time of danger, and that he does not treat the righteous as he does the wicked. When he reaches that place, Abraham is satisfied.

Lord, thank you for giving me great promises of love, acceptance, guidance, and protection. I pray that as the world watches the righteousness in its midst, it will see that your hand and your heart are committed to those who respond to your offer of grace and that your judgment awaits those who resist the patient pleading of their God.

It is obviously true that our minds cannot contain all that God is. Does that limitation diminish our trust in his response to our prayers? Do we fully accept what has been revealed in his Word and trust him to act accordingly?

HELPLESSNESS IN PRAYER

A daily devotion for June 19

Read Genesis 32:9–32.

"So Jacob was left alone, and a man wrestled with him till daybreak" (Gen. 32:24).

This is one of those intriguing incidents found frequently in the Old Testament in which some element of mystery is introduced without much explanation. Everyone who reads this asks, "Who is this masked man? Where did he come from? What is he doing?" I am sure Jacob must have felt that way too. Having sent everyone and everything across the river, he thinks he is all alone when suddenly out of the shadows steps a man who to Jacob's amazement begins to wrestle with him. As we read further, there is no doubt as to who the man is. In fact, at the end of the story, Jacob names the place of this encounter Peniel, which means "the face of God," because he says, "I have met God face to face and still survived." Here is a man who, in some strange way, in one of those Old Testament theophanies, is God himself appearing in visible form, and he wrestles with Jacob.

What does all this mean? In light of the whole story there is no question that what we have here is God's attempt to improve Jacob's prayer life with a crash course on praying. God is trying to break down Jacob's stubborn dependence upon himself. Jacob's problem was that he never trusted God to do things. He always had that feeling that if he did not do them himself, God would probably not come through. Now God is dealing with him in a defining moment. Jacob has to face up to the fact that although his prayers are eloquent, beautifully phrased, and theologically accurate, they are useless because he does not believe that God will do anything. All his trust is in himself. I meet a lot of people like that. They pray and speak in wonderful, theologically correct language but do not believe God will act. This is what Jacob is doing here. He stubbornly refuses to give up and to let God handle the situation.

I recognize myself frequently doing that. The account continues in verse 25: "When the man saw that he could not overpower him, he touched the socket of Jacob's hip so that his hip was wrenched as he wrestled with the man." That happens after hours of wrestling. Jacob has resisted, struggled, and fought back. He will not give in until at last the divine hand touches him on the thigh and puts the hip socket out of joint. That is the end of it; nobody can wrestle in that condition. All Jacob can do now is to cling in helpless dependence upon this strange wrestler. Knowing by now something of who this man is, he hangs on desperately.

Many messages about this account comment on the fact that Jacob was mighty in prayer because he wrestled with God all night long and prevailed. But it is not true that Jacob wrestled with God. It was God who wrestled with Jacob, trying to break down his stubborn self-reliance, his feeling that everything depended on him, that he had to do it or it would not get done, that God would do nothing in the situation. Furthermore, Jacob did not prevail over God by wrestling. He prevailed when his hip was broken, when he was absolutely helpless and could do nothing but hang on. That was when he prevailed with God. That is what this account is teaching us. God responds to that sense of human helplessness.

Lord, perhaps by your grace you may leave me lame that I may have a constant reminder that you are the God who acts beyond anything I can do. When I ask you to act, I should expect you to act, Lord, and not be like Jacob, working things out on my own.

Who among us does not at some time presume to control God? How does this compare with total trust in the integrity and the power of God? Are we willing to pray with Jesus, "Nevertheless, not my will but Thine be done"?

A POOR BUT GOOD PRAYER

A daily devotion for June 20

Read Numbers 11:4–34.

> "He [Moses] asked the Lord, 'Why have you brought this trouble on your servant? What have I done to displease you that you put the burden of all these people on me? Did I conceive all these people? Did I give them birth? Why do you tell me to carry them in my arms, as a nurse carries an infant, to the land you promised on oath to their ancestors? Where can I get meat for all these people? They keep wailing to me, "Give us meat to eat!" I cannot carry all these people by myself; the burden is too heavy for me'" (Num. 11:11–14).

This prayer is obviously filled with self-pity, reproach, and petulance. It is the expression of a man who feels he has been put upon. Moses comes close to rebuking and upbraiding God for giving him the job of taking care of these ungrateful people. This is one of the poorest prayers in the Bible, but it is a prayer quite like ours.

Moses had an extremely rich prayer life. His prayers have an artless eloquence, summoning up majestic thoughts about the greatness of God and reflecting man's faith and God's power to act. This, however, is surely not one of them. It is a weak prayer uttered at a time when Moses feels that God has taken advantage of him. He wants to quit, so he lays everything before God, saying, "Why ever did you give me a job like this? Where am I to get meat to give to all these people? Why should I bear them on my heart? I didn't bring them into being."

We do not often get this picture of Moses. He was a towering figure in the Old Testament, a mighty prophet and leader who affected the laws of nations for thousands of years. Therefore we tend to think of him as high above all of us in his relationship with God. We are familiar with the stories of Moses exercising the great power of God—stretching out his rod to roll back the waters of the Red Sea so that the people of Israel walked through on dry land, striking the rock so water flowed out in a parched desert to slake the thirst of the people. It is clear from many of these stories in the Bible that he was a mighty man of God.

But in this prayer we get the other side of Moses. In this and similar accounts we glimpse Moses as he lived his daily life, and the amazing thing is that when we get close to him, we see that he is a surprisingly unimpressive figure in himself. Here we see him angry and upset and feeling sorry for himself. There is nothing heroic about him at all. Moses is, by natural temperament, an irresolute, shrinking personality, distrustful of himself, easily discouraged, ready to resign and even to die when the pressure is heavy. This is the human instrument used so mightily by God.

The remarkable thing is that even this self-pitying, reproachful request of Moses was answered. It was the poorest prayer he ever prayed, far from a model of prayer, but whatever else it was, this was an attempt to draw upon divine resources. Moses recognized his insufficiency and showed an awareness of the incredible resources of God; therefore God honored his prayer and answered it. That is what prayer is, a reliance on God, which brings forth great possibilities.

> *Lord, I confess I often feel like Moses. I feel that my problems are too big for me, that my circumstances are too complex for me to work out, and I resent being asked to do so. Forgive me, Lord. Teach me that you are a God of infinite resources, of incredible wisdom, of infinite patience, and that you will work out these matters if I but trust.*

Are we quick to blame God for life's problems but slow to accept his ways and means to solving them? Could this indicate misplaced confidence in ourselves rather than confident expectation in God and his will?

PRAYER'S PRACTICALITY

A daily devotion for June 21

Read 1 Chronicles 4:9–10.

"Jabez cried out to the God of Israel, 'Oh, that you would bless me and enlarge my territory! Let your hand be with me, and keep me from harm so that I will be free from pain.' And God granted his request" (1 Chron. 4:10).

At first glance this looks like a self-centered prayer. Jabez sounds like the man who prayed, "Bless me and my wife, my son John and his wife, us four and no more." But Jabez is not being selfish. He is praying for something God wanted him to have. That is the difference between being personal and being selfish. Selfish prayers ask God for something he does not want us to have, at least not right away, making demands that show we are interested only in our own immediate welfare, our own satisfaction. But God promises great and mighty things specifically to us, so to pray for these things is not selfish but personal.

Look more closely at these four requests. First Jabez asks, "Oh, that you would bless me." What do we mean when we pray to be blessed? This is a request for a sense of relationship with God. "Blessing" is drawing near to God, finding him, knowing him personally. He is praying, "Lord, first, above all else, let me have a consciousness that you are my God, that I belong to you and that you belong to me."

Second, Jabez prays, "Enlarge my territory." This is a prayer for opportunity, for the restoration of his lost inheritance, for a place where he might gain a sense of status and respect. For us this means finding a way to break out of whatever may be limiting us, hemming us in, or enslaving us. We may feel trapped in a situation where we have no opportunity to grow, to advance, to be fulfilled and satisfied. If that is the case, this is the proper prayer to pray: "Lord, give me that opportunity."

Third, he asks, "Let your hand be with me." This prayer comes naturally to his lips as he considers his uncertain future. All of us feel this way at times. We do not know what sudden, unexpected changes may occur in our lives, and we often ask for a glimpse ahead. What we really need is not knowledge but a guide. This is what Jabez is praying for: "Lord, be with me. Accompany me into the future. Guide me and let me know that you are with me each step of the way."

His last request is, "Keep me from harm so that I will be free from pain." This young man shows a deep awareness of a tainted heredity. Jabez senses a weakness in himself that frightens him. I see this in many people. It may be a tendency toward a hot temper, which destroys many opportunities that could be used for advantage. Maybe it is avarice, a desire to acquire material goods so that you will be safe and secure, have abundance, and do what you want. Whatever it is, Jabez knows that God can handle it.

I do not think he prayed this prayer just once. This kind of prayer comes repeatedly to our lips if we are concerned about where we are and if we recognize how difficult, if not impossible, the situation looks from a human standpoint. This is the time to lay hold of the formula that Jabez found and that God used to bring him out of his circumstances.

Thank you, Lord, for a look at this young man's life. I rejoice now in the promises that surround me, the love that upholds me, and the grace that leads me along.

What are the four aspects of Jabez's prayer that we can use as guidelines in our petitions? Do we ask with bold expectation that God open and close doors so that we may glorify him by fulfilling his purpose for our lives?

PRAYER AND PEACE

A daily devotion for June 22

Read 1 Samuel 1:1–2:11.

> "In her deep anguish Hannah prayed to the Lord, weeping bitterly. And she made a vow, saying, 'Lord Almighty, if you will only look on your servant's misery and remember me, and not forget your servant but give her a son, then I will give him to the Lord for all the days of his life, and no razor will ever be used on his head'" (1 Sam. 1:10–11).

At first glance it would appear that Hannah is offering a kind of bargaining prayer—promising to give the boy back to the Lord but only if the Lord will give him to her first so she can enjoy him. It is possible to read this account that way, but if we look closely at it, we can see what is really happening here, for I am sure this is not the first time that Hannah has prayed in Shiloh for a son. All along she has dreamed of having a son of her own, a little boy to love and to cuddle, to teach him to walk, to read stories to him, to watch him grow to become a strong, fine young man, the pride of her life. She wants him for herself, and she has prayed often for that, but her prayer has not been answered.

On this occasion, however, her prayer is different. Having worked through years of barrenness and having thought deeply about the problem, she realizes for the first time something she has never known before. She sees that children are not just for parents—they are for the Lord. They are given to parents, loaned for a while, but the reason they are given is for the Lord to use. Samuel, the little boy who was ultimately born, became the man God chose to meet the need of a nation. Undoubtedly God has taught Hannah deeply through years of struggle over her barrenness, so in great distress and with intense earnestness she prays that God will have what he wants, a man for his glory and for his purposes, and that he will let her be the instrument of that blessing.

Immediately we read of a remarkable change in Hannah's heart, for the account says, "Eli answered, 'Go in peace, and may the God of Israel grant you what you have asked of him.' She said, 'May your servant find favor in your eyes.' Then she went her way and ate something, and her face was no longer downcast" (1 Sam. 1:17–18).

Immediately, God's peace has begun to guard Hannah's heart and spirit. The birth of the baby does not occur until months later, but when the baby is born she names him Samuel, which means, "Asked of God." God has granted her request, but there was peace in Hannah's heart from the moment of her prayer. This is a beautiful commentary on that well-known passage in which Paul says, "Do not be anxious about anything, but in every situation, by prayer and petition, with thanksgiving, present your requests to God. And the peace of God, which transcends all understanding, will guard your hearts and your minds in Christ Jesus" (Phil. 4:7). That is what Hannah experiences. This is the mystery of prayer that is available to us to speak peace into our hearts when we are troubled by the circumstances of our lives.

Thank you, Father, for the peace that you can give me as I yield to you in prayer. Thank you for knowing what I need and for recognizing when I need it.

Our Father wisely denies petitions motivated by self-interest. Rather than sulk or blame God, shall we ask him to refocus our hearts on his will and his glory? Have we been circumventing his peace by insisting he do things our way?

PRAYING IN THE TRUE TEMPLE

A daily devotion for June 23

Read 2 Chronicles 6:12–40.

> "Then Solomon stood before the altar of the Lord in front of the whole assembly of Israel and spread out his hands" (2 Chron. 6:12).

The great prayer of Solomon at the dedication of the temple in Jerusalem is recorded in 2 Chronicles 6:12–40. This is a unique prayer from the Old Testament. It is perhaps the only passage in the Old Testament that reports a formal prayer uttered on a great state occasion. The whole nation—or at least a great portion of it—had gathered in the courts of the temple to dedicate the new building that Solomon had erected according to the plans that his father David had drawn.

The nearest thing we would have to this scene in America today would be the inauguration of a president. As with our inauguration, on this occasion a special platform had been built for the king in the great courtyard of the temple in front of the brazen altar where the sacrifices for sin were offered. On that platform King Solomon began this prayer with a recognition of God's promise to David that Israel would never lack a man to sit upon its throne.

Solomon's prayer consists of eight wide-ranging requests concerning the temple and the place of prayer in the life of the people of Israel. Though these requests had specific applications to the Israelites, they have specific application in our own lives as well. For instance, the Jews were to face the temple when they prayed, no matter where they were in the land. This has an application to us. In the New Testament we are told that our bodies are temples of God. This truth is often missed today. It is hurtful when Christians refer to church buildings as houses of God. The New Testament never calls any building the house of God. Church buildings are not the houses of God—we are. Everywhere in the New Testament the answer to the temple of the old regime is the human body and our personal lives. We are the habitation of God by the Spirit. When we gather, the whole place becomes the temple of the living God dwelling among his people by the Spirit.

That is what makes our coming together a recognition of the presence of God in our midst. Jesus said that when two or three of us gather, he is in our midst (Matt. 18:20). What makes a church meaningful is the recognition that we gather as the temple of the living God. Considering this, Solomon's prayer becomes a marvelous teaching ministry on the place and the power of prayer in our lives.

> *Father, I pray that I may become a person of prayer, learning to communicate with the God of glory and finding in prayer with other believers the answer to the troubles that afflict us day by day.*

When we are in Christ, he is in us—we are his temples! Are we awakening to the awesome intimacy with Christ available in this relationship? Have we begun to grasp that prayer is ongoing communication with the One in whom we live and breathe and have our being?

PRAYER'S HUMILITY

A daily devotion for June 24

Read Daniel 9:1–23.

> "We have sinned and done wrong. We have been wicked and have rebelled; we have turned away from your commands and laws. We have not listened to your servants the prophets, who spoke in your name to our kings, our princes and our ancestors, and to all the people of the land" (Dan. 9:5–6).

Daniel's prayer begins with the confession of sin. But the remarkable thing is that this man, according to the record, has no sin charged against him. Never once in Scripture are we told that Daniel did anything wrong. Now I am sure he did wrong things. Certainly, sin must have appeared in his life, because Scripture tells us that no man is without sin, but the record does not give us any account of it. But Daniel confesses his own sin and the sin of his people, saying, "We have sinned; we have been wicked; we have turned away; we have not listened."

This points to something that is often missing from our own prayers. How many times do we include in them a heartfelt, honest confession of sin? There is nothing harder for us to do than to admit we were wrong, yet to do so is an honest and realistic thing. God does not ask us to confess our sins because he is trying to humiliate or to punish us. Rather, he asks us to do so because we kid ourselves, we are dishonest about ourselves, we are unrealistic about our lives, and he is the ultimate realist. God always deals with things exactly the way they are, and he says there is no way we can be helped unless we begin to do the same thing. He asks us, therefore, to start by acknowledging the areas where we have done wrong.

That is why we have the Scriptures. God's Word is like a mirror. Many of us, however, tend to ignore the Scriptures because we know this is true. If we look into the Word of God, into the mirror of the Word, we soon see exactly what we look like, and it is not always pleasant. Other people too are given to us for that reason. Since we cannot see ourselves the way we are, God graciously puts others in our lives to help us get an accurate picture. That is why it is so foolish to resist what others are telling us. If one person says something unpleasant to us, we may be able to dismiss that as coming from a twisted point of view, and we may be right. But when a half-dozen people tell us the same thing, we had better start listening, because they are revealing a truth that we cannot see. Until we see ourselves realistically, we are living in a fantasy world, messing up everything we touch, because we do not see what is really there.

The most helpful thing we can do in our prayer life, therefore, is to take a moment at the beginning of our prayer to face what the Word of God tells us is wrong in our lives—our lovelessness, our sharpness, our caustic attitudes, our tendency to defend ourselves and to put down others. This is where Daniel begins. All this is summed up in one great word found many times in Scripture, the word *repent.* When we repent we begin to set things right in our lives; we begin to deal honestly with ourselves and with others.

> *Father, I confess my sin to you. Thank you for the Word of God and for the people you have placed in my life to hold me accountable. Help me to listen and to come to you in genuine repentance and faith.*

What essential dimension in our prayers may we be avoiding? How do we respond when we are accurately confronted by others and by the Word with unconfessed sin? How does prideful avoidance affect our prayers and our communication with others?

PRAYER'S RELATIONSHIPS

A daily devotion for June 25

Read Job 42:5–10.

> "After Job had prayed for his friends, the Lord restored his fortunes and gave him twice as much as he had before" (Job 42:10).

In the book of Job, we are given clear evidence of when Job's physical problems began. They started when, after having destroyed Job's home and his wealth and killed all his children, Satan obtained permission from God to afflict him with a terrible siege of boils from head to foot. An awful series of painful, suppurating boils had turned Job into a dreadful, revolting sight. This was shattering to his self-esteem, and he groveled in the ash heap. The whole book is an account of how Job cried out in agony and despair week after week because of this. His friends pummeled him with accusations, blaming him for everything, so that he was mentally and physically tormented.

So when did Job's pain stop? This verse is the only one that offers the answer. God reversed Job's fortunes when he prayed for his friends. Even during Job's great encounter with God, recorded from chapters 40 and on, there is no mention that his agony had ceased. He was asked many searching questions by God, but he was still feeling the awful pain in his body. When he prayed for his friends, however, all that ended.

This indicates that in order for a cure to happen, Job had to deal with his natural resentment against these men. If we put ourselves in Job's place, we can understand how he must have felt. At best, he would have seen these men as a trio of self-righteous windbags who were blowing hot air. At worst, Job would have seen them as malicious slanderers who were out to destroy his reputation, because they accused him of things he never did and of attitudes he did not possess. Those were the reasons for all his trouble, they said. They assaulted him, they insulted him, and they outraged him. Job had every right by natural standards to be angry, upset, and bitter against these three so-called friends. But we cannot pray for people when we think of them in that way. To obey God, Job had to forgive these men. He had to set aside all the bitterness, the resentment, and the anger he might have felt and to deal with them as sinners just like himself. That is the beauty of this passage, because the moment Job did that his healing began.

Anger and bitterness always affect us. Holding a grudge against somebody destroys us. Jesus said this in several parables and stories in the New Testament. He clearly implied that if we do not forgive others, we subject ourselves to a terrible inner torment that will not stop until we are willing to forgive. Paul says that we are to be "Be kind and compassionate to one another, forgiving each other, just as in Christ God forgave you" (Eph. 4:32). In the Lord's Prayer, Jesus taught us that we are to forgive. Everywhere in the Scriptures there is a recognition that no healing can occur in our lives until we forgive those who have offended and hurt us.

> *Lord, thank you for being the God of truth. Nothing is hidden from you. Help me to remember that I am just as guilty as those I am angry with, that I have offended others and have offended you in many ways and that you have forgiven me. Because I am forgiven, grant to me the ability to extend a free and full forgiveness to others.*

We have been immeasurably blessed with God's gift of forgiveness, which is meant to be the gift that keeps on giving. Are we limiting the scope of God's tender mercies by failing to extend this gift to others?

PRAYER'S RESOURCES

A daily devotion for June 26

Read 2 Chronicles 14:2–16:12.

> "Then Asa called to the Lord his God and said, 'Lord, there is no one like you to help the powerless against the mighty. Help us, Lord our God, for we rely on you, and in your name we have come against this vast army. Lord, you are our God; do not let mere mortals prevail against you'" (2 Chron. 14:11).

Have you ever felt like King Asa did? Have you ever thought you were secure, with plenty of money in the bank, with good health and a future that looked rosy, and then suddenly, wham!—disaster loomed? You realized you were outnumbered, outgunned, and outclassed, up against a circumstance too big for you to handle.

Notice that the first thing Asa does is to recognize the unique ability of God to help—unique because nobody helps like God does. There is none like God to help because he knows so much more about us than anyone else does and because there are a thousand and one things he can do to set us free. King Asa also recognizes that part of the uniqueness of God is that it makes no difference to him whether we are mighty or weak. The phrase "to help the powerless against the mighty" reveals that human contribution to the victory is insignificant in God's eyes. He can use armies if he so desires, or he can use a single individual.

The second thing King Asa does is to request specific aid for the present emergency. He prays, "Help us, Lord our God, for we rely on you, and in your name we have come against this vast army." When we are confronted with a situation like that, we do not have time to pray "around the world." I once heard of a man who was invited to pray for someone who was dying in a hospital. As he stood beside the bed, the man began his prayer, "Bless the missionaries in China and India and Africa." He continued in that vein until someone stopped him and said, "I'm sorry. While you were in India the patient died." It is important to come to the point in our prayers, to deal with the specific situation as King Asa does here.

We must not tell God what to do. That is the mistake so many of us make. We have our prayers outlined, even written down. We say, "Lord, first do this. Then when that happens, do this." God's best and most frequent answer to such a prayer is to check the square that says, "None of the above." He has his own way of working. He will not give way to us. That is what makes us get so angry at God.

Third, King Asa reminds God of a divinely established relationship: "Lord, you are our God." He is saying, "We did not make you our God. You chose us. You created this relationship we have. We are your people. Therefore, if this battle is lost, you lose." That is the ground we stand on in our prayers before God. This is what King Asa is crying. Any defeat would be God's defeat. Asa stands upon that relationship. That relationship gives us boldness too. We are invited to come before God and to ask for help because we are children. We are invited to come boldly because God promises that we will obtain mercy and find grace. It is already ours to help in time of need, so we are exhorted to approach him boldly.

> *Father, thank you for allowing me to come to you in good times and in times of crisis. There is nothing too big for you, nothing that takes you by surprise. Thank you for being my God and for being a very present help in times of trouble.*

Asa's prayer illustrates three important principles for us to observe in our prayers. Do our prayers reflect our cognizance of God's character and of the ways in which he works? Do we pray expectantly, specifically, and in complete dependence upon God's power, purpose, and presence?

PRAYER'S DELAYS

A daily devotion for June 27

Read Habakkuk 1:1–3:19.

> "I will stand at my watch and station myself on the ramparts; I will look to see what he will say to me, and what answer I am to give to this complaint" (Hab. 2:1).

When we face a problem and do not understand what God is doing, we must not do what so many do and say, "Oh, I've tried faith and it doesn't work" or "I've tried God but that doesn't work" or "I've tried prayer and it doesn't work." People who make such claims don't understand their own words, because what they are saying is, "God is a liar. There is no real God." What they are saying is, "The Word of God is not true. The Bible is a fraud." They are declaring that God is faithless to his promises. But God cannot be faithless to his word. The problem is not God. The problem is us. We are so ignorant; we see so little; we understand such a minute fraction of the scope of any problem. We ought to do as Habakkuk did—get out on the watchtower and wait to see what God says. If we ask him, God will help us to understand something of what we are going through. That is what Habakkuk did, because he expected an answer. Habakkuk said he was going to wait.

God usually answers in one of three ways. Most commonly, he answers us through his Word. This is what is so valuable about reading the Word of God, especially when we are confused or troubled about how the Lord is acting. Often light will come suddenly out of a verse that seemed obscure, and we will see a new aspect of what we are facing. Perhaps an answer will come when we are listening to a message, or a verse will come to mind, and it will deal with our situation. God has given us his Word so that we might understand how he acts.

Then sometimes God answers directly in our spirit. We sense a pressure within that drives us in a certain direction; a conviction comes and settles, and we cannot shake it off. We have to be careful here, because at this point the Enemy can mimic the voice of God. But the voice of the Enemy is always nagging (to make us feel guilty) while God's Spirit speaks quietly but persistently. If this leading matches what the Word of God says, then that is the Spirit of God leading us. Paul says that "those who are led by the Spirit of God are the children of God" (Rom. 8:14). We can expect to be led along that line.

At other times God speaks through our circumstances. Doors shut, and we cannot open them, no matter how hard we try. That is God at work, shutting doors and opening others, ushering us in one direction. Often this is the way God answers. But he promises us that he will answer. He will not leave us as orphans, nor abandon us to ignorance. James says, "If any of you lacks wisdom, you should ask God, who gives generously to all without finding fault, and it will be given to you" (James 1:5). That is what Habakkuk did.

Father, I am grateful that I can wait on you, knowing that you are a faithful God and that you always answer.

How do we react to delayed or unanswered prayers? Are we responding as Habakkuk did, waiting expectantly for more complete understanding? What are three possible ways for this to unfold? While waiting, are we content to trust God, realizing he has the complete picture while ours is limited?

UNCEASING PRAYER

A daily devotion for June 28

Read Colossians 1:9–14.

"For this reason, since the day we heard about you, we have not stopped praying for you" (Col. 1:9).

Paul knows that the Colossian Christians are living in a dangerous world. A seething volcano of false teaching has begun to erupt, threatening to destroy the simplicity of the faith that is producing such beauty and liberty in their lives. Paul is in Rome, a prisoner in chains, and unable to travel to Colossae, a thousand miles east, to help them. He can do nothing physically for them. But spiritually, he is a powerful prayer warrior who can create in their midst a tremendous opportunity to know the truth that will free them and will enable them to withstand the assault of false teaching. That is what he is doing: he is praying for them.

The striking thing about this prayer is its first sentence: "For this reason, since the day we heard about you, we have not stopped praying for you." This was a continuing prayer. As far as we know, Paul had never been to Colossae. Apart from one or two among them, he did not know these believers. And yet he prays continually for them. When we encounter statements like this in Scripture it is quite fair to ask, when did he do this? Day and night Paul is chained to a Roman guard and never has a moment to himself. Awake or asleep, he is bound to his jailer. Furthermore, when he is awake, his friends are dropping by to see him to seek his counsel and instruction. He even ministers to the Roman guards, many of whom will come to Christ, as we learn in the letter to the Philippians. He is busy writing letters, too, so when does he find time to pray for the Colossians?

The answer lies in a continual life of prayer. This refers to quiet, whispered prayers and praises that flow from our hearts all day long. We use interruptions—people or events that break in unexpectedly upon our day—as calls to specific prayer. Most of us use mealtime to think of God and to voice our thanks to him. But more than food can call us to prayer. We can use the newspaper or the television set in the same way. As world decision-makers are pictured before our eyes we can breathe a quiet prayer for them by name. We can read a newspaper prayerfully, whispering to God our intercessions for those in need about whom we are reading. When we run across someone, even in an impolite way, tripping us on the bus, jabbing us with an umbrella, dodging in front of us in traffic, God may be calling that individual to our attention to inspire prayer for him.

Do we ever pray for people who cut in front of us in traffic, asking God to bless them, not to blast them? That is what this passage is suggesting: that continual prayer arises constantly as a reaction to what we are experiencing. I am sure this explains the apostle's words here. Through the day he would think of the Colossians, how they were doing and what was threatening them, and he would breathe a prayer for them. This is what he means when he says, "We have not stopped praying for you." We can pray for each other in the same wonderful way.

Lord, teach me the secret of ongoing prayer. Help me to see every event and every person in my life as an invitation to pray.

Is communication with our Father becoming a spontaneous response to all of life? Are we faithful prayer responders to the plethora of need continually surrounding us?

KNOWING GOD'S WILL

A daily devotion for June 29

Read Colossians 1:9–14.

"We continually ask God to fill you with the knowledge of his will through all the wisdom and understanding that the Spirit gives" (Col. 1:9).

The one thing Paul asks for is that the Colossians might come to understand God's will. This is the important thing to him. He knows that if they begin to understand the will of God, everything good that he desires for them will follow. Thus the chief aim of a believer's life ought to be to know God's will.

Here is where many young Christians go astray. They think the will of God is an itinerary they must discover: where God wants them to go and what God wants them to do. Most of their prayers are addressed with those thoughts in mind. What should I do today? Where should I go? Whom should I marry? But knowing God's will is about much more than simply knowing what to do. It begins with knowing who we are. Have you ever asked someone who upset you, "Who do you think you are, anyway?" We instinctively know that offensive behavior is a result of who we think we are. That is why we deliver such challenges.

God, too, knows that. The glory of the good news is that he has made us into something different than what we once were. Therefore the primary course in the curriculum of the Spirit is to learn what God has made us to be. We no longer belong to ourselves, so we are no longer to live for ourselves. Our will, our pleasure, our comfort are now secondary to what God calls us to be and what he has made us to be. The more we understand who we now are and what God has done to make us that, the more our behavior will automatically change and we will do the things that please him.

Where do we find that out? Paul answers, "Through all spiritual wisdom and understanding." Two things enable us to discover the will of God. The first is spiritual wisdom. This is wisdom that comes from the Spirit, not from the mind of man. That is what Christians need to discover: what God thinks about life. That is reality. If we want to be realistic, we must read and study the Bible to discover how God looks at things. Everything else is fantasy. If we want to live realistically, we must learn spiritual wisdom, the wisdom of God.

The second thing necessary to discover the will of God is understanding. That is the application of the wisdom we are learning to the specific circumstances of life. Understanding is a clear vision of what needs to be done. We may be struggling with problems and don't know what to do. The first thing to do is to understand how God sees those problems and what he says about them in his Word. Then as we pray and seek his face, there will come a clear vision of what needs to be done, of what steps to take or not to take. This insight doesn't result from natural abilities. It is given by the Spirit and is therefore possible for all believers. So when we open the Bible, we must pray that God will help us to understand what it says.

Teach me, Father, what it means to know your will and to live my life with wisdom and understanding.

Why is it essential to understand our identity in Christ when we seek to know God's will for our lives? Where will we find this revelation of who we are, whose we are, and why we are here? Do we need to recalibrate our search for wisdom to understand God's will for our lives?

WHAT TO PRAY FOR

A daily devotion for June 30

Read Colossians 1:9–14.

> "So that you may live a life worthy of the Lord and please him in every way: bearing fruit in every good work" (Col. 1:10).

As Paul continues his prayer for the Colossians, he mentions activities that believers can choose to do. This is instructive not only for how to pray for others but also for how to live our own lives. First, Paul prays that they may "live a life worthy of the Lord." When we understand what God has made us to be, that we are his children, cherished by him, our guilt and sin taken care of, and that God is our loving Father who protects us, guides and guards us, and when we see him in all his majesty and beauty, we will become concerned about whether our behavior reflects his beauty and about what others will think of our God when they are watching us. That is "a life worthy of the Lord." In other letters the apostle urges Christians to "walk worthy of their calling." We are to be concerned about our impact upon others—how our lives are affecting theirs and what our actions make them think about our God.

The second activity that Paul prays for is that they might seek "to please him in every way." The chief aim of every believer ought to be that he is pleasing to God, that he seeks to live in a way that delights God. What quality of life is pleasing to God? The Scripture probably puts it most effectively in a negative way. In the letter to Hebrews we are told, "Without faith it is impossible to please God!" Faith is what pleases him. Every time Jesus commended people it was because of their faith. "You have great faith," he said to the woman who pleaded with him to heal her flow of blood. "Your faith is great," he told a centurion who asked him to heal his servant. Whenever our Lord praised people it was because they believed him and acted on what he said. They didn't conform to the customs of people around them. Rather, they swam against the stream of life and stood firmly upon what he said, trusting him. That is what pleases God.

Here is the third activity Paul prays for: "bearing fruit in every good work." The "fruit," always and everywhere in Scripture, is the fruit of the Spirit: love, joy, and peace in our relationships and in our actions regarding others; concern, compassion, encouragement, and help in times of stress, bringing a word of peace into a troubled, hostile atmosphere. "Blessed are the peacemakers for they shall be called the children of God." That is what Paul is talking about: "bearing fruit in every good work."

> *Father, today as I walk with you help me to live a life worthy of you, pleasing you in every way and bearing fruit in every good work.*

What are three instructive ways to pray for our lives and for the lives of others? Are we aware of the significance of these prayers in terms of their life-changing effects?

ACTS 13–28

Turning Point
An introduction for the month of July

The thirteenth chapter is a turning point in the book of Acts. It is what Winston Churchill would have called one of the hinges of history. It marks the beginning of the third phase of our Lord's Great Commission. In the opening chapter of this book, before he ascended into the heavens, Jesus said to his disciples, "You shall receive power after the Holy Spirit is come upon you, and you will be witnesses of me" (Acts 1:8 RSV). Then he outlined geographically how that witness should proceed, beginning in Jerusalem, continuing on to Judea and Samaria, and finally moving into the uttermost parts of the earth.

In chapter 13 we see the beginning of the last phase, the journey into the uttermost parts of the earth. It is also the beginning of the apostleship of Paul. Up to this time, though he was called to be an apostle when he was converted on the road to Damascus, he has never acted as an apostle. Now, eleven or twelve years after his conversion, he begins to fulfill the ministry to which he was called by Jesus Christ. Perhaps the most important thing about this section is that here is found a revelation of how the Spirit of God guides his people.

THE STRATEGY OF THE SPIRIT

A daily devotion for July 1

Read Acts 13:1–12.

> "Now in the church at Antioch there were prophets and teachers … While they were worshiping the Lord and fasting, the Holy Spirit said, 'Set apart for me Barnabas and Saul for the work to which I have called them'" (Acts 13:1–2).

The turning point in the book of Acts began with a group of Christians in the church in Antioch who were exercising the spiritual gifts given to them. Listed here are men who had the gift of prophecy and men who had the gift of teaching. While these men were using their gifts, busy doing what God had equipped them to do in the church, the Spirit of God spoke to them.

Many people are looking to God to lead them in some dramatic way. They think they must go away and hole up in a cave somewhere to commune with nature in order for God to speak. Once they get away on a mountain, he will speak in some dramatic fashion and send them back with a great sense of call. Perhaps some have been waiting thirty or forty years for that to happen, and it has not happened yet. It's probably not going to happen at all, because God does not call us that way very often. Sometimes he does, but usually his call comes when we are busy exercising our gifts where we are. These men were busy employing their gifts and, in the midst of their activity, the call of the Spirit came.

I do not know how he spoke. It may have been through a prophetic utterance of one of these prophets as they were gathered worshiping and ministering. Or it may well have been that he spoke as he speaks to many today in what we have learned to call "insistent unanimity," a deep conviction shared by everyone in the group that the Spirit of God desires a certain thing. This is often the way God works. He spoke to men who were already at work doing what they knew. We can steer a ship or a car if it is moving but not when it is sitting still. God loves to see people at work in what they know to do. Then he will give them further direction.

We also see two elements of the Spirit's sovereign choice: he chose the men, and he chose the work. He said, "Set apart for me Barnabas and Saul for the work to which I have called them." He did not tell the church what that work was although he had told Barnabas and Saul what it would be. We do not find out until we read on and see what they did. But the Spirit had spoken to these men and had laid on them a deep concern to reach out to the world around. Then he said to the church, "Now set them aside for this purpose." That is the way the call of God came in this initial thrusting out toward the uttermost parts of the earth.

> *Dear Father, make me an obedient follower of the strategy of the Spirit. Teach me to trust that you will lead me and to use my gifts to serve you.*

Is the strategy of the Spirit the operating principle for how we observe and obey his calling? Do we serve with the expectancy that God will make clear his choosing of persons and their gifts and callings?

THE RADICAL WORD OF JUSTIFICATION

A daily devotion for July 2

Read Acts 13:32–39.

> "Therefore, my friends, I want you to know that through Jesus the forgiveness of sins is proclaimed to you. Through him everyone who believes is set free from every sin, a justification you were not able to obtain under the law of Moses" (Acts 13:38–39).

Paul makes a shattering statement in this message in Pisidian Antioch. Here were people who thought the Ten Commandments were the greatest word that God had ever given to men. They were trying their best to live up to them. They thought that the way to God was to obey the Ten Commandments—to do good. But now Paul declares to them that they will never find acceptance by God in that way.

Rather, Paul tells them, God has found a way to accept people even though they cannot be good enough in themselves, and that way is through Jesus Christ. This shook these people. They had never heard anything like this before! This is Paul's first recorded use of that great phrase that so frequently appears in the letter to the Romans, "justification by faith."

What does it mean to be justified? Most people think it means to have their sins forgiven. It does mean that, but it means more. Justification means to have our sins forgiven in such a way that God's honor and integrity are preserved. I served in the navy for two years and then was honorably discharged. This meant that I was separated from the navy. The military was through with me, and I was through with the military. But what I liked about this was the word *honorable.* This was an honorable discharge. I could freely show my discharge papers to anyone. There was no blot on my record. But I knew men in the navy who were dishonorably discharged. They were just as separated from the navy as was I. The navy was just as through with them as it was with me. But there was a blot on their discharge, a stain on it. They did not like to show their discharge papers to anyone.

So what Paul is saying here is this. If God forgave sin in the way that most people think he does—he is such a loving God that he says, "Oh, forget about it; that's all right; don't worry about it; you're such a great fellow, and I love you so much that I'm just going to ignore it"—then God's honor would be impugned. His character would be defiled by that kind of forgiveness. He could no longer be regarded as the God of justice and truth; he would be a partaker in our sins.

But God has found a way, through Jesus, to lay our guilt upon his own Son. Thus he can preserve his honor and character and integrity while he is rendered free to show his whole love to us. That is justification. Because of the cross, nobody will ever be able to point to God and to say, "Oh, you let people off who are guilty!" In the cross, God poured out all his justice upon Jesus. And in that cross, in the agony and the anguish of it, the world can see a picture of how faithfully God obeys his own laws. And the wonder of it is that, because of the cross, God's love is freed to be poured out to us.

> *Father, my heart is stirred as I think of the mercy that you show to me, this marvelous justification by which all that has lain heavily upon my conscience has been washed away in the blood of Jesus Christ. How wonderful this is, Lord; teach me never to forget that I have been justified.*

Have we missed the radical implications of God's righteous forgiveness? How can we do less than offer our lives in worship and gratitude for the majesty and wonder of God's amazing grace?

THE POWER OF OBEDIENCE

A daily devotion for July 3

Read Acts 14:1–10.

> "In Lystra there sat a man who was lame. He had been that way from birth and had never walked. He listened to Paul as he was speaking. Paul looked directly at him, saw that he had faith to be healed and called out, 'Stand up on your feet!' At that, the man jumped up and began to walk" (Acts 14:8–10).

Notice the amazing way God began to open up this city. Paul and Barnabas had no idea what they were going to do. They did not form a committee and say, "Well, let's see if we can get the chamber of commerce report on the city's population distribution. Then we could divide it into squares and evangelize in a systematic way." They had no plans other than to be there and to do what God sent them to do—to preach. So they walked right into the marketplace and began, trusting the Lord to have people of his choosing ready to open the door to the city.

As they proclaimed the gospel that is what happened. As Paul was preaching—probably for several days in a row—sitting in the marketplace was a man who had been lame from birth, who had never walked. He was evidently well known throughout the city, having been there all his life. He heard what Paul said and believed what Paul declared about the power of Jesus, the mighty Son of God. Paul looked at him and saw in that man's eyes the faith to believe. Suddenly, unquestionably led by the Spirit, he said to him, "Stand up on your feet." And the lame man, though he had never walked in his life, made the effort to obey. He had faith enough to try, and the moment he began to obey, the power to obey was given him.

That is exactly the way the Christian life works. It makes no difference whether the problem is physical, emotional, or spiritual; we will be held in its bondage until we begin to obey the Word of God about it. When we make the effort to obey, God will set us free. But he will never move until we obey. That is the way faith works. Because they keep waiting for him to do something before they will believe, most people are kept from seeing God at work in their lives. In fact, he has already done all that he is going to do in advance. When we believe what he says, he will give us the power to be free. This miracle is a mighty parable of the many who have been spiritually lame, unable to take a step toward God, but who have been set free to do so by the gospel. It cracked the city wide open. All the residents immediately took note of Paul and Barnabas in their midst.

> *Father, help me, like the apostles, to trust in a living God who is changing people's hearts and delivering their minds from the power of the Evil One. Help me to rejoice as I, too, see the power of obedience to the Word of God in my life.*

Which comes first, faith or obedience? What is the significance of the order? Obedience to what? Faith in what or in whom? Does the union of obedience and trust describe our daily walk with God?

PREACHING TO NONRELIGIOUS PEOPLE

A daily devotion for July 4

Read Acts 14:11–28.

> "Friends, why are you doing this? We too are only human, like you. We are bringing you good news, telling you to turn from these worthless things to the living God, who made the heavens and the earth and the sea and everything in them. In the past, he let all nations go their own way. Yet he has not left himself without testimony: He has shown kindness by giving you rain from heaven and crops in their seasons; he provides you with plenty of food and fills your hearts with joy" (Acts 14:15–17).

Here is the pattern for preaching to a nonreligious people. If you want to know how to reach your neighbors who are not interested in the gospel, who know nothing of Scripture, and who have not been to church and do not care about it, here is the way. The approach is through nature. When Paul went to the Jews, he started with the Scriptures, the truth of God that they already knew. When he went to the Gentiles, he started with nature, the truth of God that they already knew. He points out three things that ought to be plain to them if they have been thinking about their contact with nature.

First, he shows that behind creation there is one living God. He says that if they have really observed nature, they will realize that it is not controlled by a conglomerate of separate powers, all trying to compete with one another, as envisioned in the pagan pantheon. Paul is saying, "You haven't really seen nature. You haven't noticed that nature is as one; it all ties together, blending and harmonizing beautifully. It all exists and functions together because it has been made by one God, who is a living God. It is sustained and held together. It doesn't decay and fall apart but is constantly being renewed. So there is one living God." Paul declares to them that nature bears witness to God.

The second point he makes is that the one living God permits men free choice and therefore allows evil. One problem about God faced by anyone in the world today is the question of why evil is present among men. This is a constant argument of humanists and others. They say, "If your God is such a loving God, why does he permit suffering? Why does he allow evil, injustice, and war?" These pagans argued the same way. Paul answers by saying, "What you must know is that God, in generations past, allowed all the nations to walk in their own way." In other words, he gave them free will. To permit free will, he must allow evil.

Third, Paul says God will not allow it to go too far. He does not allow evil to engulf humanity and to wipe us off the face of the earth, as human evil would do in a few months' time if it were unrestrained. God has restrained it. And right in the midst of it, despite all the rejection, rebellion, blasphemy, and hatred that are poured out against him by these people whom he loves, God has shown his love by giving rain, fruit, harvest, and gladness in the family circle and joy throughout the moments of life. That is the God whom Paul preaches. What a marvelous declaration of the gospel, that God has provided all these things and thus has given witness to these people about himself! So the first onslaught of the Enemy falls back upon itself. The city is open to the gospel, and Paul is able to proclaim it in power.

Thank you, Father, for the powerful witness you have given to all people in nature.

How did the apostle Paul begin his witness to nonreligious, nonbelieving persons? What are three powerful aspects of God's character revealed in the natural world?

BETRAYING THE GOSPEL

A daily devotion for July 5

Read Acts 15:1–21.

> "Certain people came down from Judea to Antioch and were teaching the believers: 'Unless you are circumcised, according to the custom taught by Moses, you cannot be saved'" (Acts 15:1).

In the fifteenth chapter of Acts is the story of a betrayal of the gospel. Here we learn of the clear emergence of what we can only call false Christianity. We will never understand Christianity until we understand that there are always present, in any so-called Christian gathering, manifestations and representatives of both true and false Christianity. Unfortunately, false Christianity is believed by millions who think they have understood the true and have rejected the false. Therefore their minds are closed to the truth when it comes. Here we see the first emergence of that kind of false Christianity unthinkingly accepted by millions of people today.

It all began with the introduction of a plausible and attractive heresy that came disguised as Christianity. Luke says that certain Jewish brethren, ostensibly Christians, came down from Jerusalem to Antioch. They circulated among the Gentile believers, who had just emerged from raw paganism, who had been idolaters, and who had been devotees of the licentious and sexually immoral practices of the pagan temples. These Gentiles had been hopeless in their outlook toward the future beyond this life and had been sunk in despair and darkness, but then God had saved them. They were now rejoicing in Christ.

But these Jewish brethren came to them and said, as Luke quotes them here, "Unless you are circumcised, according to the custom taught by Moses, you cannot be saved." This introduced an issue that split the church in Antioch wide open. They were really saying, "To become a Christian, you must first become a Jew. Unless you become a Jew, you are a second-class Christian, if a Christian at all." Thus they challenged the gospel of the grace of God. So the first serious strife within the church was over race and ritual—over the question of Jews versus Gentiles and of circumcision as the sign of acceptance.

This issue has long ago passed away as a concern for us, but the principle behind it remains. The Enemy has simply changed the players on the program. I was shocked at the reply a young couple gave to my suggestion that they visit another couple who were newcomers to our church. They looked at me and said, "Oh, no. You don't want them. They're not our kind of people." That was a denial of the universality of the church and of its inclusion of all types, ages, backgrounds, and races. Not only people but also rituals often become bones of contention today. Substitute baptism for circumcision and you bring the issue right up to date. Many think people cannot become Christians unless they are baptized. These external issues are the things that Christians split over today. And that was what was occurring in Antioch.

Forgive me, Father, for those times I have denied the universality of the church. Teach me to accept and to embrace those who put their trust in you.

What was the first serious challenge to the gospel of grace in the early church? How do issues of race and ritual continue to undermine authentic Christianity in the church and in our personal experience?

A SHARP DISAGREEMENT

A daily devotion for July 6

Read Acts 15:22–41.

> "Some time later Paul said to Barnabas, 'Let us go back and visit the believers in all the towns where we preached the word of the Lord and see how they are doing.' Barnabas wanted to take John, also called Mark, with them, but Paul did not think it wise to take him, because he had deserted them in Pamphylia and had not continued with them in the work. They had such a sharp disagreement that they parted company" (Acts 15:36–39).

This a quarrel between Barnabas and Paul has fascinated many. They could not agree whether to take young John Mark with them again. Barnabas was his cousin and wanted to give the young man another chance. But Paul did not want to take the chance because the work was important and dangerous, and he did not think it wise to take someone they could not count on.

So we read the sad note: "there arose a sharp disagreement" between them. Many have asked, "Which of these men was right?" Many people have had a sharp disagreement over the answer to that question! But that is not the point. Both Paul and Barnabas were right. One was looking at the work and the other at the person. As Paul looked at the work he was perfectly right to say, "We don't want somebody who is apt to cop out on us." And he probably quoted the words of Jesus: "No one who puts a hand to the plow and looks back is fit for service in the kingdom of God" (Luke 9:62). That is right. Christian service is demanding, and those who undertake it should be prepared to stick with it to the end, for God's cause is injured by those who quit in the middle.

On the other hand, though I am sure he would have agreed about the importance of the work, Barnabas was looking at the young man. He knew Mark was gifted. Sure, he had failed, but who doesn't? Who among us does not need a second chance, does not need to have a forgiving spirit exercised toward us and to be given the opportunity to try again? So Barnabas was willing to give Mark another chance.

This indicates a normal and proper procedure by which we may know the mind of the Spirit. There are times when differing views require a separation. The will of God was that Barnabas should take Mark and go to Cyprus, because Cyprus, Barnabas's birthplace, had not been visited since the churches there had been founded. And it was God's will for Paul to take Silas and go to Syria and Cilicia, because the churches there needed his particular ministry. But it was not God's will that they should be sharp in their contention. Their quarreling was not right. It was the will of God that they should separate; it was not his will that they should quarrel. There are times when the Spirit of God leads Christians to go separate ways. But they should do so with joy and with an agreeable understanding that the mind of the Spirit has been expressed in their divergent viewpoints.

> *Teach me, Father, how to apply this practical help. When I disagree with others, help me to do it in a way that compromises neither your truth nor your love.*

What can we learn from the dispute between Paul and Barnabas? Do we receive others' opinions as ego threats? Do we honor God's work in others even when we have divergent opinions?

THE UNDERLYING PRINCIPLE

A daily devotion for July 7

Read Acts 16:1–9.

> "Paul came to Derbe and then to Lystra, where a disciple named Timothy lived, whose mother was Jewish and a believer but whose father was a Greek. The believers at Lystra and Iconium spoke well of him. Paul wanted to take him along on the journey, so he circumcised him because of the Jews who lived in that area, for they all knew that his father was a Greek" (Acts 16:1–3).

Paul is back in Lystra, the city where he had encountered the severest opposition of his first missionary journey. On that first occasion, he had led a young man to Christ. Though Timothy was still a boy, only about sixteen years old, Paul thought he observed in him gifts of ministry, perhaps of wisdom and of knowledge in the Scriptures, of teaching, and of preaching. He wanted Timothy to join him. Paul would use that marvelous means of discipling that has never been superseded, the method by which Jesus himself trained men, taking Timothy along and teaching him as they ministered together.

But there was a problem. Timothy was half Jewish, half Greek. His father was a Greek but his mother was a Jew, and according to the Jews, this made him a Jew. The Jewish people had a practical way of thinking about this. They said everyone knows who a man's mother is, but people can't be as sure of his father. So they reckoned the line of descent through the mother, and Timothy was therefore considered a Jew.

The amazing thing is that Paul circumcised Timothy while earlier he had refused to do the same to Titus. This is not recorded in Acts, but from a parallel passage in Galatians we learn that he had taken Titus, who was a Greek, with him up to Jerusalem. The Jewish brethren there wanted to circumcise Titus, but Paul absolutely refused. He was adamant because to have permitted this would have been a concession to the idea that one had to become a Jew to become a Christian.

Here is a marvelous indication of how to know the will of God. In any situation involving customs and rituals and cultural matters, the governing rule is to find the great underlying principle at stake and to act accordingly. In the case of Titus, it would have been devastating to have circumcised him. It would have meant yielding to the concept of legalism, and baptizing it as a Christian teaching, to have allowed this young Gentile, wholly a Greek, to be circumcised.

But the case of Timothy is different. He is viewed as a Jew, and in order not to offend the Jews among whom he must labor, in order to open the door of acceptance by them, Paul submits to this Old Testament ritual and circumcises Timothy. That's because here the governing principle is, "I have become all things to all people so that by all possible means I might save some" (1 Corinthians 9:22). This approach may result in two seemingly contradictory actions, but all is reconciled by the great principle underlying it.

> *Father, help me to discern your will by seeing the underlying principle and acting accordingly.*

When cultural issues are at stake, what is the best way to determine God's will? Is it safe to wing it? Is our understanding of grace versus legalism sufficient to inform us when we need to apply the defining principles?

A HEART IS OPENED

A daily devotion for July 8

Read Acts 16:11–24.

> "And on the Sabbath day we went outside the gate to a riverside, where we were supposing that there would be a place of prayer; and we sat down and began speaking to the women who had assembled. A woman named Lydia, from the city of Thyatira, a seller of purple fabrics, a worshiper of God, was listening; and the Lord opened her heart to respond to the things spoken by Paul" (Acts 16:13–14).

After proclaiming the Word of God, these disciples expected God to do something! That is the missing note among Christians in many places today. Many have given up expecting God to do anything while they expect to do everything. They expect to organize a program and carry it through. Many churches today operate in such a way that if the Holy Spirit were suddenly removed from their program, nobody would notice.

They do not expect God to do anything, but these people did. They preached the Word and then they expected God to act. They could not tell what he would do—he is always unpredictable. He has several ways of gaining access to a city, breaking open a community, spreading the gospel, and planting a church. But here we find one of the ways the Lord frequently uses: he prepared men and women in this place, people whose hearts were ready to respond to the gospel. Such a woman was Lydia who already worshiped God. She was a businesswoman who sold purple goods, who handled the purple dye for cloth that was so valuable in those days. Lydia made a good living. She had her own home, and it was large enough to accommodate Paul and his party. Her heart was ready, having been prepared by God, and she was led of God to be there and to hear.

That is one of the first principles of any Christian evangelical activity. When I have spoken to groups of non-Christians who have looked at me coldly and whose reactions I couldn't anticipate, it has been a great encouragement to realize that there are unquestionably people in the group whom God has prepared. I never doubt it, for I have always found this to be true. There are always one or two whom God has prepared. I try to talk to them and to ignore the hostile reaction of others.

This was what happened here. Lydia did not get upset by the message. She did not view it as a challenge to her Jewish faith but immediately recognized that it was the fulfillment of all her Jewish hopes. So she opened her heart and received the Lord. Thus the gospel first entered Europe through a business and professional women's association meeting.

Lord, I thank you for going before me to prepare the hearts of those with whom I share your Word.

Are we mere activists, trying to do God's work our way under our own impetus? Are we learning to expect that God will lead us to persons whose hearts he has prepared to receive the gospel?

REJOICING IN SUFFERING

A daily devotion for July 9

Read Acts 16:25–40.

> "When they had struck them with many blows, they threw them into prison, commanding the jailer to guard them securely; and he, having received such a command, threw them into the inner prison and fastened their feet in the stocks. But about midnight Paul and Silas were praying and singing hymns of praise to God, and the prisoners were listening to them; and suddenly there came a great earthquake, so that the foundations of the prison house were shaken; and immediately all the doors were opened and everyone's chains were unfastened" (Acts 16:23–26).

There is nothing unusual about an earthquake in this region. To this day, earthquakes are common in northern Macedonia. The earthquake was natural; the timing of it was supernatural. God released the earthquake precisely at the right moment and set Paul, Silas, and the other prisoners free. The most dramatic aspect of this story, though, is not the earthquake. It is the singing of Paul and Silas at midnight. Somebody has said that the gospel entered Europe through a sacred concert that was so successful that it brought down the house!

Imagine this, praising God! That is the meaning of the word *praying* used here. Paul and Silas were not asking for anything; they were praising God and singing hymns. They were not faking either. Their backs were raw and bloody, they were covered with wounds, and they had suffered a great injustice, but they exhibited no self-pity or resentment. They faced agonizing uncertainty. They did not know this delivering earthquake was coming. But at midnight they began praising God and singing hymns. I do not know what they sang. I know what I'd be singing: rescue the perishing; care for the dying. But I think they were singing, "How great thou art." Evidently they sang because they could see things that we, in our poor, blinded condition, seldom see. Paul and Silas were men of faith. When we see what they saw, our question will no longer be "Why did they sing?" but "What else could they do but sing?"

They saw first that the Enemy had panicked and had resorted to violence. They were conscious that they were in a spiritual battle, but they were delighted when they saw the Enemy reacting with alarm. That always means that he has emptied his bag of tricks. He reached the bottom of the barrel and has nothing left. Paul and Silas knew they had won. The second thing they saw was that God, in his resurrection power, was at work in the situation. Resurrection power cannot be stopped. All attempts to oppose it, or to throw obstacles in its path, are turned around and used as opportunities for advancement. Paul and Silas knew that, and so they were assured that they had won.

The third thing they understood was that suffering is absolutely necessary to Christian maturity. We will never grow up, we will never be what God wants us to be, without some form of suffering. When we learn that, we will stop griping and bewailing our estate. When we run into suffering we will rejoice. Paul and Silas saw that the foe had been defeated, that the work was established, and that they had gained spiritual benefits. So they began to rejoice, to sing, and to thank God for what they had seen. And God was so excited by this that he said, "I can't hold still. I'm going to shake the place up a little bit!" It blesses the heart of God to see men act this way, and so the prison was opened.

Father, teach me the perspective that Paul and his friends had so that I might rejoice in my suffering, knowing that you will use it to grow and mature me.

Do our comparatively minimal hardships produce self-pity or praise of God? What are three perspectives we need if we experience persecution for our faith? Are we spiritually equipped to experience severe persecution and life's inevitable hardships?

NOBLER

A daily devotion for July 10

Read Acts 17:1–15.

> "The brethren immediately sent Paul and Silas away by night to Berea, and when they arrived, they went into the synagogue of the Jews. Now these were more noble-minded than those in Thessalonica, for they received the word with great eagerness, examining the Scriptures daily to see whether these things were so" (Acts 17:10–11).

Luke draws a sharp contrast between the rabble in Thessalonica, whom Paul and his friends had encountered earlier in chapter 17, and these Jews in Berea, who were nobler. In what did their nobility consist? Well, not merely in receiving the word but also in checking it out with the Scriptures. A noble person is one who has not only an open mind but also a cautious heart. He will not accept a teaching unless he checks it with the Scriptures.

That is what the Scriptures are for. They are our guide so that we can tell what is true and what is false, what is right and what is wrong. And unless we Christians do this, we are lost in a sea of relativism and do not know what is right or what is wrong. Our minds become confused and blinded, and we can be misled and manipulated, as the rabble manipulated the crowd in Thessalonica—unless we have the nobility to check things out according to the Scriptures. That is what these Jews did, and it was a tremendous help. They checked up on the apostle Paul.

The value of this story for us, and the reason Luke includes it, is that it teaches us the necessity of testing any man's word. We must not listen to just one man's tapes or read only one man's books or messages. That is a dangerous practice. We will be misled by his errors, and we will not know how to recognize them. We must never become the acolytes of a single man. We must check whatever we read with what is in the Scriptures and with other teachers. It is essential to establish what the Word of God says. That is the authority. How delighted Luke is to commend these Bereans for their nobility in doing this very thing!

Thank you for your Word, Lord. I ask that you give me a noble heart to study your Word and to take it and it alone as my guide and my authority.

What characterized the nobility of the Berean Christians? Is it safe and prudent to follow one man's teaching exclusively? What is a certain safeguard against confusion from teachings contrary to the Word of God?

CONFRONTING IDOLATRY

A daily devotion for July 11

Read Acts 17:16–34.

> "The God who made the world and all things in it, since He is Lord of heaven and earth, does not dwell in temples made with hands; nor is He served by human hands, as though He needed anything, since He Himself gives to all people life and breath and all things" (Acts 17:24–25).

What is Paul saying here? First, that God is the maker and not the one who was made. God was not created by man; he is the One who makes man and everything else that exists in the universe. He is the originator of all things.

We have not moved far from ancient idolatry. In the ancient world, people took a piece of gold or silver or wood and formed an idol, thus worshiping the works of men's hands. Today we don't use images, but we still see men worshiping themselves, projected to infinite proportions. Man simply thinks of himself, projects this into infinity, and worships that. That is his god. That is exactly what idolatry did. Paul points out that this is not in line with reality. God is not the projection of man; God is greater than man. God originated man. Everything that exists came from his hands. He is the maker and not the made.

Second, God is the giver and has no needs. He is not looking for anything from man, as idolatry and paganism taught. People had to bring gifts to the gods; they had to do things for their gods, to propitiate them and to sacrifice to them. People today are doing the same. The gods of people today also make demands upon them. We must not think that we are free from idolatry, for if a god is the most important thing in our lives, the thing we give our time and effort and energy, to the thing we live for, then we have many gods even today.

Money is a god for some. Fame is a god for others. Our children can be our gods. We can be our own gods; we can worship ourselves. I am appalled at the number of people today who worship America and enthrone it as the highest value in life, the thing for which they would give their lives, the only thing worth living for. These are the false gods that people everywhere worship. They make continual demands upon us. They do nothing for us, but we must work for them.

Paul cancels all this out. He says the real God is one who gives, who pours out. He does not need anything from us. He does not live in temples made by man. I am sure Paul pointed to the Parthenon as he said that, for it was regarded as the home of Athena, the goddess for whom the city was named. God does not live in places like that, Paul said, but he is the one who made us and everything about us, and there is nothing we can give him that he needs. He is, rather, giving himself continually to us.

> *Father, I know how I have tried to satisfy the emptiness within with some lesser concept than you. I can never do so and am therefore rendered restless and unhappy, never finding what I seek. I pray that this great message may have its effect on me as it did on Athens, that our darkened society will be set free from its bondage to materialism, and that we will become what you intended us to be.*

Are we willing to honestly evaluate, to courageously confront, and to name our personal idols? Do we see our idols as affronts to the presence and power of Christ in us and through us? Are we sacrificing our lives to those idols—lives purchased and legitimately owned by Christ, who died for us?

ENCOURAGEMENT FROM THE LORD

A daily devotion for July 12

Read Acts 18:1–22.

> "And the Lord said to Paul in the night by a vision, 'Do not be afraid any longer, but go on speaking and do not be silent; for I am with you, and no man will attack you in order to harm you, for I have many people in this city'" (Acts 18:9–10).

When he appeared to Paul in this night vision, the Lord said, "Stop being afraid, but keep right on speaking." This reveals that Paul was indeed becoming afraid. This is quite understandable, for a familiar pattern was developing. He had seen it before many times. Paul had come to the synagogue and spoken to the Jews. They had rejected his message. He turned to the Gentiles and received an immediate response, a great flood of people accepting Christ. This aroused the anger and hostility of the Jews, and he knew that the next step was trouble.

Is that not beautifully descriptive of Paul's humanity? We sometimes think of him as being bold and fearless—yet he suffered just as we do from apprehensions, forebodings, and fears. In fact, in a letter to these Corinthians he says so. He says, "When I came to you … I was with you in weakness and in much fear and trembling" (1 Cor. 2:1, 2:3 RSV). He was very much afraid of what would happen to him in Corinth.

The reason was that the city was responding to the gospel, and the strongholds of evil were being broken down. The life of the city was being disrupted by the awakening, which was spreading because of Paul's teaching. I find many churches today that measure their success by what is going on in the congregation, but that is not the mark of success. The church is successful only when things start happening in the world. The Lord Jesus said, "You are the salt of the earth … you are the light of the world" (Matt. 5:13–14 RSV). God is aiming at the world. Until a change begins in the community, the church is a failure.

This is so evident in our day. It bothers me greatly to visit a city and to find it filled with church buildings but also to discover that the city is locked into patterns of violence and hatred. This tells me that there is something wrong with the churches of that city, for God always aims at the world. All the evils of our modern day were present in Corinth. But now this revolutionary message of the gospel was striking at the core of the city's life, breaking down the patterns of evil that had locked men and women into bondage. As Paul saw this beginning to happen he knew that he faced danger.

This is why the Lord appeared to him. How gracious and reassuring are his words: "Paul, don't let your fears grip you! Stop being afraid and don't keep silent, but keep right on preaching, because I am going to protect you. No one will hurt you, for I have a lot of work for you to do yet in this city." Among the Lord's most encouraging words are, "I have yet many people in this city." They had not yet become Christians—but the Lord knew they were there. There is nothing more encouraging to me when entering a strange situation than the realization that God has brought me there because he already knows certain people in this place will respond to what I have to say. So it was with the apostle. He was greatly strengthened, and for a year and a half he was able to preach the truth until there was a great stirring in this city.

> *Father, thank you for this encouraging account, for I know that you are at work today just as you were then. Lord, help me to stay committed to the task you assigned me when you gave me spiritual gifts and the power of your resurrection.*

Paul's experience tells us that fear is common to man. Paul was faithfully fulfilling God's calling when God promised his protective care. Are we boldly following God's calling to reach out to unbelievers with his message of hope and redemption, confident in his promise to be with us always?

HALFWAY CHRISTIANS

A daily devotion for July 13

Read Acts 18:23–19:7.

"Paul passed through the upper country and came to Ephesus, and found some disciples. He said to them, 'Did you receive the Holy Spirit when you believed?'" (Acts 19:1–2).

When Paul arrived in Ephesus he found men and women who had been told about Jesus, at least to the extent of the baptism of John. He obviously thought they were Christians when he first met them. But as he watched them, he observed that something was missing, and I am sure there was puzzlement in his voice when finally he asked them, "Did you receive the Holy Spirit when you believed?" This question indicates that the normal Christian pattern is that the Spirit is given immediately upon belief in Jesus Christ. There is no suggestion here that the Spirit of God is given after a long period of belief in Christ.

Many people believe in Jesus but do not show much evidence of the work of the Holy Spirit. When I speak in many churches in our land today, I want to say to the people, "Did you receive the Holy Spirit when you believed?" There is no sign of it.

The Holy Spirit is given upon belief in the Lord Jesus, but that does not stop with one act of believing. We are to keep on believing in the Lord Jesus and thus to manifest his power and his vitality in our lives. That continual act of believing releases the freshness of the Spirit in our lives. Paul says to the Colossians, "As you received Christ Jesus the Lord, so live in him" (Col. 2:6 RSV). In other words, "As you received him by an act of believing, keep on believing, walk in him, live in him, so that you might demonstrate the power of the Holy Spirit."

So what is wrong if there is no evidence of the working of the Spirit, none of the joy, none of the grace, none of the power? This means we are not believing in him. We believed in him once, but that believing has ceased. There is now no sense of expectancy, no fresh anticipation of his working in our lives today.

Are there signs of the Spirit of God in our lives? Are his presence, his power, his working, the freshness, the vitality, the enthusiasm, the excitement of the Spirit visible in our Christian lives? If not, we have ceased believing in Jesus. This expectation of his working is essential, for he makes himself available to us continually, moment by moment, to fulfill every demand life makes upon us, as we expect him to do. That note of expectancy is the sign of faith that marks the difference between the sterility, the deadness, and the dullness of religiosity without the Spirit and the fullness, the freshness, the vigor, and the power of a Spirit-filled life. So this question, addressed to these halfway Christians of long-ago Ephesus, still has meaning for us today as we understand the need for a continual act of faith in the Lord Jesus.

Lord Jesus, how frequently I fail to understand the truth of your promise that you have come to live within me. Grant to me anew, Lord, the faith to lay hold of this promise and to make it visible in my life.

Have we settled for being halfway Christians, absent evidence of the power of the Holy Spirit? What is the key to releasing the freshness and the vitality of his power in and through us? Is our daily walk characterized by believing in God's Word and in his indwelling presence?

OFF, WITCHCRAFT!

A daily devotion for July 14

Read Acts 19:8–20.

> "Many also of those who had believed kept coming, confessing and disclosing their practices. And many of those who practiced magic brought their books together and began burning them in the sight of everyone; and they counted up the price of them and found it fifty thousand pieces of silver. So the word of the Lord was growing mightily and prevailing" (Acts 19:18–20).

Luke mentions two movements here. The first involved the believers who began to clean up their lives and who divulged their hidden practices, confessing what they had been doing in private. Obviously these were relatively new Christians, and perhaps they had never thought that anything was wrong with these practices. But as they sat under the teaching of the apostle and saw the kingdom of God and how God longs to set people free, they began to see that what they had been doing—the astrology, the reliance on horoscopes, and all their other superstitious practices—had held them in bondage. These were the reasons they remained weak, fearful, and distressed. So they confessed all this and therefore were freed from their bondage.

That, in turn, precipitated another movement. The unbelievers around them in the city took a second look at their own practices. Many of them who had practiced magic arts brought their books and burned them when they became Christians under the influence and the power of the gospel, and thus they were set free from their own deadly delusion.

This illustrates how light breaks forth through the church. When the church straightens out and cleans up its life and acts and lives as God has called people to do, the world will begin to see itself as it is, to see what is wrong, and to start straightening up and being freed from the practices that are darkening and blinding it. This is what happened here. These people surrendered all their occult literature, and that was a costly thing to do. They totaled up the value of the books and the paraphernalia brought to be burned, and it came to fifty thousand pieces of silver. That is about ten thousand dollars, a tremendous sum in those days. This meant that these people were forsaking their livelihoods. They were completely changing the pattern of their lives as they saw that they could no longer practice the occult and live as Christians too. Their action revealed how willing they were to be free from this terrible practice.

In Ephesus, Paul and the other Christians, by the power of the truth, broke through this deception. They assaulted this stronghold of evil. They cracked it wide open so that Luke says, "The word of the Lord was growing mightily and prevailed." That is how a church ought to operate—in the power of the Spirit and by the authority of the Word. There are strongholds like this all around us today, bastions of darkness: drugs, witchcraft, homosexuality. How desperately this situation needs the assault of truth and of light. God longs to deliver people from these strongholds, and he has given the church this power.

> *Father, I see the powers of darkness holding people enthralled, locking them into misery and heartache, superstition and fear, hostility and emptiness. Lord, help me to understand that I live in a strategic time and to give myself to the exciting, glorious battle against these powers of darkness.*

Are we faithfully and transparently confronting any and all evil practices in our lives? Are we committed to being set free and to sharing that freedom with others, regardless of the cost in worldly goods or prestige?

CHRISTIANITY IS DANGEROUS

A daily devotion for July 15

Read Acts 19:21–20:1.

> "After the uproar had ceased, Paul sent for the disciples, and when he had exhorted them and taken his leave of them, he left to go to Macedonia" (Acts 20:1).

Paul is eager to explain to the Christians this tumult that has just taken place in Ephesus. There is something about it he does not want them to miss, so he calls them together and exhorts them before he leaves. Luke does not tell us the message of that exhortation, but I believe that Paul does. A passage in his second letter to the Corinthians refers to this occasion. Paul says, "For we do not want you to be ignorant, brethren, of the affliction we experienced in Asia; for we were so utterly, unbearably crushed that we despaired of life itself" (2 Cor. 1:8 RSV).

Put yourself back with the apostle amid this tremendous uproar. It had appeared for a while that the gospel had so triumphed in Ephesus that Paul could think of leaving for other places. Then this riot suddenly occurred, seeming to threaten the entire cause of Christ and putting the Christians in great danger. Paul is crushed and distressed. His life is in danger. This crowd is so wild, so uncontrollable, that for a few hours it looks as though these people might sweep through Ephesus and wipe out every Christian there. Paul says, "We were so utterly, unbearably crushed that we despaired of life itself. Why, we felt that we had received the sentence of death" (2 Cor. 1:8–9 RSV). He cannot see any way out. It looks as if he has reached the end of the road. But God has a purpose: " to make us rely not on ourselves but on God who raises the dead" (2 Cor. 1:9 RSV).

That is the heart of the Christian message, as Paul goes on to explain in this letter. "Our sufficiency is not of ourselves," he says (2 Cor. 3:5). His explanation to these young converts in Ephesus was unquestionably along this line. He was saying to them, "God has sent this event. He has allowed it to happen to teach us that he is able to handle things when they get far beyond any human control. When our circumstances get way out of order, far beyond our own resources, God is able. He has taught us this so that we will not rely on ourselves but upon him who raises the dead, who works in us to do exceedingly more than all that we could ask or think, according to the power at work within us."

What an awareness this apostle had of the fantastic strength of the body of Christ working together, praying together, supporting one another, upholding each other in prayer, and thus calling into action the mighty power of the God of resurrection, who can work through the most unexpected instruments to quiet a situation, to hold a crowd in restraint, to stop the surging emotions of people whose reasoning has been short-circuited, to hold them within limits, and to bring the whole affair to nothing! This is the might of our God.

This is what we can learn from this situation as we too encounter times of danger, pressure, and trouble. The difficulties that strike suddenly in our lives, the pressures we must endure, the catastrophes that come roaring in out of the blue—these are sent so that we might rely not on ourselves but on God.

Thank you, Father, for the trials and difficulties you bring into my life, which teach me to depend not on myself but on you.

"Safety first" is not the Christian motto! Do we need to be disabused of the notion that authentic Christian living means immunity from hardship, persecution, and suffering? Are we taking up the whole armor of God, trusting him to do battle through us, or are we resisting the adventure to which we are called?

FALLEN ASLEEP

A daily devotion for July 16

Read Acts 20:2–12.

> "On the first day of the week, when we were gathered together to break bread, Paul began talking to them, intending to leave the next day, and he prolonged his message until midnight. There were many lamps in the upper room where we were gathered together. And there was a young man named Eutychus sitting on the window sill, sinking into a deep sleep; and as Paul kept on talking, he was overcome by sleep and fell down from the third floor and was picked up dead. But Paul went down and fell upon him, and after embracing him, he said, 'Do not be troubled, for his life is in him'" (Acts 20:7–10).

This story has several interesting aspects. We have the first mention of believers worshiping on the first day of the week, Sunday. Thus early in the Christian era they had shifted from Saturday to gathering on the day of our Lord's resurrection. They evidently had met here for a communion service, and the apostle seized the occasion to teach them from the Scriptures. In his last evening there, before they gathered at the Lord's Table, he took time to teach them further from the Scriptures. He went on at considerable length, prolonging his speech until midnight.

This has always been an encouraging passage to pastors. It reveals that even the apostle Paul had people go to sleep on him. Someone has said that the art of preaching is speaking in other people's sleep. This was certainly the case here. At any rate, Eutychus fought a losing battle against falling asleep. Luke, with his physician's eye, is easy on him. He tells us that there were many lamps in the upper chamber, and each was burning up oxygen. So with the loss of oxygen in the atmosphere, the late hour, and perhaps a long week's work behind him, this young man was unable to hold out during Paul's lengthy message. He was seated in a window and fell into a deep sleep as Paul droned on, and so he fell from the third floor and was taken up dead.

Some question whether he actually died. But the issue is settled by a physician's testimony. It is Doctor Luke who says that believers took him up dead. So when Paul fell over him, embraced him, and said, "Do not be alarmed, for his life is in him," he did not mean Eutychus hadn't died. He meant that his life had returned to him. Thus God used Paul in the great miracle of raising this young lad from the dead.

Peter was involved in a similar miracle in the case of Dorcas. It was all the more remarkable in that she had been dead for several hours by the time he prayed for her. The ministries of these mighty apostles of God were confirmed by these miracles, including this one of raising a young man from the dead.

> *Father, as I face life with its uncertainties, dangers, and possibilities, I pray that I may be alert to you and to my need for others within the body of Christ. Strengthen and surprise me with moments of joy that I could not have anticipated but that are your delight to give.*

Perhaps this incident will facilitate our awareness of many who have fallen asleep in their walk with Christ. Are we available to be used by him as he pursues them with his resurrection power?

THE MAIN THING

A daily devotion for July 17

Read Acts 20:13–38.

> "Be on guard for yourselves and for all the flock, among which the Holy Spirit has made you overseers, to shepherd the church of God which He purchased with His own blood" (Acts 20:28).

The primary responsibility of an elder or a pastor is to teach the Scriptures, to feed the flock. If he is not doing that, he is failing miserably in his job. It is the truth that changes people. If the Scriptures are not being taught, people are not being changed. They are struggling in their own futile ways, and nothing is being accomplished. So the primary job of elders and of pastors is to set the whole counsel of God before the people.

They are to begin with themselves, says the apostle, by obeying the truth that they themselves learn. Their authority comes from this. Only obedience to the truth that they teach gives them the right to instruct others. Even the Lord Jesus operated on that basis. He told his disciples on one occasion, "If I do not do the works of my Father, do not believe me" (John 10:37). That is, "If what I am doing is not in exact accord with what I am saying, don't believe me!"

Would you dare say that to your children? Or to your Sunday school class? Or to others who observe you as a Christian? "If what I am doing is not in line with what I teach, don't believe me. I have no authority over you." But if your actions are in accord with your teaching, power is inherent in that obedience.

So these pastors and elders are to begin with themselves and to teach the Word. Their responsibility is to the Holy Spirit, not to the denomination or to the congregation. The Spirit has set them in their offices and has equipped them with gifts. He who reads the heart is judging their lives, so it makes no difference what anybody else thinks. They are responsible to follow the Holy Spirit in what he has given them to do.

Notice how Paul underscores the fact that theirs is a precious ministry. They are to feed the church of the Lord. Nothing is more precious to God in all the world than the people of Christ, the body of Christ. In God's sight, the most valuable thing on earth is his church. "He purchased it with his own blood," and he loves it earnestly. Therefore it has highest priority in his schedule and his emphasis. What concerns the church is the most important thing in the world today. I wish we could see that truth as the apostle understood it.

> *Father, how grateful I am for your Word. How graciously it teaches me, especially through the other members of the body. Please protect and encourage all those you have called to teach your Word.*

The emphasis on teaching and obeying God's Word is critical to private and public Christian witness. Are we instead trying to impress people with our credentials and our skills? Do we need to reassess what is the main thing in our walk and in our talk?

PAUL'S MISTAKE

A daily devotion for July 18

Read Acts 21:1–16.

> "As we were staying there for some days, a prophet named Agabus came down from Judea. And coming to us, he took Paul's belt and bound his own feet and hands, and said, 'This is what the Holy Spirit says: "In this way the Jews at Jerusalem will bind the man who owns this belt and deliver him into the hands of the Gentiles"'" (Acts 21:9–11).

This is a rather painful scene. In Caesarea they visited the home of Philip the evangelist. There Agabus, a prophet of the Lord, in a dramatic, visual way, took Paul's sash from around his waist, bound his own feet and hands, and said, "This is what the Holy Spirit is saying to you, Paul. If you go on to Jerusalem, this is what will happen to you. You'll be delivered into the hands of the Gentiles. They will bind you, and you'll be a prisoner."

This was the last effort made by the Holy Spirit to awaken the apostle to what he was doing. Agabus was joined in this by the whole body of believers. The entire family present urged him not to go, Luke included. We read in verse 12, "When we had heard this, we and the local residents begged him not to go up to Jerusalem." So even Paul's close associates recognized the voice of the Spirit to which the apostle seemed strangely deaf. He refused to listen.

And in Paul's reply we can detect that without quite realizing what has happened, he has succumbed to what we call a martyr complex. Paul said in verse 13, "What are you doing, weeping and breaking my heart? For I am ready not only to be bound, but even to die at Jerusalem for the name of the Lord Jesus." These words were brave and sincere. He meant every one of them. We can find no fault with the courage he expressed. But it was not necessary for him to go, and the Spirit had told him not to go.

Here we see what can happen to a man of God when he is misled by an urgent hunger to accomplish a task that God has not given him to do. The flesh had deceived Paul, and evidently he saw himself as doing what the Lord did in his final journey up to Jerusalem. The gospel accounts say that Jesus steadfastly set his face to go there, determined despite all the pleading and the warnings of his disciples. Paul must have seen himself in that role. But Jesus had the Spirit's witness within that this was the Father's will for him, while Paul had exactly the opposite. The Spirit had made crystal clear that he was not to go to Jerusalem.

When Paul refused to be persuaded, his friends said, "Well, may the will of the Lord be done." That is what we say when we do not know what else to say. That is what we pray when we do not know how else to act. They were simply saying, "Lord, it is up to you. We can't stop this man. He has a strong will and a mighty determination, and he's deluded into thinking that this is what you want. Therefore, you will have to handle it. May the will of the Lord be done."

Father, thank you for recording so faithfully even this failure by the apostle. This helps me to see how I must rely not upon the arm of the flesh but upon the arm of the Spirit. Teach me to walk in obedience, Lord, and not to undertake ventures that would merely fulfill my own desires.

The guidance of the Holy Spirit is intimate and personal, yet he often uses godly counsel from others to validate God's will. Are we learning to be alert to the inner witness while remaining open to confirmation from our brothers and sisters in Christ?

FREEDOM IN CHRIST

A daily devotion for July 19

Read Acts 21:17–26.

> "And when they heard it they began glorifying God; and they said to him, 'You see, brother, how many thousands there are among the Jews of those who have believed, and they are all zealous for the Law; and they have been told about you, that you are teaching all the Jews who are among the Gentiles to forsake Moses, telling them not to circumcise their children nor to walk according to the customs'" (Acts 21:20–21).

Many have misread this and concluded that Paul set aside Moses and the law, that he rejected circumcision as of no value. That charge is false. Paul never taught Jews to abandon Moses or not to circumcise their children. What he strongly taught was that the Gentiles should not be made subject to Jewish provisions. He would not allow them to come under the Jewish law and insisted that they did not have to follow any of these provisions. But he did not set aside the ritual for the Jews.

Rather, he told them that this was all symbolic and that it was all pointing toward Christ. The rituals they were performing and the sacrifices they were offering were all telling them of Jesus. The Lord's coming had fulfilled and filled out the picture that the Old Testament sacrifices had drawn. Thus, in carrying them out, the Jews were simply retelling themselves of the coming of the Lord Jesus.

These observances were much like the Lord's Table is for us today. When we take communion, we are dealing with symbols. There is a sense in which those symbols are telling again the story of the life, death, and resurrection of Jesus. Doing this does not make us any better, but it reminds us. This was the function of these Jewish rituals. They were reminders of what the Lord Jesus had come to do. All through the book of Acts we see Jewish Christians entering the temple and offering sacrifices, just as the Lord had done. There is no suggestion that they should have stopped or that it was wrong for them to do this. Until God took the sacrifices away, they were permitted this means of expression. The sacrifices ended when the temple was destroyed in AD 70, when the words of Jesus were fulfilled and Roman armies laid siege to Jerusalem (Matt. 24:66). The city was taken and the Jews were carried away captive, exactly as the Lord Jesus said. But that was several years in the future from this point in history.

Paul's practice was that when he was with the Jews, he became as a Jew; when he was with the Gentiles, he became as a Gentile, and when he was with the weak, he limited himself and became as weak as they so that he might reach them on their level. He was simply declaring again the freedom he had in Christ. He was free to live as a Gentile among the Gentiles, free to live as a Jew among the Jews, free from the law but free also to keep the law if there were advantages to be gained by so doing.

> *Thank, you, Father, for the freedom you give me to become all things to all men so that more might be won for you. Give me wisdom as I seek to practice this with those around me.*

Learning the distinguishing principles between law and grace will free us to demonstrate them to others. Are we dedicated to learning these truths so that we may freely and responsibly apply them to our relationships?

STRUCK DOWN, BUT NOT DESTROYED

A daily devotion for July 20

Read Acts 21:27–40.

> "As the soldiers were about to take Paul into the barracks, he asked the commander, 'May I say something to you?' 'Do you speak Greek?' he replied. 'Aren't you the Egyptian who started a revolt and led four thousand terrorists out into the wilderness some time ago?' Paul answered, 'I am a Jew, from Tarsus in Cilicia, a citizen of no ordinary city. Please let me speak to the people'" (Acts 21:37–39).

How remarkable that Paul asks to speak to this enraged mob that was ready to tear him limb from limb! If I had been in his shoes I would have been trying to get out of there as fast as possible, quite content to let the mob go. But Paul recognizes this as his opportunity. He has come to Jerusalem determined to speak to his nation. Out of the urgency of his love for the Jews, he wants to be the instrument to reach this stubborn crowd. So he seizes the only chance he has, hoping the Lord will give him success.

The tribune is startled when Paul addresses him in Greek, because this rough Roman officer thought he knew who Paul was. He thought he was that Egyptian who, according to Josephus, a year or so earlier had led a band of desperate men out to the Mount of Olives, promising them that he had the power to cause the walls of Jerusalem to fall down at his command. He was unable to deliver on his promise, and the Romans had made short work of the rebels, killing most of them, but the Egyptian leader had escaped.

But when this tribune heard the cultured accents of Greece he knew that Paul was no assassin. (The rebels were called that because they had concealed daggers in their cloaks, and as they mingled among the people they would strike without warning, killing people at random in cold blood. They were terrorists, trying to strike fear into the Jewish populace and thus to overthrow the Roman government.) And so, impressed by something about the apostle, the tribune lets him speak to this crowd. Amazingly, when Paul indicates with his hand that he wants to speak, a great hush falls.

Reviewing this account, I cannot help but think of a phrase Paul uses in his second letter to the Corinthians: "struck down, but not destroyed" (2 Cor. 4:9 RSV). God will sometimes let us encounter great difficulty, but he never abandons us. He never leaves us alone. He always gives us the power and the courage we need to face our opposition. He finds a way to work everything out and uses it for his glory. God never abandons his people!

> *Thank you, Father, for this wonderful example of how you gave courage and boldness to one who was in great trouble. Grant me the same boldness!*

When we feel struck down by circumstances resulting from our attempts to serve others with the gospel, what will save us from feeling destroyed? Are we learning to count on God's faithful presence with us, in us, and on behalf of his work through us?

TO KNOW HIS WILL

A daily devotion for July 21

Read Acts 22:1–29.

> "A man named Ananias came to see me. He was a devout observer of the law and highly respected by all the Jews living there. He stood beside me and said, 'Brother Saul, receive your sight!' And at that very moment I was able to see him. Then he said: 'The God of our ancestors has chosen you to know his will and to see the Righteous One and to hear words from his mouth. You will be his witness to all people of what you have seen and heard. And now what are you waiting for? Get up, be baptized and wash your sins away, calling on his name'" (Acts 22:12–16).

Paul recounts his conversion experience to the enraged mob. Though these people were ready to kill him, Paul wants to be the instrument to reach this stubborn crowd. So he seizes the only opportunity he has, hoping the Lord will give him success, and he tells of his conversion and specifically the role that Ananias played.

This event is etched into the apostle's memory. Though it occurred thirty years before, he has never forgotten a single detail. This was the moment he was chosen to be an apostle, and Ananias conveyed the commission to him. It had three parts, three aspects of ministry.

First, Paul was chosen to know the will of God. That did not involve where God wanted him to go or what God wanted him to do. Paul had to learn that the will of God is a relationship to his Son. When Paul understood that, he had all the power he needed to do anything God asked him to do.

So many young Christians struggle with this point. They think that God's will is some kind of itinerary they must discover and that if they can find where God wants them to go and what he wants them to do next, they can do his will. No. The Scriptures make clear that the will of God is a relationship. It is an attitude of expectancy that Jesus Christ, living in us, will work through us. When we expect him to do that, we are in the will of God. Everything we do is in the will of God. We may do anything we like, then, because it will be in God's will unless the Holy Spirit within us indicates otherwise, according to his Word. That is what Paul learned—the power by which a Christian lives his life.

Next, Paul looks back and says, "This is what made me an apostle. I have seen Jesus Christ many times. He has appeared to me and talked to me. He told me the things that the other apostles learned when they were with him as disciples. That is how I know these things." Motivated by the love of Jesus Christ and an awareness of the majesty of his person, Paul pushed on ceaselessly, out into the far regions of earth, performing his apostolic ministry.

Finally, Paul heard from the Lord's mouth what his message was to be—to declare what Jesus Christ had said to him. It was the same message Jesus had given to the Twelve in the days of his flesh. That is how they knew that Paul was a true apostle—because he knew what they knew. That constitutes the same message that God has for all of us today—the words of his mouth, which Jesus had given to the apostle Paul.

> *Father, thank you for commissioning me to bear witness to your great work in my life. Help me to be faithful to that call.*

What are three vital aspects of Paul's calling that apply to all who seek to know and to follow God's will? Do we attempt to define or limit his will to a specific place or a particular activity?

WHEN THE FLESH RULES

A daily devotion for July 22

Read Acts 23:1–5.

> "Paul looked straight at the Sanhedrin and said, 'My brothers, I have fulfilled my duty to God in all good conscience to this day.' At this the high priest Ananias ordered those standing near Paul to strike him on the mouth. Then Paul said to him, 'God will strike you, you whitewashed wall! You sit there to judge me according to the law, yet you yourself violate the law by commanding that I be struck!' Those who were standing near Paul said, 'How dare you insult God's high priest!' Paul replied, 'Brothers, I did not realize that he was the high priest; for it is written: "Do not speak evil about the ruler of your people"'" (Acts 23:1–5).

What a left-footed beginning! There is a noticeable reckless audacity about the apostle in his introduction. He seems almost careless about the consequences of what he says—like a man burning his bridges behind him. I suspect that Paul is aware by now that he has blundered into an untenable situation, and so he is trying to bull his way through, no matter what.

He does not begin with his usual courtesy. The customary address to the Sanhedrin was a standardized form that began, "Rulers of Israel and elders of the people." Paul does not employ that but instead puts himself on the same level with these rulers, addressing them simply with the familiar term *brothers*. That is an offense to these Jews. He also implies that there is no possible ground for complaint against him. This was certainly true. Yet Paul seems to imply that there is no reason for this meeting at all, that it is absurd to have called this council together.

So for this seeming impudence, the high priest commands that he be slapped across the mouth. That was an unusually degrading form of insult to an Israelite, and Paul's anger flashes out at this offense. He whips back this sharp, caustic retort: "God shall strike you, you whitewashed wall!" That was a typically Judaistic way of calling the high priest a bloody hypocrite. It certainly is not the most tactful way for a prisoner to address a judge. Paul likely recognized who Ananias was, but he did not know that Ananias had recently been appointed high priest. The moment it is pointed out to him that Ananias is indeed the high priest, Paul is repentant, for he recognizes that he is in the wrong. He apologizes, for the law says that the office deserves respect, even if the man does not.

This should not surprise us. The apostle has gone to Jerusalem in direct disobedience of the Holy Spirit. He has thereby put himself in the position of being mastered and controlled by the flesh, that principle of evil inherent in every one of us. Remember that Paul himself is the one who tells us that if we yield ourselves as servants to the flesh, we become the servants of what we obey (Rom. 6:16). In other words, if we give way to the flesh in one area, other areas of our lives will be affected. If we give way, the flesh always carries us further than we want to go. It sits at the controls of our lives and rules us whether we like it or not. No matter what we try to do, it all comes out fleshly.

Father, reveal to me the areas in which I have allowed the flesh to be in control. Teach me to walk not in the flesh but in the Spirit.

Are we acknowledging the reality of lifelong encounters with the flesh, that inherent principle of evil? Are we learning to recognize its subtleties, invoking and submitting to the power of Christ's indwelling life?

RESTORATION!

A daily devotion for July 23

Read Acts 23:6–35.

> "The following night the Lord stood near Paul and said, 'Take courage! As you have testified about me in Jerusalem, so you must also testify in Rome'" (Acts 23:11).

What the Lord Jesus in effect says as he appears to the apostle is, "Cheer up, Paul." That is certainly a revelation of the state of Paul's heart at this time. He is anything but cheerful. He is defeated and discouraged, wallowing in an awful sense of shame and failure, but he is not abandoned. Isn't it wonderful that the Lord comes now to restore him to his ministry?

I am sure that Luke does not give us the full account of what transpired between Paul and his Lord on that night. But there is enough here that we can see what our Lord is after. He restores Paul to usefulness. He promises Paul success in the desire of his heart, which was second only to his desire to win his kinsmen: that he might bear witness for Christ at the heart of the empire, the capital of the Gentile world. Paul had announced that after he went to Jerusalem, he must go to Rome. And as he wrote to the Roman Christians, his prayer was that he might be allowed to come to them. The Lord Jesus now gives that mission back to him.

And yet the form he employs contains a hint of the limitation that Paul had made necessary when he disobeyed the Spirit of God. The Lord Jesus puts it this way: "As you have testified about me in Jerusalem, so you must bear witness also in Rome." The emphasis here is upon the manner in which this witness will go forth. "In the way that you bore witness to me in Jerusalem, in that same way you must bear witness in Rome." And how had Paul testified in Jerusalem? It was as a prisoner—chained, bound, limited.

This encounter with the Lord Jesus must have been a wonderful moment for Paul. The Lord restored him to spiritual health, as he often must do with us. Have you ever been in this circumstance? Have you ever disobeyed God, knowing that you shouldn't have but wanting something so badly that you've gone ahead anyway? How wonderful to have the Lord ready to restore you. I have been there too, so I know how God can tenderly deal with us and bring us back to a place of being yielded.

After this Paul is his usual self again. From here on the things he says and does have that same wonderful infusion of the Spirit's power that makes unusual things happen. And from Rome he will write some of his greatest letters—letters filled with power that are still changing the history of the world. The joy of the Lord is back in his heart. The glory returns to his ministry. The love of Jesus Christ fills him, empowering and enriching him. That is the glory of being a Christian. We can be forgiven. We do not have to wait. And we do not have to pay for anything. We do not have to try to placate God in some way because of what we have done. We must make things right, as far as we can, with anyone we have wronged—but we can be forgiven and all the glory of our relationship with the Lord restored.

Father, thank you for your restoring love, for never abandoning me, and for keeping me and bringing me back.

How do we respond to God's incomparably tenacious and enduring love? Do we receive such love with deep, humble gratitude? Do we frustrate this love with our futile efforts to repay him—assuming that to be possible? Or do we persist in defying his love by refusing his sovereign and wise authority?

DISCIPLINE OF DELAY

A daily devotion for July 24

Read Acts 24:1–23.

> "Then Felix, who was well acquainted with the Way, adjourned the proceedings. 'When Lysias the commander comes,' he said, 'I will decide your case.' He ordered the centurion to keep Paul under guard but to give him some freedom and permit his friends to take care of his needs" (Acts 24:22–23).

This is an account of one of God's inscrutable delays, which often afflict us. We think that something we want to have happen is just around the corner. Then as we move toward it we find that it seems to move away from us, to recede from us, to elude us. Sometimes it takes us months or years to reach a point that we thought was right there. These circumstances raise questions in our minds and hearts. So it is with the apostle. Here we begin to see God's discipline of delay.

Felix doesn't need to have Lysias come down. He has already received from him a letter exonerating Paul. But he uses this as an excuse so that he might hear something more from the apostle. Felix's curiosity has been awakened. As Luke tells us, he knows something about Christianity, and he wants to hear more. So he retains Paul in custody, even though he has every legal right to set him free.

We shouldn't blame Felix, because he is being used as an instrument to carry out God's purposes with Paul. This is the work of a loving, heavenly Father who is concerned with a beloved son. Remember that Paul, by disobedience despite the consistent warnings of the Holy Spirit, had chosen the pathway that led to bonds and imprisonment. He had disobeyed the direct command of the Spirit that he should not go up to Jerusalem.

There is an important lesson here for us. When we disobey God and are later forgiven, as Paul was forgiven and restored, that forgiveness does not change the pathway we have chosen. God doesn't eliminate the trials and the difficulties we have deliberately assumed. But forgiveness restores to that pathway all the power and the joy that we experienced before walking in disobedience. This is what happens here with Paul. When he was restored to the fellowship of Jesus by the Lord's appearance to him in prison in Jerusalem, that pathway of imprisonment was not canceled. He remains a prisoner, and ahead of him lie two long, weary years of waiting in Caesarea and three more in Rome as a prisoner of the Lord. God doesn't eliminate that, but he does transform it into a fruitful experience for the apostle.

That is the point this whole section is making for us. We see Paul now going ahead, bound as a prisoner, yet finding that God's power and glory can work in him just as freely through the channel of imprisonment as they did when he was free. The imprisonment was not comfortable. It added a good deal of agony and heartache to the apostle's experience. But he accepted it as God's provision for him and found it to be no less the instrument of God's working and power than anything else he had experienced before.

> *Father, thank you for this lesson from the life of this mighty apostle. How faithfully you dealt with him! How deeply he learned these truths! How faithfully he passes them on to me so that I might learn to accept your delays not as denials but as opportunities for enrichment and advancement.*

Time management is a learned discipline. Are we resentful that God has the last word? Or are we learning to rest in his sovereign wisdom and his ways?

THE JUDGMENT TO COME

A daily devotion for July 25

Read Acts 24:24–27.

> "Several days later Felix came with his wife Drusilla, who was Jewish. He sent for Paul and listened to him as he spoke about faith in Christ Jesus. As Paul talked about righteousness, self-control and the judgment to come, Felix was afraid and said, 'That's enough for now! You may leave. When I find it convenient, I will send for you.' At the same time he was hoping that Paul would offer him a bribe, so he sent for him frequently and talked with him" (Acts 24:24–26).

Paul told Felix about the judgment to come. A time will come when every life will be evaluated, when each human being will suddenly find himself standing naked before God, with all his life laid out for everyone to see. Then to all will be evident the value, or the lack of it, of that life. Jesus spoke of this. He said that there will come a time when what is spoken in secret shall be shouted from the housetops and when what is hidden shall be revealed. All the secrets of the heart and everything done in secret shall be displayed.

Undoubtedly Paul pointed out to Felix that God is aware of the hearts of men; he does not merely read the outside. We are content if we can fool people by the exterior of our lives. But Paul laid before the governor the fact that he was dealing with a God who reads the heart. Wouldn't it be interesting if we had a television camera that could record thoughts? Suppose that this camera was on you and that all the thoughts running through your mind this last hour were recorded on videotape. What would you think if it was announced that next Sunday morning at church this would be played back on a screen?

That is exactly what God is talking about—a time when everyone will see the life of everyone else, exactly as it was, with nothing hidden, nothing covered over, all of it there. Then the great question will be: "What did you do with Jesus Christ?" When Paul reasoned this way before the governor, he was afraid. It all came home to him. The logic of it hit him right between the eyes. But this was his response: "That's enough for now! You may leave. When I find it convenient, I will send for you." Felix procrastinated. He had a hunger for God, but he also wanted money from Paul.

Jesus said, "Seek ye first the kingdom of God, and his righteousness, and all other things shall be added to you" (Matt. 6:33 KJV). But you can't put them on the same level of priority. You can't want God and money. That is what destroys men. That is what blinded this man so that he could not see the importance of this moment. He had one of the greatest opportunities ever afforded a human being—to spend hours with the apostle Paul—but he passed it by. "Go away," he said, "until I have a more convenient time." Are there any sadder, more pathetic words? And though Felix called Paul to him and talked with him often, he was never afraid again. That is the danger that men face when they are confronted with the reality of Jesus Christ and do nothing about it. Their hearts are hardened.

Thank you, Lord Jesus, for making provision to have your righteousness cover me on the day of judgment.

Do we welcome full disclosure of our sinful thoughts and actions so that we may experience God's amazing, gracious forgiveness? Does unbroken communion with him trump prideful cover-ups?

BY FAITH IN ME

A daily devotion for July 26

Read Acts 25:1–26:23.

> "Now get up and stand on your feet. I have appeared to you to appoint you as a servant and as a witness of what you have seen and will see of me. I will rescue you from your own people and from the Gentiles. I am sending you to them to open their eyes and turn them from darkness to light, and from the power of Satan to God, so that they may receive forgiveness of sins and a place among those who are sanctified by faith in me" (Acts 26:16–18).

Here is the heart of Paul's message before King Agrippa—his own transforming experience with Jesus Christ. In a nutshell he lays the good news out before the king. What a marvelous declaration of the gospel! Here from the words of Jesus himself, as Paul recalls hearing them on the road to Damascus, is an accurate analysis of the problem with humanity. What is the matter with people? "They are blind," Jesus says, "blind and living in darkness."

Two thousand years later that is exactly what remains wrong with our world. People do not know where to turn; they do not know where the answers lie. They do not even know how to analyze the problems accurately; they cannot see what is happening. They cannot predict the end of courses they adopt or of the forces they loose. They do not know where they are going. They are utterly blind, like men staggering around in a dark room, groping to find their way. This sense of being lost pervades our society. Two thousand years later we can see the truth of Jesus's words. How accurately he analyzes the problem!

Then the Lord Jesus analyzes why men are blind. "Because," he says, "they are under the power of Satan." Behind the darkness is the great enemy of humanity, who is distorting the thinking of men, clouding their eyes, and spreading widespread delusions. He has loosed into this world a great flood of lying propaganda. And everywhere today men and women have believed these delusions and lies.

We hear them on every side. All the commonly accepted philosophies of our day reflect the basic satanic lie that we are adequate and independent, able to run our own affairs. We also hear that if we live for ourselves, take care of "number one," we will find advancement and fulfillment in life. And we hear that material things can satisfy us, that if we get enough money, we will be happy. All these lies permeate our society. That is the power of Satan.

The power of the gospel is that it turns men from the power of Satan to the power of God, from darkness to light. God has found a way to forgive men's sins, to wipe out all the guilt from the mistakes of the past, from all that they have done in their ignorance and enslavement to the lying propaganda of Satan, and to give them a resource from which they may live in fulfillment and strength. That is what Jesus means by "a place among those who are sanctified." How do you get this? Jesus says precisely, "By faith in me." That is why we believe him when he says, "I am the way, the truth, and the life; no man can come unto the Father but by me." We have no other choice, because it was Jesus himself who said that all this happens "by faith in me." Wherever men have turned to him, they have indeed turned from darkness to light and from the power of Satan to the power of God.

Father, how grateful I am that this same mighty, delivering power is just as available to people today, that you can turn them from darkness to light and from the power of Satan to God, forgive their sins, set them free, and give them an inheritance, a new position, a new resource from which they may live.

Have we been so affected by Jesus, the Light of the World, that we are passionate to spread his light into the deep, dark blindness that holds this world hostage to the Enemy? Do our lives demonstrate the transcendent wisdom and power of Jesus? Are we spreading the fragrance of Jesus everywhere?

THAT YOU MAY BECOME WHAT I AM

A daily devotion for July 27

Read Acts 26:24–32.

> "'King Agrippa, do you believe the prophets? I know you do.' Then Agrippa said to Paul, 'Do you think that in such a short time you can persuade me to be a Christian?' Paul replied, 'Short time or long—I pray to God that not only you but all who are listening to me today may become what I am, except for these chains'" (Acts 26:27–29).

As Paul continues speaking to Agrippa, he says, "King Agrippa, do you believe the prophets? I know that you believe." He is saying, "You know the historical facts of Jesus's life. You believe the prophets. So put the two together. What did the prophets say the Messiah would do? Where does that drive you? Jesus fulfilled what the prophets wrote."

At this point the enslaved king, mastered by his own lusts, is confronted with the issue. You can see him squirming on his throne. Unfortunately, his answer is to turn his back on what Paul says. It is a little difficult to understand exactly what he replied. The Greek is a bit obscure. Certainly he didn't say what we have in the King James Version: "Almost thou persuadest me to be a Christian." He was not saying, "You've almost got me, Paul. You almost have me convinced." Many a message has been preached on that theme, as though Agrippa had almost reached the point of becoming a Christian. It is much more likely that he said with almost sneering sarcasm, "Do you really think that in this short a time you're going to make me a Christian? You've got to do a lot more than that if you're going to make me a Christian!"

Paul's reply is magnificent. With a heavy heart he says, "King Agrippa, whether I spend a short time or a long time with you, I just want you to know that the hunger of my heart is that not only you, on your throne with your wife beside you, but everyone in this room can be like I am—except for these chains." This is a magnificent answer! It is hardly the answer of a prisoner, is it? As Paul stands there he says, "I wish you could be like I am. I wish you had the peace, the liberty, the power, and the joy of my heart and my life."

What an appeal out of a great heart! What a revelation of the greatness of the gospel! It can rise above every circumstance and fill the heart with joy so that a man in chains, a prisoner, can stand before a king and say, "Even though you are a king and you have all that wealth can buy, I would gladly recommend that you become like I am, so great is this glorious liberty in Jesus Christ." That this chained prisoner could challenge a king upon his throne and offer to trade places with him is a marvelous example of the freedom that the gospel gives.

But remember that Agrippa is a Herod. He is an Edomite, a descendant of Esau, who stands throughout Scripture as a mark of the independent spirit that refuses help from God, that turns its back upon all the love of God poured out to reach us and in arrogance refuses God's grace. That is what this king does. And now he fades from history. He is the last of the line of the Herods. But Paul's great words ring in our ears down through the centuries. There is nothing like the liberty of Jesus Christ. No external condition of wealth or prestige or power is worth a snap of the finger compared with the freedom, the power, and the joy that a man can find in Jesus Christ.

Father, thank you for the freedom you give me in Christ, a freedom so great that no human circumstance can rob me of my joy in you. Please let this freedom and joy make me unashamed of the gospel like Paul.

Are we unfettered from our circumstances, liberated by the transcendent power of our indwelling Savior and Lord? Are we claiming the liberating practice of Christ's presence as the essence of life?

SECRET STRENGTH

A daily devotion for July 28

Read Acts 27:1–26.

> "After they had gone a long time without food, Paul stood up before them and said: 'Men, you should have taken my advice not to sail from Crete; then you would have spared yourselves this damage and loss. But now I urge you to keep up your courage, because not one of you will be lost; only the ship will be destroyed. Last night an angel of the God to whom I belong and whom I serve stood beside me and said, "Do not be afraid, Paul. You must stand trial before Caesar; and God has graciously given you the lives of all who sail with you." So keep up your courage, men, for I have faith in God that it will happen just as he told me'" (Acts 27:21–25).

The twenty-seventh chapter is a fascinating account by Luke of Paul's voyage to Rome and of the shipwreck that occurred on the way. Luke has taken note of the distress of these men. They had for many days been so upset and anxious over the outcome of this voyage that fear had destroyed their appetites and they had not eaten. But Paul stands before these men and announces with absolute conviction, "There will be no loss of life among you but only of the ship." His reason for saying so is that an angel had come to him the night before and had encouraged him with the message that he would stand before Caesar and that he was not to be afraid. Fear had begun to creep even into the apostle's heart, but he was reassured by the angelic messenger. Furthermore the angel had said, "God has given you all those who sail with you." Paul had been praying that the sailors and soldiers accompanying him would be spared as well as that his own goal would be accomplished on this trip. God heard his prayer and granted him their lives.

Notice the tremendous power that a man of faith exercises through the instrument of prayer. God does such mighty things if we will but ask him. He stands ready to grant us much, much more than we have ever imagined. I have often said that the church is the secret government of earth and that it has power to control the events reported in our newspapers. We sometimes feel that we are just helpless pilgrims drifting through this age, waiting to get to heaven. But the Scriptures never portray Christians that way. We are intimately related to the events happening around us, and we have great control over them. Here God granted this one man, because of his prayer, the lives of the 275 individuals who sailed with him. They were spared because Paul prayed for them. What a revelation of the power of prayer!

Notice also the secret help given to the believer in time of distress. Paul was exposed to the same peril as the others, and yet God strengthened him with a word of encouragement during the trial. He didn't remove him from it. The storm was no less severe for Paul than it was for anyone else. The danger was just as evident, the waves were just as high, the darkness just as intense. Everything was exactly the same except that God granted him an encouraging word, a secret knowledge that the others did not possess. He didn't lessen the pressure, but he gave an inward reassurance that enabled Paul to stand out from the rest of the men.

This reveals what the Christian faith is all about. It is a way of discovering resources that others do not know about, making it possible for us to live and to act and react differently from those around us. That is the characteristic of Christianity. That is what it is supposed to be like all the time.

Father, thank you for the hidden resources you provide through prayer and faith amid the storms of life. Teach me to draw from these resources that I might react differently from those around me.

Fear is the natural, instinctive reaction to life's threatening circumstances. What is the supernatural antidote to fear available to us through believing prayer? Are we succumbing to fear or choosing to conquer our fears through prayer in deepening awareness of God's presence and peace?

SAFE ON THE SHORE

A daily devotion for July 29

Read Acts 27:27–44.

> "When daylight came, they did not recognize the land, but they saw a bay with a sandy beach, where they decided to run the ship aground if they could. Cutting loose the anchors, they left them in the sea and at the same time untied the ropes that held the rudders. Then they hoisted the foresail to the wind and made for the beach. But the ship struck a sandbar and ran aground. The bow stuck fast and would not move, and the stern was broken to pieces by the pounding of the surf. The soldiers planned to kill the prisoners to prevent any of them from swimming away and escaping. But the centurion wanted to spare Paul's life and kept them from carrying out their plan. He ordered those who could swim to jump overboard first and get to land. The rest were to get there on planks or on other pieces of the ship. In this way everyone reached land safely" (Acts 27:39–44).

As Paul had been told by God, not a single life is lost. Verse 44 reads almost as a sigh of relief at the end of this chapter: "In this way everyone reached land safely." We can heave that sigh along with them. But now we have questions to answer: Why do shipwrecks come to us when we are doing the will of God? Why is it that Christians face this kind of difficulty?

The Scriptures give us several answers. First, these difficulties are the result of satanic opposition. In his letter to the Romans Paul said that he had tried many times to go to Rome and had been prevented by Satan. The Enemy did not want this mighty apostle, coming in the power of the risen Lord, to move into this city and to start breaking down the stronghold of darkness by which he controlled the entire civilized world. So he delayed Paul every way he could. We will never understand the meaning of the difficulties in our lives if we do not set them against the background of satanic opposition.

It is also well to remember that God had permitted all this. God is greater and stronger than Satan. He could have made the winds fair and had them blow in the right direction. Scripture suggests some reasons God does not always intervene to prevent Satan's work. One is that there were lessons in this for the others who sailed with Paul. Imagine what they learned of a different way of life as they watched this man of faith confronting the same perils they were facing. A baffling element kept him stable despite these circumstances. Repeatedly, he was the man who in the critical moment saved the day. He showed them a new way of life.

There were also lessons for Paul in this. He grew in faith as he learned how faithful God could be and how he could intervene, allowing things to go only so far before drawing a line at the critical moment. Paul tells us that God's strength is made perfect in man's weakness. He grew to understand more about God's love and grace as he endured these dangerous times.

Finally, there is the story of Job, which shows us that even when there is seemingly no explanation in terms of this life for the shipwrecks we suffer, there is still a victory, unknown to us, that honors and glorifies God and makes possible great progress in his kingdom.

> *Father, thank you for the reminder that life is intended to be filled with difficulties and even shipwrecks at times and that it is through these that I learn great lessons along the way.*

Are we surprised and confused when we encounter tests and trials? Are we learning to recognize the strategies of the Enemy and the power of the indwelling Christ made perfect in our weakness? Are we content that when we do not understand, God knows?

TO THE JEW FIRST

A daily devotion for July 30

Read Acts 28:1–28.

> "Three days later he called together the local Jewish leaders. When they had assembled, Paul said to them, 'My brothers, although I have done nothing against our people or against the customs of our ancestors, I was arrested in Jerusalem and handed over to the Romans. They examined me and wanted to release me, because I was not guilty of any crime deserving death. The Jews objected, so I was compelled to make an appeal to Caesar. I certainly did not intend to bring any charge against my own people. For this reason I have asked to see you and talk with you. It is because of the hope of Israel that I am bound with this chain'" (Acts 28:17–20).

In his letter to the Romans Paul said, "For I am not ashamed of the gospel, because it is the power of God that brings salvation to everyone who believes: first to the Jew, then to the Gentile" (Rom. 1:16). Paul always maintained that it was his responsibility to go to the Jew first and then to the Greek. Here we have the last account in Scripture of that priority. He invited the local Jewish leaders to come and see him. He could not go to them, because he was bound to a Roman guard. It is interesting that they responded. They didn't know him, though perhaps they had heard of him. Still, they came because he had been a member of the Sanhedrin.

Paul simply explained his predicament, pointing out that he was an innocent victim of the Jews' strange hostility toward him. He had done nothing against his nation. He himself was a Jew who longed to bless his people and to help them, but he found them antagonistic. When the Jews turned Paul over to them, the Romans wanted to let him go because they could find in him no cause for a death penalty, but the Jews objected. Paul makes clear it was the Jews who were against him, not he against them. He had no charge to bring against his nation.

Isn't that amazing? How gracious is his forgiving spirit! As we read this book we hear how Jewish zealots hounded Paul and caused trouble for him in every city he visited. They had aroused the populace against him, had beaten him, and had caused him to be scourged and stoned. But he speaks not one word of resentment against these people. He freely absolves them of any charge. Then he points out the real reason the Jews so consistently oppose him: "It is because of the hope of Israel that I am bound with this chain" (Acts 28:20). He means, by that phrase, the promised coming of the Messiah.

Is it not remarkable that now, almost two thousand years later, this is still the crucial issue in Israel—the promise of the Messiah? This issue has never been settled and never can be settled. It remains a constant thorn in the side of any Jewish community. If you want to cause a disturbance and arouse an argument, to evoke resentment and yet curiosity, you merely have to raise the issue of the Messiah and you will find today the same kind of reaction that Paul experienced. Jews immediately become deeply concerned and involved. Many, as in Paul's case, are turning to Christ as they reexamine this question. It is still a live issue in our own time.

Thank you, Father, for having a heart for all people. I ask that you open the eyes of the Jewish people to the truth that is in Jesus.

What is our response to persons who are hostile toward Christ and to our profession of faith in him? Do we follow our Lord's example, as did Paul, forgiving and praying for them?

THE END OF THE BEGINNING

A daily devotion for July 31

Read Acts 28:30–31.

> "For two whole years Paul stayed there in his own rented house and welcomed all who came to see him. He proclaimed the kingdom of God and taught about the Lord Jesus Christ—with all boldness and without hindrance!" (Acts 28:30–31).

This is what I like to call the end of the beginning. The book of Acts is just the beginning of the record of the operation of the body of Christ in the world since his resurrection and ascension. It is just the first chapter. We have come now to the last page of that chapter. The rest of the record is being written as history unfolds. Fresh and wonderful chapters are being written in our own day, ultimately to be incorporated into this account. It is a tremendous privilege and joy to be a part of this divine record.

One of the most impressive things about this last section is the two final words. The book of Acts ends with the phrase "without hindrance." That describes the freedom of the gospel. Paul was hindered, still chained day and night to a Roman guard. But he could welcome friends. He could walk around his house and his yard, and he could minister and teach there. Paul never chafed under this restraint. His letters from this period are filled with rejoicing. He never fretted about his condition, but he welcomed all who came and he sent letters back with them. During this time he wrote to Philomen and to the Ephesians, the Colossians, and the Philippians. What tremendous truths are set forth in these letters, which he had time to write because he could no longer travel abroad.

We can be grateful that God kept Paul long enough to write them; otherwise we might have been deprived of these great messages, which have changed history. Still, Paul had to appear before the emperor. In the next year or so, a great persecution broke out under the vicious Emperor Nero, one of the worst that Christians have ever experienced. But the Word was not hindered. No matter what the condition of the church, the Word of God is never bound.

Tradition and other Scripture suggest to us that at the end of a two-year period, Paul was released. Eventually he was arrested again. This time, instead of being allowed to live in a hired home, he was thrown into a dark and slimy dungeon. There he wrote his second letter to Timothy, which reflects the conditions of that confinement—cold and dank, lonely and isolated. Finally, according to tradition, he was led out one day in the early spring and taken outside the walls of Rome. There he knelt down and a sword flashed in the sun. His head was cut off, and the apostle went home to be with the Lord.

If we will be obedient to what is set forth in such clear language in the book of Acts, God will supply all the power and the vitality we need. The sweeping changes made possible by the life of Christ in his body can occur among us today just as they occurred in that first century. The power available to us is exactly the same. The conditions of the world are exactly the same. The life of the body of Christ is to go on in this century exactly as it was lived in the first. And may God grant that we will be men and women of faith, with vigor and vision, willing to move with the creative, innovative Spirit in our day and age so that we might share in the triumphs of the gospel, as recorded in Acts.

> *Father, thank you for the challenge of this book, for what it has already meant to me, and for what it can mean to me in the days and years ahead. Thank you for the challenge of the apostle's life. How I am stirred today to be faithful to the same great cause for which he gave his life!*

God's method of proclamation is through his people! Are we limiting the spread of the good news by our apathy? By deliberate disobedience? Because of fear of rejection or persecution? Do we realize the enormous consequences of our response to this incomparable opportunity?

JEREMIAH

Profile of Courage

An introduction for the month of August

Imagine yourself as that preacher. Imagine how you would feel when no one listens to you and persecution hounds you every step of the way. You feel abandoned and alone; all your friends turn from you. And if you try to quit and refuse to be this kind of a preacher, you find that you cannot quit—that the Word of God burns in your bones and that you have to speak even if you would prefer to be silent.

Now perhaps you can understand why Jeremiah, of all the prophets, was unquestionably the most heroic. Isaiah wrote more exalted passages and may have seen more precisely the coming of the Messiah and the fullness of his work. Other prophets spoke more clearly concerning future events that were to be fulfilled, but Jeremiah was outstanding among the prophets as a man of dauntless courage. For many years he endured persecution without quitting. As you read through this book you can see that here was an amazing man.

Jeremiah lived in the final days of a decaying nation. He was the last prophet to Judah, the southern kingdom. Judah continued on after the ten tribes of the north had been carried into captivity under Assyria. (Isaiah prophesied about sixty years earlier than Jeremiah.) Jeremiah appeared at the close of the reign of the last good king of Judah, the boy king Josiah, who led the last revival the nation experienced before it entered captivity. This revival was rather superficial; in fact, the prophet Hilkiah had told Josiah that though the people would follow him in his attempt to reform the nation and to return to God, they would do so only because they loved him and not because they loved God.

Jeremiah came in right in the middle of the reign of King Josiah, and his ministry carried on through the reign of King Jehoahaz, who was on the throne only about three months. Then came King Jehoiakim, one of the most evil kings of Judah, followed by the three-month reign of Jehoiachin, who was captured by Nebuchadnezzar and taken into captivity in Babylon. And Jeremiah was still around at the time of Judah's last king, Zedekiah, at the end of whose reign Nebuchadnezzar returned, utterly destroying the city of Jerusalem and taking the whole nation into captivity in Babylon.

Jeremiah's ministry covered about forty years, and during all this time the prophet never once saw any signs of success in his efforts. His message was one of denunciation and reform, and the people never obeyed him. The other prophets saw in some measure the impact of their message upon the nation—but not Jeremiah. He was called to a ministry of failure, and yet he was enabled to keep going for forty long years, to be faithful to God, and to accomplish God's purpose: to witness to a decayed nation.

YOU ARE SPECIAL

A daily devotion for August 1

Read Jeremiah 1:1–5.

"The word of the Lord came to me, saying, 'Before I formed you in the womb I knew you, before you were born I set you apart; I appointed you as a prophet to the nations'" (Jer. 1:4–5).

Is it not remarkable that when God began to talk to this young man whom he had chosen for his ministry, the first thing he did was to tell him, "I love you and have a wonderful plan for your life." Is not that what he was saying? This is the preparation of God. The remarkable thing is that this preparation began long before Jeremiah was even conceived. In other words, God said, "I started getting you ready, and the world ready for you, long before you were born. I worked through your father and your mother, your grandfathers and grandmothers, your great-grandfathers and great-grandmothers. For generations back I have been preparing you." What a remarkable revelation to this young man—that through the generations of the past God had begun to work!

When people face a crisis, they always look for a program, some method with which to attack the problem. When God sets out to solve a crisis, he almost always starts with a baby. All the babies God sends into the world, who look so innocent and so helpless—and so useless—at their birth, have enormous potential. There is nothing impressive in appearance about a baby, but that is God's way of changing the world. That is what God said to Jeremiah: "I've been working before you were born to prepare you to be a prophet, working through your father and your mother and through those who were before them."

If we read this account as though this were something extraordinary that applied only to Jeremiah the prophet, we have misread the whole passage. I often hear people say of some noted person, "When God made him, he broke the mold." That is true, but what we fail to see is that this is true of each one of us. God never made another one like you, and he never will. God never made anyone else who can fill the place you can fill and do the things you can do. This is the wonder of the way God forms human life—that of the billions upon billions who have been spawned upon this earth there are no duplicates. Each one is unique, prepared by God for the time in which he or she is to live. That is the word that came to Jeremiah to strengthen him. "Look," God said, "I have prepared you for this very hour," as he has prepared each of us for this time, for this world, for this hour of human history.

I recently heard a story concerning the death of a young man, a pastor. When he was dying of cancer, his father and his uncle, who were twin brothers, came to see him. After visiting with them a short while, he asked his uncle, "Would you mind if I talk to my dad alone?" His uncle was glad to wait in the hall. When his father came out, he said to his brother, "I want to tell you what David did while we were alone. He called me over to his bed and said, 'Can I put my arms around you?' I stooped over as best I could and let him put his arms around me. 'And now, Dad, would you put your arms around me?' I could hardly keep control of my emotions, but I put my arms around him. Then, with his arms around me, he said, 'Dad, I just want you to know that the greatest gift God ever gave me, outside of salvation itself, was the gift of a father and a mother who love God and taught me to love him, too.'"

That is what God was saying to Jeremiah. "What a gift you have! How I have prepared you for this moment through the generations that lie behind you, that you might live and speak and act in this time in history."

Thank you, Father, that you created me for a unique purpose on earth. Help me to fulfill your special purpose for my life.

Do we measure our significance by worldly approval? Are we committed to following the path of God's choosing? Are we training our children to seek God's direction for their lives?

I WILL BE WITH YOU

A daily devotion for August 2

Read Jeremiah 1:6–8.

> "'Alas, Sovereign Lord,' I said, 'I do not know how to speak; I am too young.' But the Lord said to me, 'Do not say, "I am too young." You must go to everyone I send you to and say whatever I command you. Do not be afraid of them, for I am with you and will rescue you,' declares the Lord" (Jer. 1:6–8).

Jeremiah's response is to shrink from God's call. Many a young man had done that before him. This is what Moses did and Gideon, Isaiah, and other mighty men of God. When God first laid hold of them and set them to a task, they shrank from it. Jeremiah pleads youth and inexperience and, like Moses, says he has no ability to speak. So if you ever feel that way when God calls you to a task, just remember that you are in the prophetic succession! God's servants often start out that way.

As best we can tell, Jeremiah was about thirty years old at this time. That is when young men began their ministry in Judah. Today's young people consider that over the hill, beyond the time a man is capable of doing anything. But that is when God starts. Jesus was thirty years old when he began his ministry. Yet Jeremiah feels his inadequacy, his inexperience, and his inability.

That, I think, marks the sensitivity of this young man. Throughout his prophecy we find him highly responsive and sensitive to what is happening to him. He is called to stand before kings, to thunder denunciations and judgments, to feel the sharp lash of their recrimination against him, to endure their anger and their power, and to suffer with his people as he sees them rushing headlong to self-destruction. He feels this keenly and weeps and laments. The book of Lamentations is made up of the cries of his heart as he senses all that is happening to him. Jeremiah was a sensitive young man and a sensitive prophet.

But God gives him the same answer he has given every other young person who felt this way: "Go, for I am with you. Don't worry about your voice, your looks, your personality, your ability—I will be with you. I will be your voice. I'll speak through you, give you the words. I'll give you the power to stand. I'll give you the courage. I'll be your wisdom. I'll be whatever you need. Whatever demand is made upon you, I'll be there to meet it."

We recognize that this essentially is the new covenant that Jesus makes with all of us. This is what he promises each one of us—that he will be with us in the same way. The promise that encouraged Jeremiah is the same promise made to us in the gospel—that whatever we are, whatever demand is made upon us, "Do not be afraid. Do not shrink back. Do not say, 'I can't do that.'" Remember that God says, "I will be with you, and I will make you able to do it."

Lord, I know that you call those who are not adequate, and I confess that I am among them. Teach me to put my confidence not in my own abilities but in yours.

Do we lose heart when considering the enormity of God's calling in our circumstances? Does God ever leave us alone and undefended? Do we need to reassess the power of his presence and of his provision in us as his servants?

OVER NATIONS

A daily devotion for August 3

Read Jeremiah 1:9–10.

> "Then the Lord reached out his hand and touched my mouth and said to me, 'I have put my words in your mouth. See, today I appoint you over nations and kingdoms to uproot and tear down, to destroy and overthrow, to build and to plant'" (Jer. 1:9–10).

As with Isaiah, God touches Jeremiah's mouth. Isaiah started the same way. God touched his mouth with the coals from the altar and gave him power in speaking. Jeremiah's words then become the key to his power—for this is the living, burning, shattering, building, mighty power of the word of God.

Jeremiah is set over nations and kingdoms. This is no mere poetry. The messages of this book are addressed to all the great nations of the world of that day—to Egypt, to Assyria, even to Babylon in its towering might. Jeremiah is given a word for all these nations. I believe this is repeated in every generation. Here are the nations of the world, with their obvious display of power and pomp, with leaders who are household names, marching up and down, threatening one another, so proud and assertive. But God picks out an obscure young man, thirty years of age, whom no one has ever heard of, from a tiny town in a small country, and says to him, "Look, I have set you over all the nations and kingdoms of the earth. Your word, because it is my word, will have more power than all the power of the nations."

That is a remarkable description of our heritage as Christians in Jesus Christ. James says that the prayer of a righteous man releases great power. When we pray about the affairs of life we can turn the course of nations, as the word of Jeremiah altered the destiny of the nations of his day. When we preach and proclaim the truth of God, even though we are obscure and no one knows who we are, that word has power to change the course of nations.

So Jeremiah is set amid death and destruction, but God says he will plant a hope and a healing. His word is to "uproot and to break down, to destroy and to overthrow"—and that is always the work of God. In a nation there are many things that have to be torn down—things that men trust in—just as in an individual's heart and life there are things that must be destroyed.

I talked with a young man who told me, "I don't understand what's wrong with my marriage. I'm doing everything that I know to do, but our relationship isn't right." I said to him, "Yes, I'm sure there is something wrong, and God will show it to you. There are things you're doing in your marriage that you're not aware of. Right now you are blinded to them. You think things are right, and yet they're not. All this indicates is that there are still things God needs to tear down—perhaps points of pride, moments of discourtesy that you don't recognize, habits and reactions of anxiety, anger, and frustration that you've fallen into or given way to, and you don't even know about them."

We all have areas like these in our lives. The work of God is to open our eyes to these things, to destroy them, and to root them out—and then always to build and to plant. God never destroys just to destroy; he destroys that he might build up again.

> *Father, I pray that I will find the courage of this young man so that I can stand in the day of national danger and disaster and be faithful to my calling.*

We are living in a time of crisis when truth stumbles in the streets. Will we choose to retreat from speaking the truth in love? Or will we stand in the power of our sovereign God against the destructive powers of darkness?

YOU ARE A FORTIFIED CITY

A daily devotion for August 4

Read Jeremiah 1:11–19.

> "'Get yourself ready! Stand up and say to them whatever I command you. Do not be terrified by them, or I will terrify you before them. Today I have made you a fortified city, an iron pillar and a bronze wall to stand against the whole land—against the kings of Judah, its officials, its priests and the people of the land. They will fight against you but will not overcome you, for I am with you and will rescue you,' declares the Lord" (Jer. 1:16–19).

When I was sixteen years old, I was arrested, served a warrant because it was alleged—wrongly, it was proved—that I had been hunting out of season. I remember yet how fearsome it was to receive that warrant for my arrest, to open it up, and to read these words: "The People of the State of Montana versus Ray C. Stedman." I thought, *What unfair odds! The whole population of the state of Montana against me!*

That was what the prophet Jeremiah had to face. All the people of the land, led by their kings and their priests, would be against him. But God said, "Don't you worry. You shall stand. I'll make you a stone, an iron pillar, and a bronze wall against them. Nothing will shake you." And the amazing thing is that though this young man was thrown into a dungeon where he was mired in the mud and put on a bread-and-water diet, though he was ostracized and isolated, rejected and insulted, and finally exiled to Egypt, never once when God asked him to speak did he fail to say the thing God told him to say. What remarkable courage this young man exhibited!

Through all of it, Jeremiah learned four things. He learned the sovereignty of God, his control over the nations of earth. He learned the ruthlessness of God, whose judgments would be unmerciful against his people who persisted in turning away from him. He learned the faithfulness of God always to fulfill his word, no matter what was said. Finally, he learned to suffer with the heart of God, the tenderness of God. This man suffered and wept. He lost hope for a while and cried out, "O that I had never been born!" He felt the awful hurt of his people and wept over them. But he realized that he was feeling the suffering of the heart of God over people who turned him aside and the tenderness of God that drew them back at last despite all their wandering.

Almighty God, how grateful I am that whatever I must face in this world, you will give me the grace I need to face it.

Do we want merely to know about God—or do we want to know God intimately? By what process did Jeremiah learn four essential elements of God's character? How did this knowledge of God fortify Jeremiah to endure unremitting testing and hardship?

DO YOU REMEMBER?

A daily devotion for August 5

Read Jeremiah 2:1–3.

> "The word of the Lord came to me: 'Go and proclaim in the hearing of Jerusalem: "This is what the Lord says: 'I remember the devotion of your youth, how as a bride you loved me and followed me through the wilderness, through a land not sown. Israel was holy to the Lord, the firstfruits of his harvest; all who devoured her were held guilty, and disaster overtook them,' declares the Lord"'" (Jer. 2:1–3).

This is part of the first message of Jeremiah to the nation of Judah. It highlights for us what God has to say to someone who has begun to drift away from him. Have you ever had that problem? I find there are times in my life when, without even realizing it, I have begun to lose some of the fervor, the joy, and the peace that mark the presence of God in my life.

The tragic thing about this condition, as exemplified in the nation of Judah, is that this can happen, but nobody knows what is wrong. That was happening to Judah. The people blamed God for the whole thing. That is what most of us do. Judah said it was God's fault, that he did not keep his promises, did not deliver them at the right time, did not keep the nation from its enemies as he promised. They charged God with gross misconduct and with an inability to keep his promises.

So God had something to say to this nation. He asked the people to look back and to reflect on what life was like when they began a love relationship. God said, "I remember the devotion of your youth, your love as a bride, how you followed me." In marital counseling I have dealt with couples who have been married twenty-five or thirty years but who are having difficulties. They are tense, angry, upset, and sometimes they will not speak to one another. I have had to sit down with couples like that to try to find a way to begin a healing process. Long ago I learned the best way is simply to say, "You know, before we start, I need to get acquainted with you a little bit. Tell me something about yourselves. How did you meet and where?" I can feel the atmosphere soften and their hearts expand a bit as they think back to the days when they were not angry or upset but were in love and as they remember what that meant. Half the battle is won when I can get couples thinking back to what it was like when they first knew each other.

Do you remember those first days in the relationship between you and the Lord—the wonder and the joy of love? The prophet's message here is that at such a time, the loved one is the chief priority of your life. No other relationship is more important. He is preeminent in your affection. This is what God wants you to recall. This is the first thing God says to a heart that has begun to drift: "Remember what it was like when you were secure in my affections, separate unto me, holy to me, and exclusively mine. Remember that you are the firstfruits of my harvest. Remember that you are safe, that I protect you." Do you remember your first days?

Thank you, Father, for the way you call me back to my first love with you.

"The bride eyes not her garments but her dear Bridegroom's face." Have we become so self-consumed we have lost our focus on our bridegroom? Do we need to return to our first love?

THE WAY BACK

A daily devotion for August 6

Read Jeremiah 2:5–30.

> "How can you say, 'I am not defiled; I have not run after the Baals?' See how you behaved in the valley; consider what you have done. You are a swift she-camel running here and there, a wild donkey accustomed to the desert, sniffing the wind in her craving—in her heat who can restrain her? Any males that pursue her need not tire themselves; at mating time they will find her" (Jer. 2:23–24).

If you have ever worked among horses you know what God is talking about. Here is a mare in heat, lusting. A little later on, in chapter 5, he speaks of lusty stallions that keep neighing after their neighbors' wives. God uses these vivid figures to awaken people to where they are. There is a wonderful frankness about the Scriptures that sometimes rebukes the Victorian prudishness we have inherited and often exhibit in talking about some of these things. God intended us to learn from the animal kingdom. He gave animals a different kind of sexuality than he gave us so that we might learn from them and might have a vivid picture of how we look when we lust after everything that comes along and pursue any kick, any thrill, any drive other than God. This picture must have meant a great deal to the people of Judah. They understood what an animal looks like in heat, how eager it is to be satisfied.

During my high school days I worked on a ranch in Montana. One day a group of people came out from town to go horseback riding. Among them were some schoolteachers, and one was my English teacher, who was somewhat of a prude. She was given a stallion to ride. When we were saddling up, the stallion got tremendously excited about a mare nearby. To this day I can vividly recall the bright crimson of her face as she sat on that horse and tried to restrain it while everybody else tried to pretend nothing was happening!

This is the kind of figure God holds up, saying, "That is what you're like" That is us, lusting after everything that comes by, living for kicks, wanting to be satisfied in some way. That covers everything from nonstop television, to endless golf, to the fleshpots of strip clubs, to heroin, to hate and violence. That is what happens when the heart drifts from God into degeneracy.

Father, thank you for calling me to yourself. I do not understand this, but I am grateful. I pray that when I lust after worldly things I will stop pursuing them, return to you, and remain faithful in the living of my life.

"From the best bliss that earth imparts we turn unfilled to Thee again." Are we drinking from polluted streams that can never satisfy our souls' thirst for the Lord God, the fountain of living water?

PAINFUL LOVE

A daily devotion for August 7

Read Jeremiah 7:1–34.

"While you were doing all these things, declares the Lord, I spoke to you again and again, but you did not listen; I called you, but you did not answer" (Jer. 7:13).

The first thing God does when we begin to drift is to warn us what the consequences will be. He is faithful to tell us that "Whoever sows to please their flesh, from the flesh will reap destruction" (Gal. 6:8). There is no way to escape it. Even forgiveness does not remove it. Sin will leave its scars even though the wound is healed. God warns that there will be hurt in our lives, hurt in our hearts, hurt for the loved ones around us. Then he says, "I called you, but you did not answer."

The call of God is a picture of love seeking a response, reminding us of who he is and of how much he loves us, trying in various ways to awaken a response of love and gratitude, to call us back. He is like the father in the story of the prodigal son, watching the horizon for that son to return, longing for him to come back. This is the picture of God, looking after men and women, boys and girls, being faithful to them, longing to have them back, calling them again and again. This is a picture of the patience of God. This may go on for years in some cases. All this time he asks us to pray for those like this, to reach out to them by the power of prayer.

But when that does not work, God has one step left in the program: judgment. Judgment is not his way of saying, "I'm through with you." It is not a mark of abandonment by God; it is the last loving act of God to bring us back. It is the last resort of love. C. S. Lewis put it beautifully when he said, "God whispers to us in our pleasures, speaks in our conscience, but shouts in our pains: it is His megaphone to rouse a deaf world." Every one of us knows that there have been times when we would not listen to God, would not pay any attention to what his Word was saying until one day God put us flat on our backs or allowed us to be hurt badly. Then we began to listen. That is what Jeremiah had to learn. He needed to understand that this nation had reached the place where the only thing that would heal it, the only chance it had left, was the judgment of God—allowing the pain of invasion and the loss of its national place.

This is why, earlier in the chapter, God commanded that prayer for the people cease but that preaching continue. Prayer delays judgment, but preaching hastens it. What this nation needed to restore it and heal it was judgment. So God said, "Don't delay it; don't hold me back. This is what will do the work. Radical surgery is all that is left, so stop praying."

Thank you, Father, for bringing consequences upon me when I resist you so that I learn to walk in your ways.

How do we respond when we experience the consequences of our sinful choices? Are we learning to welcome them as coming from our Father's loving heart and hand?

BOASTING IN GOD

A daily devotion for August 8

Read Jeremiah 9:1–26.

> "This is what the Lord says: 'Let not the wise boast of their wisdom or the strong boast of their strength or the rich boast of their riches, but let the one who boasts boast about this: that they have the understanding to know me, that I am the Lord, who exercises kindness, justice and righteousness on earth, for in these I delight,' declares the Lord" (Jer. 9:23–24).

What a revelation of the greatness of God! Far beyond the greatness of men, a God of wisdom and knowledge and power is at work. The prophet's heart was directed to think of that. Man's wisdom is not enough. "Let not the wise boast of their wisdom." Why not? Because man's wisdom is always partial wisdom. It never sees the whole story; never is it wide enough to take in all the factors involved. It is tunnel vision, narrow and limited. And that is why we always think we have arrived at solutions to problems only to find in a few years that the solution has only made the problem worse. Pollution is a case in point, is it not? So are warfare and all the other great problems that confront us today. Man's wisdom is not enough. It is limited.

No, we cannot trust in the wisdom of man, can we? Nor in the might of man—"let not the strong boast of their strength." Why not? Here is a man with great power and authority, a great force at his command to do what he wants—a dictator, a tyrant. Why does he not have the right to boast? Because his force is directed only at material things. It has no power to oppose an idea or a moral value.

God continues, saying, "Let not the rich boast of their riches." Why not? Because riches can buy only a limited number of things. Jesus spoke of the deceitfulness of riches. Riches give a man a feeling of power that he does not have. They give him a feeling of being loved when he is not and of being respected when he is not respected at all. Riches cannot buy love, joy, peace, and harmony. Many a rich man would give all he possesses for just a few moments of peace or joy.

Then what should we boast in? "Ah, boast in this, Jeremiah, that you know me and that you have available the wisdom of God. True wisdom is the wisdom of God, and you can correct your own faulty, frail human wisdom with my wisdom. You have the might of God at your disposal, greater than anything the world knows, a mighty moral force that is irresistible. You have riches beyond all compare, the simple riches of love, peace, joy, grace, mercy, and truth that no money can buy. Boast in this."

Father, no one has the wisdom to cope with the situations in which we live each day. I pray that I will recognize the necessity of you in my life and will stop boasting in my own resources and boast only in you.

Have we discovered that human wisdom and understanding are flawed, inadequate, and often deceptive? Do we seek first the wisdom and the guidance of God's Spirit, using his Word as our standard?

OUR PROTECTION IS IN GOD

A daily devotion for August 9

Read Jeremiah 11:1–20.

> "But, O Lord of hosts, who judges righteously, who tests the heart and the mind, let me see your vengeance upon them, for to you have I committed my cause" (Jer. 11:20).

Perhaps the central lesson of this book is what happened to Jeremiah as God prepared him to minister in a day of decay. He was called to a strange and difficult ministry. God had to toughen him for the assignments he would be given. So Jeremiah was plunged into a more difficult time than he had ever known, a troubled time for the nation.

For the third time in young Jeremiah's ministry, God sent him to the nation with a word of warning and denunciation. God told him, "Therefore do not pray for this people, or lift up a cry or prayer on their behalf, for I will not listen when they call to me in the time of their trouble" (Jer. 11:14 RSV).

This was what distressed Jeremiah so much—that God would not even let him pray for the people. He had laid a vocal quarantine on Jeremiah and had said, "I do not want you to pray, for prayer delays judgment." This had a great effect upon Jeremiah. From here on we see God's toughening of this young man in preparation for what would come.

Jeremiah found something happening that threw him into consternation. He learned that his neighbors and friends were plotting to take his life: "The Lord made it known to me and I knew; then thou didst show me their evil deeds. But I was like a gentle lamb led to the slaughter" (Jer. 11:18–19 RSV). Jeremiah realized how naive and blind he had been to trust these neighbors and friends.

"I did not know it was against me they devised schemes, saying, 'Let us destroy the tree with its fruit, let us cut him off from the land of the living, that his name be remembered no more'" (Jer. 11:19 RSV). Jeremiah was dismayed that his friends would refuse to support him and would betray him in this way. He came to the Lord and cried out, "But, O Lord of hosts who judges righteously, who tries the heart and the mind, let me see thy vengeance upon them, for to thee I have committed my cause" (Jer. 11:20 RSV).

Jeremiah did the right thing. He brought his problem to the Lord. Some of us do not bother to do that when a trial strikes. We run to somebody else. But he brought it to the Lord. Yet he was a thoroughgoing evangelical, for though he brought his problem to the Lord, he had with it a complete plan for how God ought to solve it!

Father, help me lay aside my pride and commit myself to you and to your causes, for you are my protector always.

How do we respond when God's response differs from our understanding? Do we presume to counsel him? Or have we learned that his wisdom, his presence, and his power are everything we need for every situation?

CAN YOU COMPETE WITH HORSES?

A daily devotion for August 10

Read Jeremiah 12:1–17.

> "How long will the land lie parched and the grass in every field be withered? … 'If you have raced with men on foot and they have worn you out, how can you compete with horses? If you stumble in safe country, how will you manage in the thickets by the Jordan?'" (Jer. 12:4–5).

Jeremiah cries out to God with some troubling questions on his mind. These are the standard questions people ask when things go wrong in an individual life, in the life of a community, or in the life of a nation. I heard recently that a well-known and well-liked high school girl had disappeared mysteriously a few days before and that no one knew where she was. All her high school friends prayed for her. She was a Christian, and they were sure that God would protect her. But word came that her body had been found. She had been abused and killed. These young people were stunned, and they were asking the same question: "Why? If there's a God of love and power, why couldn't he have done something about it? If he is a God of power, he could act. If he is a God of love, he would want to act. Why does he sit there and let things like this happen?" That is one of the great questions thrown at our faith. For this very reason Jeremiah is crying out to God.

God's response is interesting. In essence, he says, "Jeremiah, what are you going to do when it gets worse? If these kinds of things throw you, if your faith is challenged and you are upset and you cry out to me and ask these questions, what are you going to do when it gets much worse? Then where will you turn? What will you stand on then? If you have been running with the men on foot and have gotten tired, what will you do when you have to run against horses? And if in running through the open prairie you fall down, what will you do when you have to struggle through a hot, sweaty jungle, whose thick growth impedes your progress in every way?" These are searching questions, are they not?

We know that Jesus said that as we near the end, there will come earthquakes and famines and wars, with nation rising up against nation, and that frightening things in the sea—the roaring of the waves—would make men afraid. And he called all this "the beginnings of sorrow"—merely the beginnings. God's question to Jeremiah—and to us—is, "If faith grows cold, faint, and weak amid today's pressures, what will you do when things get worse? How will you compete with horses when you give in against men on foot?"

Jeremiah expects God to lift the burden. I think most of us are due for a shock when we reach that stage in Christian development where we expect God to work out all our problems on easy terms, and then one day he doesn't do it! That is always a shocking time, and that is where Jeremiah is right now. God does not say, "Don't worry, Jeremiah. I'll work out your problems. I'll take care of everything. You won't have any more strain. Go right back to work." He says, "Jeremiah, it's going to get worse, a lot worse; what are you going to do then?"

Lord, grant me the strength I need to be prepared for whatever may come my way. I know I don't have the strength within myself to endure, but you can strengthen me to manage even in the thickets by the Jordan.

God does not coddle our fears with false promises. Are we establishing habits of trust today that will carry us through the increasing hardships and tests of tomorrow?

HE DOES NOT BUDGE

A daily devotion for August 11

Read Jeremiah 14:1–22.

> "Then the Lord said to me, 'Do not pray for the well-being of this people. Although they fast, I will not listen to their cry; though they offer burnt offerings and grain offerings, I will not accept them. Instead, I will destroy them with the sword, famine and plague.' But I said, 'Alas, Sovereign Lord! The prophets keep telling them, "You will not see the sword or suffer famine. Indeed, I will give you lasting peace in this place"'" (Jer. 14:11–13).

Jeremiah goes on to describe the land, how the cisterns have no water, the ground is parched, there is no rain on the land, the crops are dried up, wild asses stand and pant, and there is no water in all of the land. This is part of the judging hand of God.

Once again this arouses questions in Jeremiah's heart. He asks, "Though our iniquities testify against us, act, O Lord, for thy name's sake" (Jer. 14:7 RSV). He is saying, "I understand that you have to judge this people because of their wickedness, Lord, but what about you? You're the healer; you're the God who can restore wicked people. For your name's sake, do this." "For our backslidings are many, we have sinned against thee. O thou hope of Israel, its savior in time of trouble, Why shouldst thou be like a stranger in the land, like a wayfarer who turns aside to tarry for a night? Why shouldst thou be like a man confused, like a mighty man who cannot save? Yet thou, O Lord, art in the midst of us, and we are called by thy name; leave us not" (Jer. 14:6–9 RSV).

Have you ever come to that place? Many a man of God, in the record of the Scriptures, turned away the judging hand of God by pleading for the glory of God himself. Moses did, Samuel did, and others had stood before God and said, "Regardless of what we're like, God, remember what you're like. Surely, for your name's sake you won't let this thing happen, lest your name be defiled among the nations." And this is Jeremiah's cry. That is great praying. Jeremiah is reaching out to God on the highest level of prayer possible. He calls to God in these terms, and he closes the chapter with an eloquent plea to him. Consider these words:

> Hast thou utterly rejected Judah? Dost thy soul loathe Zion? Why hast thou smitten us so that there is no healing for us? We looked for peace, but no good came; for a time of healing, but behold, terror. We acknowledge our wickedness, O Lord, and the iniquity of our fathers, for we have sinned against thee. Do not spurn us, for thy name's sake; do not dishonor thy glorious throne; remember and do not break thy covenant with us. Are there any among the false gods of the nations that can bring rain? Or can the heavens give showers? Art thou not he, O Lord our God? We set our hope on thee, for thou doest all these things. (Jer. 14:19–22 RSV)

That is great praying, is it not? But look at God's answer: "Then the Lord said to me, 'Though Moses and Samuel stood before me, yet my heart would not turn toward this people. Send them out of my sight, and let them go! And when they ask you, "Where shall we go?" you shall say to them, "Thus says the Lord: Those who are for pestilence, to pestilence, and those who are for the sword, to the sword; those who are for famine, to famine, and those who are for captivity, to captivity"'" (Jer. 15:1–2 RSV).

God does not budge an inch. Now, what are you going to do with a God like that? When God becomes that immovable, it is a great threat to faith. But God is not through with Jeremiah. Though he seems to be adamant, harsh, and unyielding and repeats his threats to the nation and refuses to be moved, he has something yet to say.

Father, regardless of my situation may I hold to your truth as being unshakable.

Do we resort to counseling God in our prayers? Are we acknowledging that his judgments are unsearchable and his ways inscrutable? Do we wrestle with God, or do we nestle in his sovereign character?

THE TRUTH ABOUT OUR HEARTS

A daily devotion for August 12

Read Jeremiah 17:1–18.

"The heart is deceitful above all things and beyond cure. Who can understand it?" (Jer. 17:9).

In those two lines we have the explanation for all the misery, heartache, injustice, and evil of life. It all stems from that. The heart, the natural life into which we were born, has two things wrong with it. First, it is desperately corrupt. This means it never can function as it was designed to do. It can never fulfill all we expect of it. It will never fulfill our ideals or bring us to the place where we can be what we would like to be. It is infected with a fatal virus and cannot be changed. There is nothing we can do about it. The heart is useless and wasted. Therefore there is only one thing it is good for—to be put to death. That is exactly what the Lord Jesus Christ did with it when he died some centuries later. He took that fatal nature, human nature, and he put it to death.

I know that many people have trouble at this point. This is the verse, among others like it in the Scriptures, that divides humanity right down the center. You either believe this verse and act according to these terms for the rest of your life, understanding this fact, or you deny it and say, "It is not true; man is basically good." It is either one side or the other. Your whole system of philosophy, of education, and of legislation, and everything else, will be determined by which one of those views you take. This is the great divide of humanity.

One of the greatest confirmations of the truth in this verse is the Constitution of the United States of America. Our founding fathers were so aware of this great fact—that man, by nature, is desperately corrupt—that they never trusted a single man, even the best of them, with ultimate power. They set up checks and balances by which any man in office, even the most admired of men, would have his power scrutinized by others. They did not trust anybody, and rightly so! No system of philosophy, of psychology, of education, will ever eliminate the evil failing of the human heart. It cannot be done. We must face life on those terms.

As if that were not bad enough, there is another quality about the heart: it is deceitful above all things. It never looks quite as bad as it really is. It has an amazing power to disguise itself and to look good and hopeful and fair—even admirable. That is what is so deceitful about the heart. This explains why, all through the centuries, men keep trying to make their hearts seem better. We want to think we are just a few steps from success. Most of the approaches of humanity are equivalent to taking a well with poisoned water and improving it by painting the pump!

The heart is clever, crafty; it can appear one way when it is quite another. We know that we have a frightening ability to hide a hateful heart under flattering words and that we can speak softly and lovingly to someone whom we utterly despise. We do it all the time. We can use a sweet tone and act and sound as if we are perfectly at ease when inwardly we are seething with rebellion. That is the heart. It has this ability. It can appear fair. It can make the most impressive vows to do better. It can promise reform and suffer hardship.

That is the heart, and the only books in the world that tell you this are the Bible and those based upon it. You will never find that information in any other source. All studies of humanity will never lead you to this revelation. This is God himself, opening up a truth that divides the world but that men must know if they are going to face life the way it really is.

Precious Lord, how I thank you for providing in the cross of Christ a way for me to be delivered from this nature, which is "deceitful above all things, and desperately corrupt."

Do we cling to the myth of our perfectibility, or do we reckon our old self crucified with Christ so that we need no longer be enslaved to it? Are we exchanging the old self-life for the indwelling life of Christ?

THE TRUE SABBATH

A daily devotion for August 13

Read Jeremiah 17:19–27.

> "But if you are careful to obey me, declares the Lord, and bring no load through the gates of this city on the Sabbath, but keep the Sabbath day holy by not doing any work on it, then kings who sit on David's throne will come through the gates of this city with their officials … But if you do not obey me to keep the Sabbath day holy by not carrying any load as you come through the gates of Jerusalem on the Sabbath day, then I will kindle an unquenchable fire in the gates of Jerusalem that will consume her fortresses" (Jer. 17:24, 27).

What a strange message to send! Why is God so concerned about the Sabbath all through the Bible and especially here in the last days of this nation? Why does he focus on the Sabbath? It is amazing how this message about the Sabbath has been distorted in the understanding of men in the church through the ages.

The Sabbath began when God ceased from the work of creation and rested on the seventh day. He ceased from all his works. He tells man all through the Scriptures that this is a picture of the life of faith and of trust in him. That life of faith is to cease from our own works and to trust in God to work for us. That is keeping the Sabbath. All the ceremonies and rituals surrounding this day illustrate for us what God intends. In the letter to the Hebrews he says, "For whoever enters God's rest also ceases from his labors as God did from his" (Heb. 4:10 RSV).

The Sabbath is a picture of how God intends us to live—not by trusting in ourselves, not by trusting in others or in what they can do but by accepting this new way of life, which is God himself living in us, God himself working through us. We must make our humanity available to him, with our minds, our emotions, our wills, and everything about us, saying, "Lord, here I am. Here's the situation in front of me, the thing I have to do. (Maybe it is my work tomorrow and all through the week. Maybe it is some special demand made upon me by my children, by my husband or my wife. Maybe it is some difficult situation to which I must respond. Lord, how do I meet it? Well, here I am, Lord. You meet it. You meet it in me. I'll do what is necessary, but I'll count on you to do it in me, and you'll be responsible for the results."

That is the Sabbath. That means you are at rest inside, because the strain is not on you but on God. You are at peace because you do not have to be responsible for what happens; he does. That is what it means to approach life at rest. That is the man who never turns dry and barren but who remains strong and fresh amid the drought and the disaster around him. That is the man or woman who remains as a green tree in the time of drought, who stands continually before God in the face of every demand and says, "Heal me, O Lord, and I shall be healed; save me, and I shall be saved."

> *Father, I pray that I may be able to enter into rest, cease from my works, let Christ live through me, and know his victory in me.*

How does our understanding of the Sabbath affect the essence of our Christian life? Are we attempting to live and to serve as Christians with restless vigor?

THE POTTER AND THE CLAY

A daily devotion for August 14

Read Jeremiah 18:1–23.

> "This is the word that came to Jeremiah from the Lord: 'Go down to the potter's house, and there I will give you my message.' So I went down to the potter's house, and I saw him working at the wheel. But the pot he was shaping from the clay was marred in his hands; so the potter formed it into another pot, shaping it as seemed best to him" (Jer. 18:1–4).

I have commented in previous messages about the many things God uses to teach his people, the remarkable visual aids that appear from time to time in this book whereby God imparts lessons to this prophet. Jeremiah was sent down to the potter's house, and there he saw three simple things, conveying to him a fantastic lesson. You may have observed the same things that Jeremiah did, for the art of making a pot has not changed through the centuries. The wheel is now turned by an electric motor, but that is about the only difference. Even this function is still controlled by the foot of the potter. The clay is the same as it has always been. The potter is the same, with his capable hands working to mold the clay into the vessel he has in mind.

What did Jeremiah see in this lesson? First there was the clay. Jeremiah knew, as he watched the potter shaping the clay, that he was looking at a picture of himself, of every man, and of every nation. We are the clay. Isaiah and Zechariah, in the Old Testament, join with Jeremiah in presenting this picture of the potter and the clay. In the New Testament we have Paul in that great passage in Romans 9, reminding us that God is the potter and we are the clay. So Jeremiah saw the clay being molded into a vessel. Then some imperfection in the clay spoiled it in the potter's hand, and the potter crumpled it up and began anew the process of shaping it into a vessel that pleased him.

Jeremiah saw the wheel turning constantly, bringing the clay against the potter's hand. The wheel stands for the turning circumstances of our lives under the control of the potter, for it is the potter's foot that guides the wheel. The lesson is clear. As we are being molded by the great potter, the circumstances of our lives bring us again and again under his hand, under the pressure of his fingers, so that he shapes the vessel according to his will.

Then Jeremiah saw the potter. God, he knew, was the great potter, with an absolute right to make the clay what he wanted it to be. Paul argues this with keen and clear logic: "Shall what is formed say to the one who formed it, 'Why did you make me like this?' Does not the potter have the right to make out of the same lump of clay some pottery for special purposes and some for common use?" (Rom. 9:20–21). Of course he has. The vessel is shaped according to the image in the potter's mind.

So Jeremiah, by watching, learned that an individual or a nation is clay in the great potter's hands. He has a sovereign right to make it what he wants it to be. He has the skill and the design to work with the clay and to bring this to pass. If there be some imperfection in the clay, something that mars the design and spoils the work, the potter simply crushes the clay down to a lump and begins again to make it a vessel according to his mind.

Thank you, Father, for creating me and for shaping me. I trust that you are sovereign in all that you do and that your purpose for me is good.

What are three principles we may learn from the visual aid of potter and vessel? Are we learning to be grateful for the potter's molding of our earthly vessels?

BREAK THE JAR

A daily devotion for August 15

Read Jeremiah 19:1–15.

> "Then break the jar while those who go with you are watching, and say to them, 'This is what the Lord Almighty says: I will smash this nation and this city just as this potter's jar is smashed and cannot be repaired. They will bury the dead in Topheth until there is no more room'" (Jer. 19:10–11).

Jeremiah was told, in the striking figure God employed for the benefit of these people, to take the potter's vessel he had bought and to dash it to pieces on a rock. As they watched it fly into smithereens so that it was impossible to reassemble it back, these people learned that they were dealing with a God whose love is so intense that he will never alter his purpose—even if he has to crush and to break them down again.

That is the way the world sees God now. People see the hell that is coming into our world. And soon it will be worse, according to the prophetic Scriptures. There will be worse signs taking place, worse affairs among men. They will cry out against God as being harsh, ruthless, and vindictive, filled with vengeance, anger, and hatred. That is all the world sees.

But the people of God are taught further truth. Jeremiah had been to the potter's house. He had seen the potter making a vessel, and he knew that love was behind this potter's pressures. He realized that when the vessel was marred, this potter was capable of crushing it down, bringing it to nothing but a lump, and then shaping it again, perhaps doing this repeatedly, until at last it fulfilled what God wanted. That was the great lesson Jeremiah learned at the potter's house and that we can learn there as well.

One of the great lessons we can learn from the New Testament's use of the figure of the potter is in the book of Acts—the incident when Judas brought back the thirty pieces of silver and flung them down at the feet of the priests after having betrayed his Lord. The priests gathered the money, took counsel together, and used the money to buy a potter's field. It was known thereafter as "the field of blood" (Matt. 27:6–10). This again is God's wonderful reminder of the heart of our potter. For if we watch this potter carefully, at work in our lives, we will find that his hands and his feet bear nail prints and that it is through the blood of the potter that the vessel is being shaped into what he wants it to be.

When we are in the potter's hands, feeling his pressures, feeling the molding of his fingers, we can relax and trust him, for we know that this potter has suffered with us and knows how we feel but is determined to make us into vessels "useful to the Master" (2 Tim. 2:21). What a tremendous lesson Jeremiah learned at the potter's house—one that can guide and guard us under the pressures of life.

> *Lord, you have used the trials and the pressures in my life to teach me to surrender to you. I invite you to use these means to continue to mold me into the person you want me to be.*

Are we learning that God's disciplines are evidence of his unquenchable love? How do we respond to this love, which helps make us whole?

JEREMIAH'S COMPLAINT

A daily devotion for August 16

Read Jeremiah 20:1–10.

> "You deceived me, Lord, and I was deceived; you overpowered me and prevailed. I am ridiculed all day long; everyone mocks me. Whenever I speak, I cry out proclaiming violence and destruction. So the word of the Lord has brought me insult and reproach all day long. But if I say, 'I will not mention his word or speak anymore in his name,' his word is in my heart like a fire, a fire shut up in my bones. I am weary of holding it in; indeed, I cannot" (Jer. 20:7–9).

Here, in poetic form, we have the thoughts of Jeremiah while he is in the stocks, waiting for what will happen on the morrow. This is a remarkable account of what the prophet thought while he was imprisoned. He was, to say the least, a profoundly perturbed prophet! Here we get another look at the honest humanity of this man, at the way he faced circumstances just as we do, fear and despair alternating at times with faith and confidence.

The first thing he feels is that God has deceived him. In a bitter cry Jeremiah charges God with having lied to him and with having taken advantage of him. Have you ever felt like that toward God? Jeremiah is probably thinking of the promise with which he began his ministry. God had called Jeremiah as a young man, and Jeremiah had objected. Remembering those words, he is saying, "What happened, Lord? What happened to your promise? You said you'd be with me to deliver me, but here I am in these miserable stocks."

That is the way the heart can easily feel toward God. Like so many of us, Jeremiah took these promises rather superficially. He read into them assumptions God never intended, and so he charges God with lying. That is the one thing God cannot do. He cannot lie. Yet Jeremiah feels, as many of us have felt, that God has failed his promise. I do not know how many times people have said to me, referring to the Word of God, "Well, I know what it says, but it doesn't work!" That is just another way of saying, "God has deceived me; God's a liar!" That was the prophet's predicament.

The second thing Jeremiah finds is that people are mocking him. They cannot answer the keenness of his logic, so they do the only thing they can do—they ridicule his person. That is always the refuge of petty minds. When people cannot handle a logical argument they attack the person and try to destroy him personally. They laugh at Jeremiah, poke fun at him, ridicule him. Mockery is hard for the human spirit to take, and this is getting to Jeremiah.

Third, he discovers an unbearable tension within himself. He says, "Lord, your word is a reproach and derision to me. I wish I had never heard it!" He wants to quit preaching, but he cannot. He is torn with this inner tension—fear and a dislike of proclaiming the truth, because it subjects him only to ridicule and scorn—and yet when he resolves to quit he finds he cannot, because the fire of God is burning in his bones and he has to say something.

Do you know anything of that? Perhaps not about public preaching—not all of us are called to that. But have you ever felt that you had to speak out? Some injustice, some moral perversity, some scandalous conduct, some loveless hypocrisy was occurring, and you could not keep quiet about it. You knew that if you spoke out you would only get into trouble and that nobody would thank you for it. You would only upset the status quo and create strife, but you could not contain yourself. Did you ever feel that way? That is what Jeremiah is experiencing here—a tremendous struggle within himself against the proclamation of the Word of God, which only creates more trouble.

Lord, thank you for allowing me to pour my heart out to you. Keep me from charging you with falsehood. Keep me, Lord, from weakness. But even when I am weak, thank you for the forgiveness and the healing that you manifest in my life.

Are we willing to stand against overt evil and to trust God's sovereign wisdom for the outcome of our witness? When life tumbles in do we question God's prerogative to determine our circumstances?

GOD'S FAITHFULNESS

A daily devotion for August 17

Read Jeremiah 20:11–18.

> "But the Lord is with me like a mighty warrior; so my persecutors will stumble and not prevail. They will fail and be thoroughly disgraced; their dishonor will never be forgotten. Lord Almighty, you who examine the righteous and probe the heart and mind, let me see your vengeance on them, for to you I have committed my cause" (Jer. 20:11–12).

Previously in this chapter, Jeremiah poured out his complaint to the Lord while he was in the stocks. But now faith comes to Jeremiah's rescue and begins to strengthen him. Faith counterattacks to uphold the tottering prophet. Jeremiah is now fighting back against the assault against him. He begins to reckon on reality, to count as truth what God had made known to him. That is the way to handle any frightening situation. You can be almost sure that the way you see it is not really the way it is. This is what you have to remember. It appears to be that way, but it is not that way. Your mind is being assaulted, your thoughts distorted by a naturalistic view of things. The only answer is to begin with God, the unchangeable One, who sees things the way they really are. Start with him and with what he has told you, work from that back to your situation, and you will see it in an entirely different light.

This is what the prophet does here. He starts with God. "The Lord is with me [that is the first thing to remember], and he is a mighty warrior [he knows how to fight, how to repel assaults]; therefore my persecutors will stumble [their plans will not work], they will not overcome me. In fact, they will be greatly ashamed, for they will not succeed." Faith reassures him that this is what will happen. And this is the correct view, because this is what does happen. And so Jeremiah cries out, "Sing to the Lord; give praise to the Lord! He rescues the life of the needy from the hands of the wicked" (Jer. 20:13).

That sounds like the account in Acts 16 of the incident in which Paul and Silas, thrown into the dungeon and thrust into stocks at Philippi, began at midnight to sing praises to God, because their faith was fastened onto him and his greatness and not upon their circumstances. This is what Jeremiah learned to do—to sing praises to the Lord.

What allowed him to do this? Perhaps Jeremiah remembered what God had said to him at the outset: "I am watching to see that my word is fulfilled" (Jer. 1:12). So even though it may take a while, even though things do not go right at first, do not be shortsighted and blame God, for he will "watch over his word to perform it."

Paul sums this up beautifully. In an hour of great turbulence he tells Timothy, "If we are faithless, he remains faithful—for he cannot disown himself" (2 Tim. 2:13).

Thank you, heavenly Father, for this reminder of your faithfulness to the prophet Jeremiah and for your faithfulness to your promises today.

What is our point of reference when evaluating life's perplexing circumstances? Are we training our minds to begin with God's truth and his faithfulness?

TRUE LEADERSHIP

A daily devotion for August 18

Read Jeremiah 22:1–23:8.

> "Do what is just and right. Rescue from the hand of the oppressor the one who has been robbed. Do no wrong or violence to the foreigner, the fatherless or the widow, and do not shed innocent blood in this place" (Jer. 22:3).

Jeremiah stands before King Zedekiah with a message that the leadership of the nation was terribly wrong. Throughout the Bible, leaders are called to be shepherds of the people, watching over and caring for them. This king and others like him had failed to do that. Leaders are to be an example of righteousness and justice before the people. It is a serious matter when elected officials do wrong, because, as Paul makes clear in Romans 13, every leader is a minister of God. He may not be a believer, but he is an agent of God and is to represent God's standard of righteousness. Therefore, when leaders of the land are guilty of wrongdoing, the effect of their wrongdoing is far greater than if they were ordinary citizens. Jeremiah was sent to tell the king that this was what was wrong in his life. Zedekiah had failed to correct the leaders of the land and to be an example of justice and righteousness.

Government leaders are also told, "Do no wrong or violence to the foreigner, the fatherless or the widow." The weak and the helpless are minority groups in any country. Jeremiah tells the king that it is his task to watch that he does no violence to them. This admonition recognizes the power of government to hurt the weak. Bureaucracy can grow large, making it easy to turn a deaf ear and to be unavailable to those in trouble. Every government must take special care to watch over the weak.

Finally, Jeremiah is given a vision of the true shepherd. For the first time in this great prophecy he looks down through the centuries and sees the coming of One who will fulfill God's ideal and who in time will return to carry it out in practice. "The days are coming," declares the Lord, "when I will raise up for David a righteous Branch, a King who will reign wisely and do what is just and right in the land. In his days Judah will be saved and Israel will live in safety. This is the name by which he will be called: The Lord Our Righteous Savior" (Jer. 23:5–6). That is the name applied to Jesus by the apostle Paul in 1 Corinthians 1:30: "Christ Jesus, who has become for us wisdom from God—that is, our righteousness, holiness and redemption." He himself is our righteousness. So the prophet sees him coming as God's rightful King, who will one day come again so that Judah will be saved and Israel will dwell securely.

> *Lord God of Hosts, may my mind and my heart be open to understand what you are doing in the nations of our day. Help me to bow before you and to become a vessel fit for your use.*

To whom are national leaders ultimately responsible? What essential characteristics does God require of these leaders? Who is the ultimate shepherd and the rightful king?

IN HIS HANDS

A daily devotion for August 19

Read Jeremiah 26:1–24.

> "Then Jeremiah said to all the officials and all the people: 'The Lord sent me to prophesy against this house and this city all the things you have heard. Now reform your ways and your actions and obey the Lord your God. Then the Lord will relent and not bring the disaster he has pronounced against you. As for me, I am in your hands; do with me whatever you think is good and right. Be assured, however, that if you put me to death, you will bring the guilt of innocent blood on yourselves and on this city and on those who live in it, for in truth the Lord has sent me to you to speak all these words in your hearing'" (Jer. 26:12–15).

This is an official gathering, a trial. Jeremiah has been impeached by the people, and the religious authorities of the nation—the priests and the prophets—are behind this. They have laid a serious charge, a charge of treason, against the prophet. These people felt that because the temple was God's house, God would defend that temple no matter what happened within it. They thought the temple was inviolate and that the city was protected because it was the city of God. They were saying, "It can't happen here!" But Jeremiah said it would happen. So they charged him with blasphemy and treason against the temple of God and the city of God.

Notice that Jeremiah makes not the slightest deviation in his response. This would have been the time, if he were so inclined, to have told these people, "Now just a minute. I want to make one thing perfectly clear! I have indeed prophesied, but I didn't mean to have it taken as seriously as you are doing. If you'll let me off, I can intercede before God for you, and perhaps he'll change his mind." But he does not say that. He does not alter his message one bit: "Amend your ways and your doings, and the Lord will repent of the evil which he has pronounced against you."

Jeremiah does what the people of God have been exhorted throughout the Scriptures to do at times like this: leave everything in God's hands. The battle is his. If we are charged unjustly, we should not try to defend ourselves. We must place ourselves in God's hands, and he will see us through. This is what Peter says about the Lord Jesus: "When he was reviled, he did not revile in return; when he suffered, he did not threaten; but he trusted in him who judges justly." This is what Jeremiah does. So often we are so concerned about defending ourselves, vindicating ourselves. We are fearful lest somebody think something wrong about us. It is perfectly all right to explain things as far as possible. But when it is evident that nobody is willing to listen, we must let God handle the matter. He knows what he is doing.

Lord, give me the courage and the faith to put everything in your hands.

When we respond to God's call to be his witnesses, do we equivocate his truth? When we anticipate the possibility of rejection and persecution, do we confidently place ourselves in God's hands?

WHO KNOWS?

A daily devotion for August 20

Read Jeremiah 29:1–32.

> "'For they have done outrageous things in Israel; they have committed adultery with their neighbors' wives, and in my name they have uttered lies—which I did not authorize. I know it and am a witness to it,' declares the Lord" (Jer. 29:23).

The closing words of the chapter are specific prophecies against false prophets among the exiles in Babylon. This was a time of terrible uncertainty. People were torn, asking, "What shall I believe?" There were many conflicting voices, many rival factions. The supreme need of the hour was for someone who knew the facts and would declare them, giving the people an indication of what to do. God says, "I am the one who knows. I know what is going on in the inner lives of these people, and I will make it known. I will bring it out." That is the voice we can trust.

God makes known his way and his will and the truth by three means in the Scriptures. The first is through history. I would commend to you the reading of history, which records all the errors that we see around us today. The solutions are also recorded. No error is introduced into the world that has not already been answered.

The second means is through current events. God is always bringing truth to life. That is why we as a nation go through difficulties. We have seen many times how everything that the nation's most powerful leaders think they can keep hidden is forced into the light. That is the way God works in the affairs of men.

And third, God makes the truth known through the direct revelation of his word, the truth found in Jesus coming to the man of God, who declares it before the people.

So in this day of confusion, of uncertainty, which voice will we listen to? The voices of the occult world around us? The false prophets who claim to have visions from God? The secular voices telling us that things are not the way the Bible says they are? Whom will we follow? What will be the guideline for our actions? The message of Jeremiah is: "God rules in the affairs of men. And if you want to know how to behave, listen to God, for he is the one who knows and who makes known."

> *Father, thank you for being the One before whom I stand naked with nothing hidden and for being the One who exposes and brings everything to light. I pray that the words of my mouth and the meditations of my heart may be acceptable in your sight.*

What are three resources that reveal to us God's way, his will, and the truth? Do his criteria inform our minds and our responses? Do we invite his penetrating scrutiny?

THE PAIN THAT HAS NO CURE

A daily devotion for August 21

Read Jeremiah 30:1–24.

> "Why do you cry out over your wound, your pain that has no cure? Because of your great guilt and many sins I have done these things to you" (Jer. 30:15).

God takes full responsibility for what happens to Israel. He says, "I have done these things to you." It is as though he stands with his hands on his hips and says to the people, "Look, I'm responsible. Any questions?" God says he has acted because of their flagrant sins.

We must not read this as though it is something remote from us. If we are inclined to say, "Oh, it's such a pity what's going to happen to Israel," we should remember that this is our story, too. This is how God works. He deals with Israel this way because this is the way he deals with everybody. We too often forget a scriptural principle reflected here. Just because judgment does not fall immediately upon people, they think they are in the clear. But Paul says, "Do not be deceived: God cannot be mocked. A man reaps what he sows. Whoever sows to please their flesh, from the flesh will reap destruction" (Gal. 6:7–8).

That is inevitable. God does not cancel that judgment by the forgiveness of sin. That is part of what we call the natural consequences of evil, the temporal judgment of God. It is never eliminated, any more than the rest of what Paul says is eliminated: "Whoever sows to please the Spirit, from the Spirit will reap eternal life" (Gal. 6:8) This is God's promise for now—not just in heaven some day but now. The joy and glory of life will come to us if we walk in the Spirit, and that is inevitable. But so is the judgment for our sin, the inevitable consequences of our selfish choices.

This means that ultimately a recompense comes to us in life for the evil we done in our flesh—whether it is blatant, sensual evil or whether it is inward evil—spiritual pride, bitterness, and all the other sins of the spirit. It makes no difference. Evil brings its own results. As someone has wisely said, "You can pull out the nail driven into the wall, but you can't pull out the nail hole."

God reminds us here that there will be pain, heartache, and trouble because of the evil of our past. The sins of our youth will catch up to us—usually in middle age! And there is no escape. As Kipling says, "The sins that they did two by two, they pay for one by one." God says this is inevitable. It is inevitable for his people Israel; it is inevitable for us as well. Yet even in that trial, God is present in his mercy and his grace.

> *Thank you, Lord, for the lesson I learn when I deal with the consequences of my poor choices. And thank you for your grace, which is sufficient even for these things.*

Are we surprised by the inevitable consequences of our sins? Are we also surprised by joy when the Spirit produces good fruit through our walk with Christ? Do we recognize both as aspects of God's sovereign initiative?

EVERLASTING LOVE

A daily devotion for August 22

Read Jeremiah 31:1–22.

> "'I have loved you with an everlasting love; I have drawn you with unfailing kindness … Is not Ephraim my dear son, the child in whom I delight? Though I often speak against him, I still remember him. Therefore my heart yearns for him; I have great compassion for him,' declares the Lord" (Jer. 31:3, 20).

As a father cannot forget his son—no matter how sharply he must reprimand him—so God remains tender toward his people. Behind the darkness and the distress is the everlasting love of God. This phrase, "I have loved you with an everlasting love," is beautiful. *Everlasting* is one of those words that baffle us. Even in the original language it is difficult to define. *Everlasting* connotes more than duration and means more than merely "eternal"; it has in it an element of mystery.

Let your mind run back over all the years of history, and you come to a place where finally you cannot think any further. Yet logic affirms that even beyond this point there has been existence and time. This is what *everlasting* means. Let your mind run into the future, and you come to the same kind of haziness, a place where you no longer can comprehend what the ages mean, where times and durations seem meaningless. That is the vanishing point in the future beyond which lie experiences for God's people that we are unable to grasp. That is the mystery of *everlasting*. The word means "beyond dimension,""greater than we can think." This is what Paul means when he wishes "that you, being rooted and grounded in love, may have the power to comprehend with all the saints what is the breadth and length and height and depth, and to know the love of Christ which surpasses knowledge" (Eph. 3:18–19 RSV).

Sometimes we get to a point where the sins of the past, and those of our mothers and fathers before us, are taking a toll upon your lives, and we are tempted to cry out, "Why? Why should this happen to me? What have I done to deserve this?" When this happens, God is at pains to remind us that in the midst of this we are experiencing his mysterious everlasting love.

He is saying to us, "Look, it may pain you, but it won't damage you. This hurt you are going through will produce in you the character that both you and I want. This will refine you, soften you, open you up, make you a human being. Instead of being callous, resistant, and self-centered, you'll become open, responsive, and selfless." That is the mysterious quality of this love, which draws us on. "I have loved you with an everlasting love; I have drawn you with unfailing kindness." In other words, "Despite the exercise of the flesh in your life, I have not let you miss out on anything that I have planned for you." That sounds strange to us, does it not? We want to escape the consequences. Instead, God leads us through them.

Thank you, Father for your love, which endures forever.

Are we learning to see God's fatherly love in his disciplines? Are we awed by the vastness of his eternal love for his children?

THE NEW COVENANT

A daily devotion for August 23

Read Jeremiah 31:23–40.

> "'The days are coming,' declares the Lord, 'when I will make a new covenant with the people of Israel and with the people of Judah ... This is the covenant I will make with the people of Israel after that time,' declares the Lord. 'I will put my law in their minds and write it on their hearts. I will be their God and they will be my people. No longer will they teach their neighbor, or say to one another, "Know the Lord," because they will all know me, from the least of them to the greatest,' declares the Lord. 'For I will forgive their wickedness and will remember their sins no more'" (Jer. 31:31, 33, 34).

This is a marvelous promise. God will do what the people could never do. Despite all their failure, he will bring them around. He will do it by a new process. First, he says, "I will put my law in their minds and write it on their hearts." That is a new motive. God will change the motivation of a person's life so that it comes from within instead of from without. The old covenant is a demand made on us from without. This is impossible for us to carry out. But the new covenant is something put within us. Love is the motive in the new covenant. We respond out of love for God, out of love for what he has done in our lives and our hearts.

The second manifestation is a new power. "I will be their God, and they will be my people." God is the strength of people's lives. He supplies all the power to act; they are the ones who do the acting. This is a beautiful description of the new covenant. Everything comes from God; nothing comes from us. We are not trying to do something for God; he is doing something for us and through us in everything we do. That is the new power.

Then there is a new family. "No longer will they teach their neighbor, or say to one another, 'Know the Lord,' because they will all know me, from the least of them to the greatest," declares the Lord. All those in the family know each other. We know the dominant drives of each life, the underlying hopes and passions, because they are all the same: that we might know God better and become like him. That is why when Christians gather, though they have never met before, they always have a basis for sharing. They know each other and share the same life.

The new covenant rests on this great platform: "For I will forgive their wickedness and will remember their sin no more." That is how God proposes to win this battle. When the law fails and we cannot respond the way we know we should, how will we win? Our worry vanishes when we understand that full provision has already been made for all our failure. God does not hold that failure against us. His love will be with us and will sustain us through the results of our folly and our failure. God is for us and will turn all the difficulty we experience to our advantage so that it makes us transformed people. That is the new covenant in action. As we learn to walk in dependence upon a new motive and a new power in a new relationship with one another, resting upon the forgiveness of God, we discover that marvelous things are happening in our lives.

> *Father, forgive me for being so sure I can make it myself. Help me to assume a poverty of spirit, which will open to me the riches of eternity.*

What are three life-changing aspects of the new covenant God makes with his people? Do we see this as God entering into our pain and our weakness and transforming us by his power and his everlasting love?

QUALITIES OF GENUINE FAITH

A daily devotion for August 24

Read Jeremiah 32:1–10.

> "Jeremiah said, 'The word of the Lord came to me: Hanamel son of Shallum your uncle is going to come to you and say, "Buy my field at Anathoth, because as nearest relative it is your right and duty to buy it." Then, just as the Lord had said, my cousin Hanamel came to me in the courtyard of the guard and said, "Buy my field at Anathoth in the territory of Benjamin" ... I knew that this was the word of the Lord; so I bought the field at Anathoth from my cousin Hanamel and weighed out for him seventeen shekels of silver'" (Jer. 32:6–9).

That is a remarkable act of faith. It belongs with those acts of faith recorded in Hebrews 11. As we examine it, we learn what it means to walk by faith. Every one of us is called to walk by faith, and certain qualities of faith are seen here.

First there is what we might call the caution of faith. Notice how the account progresses. God says to Jeremiah, in the loneliness of his prison, "Your cousin Hanamel is coming to you, offering to sell his field." A little later on the account says, "Then Hanamel my cousin came to me ... in accordance with the word of the Lord." Later still, "Then I knew that this was the word of the Lord." The important thing to see is how Jeremiah tests this impression he received.

Many of us have wondered how these Old Testament prophets were given "words" from God. Many times we find this phrase in the Scriptures: "The word of the Lord came to me." How did it come? This account suggests that the usual way God spoke to these prophets was the same way he speaks to us—through a vivid impression made upon the soul, an inner voice informing them of something.

But the great lesson to learn from this account is that this inner voice is not always the voice of God. Sometimes the god of this world can speak through that inner voice, sounding very much like God. Many a person has been tremendously injured in his faith, and has damaged the faith of others, by acting impulsively on what this inner voice has to say without testing whether it is the voice of God.

Though it acts in a remarkable way, faith does not act fanatically. Faith acts cautiously, expecting God to confirm his word. Jeremiah was no novice in the active life of faith. He knew that God would confirm his word, and he had learned to wait upon him. God confirmed the word by fulfilling the prediction he had made.

Yet with all the caution of faith, notice another quality of faith here. It is what we might call the audacity of faith. This was a thoroughly unreasonable thing to do! It was ridiculous to buy property when the city was about to fall into enemy hands. This is always a quality of faith. Faith has an apparent foolishness. We are not acting by faith if we are doing what everyone around us is doing. Faith always appears to defy the circumstances. It constitutes a risk and a venture.

Noah built an ark where there was no water and where there had never been any rain. I am sure the people of his day called him crazy Noah—building an ark out on the dry land! Abraham went on a journey without a map. People asked him, "Where are you going?" He said, "We don't know; we're just going, that's all. God is leading us." They must have twirled their fingers alongside their heads and said, "Poor Abe—he's lost his marbles!" That is the quality of faith—it acts in an apparently ridiculous way. But it acts this way because it is based on a higher knowledge. It always has a basis on which to rest. Therefore faith does not demand that we run out and do foolish, impulsive acts for no reason. The reason is higher than many people can see, but it is there.

Thank you, Lord, for calling me to walk by faith. Sometimes that means acting in ways that make no sense to the world around me. Help me to trust that you will establish your word and show yourself faithful.

What are two distinguishing elements in a walk of faith? Are we learning to recognize and to receive God's direction for our faith ventures?

FAITH AND DOUBT

A daily devotion for August 25

Read Jeremiah 33:11–44.

> "I took the deed of purchase—the sealed copy containing the terms and conditions, as well as the unsealed copy—and I gave this deed to Baruch son of Neriah, the son of Mahseiah, in the presence of my cousin Hanamel and of the witnesses who had signed the deed and of all the Jews sitting in the courtyard of the guard. In their presence I gave Baruch these instructions: 'This is what the Lord Almighty, the God of Israel, says: Take these documents, both the sealed and unsealed copies of the deed of purchase, and put them in a clay jar so they will last a long time. For this is what the Lord Almighty, the God of Israel, says: Houses, fields and vineyards will again be bought in this land'" (Jer. 32:11–15).

What a ringing testimony to the power and the greatness of God! He had said the land ultimately would be restored, and so this deed would be valid. Therefore it was to be put in a safe place. That is what Jeremiah did. He sent Baruch down to the title company and had him bring a deed to be signed. He acted before witnesses and had the witnesses sign the deed and the copy—one to be sealed in a safe deposit box, the other to be kept by Jeremiah and passed on to his heirs so that eventually they might claim title to this land. He worked in this normal way and then clearly announced the purpose of it all: "It is because God says there will be houses and fields and vineyards bought in this land again."

Faith takes no halfway measures. Jeremiah doesn't hedge his bets and tell these people, "Well, I'm just buying this property on speculation, hoping it will all work out, but it's just a gamble, a shot in the dark." No, he assures them that God has spoken and that everything he is doing is consistent with God's word.

Later in chapter 32, another quality of faith is revealed. A remarkable prayer by Jeremiah is recorded in verses 16 through 25. These are his private thoughts about this deed. Before men this prophet is bold, resolute, and confident. But before God he admits that he is not quite so sure this will all work out. He tells the Lord in verse 25, "And though the city will be given into the hands of the Babylonians, you, Sovereign Lord, say to me, 'Buy the field with silver and have the transaction witnessed.'" I am glad this account is here, because this is what we might call the doubtings of faith.

Faith always has its doubts. I once had the impression that if I doubted, I could not have faith—that faith and doubt were contrary to one another. But I gradually began to understand that this is not true. Doubt is the proof of faith. Doubt is an attack upon the faith we have. We cannot have doubts unless we have faith. Faith is the way God works, and so the Enemy is bound to attack our faith immediately when he sees us beginning to live by it. Therefore doubts will arise as a result of Satan's attempts to overthrow our faith. There is no faith without doubts.

Though he always lived by faith and though everything he did was by faith, Jesus himself was subjected to times of severe doubt. Otherwise he was not "one who in every respect has been tempted as we are, yet without sinning" (Heb. 4:15 RSV). Doubt is part of the life of faith. If you are trying to walk by faith in a promise God has given you, and you are troubled by doubts, this is the proof you are living by faith. Hang in there! Do not let your doubts overthrow you.

Father, thank you for reminding me of the kind of God you are. I rest upon your faithfulness, praying that I will be strengthened by faith to walk as the prophet walked during my own challenging times.

Are we learning to see our doubts as corollaries to our faith? Do we process our doubts through what we have proven to be true? Have we experienced the holy fear of audacious faith?

PROFANING HIS NAME

A daily devotion for August 26

Read Jeremiah 34:1–22.

> "Recently you repented and did what is right in my sight: Each of you proclaimed freedom to your own people. You even made a covenant before me in the house that bears my name. But now you have turned around and profaned my name; each of you has taken back the male and female slaves you had set free to go where they wished. You have forced them to become your slaves again" (Jer. 34:15–16).

The remarkable phrase in this passage is "you profaned my name." This was a serious charge to Jews. They had been brought up to revere the name of God. The scribes did not even dare to write the name of God without taking a bath and changing their clothes. And they never pronounced it. The four Hebrew letters used for the name of God they called "the Ineffable Tetragrammaton"—the unpronounceable or unspeakable four letters. They never spoke the name of God. Yet God's charge against this king is, "You have profaned my name." The Hebrew word translated as "profane" means "wound," "pierce," or "deface." God's charge is, "You have defaced me." They did this by failing to respect the human rights of slaves. It is an act of blasphemy against God to treat a human being as less than a person. God calls a nation to account for this.

As we think of our own national history, we can see what a heavy charge must be leveled against us. How have we treated the American Indians, the original inhabitants of this land, or the Africans we brought forcibly into our midst? We have despised them, treated them as less than human. The God of the nations says, "That is a profanation of my name. You have profaned my name when you have done a thing like that."

It is always healthy for me to remember that God's view of my spirituality, his judgment of whether I am a spiritually minded person, is based not upon how I treat my friends and those I like but on how I treat the waiter at the table, the clerk in the store, or the yardman. This is the mark of spirituality. In other words, God requires of a people that they respect the rights of all humanity. And when they violate that standard, God takes that into account.

Father, I pray that I continue to respect humanity as I live a spiritually minded life.

Are we compelled by God's love, seeing others through his eyes? How does this differ from the worldly point of view? Do we claim to represent Christ but dishonor his name by mistreating and demeaning others?

THE FEAR OF THE LORD

A daily devotion for August 27

Read Jeremiah 36:1–32.

> "So Jeremiah took another scroll and gave it to the scribe Baruch son of Neriah, and as Jeremiah dictated, Baruch wrote on it all the words of the scroll that Jehoiakim king of Judah had burned in the fire. And many similar words were added to them" (Jer. 36:32).

Judgment came against Jehoiakim not simply because he acted foolishly in burning the Scriptures but because of the condition of heart that his action revealed. We see this in one flaming sentence in verse 24: "Yet neither the king, nor any of his servants who heard all these words, was afraid, nor did they rend their garments." These men had lost the fear of God. And a nation, a people, or an individual without the fear of God faces destruction. The fear of God is based upon the sovereign power that he exercises over life. The king and his servants were shown to be stupid and senseless men who had lost their grip on reality because they had lost the fear of God.

The law of retribution is a great fact revealed everywhere—in Scripture, in history, and even in nature. This law holds that there is an inevitable consequence for doing wrong and that there is no way to escape it. Even an atheist, who does not believe in God, must conclude when he examines the laws of nature that man either obeys these laws and lives or disobeys them and dies. And man is helpless to change that. We are in the grip of forces greater than we are, and everything testifies to this. That is why we learn respect for the laws of electricity. We do not fool around with ten thousand volts of electricity, thinking we can make up the laws as we go along. We had better find out what they are first, for we disobey them at our peril.

God has implanted this reality in every part of life. How foolish and utterly stupid is the person who seeks to ignore that fact. God requires that every nation recognize his sovereign government of men and the law of retribution for evil. History has testified repeatedly that God always accomplishes what he says he will do. God rules in the affairs of men. At the height of his career, Napoleon once boldly said, "God is on the side that has the heaviest artillery"—his cynical answer to someone who asked if God was on the side of France. Then came the Battle of Waterloo where he lost both the war and his empire. Years later, in exile on the island of St. Helena, chastened and humbled, Napoleon apparently recalled what an aide had said to him just prior to that battle, "Man proposes; God disposes." This is the lesson with which life seeks to confront us. God is able to work his sovereign will—despite man. Therefore the elementary knowledge of life with which everyone ought to start is the fear of God.

Father, these words sober me. I pray that I will not point a self-righteousness finger at others but rather will acknowledge the times I have not shown you the fear worthy of your name.

Is the arrogant defiance of God in our cultural environment eroding our reverent fear of our holy God? Do we need to inventory our hearts for signs of self-righteous pride?

HEAL OUR LAND

A daily devotion for August 28

Read Jeremiah 39:1–18.

> "In the ninth year of Zedekiah king of Judah, in the tenth month, Nebuchadnezzar king of Babylon marched against Jerusalem with his whole army and laid siege to it. And on the ninth day of the fourth month of Zedekiah's eleventh year, the city wall was broken through. Then all the officials of the king of Babylon came and took seats in the Middle Gate ... When Zedekiah king of Judah and all the soldiers saw them, they fled; they left the city at night by way of the king's garden, through the gate between the two walls, and headed toward the Arabah" (Jer. 39:1–4).

In the last chapter of Jeremiah, we are told that the Babylonians burned the temple of God as well. The long-delayed hour of judgment came at last. The city was taken. The temple was burned. Reading this account, we see a certain poetic justice that is always characteristic of God's judgments. The city refused God, and he refused the city. He granted the people their desire. The temple where incense was burned to idols was itself burned. The king who would not see had his eyes put out. The people who held their slaves captives were themselves taken captive by the Babylonians. This is always the way God works. His judgment gives us exactly what we are asking for, letting us have our way—but to the fullest extent, beyond anything we would desire.

A nation must never forget that ultimately the judgment of God will come. "The mills of God grind slow, but they grind exceeding small." Sooner or later judgment will fall. No nation has the right to continue to exist when it habitually violates the requirements of God's justice. Therefore the hand of doom rests upon any nation that deliberately refuses to hear and to heed the will of God. Ultimately, judgment will come. No political manipulation will avert it. No partial compromise will delay and no defiance will evade what God has said. It will come at last—some eleventh year, ninth month, and fourth day when a breach is made in the walls of the city and judgment and destruction can no longer be averted.

Individuals and nations use several means to seek to turn aside the will of God. First, a people can ignore and refuse to listen to God, giving themselves over to things that help them forget—lives of debauchery and revelry, for example. Second, a people can persecute the prophets of God and hinder his message, developing a callous attitude against the preaching of the Word of God. Third, a people can seek to circumvent the coming catastrophe by political maneuvering and by manipulations. Finally, a people can compromise in outward ways but fall short of real submission to God. They become outwardly religious, learning the "God words" and practicing civil religion, but their hearts remain unchanged

Only one attitude will avert the judgment of God: repentance, deep humiliation before God, an understanding and acknowledgment of guilt, a willingness to recognize that we have lost our right to exist as a nation, and a cry to God that he will heal us, change us, forgive us, and heal this land. When that occurs, God assumes responsibility for recovering the nation. Despite all the damage that has been done, he will restore the years that the locusts have eaten. But if a nation ignores God, it goes down into the dust of history, as hundreds of kingdoms and nations before us have perished.

Lord, I ask you to heal us as a nation.
Heal our land, and turn us from evil.

What are four ways individuals and nations seek to avert the will of God? Since each of these is unmistakably present in contemporary culture, what is the urgently needed response for us individually and as members of Christ's body, the church?

OVERTHROW THE FLESH

A daily devotion for August 29

Read Jeremiah 45:1–5.

> "But the Lord has told me to say to you, 'This is what the Lord says: I will overthrow what I have built and uproot what I have planted, throughout the earth. Should you then seek great things for yourself? Do not seek them. For I will bring disaster on all people, declares the Lord, but wherever you go I will let you escape with your life'" (Jer. 45:4–5).

The root of all our troubles with the flesh is seeking great things for ourselves. That is behind the naiveté, the secret vengeance, the treachery and murder, the unjustified fear, the pious deceit, the baseless hopes, the misdirected blame, the insolent rebellion—all of these arise out of a heart that longs to have glory that belongs to God. That is the basic problem, is it not? As we look at this problem, we say, "Who is sufficient for these things? How can we lick this terrible enemy within?" The only answer is the cross and the resurrection of Jesus. Only these forces have ever proved able to defeat the flesh: the cross, which puts it to death, and the resurrection, which provides another life in its place. That is the glory of the gospel.

Near Watsonville, California, there is a creek with a strange name: Salsi Puedes Creek. *Salsi puedes* is Spanish for "Get out of it if you can." The creek is lined with quicksand, and the story is that many years ago, in the early days of California, a Mexican laborer fell into this quagmire. A Spaniard, riding by on a horse, saw him and shouted, "Salsi puedes!" This was not very helpful. The creek has been so named ever since.

That is what the flesh is like. We struggle to correct these tendencies, but we cannot do it. Only God has the wisdom to do it. Jeremiah's words in the tenth chapter come to mind again. He said, "I know, O Lord, that the way of man is not in himself, that it is not in man who walks to direct his steps." And we recall the wisdom of the Proverbs: "Trust in the Lord with all your heart, and lean not unto your own understanding. In all your ways acknowledge him, and he shall direct your paths" (Prov. 3:5–6 KJV).

Nothing else will do it. Your own heart will deceive you. If you follow your own desires, you will end up trapped. Only the wisdom of the Word, only an honest acknowledgment of what is happening in your life, will suffice. Bring it to God, tell him the whole thing, and trust that he put your flesh to death on his cross. Then live according to his resurrection, relying upon his power and his grace to lead you. Jesus's knowledge of this tendency of the flesh led him to include in the Lord's Prayer the little phrase that I pray every day and that I hope you will too: "Lead us not into temptation."

> *Father, I pray that you will lead me away from temptation. Lead me from this evil thing within me that I cannot escape by myself. Deliver me from evil by the power of the redeeming work of Jesus Christ.*

What are identifying characteristics of the flesh? Have we learned to recognize the root problem? Are we choosing God's glory over our own, his power over our weakness?

DEFEATING WORLDLINESS

A daily devotion for August 30

Read Jeremiah 46:1–28.

> "This is the word of the Lord that came to Jeremiah the prophet concerning the nations: Concerning Egypt: This is the message against the army of Pharaoh Necho king of Egypt, which was defeated at Carchemish on the Euphrates River by Nebuchadnezzar king of Babylon in the fourth year of Jehoiakim son of Josiah king of Judah" (Jer. 46:1–2).

This passage takes us back to the year 605 BC when Nebuchadnezzar first came up against Judah. He was met by the armies of Egypt at the city of Carchemish on the Euphrates River, and there one of the great strategic battles of all history was fought. Until then, Egypt had been the most powerful nation of the day, but Babylon broke the power of Egypt at that place. In chapter 46, Jeremiah is describing that battle in advance—how long in advance we do not know. He describes in vivid terms the march of the Babylonian army, the clash of these conflicting forces, the terrible battle that ensued, and the final defeat of Egypt. We will not take time to cover these verses, but you can read them for yourself. The language is beautiful.

In the midst of this is a characterization of Egypt. In the Scriptures Egypt is a picture of the world and of its influence upon us. Egypt was a place of tyranny and bondage for the people of Israel. They were under the yoke of a wicked and severe king who enslaved them and treated them cruelly. Yet strangely enough, after the Israelites escaped, Egypt became a place they fondly remembered and to which they wanted to return. They remembered the food, the comfort, and the ease of life there. So, for the believer, Egypt has always stood as a picture of the lure of the world—to think as it thinks, to react as it reacts, to seek one's own satisfaction, pleasure, and enjoyment instead of living for the glory of God.

When I refer to "the world" I am not talking about people or about any so-called worldly activity. That is not what worldliness is. Worldliness is an attitude that causes us to live only for our own pleasures and enjoyment. That is what Egypt symbolizes in Scripture. The character of Egypt is described for us: "Who is this, rising like the Nile, like rivers whose waters surge? Egypt rises like the Nile, like rivers whose waters surge" (Jer. 46:7–8 RSV). Every spring the Nile River rises and overflows its banks, and this restores Egypt. The prophet uses this as a picture of the way the world comes at us—in surges and waves. We think we have it licked, but pretty soon it will come at us again. Repeatedly, throughout our lives as believers on a spiritual pilgrimage, the world rises to afflict us and to lure us, seeking to betray us and to return us to bondage.

But there is another message about Egypt in verses 13 to 24, delivered by Jeremiah after he had gone into exile in Egypt. Here he describes the forthcoming invasion of Egypt by Nebuchadnezzar, which took place after Jeremiah's death. In accord with this prophecy, Nebuchadnezzar came down into Egypt and took over the land. Included in this prophecy is another characterization of Egypt: "Call the name of Pharaoh, king of Egypt, 'Noisy one who lets the hour go by'" (Jer. 46:17 RSV).

Isn't that a strange name to give somebody? That is the characterization of Egypt—and the world. This is one of the ways we can recognize the world: it loves noise because it does not want to stop and to think. It loves to kill time. The world comes at us constantly, trying to get us to think only in terms of immediate pleasure and indulgence and to forget that this leads to slavery. So God punishes Egypt. That is the message here.

Thank you, Father, for the faithfulness of your word. Teach me to stand against the world and to stay faithful to you in this day of moral dissolution.

Are we learning to identify worldly attitudes by comparing them with God's Word of Truth? Have we succumbed to the worldly distraction of noise?

BABYLON!

A daily devotion for August 31

Read Jeremiah 50:1–51:64.

Chapters 50 and 51, two of the longest in the book, are devoted to the destruction and overthrow of Babylon. Everywhere in Scripture Babylon is a symbol of the great enemy of God, especially as the Devil uses false religious authority to claim earthly prestige and power.

Babylon began in the tower of Babel after the flood. Men erected a tower to ascend into the heavens and to become like God. Under Nimrod Babylon became the mother of harlots and of the abominations of the earth. It became the fountainhead of idolatry and began to export these ideas throughout the world. The Babylonians did this so that they might make a name for themselves (Gen. 11:4). Babylonianism is the attempt to gain prestige or status in the eyes of the world by religious authority. Every religion in the world seeks that. Whole systems of religion have been seized, and these systems seek to gain great authority, to be known as princes and kings and powers in the world today. It all began with the tower of Babel.

Just as Babylon was the great destructive power against Judah, so Babylon's turn would come. Out of the north, the Medes and the Persians would descend on Babylon and overthrow this great kingdom. Despite its tremendous walls, its vast palaces, its ornate hanging gardens, its huge size, and its great armies, God declared that the greatest power in the world of that day would be annihilated.

Many say that Babylon must be built again because of the prophecies in the book of Revelation that refer to Babylon. But the reference there is to "Mystery Babylon the Great" (Rev. 17:5 KJV), so this is not the city but that for which it stands—the idolatrous practices and the blasphemous assumption of power by religious authority. That is what will be destroyed, as Revelation says. Yet here in Jeremiah 51, we are given a description of the destruction of this city, which is used again in Revelation.

Babylon symbolizes the Enemy arrayed against us —the Devil—and the two channels through which he attacks us—the world and the flesh. These are forces with great power, bringing to pass all the terrible things recorded in our daily newspapers. God is adequate for all of them. Jesus speaks of these troubles in the world, assuring us, "But take heart. I have overcome the world" (John 16:33). Faith in a living God can overcome the power of the world, can beat back the deceitfulness of the flesh, and can overcome the roar of the Devil in our lives so that we can stand free from the bondage of this age. Babylon shall sink and never rise again.

Thank you, Lord, for the promise that you will defeat the forces arrayed against me, symbolized forever by Babylon. Help me to walk by faith in the victory you have promised and have given me in Christ.

What evil worldly power is symbolized by Babylon? Have we learned to identify this power as we encounter media reports of worldwide terror and suffering? To whom do we turn for personal deliverance and ultimate worldly triumph?

September

ROMANS 1–8

From Guilt to Glory
An introduction for the month of September

I don't know of any letter more foundational than Paul's letter to the Romans. It is unquestionably the greatest of all of his letters and the widest in scope. It offers intense and penetrating insight into the understanding of truth; therefore, it is one of the books of the New Testament with which every Christian ought to be thoroughly familiar. If you haven't mastered the letter to the Romans and aren't able to think through this book without a Bible before you, I urge you to set that as your goal.

Master the book of Romans—be so acquainted with it that you can outline it and think of its great themes without looking at a Bible. That requires reading it, studying it, and thinking it through in careful detail. It is safe to say that Romans is probably the most powerful human document ever penned.

I cannot help but think of the great documents of our American history, such as one of the original copies of the Constitution and Thomas Jefferson's copy of the Declaration of Independence. We value these great documents. In many ways, our freedom rests upon them, and we Americans rightly honor and respect them. But even these great documents of human liberties cannot hold a candle to the impact the epistle to the Romans has had upon human history.

Paul's letter to the Romans was written about AD 56–58, somewhere around the middle of the first century when the apostle was in Corinth on his third missionary journey. As you read this letter, you can catch glimpses of the conditions in Corinth. This Greek city was located at the crossroads of trade in the empire. It was one of the notoriously wicked cities in the Roman world, and much of that atmosphere is characterized in the letter to the Romans.

This letter was written only about thirty years after the crucifixion and resurrection of the Lord Jesus. The memory of the cross was still sharply etched in the minds of Christians all over the Roman Empire. This letter was sent to them to teach them, to instruct them, and to bring to their remembrance the meaning of these fantastic events that had so startled and amazed men in that first century.

REGARDING HIS SON

A daily devotion for September 1

Read Romans 1:1–7.

> "Paul, a servant of Christ Jesus, called to be an apostle and set apart for the gospel of God—the gospel he promised beforehand through his prophets in the Holy Scriptures regarding his Son, who as to his earthly life was a descendant of David, and who through the Spirit of holiness was appointed the Son of God in power by his resurrection from the dead: Jesus Christ our Lord" (Rom. 1:1–4).

At the heart of Paul's argument is a person: Jesus Christ, our Lord. That is the theme of the epistle to the Romans, as it is the theme of all Paul's writings and of all the New Testament. Union in Christ is the central truth that God wants us to see. As Paul wrote, "Christ in you, the hope of glory" (Col. 1:27). That is the great truth from which all others flow.

Sometimes Bible teachers identify certain major tenets flowing from that truth as being the central truth. For instance, they emphasize justification by faith or sanctification—that is, solving the problems of sin. But these themes all stem from the great central theme—union with Christ. We are not simply followers of a philosophy, or even of a philosopher, but of a savior, a redeemer, a person—and he must be central in all things.

In his introduction, Paul points out that the Lord was promised to us; he came as predicted in the Old Testament. The gospel was promised beforehand through the "prophets in the Holy Scriptures regarding his Son." One of the most important things that we can learn about our faith is that it comes to us through the anticipation and the prediction of centuries of teaching and preaching.

When the Lord Jesus comes, he is presented to us in two unique ways. First, concerning his human nature, the apostle says he was a descendant of David. The Greek says he comes of the sperm of David, emphasizing his intense humanity.

Second, Paul proclaims the deity of him who "was appointed the Son of God in power." The apostle begins with the phrase "the Son of God," which unmistakably declares the deity of our Lord. Three things marked the deity of Jesus. First, there was power; he came by power. This refers to the miracles that he did. Second, he came by the spirit of holiness. I've always been concerned about the word *holiness* because I find many of us misunderstand it. We think of it as something bad, but we can recapture the meaning if we use a similar term that comes from the same root, the word *wholeness*. Paul is saying that when Jesus came, he was a whole person. He demonstrated whole humanity—humanity as it was intended to be. That is how we are called to live. The glory of the good news is that God's goal for us is to make us whole so that we can walk amid the pressures, the turmoils, and the tragedies of this world and handle them as whole persons—holy persons. Jesus demonstrated that wholeness and supplies us with it in himself.

The third great mark of Jesus's deity was the resurrection; his deity was authenticated "by his resurrection from the dead." That is where our faith ultimately rests. We can have confidence that God has told us the truth, because of the unshakable fact that he raised Jesus from the dead. No one can remove that fact from the annals of history. It happened, our faith rests on it, and whenever unbelievers try to shake our faith, we should ask them to explain the resurrection. Ask them how they account for it—because it cannot be explained away. It is the immutable truth through which God has broken into our time, and he rests the whole story upon that great truth.

> *Thank you, Father, for sending your Son and for giving me the joy of knowing him and of seeing his life manifest through me.*

What is the central theme of Romans? What are three powerful proofs of Christ's deity? Are the Lord Jesus Christ and our union with him the central theme of our lives and of our verbal witness?

NOT ASHAMED

A daily devotion for September 2

Read Romans 1:8–17.

> "For I am not ashamed of the gospel, because it is the power of God that brings salvation to everyone who believes: first to the Jew, then to the Gentile. For in the gospel the righteousness of God is revealed—a righteousness that is by faith from first to last, just as it is written: 'The righteous will live by faith'" (Rom. 1:16–17).

The quotation from Habakkuk that Paul uses is the great fact that he is expounding in the gospel. He is not ashamed of it, and that is a way of saying that he is proud of it.

Paul especially is not ashamed of the gospel in Rome because the Romans appreciated power, just as Americans do. The Romans prided themselves on their power. With their military power, they could conquer all the nations that stood in their path; they had a tremendous program of road-building; they produced some of the greatest lawmakers in history; they had the power to write literature and to create art. But Paul knew that the Romans were powerless when it came to changing hearts. They were powerless to eliminate slavery. They were powerless to change the stubborn, hostile, hateful hearts of men and to eliminate violence. Paul says that is why he is so proud of the gospel—because it is the power of God to do the things that men cannot do. We never need to apologize for the gospel. It is absolutely without rival.

Paul is not ashamed of the gospel because it reveals a righteousness from God. *Righteousness* is an old word that we don't much understand. I would substitute for it the word *worth*, a worth before God, a sense of acceptance before him that he has given to us. We can't earn it, we certainly don't deserve it, but he provides it. God accepts us because of the gospel, because of the good news of the work of Jesus Christ on our behalf. Therefore, it is something that anybody can have, and it is complete and perfect.

The last thing Paul says is that righteousness is received by faith. It is not something we can ever earn, but it is something we can take anytime we need it, and that is good news. Our worth before God is not simply something we receive once by faith at the beginning of our Christian lives. It is also something we remind ourselves of every time we feel depressed, despairing, discouraged, or defeated. God has loved us and restored us, and we have perfect standing in his sight. He already accepts us and loves us as much as he possibly can; nothing more can be added. That is the righteousness revealed in the gospel by faith to all who believe, no matter what their background or training may be.

> *Father, I pray that I may understand how hopeless, how dark, and how bitter my condition would be were it not for the gospel of your grace. Help me to know that nothing could have saved me from the wicked machinations of the Evil One had it not been for the intervention of the gospel of grace.*

When we consider the magnitude of God's gift of unearned, undeserved righteousness, are we responding with gratitude and worship? How does this knowledge affect our hearts and our actions?

SUPPRESSING THE TRUTH

A daily devotion for September 3

Read Romans 1:18–23.

> "The wrath of God is being revealed from heaven against all the godlessness and wickedness of people, who suppress the truth by their wickedness, since what may be known about God is plain to them, because God has made it plain to them. For since the creation of the world God's invisible qualities—his eternal power and divine nature—have been clearly seen, being understood from what has been made, so that people are without excuse" (Rom. 1:18–20).

Here we see the cause of the wrath of God. The apostle explains that it is "the godlessness and wickedness of people, who suppress the truth by their wickedness" that cause God's wrath. Life's tragedies stem from men's attitudes and the actions that follow. Notice the order of this—godlessness and then wickedness. A godless attitude produces wicked actions, and that is why the wrath of God is being revealed constantly from heaven against man. What is godlessness? Godlessness isn't necessarily atheism, the belief that God doesn't exist. Godlessness is acting as though he doesn't exist. This thinking doesn't necessarily deny that there is a God, but it never takes account of him; it doesn't expect him to be active.

Godlessness brings unrighteousness or wickedness, selfish and hurtful acts of men toward one another. We act selfishly and hurt each other because we disregard God and expect no consequences. That is Paul's analysis. By means of these hurtful and selfish acts, the truth is suppressed.

Here we are in a world where truth from God is breaking out all around us, but we are busy hiding it, suppressing it, keeping it from being prominent and dominant in our thinking. Life has turned tragic in so many cases because the world is deprived of the truth that is necessary for life, liberty, and godliness. The truth that is suppressed is the existence of a God of eternal power and majesty.

How has God made truth plain? The Scripture says he has revealed himself to man. Truth is not a vague, invisible, difficult thing to comprehend; it is clearly seen. God himself has insured that. How? The Scriptures say, "It is seen in that which is made," in creation. From the creation of the world it has been visible, always and everywhere present. No one is left out—all can read this revelation of God if they want to do so. This argument from creation's design and order has never been refuted. Those who disregard God cannot explain this away, because the truth about him is breaking out everywhere around us.

Thus, says the Scripture, people are without excuse. No one who wants to find God need miss him.

Father, help me not to suppress the truth but to bow before you as my Creator and my Redeemer.

Blatant suppression of truth in the public square is undeniable. What about our lives? Are we suppressing God's truth by neglecting to know and to obey the revelation of truth in his Word?

GOD GAVE THEM OVER

A daily devotion for September 4

Read Romans 1:24–32.

> "Therefore God gave them over in the sinful desires of their hearts, to sexual impurity, for the degrading of their bodies with one another" (Rom. 1:24).

The wickedness at work among human beings follows a process that is identified in this passage by the thrice-repeated phrase "God gave them over." This phrase reveals what is going on in our culture. The first mark of wickedness in a godless society is widespread sexual immorality—the degrading, or the dishonoring, of the body. Many people think this account describes all the evil things men do and then says that God washes his hands of evil people because they are so filthy. That is not what this says. But because men run after other gods and refuse the testimony of their own hearts and do not glorify or thank the true God, he removes his restraints from society so that what is done in secret becomes open and acceptable. That is the mark of the wrath of God at work. The first sign of wickedness in a civilization is that sexual immorality becomes widely accepted.

You may ask, "Why is it that sex always seems to be singled out as the sign of God's judgment?" Many Christians have wrongly concluded that sexual sins are the worst transgressions. But that is not true. This passage in Romans bears that out. It begins with sexual impurity and proceeds to sexual perversity. However, the final result is not sexual sins but sins of the spirit. Widespread animosity, hatred of the heart—these are the worst sins. God has a good reason for allowing sexual practices to come to the surface. He permits this to show us what is going on in our spiritual lives. This highlights the fact that sex is linked with worship. Sex is a desire to possess another body and to be possessed by another. It is a deep-seated craving inherent in every human being.

We have all heard the statement "Girls give sex in order to get love; boys give love in order to get sex." This is true, superficially. But what both are really after is not sex at all; they are after worship. They want to worship and to be worshiped. They want a sense of total fulfillment, a oneness, an identity. Only God can give that fulfillment. Only God can satisfy that deep longing for complete identity and unity with another person. That is what we call worship. When we worship, we are longing to be possessed of God and to possess him fully. Jesus offers the perfect description of the best relationship with God possible for a believer: "You in me, and I in you" (John 14:20).

When people think they will find that fulfillment in sex, God says to them, "Look, it won't work. But you won't believe that until you try it out." So he removes the restraints and allows immoral sexual practices to become widely accepted, understanding that men indulging in these things will finally find themselves just as dissatisfied, empty, and hopeless as they were when they started. Thus they will learn that worshiping God is the only way by which people find fulfillment.

Father, I see how accurately these words describe our own times. I am grateful that you have not forsaken this world and that the message of truth and light is still as available as ever.

Do we react to the prevalent cultural immorality with self-righteous condemnation? Does it increase our awe and our gratitude for God's grace and therefore our compassionate care for others?

SINFUL MORALITY

A daily devotion for September 5

Read Romans 2:1–11.

> "You, therefore, have no excuse, you who pass judgment on someone else, for at whatever point you judge another, you are condemning yourself, because you who pass judgment do the same things" (Rom. 2:1).

Here Paul talks about those who pass judgment on others. The apostle makes two points about these people. First, he says that they know the difference between right and wrong; otherwise they would not presume to judge. Paul's second point is that these people are guilty because they are doing the same things themselves. The judges are as guilty as the ones who are being accused.

Whenever moral people, those who pride themselves on a degree of righteousness and a standard of ethics, read a statement like this, they are taken by surprise. "What do you mean? How could this be?" I will use myself as an illustration, simply because I am such an excellent example of what the rest of us are like. I see three ways by which I try to elude the fact that I am guilty of the things that I accuse others of doing.

First, I am congenitally blind to many of my faults. I do not see that I am doing the same things that others are doing, and yet other people can see that I am. We all have these blind spots. One of the greatest lies of our age is the idea that we can know ourselves. We often argue, "Don't you think I know myself?" The answer is, "No, you do not know yourself. You are blind to much of your life." We can be unaware of hurtful and sinful areas.

I caught myself the other day saying to someone, "Relax! Take it easy!" It was only after hearing my own voice that I realized I was not relaxed and I was not taking it easy. Have you ever lectured your children on the sin of procrastination? Then did you barely get your income tax report in on time or not get it in at all? We are congenitally blind to many of our own faults.

A second way we try to elude the fact that we are guilty of the things we accuse others of doing is by conveniently forgetting the wrong we have done. We may have been aware of our sin at the time, but somehow we assume that God will forget it and that we do not have to acknowledge it in any way. As the sin fades from our memory, we think it fades from his as well. Consider our thought life. In the Sermon on the Mount we learn that if we hold a feeling of animosity and hatred against someone, we are guilty of murder just as though we had taken a knife and plunged it into that person's breast. We think these things will go unnoticed, but God sees them in our hearts. He sees all the actions that we conveniently have forgotten. We, who condemn these things in others, find ourselves guilty of the same things. Isn't it remarkable that when others mistreat us we always think this is a serious matter requiring immediate correction? But when we mistreat others, we tell them. "You're making so much out of a little thing!"

The third way we try to elude the fact that we are guilty of the things we accuse others of doing is by cleverly renaming these things. Other people lie and cheat; we simply stretch the truth a little. Others betray; we simply protect our rights. Others steal; we borrow. Others have prejudices; we have convictions. Others murder and kill; we exploit and ruin. Others rape; we pollute. We cry, "Those people ought to be stoned!" Jesus says, "He that is without sin among you, let him cast the first stone" (John 8:7). Yes, we are all guilty of the same things we accuse others of doing.

> *Father, thank you for being the God of truth. You do not deceive or delude; you tell the blunt, stark truth that I might know exactly what I am and what I can do about it. Save me, Lord, from the folly of trying to protect, to rationalize, and to justify these areas of evil in my life. Grant me the grace to confess and to be forgiven.*

What three personal considerations do we need to take seriously before judging the sins of others? Are we open to the conviction of the Holy Spirit and to the instruction of the Word regarding our sins of heart and mind?

ACCORDING TO LIGHT

A daily devotion for September 6

Read Romans 2:12–29.

> "All who sin apart from the law will also perish apart from the law, and all who sin under the law will be judged by the law. For it is not those who hear the law who are righteous in God's sight, but it is those who obey the law who will be declared righteous. (Indeed, when Gentiles, who do not have the law, do by nature things required by the law, they are a law for themselves, even though they do not have the law. They show that the requirements of the law are written on their hearts, their consciences also bearing witness, and their thoughts sometimes accusing them and at other times even defending them.) This will take place on the day when God judges people's secrets through Jesus Christ, as my gospel declares" (Rom. 2:12–16).

Here we are dealing with the question of what to do about the people who have not heard the gospel. What about those who live where the Bible is unknown or those who follow a religion that makes no reference to the life, death, and resurrection of Jesus Christ? In this passage Paul says that their problem is that they defile their consciences. These people will be judged by their own standards. God judges men not according to what they do not know but according to what they do know.

In Romans 2:9–10, Paul also says the judgment of God is according to light. He will not judge all mankind on the basis of the Ten Commandments, but people will be judged according to light. That means that God will say to the individual, "What did you think was right and wrong?" When the individual answers, God will then ask, "Did you do the right and not the wrong?" By that standard everyone fails. Paul makes that clear: "All who sin apart from the law will also perish apart from the law." The fact that such men never heard the Ten Commandments, or anything else in the Bible, does not mean they will be acceptable in God's sight. They will perish not because they did not hear but because what they did know was right they did not do.

Here we have a revelation of what goes on in the primitive world. Men and women who have never heard anything about the Bible nevertheless are subject to judgment because they have truth written in their hearts. They know what is right and wrong. They show it in their lives. People say, "Let your conscience be your guide." That is a recipe for unhappiness. If that is all you have, it is a certain way of plunging into a life that alternates between fear and momentary peace.

Thank you, Lord, for providing a way for me to be forgiven of the sins I have committed against my conscience. Thank you for Jesus!

When we understand the cost of rejecting the light of conscience, do we feel a deeper gratitude for the price paid for our forgiveness? Do we realize the urgency of spreading the light of the gospel to those who have never heard the message of God's grace?

TOTAL WIPEOUT

A daily devotion for September 7

Read Romans 3:1–20.

> "Now we know that whatever the law says, it says to those who are under the law, so that every mouth may be silenced and the whole world held accountable to God. Therefore no one will be declared righteous in God's sight by the works of the law; rather, through the law we become conscious of our sin" (Rom. 3:19–20).

When we read this terrible description of the human race as God sees it, we find it almost impossible to believe that he will not say, "Enough! Wipe them out!" If all he sees is wretchedness, misery, deceit, hypocrisy, vulgarity, profanity, slander, and all the other evil things that are in every heart, our natural instinct is to say, "Then God doesn't want us." But the amazing thing is that across this kind of verse he writes, "God so loved the world that he gave his only begotten Son" (John 3:16 KJV). God did not send the law to destroy us (and this is crucial); he sent the law to keep us from false hope.

It is terrible to be heading down a road to an important destination, thinking we are on the right track and spending all the time necessary to get there, only to discover that the road peters out into nothingness. We find we have been on the wrong track and it is too late to go back. That was what was happening to humanity. So God, in his loving kindness, has given us the law to keep us from taking a false path. Though the law condemns us, that condemnation makes us willing to listen so that we find the right path.

Paul says the law does three things to us. First, it stops our mouths; we have nothing to say. A clear sign that someone is close to becoming a Christian is that the person will shut up and stop arguing back. Self-righteous people are always saying, "But this," "But I," "Yes, but I do this and I do that." They are always arguing. But when they see the true meaning of the law, their mouths are shut.

Second, Paul says, "The whole world is held accountable to God." That makes us realize there is no easy way, no way by which death will suddenly dissolve all things into everlasting darkness, forever forgotten. The whole world must stand before God. Hebrews puts it starkly: "It is appointed unto men once to die, but after this the judgment" (Heb. 9:27 KJV).

Finally, the law clearly reveals what sin is. What does the law want of us? Jesus said that all the law is summed up in one word: love. All the law asks us to do is to act in love. All the things the law states are simply loving ways of acting. When we face ourselves before the law, we have to confess that many times we fail in love. That is what the law wants us to see, because then, when all else fails, we are ready to listen to what follows.

Father, thank you for loving me enough to block all other ways—to tell me they are wrong and do not lead anywhere—so that I give up trying to make myself good enough to belong to you. Help me to take the only way that has ever been provided, a righteousness that I never earned but that is given me because I believe the Lord Jesus.

What are three essential purposes of the law? Since the greatest of these is love, what is the prime example of love? Can we generate that quality of love? What is the sole source available to us?

BUT NOW …

A daily devotion for September 8

Read Romans 3:21–26.

> "But now apart from the law the righteousness of God has been made known, to which the Law and the Prophets testify" (Rom. 3:21).

This is what Paul elsewhere calls "the glorious gospel of the blessed God" (1 Tim. 1:11), the good news that God announces to us, which consists of a gift that he gives us—the righteousness of God himself. This word *righteousness* is highly misunderstood in our day. Often it is associated with behavior. If people are behaving in a right way, we say that they are behaving righteously. But in discussing righteousness, the letter to the Romans does not directly touch on behavior. Righteousness is not what we do; it is what we are! That is even more important, because our behavior stems from what we are. The gift Paul is talking about, the gift from God, is that of a righteous standing.

But the real meaning underlying this word, as we understand it today, is found in the word *worth.* People everywhere are looking for a sense of worth. Psychologists tell us that a sense of worth is the most essential element in human activity and that without it we cannot function as human beings. Therefore, whether we know it or not or describe it in these terms, we are all looking for a sense of worth. But the gospel announces that it is given to us. What other people work all their lives to achieve is handed to us at the beginning when we believe in Jesus Christ. According to the gospel, we cannot earn it, but it is given to us.

Millions of people today openly acknowledge that they need help and come looking for it. Others never ask, but behind their smiling facades and confident airs lie insecure hearts and a consciousness of deep self-doubt. This is humanity's basic problem. The gospel, therefore, deals with something tremendously significant. It does not deal only with what happens when we die. This is one of the reasons many churches today are half-empty: so many people do not know that the gospel is all about self-worth. Far deeper than the need to feel that some human being loves us is our need to know that God loves us, that we are acceptable in his sight, and that we have standing and value to him. Something about us, that bit of eternity planted in our hearts by God, bears witness to us that this is the ultimate issue. Somehow life can never be satisfying if that question is not settled.

God is offering a gift of righteousness—his own perfect righteousness, a perfect value that cannot be improved upon. By faith in Jesus Christ, he gives us a sense of worth and of acceptance, and there could be no better news for mankind.

Thank you, Father, for knowing my deep need for a sense of worth and for providing it through the work of Jesus.

How do we answer the question, "Who am I?" Do we live as persons of worth because of God's amazing, undeserved gift of his righteousness? Or do we continue to vainly seek worldly affirmation?

NO BOASTING

A daily devotion for September 9

Read Romans 3:27–31.

> "Where, then, is boasting? It is excluded. Because of what law? The law that requires works? No, because of the law that requires faith. For we maintain that a person is justified by faith apart from the works of the law. Or is God the God of Jews only? Is he not the God of Gentiles too? Yes, of Gentiles too, since there is only one God, who will justify the circumcised by faith and the uncircumcised through that same faith" (Rom. 3:27–30).

Paul raises and answers three simple questions to show us the natural results of this tremendous acceptance that God gives us in Jesus Christ. First, "Who can boast?" Absolutely no one. How can we boast when everyone receives the gift of grace without any merit on his part? This means that any basis for self-righteousness is eliminated, and that is why this is the ugliest sin among Christians. When we look down on people who are involved in homosexuality, greed, or gambling—when we begin to think that we are better than they are—we have denied what God has done for us. All boasting must be excluded. There are no grounds for anybody to say, "Well, at least I've never done that." The only basis for acceptance is the gift of grace.

Second, Paul asks, "Is anyone excluded from grace, Jew or Gentile?" The answer is no! God has no most-favored nation; they are all alike before him. Paul argues, "Is God the God of Jews only? Then there must be two Gods—one for the Jews and one for the Gentiles. But that cannot be; there is only one God; God is one." Therefore he is equally the God of the Gentiles and the God of the Jews, because both must come on exactly the same grounds. This is the wonderful thing about the gospel. All mankind is leveled; no one can stand on any other basis than the work of Jesus Christ.

Paul's third question is, "Does this cancel out the law or set it aside? Do we no longer need the law?" His answer is, "No, it fulfills the law." The righteousness that the law demands is the very righteousness given to us in Christ. So if we have it as a gift, we no longer need to fear the law, because the demands of the law are met. But this is not something for which we can take credit; indeed, whenever we act in unrighteousness after this, the law comes in again to do its work of showing us what is wrong. That is all the law is good for. It shows us what is wrong. But now instead of condemning us, all the hurt accomplished by our sin is relieved again by the grace of God, the forgiveness of God.

Receiving God's forgiveness is not something we do only once; it is something we do repeatedly. It is the basis on which we live, constantly taking fresh forgiveness from the hand of God. John's letter puts it this way: "If we confess our sins, he is faithful and just to forgive us our sins, and to cleanse us from all unrighteousness" (1 John 1:9 KJV). That is God's gift, and we must continually take it afresh from his hand. When we find ourselves slipping into self-righteousness, when we find ourselves looking down our noses, when we find ourselves filled with pride and acting in arrogance—critical, calloused, and caustic or bitter and resentful toward one another—our relationship to a holy God is not affected if we acknowledge that we have sinned. We can come back, and God's love is still there. He still accepts us and highly values us.

That is what God's gift of righteousness means to us. It is wonderful news indeed that we never need fear. The God of ultimate holiness, the God who lives in holy light, whom we cannot begin to approach, has accepted us in the beloved, and we stand on the same ground of worth that he does.

Heavenly Father, these words are so remarkable I can hardly believe them. I pray that I may live on this basis, enabling me to forgive and to be tenderhearted and loving toward others, knowing that I already have this gift in Jesus Christ our Lord.

Do we view self-righteousness as an egregious denial of God's undeserved assignment of his righteousness to us? How then should we think and act toward others? What is the basic and prevailing purpose of the law?

THE FATHER OF FAITH

A daily devotion for September 10

Read Romans 4:1–12.

> "What then shall we say that Abraham, our forefather according to the flesh, discovered in this matter? If, in fact, Abraham was justified by works, he had something to boast about—but not before God. What does Scripture say? 'Abraham believed God, and it was credited to him as righteousness'" (Rom. 4:1–3).

Paul says that Abraham our forefather discovered two ways to gain worth. One, Paul suggests, is by works. Abraham was a man of good works. In Genesis, Abraham was an idolator and worshiped the moon goddess. But he was not deliberately seeking to evade God. He worshiped in ignorance. In the midst of that condition God appeared to him and spoke to him. Abraham believed God, responded to his call, and set out on a march without a map. He trusted God to lead him to a land he had never seen before, to take care of his family, and to fulfill his promises. So Abraham appears in the Scripture as a man of great works.

Paul admits that if Abraham was righteous because of works, he had something to boast about. Works always give us something to boast about. We can look at the record; we can show people what we have done and why we ought to be appreciated. We may not boast openly, but we all have subtle ways and clever tricks to reveal information so people can see what we have done. We can drop a hint about an accomplishment, hoping people will ask more about it. Somehow we manage things so that others know we are people of significance. That is the way the world is today and the way it was in Abraham's day.

That may work before men but not before God. God is never impressed by that kind of performance. God, who sees the heart, is not looking at outward performance. He knows the selfishness, the greed, the grasping, the ruthlessness with which we cut people out and harm those we profess to love. He sees all the maneuvering and manipulating, the clever arranging that goes on in our lives and in our hearts. Therefore that beautiful performance is utterly invalid to God. That is why the sense of righteousness that results from our performance before men never lasts. It is but a temporary shot in the arm that we need to repeat again and again, almost as though we are addicted to it. But it will always let us down in the hour of crisis. Only the righteousness that comes from God is lasting and will work—not only in time but for all eternity. That is what Abraham discovered. He learned that righteousness that comes from performance is worthless.

How did he discover this? Paul refers to the fifteenth chapter of Genesis where God appeared before Abraham. He took him out one night and showed him the stars in the heavens. "Abraham, look up!" Abraham looked up into the stillness of the night, with the stars blazing in all their glory. God said to him, "If you can number those stars, you can number your descendants. Their number will be far more than all the stars of heaven." Paul says, "Abraham believed God, and it was reckoned to him as righteousness"—self-worth, standing before God, acceptance, a sense of love and of value in the sight of God.

The passage says, "Abraham believed God," but we have to be careful. Interestingly enough, when James quotes this passage he says, "Abraham believed God, and it was credited to him as righteousness," then he adds, "and he was called God's friend" (James 2:23). That is acceptance, isn't it? Abraham became God's friend, not because he behaved so well or because he was a godly man and obeyed God. He became the friend of God because he believed God's promise. Abraham is a beautiful example of what Paul is talking about here in Romans.

> *Father, forgive me for any lingering desire in my heart to try to earn a standing before you, for any hungering after the righteousness that comes from men. Help me to live by faith as Abraham did.*

Does our standing with our holy God differ from that of Abraham? How does this affect our walk of faith? Do we continue to earn our worth by doing good works?

THE FAITH OF OUR FATHER

A daily devotion for September 11

Read Romans 4:13–25.

"He is our father in the sight of God, in whom he believed—the God who gives life to the dead and calls into being things that were not. Against all hope, Abraham in hope believed and so became the father of many nations, just as it had been said to him, 'So shall your offspring be.' Without weakening in his faith, he faced the fact that his body was as good as dead—since he was about a hundred years old—and that Sarah's womb was also dead. Yet he did not waver through unbelief regarding the promise of God, but was strengthened in his faith and gave glory to God, being fully persuaded that God had power to do what he had promised" (Rom. 4:17–21).

Paul tells us here what faith is. First, he says the key is the object of faith. Abraham, Paul says, believed God, and so God is the object. The quality of our faith depends upon the object in which we have placed our trust. The amount of faith has nothing to do with it. That is why Jesus told us that even if we have a tiny faith, like a grain of mustard seed, it will work. The object of our faith is the important thing. The size of our faith doesn't matter; what matters is how big our God is! Two things about this God helped Abraham tremendously. First, he is the God who gives life to the dead, who takes things that once were vibrant and full of life, but have died and become hopeless, and brings them to life again. Second, he is the God who "calls things that are not, as though they were." He calls into existence the things that do not exist. He is a creative God.

Notice also the obstacles to faith. Whenever we have faith or are called to exercise it, there are obstacles. Abraham teaches us this. First, he faced hopeless circumstances. Abraham saw his hundred-year-old body and the barrenness of Sarah's womb. She was ninety years old and had never had a baby. They had been trying for years and years, and no baby had come. Now here is the beauty of Abraham's faith. Paul says that he faced the facts. I love that. Many of us think that faith is evading the facts—escapism, a dreamy idealism that never looks at reality, a fanciful adventuring in which we hope everything will work out. It is never that!

But verse 20 says, "Yet he did not waver through unbelief regarding the promise of God." That is, the promise itself was the second obstacle to faith because it was too good to be true! It was beyond belief that God would make Abraham heir of all the world and give him a standing before God that he didn't deserve. It was too good to be true, so it was an obstacle to faith. Isn't that interesting?

Father, thank you for this example of Abraham. What a tremendous model of faith he is. By his example, he has taught me how to trust despite the circumstances that surround me when I have a God who promises to come to my aid and who cannot fail.

When our faith is weak and subject to attack, what are two facts about God that will reassure us and will stabilize our trust in him? Do we need more faith, or is our God too small?

PEACE WITH GOD

A daily devotion for September 12

Read Romans 5:1–2.

> "Therefore, since we have been justified through faith, we have peace with God through our Lord Jesus Christ" (Rom. 5:1).

The first thing that we learn as Christians is that we are justified by faith. To help us understand what that means, the apostle used the example of Abraham in chapter 4. Before the law was given, Abraham was justified by faith. He was declared to be acceptable to God. He was God's friend. Abraham didn't earn that. He was given that at the beginning of his relationship with God when he believed God. That is what faith means. When Abraham believed that God could and would do what he had promised, Abraham was declared the friend of God and entered into that close relationship with God that characterized his life. That is what it means to be justified by faith. We receive this through no merit on our part but by faith alone by believing God's promise, according to the work of his Son. That is justification.

Then, Paul says, there is a way by which we can test whether we really believe that and have been justified by faith: "Since we have been justified by faith, the sure result is that we have peace with God." As we think about our lives and about our relationship with God, if we really have believed that God justifies the ungodly, we will have peace with him. We are in his family. The war is over. All the conflict between us and God is ended.

I was in Honolulu when World War II ended. We had experienced the excitement and joy of VE Day some months before when the war had ended in Europe, but that was a long way from the South Pacific. Though we were glad that the battle in Europe had ended, we still had a war to fight. Out in the South Pacific there were many bloody battles yet to come. I will never forget the day it was announced that a peace treaty with Japan had been signed. All over the world, the war was at an end. In Honolulu the people poured out into the streets. Thousands of people jammed the beaches and streets of the city, rejoicing because they were at peace. That is what happens in the heart when we understand that we have been justified by faith. The war is over, and we are at peace with God. All conflict has ceased.

If you do not have that sense of peace, the way to get it back is not by working on your feelings but by reviewing your justification. Go over the facts again, and remind yourself of what God has declared. Then your faith will be restored and you can handle these doubts and fears. If you have peace with God, you have an answer to the accusation of your conscience when you sin.

Many young Christians, in that glory and first flush of love in their relationship with the Lord, think they will not sin again. They cannot imagine doing the things they once did. But eventually they will be back doing some of those things. Perhaps they will not return to all that they formerly did, but they will fall back. If you are in that situation, how do you reply when your accusing conscience says, "Are you a Christian? Could you possibly be a Christian and act like this?" That is where justification by faith comes in. You remind yourself, "My standing and my acceptance by God do not depend upon me. Even my sin doesn't cancel it out. The whole essence of this truth is that God has found a way to put aside my sin by faith in the work of his beloved Son on my behalf. In that truth, Lord, I confess my sin and put my trust in you."

> *Thank you, Father, for these riches that are given so freely in Jesus. I don't deserve them, but I have them because I have believed your great and mighty promise. I have peace with you. I have been reconciled. I have acceptance in your presence and continual access to your help.*

What is the alternative to our feelings when we are anxious and fearful about our relationship with God? Does peace with God depend upon us? Do we need to review the facts about our justification by faith?

REJOICING IN SUFFERING

A daily devotion for September 13

Read Romans 5:3–10.

> "Not only so, but we also glory in our sufferings, because we know that suffering produces perseverance; perseverance, character; and character, hope. And hope does not put us to shame, because God's love has been poured out into our hearts through the Holy Spirit, who has been given to us" (Rom. 5:3–5 NIV).

It is clear from this that Christians are expected to experience suffering. Those who think that becoming a Christian will remove them from suffering have been seriously misled, for the Scriptures teach that we are to expect suffering.

The Greek word for *suffering* is translated as "tribulation, something that causes distress." This can range from minor annoyances that we experience every day to major disasters that come sweeping down out of the blue and leave us stricken. These are the sufferings that we might endure, the tribulations.

According to Romans 5, the Christian response to suffering is to rejoice: "Not only so, but we rejoice in our sufferings." Here is where many people balk. They say, "I can't buy that! Do you mean to say that God is telling me that when I am hurting, I am expected to rejoice in that? That is not human, not natural!"

How do we get to the place where we can rejoice in suffering? The apostle's answer is, "We rejoice in suffering because we know." We rejoice not because it's such a great feeling to be hurt but because we know something about suffering. It is something our faith enables us to know, a kind of inside information that others do not share.

Paul says we know what suffering produces. Suffering accomplishes something. It is productive. We know it works, and that is what makes us rejoice. Watch a woman in labor. If you have any empathy, you can't help but feel deeply hurt with her because she is going through such pain. And yet there usually is joy in the midst of it because she knows that childbirth produces children. Many women will gladly go through childbirth because they want children. Suffering results in something worthwhile.

The apostle says suffering produces three things. First, it produces perseverance. In some versions the word is *patience*. The Greek word means "to abide under, to stay under the pressure." Pressure is something we want to escape, but suffering teaches us to persist in the face of it. The best translation I can think of is the word *steadiness*. Suffering produces steadiness.

Second, steadiness produces character. The Greek word for *character* carries with it the idea of being put to the test and approved, of being shown to be reliable. We finally learn that we are not going to be destroyed, that things will work out. People start counting on us. They see strength in us, and we become more reliable.

Third, we find that reliability produces hope. The hope is that we will share the glory of God, which is God's character. We have the hope that God is producing the image of Christ in us. This hope is a certainty, not just a possibility. We are being changed. We are becoming more like Jesus. We can see that we are more thoughtful, more compassionate, more loving. We are being mellowed. We are becoming like Christ—stronger, wiser, purer, more patient. God is transforming is into the image of his Son.

> *Thank you, Lord, for giving me a deep sense of joy through the pressure and the testing. I trust that you will release your love into my heart to steady me, to enfold me, and to keep me strong and rejoicing.*

Are we surprised by suffering? Did Jesus promise or demonstrate a trouble-free life? What inside information about the goal of suffering produces joyful expectation?

ONE MAN

A daily devotion for September 14

Read Romans 5:11–21.

> "For if, by the trespass of the one man, death reigned through that one man, how much more will those who receive God's abundant provision of grace and of the gift of righteousness reign in life through the one man, Jesus Christ!" (Rom. 5:17).

Paul's argument is that Adam's transgression permitted death to reign over the whole race. This involves more than just the funeral held when someone's life on earth has ended. True, that funeral happens because of Adam's trespass, but there is more to it than that. Not only does death come to us at the end of our lives because of Adam, but it reigns throughout our lives because of him. Paul is talking about forms of death other than the mere cessation of life.

Life is love, joy, and excitement. It is vitality, enrichment, and power; it is fulfillment in every possibility of our being. That is life. Death is the absence of life. Death is emptiness, loneliness, misery, depression, boredom, and restlessness. How much of your life is made up of death? A lot of it, right? Some people never seem to have anything but death in their lives. Death reigns because of Adam's transgression.

Paul is saying that Christ's death provides such abundant grace and loving acceptance, which are continually available, that all who are in him can reign in life now. We can have life amid all the pressures, suffering, and troubles. Our spirits can be alive and joyful—experiencing fulfillment and delight. Life in the midst of death! We reign in life now. Love, joy, peace, and glory fill our hearts despite all the heartaches and the pressures of life.

Paul draws this parallel so that we might see how much more we have in Jesus than we ever had in Adam. What we lost in Adam, we regain in Jesus, plus so much more. Just as a climber on a mountaintop can dislodge a pebble that rolls downward and accumulates others until it launches an avalanche that moves the whole mountainside, so Adam's sin in the garden of Eden dislodged a pebble that created an avalanche of sin and death that has swept through humanity. But Paul tells us Jesus has launched an avalanche of grace, and in him there is ample counteraction against all that Adam has brought.

Adam has ruined us all. Only Christ can set us free. Sin and death will never loose their hold on us except at the command of Jesus Christ. Therefore, the one to whom we look is the Lord Jesus, who broke the terrible death grip on us and set us free—Jesus, the head of a new race, the beginning of a new humanity. Jesus is Lord. As we see him thus, we discover what the Scriptures say, that the blessed Lord, who broke through death and sin, has come to live within us, to give himself to us, and to infuse us with his strength and purity, his wisdom and power. All that he is has become available to us. Thus we rejoice in God through our Lord Jesus Christ.

By your Spirit, Father, I rejoice in the Lord Jesus Christ because he has broken the shackles of death and sin that held me. He has set my spirit free and has given me the opportunity to draw from him the grace and mercy I need every day.

What is a dimensional description of death? Of life? As we walk through the valley of the shadow of death, are we living in the fullness of life in Christ that is our inheritance?

DEAD TO SIN

A daily devotion for September 15

Read Romans 6:1–2.

> "What shall we say, then? Shall we go on sinning so that grace may increase? By no means! We are those who have died to sin; how can we live in it any longer?" (Rom. 6:1–2).

Shall we go on sinning so that grace may increase? Notice three things about this question. First, the question is logical. It is a good one, the kind that ought to be asked at this point. Something about the grace of God immediately raises this issue. If sin is so completely taken care of by the forgiveness of Christ, then we don't need to worry about sins, do we? They won't separate us from Christ, so why not keep on doing them? It is a perfectly logical question.

But second, notice that our very nature would have us raise this question. It is not only logical but natural. That is because sin is fun, isn't it? We like to do it. Otherwise we wouldn't keep on doing it; we would not get involved in it. We know sins are bad for us, but we take pleasure in them. Therefore, any suggestion that we can escape the penalty for our sin and still enjoy the action arouses considerable interest in us.

We must understand that Paul is talking about a lifestyle of sin, not just an occasional failure. He is talking about Christians who continue absolutely unchanged in the lifestyle they lived before they were Christians. The word he uses for "go on sinning" is in the present continuous tense. It means the action keeps on happening. Paul is talking about a habitual practice. Can we go on living this way?

Finally, notice that this question is put in such a way as to sound rightly motivated and even pious. "Shall we go on sinning, so that grace may increase?" This suggests that our motivation for sinning is not just our own satisfaction—we are doing this so that grace may increase. God loves to show his grace. Therefore, if we go on sinning, he will have all the more opportunity. This question is not asked by a complete pagan but by someone who seems intent on the glory of God. Having said that, we come now to Paul's answer.

Paul immediately reacts with a positive statement, bluntly put: "By no means! We are those who have died to sin. How can we live in it any longer?" This does not mean that sin is dead in us. It doesn't mean that we have reached the place where we cannot sin. Neither does Paul mean that we are dying to sin, that we are gradually changing and growing, and that there will come a time when we will outgrow all this evil. He doesn't mean that at all. Again, we must face clearly the statement the apostle makes. He puts it in a once-and-for-all way: we died to sin. It is impossible for our lifestyle to continue unchanged when we become Christians. That's because a change has occurred deep in the human spirit. And those who protest and say they can go on living in the old way are simply revealing that there has been no change in their spirit, that there has been no break with Adam. They are still in the same condition.

Thank you, Father, for the grace of our Lord Jesus, who has the power to break the grip of death upon my life.

Are we using God's grace as a pretext for continuing in our sins? What are three reasons we continue this self-deception? Are we choosing to live in Christ's resurrection life rather than in sin and death in Adam?

TRUE BAPTISM

A daily devotion for September 16

Read Romans 6:3–7.

> "Or don't you know that all of us who were baptized into Christ Jesus were baptized into his death? We were therefore buried with him through baptism into death in order that, just as Christ was raised from the dead through the glory of the Father, we too may live a new life" (Rom. 6:3–4).

When I was a boy in Montana, I had a horse that could smell water from farther away than any animal I ever saw. There are people who are like that. Whenever they read these passages and see the word *baptism*, they smell water, but there is no water here. This is a dry passage.

This passage deals with the question of how we died to sin, how we became separated from Adam, and how we became joined in Christ. No water can do that. This change requires something far more potent than water. This passage is, therefore, a description of what is called "the baptism of the Holy Spirit." Paul wrote to the Corinthians, "For we were all baptized by one Spirit into one body—whether Jews or Greeks, slaves or free—and we were all given the one Spirit to drink" (1 Cor. 12:13). He says twice that all believers were baptized into one body. We were placed into Christ. We are not Christians if that isn't true of us. People today who say we need to experience the baptism of the Holy Spirit after we become believers do not understand the Scriptures. There is no way to become a believer without being baptized with the Spirit.

In this passage Paul makes several points about the baptism of the Spirit. First, he says that we are expected to know about it. "Don't you know?" Paul asks. He expects these Roman Christians, who had never met him or been taught in person by him, to know this fact. This is something new Christians ought to know.

The apostle also says, "This is how we died to sin." The great statement of this passage is that when we became Christians, we died to sin. Paul is still discussing the question, "Can a believer go on sinning?" "No," he answers, "because he died to sin." How did we die to sin? Paul explains that the Spirit took us and identified us with all that Jesus did. That means that somehow this is a timeless event. The Spirit of God is able to ignore the two thousand years since the crucifixion and the resurrection and to identify us with that moment when Jesus died, was buried, and rose again from the dead. We participate in those events. That is clear.

Therefore this is not theological fiction; it is fact. Adam sinned, and we sin. Adam died, and men ever since have died. The apostle is saying that what was true in Adam has now been ended and that now we are in Christ by faith in him. Once Adam's actions affected us, but now what Christ did becomes our actions as well. Christ died, and we died; Christ was buried, and we were buried with him; Christ rose again, and we rose with him. So what is true of Jesus is true of us. Here Paul is dealing with what is probably the most remarkable and certainly the most magnificent truth recorded in the pages of Scripture. It is the central truth God wants us to learn. We died with Christ, were buried, and rose again with him. That union with Christ is the truth from which everything else in Scripture flows. If we understand and accept this as fact, which it is, everything will be different in our lives. That is why the apostle labors so to help us understand this.

Lord, thank you for this assurance that,
having been baptized in the Holy Spirit,
I am dead to sin and alive to you.

Can water baptism bring us out of our death in Adam and into new life in Christ? What is its purpose? What essential and transforming truth does the baptism of the Holy Spirit signify?

A NEW MASTER

A daily devotion for September 17

Read Romans 6:8–14.

> "For sin shall no longer be your master, because you are not under law, but under grace" (Rom. 6:14).

Paul brings in the law because he is dealing with one of the most basic problems of the Christian struggle, the thing that often depresses and discourages us more than anything else—the sense of condemnation we feel when we sin. The law produces condemnation. The law says that unless we live up to this standard, God will not have anything to do with us. This idea has been so engrained in us that when we sin, even as believers, we think God is angry and upset with us and doesn't care about us. We think that way about ourselves, and we become discouraged, defeated, and depressed. We want to give up.

But Paul says that is not true. Believers are not under the law, and God does not respond that way toward us. We are under grace. God understands our struggle. He is not upset by it; he is not angry with us. He understands our failure. He knows that we will struggle and that we will sometimes fail. He also knows that he has made full provision in Christ for us to recover immediately, to pick ourselves up, and to continue climbing up the mountain. Therefore, as his beloved children, we don't need to be discouraged, and we won't be.

Sin will not be our master because we are not under law and condemnation but under grace. And even though we struggle and fail, if we return to God and ask his forgiveness, accept it from him, remember that he loves us, and go on from there, we will win.

I will never forget how, as a young man in the service during World War II, I was on a watch one night, reading Romans. This verse leaped out of the pages at me. The Spirit made it come alive, and I saw the great promise that all the things I was struggling with as a young man would ultimately be mastered—not because I was so smart but because God was teaching me and leading me into victory. I walked the floor, my heart boiling over with praise and thanksgiving to God. I walked in a cloud of glory, rejoicing in this great promise: "Sin shall no longer be your master, because you are not under law, but under grace."

Looking back across the years since that night, I can see that God has broken the grip of the things that mastered me. Other problems have arisen with which I still struggle. But the promise remains: "Sin shall no longer be your master, because you are not under law, but under grace."

> *How grateful I am, Father, for this word of assurance that as one who is in Christ I need not be discouraged and need not fail, for nothing can separate me from the love of God that is in Jesus Christ our Lord.*

When our sins are exposed by the law, where do we go with our burden of guilt? Are we learning to live in the forgiveness and the liberating power of God's grace? Are we captured by God's unrelenting love?

A NEW HUSBAND

A daily devotion for September 18

Read Romans 7:1–6.

> "Do you not know, brothers and sisters—for I am speaking to those who know the law—that the law has authority over someone only as long as that person lives? For example, by law a married woman is bound to her husband as long as he is alive, but if her husband dies, she is released from the law that binds her to him. So then, if she has sexual relations with another man while her husband is still alive, she is called an adulteress. But if her husband dies, she is released from that law and is not an adulteress if she marries another man" (Rom. 7:1–3).

Paul uses an illustration to teach us the way to be free from the law. The woman is us. She has two husbands, one following the other. Notice what the death of the first husband does to the woman's relationship to the law. When the first husband dies, not only is she released from him, but she is released from the law. If her husband dies, the law can say nothing to her as to where she can go, what she can do, and who she can be with. She is released from the law. The death of the husband makes the woman dead to the law.

The first husband is Adam, the old life into which we were born. We were linked to it, married to it, and couldn't get away from it. A woman married to an old, cruel husband can't do much about it. While she is married she is tied to that husband. She cannot have a second husband while she is married to the first. She is stuck with number one, and she must share his lifestyle of bondage, corruption, shame, and death. That is why we who were born into Adam have to share the lifestyle of fallen Adam.

If this woman, while married to her first husband, tries to live with another—for this lifestyle is sickening to her—she will be called an adulteress. Who calls her that? The law does. The law condemns her. Only when the first husband dies is she free from that condemnation of the law and able to marry again. When she does, the law is absolutely silent; it has nothing to say to her. Verse 4 says, "So … you also died to the law through the body of Christ, that you might belong to another, to him who was raised from the dead, in order that we might bear fruit for God."

What a fantastic verse! Here is the marvelous declaration of the gospel of our Lord Jesus. Notice how Paul draws the parallel: "So … you also." We fit right into this. The key words here are "you also died to the law through the body of Christ." "The body of Christ" refers to the death of the Lord Jesus on the cross.

Paul is referring to what the Scriptures say in many places—that on the cross the Lord Jesus was made sin for us. He took our place as sinful humanity on the cross. In other words, he became that first husband, that Adamic nature to which we were married. When he became that, he died. When he died, we were freed from the law.

The law has nothing to say to us anymore. We are free to be married to another, no longer to our Adam-like flesh but instead to the risen Christ. Our first husband was crucified with Christ; our second husband is Christ, now risen from the dead. We now share his name. We share his power. We share his experiences. We share his position, his glory, his hope, his dreams—all that he is, we now share! We are married to Christ, risen from the dead. The law, therefore, has nothing to say to us.

> *Thank you for this Father. I pray that I may understand more fully that I am not under condemnation. Even though I struggle and don't always act on the principles revealed to me, you don't reject me or cast me aside.*

How did Christ's death change our relationship to the law? How did Christ's resurrection change our identity? How does this profoundly affect the way we deal with sin and guilt?

THE CONTINUING STRUGGLE

A daily devotion for September 19

Read Romans 7:7–25.

> "For I know that good itself does not dwell in me, that is, in my sinful nature. For I have the desire to do what is good, but I cannot carry it out. For I do not do the good I want to do, but the evil I do not want to do—this I keep on doing. Now if I do what I do not want to do, it is no longer I who do it, but it is sin living in me that does it" (Rom. 7:18–20).

Paul says that as a Christian, redeemed by the grace of God, there is now something within him that wants to do good, that agrees with the law (because the law describes God's holy nature), that says the law is right. Something within says what the law tells him to do is right, and he wants to do it. But there is something else in him that rises up and says "No!" Though he is determined not to do what is bad, when he finds himself in the wrong circumstances, his determination melts away, his resolve is gone, and he ends up doing what he had sworn he would not do.

So what has gone wrong? Paul explains, "It is no longer I who do it; it is sin living in me." Isn't that strange? There is a division within our humanity. There is the "I" that wants to do what God desires, but there is also the sin that dwells in us. Human beings are complicated creatures. We have within us a spirit, a soul, and a body. These are distinct. Paul is suggesting that the redeemed spirit never wants to do what God has prohibited. It agrees with the law that it is good. And yet there is an alien power, a force that he calls sin, a great beast that lies still within us until touched by the commandment of the law. Then it springs to life, and we do what we do not want to do.

This is what we all struggle with. The cry of the heart at that moment is, "What a wretched man I am! Who will rescue me from this body of death?" (Rom. 7:24). Right here we arrive at where the Lord Jesus began the Sermon on the Mount: "Blessed are the poor in spirit, for theirs is the kingdom of heaven" (Matt. 5:3). Blessed is the man who comes to the end of himself. Blessed is the man who understands his spiritual bankruptcy, because this is the point—the only point—where God's help is given.

This is what we need to learn. If we think that we can use something in ourselves to work out our problems, if we think that our wills are strong enough, that we can control evil in our lives simply by determining to do so, we have not come to the end of ourselves yet. The Spirit of God simply folds his arms to wait and lets us go ahead and try it on that basis. And we fail miserably—until at last, out of our failures, we cry, "O wretched man that I am!" Sin has deceived us, and the law, as our friend, has come in and exposed sin for what it is. When we see how wretched it makes us, we are ready for the answer, which comes immediately in verse 25: "Thanks be to God—through Jesus Christ our Lord!"

Who will deliver us from this body of death? The Lord Jesus has already done it. We are to respond to the feelings of wretchedness and failure, to which the law has brought us because of our sin, by reminding ourselves immediately of the facts that are true of us in Jesus Christ. We are no longer bound to our sinful flesh by the law. We are married to Christ risen from the dead. We must no longer think, *I am a poor, struggling, bewildered disciple, left alone to wrestle against these powerful urges.* We must now think, *I am a free son of God. I am dead to sin and dead to the law because I am married to Christ. His power is mine right at this moment. Though I may not feel a thing, I have the power to say no and to walk away and be free in Jesus Christ.*

> *Thank you, Father, for the simple and clear teaching of this passage. Help me to understand that I am freed from the law once it has done its work of bringing me to the knowledge of sin. I cannot control myself by that means or deliver myself from evil, but I can rest upon the mighty deliverer who will set me free.*

What is the purpose of the law? What effect does our new identity as Christ's bride have on our desire to live lives pleasing to him? Do we have the power to resolve the continuing conflict of spirit versus soul and body? Are we surrendering our incompetence to his all-surpassing power?

NO CONDEMNATION

A daily devotion for September 20

Read Romans 7:25–8:2.

> "So then, I myself in my mind am a slave to God's law, but in my sinful nature a slave to the law of sin. Therefore, there is now no condemnation for those who are in Christ Jesus" (Rom. 7:25–8:1).

Paul says, "I want to do good. I believe in it. I delight in God's law—God's holy nature—in my inner being. I am changed; I agree that the law is good, but I find I can't do it." In his mind Paul is awakened to the value and the righteousness of God's law, but set against that is the sin in his flesh that takes hold of him and makes him a slave to the law of sin, even though he does not want to be.

How does Paul break this hold? He is saying though we struggle at times, there is no condemnation of those who are in Christ Jesus. The reason for this is given in one little phrase: "in Christ." That goes back to our justification by faith. We came out of Adam, we are in Christ, and God will never condemn those who are in Christ. We have to understand what "no condemnation" means. Certainly, the most basic element is that there is no rejection by God. He does not turn us aside or kick us out of his family. If we are born into the family of God by faith in Jesus Christ, the Holy Spirit has come to dwell within us, and he will never leave us.

Another thing "no condemnation" means is that God is not angry with us when this struggle comes into our lives. We want to be good, or we want to stop doing bad, but when the moment of temptation comes, we find ourselves overpowered and weak, and we give way. Then we hate ourselves. We go away frustrated, thinking, *Oh, what's the matter with me? Why can't I do this thing? Why can't I act like I want to?* But though we may condemn ourselves, God does not. He is not angry with us about that.

The beautiful figure is that of a tender, loving father, watching his little boy take his first steps. No father ever gets angry with his little son because he doesn't get right up and start running around the first time he tries to walk. If the child stumbles and falters, the father helps him; he doesn't spank him. He lifts him up, encourages him, and shows him how to do it right. And if the child has a problem with his feet—maybe one foot is twisted or deformed—the father finds a way to relieve that condition and to help him learn to walk. That is what God does. He is not angry when we are struggling. He knows it takes awhile—quite awhile at times. And even the best of saints will, at times, fall. This was true of Paul, it was true of the apostles, and it was true of all the prophets of the Old Testament. Sin is deceitful and it will trip us at times. But God is not angry with us.

> *Heavenly Father, I am forever grateful that you are slow to anger when I continue to follow after the things of this world. Thank you for your patience and for the abundance of grace I receive each day.*

What do we do with the guilt inevitably resulting from our sin and our failure? Do we seize the prepaid gift of God's forgiveness? Do we then live free from condemnation and submit to the quality control of his Spirit?

GOOD NEWS

A daily devotion for September 21

Read Romans 8:3–4.

> "For what the law was powerless to do in that it was weakened by our sinful nature, God did by sending his own Son in the likeness of sinful man to be a sin offering. And so he condemned sin in the sinful man, in order that the righteous requirement of the law might be fully met in us, who do not live according to our sinful nature but according to the Spirit" (Rom. 8:3–4).

This is a beautiful description of the good news in Jesus Christ. Paul says the law is powerless to produce righteousness. It cannot make us good—no way. It can demand and demand, but it cannot enable and it never will. This, by the way, is why nagging somebody never helps. Nagging is a form of law, and God will not let the law nag us, because that doesn't help. It only makes things worse. If we nag a spouse or a child, we will find that the same thing happens. Nagging only makes things worse. The reason, Paul says, is because the law only stirs up the power of sin. It releases this force, this beast within us, this powerful engine that takes over and carries us where we don't want to go. That is why nagging, or any form of the law, will never work. It is not because there is anything wrong with what is being said. It is because of the weakness of the flesh that it cannot work. Paul says, "The sting of death is sin, and the strength of sin is the law" (1 Cor. 15:56). The law keeps sin going; it stirs it up.

To break through this vicious circle, Paul says, God sent forth his own Son. There is a beautiful tenderness about this. He sent his own Son. He did not send an angel; he did not send a man. He sent his own Son as a man, in the likeness of sinful flesh. Notice that. He did not send him just in the likeness of flesh but in the likeness of sinful flesh. Jesus had a body like ours. Since sin has been done in the body, it must be judged and broken in the body. Therefore, Jesus had a body. But it was not just a body of sinful flesh but the likeness of sinful flesh. It was like our sinful bodies, in that it was subject to infirmities (Jesus was weak, hungry, and weary), but there was no sin in him. Paul carefully preserves that idea here.

In that body of flesh, without sin, Jesus became sin. As we read here, he was made an offering for sin. And in the mystery of the cross, which we can never understand, no matter how long we live, the Lord Jesus, at the hour of darkness, gathered into himself all the sins of the world, all the terrible, foul injustice, crime, and misery that we have seen throughout history, from every person, and brought them to an end by dying. The good news is that somehow, by faith in him, we get involved in that death.

Father, thank you for showing me that the way out of my struggle with sin is not to force myself to be different but to see that I already am different. I have been cleansed and made whole in Jesus Christ. He is my life, and I belong to him and always will. Help me to believe that and to act that way.

Are our lives being sculpted by the power of God's amazing grace? Do we live as ones liberated from the dead works of performance and demand? Is this freedom evident in our relationships with others? Are we responding with awe and gratitude to the mystery and the reality of God's gift in his Son?

TWO POSSIBILITIES

A daily devotion for September 22

Read Romans 8:5–8.

> "Those who live according to the flesh have their minds set on what the flesh desires; but those who live in accordance with the Spirit have their minds set on what the Spirit desires" (Rom. 8:5).

As Christians we face two possibilities that will determine if we manifest the righteousness of God: whether we walk according to the Spirit or according to the flesh. The deciding factor is what we set our minds on—what we think about all through the day, what is important to us. Do we adopt the viewpoint of the flesh, which governs the thinking of the world? Or do we choose the viewpoint of the Spirit—God's viewpoint—on life? What we do with our thinking is the determining factor. Where we set our minds will make the difference.

What is the mindset of the person who lives according to the flesh? We need only look around to see what that is. It is the natural viewpoint of life. People want to make money because money provides comforts and conveniences that we would like to have. People want to have fun. People want pleasure, money, and fame. They will give their right arm to gain influence and prestige. People desire to fulfill themselves. They want to manifest every capability within them. That is what the world lives for. And it wants it all now, not later. That is the natural point of view.

There is nothing wrong with that unless that is all we want. If that is all we want, then it is very wrong. This is what the Scriptures help us to see—that there is another point of view, which is life viewed according to the Spirit. "Ah," some say, "I know what that means! That means you have to forget about making money and having fun and fulfilling yourself. All you do is memorize Scripture and think about God all day long. You go around reciting Scripture verses and telling people what is wrong with their lives."

Many people think that is what we are talking about when we say that we are to have our minds set on the things of the Spirit. But if we see people like that, we soon discover that kind of life does not produce the results this passage tells us should be there. That is only another form of being run by the flesh—it's a religious form of it, but it is the same thing.

What does it mean, then, to have our minds set on the Spirit? It means that in the midst of making money, having fun, gaining fame, and fulfilling ourselves, we are primarily concerned with showing love, helping others, speaking truth, and, above all, loving God and seeking his glory. The trouble with the world is that it is content with just making money, having fun, and fulfilling itself—that is all it wants. But the mind set on the Spirit desires that God be glorified in all these things. When our minds are set on the Spirit we look at life's events from God's point of view, not from the world's. Our value system is changed and it touches everything we do. The important thing in seeking to fulfill our needs is that God be glorified. That is what makes the difference. That is the mind set on the Spirit. It does not remove us from life—it puts us right back into it. But it does that with a different point of view.

> *I am grateful, Lord, that even though I struggle in Christ Jesus there is no condemnation for me. Grant me the mindset of the Spirit.*

Is the chief end of our lives the glory of God and our enjoyment of him? How does this affect our reactions to losses and gains of earth's treasures and pleasures? Do we need to seriously reassess our priorities?

THE SPIRIT AND THE BODY

A daily devotion for September 23

Read Romans 8:8–13.

> "But if Christ is in you, then even though your body is subject to death because of sin, the Spirit gives life because of righteousness. And if the Spirit of him who raised Jesus from the dead is living in you, he who raised Christ from the dead will also give life to your mortal bodies because of his Spirit who lives in you" (Rom. 8:10–11).

Notice the helpful teaching about the Spirit here. He is called the Spirit of God and the Spirit of Christ. Then Paul makes clear that the Spirit is the means by which Jesus Christ himself is in us. By means of the Holy Spirit, Christ is in us. And if Christ is in us, our bodies are dead because of sin.

The problem is, our bodies are yet unredeemed. As a consequence, they are the seat of the sin that troubles us so. And the sin that is in us—still there in our bodies—affects the body. That is why the body lusts, the body loves comfort, and the body seeks after pleasure; that is why our minds react with hate, bitterness, resentment, and hostility. Sin finds its seat in the body. That is why our bodies keep growing old. They are dying because of sin.

But that is not the final answer for the Christian. The spirit in the Christian is alive because of the gift of righteousness. Christ has come in, and we are linked with him. Paul puts it beautifully in 2 Corinthians 4:16: "Though outwardly we are wasting away, yet inwardly we are being renewed day by day." That is the joy of being a Christian. Though the body, with the sin that is within it, gives us difficulty, tempting us, confounding us at times, the spirit is alive because of righteousness. Sin has its seat in the physical body, and it rises up like a powerful beast. But we have an answer. It is put beautifully in 1 John 4:4: "The one who is in you is greater than the one who is in the world." The Spirit of God within us is stronger than the sin that is in our bodies. Therefore in Christ, we have strength to control the body.

Unfortunately, many commentators say that verse 11 refers to the promise of the resurrection at the end of life when God will make our bodies alive. But that is not what Paul is saying. He is talking about the Spirit in us giving life to our mortal bodies. A mortal body is not yet dead. A mortal body is subject to death. It is dying, but it is not yet dead. Therefore, this verse does not pertain to the resurrection. Later on Paul will come to that, but here he is talking about what the Spirit does in us now. He says that though sin in our mortal bodies will tempt us severely and at times rise up with great power, we must never forget that because our human spirit has been made alive in Jesus Christ and because the Spirit of God dwells in us, we have the strength to say no to that expression of evil.

We cannot reverse the processes of death—no one can. Our bodies will die. But we can refuse to let the members of our bodies become the instruments of sin. We can refuse, by the power of the Spirit within, to let our members be used for that purpose. We don't have to let our eyes look at wrong things. We can say no. We don't have to let our tongues say evil, hurtful, sarcastic, and vicious things. We can say no to that. We don't have to let our ears hear things that are hurtful. We don't have to let our hands be used for wrong purposes. We don't have to let our legs and feet lead us into places where we ought not to be. We have been made alive in Jesus Christ, and the Spirit of God himself dwells in us!

> *Father, you have made me alive through your Spirit. Teach me to yield to him rather than to my flesh.*

Describe the radical differences between the two mindsets. What are the two sources of power controlling them? What response to sin's slavery is characteristic of those led by the Spirit of God? What is the result of choosing to live according to the sinful nature? Shall we then choose life?

CHILDREN OF GOD

A daily devotion for September 24

Read Romans 8:14–15.

> "For those who are led by the Spirit of God are the children of God. The Spirit you received does not make you slaves, so that you live in fear again; rather, the Spirit you received brought about your adoption to sonship" (Rom. 8:14–15).

We are all creatures of God by natural birth, but Paul is careful to use a different term in Romans. Here the description is "children of God." We are in the family of God, and this is a distinctive term. God intends for us to return to this truth when we are in trouble. If we are having difficulty with our behavior—whether we are not doing what we want to do or doing what we don't want to do—the way to handle the problem is to remind ourselves of what God has made us to be.

In other words, in our struggle with sin, we are not slaves, helplessly battling against a cruel and powerful master; we are sons and daughters of the living God, with power to overcome the evil. Though we may be temporarily overcome, we are never ultimately defeated. That cannot be, because we are children of God. That is why Paul could say, "Sin shall not have dominion over you, for you are not under law but under grace" (Rom. 6:14 KJV). In this gracious relationship, we are made children of the living God. No matter what happens to us, that is what we are. Nothing can change that.

It is also important for us to see how we become children of God. Paul says the Spirit of God found us and adopted us into God's family. Some may say, "What do you mean when you say we are adopted into the family of God? I have been taught that I was born into the family of God." Both of these are true. We are both adopted and born into the family of God. He uses both terms because he wants to highlight two different aspects of our belonging to his family. We are said to be adopted because God wants us to remember always that we are not naturally part of his family. We are all children of Adam by natural birth. We belong to the human family, and we inherit Adam's nature—all his defects, all his problems, all the evil that came into his life by his disobedience. So by nature we are not part of God's family. This is just like those today who were born into one family but were taken out of that family and were adopted into another family. From then on they became part of the family that adopted them.

This is what has happened to us. God has taken us out of our natural state in Adam and has made us children of God. He reminds us that we are in his family by adoption so that we might never take this for granted or forget that if we were left in our natural state we would not have a part in the family of God. It is only by God's grace that we come into his family.

But it is also true that we are born into God's family. Once we have been adopted, because God is God, he not only makes us legally his children but allows us to partake of the divine nature and we are born into his family. Peter puts it this way: "We have been made partakers of the divine nature" (2 Peter 1:4 KJV). So by God's grace we are as much a part of his family as if we had originally been born into it.

There is nothing more wonderful to remind ourselves of each day than this great fact: if we are Christians, we are children of the living God, adopted and born into his family. Because we are his children, God loves us, protects us, provides for us, plans for us, hears us, claims us and openly acknowledges us.

> *Thank you, Father, for making me your child. I have been both born into your family and adopted!*

Have we made the critical transition in mindset from our identity in Adam to our identity as children of God in his family? Think of some of the resulting vital distinctions in perspective toward life, death, and calling.

ASSURANCE

A daily devotion for September 25

Read Romans 8:15–17.

"And by him we cry, 'Abba, Father.' The Spirit himself testifies with our spirit that we are God's children" (Rom. 8:15–16).

What Paul describes here is our deepest level of assurance. Beyond the emotions is a deep conviction born of the Spirit of God himself, an underlying awareness that we are undeniably part of God's family. We are the children of God. This is the basic revelation to which our emotions respond with the cry, "Abba, Father." That is our love for him, but even more this is his love for us. This is what Paul refers to in Romans 5 when he speaks of the love of God "which is shed abroad in our hearts by the Spirit of God, the Holy Spirit which is given unto us" (Rom. 5:5 KJV).

As I look back on my own life, I can understand how this is true. I became a Christian when I was about eleven years old at a Methodist brush arbor meeting. I responded to the invitation and, with others, knelt down in front and received the Lord. I had a wonderful time of fellowship with the Lord that summer and the next winter, and there were occasions when I was overwhelmed with a sense of the nearness and dearness of God. I used to sing hymns until tears came to my eyes as those old words spoke to the relationship that I had with God. Then I used to preach to the cows when I brought them home. Those cows were a great audience, by the way—they never went to sleep on me.

But that fall we moved from the town where I had Christian fellowship to a town in Montana that didn't even have a church. Gradually, because of that lack of fellowship, I drifted away from that relationship with God and fell into all kinds of ugly and shameful things—sinful habits of thought and activity. I even developed liberal attitudes toward the Scriptures. I didn't believe in the inspiration of the Bible. I argued against it, and during high school and college I was known as a skeptic. But all through those seven years I had a relationship with God I could not deny. Somehow I knew, deep down inside, that I still belonged to him, and there were things I could not do, even though I was tempted. I could not do them because I felt that I had a tie with God. This was that witness of the Spirit. Calvin called it "the testimonial of the Spirit," which we cannot deny and which is especially discernible in times of gross sin and despair. As John says, "If our heart condemn us, God is greater than our heart" (1 John 3:20 KJV). He knows all things. There is a witness born of the Spirit that we can't shake, that is there along with the ultimate testimony that we belong with the children of God.

This is where to begin when you get into trouble. Return to this relationship. Remind yourself of who you are. You can see it in your experience as you look around. You are led by the Spirit of God. You can feel it in your heart. There are times when your emotions are stirred by the Spirit, and you can sense at the level of your spirit that you belong to God.

Father, help me to understand these things. Thank you for the work of the Spirit. What a wonderful thing it is that you have called me a child of the living God. Help me never to forget it and to be worthy of such a calling.

Our adoption as God's children is far from simply theoretical, so what response does it evoke from us? Do our lives bear witness to our shared inheritance with Christ? How do we share in his sufferings?

OUR PRESENT SUFFERINGS

A daily devotion for September 26

Read Romans 8:18–25.

> "I consider that our present sufferings are not worth comparing with the glory that will be revealed in us" (Rom. 8:18).

The theme of this verse and the next nine verses is that incomparable glory lies ahead—glory beyond description, greater than anything we can compare it with on earth. A magnificent and fantastic prospect awaits us. A rumor of hope runs all through the Old Testament, through the prophetic writings, and into the New Testament. This rumor speaks of a day that is coming when all the heartache, injustice, weakness, and suffering of our present experience will be explained and justified and will result in a time of incredible blessing upon the earth. The whisper of this in the Old Testament increases in intensity as it approaches the New Testament where we come to proclamations like this that speak of the incomparable glory that lies ahead.

We tend to make careful note of our suffering. I received a letter from a man who had written out in extreme detail a report on his recent operation. He said he'd had to listen to all the reports of other people's operations for years, and now it was his turn! We record the specifics of our sufferings, but here the apostle says, "Don't even mention them! They are not worthy to be mentioned in comparison with the glory that is to follow."

That statement would be just so much hot air if it didn't come from Paul. Here is a man who suffered intensely. He was beaten, stoned with rocks, chained, imprisoned, shipwrecked, starved, and was often hungry, naked, and cold. Yet this apostle takes pen in hand and says, "Our present sufferings are not worth comparing with the glory that shall be revealed in us." The glory that is coming is incomparable in intensity.

Our sufferings hurt us, I know. I am not trying to make light of them or to diminish the terrible physical and emotional pain that suffering can bring. It can be awful, almost unendurable. Its intensity can increase to such a degree that we scream with terror and pain. We think we can no longer endure. But the apostle is saying that the intensity of the suffering we experience is not even a drop in the bucket compared with the intensity of glory that is coming. We can see that Paul is straining the language in trying to describe this fantastic thing that is about to happen, which he calls the revelation of the glory that is coming.

This glory is not only incomparable in its intensity but incomparable in its locality. It will not be revealed to us but in us. The word Paul uses means "into us." This glory will not be a spectator sport; we will not sit up in some cosmic grandstand and watch an amusing or beautiful performance in which we have no part. We are to be on the stage. We will be involved in it. This glory will be "revealed into us," and we will be part of it.

This is the incredible glory that God has prepared for those who love him, that he has given to us—not because we have been faithful, not because we have earned it, but because we are heirs of God and coheirs with Christ. All Christians suffer. There are no exceptions. If we are true believers in Jesus Christ, we will suffer. But we are not only given the privilege of suffering with him now but also of sharing in his glory, which is yet to come. We can endure the suffering and even triumph in it, because we see the glory that is to follow.

> *Lord, thank you so much for the glory that awaits me. Help me to endure suffering with joy because of the hope you have given me.*

What effect does the expectation of promised glory have on our view and our experience of suffering? Did the apostle Paul's suffering make him more or less self-focused?

ALL THINGS

A daily devotion for September 27

Read Romans 8:26–28.

> "In the same way, the Spirit helps us in our weakness. We do not know what we ought to pray for, but the Spirit himself intercedes for us through wordless groans. And he who searches our hearts knows the mind of the Spirit, because the Spirit intercedes for God's people in accordance with the will of God. And we know that in all things God works for the good of those who love him, who have been called according to his purpose" (Rom. 8:26–28).

Never separate these verses. The Spirit prays according to the mind of God, and the Father answers by bringing into our lives the experiences that we need and allowing us to work through them. These are always just what we require.

That means that even the trials and the tragedies that happen to us are an answer from the Father to the praying of the Spirit. We may be in an automobile accident. Someone may steal our purse or our wallet. We may find our house is on fire. There are a thousand and one possibilities. We need to understand that these things do not happen by accident. They happen because the Spirit that is in us prayed and asked that the Father allow them to happen—because we or someone close to us needs what God will accomplish in them. These are the results of the praying of the Spirit.

The joys, the unexpected blessings, and the unusual things that happen to us are also the result of the Spirit's praying. The Spirit is praying that these things will happen; he is voicing the deep concern of God for our needs. Out of this grows the assurance that no matter what happens, God will use for good. This verse does not say that everything that happens to us is good. It does say that whether the situation is bad or good, it will work out for our good if we are loved and called by God. What a difference that makes as we wait for the coming of the glory! God is working out his purposes within us.

Paul is telling us here that we can wait with patience because nature testifies to God's glorious coming. Our experience confirms it as well. We can't tell what it is specifically, but we are being prepared for something. One of these days, at the end of our lives, if not before, we will step out of time into an incredible experience of glory, something that defies description—a glory that Christ shares and that we all shall share with him.

This is what God is preparing us for. No wonder the apostle closes this passage with one of the greatest paeans of praise in the Scriptures in verses 31 to 39. As we suffer now, what a blessing and what a help it is to remember the glory that has been granted to us. We have been counted worthy to suffer for God's name that we may also share in the glory that is to come.

Thank you, Father, for these mighty promises. I pray that I may understand them and thus be able to endure patiently and with thanksgiving what I am going through now, knowing that this suffering is producing glory.

In what ways does this promised partnership with the Spirit change our perspective on our prayers? Are we learning to confidently receive all aspects of our lives as God's loving, perfect will?

FROM ETERNITY TO ETERNITY

A daily devotion for September 28

Read Romans 8:29–30.

> "For those God foreknew he also predestined to be conformed to the likeness of his Son, that he might be the firstborn among many brothers. And those he predestined, he also called; those he called, he also justified; those he justified, he also glorified" (Rom. 8:29–30).

These are the five steps that God takes, stretching from eternity to eternity—far greater than any of our lives would suggest. The first step is that God foreknew us. A lot of people talk about how God foreknew what we were going to do or foreknew that we would believe in Christ. This passage doesn't deal with that. This passage is concerned with the question of existence. It tells us that from among the tremendous number of human beings who have been spawned on this earth since the creation of man, God foreknew that you and I would be there—as well as all the believers who have preceded us or who will follow us throughout history.

The next step, Paul says, is that God predestined. "Ah," some say, "I know what that means! That means God looked over the whole group and said, 'Now these will go to hell, and those will go to heaven.'" Predestination has nothing to do with going to hell. Predestination has to do only with believers. It simply tells us that God has selected beforehand the goal toward which he is going to move every one of us who believes in Christ. That goal is conformity to the character of Christ. Everything that happens to us focuses on that one supreme purpose.

The third step is that God called us. This is where we get into the act. I could not begin to describe the mystery and the wonder involved in this. This means that the Holy Spirit somehow begins to work in our lives. We may be far removed from God, we may have grown up in a non-Christian family, we may be involved in a non-Christian faith, or we may be from a Christian home. It makes no difference. God begins to work and he draws us to himself.

Fourth, those God called, he justified. Justification is God's gift of worth. Those who are justified are forgiven, cleansed, and given the position before him of being loved, accepted, wanted, and endeared. By the cross, God was freed to give the gift of righteousness. Had he given it apart from the cross, he could have been properly accused of condoning sin—but the cross freed him. It established his righteous justice on other grounds so that he is now free to give to us the gift of worth without any merit on our part.

Then, finally, those God justified, he also glorified. Paul writes as though this has already happened. It has already begun, and God counts it as true. Glorification is the exciting day that all of creation is anticipating when God will suddenly pull back the curtains on what he has been doing with the human race. All at once, the children of God will stand out in glory.

Those whom God foreknew, before the foundation of the world, he also predestined to conform to the likeness of his Son. The same number of people he called, and the ones he called, he also justified. The ones he justified, he also glorified. No one is lost in the process, because God is responsible for it. It will involve pain and toil, but it will happen, because what God sets out to do he does—no matter what it takes.

Father, I am so grateful for your eternal purposes, which allow me to rest in deep gratitude for your grace and mercy.

What are five aspects of God's eternal plan for those called according to his purpose? How does this radically change our time-management perspectives?

WHO CONDEMNS YOU NOW?

A daily devotion for September 29

Read Romans 8:31–34.

> "Who will bring any charge against those whom God has chosen? It is God who justifies. Who then is the one who condemns? No one. Christ Jesus who died—more than that, who was raised to life—is at the right hand of God and is also interceding for us" (Rom. 8:33–34).

This is a reminder of the work that God has done. We love God when we trust in the full effect of his work on our behalf. Paul is looking back over the letter and sees two great works that God has done. The first is justification. "Who will bring any charge against those whom God has chosen?" Who can? It is God who justifies. Justification means that no one anywhere can accuse us successfully before God.

The Devil is the accuser of the brethren. He will constantly try to accuse us. This verse tells us that we must not listen to his voice. We must not listen to these thoughts that condemn us, that put us down, that make us feel that there is no hope for us. These thoughts will come—they cannot be stopped—but we do not have to listen to them. We know God is not listening to these accusations. Who can condemn us when God justifies us? Therefore we refuse to be condemned. We don't do this by ignoring our sin, trying to cover it over, or pretending that it isn't there. We do it by admitting that we fully deserve to be condemned, but that God, through Christ, has already borne our guilt. That is the only way out. That is why Christians should not hesitate to admit their failure and their sin. We will never be justified until we admit it. But when we admit it, we also can comprehend the full glory of the fact that God justifies the ungodly so that there is no condemnation.

Then Paul raises the question, "Who is he that condemns? Who is going to do this?" The only one who has the right is Jesus—and Jesus died for us. And more than that, he was raised to life for us, he is now at the right hand of God in power for us, and he is also interceding for us. So there is no chance that he is going to condemn us. This is a reference to the power that we have by which we take hold afresh of the life of Jesus. Not only is our guilt set aside, but we have power imparted to us —his life in us, his risen life made available to us now. So we can rise up and say no to the temptations that surround us and the habits that drag us down; we can be victors over them. That is not a mere dogma; we are in touch with a living person. That is the glory of Christianity. The unique distinction of Christians is that we have Jesus.

I am grateful, Lord, that because of all that you have done for me in Christ there is no one who can condemn me.

Are we being held hostage to condemnation instigated by the Enemy? What response to God's forgiveness allows us to fully experience freedom from condemnation? What power is available to withstand the temptations and the accusations from the Enemy?

HOW TO LOVE GOD

A daily devotion for September 30

Read Romans 8:35–39.

"Who shall separate us from the love of Christ?" (Rom. 8:35).

How do we love God? We love him by answering this question. Who or what will separate us from the love of Christ? Is there any force that can come between us and Jesus? Who can remove us from Christ once we fully come to him? Paul says, "Let's take a look at the possibilities."

First, can all the troubles and the dangers of life separate us from his love? "Shall trouble or hardship or persecution or famine or nakedness or danger or sword?" (Rom. 8:35). That is life at its worst. Will that do it? Will hardship do it? That means the tight, narrow places we have to pass through sometimes. Will persecution do it? That is hurt deliberately inflicted on us because we are Christians. Will famine or lack of money do it? Will nakedness or lack of clothes? Will danger or threat to our lives? Will the sword (war, riot, uprising) do it? "No," Paul says. "In these we are super conquerors." Why? Because rather than dividing us from Christ, they draw us closer to him. They make us cling harder. They scare us and make us run to him. When we are independent and think we can make it on our own, these things strike, and we start whimpering and running for home, and we stay even closer to the nest. We can never be defeated then, so we are more than conquerors.

What about supernatural forces? What about people and power, demons and strange forces? "For I am convinced that neither death nor life, neither angels nor demons, neither the present nor the future, nor any powers, neither height nor depth, nor anything else in all creation, will be able to separate us from the love of God that is in Christ Jesus our Lord" (Rom. 8:38–39). Nothing is left off of that list, is it? Everything is there—demons and dark powers, black magic and angels, truth and error, death and life—whether in this creation or any other creation. Paul takes everything in and says that nothing, no being or force, is capable of separating us from the love of Jesus Christ our Lord.

So we love God when we say, "If God be for us, who can be against us?" We love God because of what he has done for us, and the nature of that commitment is that he loves us. Nothing can separate us from that. This is the high point of the letter. Obviously, Paul cannot go beyond this, and neither can we. What can we say? What can we do but love when we are confronted by a God like that?

Father, thank you for the security you give in your great love. Let your love be the thing that fuels my love for you through the challenges of life.

Is it fair or accurate to assess God's love by comparing it with our fragile, conditional human love? Do we respond to his unrelenting love by loving him with all our hearts, souls, and minds? Do we in gratitude extend his love to others?

1 CORINTHIANS

Epistle of the Twenty-First Century
An introduction for the month of October

Paul is writing this letter from Ephesus in about AD 56 or 57. He had founded the church in Corinth about five years before that when he had come alone, driven out of Macedonia by the persecution there. He had left Timothy and Luke behind and had gone to Athens and then from there to Corinth. After founding the church, which took about two years during his ministry, the apostle left and went on other journeys. Now he is in Ephesus, and word has come to him that there is difficulty in the church in Corinth.

Paul wrote a letter to the Corinthians, referred to in the ninth verse of the fifth chapter, which has been lost to us. All we know of it is what the apostle says there, that he wrote the letter to the Corinthians telling them that they should not keep company with those who had fallen into immorality. Subsequently, a group of men had come from Corinth to visit him in Ephesus (they are identified in the final chapter of this letter as Fortunatus, Stephanas, and Achaicus), and they had evidently brought word of further troubles there. They had also brought a letter from this church asking the apostle to answer questions that its members had. This letter that we now have, 1 Corinthians, is his answer to that letter and to the reports that he had received from the Corinthian church.

This letter is remarkably different from all the other letters the apostle wrote. Most of them begin with a lengthy doctrinal section in which Paul teaches great truths and close with a practical section in which he applies what he is teaching. But here, right from the beginning, he plunges into the problems of the church, interspersing practical doctrine with revelations of truth throughout the letter.

This is certainly the most practical of all Paul's letters. Even in the opening greeting, his concern for the church with its problems is clearly reflected. The letter begins with an emphasis upon his apostleship: "Paul, called by the will of God to be an apostle." That was necessary because there were people in Corinth who were ready to challenge that fact since he had not been one of the original twelve disciples. His apostleship was called into question, and some were wondering if he were not even a false apostle, so Paul has to defend his role in the letter. Therefore, he puts his apostleship first as he writes.

CALLED INTO FELLOWSHIP

A daily devotion for October 1

Read 1 Corinthians 1:1–9.

"God is faithful, who has called you into fellowship with his Son, Jesus Christ our Lord" (1 Cor. 1:9).

This is the key verse of 1 Corinthians. The rest of the letter revolves around it. This verse declares that God had called the Corinthians to an important relationship and that the church was experiencing problems because they had not understood the implications of their calling and of the personal relationship they had with Jesus himself. As a result, beginning with the next verse, the apostle has to deal with divisions, scandals, lawsuits, immorality, drunkenness, and quarreling. It is clear that despite the fullness of provision the Corinthians had received, they were experiencing a great failure in the church. They had the ability to do all these mighty things in the Spirit, but not much was happening out in the city. Instead of the church making an impact on Corinth, Corinth was making an impact on the church. All the ugly attitudes and actions of the city were beginning to infiltrate into the church, and instead of the church changing the city, the city was changing the church.

This reminds me of Peter Marshall's vivid description of contemporary Christians. He says, "Christians are like deep-sea divers encased in suits designed for many fathoms deep, marching bravely forth to pull plugs out of bathtubs!" The problem was the Corinthians' lack of understanding of what it meant to have Jesus Christ living among them. The major struggle of most churches is right at this point. They have lost the sense that Jesus is among them, that they have an individual relationship with the Lord of glory himself. They no longer live their lives in the awareness and the excitement that they are partners with Christ in everything they do. When that truth begins to fade from the Christian consciousness, all these troubles that the Corinthians were experiencing begin to arise. This letter is written to call them back to an awareness of what it means to have fellowship with Christ.

Fellowship with Christ is the work of the Holy Spirit. It is his task to take the things of Christ and to make them known to us, to make the person of Jesus real in our daily experience. That is what Paul is talking about here—Christ made real to the heart, enabling him to satisfy the thirsts of the soul; Christ providing the power that it takes to meet the demands of both the law and the love of God. Fellowship with Christ is not only direction in what to do, but it is dynamic—it is how we are able to do it.

Often churches fall into the habit of trying to obey the Lord with no awareness of the great provision he has made. He gives us not only guidance but resources. He offers not only an understanding of life but an undergirding so that we might act. Christ not only sets a program before the church but provides the power to carry it out. That is what these Corinthians lacked. That is what we lack. When we forget this, we drift into that syndrome of recognizing the Lord on Sunday and from Monday through Saturday living our lives without any recognition of his presence with us. He is Lord of only a part of our lives. If he is not Lord of our lives all day long, he is Lord only of the margins, only of the weekends. The church is called to an understanding of Christ's presence in the human heart to supply to it that sense of adventure that opens doors in unusual and unanticipated ways and that lends color to life.

Lord, may my heart be always willing to return to fellowship with the Lord Jesus and to rely completely on the indwelling of your Spirit.

What is the primary aspect of our calling as Christ's ones? Are we giving preeminence to anything less than our privileged and necessary fellowship with him?

BEHIND DIVISIONS

A daily devotion for October 2

Read 1 Corinthians 1:10–17.

> "I appeal to you, brothers and sisters, in the name of our Lord Jesus Christ, that all of you agree with one another in what you say and that there be no divisions among you, but that you be perfectly united in mind and thought" (1 Cor. 1:10).

Paul always expresses great concern about the possibility of a split in the church. In a similar passage in his letter to the Philippians he says, "So if there is any encouragement in Christ, any incentive of love, any participation in the Spirit, any affection and sympathy, complete my joy by being of the same mind, having the same love, being in full accord, and of one mind" (Phil. 2:1–2 RSV). In writing to the church at Ephesus, he exhorted the elders there to be careful to "maintain the unity of the Spirit in the bond of peace" (Eph. 4:3 RSV).

Church unity is a crucial matter. Paul puts it first in the list of problems he has to deal with in Corinth. Many of the other problems flowed out of this division within the congregation. In verse 10 he briefly shows us the basis for unity and the nature of unity in a church. The basis is the name of our Lord Jesus Christ. "I appeal to you," he says, "in the name of our Lord Jesus Christ." The Corinthians' relationship to Christ was the unifying factor in the church. There is no other name big enough, great enough, glorious enough, and powerful enough to gather everybody together despite diversity of viewpoints, differences of background, or status in life than the name of Jesus. That is why the apostle appeals to it. He recognizes that we share a common life if we have come to Christ; we are brothers and sisters because we have his life in us. He is always the ground of unity. And more than that, we have a responsibility to obey him, to follow his lordship. Therefore, the only way to get Christians to agree is by setting before them the person of the Lord Jesus.

Paul says unity means being "perfectly united in mind and thought." That does not mean that everybody has to think alike. With all the differences among us, it is impossible to get people to think alike. The church is never called to have everybody think exactly alike. Yet the apostle says the Corinthians are to be of united in mind. How can that be? The letter to the Philippians helps us here. Paul says, "Let this mind be in you which was also in Christ Jesus" (Phil. 2:5). He goes on to describe for us the mind of Christ, which is a willingness to give up rights and privileges, to give in, and to take a lower place. Then comes that great Christological passage where he describes how Christ, "though he was in the form of God, did not count equality with God a thing to be grasped, but emptied himself, taking the form of a servant, being born in the likeness of men. And being found in human form he humbled himself and became obedient unto death, even death on a cross" (Phil. 2:6–8 RSV).

That is the mind Paul is talking about. Harmony reigns in a congregation when everybody decides to put the things of Christ first and is willing to suffer loss that the honor and glory of Christ might be advanced. That is always the unifying factor in a church, and that is the mind we should have, the mind that does not consider itself the most important thing.

> *Thank you, Father, for your Word. Let it do its great work of cutting down and eliminating from my life the things in which I take pride and that separate me from others. Help me to judge these in the light of the cross and to walk before you in unity with my brothers and sisters in Christ.*

Are we confusing equality with authentic unity in Christ? Do we need to rethink our personal responsibility for building walls of separation and disunity, choosing rather to be peacemakers?

GOD'S NONSENSE

A daily devotion for October 3

Read 1 Corinthians 1:18–25.

"For the message of the cross is foolishness to those who are perishing, but to us who are being saved it is the power of God. For it is written: 'I will destroy the wisdom of the wise; the intelligence of the intelligent I will frustrate'" (1 Cor. 1:18–19).

The theme of this section is the power of the cross, and Paul will show clearly what the cross does in human thinking and in human affairs. The cross has become the symbol of Christianity. Women wear it on chains around their necks; we use it as a decoration. We have become so familiar with the cross that we have forgotten much of the impact it had in the first century. It was, for these early Christians and for those among whom they lived, a horrible symbol. If these Christians had used it as a symbol it would have made people shudder. We would get much closer to its early impact if we substituted a symbol of an electric chair for the cross. Wouldn't it be strange driving across this country to see electric chairs atop church steeples?

The cross is significant in Christianity because it exposes the fundamental conflict of life. The cross gets down below all our surface attempts at compromise and cuts through all human disagreement. Once we are confronted with the cross and its meaning, we find ourselves unable to escape that central question of life: whether we are committed to error or committed to truth.

We must understand what Paul means by "the word of the cross." First of all, this means the basic announcement of the crucifixion of Jesus. There are many religious groups founded upon various philosophical concepts. Christianity, however, does not start with philosophy but with facts of history that cannot be thrown out. One of them is the incarnation of Jesus, the fact that he was born as a man and came among us. Another of the great facts of our faith is the crucifixion. Jesus died. The crucifixion took place at a certain point in history and cannot be evaded. This is part of the word of the cross. Jesus did not deserve it, but by the judgment of the Romans and the Jews he was put to death for a crime that he did not commit.

Paul is pointing to the judgment that the cross makes upon human life. When we say that Jesus was crucified we are saying that when the finest man who ever lived takes our place, he deserves nothing but the instant judgment of God. And that is a judgment on all of us. That is what people do not like about the cross. It condemns our righteousness. It casts aspersions on all our good efforts.

The word of the cross always produces two reactions. First, the word of the cross is foolishness to those who are perishing. It is silliness, absurdity, nonsense, to them. If you have ever tried to witness to somebody who has a sense of self-sufficiency, you have discovered the folly of the cross. If you tell such a person that all his efforts and his impressive record of achievement are worth nothing in God's sight, you will immediately run into the offense of the cross.

The other reaction is that the cross is the power of God to those of us who are being saved. To us who are being saved, the cross is the key to the release of all God's blessing in human life. It is the way to experience God's healing in the heart, deliverance from the reign of sin, and the entry into wholeness, peace, and joy. The cross is an inescapable part of that process.

Thank you, Father, for the cross. Thank you that I no longer have to prove myself worthy of your love and that through the cross you are changing me into the likeness of Christ.

What are the two inescapable implications of the cross of Christ? What provision does Christ's sacrifice make for us to live as new creations in the liberty of forgiveness and the power of his indwelling life?

NOT MANY

A daily devotion for October 4

Read 1 Corinthians 1:26–31.

> "Brothers and sisters, think of what you were when you were called. Not many of you were wise by human standards; not many were influential; not many were of noble birth. But God chose the foolish things of the world to shame the wise; God chose the weak things of the world to shame the strong. God chose the lowly things of this world and the despised things—and the things that are not—to nullify the things that are, so that no one may boast before him" (1 Cor. 1:26–29).

The apostle is dealing with the wisdom of the world versus the inscrutable, marvelous wisdom of God. The believers of ancient Corinth were exalting the wisdom of the world. The Greek custom of philosophizing about everything had penetrated the church, and they were dividing into factions, following certain men, quarreling, boasting, and glorying in men's ability, power, insight, and wisdom.

To deal with this the apostle shows us how God works. He presents a simple contrast and uses the Corinthians themselves as exhibit A. He says, "Look at yourselves. Consider your own call, and look what has happened in your lives." He then points out two obvious but important facts they were evidently overlooking. First, he says, "There are not many mighty among you, are there?" Fortunately, Paul does not say "any mighty." Lady Hamilton, an evangelical believer among the English nobility in the early part of the twentieth century, used to say she was saved by an *m*, because if Paul had said there were not any mighty or any nobles in the church, she would not have made it, but the added *m* allowed her admission. In Corinth there were only a few believers who had standing in the community. Many may have been slaves, and most were plain, ordinary people.

Some of them were weak, the apostle says; they had no political or military clout; they were not men of influence and had no "in" at city hall. They were apparently without power to affect life around them, but God chose them. The church was made up of what we would call the working classes—artisans, tradesmen, the little people of the world. So if you feel that nobody recognizes you, rejoice that you are a Christian, because power and influence are not necessary to be greatly used by God. He delights in setting aside the impressive things of men.

This does not mean that God does not often use people of stature as well. He does, but only, remarkably enough, when they have learned that their usefulness does not derive from their position or their abilities but from his presence in their lives. Is it not strange that we think so highly of the wisdom of the world when God thinks so little of it? Jesus said once, "That which is highly esteemed among men is abomination in the sight of God" (Luke 16:15 KJV), and all that Paul is saying here seems to flow from that fact. God works in different ways, and what men put great store by, and emphasize as so necessary, is often set aside totally by God; it is abomination in his sight.

I am thankful, Father, that although there was nothing to commend me, you have called me to be your child.

Do we base our worth on the message from the cross or on worldly wisdom? What is the essential difference between God's wisdom and the world's legalistic system of human achievement?

GOD'S WISDOM

A daily devotion for October 5

Read 1 Corinthians 2:1–5.

> "I came to you in weakness with great fear and trembling. My message and my preaching were not with wise and persuasive words, but with a demonstration of the Spirit's power, so that your faith might not rest on human wisdom, but on God's power" (1 Cor. 2:3–5).

This ought to be one of the most encouraging passages to any of us who have tried to be Christian witnesses. Speaking of the things of Christ and the things of God is easy in a church gathered with Christian friends, because nobody objects. However, try to talk about these things with unbelievers, people who are committed to the philosophy of taking care of number one and who are seeking fame and fortune, and the task becomes difficult. A believer will feel much personal weakness, fear, and trembling. That is the way Paul felt, and this ought to be an encouragement to us.

He felt like this is because what he was telling these people was not in line with what the world wants to hear about itself. He did not massage the ego of man or make him sound incredibly important. Paul deliberately rejected that approach because it does not help man. Instead, he spoke about the judgment of God upon the thinking, the attitudes, and the wisdom of man, and this left him feeling rejected. Paul came to Corinth, but there was no great ego-pleasing reception for him; there were no dinners; there was no Academy Award given to him.

He tells us he felt fearful, weak, and ineffective. He felt his words were not outstanding; he felt he did not impress anybody with the way he preached. Have you ever felt that way? I have many times. I have sat down with somebody to witness to him and have felt as if I had two tongues that were stumbling over one another. I did not seem to have the right answers. I could talk only about how things affected me; I felt like I was doing nothing effective. Yet Paul was not discouraged. In the book of Acts we are told that after he had been in Corinth for a few months the Lord Jesus appeared to him in a vision, strengthened him, and said, "Do not be afraid, but speak and do not be silent … and no man shall attack you to harm you" (Acts 18:9–10). Paul was afraid he would be beaten up as he had been in other cities. He was afraid of being branded a religious fanatic. He did not like those feelings. Nevertheless he faithfully began to talk about Jesus Christ.

Soon there was a second visible result. Paul calls it the "demonstration of the Spirit's power." As Paul with his great sense of weakness told the facts out of the simple earnestness of his heart, God's Spirit began to work and people started coming to Christ. We read the account in Acts. First, the rulers of the synagogue turned to Christ, and then hundreds of the ordinary people of Corinth became Christians. Soon there was a great spiritual awakening, and before the city knew what had happened, a church had been planted in its midst and a ferment was running throughout Corinth. I believe that this working through our human inadequacy is God's perennial way of evangelism.

Does that encourage you? It does me. You may sit down with somebody over a cup of coffee and hardly know how to speak, but you stammer out some word about what Jesus Christ has meant to you, and the earnestness in your face and the love and compassion in your heart come through in that simple way and somebody is touched who would never have been reached by eloquent oratory or rhetoric. That is what Paul is talking about, the simplicity of the approach. He knew what he was doing, because he was simply being honest with these people. He was telling them what was true about their lives.

> *Father, thank you for filling me with the glory of the truth and of life, of hope and of courage, of faith and of fulfillment. I pray that, despite fear and trembling, I may be willing to speak for you.*

Do we fall apart when our attempted witness is received with rejection and skepticism? Are we learning to speak the truth with compassion? Do we count on the power of God rather than our own human resources?

GOD'S TEACHER

A daily devotion for October 6

Read 1 Corinthians 2:6–16.

> "These are the things God has revealed to us by his Spirit. The Spirit searches all things, even the deep things of God. For who knows a person's thoughts except their own spirit within them? In the same way no one knows the thoughts of God except the Spirit of God" (1 Cor. 2:10–11).

This passage tells us that a mighty teacher come from God, the Holy Spirit, will instruct us with the Word of God and lead us into his truth. He will expose us to the "secret and hidden wisdom of God" (v.7), changing our lives. When we discover that wisdom, life will be exciting and adventurous, like nothing we ever imagined, for this truth is designed to set us free, to let us be the men and women God designed us to be.

Notice how the apostle first underscores the spirit's knowledge: "No one understands the things of man except the spirit of man which is in him." Have you ever tried to talk to your plants? We are told that plants can respond to our moods and reflect our attitudes. I know a woman who prays over each plant. I don't know what this does for the plants, but it probably helps her a great deal. But plants do not talk back. Life is constructed at various levels. We have plant life, we have animal life, then human life, angelic life, and finally, divine life. The higher can reach down to encompass the lower, but the lower cannot reach up to the higher. That is Paul's argument here. Though no animal can reach into the realm of human relationship and converse with us, other human beings like ourselves can.

Now here is this great God in our universe, this fantastic being of infinite wisdom and mighty power. How can we know anything about him? Paul's answer is that we cannot except when he discloses himself to us. We cannot find out about God by searching. Man by wisdom does not know God. Man by investigation of all the natural forces of life will never find his way to the heart of God. He must open himself to us. God has done this by means of his Spirit—the Spirit has come to teach us about God.

The Lord Jesus appeared as a man so that we might have a visible demonstration of what God is like. What is God like? The simplest answer is to say he is like Jesus. It is the work of the Spirit to show us what Jesus is like. Jesus said, "He will take of the things of mine and show them unto you" (John 16:14 KJV). We can read the record of the Gospels and read the historical record of Jesus, but the living Lord does not stand out from the pages through mere reading. Only when the Spirit illuminates those pages and makes them vivid and real do we confront the living, breathing Christ. That is the work of the Holy Spirit.

> *Father, how grateful I am for this mighty teacher, the Spirit of God, sent from you into my heart to instruct me about the things of Jesus and to give me his life that I might live in a new and different way.*

Where can we go when our efforts to know God by means of human wisdom fail? Have we realized the power of God's self-disclosure as the Holy Spirit reveals him in the person of Jesus Christ?

GOD'S SERVANTS

A daily devotion for October 7

Read 1 Corinthians 3:1–9.

> "What, after all, is Apollos? And what is Paul? Only servants, through whom you came to believe—as the Lord has assigned to each his task. I planted the seed, Apollos watered it, but God has been making it grow. So neither the one who plants nor the one who waters is anything, but only God, who makes things grow" (1 Cor. 3:5–7).

Paul is writing of the true view of ministry and ministers, and he does not mean by ministers only the apostles or a select group called clergy or pastors. This is a devilish idea that has possessed the church. Many see the clergy as different people with a special pipeline to God. That idea is never found in Scripture. No, in Scripture all Christians are in the ministry, everyone without exception. All are given gifts by the Spirit. All are expected to have a function, a service God uses. It need not come in the meeting of the church. It can be out in the world anywhere we are.

But how are we to view one another? As big shots striving to see who can get the most recognition, as dignitaries with special dress to indicate our rank and style of life? Are we to be the heavies, the bosses, the brass? No. Paul says we are servants; that is all. All of us are servants of Christ. That is the highest rank possible in the church, and everybody has it from the start. Thus, there is no need for competition or rivalry. Jesus told us what our attitude is to be: "The Son of Man," he said, "came not to be ministered unto but to minister, and give himself a ransom for many" (Matt. 20:28, Mark 10:45 KJV).

How do we think of ourselves when we come to church? What is our reason for coming? Is it to be ministered unto? Do we attend this assembly so that we might have a blessing or so that we might be a blessing? The attitude of a servant is always, "What can I do for another?" In the process we will find ourselves abundantly ministered unto. But we hear so much of this cult of the self-life today that insists that everything meet our needs. That is preeminent. Now that is the world's thinking, isn't it? The apostle is telling us that this thinking will mean nothing but trouble in the church, creating divisions and factions. We must come to see each other as servants of Christ, ministering to one another as God gives opportunities to do so. This is what the Lord demonstrated for us. Are we in competition? "No," says Paul, "we're in cooperation. I planted, Apollos watered, but God gave the growth. We are doing different things, but we need both of them."

One of the glories of the church is that nobody does the same thing. Churches that try to turn out people who all look alike, dress alike, carry the same kind of notebook, speak the same kind of language, and use the same version of the Bible are missing what God has in mind, because we are all to be different, yet needing one another and working together. The evangelist plants; the Bible teacher waters. Which is more important, Bible teaching or evangelizing? Paul's answer is, "Neither!" God can do away with both of those. The important thing is not what either can do but what God alone can do—take that truth and change lives with it. Evangelists cannot do that. Bible teachers cannot do that. Only God gives increase. Only God opens minds, changes hearts, and makes people different. That is what we ought to emphasize instead of attaching such importance to our methods, to our abilities to do this and that, and to the demands that some people make for training. All of that emphasizes the people, not the God who gives the increase.

Lord Jesus I ask you to take my life and to use me where I work and where I live. I know this is what you love to do, and I ask that you will grant me the grace to understand how to do this and to yield myself to you.

What is the highest rank possible in the body of Christ? Does this leave room for competition, comparisons, or pedestals? Do we serve with expectation of increased status? Whose power produces growth and fruit from serving?

GOD'S BUILDERS

A daily devotion for October 8

Read 1 Corinthians 3:10–15.

"If what has been built survives, the builder will receive a reward. If it is burned up, the builder will suffer loss but yet will be saved—even though only as one escaping through the flames" (1 Cor. 3:14–15).

Paul says, "We must all appear before the judgment seat of Christ" (2 Cor. 5:10), and John describes the Lord before whom we will appear, saying, "His eyes are like a flame of fire" (Rev. 1:14). Those searching eyes will examine all of our lives to see what we have used to build them. Paul says, "Then we shall receive the things done in the body whether they be good or bad" (2 Cor. 5:10)—whether they are built on the revelation of the mind and the Spirit of God or whether they reflect the philosophies of the spirit of the age.

What are we building with? If it is good it will endure; it will stand the test, and we will be given a reward. What is the reward? There are a lot of guesses because the Scriptures do not tell us flat out, but I think there are hints. Paul wrote to the Thessalonians, "Are you not our crown of rejoicing?" (1 Thess. 2:19 KJV). I think the reward will be endless joy over having spent our lives in a way that counts.

At the end of a game members of the winning team go crazy. Grown men jump on each other's backs; they pound one another, hug one another, and even kiss one another. They are filled with joy because the efforts they put forth produced results and this was satisfying to them. This was their reward. But members of the losing team do not jump around and slap one another on the back. Sadness and gloom prevail; they are ashamed because all their efforts were to no avail. All their work was wasted. All of us shall have some of both in our lives. Every Christian will have gold, silver, and precious stones; God guarantees this by having come into our lives. But we will also have a lot of wood, hay, and stubble accumulated by following the philosophy of the flesh instead of the Spirit.

What will our lives count for? All of us are investing our lives in something. We cannot live without making an investment. What is it in? Will it stand the test? In the great day when all the universe sees things the way they are, will we be filled with joy that our lives were invested in what stood the test and contributed to the glory of the Lord? Or will we be ashamed that we wasted years making an impression on people when this empty building was burned up in the fire? I know there are people who do not like this kind of preaching. They say we ought to preach the grace of God, but the Scriptures teach us that we have some choice in this matter. Will our lives be lived on the basis of gold, silver, and precious stones, growing out of that revelation of God by the Spirit, or will they reflect the empty, vain philosophies of the world so that we live only for pleasure, fame, and power?

Lord, I know that these words are not sent to condemn me but to encourage me to choose the right path and to invest my life in ways that will fulfill the promise that you have given me. Help me to manifest this increasingly as I go on day by day, guided and guarded by your Spirit.

Are we going for the gold, following the wisdom of our master architect's plan and purpose? When crunch time comes, will our life assessment bring honor to him and resulting joy to us, his building?

ALL THINGS ARE YOURS

A daily devotion for October 9

Read 1 Corinthians 3:16–23.

> "All things are yours, whether Paul or Apollos or Cephas or the world or life or death or the present or the future—all are yours, and you are of Christ, and Christ is of God" (1 Cor. 21–23).

Paul is showing us what happens when we choose the wisdom and the ways of God. We end up gaining the whole world. That is what Jesus said: "The meek shall inherit the earth" (Matt. 5:5). What a great and broad vista opens up to us in these words! After all, the trouble with the world is that if the world, or the worldly church, offers us something—fame, pleasure, honor, or wealth—and we want it badly enough, we will probably get it. But that is all we will get.

Jesus said that if we do our giving to be seen by men we have our reward (Matt. 6:5). That is it. We will never get another one; nothing will be waiting for us beyond, no treasure laid up in heaven. If we do our praying to be heard by men so that we get a reputation for piety and godliness, we will get the reputation, but that is all we will get. The world is narrow; it is withered and limited in its approach. But, as Paul reveals here, those who choose God never lose.

This is right in line with Jesus's great principle: "If you save your life you will lose it, but if you give up your life for my sake you will save it" (Matt. 16:25, Mark 8:35). Paul looks around and says, "He who lets God choose ends up with everything. Why do you divide between Paul and Apollos and Cephas and choose one among them? You can have them all. They are all yours. Paul, who planted—his whole ministry is yours. Apollos, the waterer—his ministry is yours; you can get the benefit of it. Cephas, the rock—anything of value in his ministry is yours. In fact the whole world is open to you. Led by the Spirit of God, you can go anywhere you want, and God will give you things that money cannot buy."

I have had the experience many times of enjoying things that millionaires own but that I get to use and they do not. The world is ours. Life with all its possibilities is open before us. God can lead us into where the real living is. Even death with its threat is already mastered; it is already ours. When we come to it, it will minister to us—not take from us. It will bring us into glory. The present, the future, all things are ours because we are Christ's, and because Christ is God's, everything he owns is ours. All things belong to us because we belong to the One to whom all things belong.

That is an incredible vista, isn't it? And yet those words are true. That is what God has in mind for his people. Do we have the faith and the courage to set aside the lifestyle of the world around us, with all its demands for conformity, and to walk with God? When we do, all that God possesses becomes ours. We become children of a heavenly being who makes it all available to us.

Lord, thank you for opening this vista of life in which all that you possess becomes mine.

Are we open and willing to receive our full inheritance in Christ? Are we learning to receive and use his good gifts at his discretion and with thankfulness for his perfect provision for our needs?

STEWARDS OF THE MYSTERIES OF GOD

A daily devotion for October 10

Read 1 Corinthians 4:1–7.

> "This, then, is how you ought to regard us: as servants of Christ and as those entrusted with the mysteries God has revealed. Now it is required that those who have been given a trust must prove faithful" (1 Cor. 4:1–2).

A minister of Christ is a steward entrusted with what Paul calls "the mysteries God has revealed," the hidden wisdom of God, valuable truths found in the revelation of the Word of God and nowhere else. Ministers are responsible for continually dispensing these truths to the congregation so that lives are changed and lived on the basis of this remarkable wisdom. These are truths about life, about our families, about God, and about ourselves. They lie beyond all secular research and opinion polls; they are undiscoverable by natural reason or by observation. These mysteries, when understood, are the bases upon which all God's purposes in our lives are worked out.

Paul says that stewards are to be found faithful. They must be faithful at dispensing the mysteries so people understand them. You may fail at many things as a teacher, a preacher, or a leader of a class. You may not make it in many areas, but do not fail in this one. Be sure that you are setting forth the mysteries of God. That is what stewards will be judged on.

Here are some of these mysteries. There is the "mystery of the kingdom of God" (Mark 4:11 KJV). This refers to God at work in history, how he is using the events of our day and of days past to carry out his purposes. There is the "mystery of iniquity" (2 Thess. 2:7 KJV), of lawlessness. We must continually be reminded of why we are never able to make any progress in solving human dilemmas—why every generation repeats the struggles and difficulties of the previous generation. Then there is the counteraction to that—the "mystery of godliness" (1 Tim. 3:16 KJV). This is the remarkable secret that God has provided by which a Christian is enabled to live amid the pressures of the world with all of its illusion and all of its danger, not to run away from it but to refuse to conform to it and to do so in a loving, gracious way. The secret is an imparted life—"Christ in you, the hope of glory" (Col. 1:27 RSV). Christ in us, available to us—his life, his wisdom, his strength, his power to act—enables us to do what we do not think we can do at the moment. But when we choose to do it, we find the strength to perform. That is the mystery of godliness, the most life-transforming doctrine ever set before man, radical in its effect.

Then there is the "mystery of the church" (Eph. 3:1–6), the strange new society that God is building that is to demonstrate a totally different lifestyle before a watching world, to repel the impact of the world upon it, and instead to have an impact upon the world and to change it. Those called to teach this in a church congregation are stewards of that mystery, entrusted to set it out and to help people to face the facts of life without fear or favor so that all can experience both the ecstasy and the agony of Christianity.

Thank you, Lord, for these insightful words that help me to understand how the church functions. Help me to support those who teach and preach and to hold them up in prayer before you.

Whether we teach or are being taught, we need to know the four mysteries revealed only in Scripture. Can we identify them? Are we giving priority to learning and sharing this transcendent truth?

COMPLACENCY

A daily devotion for October 11

Read 1 Corinthians 4:8–21.

> "Already you have all you want! Already you have become rich! You have begun to reign—and that without us! How I wish that you really had begun to reign so that we also might reign with you!" (1 Cor. 4:8).

The seat of the problem in Corinth was believers' love of human wisdom, their hunger for the world's approval, and the pride they took in their own accomplishments, which they felt merited that approval. Paul saw several things in Corinth that told the story for him. He had seen the divisions among believers. The congregation had split up into little cliques gathering around certain teachers. They were telling everyone how great a church they were, how tremendous were their meetings, and taking credit as though this were something they had thought of and had planned and worked out. There was jealous strife and infighting in the congregation and the leadership, and finally there was a complacent spirit. A lot of exciting things were going on, but believers had a smug satisfaction about being the way they were.

What do complacent Christians look like? Paul points to their sense that they have arrived. You meet people like that today. Some seem to feel they have it made; they have learned the whole truth; there is nothing you can tell them that they have not already learned; they think of themselves as rich.

Many things can give a Christian a sense of being rich and make him complacent. In Laodicea the problem was material possessions. "We are increased with goods," the Laodiceans said, "and have need of nothing. We have a tremendous budget; we have plenty of money; we can do what we want; we do not even need God anymore" (Rev. 3:17). They prided themselves on how affluent they were, and this made them complacent. Thus the Lord had to say to them, "You have no idea what you are really like—you are poor and blind, pitiable and naked, and spiritually poverty-stricken." Affluence can do that to a church.

Sometimes prominence produces complacency. People attending a large church that is known worldwide and has a reputation as a missionary church, a Bible-teaching church may soon begin to think, *We have arrived; we have no further to go*, and the pride of complacency begins to appear.

In Corinth, however, the problem was none of these. Here believers became complacent because they possessed all the gifts of the Spirit. At least twenty-one gifts of the Spirit can be detected in the Scriptures, and all of them were present in Corinth. That is amazing because today we are told that the trouble with the church is that it does not have enough knowledge and experience with the gifts of the Spirit. But here was a church that had them all. The Corinthians had tongues, miracles, healings, and prophecies plus a lot of what they regarded as lesser gifts—the gifts of helps and administrations, wisdom and knowledge, teaching, service, and giving. That was what made them complacent: they felt rich because they had all the gifts of the Spirit, and so they were self-satisfied.

I am sure their meetings were interesting. Nobody wanted to stay away, because lots of things were happening, but the church was in danger. Paul saw it and wrote to the Corinthians to point this out. That is the mark of complacent Christians: the feeling that they have arrived.

> *Father, thank you for a father's love, which rebukes and chastens. "Those whom I love I rebuke and chasten." Help me to cleanse my life of whatever introduces complacency and pride.*

Has affluence resulted in complacency or self-satisfaction in our lives? Are we aware of the serious erosion in our worship and our serving? Are we ready to be rerouted into authentic and effective discipleship?

SCANDAL IN THE CHURCH

A daily devotion for October 12

Read 1 Corinthians 5:1–13.

> "I wrote to you in my letter not to associate with sexually immoral people—not at all meaning the people of this world who are immoral, or the greedy and swindlers, or idolaters. In that case you would have to leave this world. But now I am writing to you that you must not associate with anyone who claims to be a brother or sister but is sexually immoral or greedy, an idolater or slanderer, a drunkard or swindler. Do not even eat with such people. What business is it of mine to judge those outside the church? Are you not to judge those inside? God will judge those outside. 'Expel the wicked person from among you'" (1 Cor. 5:9–13).

Paul refers to a letter that he had written to the Corinthians, a letter lost to us. In it, he had evidently said something about not associating with immoral people, and the Corinthians had taken this to mean (as many Christians seem to feel today) that they were to have nothing to do with unbelievers who lived immoral lives.

I am amazed at how the attitude that Paul was attempting to correct has pervaded the evangelical world. I meet people who refuse to allow anybody who is not a Christian into their homes—people who want nothing to do with anyone who lives in a way that is offensive to the Lord. In my early pastorate I asked a couple to open their home for a Bible class. The lady looked horrified and said, "Oh! I could never do that." I asked, "Why not?" "Why," she said, "people who smoke would come in. My home is dedicated to God, and I am not going to have any smoking going on there."

That misunderstanding is just what Paul is talking about. We cannot avoid the world—we were sent into it. The Lord Jesus told his disciples, "Behold, I send you forth as sheep in the midst of wolves" (Matt. 10:16 KJV). That is where we belong. Their habits may be offensive to us, but that is understandable. We do not have to pronounce judgment on them; God will do that. We are to love them and to understand that they do not have any basis of knowledge for a change. We are not to demand it of them before we begin to show friendship and love and to reach out to help them see their need for the One who can answer the hunger of their hearts. What we offer the world is the gospel, not condemnation but the good news.

As for the church, we are to judge it for specific wrongdoings. Notice how Paul lists them. We are not to judge fellow Christians because they are hard to live with, impatient, or obnoxious. But if they are immoral, greedy, idolaters, revilers, drunkards, or robbers, then they are to be judged by the actions of the church, even to the point of social pressures. "Do not even eat with them," Paul says. If they will not listen, we should withdraw from them. The ultimate penalty is exclusion, as he has indicated in this passage.

What health would return to the world and to the church if the church behaved this way! The church is letting the world go downhill rapidly by failing to maintain the standards that God has given us here. The purpose of a passage like this is to call us back to what God has given us and to recognize the unique position the church holds in the world when it begins to walk in the beauty of holiness and to enjoy the privileges that God has provided. When we live in victory over the forces that destroy others, people see that there is meaning, purpose, and reason for the salvation we profess to have.

Thank you, Father, for telling the truth about me. You are the God of truth. You do not spare me, and you do not condemn me either. You do not wipe me out, but you do tell me the truth. I see a loving father's concern behind this. Help me to judge my life in these areas according to your Word and to walk in its light and its power.

Do we share God's care about the spiritual health of his body? Are we judging non-Christians rather than targeting our individual and united godliness? What may be preventing our effective witness beyond the church walls?

THE WRONG WAY TO RIGHT WRONGS

A daily devotion for October 13

Read 1 Corinthians 6:1–11.

> "If any of you has a dispute with another, do you dare to take it before the ungodly for judgment instead of before the Lord's people? Or do you not know that the Lord's people will judge the world? And if you are to judge the world, are you not competent to judge trivial cases? Do you not know that we will judge angels? How much more the things of this life!" (1 Cor. 6:1–3).

The apostle does not use the word *stupid* here, but his implication is that these people are foolish for doing what they are doing. They are obviously engaging in lawsuits, dragging their quarrels before the Roman courts, having all their dirty linen washed in public and their disputes settled by secular bodies. This, the apostle tells them, is foolish, and he has two reasons for saying this.

First, he implies that this is an act of audacious boldness. "Dare any one of you having a grievance against his brother take it to a law court to settle?" His clear implication is that this is an outrageous act, a daring thing to do. Paul implies that by the words he uses—that one who does this is uncaring; he has reached the point where he does not care what anybody thinks or feels, and he is acting regardless of the injuries that may be done to others. In the two questions he asks, Paul then suggests that anybody who does such a thing is an ignorant person. "Do you not know that the church is going to judge the world, and do not you know that the church is going to judge angels?"

These questions imply that the Corinthians ought to have had a certain degree of knowledge. "Do you not know," he says, "that the saints will judge the world?" Surely he is referring to those passages in the Gospels and in the Epistles where we are clearly told that when the Lord returns the saints will share the throne of judgment with him. We are to rule and to reign with Christ, entering into judgment with him. We are not told whether we will be assigned a little throne to sit on, will have a certain number of people come to us, or will divide up according to the alphabet. We are, however, to enter into the mind and the heart of God as he examines the motives and the hearts, the thoughts and the innermost desires and urges of men. In chapter 4, Paul said that we are not to judge before the Lord, who will examine the hidden things of the heart. But we are learning how to do that, and that is the point Paul raises here. He does not mean to put down the systems of justice practiced in that day or in any day. Paul admired and honored Roman law—he himself called upon it for defense on occasion—but he is saying that human law by its nature must deal with trivial, superficial things, with actions and not with urges and deep, hidden motives.

Then the apostle goes even further and says, "Do you not know that we are to judge angels?" Just think of that! We do not know much about angels. They are beings of a higher order than we are. They are different in nature from us, and yet the amazing statement of Scripture is that God is preparing a people who will be so capable of delving into the motives, the hidden desires, and the urges of all beings that some day they will sit with him in judging the fallen angels. So Paul is arguing, "Is it not rather ridiculous that you people who are going to have to deal in such difficult, hidden, and subtle matters as the judgment of the world and of angels cannot even settle these little squabbles among yourselves?" This is almost like having a mathematician who works with supercomputers call in a ninth-grader and ask him for help in balancing his checkbook. It's ridiculous, isn't it?

Father, help me to understand more thoroughly the great sweep of Scripture extending even beyond this life where I am now learning principles that I will put into practice in the life to come.

Are we maximizing the trivial and the momentary while trivializing the essential and eternal events of our lives? Are we viewing God's equipping and training as preparation for the time to come?

WHAT ARE BODIES FOR?

A daily devotion for October 14

Read 1 Corinthians 6:12–20.

> "Do you not know that your bodies are temples of the Holy Spirit, who is in you, whom you have received from God? You are not your own; you were bought at a price. Therefore honor God with your bodies" (1 Cor. 6:19–20).

This passage tells why sexual immorality is different from other sins. Here again Paul is reflecting on how human nature is different from animal nature. It has the unique and marvelous capacity to hold God, to be intimately related to his greatness, his majesty, and his glory, to have God within. The body is a temple—God dwelling in something transforms it into a temple. But sexual immorality defiles that temple. It offers the temple to another. It brings the body of that person who is the temple into a wrong union, and therefore, it is basically the sin of idolatry. That is why in Colossians and other places the apostle speaks of "covetousness, which is idolatry." He means sexual covetousness, the desire for another person's body, and identifies this as a form of idolatry.

Idolatry, the worship of another god, the substitution of a rival god, defiles the temple. That is why sexual immorality has an immediate and profound though subtle effect upon the human psyche. It dehumanizes us. It animalizes us. It brutalizes us. Those who indulge in it grow continually more coarse and less sensitive, have less regard for the welfare of others, and are more self-centered and more desirous of having only their own needs met. Their attitude says, "I couldn't care less about the rest of you." That is what fornication does.

I have seen it destroy young people's relationships. A beautiful young couple came to me. Both of them were Christians and had formed a close friendship. They were growing in the Lord and heading for marriage, and then something happened. They began to fight. Finally, they brought one of their quarrels to me, and in the process of working it out I said to them, "Are you having sex together?" They admitted they were. I said, "Well, this is the result. It is destroying your relationship." But they did not believe me and they went on. Sure enough, they soon ended it with great brokenness and hurt on both sides—a painful episode remaining in each of their lives. This is what sexual immorality does.

Paul closes with a beautiful summary: "You are not your own; you were bought at a price." That is basic Christian truth. This is something every Christian ought to remember every day of his life. We have no final right to ourselves. God has ordained that we should face decisions that only we can make. He does not take away our right of choice. He does not turn us into robots, but he says we will have to account for the decisions we make.

God has bought us; he owns us and we are his by right of creation and of purchase. Thus he reserves the right to take from our lives whatever is harmful to us whether we like it or not, to give us both blessing and trouble as he sees that we need each, and to guide us as a loving Father to the place where we recognize that he owns us, that we belong to him. God is honored when any Christian lives on that basis. That's why he says, "Honor God with your bodies." This is what makes the world see that there is something different about Christians—they have discovered the secret of their humanity. God has come to dwell in his temple again, and that temple should be maintained without defilement, without offering it to another, except as God has ordained in the beautiful sacrament of marriage.

Lord, thank you for these searching words. Help me to manifest before the watching world the beauty of holiness and the joy of a life that walks in close communion with a God who dwells within.

Do we value the high privilege of living as tenants in God's temple? How does sexual immorality defile God's temple? Do we worship the occupant rather than the owner of God's temple?

SEX IN MARRIAGE

A daily devotion for October 15

Read 1 Corinthians 7:1–9.

> "The husband should fulfill his marital duty to his wife, and likewise the wife to her husband. The wife does not have authority over her own body but yields it to her husband. In the same way, the husband does not have authority over his own body but yields it to his wife. Do not deprive each other except perhaps by mutual consent and for a time, so that you may devote yourselves to prayer. Then come together again so that Satan will not tempt you because of your lack of self-control" (1 Cor. 7:3–5).

The major thrust of this paragraph is that sex in marriage is designed for the fulfillment of each partner. Paul does not say to the husband and the wife, "Demand your own sexual rights." He never puts it that way, and yet I have been involved in scores of marriage cases in which a major problem was that one partner, usually the man, demanded his sexual rights from the other. Nothing is more destructive to marital happiness than that. To misread the passage that speaks of the wife not ruling over her own body as giving license to the husband to demand sex whenever he wants it is to destroy the beauty of sex in marriage.

Understanding that would make a big difference in many marriages, and it's easy to see why. In marital relations, you need another to minister to you. God has designed this sexual relationship to teach us how to fulfill the basic law of life, which Jesus put in these terms: "If you attempt to save your life you will lose it" (Matt. 16:25). If you try to meet your own need, if you put that first in your life, you will lose everything you are trying to gain. Instead of finding fulfillment you will find emptiness, and you will end your years looking back upon a wasted experience. You cannot get fulfillment that way.

That is not merely good advice—that is a law of life as inviolable as the law of gravity. The only way to meet your needs and to fulfill yourself is to fulfill another's needs. Throw your life away, Jesus said, and you will find it. That is what sex is all about. It is designed not to have your needs met but to meet another's needs. Thus marriage offers a beautiful reciprocity. By devoting yourself to the enjoyment of your mate and to giving him or her the most exquisite sense of pleasure that you can, you find your own needs met.

This is why God designed us to need someone else to fulfill us sexually. That is why unresponsiveness in a sexual partner always creates a deep-seated problem in a marriage and a rift occurs. God has given us the ability to offer a gift of love and to respond to another person, and the joy of doing so is what creates the ecstasy of sexual love in marriage.

So important is this to marriage that the apostle goes on to say that it takes precedence over everything else in married life except an occasional spiritual retreat for prayer. "Do not refuse one another except perhaps by agreement." If you are going to do this, it must be a mutual decision. You must not give up or deny your partner the right to this kind of enjoyment. To unilaterally refuse to involve yourself in a sexual union in marriage is to violate God's command and to severely hurt the marriage. This can be such a dangerous thing in marriage that Paul says, "Be careful. Don't continue it very long, and come together again, lest Satan be given an advantage over you." Those are wise words, and Paul underscores here much that is causing problems in marriages today.

> *Father, thank you for your frankness in dealing with these matters. Teach me, Lord, the beauty, the glory, and the joy of sexuality. Help me to learn how to express it in ways that give honor to you and that fulfill your divine intention for me.*

Is our perspective toward sexual intimacy in marriage consistent with the basic spiritual principles for all of life? Do we need to examine the inconsistencies and the ways in which they may be unloving and ungodly?

WITH GOD

A daily devotion for October 16

Read 1 Corinthians 7:10–24.

> "Were you a slave when you were called? Don't let it trouble you—although if you can gain your freedom, do so. For the one who was a slave when called to faith in the Lord is the Lord's freed person; similarly, the one who was free when called is Christ's slave. You were bought at a price; do not become slaves of human beings. Brothers and sisters, each person, as responsible to God, should remain in the situation they were in when God called them" (1 Cor. 7:21–24).

Paul is dealing here with the common problem of slavery in that day, and what he says is interesting. Basically, he argues, "To be a slave or to be free is not the overriding consideration of life. It is what you are inside that counts." In the novel *Roots* and in the television portrayal of that book, it was evident that some of the slaves who were believers in Christ were much nobler, more loving, more compassionate, more understanding, and demonstrated more integrity than their free masters. This passage tells us that faith in God is the true freedom.

Paul is not denying the possibility that God may so arrange things that an opportunity for freedom arises. If so, "Take it," he says. This is a gift from God. Though it is revolutionary, Christianity is not designed to be radically so. It does not entail a violent overthrow of systems of the past, but it is designed to free from within. This is what the apostle is saying. So if you are in a situation that is difficult to handle and hard to bear, remember that this is only external; it is only temporary, and you can be free in Christ in a most beautiful, effective, and influential way.

The key words in verse 24 are "with God." Regardless of what your situation may be, even if you cannot change it, even if you are involved in a so-called difficult marriage, remember that God is able to meet you right where you are and to fill your life with love, joy, and peace despite the struggles. The struggles themselves will help you if you understand them as God's choice for you. So Paul says, "Do not become slaves of human beings." You become a slave when you conform to the world, when you let worldly opinions shape your judgments about what you ought to be in marriage or about whether you should get a divorce. You become a slave to men instead of to the Lord when you do that. When you follow after teachers in the church and think of one as being better than another, you become a slave of men. When you give way to secular pressures to sexual infidelity, you become a slave of men. Do not become slaves of men, Paul says, but remain where you are, "with God."

Thank you, Father, for the grace that helps me live in the difficult situations in which I find myself.

What are some habits and/or emotional commitments that may enslave us? What are some specific ways in which God's rightful ownership sets us free?

THE TIME IS SHORT

A daily devotion for October 17

Read 1 Corinthians 7:25–40.

> "What I mean, brothers and sisters, is that the time is short. From now on those who have wives should live as if they do not; those who mourn, as if they did not; those who are happy, as if they were not; those who buy something, as if it were not theirs to keep; those who use the things of the world, as if not engrossed in them. For this world in its present form is passing away" (1 Cor. 7:29–31).

All Paul says here hangs on the words "the time is short." While he did anticipate the Lord Jesus Christ returning in his lifetime, Paul recognizes the brevity of life. The longer we live the more we sense how time seems to fly. As someone has said, "About the time your face clears up, your mind begins to go." That's how life seems to be.

Christians aren't the only ones who see that; non-Christians also speak of the shortness of time, and their reaction is, "Well, if life is short, so let's grab all we can. Let's live life with gusto. There is nothing beyond, so let's have pleasure now." Their philosophy seems to be, "If you are going to be a passenger on the *Titanic* you might as well go first class. Live it up. Eat, drink, and be merry, for tomorrow we die." But that's not to be the Christian's philosophy, Paul tells us.

Clearly the Christian response is, "Use your short time for eternal purposes. Be sure that your goal is not just making a living but making a life." That's what Paul counsels, and it's why he says, "Let those who have wives live as though they had none." He is not encouraging us to neglect our spouses or our responsibilities to our children and our homes. He is saying that we are to keep things in proper focus. We must not let maintaining our homes be the major reason for our existence or give all our time to enjoying this present life. Life has higher demands and higher challenges.

Therefore, even marriage, God-given and beautiful as it is, is not the highest choice an individual can make. If some choose not to marry, to instead pursue other standards, especially spiritual involvement, their choice should be affirmed as good and proper. No one should put them down for it. So Paul advises us, "Do not let things that the world lives for become the center of your life." Joys and sorrows are seen quite differently from the viewpoint of eternity. Success in business is not life's greatest aim, for all in this world is passing away, even its fame and its glory.

I once visited the museum tomb of General Douglas MacArthur, a great American hero from my day. I remembered his welcome in San Francisco when he finally returned home after World War II and the ticker-tape parades he received there and in New York. Cabinets held his medals and memorabilia, letters he had written, and uniforms he'd worn. All were gathering dust, and paint was peeling from the ceiling. Standing there I suddenly and deeply sensed the fading glory of earth. I compared it with what the Scriptures say awaits the believer in Jesus Christ: that "exceeding weight of glory" (2 Cor. 4:17), which Paul says is beyond all comparison. It is something so fantastic, so mind-blowing, so unbelievable that nothing on earth can remotely compare to what awaits those who have found God's purposes and realized his fullness in this life. How tawdry this tomb seemed. The glory of MacArthur was nothing compared with the glory of the simplest believer in Christ. How important therefore it is to pursue that kind of glory rather than empty baubles that gather dust. That is Paul's point: this present world is passing away.

> *Thank you, Father, for the hope I have in you. Nothing in this short life can compare with what you have in store for me. Help me live not for things that are passing away but for what will last for eternity.*

Whether brief or long, time is given us by God with a view to eternity. Are we investing this priceless gift in the tawdry and perishable things of earth or in the timeless, imperishable, and invaluable purposes of God's perfect will?

FOR LOVE'S SAKE

A daily devotion for October 18

Read 1 Corinthians 8:1–13.

"Now about food sacrificed to idols: We know that 'We all possess knowledge.' But knowledge puffs up while love builds up" (1 Cor. 8:1).

Animals were sacrificed in pagan temples. Like the Jews, the pagans reserved some of this meat for their priests and for public sale. So the best meat markets in Corinth were right next to idol temples. Everyone in town knew that if you ate some of that meat you were eating meat that had been offered to an idol. So the question arose among Christians, "If a Christian eats meat offered to an idol is he somehow participating in the worship of that idol?"

A group within the church was saying, "Yes, that's exactly what happens. When these pagans see a known Christian sitting in the public restaurant next to the temple, enjoying a steak that had been offered to the idol, they will think that person agrees with the pagan ideas about that idol. As a consequence, that Christian is giving a false testimony; he is not clearly declaring that Christ has replaced all idols. Furthermore, he is causing weak Christians to stumble, ones who might easily be led back into worship of an idol by their actions."

But another party said, "No, that's not true. An idol is nothing but a piece of wood or stone. How can you worship something that does not exist? How can we deliver people from their idolatrous ways if we act as if there is something to this? It is better that we act according to the knowledge of reality that God has brought us in Christ. Let's enjoy our freedom and eat this meat without any question. It is perfectly good meat, and it would be wrong not to use it." So there was a division in the church.

Paul argues that such problems cannot be solved merely by declaring that we know something to be true and are therefore free to act. "No," Paul says, "knowledge or doctrine alone is not enough. We need love. Knowledge puffs up, but love builds up. Love looks at somebody else's situation, not always at our own." Knowledge, in other words, is self-centered, but love reaches out to include others in our thinking.

Dr. H. A. Ironside gave an illustration of this. He was at a picnic with other Christians, including a convert from Islam. A girl brought a basket of sandwiches to this man and offered one. He said, "What kind are they?" She said, "All we have left are ham or pork." He said, "Don't you have any beef?" She replied, "No, they're all gone." "Well," he said, "then I won't have any." Knowing he was a Christian, she said, "Well, sir, I am really surprised. Don't you know that as a Christian you are freed from food restrictions, and you can eat pork or ham or whatever you like?" He said, "Yes, I know I am free to eat pork, but I am also free not to eat it. I'm still involved with my family in the Middle East, and I know that when I go home each year and come to my father's door, the first question he will ask is, 'Have those infidels taught you to eat the filthy hog meat yet?' If I have to say, 'Yes, Father,' I will be banished from that home and have no further witness in it. But if I can always say, 'No, Father, no pork has ever passed my lips,' then I have admittance to the family circle, and I am free to tell them of the joy I have found in Jesus Christ. Therefore I am free to eat or I am free not to eat, as the case may be."

That story puts this problem in proper perspective. We do not have to claim our right to freedom based on knowledge. We are free to give up our rights anytime the situation warrants. Though we have rights, we also have the right, for the sake of love, not to exercise them.

Help me, Father, to act in love in what I do and not to act merely in knowledge. Thank you for the truth that sets me free and also for the love that restrains me and makes me consider the welfare of others.

God's love sets us free to make loving choices. Do our relationships demonstrate thoughtful responses that originate in godly love?

DUTY AND DELIGHT

A daily devotion for October 19

Read 1 Corinthians 9:1–23.

> "For when I preach the gospel, I cannot boast, since I am compelled to preach. Woe to me if I do not preach the gospel! If I preach voluntarily, I have a reward; if not voluntarily, I am simply discharging the trust committed to me. What then is my reward? Just this: that in preaching the gospel I may offer it free of charge, and so not make full use of my rights as a preacher of the gospel" (1 Cor. 9:16–18).

Paul is saying that faithfully preaching the gospel without charge gives him no sense of pride or of achievement. On the contrary, he has no choice about preaching the gospel. "I am compelled to preach." In other words, "If I do not preach I am miserable. I have no choice in this matter. I would much rather preach than face what I know I would experience if I do not: the lash of my conscience, the sense of failing to do what God has called me to do. I cannot live with that. Woe to me if I preach not the gospel. If I do it willingly, I gain a reward. If I accept this commission from God and joyfully do what he tells me to do, it is to my great advantage. I enjoy it, but whether I like it or not, I must do it."

There is nothing wrong with a sense of duty, the feeling that God has given us a job to do and that we must do it whether we like it or not. Many of us are uneasy with that kind of motivation, but Paul felt it. He said, "There is no choice for me in the matter of preaching. Whether I like it or not I have a commission to fulfill, and if I want my life to be worth anything at all, I had better do it."

But that is not why he does it without charge. He tells us the reason in verse 18: "What then is my reward? Just this: that in preaching the gospel I may offer it free of charge, and so not make full use of my rights as a preacher of the gospel." He is saying that the thing that motivates him, the thing that drives him to work late hours at night making tents so he can earn a living and will not have to be supported by anybody in the church in Corinth, is the sheer delight it gives him to bless and to enrich others without taking a penny in return. Paul is experiencing the joy of giving.

I was invited by some missionaries to go to the south of France to hold a Bible conference. They needed to be refreshed from the Word of God, but I knew that they could not afford my appearance, and they told me so when they called. They said, "We cannot afford to give you an honorarium." I said, "That is all right with me. I will come anyway. Can you meet the expenses of the trip?" They said, "We will try." I knew that they were going to try out of meager salaries, since they lived in an area with one of the highest costs of living in the world.

So I went to France. Through a miscommunication I was not met at the airport in Lyon, and I sat there for twenty-four hours waiting to be picked up. I finally reached the conference ground, and we had a great three or four days together feasting on the Word of God. I saw the missionaries' spirits blessed as they heard the truth. At the close of the conference they came to me and said, "We have put together a check from all of our contributions here. We do not know if it is enough, but it is all we have got, so here it is." It was not enough, hardly covering half of my expenses. But I had the exquisite pleasure of turning the check over, endorsing it, and handing it back, saying, "Use this to establish a fund to have more speakers minister to you." To see the joy and the surprise in their faces was all the reward I needed. I went away richly repaid for that ministry.

Lord, teach me to be giving and generous, not always asking, "What's in it for me?" Help me not to be squeezed in the mold of the world. Teach me to be like you, Lord, to give freely and gladly even though I receive nothing in return.

Is a price tag attached to our service to others? Do we give and serve with grace and with gratitude to the Lord Jesus Christ, who gave all that we may have eternal riches?

NO TEMPTATION

A daily devotion for October 20

Read 1 Corinthians 9:24–10:13.

> "No temptation has overtaken you except what is common to mankind. And God is faithful; he will not let you be tempted beyond what you can bear. But when you are tempted, he will also provide a way out so that you can endure it" (1 Cor. 10:13).

Oh, what an encouragement this is! Paul writes this that we might understand three specific things about our testings. First, they are common to all. When we are under testing nothing is harder to believe than that. We all think, *Why isn't this happening to others? They deserve it so much more than I do. Why is it happening to me?* In fact, everybody goes through this. We are not permitted to witness the martyrdom of others, but we will not be allowed to miss ours. No one is left out. Trials are common to all. Their time is coming, if it has not already arrived, so we must never allow ourselves to think that what is happening to us is unique. It is not at all, and the minute we start inquiring around, we will find a dozen others have gone through the same thing.

Second, throughout our trials, God is faithful, and he will not allow us to be tested beyond our strength. Again, that is hard to believe, is it not? We say, "Well, it has already happened. I am already beyond my strength." But we are not. We just think we are. God knows our strength more than we do. He knows how much we can handle and how much we cannot. One of the basic principles of training for an athletic contest is to aim to do things we do not think we can do right now, to put more pressure on ourselves than we think we can handle. And we discover we can handle it. This is what God does with us. He puts the pressure on, but it is controlled pressure. It will never be more than we can handle as long as we understand the third thing.

The third thing is the conquering grace that he provides, the way out that is always present, never failing. What is that way of escape? It is dependence. Discipline is necessary, but so is dependence. The heroes and the heroines of faith throughout the Old Testament have taught us that in the hour of testing God strips away all human support so that we may learn that he is enough. "God is our refuge and our strength, a very present help in time of trouble" (Ps. 46:1), and we will never discover that until everything else has been taken away. Then we begin to see that God can hold us steady. He himself is the way of escape, and that is why he puts us through pressures and testings.

Lord, I pray that this may be my experience in the days that lie ahead in this troubled world.

What three aspects of our trials and our temptations are assured to us as God's people? How do these address our complaints as well as our confidence in God's purposeful ending?

IDOLATRY

A daily devotion for October 21

Read 1 Corinthians 10:14–11:1.

"Therefore, my dear friends, flee from idolatry" (1 Cor. 10:14).

There were many idol temples in Corinth. On the hill behind the city was the temple of Aphrodite where male and female prostitutes plied their trade in the name of the worship of Venus, the goddess of love. Other temples were scattered within the city; their ruins are visible today. These Christians had once been idol worshipers, bowing down before these images, their lives controlled by the fear and the philosophy of the Greek and the Roman pantheons of gods.

I do not think that the apostle fears that these Christians will again bow down to idols. What he has in mind is not bowing and scraping before an image but succumbing to the temptation to enjoy again the atmosphere found at the idol temple. A great deal of fun was attached to idolatry, and some of the Corinthians were hoping to hang on to this. Everyone regarded the temples as the most exciting places in town. There people could get the best food, served up in open-air restaurants. There they had the wildest music and all the seductive pleasures of wine, women, and song. If Corinthians wanted to enjoy themselves, they went to the temples.

Paul is concerned that these Corinthians, in seeking to enjoy the normal pleasures of life, may indulge in them to such a degree that they will find themselves lured back into belief in these idols and their power. Idolatry is not something we do outwardly with our bodies. Idolatry occurs whenever anyone or anything becomes more important to us than the living God. This is the greatest temptation we all face. When we fall into a place where something becomes of greater importance to us and more controlling in our lives than God, we have succumbed to idolatry.

How easily this kind of idolatry happens to us today! We can get so wrapped up in sports, for instance, that we live for them; they take over our lives. When dancing becomes more than recreation but is something we cannot put aside, it becomes idolatry. Skiing can do the same thing. Fishing can keep us away from ministry. Television robs us of Bible study. Gourmet eating that demands too much attention and too much money is a form of idolatry. These things are not wrong in themselves, but it is easy to fall prey to them. They lure us into more and more involvement until, before we know it, they are more important to us than God. That is idolatry. We have a new god, a new love, and a new master.

Lord, I live in a dangerous world. I often forget that, thinking I can go along with many of these things, and I find myself beginning to be drawn away, losing my fervor for the things of God. Help me at that moment, Lord, to flee idolatry.

Are we giving first priority to the indwelling life and love of the Lord Jesus Christ? Are we allowing other interests to deceive us and to detract from loving him with all our heart, mind, and soul?

HEADSHIP

A daily devotion for October 22

Read 1 Corinthians 11:2–16.

"But I want you to realize that the head of every man is Christ, and the head of the woman is man, and the head of Christ is God" (1 Cor. 11:3).

Even in the ancient world, the head was understood to be the control center of the body. That is what the head on the body does; it runs the body; it is in charge; it is the body's direction setter. Used figuratively, the word *head* primarily connotes leadership, and that is Paul's meaning in this passage. This is clear from the three uses that the apostle makes of the word here.

The first one is "the head of every man is Christ." This is a declaration of Christ's right to lead the whole human race. He is the leader of the race in the mind of God, and ultimately, as Scripture tells us, there will come a day when all humanity shall bow the knee and confess that Jesus Christ is Lord (Rom. 14:11, Phil. 2:11). So whether we know it or not, Christ is our head, and we are responsible to follow him. That is the whole objective of life for any person who wishes to fulfill his humanity.

Move down to the third level of headship mentioned here, "the head of Christ is God." Here we have a manifestation of headship demonstrated for us in history. Jesus, the Son of God, is equal to the Father in his deity. Nevertheless, when he assumes humanity, he submits himself to the leadership of the Father. Everywhere Jesus went he declared that he always did those things that pleased his Father. He even said, "My Father is greater than I" (John 14:28). That statement does not challenge the equality of the members of the Godhead, but when Christ became man he voluntarily consented to take a lower position than the Father. It is in that sense that he says, "My Father is greater than I."

Those two headships help us to understand the meaning of the central one, "the head of the woman is man." The Revised Standard Version says, "The head of the woman is her husband," because the subsequent passage has in view a married woman. Headship is most visible in marriage in which a woman voluntarily undertakes a support role. The man is to be leader, and she assumes this support role to help him fulfill the objectives of their life together as Christ, his head, makes clear. If the woman does not want to do that, she is perfectly free to forgo that role. No woman should get married if she does not want to do that. If she wants to pursue her own objectives, she has every right to do so. But then she ought not to get married, because marriage means that she is willing to recognize her husband as the leader of the two.

In turn, the man is to discover the secrets God has put into his wife and to encourage her so that she will be all that she is capable of being. This is the argument of Ephesians 5. They are one and no man hates his own flesh. If he hurts his wife he hurts himself. There is no way that he can achieve the fullness of his manhood in marriage apart from encouraging his wife to use all the gifts God has put in her. This is the reciprocal relationship in marriage seen in Scripture. This creates the beauty of every wedding. When a man and a woman stand together to be married, the marriage ceremony has for centuries recognized that she is giving herself to him, and he promises to treat that gift with kindness, tenderness, and loving care.

Lord, I pray that I will remember that my views of life are often shallow and inadequate. However, when I conform to the divinely given order I find myself opening a door into joy, love, and peace such as I never imagined. Your yoke is easy and your burden is light.

Do we need to revisit our view of headship? Does our concept of submission equate with our Lord Jesus's submission to the Father? Do we then value it as a privileged and holy calling?

THE LORD'S SUPPER

A daily devotion for October 23

Read 1 Corinthians 11:17–34.

> "For I received from the Lord what I also passed on to you: The Lord Jesus, on the night he was betrayed, took bread, and when he had given thanks, he broke it and said, 'This is my body, which is for you; do this in remembrance of me.' In the same way, after supper he took the cup, saying, 'This cup is the new covenant in my blood; do this, whenever you drink it, in remembrance of me'" (1 Cor. 11:23–25).

Paul passes on to the Corinthians and to us our Lord's emphasis upon two remarkable symbols, the bread and the cup. After the Passover feast, Jesus took the bread, and when he had broken it, to make it available to all the disciples, he said to them, "This is my body." Unfortunately some have taken that to mean that he was teaching that the bread becomes his body, but looking at the story of the upper room, it is clear that he meant this in a symbolic sense. If his meaning was literal, then there were two bodies of Christ present in the upper room, one in which he lived and by which he held the bread, and the bread itself. But clearly our Lord means this as a symbol. "This represents my body, which is for you."

The words were not "broken for you," as some versions have it. That is an inaccurate rendering. It is not broken for us. The Scriptures tell us that not a bone of his body was broken. Rather his body is intended for us to live on; that is the symbolism. Thus when we gather and take the bread of the Lord's Table, break it, and pass it among ourselves, we are reminding ourselves that Jesus is our life: he is the One by whom we live. As Paul says, "I am crucified with Christ: nevertheless I live; yet not I, but Christ liveth in me: and the life which I now live in the flesh I live by the faith of the Son of God, who loved me, and gave himself for me" (Gal. 2:20 KJV).

This is what the bread symbolizes—that Christ is to be the power by which we obey the demands of God to love one another, to forgive one another, to be tender, merciful, kind, and courteous to one another, not to return evil for evil but to pray for those who persecute and misuse us. His life in us enables us to be what God asks us to be. We live by means of Christ.

Following that, our Lord took the cup. The wine of the cup symbolizes his blood, which he said is the blood of the new covenant, the new arrangement for living that God has made by which the old life is ended. That is what blood always means. It is the end of the old life in which we were dependent upon ourselves, lived for ourselves, and wanted only to be the center of attention. That is what the cup means. We agree to that; we are no longer to live for ourselves. We do not have final rights to our lives, and the price is the blood of Jesus. Therefore, when we take that cup and drink it, we are publicly proclaiming that we agree with that sentence of death upon our old life and believe that the Christian life is a continual experience of life coming out of death.

Power with God comes only when we die to the wisdom and the power of man. We give up one so that the other may be manifest within us. That is what the cup means. It is a beautiful picture of what Jesus said of himself, "Except a corn of wheat fall into the ground and die, it abides alone" (John 12:24 KJV). Nothing is more descriptive of the emptiness of life than that phrase "abides alone"—lonely, restless, bored, miserable. That is the life that tries to live for itself, its own needs, and its own rights, but the Christian life is one in which that is freely surrendered. If the corn of wheat falls into the ground and dies, it will bring forth much fruit, and by our participation in the cup this is what we are declaring.

Lord Jesus, thank you for giving up your life that I might have new life in you.

When we partake of the symbols of bread and wine, do we honor the richly profound reality they represent? Does our gratitude for Christ's indwelling life find expression in sacrificial love, no longer living for self-interest but for him who gave himself for us?

HOW THE BODY WORKS

A daily devotion for October 24

Read 1 Corinthians 12:1–31.

> "Just as a body, though one, has many parts, but all its many parts form one body, so it is with Christ. For we were all baptized by one Spirit so as to form one body—whether Jews or Gentiles, slave or free—and we were all given the one Spirit to drink" (1 Cor. 12:12–13).

In this chapter, the apostle begins to use an analogy that will help us understand how the church is designed to function. He places before us a human body and draws lessons from it all through the rest of the chapter as to its parallel with the functioning of the body of Christ. It is more than a mere figure of speech to say that the church is the body of Christ. God takes this seriously, giving us the human body as a visual aid to live in, to walk around in, and to examine as we think through the meaning of the church as the body of Christ.

That is where Paul begins. "Just as the body is one and yet has many members," he says, "so also it is with Christ." Notice it is not "so also it is with the church," because it is the church and Christ that constitute the body of Christ. The body is divided into two major sections, the head and the torso. The head is the control center of the body, while the torso is the biggest part of it and the part to which the members—the arms, the legs—are attached. This design helps us understand how the church is to function, for the whole body plus the head constitute the body of Christ.

To declare, as Paul does, that we are part of Christ is an amazing statement. We constitute the means by which Christ functions in the world, and it is important to keep that concept in mind if we want to understand how the church works. It is a body with many members, and yet it is only one body. It is not many bodies, many denominations. They are all tied together by sharing the same life, and they are tied with the head so that they function as his means of expressing his life in this world.

Paul answers the question, "How did we get into that body?" We were not born into it as infants; the body of Christ does not consist of everybody in the world, only certain ones. His answer is clear: "For by one Spirit we were all baptized into one body." That is the "baptism with the Holy Spirit" predicted by John the Baptist and by Jesus himself, fulfilled for the first time on the day of Pentecost and continually fulfilled ever since whenever people believe in Jesus. They are baptized then by the Spirit into the body of Christ and made part of the living Christ as he has been working in the world through all these centuries.

The church is not just a group of religious people gathered to enjoy mutually desired functions. It is a group of people who share the same life, who belong to the same Lord, who are filled with the same Spirit, who are given gifts by that Spirit, and who are intended to function together to change the world by the life of God. That is the work of the church.

Thank you, Father, for making me part of the body of Christ. I have been baptized into one body and made to drink of one Spirit. I pray that on that basis I may fulfill my function in life to be your instrument right where I live and work.

Have we given serious consideration to the church as the body of Christ on earth? How does this affect our mission and the power and wisdom we receive from Christ our head?

THE SUPREME PRIORITY

A daily devotion for October 25

Read 1 Corinthians 13.

> "If I speak in the tongues of men or of angels, but do not have love, I am only a resounding gong or a clanging cymbal. If I have the gift of prophecy and can fathom all mysteries and all knowledge, and if I have a faith that can move mountains, but do not have love, I am nothing. If I give all I possess to the poor and give over my body to hardship that I may boast, but do not have love, I gain nothing" (1 Cor. 13:1–3).

Analyzing those words is like taking a beautiful flower and tearing it apart. But some analysis is necessary to fully grasp what Paul is saying here. We should remember that this chapter on love fits beautifully with what the apostle talked about in the previous section. In chapter 12 Paul discussed the gifts of the Spirit. In chapter 13 we come to the fruit of the Spirit. Paul introduces it with a hint that the fruit of the Spirit far outweighs the gifts of the Spirit. That we become loving people is far more important than whether we are active, busy people. Both are necessary, but one is greater than the other. Paul has said so: "I will show you a still more excellent way." That is the way of love.

I call this the "fruit of the Spirit" because in the letter to the Galatians Paul details for us what the fruit of the Spirit is. It is love, joy, peace, patience, kindness, goodness, faithfulness, gentleness, and self-control (Gal. 5:22–23). All of those qualities are manifestations of love. This chapter sets forth that quality of love that is the work of the Spirit of God within us reproducing the character of Christ. Once we have love all these other qualities that are part of the fruit of the Spirit are possible for us. If we have the love of God in our hearts, we can be patient, peaceful, good, loving, faithful, gentle, and kind.

The word *love* is not the Greek word *eros*. That word is used to describe erotic love. And the word here is not *philia*, which means affection or friendship. Paul is talking about *agape*, a commitment of the will to cherish and to uphold another person. This is the word used to describe the love of God. It is a word addressed to the will. It is a decision that we make and a commitment that we undertake to treat another person with concern, with care, and with thoughtfulness and to work for his or her best interests. That is what love is, and this is what Paul is talking about.

This kind of love is possible only for those who first love God. Any attempt to exercise love like this without first having loved God will result in a fleshly love. There are two great commandments. The first is to love the Lord with all your heart. The second is to love your neighbor as yourself (Matt. 22:37–39). We try to turn that around. Many of us are trying to love our neighbor without having loved God, and it is impossible to do that. It is "the love of God shed abroad in our hearts by the Holy Spirit," as Paul puts it in Romans 5:5, that fulfills the definition given in this chapter. We cannot love other people until we love God.

Love for God is not difficult, because all we need to do is be aware of how he has loved us. Above all else he has loved us in having given his Son for us, having redeemed us and forgiven us. Our guilt is taken away. By these means God has called us to himself and given us a standing before him as his children. To remember all that is to be stirred with love for God. When we love God we awaken our capacity to love people. Love is a supernatural quality. God alone can give this kind of love. God alone can lead us to choose to love somebody who does not appeal to us. Yet that is what God's love is. That is what is so desperately needed and so beautifully described in this passage. It can come only as we love God and as love is awakened within us by the Holy Spirit.

> *Lord, I pray that the gift of love may be manifest in my life.*

Are we long on good works and good intentions but short on love? What does this infer about our intimacy with our God, who is love? Are we looking for something less than genuine love in all the wrong places?

THE VALUE OF PROPHECY

A daily devotion for October 26

Read 1 Corinthians 14.

"Follow the way of love and eagerly desire gifts of the Spirit, especially prophecy. For anyone who speaks in a tongue does not speak to people but to God. Indeed, no one understands them; they utter mysteries by the Spirit. But the one who prophesies speaks to people for their strengthening, encouraging and comfort" (1 Cor. 14:1–3).

This passage is tied to the love chapter. Love is to be the basic, biblical reason for exercising a spiritual gift. Love is the hunger to reach out for someone else's benefit. That is the controlling theme throughout this chapter in the discussion of tongues and prophesying. Love is building up someone else. To that end, "desire spiritual gifts" so that they may be a means of helping others and fulfilling love.

Clearly the one spiritual gift that is most effective in that direction is prophesying. The gift of prophesying is not predicting the future. That may occasionally be an element in it, but prophesying is the explanation of the present in the light of the revelation of God. Today we would call this biblical preaching, which unfolds the mind of God and applies it to the daily struggles of life. That is prophesying. That is the gift for a congregation to desire above all others.

From verse 2 through verse 5, Paul compares the gifts of prophecy and tongues. Anyone who speaks in tongues is not understood in a congregation, because he speaks "mysteries in the Spirit." He is speaking in a language that people do not understand. In Corinth people would stand up and speak in these languages, perhaps recognizable as languages used somewhere nearby (as on the day of Pentecost), but the people there did not understand these languages, and so they could not know what the speakers were saying.

In contrast, Paul now describes the gift of prophesying, which he says has three effects. First, it builds people up. The word is *oikodomen* in the Greek; *oiko* means "house," and *domen* means "to build." To build a house on a solid foundation is the idea, and the work of prophesying gives people a foundation. A major problem among Christians today is the struggle they have with a sense of their true identity. Many people are emotionally torn apart because they do not understand that they are new creatures in Christ; they are no longer what they once were. But they still feel at times that they remain what they once were, and they react accordingly. They cannot escape this up-and-down experience. Prophesying corrects that. It teaches us who we are in Christ.

The second thing prophesying does is strengthen people. This word "strengthened" is the word from which we get the word *paraclete*, one of the titles of the Holy Spirit. He is the strengthener of God's people. A paraclete is "one called alongside" to support, steady, and strengthen another.

The third ministry of prophesying is that of comforting. Still a third Greek word is used here, *paramuthian*, which means to empathize, to put yourself in the place of others, to understand the pressures they are under. It means to be able to feel with them and to encourage them with the fact that you know how they feel. That is what the work of prophesying is inclined to do. We have all had the experience of listening to a text from Scripture expounded and feeling that this spoke directly to our basic problem. That is what prophesying does. You can see how useful and how important it is to have this gift exercised in a church.

Thank you, Father, for the ministry of the Word of God in my life. I pray for those who expound it that they might be your messengers to a needy people.

What is the primary aim in the exercise of spiritual gifts? In what ways does the gift of prophesying, as in exposition of the Word of God, fulfill this basic purpose?

OF FIRST IMPORTANCE

A daily devotion for October 27

Read 1 Corinthians 15:1–4.

> "For what I received I passed on to you as of first importance: that Christ died for our sins according to the Scriptures, that he was buried, that he was raised on the third day according to the Scriptures" (1 Cor. 15:3–4).

There are three elements of the gospel. First, Christ died for our sins according to the Scriptures. Isn't it amazing that Paul does not mention a word about the life of Jesus? That is startling, but that is where the gospel begins. And he does not simply say, "Christ died." Ask people today what the gospel is, and they will often say, "Well, Jesus lived and died." No, that is not the gospel. Everyone believes that Jesus died. Go to any of the modern presentations of the life of Jesus, and you will find they all end at his death. But there is no good news in that. The good news is Christ died for our sins. The Scriptures tell us that his death accomplished something for us. It changed us; it delivered us; it set us free. That death had great significance in the mind and heart and eyes of God, and that is the good news. As Peter puts it, "He himself bore our sins in his body on the tree" (1 Peter 2:24 RSV). Or, to use Isaiah's words, "He was wounded for our transgressions, he was bruised for our iniquities: the chastisement of our peace was upon him; and with his stripes we are healed" (Isa. 53:5 KJV).

The second element of the gospel is that Jesus not only "died for our sins according to the Scriptures" but that he was also "buried." Why does Paul include the burial of Jesus? Is it not enough that Jesus died and rose again? The reason he does this is that when the disciples took the body of Jesus down from the cross, they showed their acceptance of his death. Did we realize how hard it was for them to accept this fact? They did not want to believe it when he himself told them that this would happen. When it happened they went away stunned and unbelieving. But somewhere along the line some realist among them faced up to the truth and said, "We have got to go get his body and bury him." Joseph of Arimathea came forward and offered a tomb, and with loving hands they took Christ's body down from the tree. They wrapped it in grave clothes and bound it tightly. They embalmed Jesus with spices, and then they placed him in a tomb where he lay for three days and three nights. There is no question that the disciples believed that he was dead. They could never have entertained any idea that he had merely fainted on the cross or fallen into a coma, for they themselves had performed the burial service. That is why Paul adds that here. It marked the disciples' acceptance that Jesus was dead.

But the third element is that "he was raised on the third day according to the Scriptures." It was anticipated that Jesus would die; it was equally anticipated that he would rise again from the dead. On the third day, to the amazement of the disciples, he fulfilled all predictions. Jesus was not merely resuscitated (that is, returning to the life he had before) but resurrected. That means he came back to a life he had never lived before—a glorified life—and yet in the amazing mystery of the resurrection, this was the same Jesus with the wounds in his body that they could touch and see for themselves.

That is the story of the gospel—three basic facts. These are not doctrines; these are not philosophies; these are not ideas that men have had about what God should be like. These are events that occurred in history. They cannot be eliminated or evaded. There they are. These facts have changed the history of the world. Our faith does not rest upon mere philosophy but upon events that have occurred and that cannot be taken away from us.

Heavenly Father, thank you for the marvel of the gospel. Help me to understand that this is to be the center of my life, that the most basic thing about me is my faith in this good news.

Have we grasped the importance of the three elements of the gospel that are essential to our faith? Do we see them as historic facts that give total authenticity to our lives and to our witness?

WHAT IF?

A daily devotion for October 28

Read 1 Corinthians 15:5–19.

> "And if Christ has not been raised, our preaching is useless and so is your faith. More than that, we are then found to be false witnesses about God, for we have testified about God that he raised Christ from the dead. But he did not raise him if in fact the dead are not raised. For if the dead are not raised, then Christ has not been raised either. And if Christ has not been raised, your faith is futile; you are still in your sins. Then those also who have fallen asleep in Christ are lost. If only for this life we have hope in Christ, we are of all people most to be pitied" (1 Cor. 15:14–19).

Paul considers the question, "What if?" What would the world be like if Jesus had not been raised? Six history-changing facts would have followed if Jesus had not risen. First, without the resurrection all preaching would have been a waste of time. All the messages we have ever heard or read, all the Christian books we have read, all radio and television broadcasts of the gospel we have listened to would have been a total waste of time had Jesus not risen from the dead.

Second, without the resurrection, all Christian faith would be useless. What would be the point of coming to church every Sunday morning, of going to a Bible study, of reading the Scriptures, or of trying to believe that God is there to help us? All that would be worthless. It would be only a kind of religious game. Life would be reduced to grim realities, with no hope now or later.

Third, if the resurrection is untrue, the apostles would be the world's greatest liars. They would deserve to be treated as arch deceivers rather than as honored men of integrity and truth. They would hypocrites, and worse than that they would be deceivers who have led us into gross darkness and error. After twenty centuries of the preaching of these things, they would undoubtedly have won the title of the world's greatest liars. That is what Paul says, and that conclusion is unavoidable if there is no resurrection, because the apostles staked their reputation on the fact that Jesus had risen from the dead.

The fourth point is even worse. If Christ is not raised, then all our sins are still with us. This means that even granting that there is a God, we must stand at last before him and give an account of all we have done. And there would be no way of escaping the justice with which God would deal with sin. There would be no hiding place, no hope for mercy, no loving Christ to say, "I've paid the penalty for you; I've taken your place; I've loved you and given myself for you."

The fifth thing, Paul says, is that "those also who have fallen asleep in Christ are lost." We would never again see all those loved ones who we thought had gone on to be with the Lord, whom we hoped to meet again. Our children, our parents, our friends, those who have been taken suddenly, those to whom we bid a weeping farewell with the hope that one day we would meet them again in glory—we would never see them again. A terrible silence would fall; they would be gone forever.

Finally, the sixth fact: "If for this life only we have hoped in Christ, we are of all people most to be pitied." Even the present would be changed. We would have to give up our beautiful dream and go back to coldness, selfishness, drabness, grimness, and darkness. All of this would be made worse by the fact that we once thought we had escaped; we once thought we had a hold of something so marvelous that it gave us great joy and peace and glory and blessing. But if there is no resurrection all this would crumble and be taken away from us; our darkness would be all the darker for that.

Thank you, Lord, for the hope and the purpose that the resurrection of Jesus gives me.

The resurrection of Jesus Christ is crucial to the Christian faith, which has changed the course of world history. Consider at least six major life-altering effects that would result if Christ had not risen from the dead, and be awed by this vast, historic reality!

THEN COMES THE END

A daily devotion for October 29

Read 1 Corinthians 15:20–58.

> "Then the end will come, when he hands over the kingdom to God the Father after he has destroyed all dominion, authority and power. For he must reign until he has put all his enemies under his feet. The last enemy to be destroyed is death" (1 Cor. 15:24–26).

Notice that the reign of Christ does not begin after he subdues his enemies, although we often think that way. The biblical truth is that he does reign and that he shall continue to reign until his enemies are made his footstool. I know of nothing that has more power to steady us in times of pressure and to undergird us in times of discouragement, defeat, and oppression than the realization that Jesus now reigns. He is in control now. When we run up against oppressive governments, severe limitations on our freedom, and violent persecution of the Christian faith, we are to remember that all this takes place under the overall authority of Jesus Christ, who, after his resurrecton, said, "All power is given unto me in heaven and in earth" (Matt. 28:18 KJV). He permits these things to happen to accomplish his purposes, just as in the Old Testament God raised up the Babylonians and the Assyrians and brought them against Israel. He allowed Jerusalem to be conquered and the Israelites to be taken into captivity, not because that was the way he wanted things to happen on earth but because that was necessary to teach his people the lessons they needed to know. God brings these things to pass for our sake, and they happen under the authority of Christ.

Now the apostle says, "The last enemy to be destroyed is death." This can be seen to be true in both an individual and a universal sense. Universally, death will never disappear from this earth until we come to that moment, described in the book of Revelation, when a new heaven and a new earth come into existence.

But there is a sense in which this is individually true of us right now. We are experiencing a continual reciprocation of death, out of which comes life. We are all fighting battles, and at times we fail, falter, and are overcome. We give way to worry, impatience, anger, malice, and lust. Sometimes we struggle against these things with great effort; other times we give in quickly. But we are all engaged in a great battle in which we are assaulted continually with temptations to yield and to fall into death. Yet even in times of failure, by the grace of God's forgiveness we are restored. Life is handed back to us, and we go on to walk for a longer time without failure until gradually we gain victory over evil habits and evil attitudes. Life, therefore, is a continual experience of life coming out of death, of pain leading to joy, and that will never end as long as we are in this present life.

But there will come a time when this body will die, and death then is destroyed for us. "The last enemy to be destroyed is death." Once we pass through the experience of death into resurrection, like our Lord himself, we shall never die again. Christ having once died, Paul says in Romans, never dies again, and we share his existence. He is the firstfruits of the great harvest of which we are a part.

I am thankful, Lord, that the day will come when there will be no more death, no more mourning, and no more pain.

Are we daily claiming the privilege of the Lord Jesus's sovereign reign both over us and over the world? Are we living in the power and the wisdom of Christ's indwelling presence, trusting him to resolve the tension between death and life in daily experience?

THE FIRST DAY OF THE WEEK

A daily devotion for October 30

Read 1 Corinthians 16:1–9.

> "Now about the collection for the Lord's people: Do what I told the Galatian churches to do. On the first day of every week, each one of you should set aside a sum of money in keeping with your income, saving it up, so that when I come no collections will have to be made. Then, when I arrive, I will give letters of introduction to the men you approve and send them with your gift to Jerusalem. If it seems advisable for me to go also, they will accompany me" (1 Cor. 16:2–4).

Paul is talking about the collection being made in many churches to send to the troubled church in Jerusalem. Paul is anxious that these Gentile churches should have a part in helping the afflicted saints in Jerusalem. This is a beautiful picture of the way the church is one all over the earth. What happens to our brothers and sisters in other corners of the earth ought to be of immediate concern to us., so Paul exhorts the churches in Corinth and other places to meet that need. In doing this, he gives us wonderful principles to govern our giving.

First, giving is a universal practice. This was not just something that the Corinthians had to do. Everywhere Paul went, wherever he founded a church, he taught believers to give, because giving is an essential part of Christianity. It is not an option; it is something every Christian must do.

The second principle is that giving is to be done every week. This is one of the first indications we have that Christians had begun to gather regularly to worship, to pray, and to give on the first day of the week, Sunday. The Jewish day of worship is Saturday. These Christians had forsaken that and had begun to worship on the first day of the week.

Third, giving is a personal act. Paul says "each one of you." He does not leave anybody out. Even children ought to be taught to give. It may be only a few pennies, a nickel, or a dime, but on every Sunday there ought to be a gift from every Christian. It is not the amount that is important but the regularity of giving, which is a continual reminder that we have freely received and therefore freely give. So each one is to do this. It is, in that sense, not an option.

Fourth, Christians are to save it up. Paul refers to the fact that people in this culture got paid every day. They were to put aside each day a certain amount of money so that on Sunday they would have a larger amount to bring to the services and to contribute to the needs of others.

Then a fifth principle is to give "in keeping with your income." That means giving according to the way God has given to you. Has he poured out abundantly? Then give abundantly. Are you having a hard time and barely making it? Then your gift can be reduced proportionately. It ought to be something, but it can be very little because God is not interested in the amount. He is only interested in the motive of the heart in giving.

The sixth principle is critical. Paul says do this "so that when I come no contributions need to be made." Paul knew that when he was present, he had a tremendous effect on people. He did not want their giving to come because they were moved by his preaching or in any other way pressured into giving.

The seventh principle is seen in verses 3 and 4: "When I arrive, I will give letters of introduction to the men you approve and send them with your gift to Jerusalem. If it seems advisable for me to go also, they will accompany me." Giving should be done responsibly. Paul is careful not to take this responsibility himself. What a contrast this is with people today who exhort us to give and then take the money themselves, never giving an accounting for it.

> *Thank you, Father, for the practicality of this section. I pray that I might apply these principles and be generous with all that you have given me.*

What are seven basic principles for the practice of giving? Are we learning that as Jesus said, "It is more blessed to give than to receive"? Joy results from spontaneous compassion and from simple obedience.

THE CARE AND FEEDING OF FELLOW WORKERS

A daily devotion for October 31

Read 1 Corinthians 16:10–24.

> "Now about our brother Apollos: I strongly urged him to go to you with the brothers. He was quite unwilling to go now, but he will go when he has the opportunity" (1 Cor. 16:12).

That is a most remarkable verse, especially in view of the attitude many today have that the apostles were, in a sense, generals in the army of the Lord, sending out people, ordering them here or there, and commanding these younger Christians to go at their beck and call. But we do not find that here. This verse indicates that Paul does not command Apollos; he has no authority over him. He simply urges him. In several places in the New Testament we are reminded by the apostle that he was not lord over anybody else.

Lording it over the brethren is one of the great curses of the church today. Some men assume, for instance, that the office of pastor gives them authority over other people. But notice that Paul respects the personal freedom of Apollos to be directed by the Lord, even as he himself is. He does not tell Apollos what he must do. Apollos says it was not his will to come, and Paul accepts that. Apollos was also operating under the direct control of God. This is true not only of leaders such as Paul and Apollos but of all Christians. Perhaps the clearest word on this was spoken by the Lord himself when he said, "For you have one teacher and you are all brothers" (Matt.23:8).

The church must return to that sense of being brothers with one another, not in position over one another but working together. I find Christians everywhere under the authority of men who seem to be dictators—much like Diotrephes, whom John mentions in one of his letters, who loved to have preeminence among them (3 John 1:9). Believers must understand that no pastor has the right to tell them what they can do with their spiritual gifts and that no pastor has the right to tell them that they cannot have a meeting in their home and teach the Word of God to whoever will come and listen.

Perhaps they should listen to him as a wise brother who understands the nature of truth and who can give them helpful suggestions. But no pastor ever has the right to tell other Christians that they cannot follow the leading of the Lord as to their ministry. Paul makes that clear in this passage.

Observe how he supports Apollos in this. Apollos will come, he says, "when he has opportunity." Paul, Apollos, and Peter were three men around whom factions were gathering in this church. Perhaps Paul wanted Apollos to go because he thought it might improve that situation. But that may have been the reason Apollos did not want to go. He might have feared that his visiting Corinth would aggravate the tendency of the Corinthians to cluster around an individual. So he chose not to go, and the apostle supported him. This is a helpful glance into New Testament life.

> *Lord, thank you for your Word. Teach me to listen to you and to pray for those around me who are called to shepherd the flock of God.*

Does command-control leadership have biblical authorization? Are we honoring the Holy Spirit's prerogative in our fellow believers with prayerful support?

ROMANS 9–16

From Guilt to Glory— Exhibited and Experienced
An introduction for the month of November

A verse in the book of Jeremiah comes to mind as we begin to study the second half of Romans. When Jeremiah was troubled about things that were happening to him, he came to God and told him how he felt. Instead of comforting him as Jeremiah thought he would do, the Lord said to him, "If you have fainted when you run with footmen, how will you contend with horses?" (Jer. 12:5). If you had difficulty handling Paul's arguments in chapters 1 through 8 of Romans, what are you going to do now that we are in the ninth chapter? For, in this chapter, the apostle brings before us some of the toughest questions ever faced by man as he contemplates God's workings. All the bitter and denunciatory accusations that man brings against God are dealt with squarely in this chapter.

Chapters 1 through 8 constitute the first major division of the letter and concern Paul's explanation of the gospel of the grace of God, the full plan of redemption as God has worked it out. It is a marvelously brilliant explanation—the best, the most accurate, the most theologically complete that we have in the Scriptures. Then in chapter 9, the second division begins. Paul has been talking about the grace of God and the gospel of God, and he has given an explanation of these things, but now he goes back over them again. This time, though, his purpose is not to explain the gospel but to exhibit it. These chapters are an exhibition of the grace of God.

The Wax Museum at Fisherman's Wharf in San Francisco displays scenes from historic moments and the wax figures of renowned characters from national and world history. Those figures help me to grasp more clearly what those historical events were like. This is what we have in these chapters of Romans. They demonstrate—in terms of people—how God works in human history, how he redeems and saves.

In chapters 1 to 8, the apostle has declared that man is helpless to save himself. There is not a thing we can do to save ourselves. We have power to choose, we are expected to choose, and we are free to choose, but nevertheless, as Paul has made clear, God is behind it all. We don't understand that, and so in chapters 9 to 16 Paul turns the spotlight on Israel to demonstrate just how God works. We will learn many important things from this section of the epistle to the Romans.

The story of Israel is sad and rather sobering. Here was a nation that counted itself as having an inside track with God and saw itself as the people of God, the chosen nation close to God, with advantages no other nation had. The Israelites regarded themselves as having a specially privileged position with God. Yet Paul begins this section with a clear acknowledgment that this nation is far away from God. Despite all the possibilities that this people enjoyed, they are a long way from the Lord.

JACOB I HAVE LOVED

A daily devotion for November 1

Read Romans 9:1–13.

"Just as it is written, 'Jacob I loved, but Esau I hated'" (Rom. 9:13).

Many have struggled over those words. But all the apostle is saying is that it is clear from this story that ancestry makes no difference (these boys had the same father) and that what they do in their lives ultimately will not matter. Before they were able to make choices—good or bad—God had said to their mother, "The elder shall serve the younger." By that he implied not only that there would be a difference in the nations that followed (the descendants of these two men), and that one would be in the place of honor and the other wouldn't, but also that the personal destinies of the two were involved. That is clear from the record of history. Jacob forevermore stands for all the things in men that God honors and wants them to have. Jacob was a scheming, rather weak character—not very lovable. Esau, on the other hand, was a rugged individualist—much more admirable when he was growing up than was his brother. But Jacob was the one who was brought to faith, and Esau was not. God uses this as a symbol of how he works.

I once heard of a man who told a noted Bible teacher, "I'm having trouble with this verse, 'Jacob have I loved, but Esau have I hated.' How could God ever say, 'Esau have I hated'?" The Bible teacher said, "I have trouble with that verse, too, but my problem is not quite the same. I have no trouble understanding the words 'Esau have I hated.' What bothers me is how God could ever say, 'Jacob have I loved'!" Read the life of Jacob and you will see why.

We must not take the word *hated* to mean God disliked Esau and would have nothing to do with him and treated him with contempt. That is what we often mean when we say we hate someone. Jesus used this word when he said, "Except a man hate his father and mother and brother and sister and wife and children and houses and land, and even his own life, he cannot be my disciple" (Luke 14:26). Clearly he was not saying that we have to treat our mothers and fathers and wives and children and our own lives with contempt and disrespect. He clearly meant that he is to have preeminence. Hatred, in that sense, means to love less. We are to love these less than we love him.

God didn't hate Esau in the sense we usually employ that word. In fact, he blessed him. He made of him a great nation. He gave him promises that he fulfilled to the letter. What these verses imply is that God set his heart on Jacob to bring him to redemption, and all Jacob's followers would reflect the possibilities of that. As Paul has already argued, those followers were not all necessarily saved by that, but Jacob would forever stand for what God wants men to be, and Esau would forever stand as a symbol of what he does not like.

What Paul is teaching us here is that God has a sovereign, elective principle that he carries out on his terms. Here are those terms. Salvation is never based on natural advantages. What we are by nature does not enter into the picture of whether we will be redeemed. Second, salvation is always based on a promise that God gives. This is why we are exhorted in the Scriptures to believe his promises. This includes, in some mysterious way, the necessity that we be confronted with those promises and give our voluntary submission to them. The third principle is that salvation never takes any notice of whether we are good or bad. Never! That is what was established here. These children were neither good nor bad, yet God chose Jacob and passed over Esau.

Father, again I must admit I don't understand very much. I am a finite creature, and I cannot fully understand how you act. But I believe you are faithful. Help me to be open and teachable in spirit that I might recognize the marvelous grace that has reached out and found me.

What are three sovereign elective principles in God's plan of redemption? Does our finite understanding allow us to question God's sovereign choices?

LET GOD BE GOD

A daily devotion for November 2

Read Romans 9:14–21.

> "What then shall we say? Is God unjust? Not at all! For he says to Moses, 'I will have mercy on whom I have mercy, and I will have compassion on whom I have compassion.' It does not, therefore, depend on human desire or effort, but on God's mercy. For Scripture says to Pharaoh: 'I raised you up for this very purpose, that I might display my power in you and that my name might be proclaimed in all the earth.' Therefore God has mercy on whom he wants to have mercy, and he hardens whom he wants to harden" (Rom. 9:14–18).

This passage delivers a clear message. Salvation is not based on human effort—it is God who chooses. The ultimate reason for God's choice of anyone is that he chooses whom he wants. This is the truth about God that people dislike the most. We must face the fact that God is a sovereign being. He is not answerable to anyone. We don't like that, because to us sovereignty is always connected with tyranny. To trust anyone with that kind of power is to put ourselves in the hands of someone who might destroy us. We fight that in our national life, we fight it in our family life, and we fight it in our individual relationships. We do not trust anyone with absolute power over us. It is no wonder that when we are confronted by a God with absolute power, we are troubled. But if God had to give an answer to anyone, the person to whom God had to account would become God. The core of God's nature is that he does what he pleases. We must get rid of the idea that his sovereignty will be destructive to us. As we will see, his sovereignty is our only hope!

God declares his sovereignty. He says to Moses, "I will have mercy on whom I have mercy, and I will have compassion on whom I have compassion" (Ex. 33:19). Moses was an example of God's choice to bless someone. Who was Moses that God should choose him? He was nobody, a murderer and a fugitive from justice who for forty years lived in the desert. But God made him his messenger and gave him a name known throughout history. Why? God chose to do so.

God demonstrated his sovereignty with Pharaoh as well. He took a man who was no better than Moses and put him on a throne and gave him authority over all of Egypt. Then, when Moses confronted him, God allowed Pharaoh to continue to resist God's will. God could have stopped him, but he didn't. He allowed him to do what all men do by nature—resist God. So Pharaoh held out against God, and God allowed this so that he might demonstrate his power and attract the attention of men everywhere to his greatness.

That bothers us. We think anybody who boasts about his greatness, who tries to get people to think about how great he is, is conceited. We don't like such people. But in our tendency to think of God as nothing but an enlarged man, we attribute to him our own motives. When a man does this, he is destructive and must necessarily put others down to elevate himself. But what God does is necessary to the welfare and benefit of his creatures. The more we understand the goodness and the glory of God, the richer our lives will be. So when God invites us to think about his greatness, it is not because his ego needs to be massaged; it is because we require that for our welfare. Therefore God finds ways to do it, and he uses people even to resist his will so that there might be an occasion to display his greatness and his power.

Sovereign God, thank you for your place on high above all, for your plans to make yourself known through humankind, and for your perfect justice.

The concept of God must recognize him as the ultimate authority. Can we trust the sovereign authority of God, who is love?

WHY PEOPLE STUMBLE

A daily devotion for November 3

Read Romans 9:22–33.

> "What then shall we say? That the Gentiles, who did not pursue righteousness, have obtained it, a righteousness that is by faith; but the people of Israel, who pursued the law as the way of righteousness, have not attained their goal. Why not? Because they pursued it not by faith but as if it were by works. They stumbled over the stumbling stone. As it is written: 'See, I lay in Zion a stone that causes people to stumble and a rock that makes them fall, and the one who believes in him will never be put to shame'" (Rom. 9:30–33).

God says there is a way to tell whether you are being drawn by the Spirit unto salvation or whether you are being permitted by God to remain where you are, lost and condemned: The way you can tell is by what you do with Jesus. God has planted a stone in the midst of society. When you walk down a path and come to a big flat rock in the middle of the path, there are two things you can do. You can stumble over it, or you can stand on it. That is what Jesus is—a stone planted by God.

The Jews, who determined to work out their salvation on the basis of their own behavior, their own good works before God, stumbled over the stone. That is why the Jews rejected Jesus and why they reject him to this day. They don't want to admit that they need a Savior, that they are not able to save themselves. No man is able to do this. But those who see that they need a Savior have already been drawn by the Spirit of God, awakened by his grace, and made to understand what is going on in their lives. Therefore, their desire to be saved, the expression of their need for a Savior, causes them to accept Jesus. They stand upon that stone. Anyone who comes to God on that basis will never be put to shame. God says that is the testing point.

The crisis of humanity is Jesus. You can be extremely religious, you can spend hours, days, or an entire lifetime following religious pursuits and apparently honoring God, but the test will always come: what will you do with Jesus? God put him in the midst of human society to reveal those he has called and those he has not. Jesus taught this plainly: "No man can come to me except the Father who has sent me draw him" (John 6:44) and "All that my Father has given me shall come to me. Him that comes to me I will never, never cast out" (John 6:37 KJV).

So what is left for us? To respond to Jesus and to thank God that we are not only doing what our hearts and our consciences urge us to do but that we are responding in obedience to the drawing of the elective Spirit of God, who in mercy has chosen to bring us out of a lost humanity.

> *Father, how this makes me realize afresh how desperately dependent I am upon your saving grace. I did not save myself—I could not. I did not even initiate the desire to be saved—that comes from you. But I thank you for calling me, for redeeming me, and for bringing me to you at infinite cost to yourself. Thus I give myself anew to you today.*

Are we investing our lives in short-term approval for performance? The person and the saving grace of the Lord Jesus represent a crisis for us. Have we consented to his reign, the redeeming power of his presence?

THE NEED TO BE SAVED

A daily devotion for November 4

Read Romans 10:1–4.

> "Brothers and sisters, my heart's desire and prayer to God for the Israelites is that they may be saved" (Rom. 10:1).

In Romans 10:1–4 Paul expresses his intense passion that many within the nation Israel will be saved. I do not think there is any word in the Christian vocabulary that makes people feel more uncomfortable than the word *saved*. People cringe when they hear it. Perhaps it conjures up visions of hot-eyed, zealous buttonholers—usually with bad breath—who walk up and grab you and say, "Brother, are you saved?" Or perhaps it raises visions of a tiny band of Christians at a street meeting in front of some saloon singing, "Give the winds a mighty voice. Jesus saves! Jesus saves!" Whatever the reason, people are bothered by this word.

I will never forget the startled look on the face of a man who came up to me in a movie theater. The seat beside me was vacant, and he said, "Is this seat saved?" I said, "No, but I am." He found a seat across the aisle. Somehow this word threatens all our religious complacency and angers the self-confident and the self-righteous alike.

And yet, when we turn to the Scriptures we find that this is an absolutely unavoidable word. Christians have to talk about men and women being saved, because the truth is that men and women are lost. There is no escaping the fact that the Bible clearly teaches that the human race into which we are born is a lost race. This is why the good news of John 3:16 is that, "[16] For God so loved the world, that he gave his only begotten Son, that whosoever believeth in him should not perish, but have everlasting life." (John 3:16 KJV).

We can never deal realistically with life until we face up to this fundamental fact: people are not waiting until they die to be lost—they are already lost. The grace of God reaches down, calls us out of that lost state, and gives us an opportunity to come to Christ and be saved. Therefore *saved* is a perfectly legitimate word to use. It makes us uncomfortable only when we refuse to face the fact that men and women are lost. They are born into a perishing race in which their humanity is being put to improper uses and is gradually deteriorating and falling apart, and they face an eternity of separation from God. These are the facts as the Scriptures declare.

Lord, thank you for the simple but marvelous miracle of salvation.

Why are many offended by the word *saved*? Since it is the realistic assessment of everyone who has entered by faith into God's saving grace in Jesus, is it our heart's desire and prayer that the lost be saved?

HOW TO BE SAVED

A daily devotion for November 5

Read Romans 10:5–11.

> "If you confess with your mouth that Jesus is Lord and believe in your heart that God raised him from the dead, you will be saved. For it is with your heart that you believe and are justified, and it is with your mouth that you profess your faith and are saved. As Scripture says, 'Anyone who believes in him will never be put to shame'" (Rom. 10:10–11).

That is the clearest statement in the Word of God on how to be saved. Paul makes it simple. He says that it begins with the confession of the mouth: "Jesus is Lord." We shouldn't twist those words to mean that we must stand up in public somewhere and announce that we believe Jesus is Lord before we are saved. Paul does not mean it that way, although he does not exclude that. He means that the mouth is the symbol of the conscious acknowledgment to ourselves of what we believe. This means we have come to the place where we recognize that Jesus has the right to lordship in our lives. Prior to this point we have been lords of our lives and have run our own affairs. We have decided we have the right to make our own decisions according to what we want. But there comes a time as God's Spirit works in us when we see the reality of life as God has made it to be, and we realize Jesus is Lord.

He is Lord of our past, to forgive us of our sins; he is Lord of our present, to dwell within us and to guide and to control every area of our lives; he is Lord of our future, to lead us into glory at last; he is Lord of life, Lord of death, and Lord over all things. He is in control of history. He is running all human events. He stands at the end of every path on which men go, and he is the ultimate One we all must reckon with. That is why Peter says in Acts 4:12, "Salvation is found in no one else; for there is no other name under heaven given to men by which we must be saved."

We cannot read the book of Acts without recognizing that the basic creed of the early Christians was "Jesus is Lord." These days we hear a lot about mantras, words that we are supposed to repeat when we meditate. I suggest we adopt this as a mantra: Jesus is Lord. We should repeat it wherever we are to remind ourselves of this great truth. When Peter stood up to speak on the day of Pentecost, this was his theme: Jesus is Lord.

When God has led you to the place where you are ready to say to yourself, *Jesus is my Lord*, he then acts conclusively. Through that confession God does something. No man can do it, but God can. He immediately brings about all that is wrapped up in the word *saved*. Your sins are forgiven. God imparts to you a standing of righteous worth in his sight. He gives you the Holy Spirit to live within you. He makes you a child in his family. He gives you an inheritance for eternity. You are joined to the body of Christ as a member of the family of God. You are given Jesus himself to live within you, and you will live a life entirely different than you lived before. That is what happens when you confess with your mouth that Jesus is Lord and believe in your heart that God raised him from the dead.

> *Father, I am grateful for these clear words from Paul. Today I reaffirm by confession that Jesus is Lord.*

Is our verbal confession congruent with our acceptance of Jesus as Lord? Do we need to review the radical implications of our inheritance as Christ's disciples? Is Jesus in reality Lord of our body, soul, and spirit?

KINDNESS AND STERNNESS

A daily devotion for November 6

Read Romans 11:1–24.

> "Consider therefore the kindness and sternness of God: sternness to those who fell, but kindness to you, provided that you continue in his kindness. Otherwise, you also will be cut off" (Rom. 11:22).

Paul speaks of the kindness and the sternness of God. If you come to God needy and repentant and acknowledge that you need help, you will always find him to be loving, gracious, open-armed, ready to help you, ready to forgive you, ready to give you all that you need. But if you come to God complaining, excusing yourself, justifying what you've been doing, and trying to make yourself look good in his sight, you will always find that God is as hard as iron, as merciless as fire, and as stern as a judge. God will always turn that face toward those who come in self-pride and in justification through their own strength.

This is the secret of the mystery of Israel and its blindness today. As long as the Jews come to God in that manner, they will always find a hard, iron-willed, stern God. But as Zechariah the prophet describes, when Jesus appears and they look at him whom they pierced and they ask, "Where did you get these wounds in your hands?" he will say, "These are those which I received in the house of my friends" (Zech. 13:6). Then in repentance they will mourn for him as one mourns for an only child, and the mourning of Israel that day will be like the mourning for King Joash in the battle of Jezreal. The whole nation will mourn. Then God will take that nation, and it will replenish the earth. This is what Paul looks forward to.

This is a reminder to our hearts of the faithfulness of God. His promises will not fail. God's purposes will never be shortchanged. He will accomplish all that he says he will do. Though it may be a long way off, and though it may lead through many trials, temptations, hurts, and heartaches, what God has said he will do, he will carry through. On that basis we can enter each day with a deep awareness of the faithfulness of our God.

> *Thank you, Father, for your faithfulness. Thank you for being the God of glory and the God of mercy. I stand amazed at both your kindness and your sternness. Lord, teach me that you are not someone I can manipulate. Help me to bow before you in humble adoration at the grace that reaches out to me when I am ready to admit my need and to come before you trembling and contrite.*

Kindness and sternness are integral qualities of God's character, each necessary to the full expression of his love. What are the appropriate responses to his kindness and to his needed sternness?

THE MYSTERY OF THE JEWISH PEOPLE

A daily devotion for November 7

Read Romans 11:25–32.

> "I do not want you to be ignorant of this mystery, brothers and sisters, so that you may not be conceited: Israel has experienced a hardening in part until the full number of the Gentiles has come in, and in this way all Israel will be saved" (Rom. 11:25–26).

The most striking thing about this passage may be that Paul calls the Jews' resistance to the gospel a mystery. He doesn't mean that it is difficult to understand. Paul means that this is a supernatural phenomenon that has to be revealed to us. We can't explain it with the normal reasons for resistance to the gospel.

If you have had occasion to witness to a Jewish person, perhaps you have run up against what seemed to be a rock wall of indifference and resistance to what you were saying. If so, you may well have been experiencing what Paul is talking about here, a strange hardening toward the gospel by the Jewish people. This is not because the Jews are inferior in intelligence—they are among the most intelligent of people. It is not because they don't want God; they are among the most religious of all people. Ordinarily you would think they would be open to hearing the good news of how God, in grace, is ready to reach men, to change them, to dwell in them, and to enrich their lives. And yet those who go among the Jews often find this strange resistance, this anger awakened by the preaching of the gospel.

Paul says three things about this hardness. First, it is a hardening "in part." That is, not all Jews are afflicted this way. We are not told here what portion of Israel will be hardened—whether 10 percent or 90 percent. All we are told is that there will be some Jews who simply will not receive the gospel. I have been to Israel five times, and I am always amazed at how resistant the Jews there seem to be to the claims of the Lord Jesus. But Paul tells us that this hardening is limited in time. It will not go on forever. A hardening of the heart has happened "until the full number of the Gentiles come in." So this is not something that the Jews are bound to experience forever.

What does "the full number of the Gentiles" mean? When Paul uses this phrase, he is talking about a Gentile church that will become so rich and full in its spiritual riches that it will awaken the envy of Israel. God turns to the Gentiles so that he may arouse the Jews to envy. Anyone who reads church history knows that there hasn't been a great deal in Gentile churches that would awaken the Jews to envy! Often the Jews have been oppressed and persecuted—all in the name of Jesus Christ—by those who profess to be Christians. But this is still a hopeful thing for us. It means that a day is coming when the Gentile churches will be enriched with such spiritual blessing that the Jewish people will say, "We want that!" And they will be open as never before to the gospel of the grace of God.

Though we may be treated as enemies, we must remember that the Jewish people are loved by an unchanging God. He loves every Jewish person without exception. No matter how stubborn or resistant they may be, he has set his love upon them. The nations of the world had better not forget that God still has chosen the Jews.

> *Lord, I thank you for the love you have bestowed on all nations across the centuries. This is a great reminder that no matter the difference in beliefs, both Jews and Gentiles can fully understand and be open to the gospel of God's grace.*

Has God repudiated his investment in Israel? Can we recognize God's kindness and his severity in Israel's ongoing saga? Can we also see how our redemption is entwined with that of the Jews?

OUR GREAT AND GLORIOUS GOD

A daily devotion for November 8

Read Romans 11:33–36.

> "Oh, the depth of the riches of the wisdom and knowledge of God! How unsearchable his judgments, and his paths beyond tracing out! 'Who has known the mind of the Lord? Or who has been his counselor? Who has ever given to God, that God should repay them?' For from him and through him and for him are all things. To him be the glory forever! Amen" (Rom. 11:33–36).

This reminder of the strange ways God works awakens within Paul a tremendous outburst over God's inscrutable wisdom and his ways with men. The apostle is amazed at what he calls the deep riches of God's wisdom and of his ways. They are beyond human exploration. There is no way we can finally fathom God.

Some struggle to put God in a box where they can get hold of him and analyze him. But if they succeed in that, they have reduced God to the size of a man. God is greater than man. He is beyond us. Our minds cannot grasp the greatness of God! We can understand what he tells us about himself, but there is much more that we cannot know. There are depths of riches. That is why we are always being surprised by God if we trust him. He is always enriching us in ways that we don't anticipate.

Then Paul speaks of God's "unsearchable judgments." For instance, it is clear from Scripture that nothing God ever planned interferes with human responsibility. We are free to make choices. We know it. We feel ourselves free to decide to do this or that, to do good or bad. And yet the amazing thing is that nothing humans ever do can frustrate God's sovereign plan. No matter what we do, whether we choose this or that with the freedom of choice we have, ultimately everything works to accomplish what God has determined shall be done. That is the kind of God we have.

Paul is not only impressed with God's inscrutable wisdom and ways, but he contrasts these with the impotence of man. He asks three searching questions. His first one is, "Who has known the mind of the Lord?" What he is asking is, "Who has ever anticipated what God is going to do?" Have you ever been able to figure out how God will handle the situations you get into? We all try, but things never turn out quite the way we think they will. There is a little twist that we never could have guessed.

Paul's second question is, "Or who has been his counselor?" Who has ever suggested something that God has never thought of? Have you ever tried that? I have sometimes looked at a situation, have seen a way to work it out, and have suggested to God how he could do it, thinking I was being helpful. But it turned out that he knew things I didn't know and was working at things that I never saw and couldn't have seen. God's solution was right, and mine would have been wrong.

Paul's last question is, "Who has ever given to God, that God should repay him?" That is, "Who has ever given God something that he didn't already have?" Paul says, "Everything we are and have comes from him. He gives to us; we don't give to him." He concludes with this great outburst: "For from him and through him and to him are all things. To him be the glory forever! Amen." God is the originator of all things; all things come from him. He is the sustainer of all things; they all depend on him. As C. S. Lewis puts it, "To argue with God is to argue with the very power that makes it possible to argue at all!" He is the end purpose. All things will find their culmination in God. He is why all things exist. Therefore, "to him be the glory forever! Amen."

Thank you, Father, for this look at something of the wonder of your being. How far beyond my stumbling words your greatness is! How mighty and vast you are, Lord, how powerful among the nations of earth.

What significant changes in attitude and action would result if this grand and glorious doxology were the basic, day-by-day guide in our lives? Worship? Humility? Trust? Joyful surrender to God's will?

OFFER YOUR BODY

A daily devotion for November 9

Read Romans 12:1–3.

"Therefore, I urge you, brothers and sisters, in view of God's mercy, to offer your bodies as a living sacrifice, holy and pleasing to God—this is your true and proper worship" (Rom. 12:1).

That is what we sing in that great hymn "When I Survey the Wondrous Cross." Its final line is, "Love so amazing, so divine, demands my soul, my life, my all."

That is what Paul urges us to do here. He says God wants us to make our bodies available to him. When Paul says "offer your bodies," he uses what the Greeks call the aorist tense. That means this is something we do once and for all; it is not something we do over and over again. We do it once, and then we spend the rest of our lives on that basis. So there comes a time when God wants us to bring our bodies to him.

It amazes me that God would ever want our bodies. Why does he want my body? I can hardly stand it myself at times! But God says, "Bring your body." Paul has been talking about the body all the way through this section of Romans. He tells us the body is the seat of what he calls "the flesh," that antagonistic inclination within us that does not like what God likes and does not want to do what God wants. We all have it, and somehow it is located in or connected with the body. Our bodies are a source of temptation. It grows weak and wobbly. That God would want this is amazing! And yet he does.

Some of us, I know, feel like saying, "Lord, surely you don't want this body! Let me tell you something about it. It smells and snores. It has a bad heart, Lord. It has a dirty mind. You don't want this body. I have trouble with this body. It is always tripping me up. My spirit is great, and I worship you with my soul—but the body, Lord, that's what gets me down!" But the Lord says, "Bring your body. I know all about it. I know more about it than you do. I know all the things you tell me about it plus some things you haven't learned yet. By means of the blood of Jesus and by the work of the Holy Spirit, I have made it holy and pleasing to myself."

That is the beautiful appeal of this verse. Paul doesn't say we have to get cleaned up, straighten out our lives in every way, and become perfect before we can offer ourselves to God. He says, "I urge you, brothers and sisters, in view of God's mercy, to offer yourselves as living sacrifices. Bring your bodies [the Greek word means 'your bodies,' not 'yourselves'] as a living sacrifice unto God." We must bring them just the way they are, with all the difficulties and the temptations they present! That encourages me greatly. All the other religions in the world tell us that somehow we have to straighten out our lives first and then offer them to God. He never talks that way. He says, "You come to me just the way you are. I am the answer to your problems; therefore, you must start with me. You can't handle those problems yourself. Don't think you have to get them straightened out. Come to me because I have the answers for your problems."

Thank you, Father, for inviting me to come to you just as I am with my whole self, including my body.

How essential to the whole and integrated person is the surrender of our bodies? How does the sacrifice of our bodies affect our spiritual worship? How does it fulfill God's perfect will?

WHO AM I, LORD?

A daily devotion for November 10

Read Romans 12:3–8.

> "For by the grace given to me I say to every one of you: Do not think of yourself more highly than you ought, but rather think of yourself with sober judgment, in accordance with the faith God has distributed to each of you" (Rom. 12:3).

Paul tells us to think about ourselves. Many people get the idea that the Christian life consists of never thinking about themselves. Because we know that we are to reach out to others, we think that there is no place for thinking about ourselves. That is wrong. It is true that some Christians have abused this advice to such a degree that all they think about is themselves. I know Christians who are forever taking their spiritual temperature, feeling their spiritual pulse, and worrying about their spiritual condition. It is wrong to think continually of nothing but ourselves, but it is quite right to take time occasionally to evaluate ourselves and where we are in our Christian life. In fact, Paul exhorts us with his apostolic authority to do so. "By the grace given to me," the gift of apostleship, based on that office, he exhorts every one of us to take time to think through who we are.

Paul stresses that we have to do this in a way that avoids overrating ourselves. "Do not think of yourself more highly than you ought." He mentions this first because this is such a natural tendency with us. But feelings can change a thousand times a minute. They are dependent upon many factors over which we have no control. The most foolish thing in the world is to judge ourselves on the basis of how we feel at any given moment. Feelings aren't wrong, but we shouldn't use them as the basis for evaluating ourselves. Instead we should look at how God sees us. That is reality—what God says we are. This is a twofold evaluation, as the apostle makes clear in this verse.

First, he says, "Do not think of yourself more highly than you ought, but think of yourself with sober judgment." What does it mean to think soberly about ourselves? Surely that refers to the teaching of the Scriptures that we are all fallen creatures. We all have within us the flesh, which is not to be trusted at all. As long as we are in the flesh, in the body, we will have fleshly struggles. There will be something in us that we can't quite trust. There will be temptations, wrong thoughts, and distorted attitudes in our lives. And they will always be there.

But then, second, Paul tells us to think with "the measure of faith that God has distributed to each of you." We must reflect on all God has told us about what has happened since we have come to Christ. The degree to which we trust what God has said about us will give us confidence, courage, and ability—through Christ's life within us—to function every day. What has God said about us? Let's look back at all the tremendous truth given in the first eight chapters of Romans. We are no longer in Adam, in our nature or spirit, but are now united with Christ. He lives within us; his power is available to us. The Holy Spirit has come to enable us to say no to all the evil forces and temptations that we face so that sin shall not have dominion over us, for we are not under the law but under grace. That is the way to think about ourselves. We must always be on guard because of the evil of the flesh within us, but we can always win because of the grace of God, the righteousness of Jesus Christ, and the gift of the Holy Spirit that we have.

Father, help me to discover who I am before you and then to accept that so that I may bless your heart and fulfill my life.

Who or what is defining our personal identity? Pop psychology? The news media? Our relationships? Are we experiencing the transforming freedom of God's rightful ownership?

SINCERE LOVE

A daily devotion for November 11

Read Romans 12:9–13.

> "Love must be sincere. Hate what is evil; cling to what is good. Be devoted to one another in love. Honor one another above yourselves. Never be lacking in zeal, but keep your spiritual fervor, serving the Lord. Be joyful in hope, patient in affliction, faithful in prayer. Share with the Lord's people who are in need. Practice hospitality" (Rom. 12:9–13).

This passage describes love among Christians. It consists of six things. First, Paul says, "Hate what is evil; cling to what is good." Hate what is evil in people, but don't reject the person because of the evil. God loves that person. He or she is made in the image of God. True love learns to hate evil but not to reject the good. Hypocritical love, love that pretends to be Christian, does the opposite.

Second, love remembers that relationship, not friendship, is the basis for concern. That is why Paul says, "Be devoted to one another in brotherly love." He doesn't refer to anyone who is in need but to our brothers and sisters. The basis of concern for one another is not that we know each other well or enjoy one another. It is that we are related to one another. If we are Christians, we know that we already have a tie that ought to evoke care for one another. We are brothers and sisters, and so we treat each other warmly and with acceptance.

Third, Paul says that true love regards others as more deserving than ourselves. "Honor one another above yourselves." I like the J. B. Philips translation here. He says, "Be willing to let other men have the credit." If we don't care who gets the credit, then we can enjoy ourselves and do all kinds of good deeds. We can be glad that the work is done and stop worrying about who gets the credit. Our flesh doesn't like that. It is eager to be recognized, but the Word tells us that real love will not act that way.

Fourth, real love retains enthusiasm despite setbacks. "Never be lacking in zeal, but keep your spiritual fervor, serving the Lord." One of the most noticeable marks of a Christian walking in the Spirit is that he retains enthusiasm, always rejoicing in hope. He never lets his spiritual zeal fades but maintains it. The Lord cannot put up with lukewarmness (Rev. 3:16). It is nauseating to him. He will spew us out of his mouth if we are indifferent, neither hot nor cold.

Fifth, true love rejoices in hope. "Be joyful in hope, patient in affliction, faithful in prayer." We can rejoice in hope because we are patient in affliction, and we are patient in affliction because we have been faithful in prayer. So when trials come, we must begin with prayer. If we are faithful in prayer, we will hang in there, not getting impatient, angry, or resentful but quietly waiting for God to accomplish what he had in mind in these trials. We will rejoice in hope because we know that God has a thousand and one ways of working things out.

Then, six, true love responds to needs. "Share with God's people who are in need. Practice hospitality." These days when we have so much social help available—unemployment insurance, Social Security, welfare, Medicare—we tend to forget that there are still human needs and that we have a responsibility to meet them. We need to be reminded that people are still hurting and that it is a direct responsibility of Christians to care for one another's needs.

Lord, thank you for how you have loved me. Teach me to love my brothers and sisters in Christ in the same way.

Our love for one another is defined by godliness and sincerity as opposed to pretense and hypocrisy. In expressing authentic love, to whom shall we look for an example, for motivation, and for enabling grace?

WHOM TO BLESS

A daily devotion for November 12

Read Romans 12:14–21.

"Bless those who persecute you; bless and do not curse" (Rom. 12:14).

Paul describes the kind of love we should show to a non-Christian world. He gives practical help on this. Love speaks well of its persecutors. That is getting right down to where the rubber meets the road, isn't it? That means we don't bad-mouth people who are not nice to us. We don't run them down or speak harshly about them to others, but we speak well of them. We find something that we can approve, and we say so to others. I confess that is not my natural reaction. When somebody persecutes me, I persecute back! At least I want to. But this is what the Word tells us we should not do. This applies to such practical areas as traffic problems. Have you ever been persecuted in traffic? It happens all the time. Somebody cuts you off, and you want to roll down the window and shout at this person. But according to the Word, you are not supposed to do this. Now, it doesn't tell you what to call the other driver, but it does tell you to bless that person.

In verse 17 Paul says, "Do not repay anyone evil for evil. Be careful to do what is right in the sight of everybody." In verse 19 he adds, "Do not take revenge, my friends, but leave room for God's wrath, for it is written, 'It is mine to avenge, I will repay,' says the Lord." Revenge is one of the most natural of human responses to hurt, injury, or bad attitudes. We always feel that if we treat others according to the way they have treated us, we are only giving them justice. We can justify this so easily. "I'm only teaching them a lesson. I'm only showing them how I feel. I'm only giving back what they've given me." But any time we argue that way we have forgotten the many times we have injured others without getting caught. But God hasn't forgotten.

This always puts us in the place of those Pharisees who, when the woman maybe caught in adultery, were ready to cast stones and put her to death. Jesus said to them, "He that is without sin among you, let him cast the first stone" (John 8:7). That stopped them all dead in their tracks, because there wasn't one of them who wasn't equally as guilty as she. They needed to be judged too. We must never carry out revenge, because we are not in the position of a judge. We, too, are guilty. We need to be judged. Therefore, Paul's admonition is, "Don't try to avenge yourself." We will only make a mess of it. The inevitable result of trying to get even with people is that we escalate the conflict.

When I was in school in Montana, I used to watch the cows in a corral. They would be standing there peacefully, and then one cow would kick another cow. Of course, that cow had to kick back. Then the first cow kicked harder, missed the second cow, and hit a third. That cow kicked back. I watched that happen many times. A single cow, starting to kick another, soon had all the cows kicking and milling and mooing at one another, mad as could be. This happens in churches, too.

Paul gives two reasons we should not avenge ourselves. One is because God is already doing it. "Leave room for God's wrath." God knows we have been insulted or injured, and he is already doing something about it. Second, God alone claims the right to vengeance because he alone can work it without injury to all concerned. He will do it in a way that will be redemptive. He won't injure the other person but will bring him out of it. We don't give God a chance when we take matters into our own hands. Paul says that is wrong. It is wrong because we don't want that person to be redeemed; we want him to be hurt. We get angry because God hasn't taken vengeance in the way that we would like. Paul reminds us that God is already avenging, so we should leave him room.

Lord, teach me the hard lesson of blessing and loving those who have done me wrong. Thank you for loving me first in that same way.

Do we resist blessing those who mistreat us? Are we willing to leave matters in God's hands so he may apply vengeance according to his wisdom? Will we thus leave room for his redemptive action?

GOD AND GOVERNMENT

A daily devotion for November 13

Read Romans 13:1–5.

> "Everyone must submit himself to the governing authorities, for there is no authority except that which God has established. The authorities that exist have been established by God" (Rom. 13:1).

When Paul refers to governing authorities, he uses a phrase that can best be translated as "the powers that be." He is not just talking about heads of state; he is talking about all levels of authority, all the way down to the local police. He tells us that the thing we must remember about these governmental offices is that they are, in some way, brought into being by God himself.

I often hear people ask, "Which form of government is the best? Which is the one God wants us to have?" We Americans would love to think that democracy is the most God-honored form of government. But I don't think we can establish that from the Scriptures. In fact, the Scriptures reflect various forms of government. People ask, "Which government is the best kind? Is it a monarchy? An oligarchy? Is it a republic? A democracy?" The answer of Scripture is not necessarily any of these. It is whatever God has brought into being. This will be what is best for that place and time in history. God has brought it into being, considering the makeup of the people, the degree of truth and light disseminated among them, and the prevailing moral conditions. For that condition, for that time and place, God has brought into being a particular government.

That government can change. God doesn't ordain one form of government to be continued forever. If the people grow toward the understanding of truth, and morality prevails in a community, the form of government may well take on a democratic pattern. Where truth disappears, government seems to become more autocratic. But the apostle says that whatever form of government we find, God is behind it. We shouldn't think of any state or of any government as something that in itself is opposed to God, because it isn't.

This truth is not confined to the New Testament. In the book of Daniel, the prophet stood before one of the greatest monarchs the world has ever seen, one of the most autocratic of kings, and told him, "God changes times and seasons, God removes kings, and he sets up kings" (Dan. 2:21 RSV). Daniel made clear that God has a hand in whatever is happening on the earth at a particular time. Sometimes we are tempted or even taught to think of God as being remote from our political affairs, as being off in heaven and turning a morbid eye on us human beings struggling with our political problems down here. But God is not on some remote Mount Olympus; he is right among us, involved in the pattern of governments; he raises up kings, puts down others, and changes forms of government.

When Paul wrote this letter to these Christians, they were living in Rome, the capital city of the empire. Rome had already passed through several forms of government. It had been a monarchy, a republic, a principate, and now it was an empire. Nero had just begun his reign as the fifth emperor of Rome when Paul wrote this letter. Paul is telling these Christians that whatever form of government may be in control, they are to remember that God is behind it.

Father, thank you for these practical words. Help me to be a good citizen, trusting that you raise up and bring down leaders to accomplish your purposes.

A particular form of government cannot be counted on to uphold righteousness. To whom are we ultimately responsible? What is our responsibility toward government that God permits?

TAX DAY

A daily devotion for November 14

Read Romans 13:6–7.

> "Give to everyone what you owe them: If you owe taxes, pay taxes; if revenue, then revenue; if respect, then respect; if honor, then honor" (Rom. 13:7).

Here the apostle is dealing with our response to the demands of government. We haven't the right to withhold taxes if the government doesn't use them quite the way we think it should. Governments are made up of fallible men and women just like us, and we can't demand that the government always handle everything perfectly. Therefore Paul tells these Romans, who had the same problems we have with taxes, "If you owe taxes, pay them."

The apostle is clearly making the point that we shouldn't resent these powers of government. This is all set within the context of his earlier advice: "Be not conformed to this present age" (Rom. 12:2). We shouldn't act like everybody else does about taxes. The world grumbles and groans over paying taxes. We have a right, of course, to protest injustice and to correct abuse. There is no question about that. But we shouldn't be forever griping about the taxes we have to pay.

I don't offer any defense for the gross injustices that prevail in our American system. But we can meet for worship without hiding behind closed doors and we have relative freedom from attack on the streets because of a government that God has brought into being. I want to make every effort I can, as a good citizen, to improve this government and to see that it does things better. But we can thank God for the privilege of paying our taxes. This is what the apostle is after. He wants us to have a different attitude than the world around us about these matters. We are not to come on with gimlet-eyed fanaticism, attacking the government and seeking to overthrow it because it doesn't behave quite as we think it ought. Rather, we are to understand that God has brought it into being and that he will change it if the hearts of the people of the land warrant that.

Somebody has well said, "Every nation gets the government it deserves." And so as we pay our taxes, let us do so cheerfully. We should remember that the apostle says not only that we are to pay our taxes but that if we owe respect, we are to give that; if honor, to give that. We must never forget that the worst of governments are better than anarchy and serve functions that God himself has ordained.

Therefore let us respond as Christians with cheerfulness and gladness for what we can do under God, and let us do so with such an attitude that people will see that there is something different about us. Thus we commend ourselves to God and to the people around.

> *Father, help me to be faithful to my responsibility to show honor to those to whom honor is due and respect to those who deserve it.*

The taxation burden tests our willingness to respond out of obedience to the Word. Do we seek to respond to this pressure as dutiful and thankful servants of Christ?

A DEBT OF LOVE

A daily devotion for November 15

Read Romans 13:8–10.

> "Let no debt remain outstanding, except the continuing debt to love one another, for whoever loves others has fulfilled the law" (Rom. 13:8).

Have you ever struggled to obey the Ten Commandments? Have you found it difficult to face up to obeying these demands that you shall not murder or lie or steal or commit adultery? Well, Paul says it is simple. All you have to do is love. Act in love toward people and you won't hurt them. The solution to all the problems you struggle with is this one thing. Have you ever thought of what would happen in this world if people could be taught how to love—and then did it?

The first result that occurs to me is that all the impending divorces would be happily resolved. Couples ready to split up because love has left their marriages could get back together and learn how to work out their problems. Furthermore, if we could teach people how to love we wouldn't fight wars. Think of how much energy and money are being expended to produce an endless array of armaments simply because we can't trust people to love each other. If we could love each other, there would be no more crime. The streets of all the great cities of our land would feel safe and secure. If there weren't any crime, we wouldn't need any prisons. All the money we spend on prisons and reformatories could be spent on something more useful. We wouldn't need any courts or police. We need all these things because we are so deprived in this ability to love.

This passage tells us that the ability to love—that and nothing less—is the radical force that Jesus Christ has turned loose in this world by his resurrection. It has the power to radically change the world. Paul implies that this must start with us. If we are Christians, if we know Jesus Christ, we have the power to love. We don't have to ask for it; we've got it. If we have Christ, we can act in love, even though we are tempted not to do so. Therefore, Paul says that when we come up against difficult people, we must remember that our first obligation is to love them.

Paul says plainly that we are to think of this as our obligation to everyone. I wonder what kind of radical things would happen among us if we began living on this basis. Every day, with every person we meet, we would say to ourselves, *I need to show some love to this person. No matter what else happens, I have an obligation to pay him that debt.* I have owed money to people, and I have noticed that whenever I have met them, that is the first thing that has come into my mind. I have remembered the debt that I owed them and wondered if that was what they were thinking about too. This is what Paul says we are to do about love. We are to remember that we have an obligation to love every person.

This applies to our neighbor. Who is our neighbor? We think immediately of the people who live on each side of us, but this includes everyone. The people we meet in business and while shopping are our neighbors. Wherever we are, the people we make contact with are living right beside us and are our neighbors for that moment. Since we have the ability to love, we are to love our neighbors as ourselves. The butcher, the baker, the Cadillac maker—it makes no difference. They are all our neighbors.

> *Jesus, come in and be my Lord. Rule in my life and give to me this amazing ability to love.*

Do we see our calling to love our neighbor as the expression of Jesus Christ's radical love? Where can we this day begin to pay off our debt of love, trusting him to love through us?

PUT ON THE LORD JESUS CHRIST

A daily devotion for November 16

Read Romans 13:11–14.

> "Rather, clothe yourselves with the Lord Jesus Christ, and do not think about how to gratify the desires of the flesh" (Rom. 13:14).

When I got up this morning I put on my clothes. I did this with the intention that they would be part of me all day, that they would go where I go and do what I do. They will cover me and make me presentable to others. That is the purpose of clothes. In the same way, the apostle is saying to us, "Put on Jesus Christ when you get up in the morning. Make him a part of your life that day. Intend that he go with you everywhere you go and that he act through you in everything you do. Call upon his resources. Live your life in Christ."

These words have forever been made famous by their connection with the conversion of Saint Augustine. He was a young man in the fourth century who lived a wild, carousing life, running around with evil companions, doing everything they were doing. He forbade himself nothing, went into anything and everything. And, as people still do today, he came to hate himself for that. One day Augustine was with a friend in a garden, and he walked up and down, bemoaning his inability to change. "O, tomorrow, tomorrow, tomorrow! How can I free myself from these terrible urges within me that drive me to the things that hurt me?" In his despair, he suddenly heard what he thought was the voice of a child—perhaps some children were playing in the garden next door—and the voice said, "Take and read; take and read."

Augustine could not remember any children's games with words like that, but the words stuck. He went back to the table and found lying on it a copy of Paul's letter to the Romans. He flipped it open, and these were the words he read: "Let us behave decently, as in the daytime, not in orgies, and drunkenness, not in sexual immorality and debauchery, not in dissension and jealousy. Rather, clothe yourselves with the Lord Jesus Christ" (Rom. 13:13–14).

Augustine said that at that moment he opened his life to Christ. He had known about him but had never surrendered to him. But at that moment he did, and he felt Christ's healing touch cleansing his life. He was never the same man again. He went on to become one of the greatest Christians of all time.

That is what Jesus Christ is capable of doing. He gives us all the power to love. If we but choose to exercise this power at the moment it is needed, we can release in the world this radical force that has the power to change everything around us. It will change our homes, our lives, our communities, our nations, the world—because a risen Lord is available to us to live through us. I love J. B. Philips's translation of this last verse: "Let us be Christ's men from head to foot, and give no chance to the flesh to have its fling" (Rom. 13:14 J. B. Philips). That is the way to live.

> *Thank you, Father, for the freedom and the power you have given me to clothe myself with Christ and to stop gratifying the desires of my flesh.*

Have we grasped the inestimable privilege of being clothed with the life and the love of the Lord Jesus Christ? Is this becoming a habit of heart and of mind?

DEBATABLE ISSUES

A daily devotion for November 17

Read Romans 14:1–4.

> "One person's faith allows them to eat everything, but another, whose faith is weak, eats only vegetables" (Rom. 14:2).

This issue arises out of the background of the early church when there was a moral question about eating meat. Not only did the Jews place restrictions on certain forms of meat—they did not eat pork, and even beef and lamb had to be kosher—but animals had to be slain in a certain way. So a Jew, or even one raised as a Jew, after becoming a Christian, always had great emotional difficulty in eating meat. In Rome and in other pagan cities there was also the debate over eating meat that had been offered to idols. Some Christians said that doing that was tantamount to worshiping the idols. Other Christians said, "Oh, no. How can that be? Meat is meat. The fact that someone else thinks of it as offered to idols does not mean that I have to." So there was a problem in the church.

As with every issue of this type, there were two viewpoints. There was a liberal, broad viewpoint that said it was perfectly all right to do this, and a stricter, narrower viewpoint that said it was wrong. The debate over many of our modern problems is divided in this way. Should we drink wine and beer? Should we go to the movies? Should we dance? What about work on Sunday? Let us be clear that Scripture leaves no room for debate about these areas. It is always wrong to be drunk. It is always wrong to commit adultery or immorality. These things are clearly sinful. In both the Old and New Testaments, God has spoken and has judged in these areas. Christians are exhorted to rebuke, to exhort, to reprove, and, if necessary, even to discipline one another according to patterns set out in the Scriptures. This is not judging each other in those areas.

But many other areas are left open, and the amazing thing to me is that Scripture does this. Paul will not give yes-or-no answers about some of these things, because God does not do so. In some areas, in other words, God wants to let individuals decide what to do. He expects their decisions to be based upon their deep convictions, but these choices are up to them.

Paul calls the liberal party strong in the faith and the narrow party weak in the faith. Therefore, the mark of understanding truth is freedom. That is why Paul says those who understand truth clearly are strong in the faith, while those who do not understand it clearly are weak in the faith. They are weak in the faith because they have not yet discovered the meaning of Christian freedom; they see Christianity as a set of rules. Also, they have not yet liberated themselves from a belief in the efficacy of works. In their hearts they believe that they can gain God's favor by doing certain things and abstaining from others. Basically, they are still trying to earn a right relationship with God and have not yet accepted the way of grace.

That is the problem of a Christian who does not yet fully understand the freedom that Christ has brought him, who struggles with things like certain meats, and who feels limited in his ability to indulge in or to use some of them—while others feel free to do so. One is strong in the faith; the other is called weak in the faith. Every church has these groups. Paul puts his finger precisely on the natural attitudes that each group would have toward each other. These attitudes must be avoided if we are to accept one another as he urges.

Father, teach me to accept and to love my brothers and sisters in Christ and to refrain from judging in debatable matters.

Are we honoring our fellow believers when their opinions differ from ours? How does God use our choices to teach and to train us?

READING HEARTS

A daily devotion for November 18

Read Romans 14:5–12.

> "One person considers one day more sacred than another; another considers every day alike. Each of them should be fully convinced in their own mind. Whoever regards one day as special does so to the Lord. Whoever eats meat does so to the Lord, for they give thanks to God; and whoever abstains does so to the Lord and gives thanks to God. For none of us lives for ourselves alone, and none of us dies for ourselves alone. If we live, we live for the Lord; and if we die, we die for the Lord. So, whether we live or die, we belong to the Lord" (Rom. 14:5–8).

Paul is saying that God can read hearts and we cannot. These differences of viewpoint arise out of honest convictions that God sees, even though we cannot. Therefore, an individual is not simply being difficult when he does not agree with us. He is acting based on what he feels is right, so we should trust him on that. We must believe that he is as intent on being real before God and as true to him as we are, and if he feels able to indulge in things we think are not right, we should at least see him as doing so because he feels that God is not displeased with him on that basis. Or, if he does feel limited and thinks he should not do certain things, we should not get upset with him because he has not yet entered freedom. We must remember that he feels that God would be displeased if he did those things. The apostle makes clear that every person should have that kind of a conviction. "Let every man be fully persuaded in his own heart" (Rom. 14:4 KJV).

Paul says that God sees both of these people and both of these viewpoints as honoring him. The one who thinks Sunday is a special day that ought to be kept different from all other days is doing so as unto the Lord. Therefore we should respect that viewpoint. Another says, "When we are in Christ, days mean nothing. They are not set aside for any special purpose. Therefore, I feel every day is alike, and I want to honor the Lord on every day." We should not feel upset at that. He is doing so out of a deep conviction of his heart.

The one who drinks wine gives thanks to God for the taste of it, and it is perfectly proper that he does so. The one who says, "No. I cannot drink wine, but I can drink coffee," gives thanks for the coffee. The coffee may do as much physical harm as the wine, but neither activity presents a moral question. The question is what the heart is doing in the eyes of God.

I heard some time ago of a girl who was a converted nightclub singer, a fresh, new Christian, who was asked to sing at a church meeting. She wanted to do her best for the Lord, whom she had come to love, and so she dressed up the best way she knew how and sang a song that she thought was expressive of her faith. She did it in the style of a nightclub singer. Somebody came up to her afterward and ripped into her, saying, "How can you sing a song like that and claim to be a Christian? God could never be happy with a Christian who dresses the way you do, and to sing in a nightclub style must be offensive to him." The poor girl was so taken aback that she stood frozen for a minute and then broke into tears, turned, and ran. That was a wrong and hurtful thing to do to her. Granted, later on she might have changed her style, but God only had the right to change her. Her heart was right, and God saw the heart and honored it. He was pleased with her.

Father, help me to see where I have been usurping your place. Help me to stop that and to begin to answer only for myself before your throne, upholding and praying for my brothers and sisters if I feel they need it. Grant to me, Lord, that illuminating understanding of truth that sets me free.

Are we qualified to change others' hearts? Shall we consider it off limits for us to judge their motivations or conclusions? What is our recourse when we see what we deem erroneous choices?

WHAT MATTERS

A daily devotion for November 19

Read Romans 14:13–18.

> "Therefore, do not allow what you consider as good to be spoken of as evil. For the kingdom of God is not a matter of eating and drinking, but of righteousness, peace and joy in the Holy Spirit, because anyone who serves Christ in this way is pleasing to God and receives human approval" (Rom. 14:16–18).

If you create division by arguing so hard for your rights or for your freedom, you are distorting the gospel. The word Paul uses for *evil* means "blaspheme." You are causing the good news about Christ to be blasphemed because you are making too much of an issue over a minor matter. You are insisting that your rights are so important that you have to divide the church over them. That says to a watching world that Christianity consists of doing or not doing a certain thing.

I heard of a church that got into an argument over whether there ought to be a Christmas tree at its Christmas program. Some thought that a tree was fine; others thought it was a pagan practice, and they got so angry at each other that fistfights broke out over the issue. One group dragged the tree out, and then the other group dragged it back in. They ended up suing each other in a court of law, and the dispute was spread in the newspapers for the entire community to read. What else could non-Christians conclude other than that the gospel consists of deciding whether to have a Christmas tree?

That is wrong. The main point of the Christian faith is not eating or drinking or Christmas trees. The main point is righteousness, peace, and joy in the Holy Spirit. A non-Christian, looking at a Christian, ought to see these gifts, not disputing and fighting and law courts. The word *righteousness* means that because of Christ's death for us, we are loved and accepted by him. The world ought to see us confident about who we are, with an underlying assurance that shows we have a basis for self-acceptance that the world knows nothing about.

Another thing the world ought to see is peace. That is evident in a calmness, in a serenity undisturbed by the minor irritations of the moment. This is the quiet assurance that God is present in a situation, that he will work it out for his glory, and that we need not get upset or angry. It is hard for the world to get the impression of peace and calm if two people are screaming at one another. That does not look like peace.

The third element is joy, a delight in life that always finds it worthwhile, even though it may be filled with problems. Joy does not come from circumstances. I met a woman who had been lying in bed for thirteen years. She had such severe arthritis that her joints were disconnected and she could not raise her hands. But the smile on her face was an outstanding witness to the fact that joy of this kind is a gift from God. It comes out of relationship, not out of circumstance.

Paul is saying that if we have discovered this, we can easily give up some momentary indulgence that we enjoy if it is going to cause others to act contrary to their consciences. Sometimes when we enter a main highway, we see a sign that says, "Yield." I wish we could make one of those and put it up in our dining rooms. That is a Christian philosophy—to yield, to give way. We should not insist on our rights under these circumstances.

I am thankful, Father, that there is a way of working out problems, peacefully and joyfully, "preserving the unity of the Spirit in the bond of peace."

What is the threefold evidence of one who is intentionally walking in the Spirit? How does the alternative violate the gospel and invalidate our witness to the world?

CONVICTION BASED ON GOD'S WORD

A daily devotion for November 20

Read Romans 14:19–23.

> "So whatever you believe about these things keep between yourself and God. Blessed is the one who does not condemn himself by what he approves" (Rom. 14:22).

Paul does not mean that you are to keep quiet about your liberties and to leave the issue between yourself and God. He is saying, "If you have faith, have it between yourself and God." Let God's Word, and nothing else, be the basis for your faith. Be sure that you are not acting out of pride, because you want to show off how free you are. Make sure you are acting because God has freed you by his Word. If you base your action on that, your conscience will be free. You will not feel guilty and troubled over whether you are acting beyond what the Word of God says. You will be happy, free, and blessed. But if you have not settled this question based on Scripture but are acting only because you want to indulge yourself, if you like this thing but are still a bit troubled by it, you will be condemned by your conscience for this action. And if you are condemned by your conscience, you will feel guilty. And if you act though you feel guilty, you are not acting out of faith, and therefore you are sinning. This is Paul's argument.

"Without faith, it is impossible to please God" (Heb. 11:6). Faith means believing what God has said. You must base your actions on what the Word of God declares—not about any specific thing but on the great principle of freedom that it sets forth. If you understand that, fine, Paul says. But be sure that you are acting not out of pride, not out of self-indulgence, but out of a deep conviction that rests upon the Word and the revelation of God.

To sum up, Paul makes three points. First: Do not deliberately shock your brothers or sisters or cause them to stumble. Do not deliberately do things that will offend them or even make them feel uncomfortable. Think about them, not about yourself. Second: Give up your right when it threatens the peace or hinders the growth of another individual. Be alert to judge in that area. Third: Never act from doubt. Act only from conviction by the Word and by the Spirit of God. If problems are all settled on that basis, you will be moving gradually toward the great liberty that we have as children of God.

What will happen in the eyes of the watching world? Christians will be seen to be free people, not controlled by scruples that limit them in their enjoyment of God's great gifts. Yet these things will not be of such importance that they are put at the heart and center of everything. The world will see that the heart of the gospel is righteousness, peace, and joy in the Holy Spirit, the gifts of God. Those gifts, then, are the basis for freedom in all these areas. But you are just as free to say no to the exercise of a gift as you are to say yes. That is true freedom. You are not free if you think you have won your rights. That is not freedom. Freedom is the right to give up your rights for good and proper cause. That is what the watching world will begin to see.

Teach me, Lord, to walk softly before you in this, with a concern for my brother and my sister, to be patient and to learn to enjoy my liberties only as they do not injure another.

What three conclusions summarize God's Word to us concerning our attitudes and our behavior over debatable issues? What is authentic freedom when the issue is our rights?

THE WISE USE OF LIBERTY

A daily devotion for November 21

Read Romans 15:1–6.

> "Now we who are strong ought to bear the weaknesses of those without strength and not just please ourselves. Each of us is to please his neighbor for his good, to his edification" (Rom. 15:1–2).

There are two thumbnail rules to follow when you have to make a quick decision about whether to insist on liberty in a certain area or to give way to someone else's qualms, prejudices, or differing viewpoint.

The first rule is to please your neighbor rather than yourself. Do not insist on your way of doing things; be quick to give in. This is what love does. Love does not insist on its own rights, Paul tells us in 1 Corinthians 13. Therefore, if you are loving in your approach, you will adapt to others.

The second rule, however, is that you should be careful that in yielding you do not allow your neighbor to be confirmed in his weakness, that you do not leave him without encouragement to grow or to rethink his position. We are to seek to build one another up. If we do nothing but give in to people's weaknesses, the church eventually ends up living at the level of the weakest conscience in its midst. This presents a distorted view of Christian liberty, and the world gets false ideas about Christianity. So you must help to balance the situation. Please your neighbor, but for his own good, always leave something to challenge his thinking, to make him reach out a bit and possibly change his viewpoint.

A man came to see me and told me he was a teacher in a Christian school. He had been asked by the board to enforce a rule prohibiting students from wearing their hair long. He did not agree with the rule, so he found himself in a dilemma. The board had told him that if he did not enforce the rule, he would lose his job. If he did enforce it, he would upset the students and their parents, who felt that this was a matter that did not merit such attention. Our culture has long since changed from regarding long hair as a symbol of rebellion, so this man found himself between a rock and a hard place. His plea to me was, "What shall I do?"

My counsel was that we should not push our ideas of liberty to the degree that they would upset the peace. So I told him, "For the sake of peace, go along with the board and enforce the rule for this year. But make a strong plea to the board to rethink its position and to change its viewpoint. At the end of the year if the board is unwilling to do that, you might well consider moving to a different place. That way you would not be upsetting things and creating a division in the school."

That illustrates what Paul is saying. People can lose sight of the main objective of being together as Christians, and they get so focused on these issues that a church can split right down the center. Or these issues will create such bickering and dissension within the group that the atmosphere of the church is changed. Paul tells us that this is not necessary since things can be done to solve these problems.

> *Father, thank you for the freedom that you give. I pray that we who regard ourselves as strong may be willing to bear the burdens of the weak. May your people manifest a spirit of unity to a world that knows no way to get divergent factions together.*

Are we committed to pleasing our neighbors for their good? How will we discern the good that is needed? Do we have increased awareness of our need for discernment from the Word, both written and dwelling in us, God's people?

ACCEPT ONE ANOTHER

A daily devotion for November 22

Read Romans 15:7–13.

> "Therefore, accept one another, just as Christ also accepted us to the glory of God. For I say that Christ has become a servant to the circumcision on behalf of the truth of God to confirm the promises given to the fathers, and for the Gentiles to glorify God for His mercy; as it is written, 'Therefore I will give praise to You among the Gentiles, and I will sing to Your name'" (Rom. 15:7–9).

If you have been involved in a church fight, you know that tempers can get hot. People can get very upset, and factions can form; divisions and feuds break out.

Yet I have never heard of a church fight any worse than the one that Jews and Gentiles had in Paul's day. The Jews held the Gentiles in contempt; they called them dogs. They would have nothing to do with them. The Jews even regarded it as sinful to go into a Gentile's house, and they would never dream of eating with a Gentile. In the book of Acts, Peter got into serious trouble with his Jewish friends because he visited the home of Cornelius and ate with him. Peter was able to justify his conduct to his friends only by showing them that the Holy Spirit had sent him there.

Of course, if the Jews felt that way about the Gentiles, the Gentiles paid them back in kind. They hated the Jews. They called them all kinds of names. This is where modern anti-Semitism was born. These opposing factions hated each other and would have nothing to do with one another.

Yet Paul says God heals that kind of division by the work of Jesus. How does Jesus do it? A more literal translation of the text is that "he became a minister of circumcision." The apostle is arguing that the Lord healed this breach between the Jews and the Gentiles by giving in and limiting his own liberty. He who designed the human body consented to circumcision. Jesus consented to that and limited himself in that way. He became a circumcised Jew. He who declared in his ministry that all foods are clean, and thus gave clear evidence that he understood the liberty that God gives us in the matter of eating, never once ate anything but kosher food. He limited himself to the Jewish diet, even though he declared that all foods were clean.

He who was without sin insisted on a sinner's baptism. He came to John, and John said, "Why are you coming to me? I need to be baptized by you. You do not need to be baptized." Jesus said, "Allow it to be so, for in this way it becomes us. It is fitting for us to fulfill all righteousness" (Matt. 3:15). So he who had no reason to be baptized consented to be baptized. He who longed to heal the hurts of the world said that when he came, he limited himself to the lost sheep of the house of Israel.

Paul says that by limiting himself Jesus broke the back of the argument and of the contempt between the Jew and the Gentile. He reached both Jews and Gentiles to the glory of God. Paul is saying that in the death and the resurrection of Jesus, God showed his faithfulness to the Jews in fulfilling the promises made to the patriarchs and that he showed his mercy to the Gentiles, saving them who were without any promises at all. Thus the two, Jew and Gentile, shall fully become one, just as the Scriptures predict.

Paul is telling us, "You do not need to separate; you do not need to fight; you do not need to sue one another. You can work out your problems, and God is honored and glorified when you do."

Thank you for the miracle of unity in Christ. I ask that it be preserved in the name of the Lord Jesus.

Jesus's example is the answer to the question, "What would Jesus do?" The cross was the price he paid for our acceptance. Are we yielding our rights in order to accept others for Jesus's sake?

FULL OF GOODNESS AND KNOWLEDGE

A daily devotion for November 23

Read Romans 15:14.

"And concerning you, my brethren, I myself also am convinced that you yourselves are full of goodness, filled with all knowledge and able also to admonish one another" (Rom. 15:14).

In this chapter of Romans, Paul gives us a little further insight into the church in Rome. In verse 14, he mentions three great qualities that this church possessed.

First, he says, "I am convinced, my brothers, that you yourselves are full of goodness." That is, their motives were right. They had come to the place where they were motivated by a sense of goodness. Certainly, the church in Rome was a responsive church, a compassionate church. It reached out to people who were in need. It responded to those who had hurts, burdens, and concerns. This is one of the qualities I most appreciate about a congregation. Whenever a need is shared, there is always a compassionate response.

The second thing that the apostle says is that Rome's Christians were complete in knowledge. That is remarkable. Here was a church to which Paul did not need to give any new theology. He acknowledges that this church had it already. Though Romans is one of the most deeply penetrating theological treatises in the New Testament, Paul did not write it because these people did not know these truths.

The apostle emphasizes certain themes in this letter. One is justification by faith, the gift of worth in God's sight. This gift cannot be earned. It is a gift because of the work of Jesus Christ for us. Rome's Christians also understood the nature of the flesh and the need for sanctification. They knew that although they had been redeemed, they were still possessed of fallen bodies. The flesh was still there, giving them trouble. We all struggle with the flesh. Young Philip Melancthon, the colleague of Martin Luther, once wrote to Luther and said, "Old Adam is too strong for young Philip." These people in Rome understood this truth, and they knew that this would be the struggle of their Christian lives. Paul did not have to tell them that; they knew it before he wrote. But they also knew that God is working out a great plan, that he is creating a whole new humanity, and building a new creation. Amid the ruins of the old, he is producing a new man, and they were part of it. Finally, they understood the great themes of glorification and of the eternal ages to come.

The third thing the apostle had to say about this church was that its members were competent to instruct one another. In a sense, he was saying, "You are able to counsel one another." That is a remarkable thing. This is the answer to all the terrible pressure placed upon pastors, who are expected to solve all the problems of their congregations and to counsel everyone. That was never God's intention. His plan is that the whole congregation be involved in the work of counseling. The whole congregation is to be aware of what is going on with neighbors and friends and brothers and sisters and to do something about meeting their problems. This is done by the imparting of the gifts of the Spirit. So the church in Rome had the right motives; the people had complete knowledge and the full range of gifts, so they were able to do many things within their church community and in the city of Rome.

Thank you, Father, for all the gifts of goodness and knowledge and instruction that you have given to your people to use in serving and loving one another.

Three great doctrines of the faith were known by the church in Rome. Are we being equipped to serve and to counsel others with the gifts of godly insight and knowledge?

A BOLD REMINDER

A daily devotion for November 24

Read Romans 15:15–16.

> "But I have written very boldly to you on some points so as to remind you again, because of the grace that was given me from God, to be a minister of Christ Jesus to the Gentiles, ministering as a priest the gospel of God, so that my offering of the Gentiles may become acceptable, sanctified by the Holy Spirit" (Rom. 15:15–16).

You would think that people who were theologically knowledgeable, able to instruct and to counsel one another in the deep problems of life, and filled with a spirit of goodness and compassion would hardly need anything more said to them. Yet it is to such people that Paul addresses his letter to the Romans. He says they need three other things.

First, they need a bold reminder of the truth. I saw a man the other day with a string around his finger. The string was to remind him of something. The ease with which we forget things is somehow built into our humanity, and one of the greatest proofs of the fall of man is that we have such a hard time remembering what we want to remember, yet we so easily remember what we want to forget! We even need to be reminded again and again of these great themes of the gospel. That is why Paul says, "You need your mind renewed by the Holy Spirit" (Rom. 12:2). That is one reason to gather every Sunday. We need to have our minds renewed. We need to be called back to a vision of reality.

Living out in the world and working every day among non-Christians, it is easy to be sucked into worldly attitudes. It is easy to get the idea that life is designed to be a pleasant picnic, that we can work toward the day when we can retire and enjoy ourselves. I find that attitude prevalent among people everywhere, but that is not what the Bible says. The Bible says we are in the midst of a battle to the death against a keen and crafty foe. He wants to discourage us and to defeat us, to make us feel angry and hostile. He knows how to do it, and he never lets up. This life is not designed to be a time of relaxation. There are times when we need recreation and vacations, when we can slow down a bit. But we never see Paul talking about quitting the battle. We cannot quit as long as life continues. So Paul tells us that we need to be reminded day by day and week by week that we are in a battle and that we have a crafty foe.

The second thing the apostle says the Christians in Rome need is a priestly ministry. He tells them, "You not only need to be reminded of the truth, but you need an example to follow. You need somebody you can see doing this kind of thing. That is what pastors have the privilege of doing. They are called by God not only to be examples of leadership but also to be like priests working in the temple, awakening among people a sense of worship, a sense of the greatness of God"

The third thing Paul says they need is that "the Gentiles might become an offering acceptable to God, sanctified by the Holy Spirit." Every congregation needs this. We need to labor, to pray, to counsel, to evangelize. But all of the activity of the Christian life is of no avail if it is not sanctified by the Holy Spirit, if it does not have in it that touch of God, that unction from on high, that divine wind blowing upon the dead bones and making them come to life. Paul reminds Rome's Christians of the ministry of prayer and of the need to remember that God himself must touch something—otherwise it is dead and useless. So Paul calls this church back to this tremendous reality. These people had so much, but they needed this as well.

> *Lord, continue to remind me of my need for these three things. I continue to need a bold reminder of the truth, a priestly example, and the sanctifying work of the Holy Spirit. Thank you for being more than willing to provide these things.*

Has the daily exposure to worldly affairs and ideas diverted our minds from our heritage of truth and love? Have we settled into complacency when that knowledge and goodness are so urgently needed?

PIONEERS OR SETTLERS?

A daily devotion for November 25

Read Romans 15:17–29.

> "Therefore in Christ Jesus I have found reason for boasting in things pertaining to God. For I will not presume to speak of anything except what Christ has accomplished through me, resulting in the obedience of the Gentiles by word and deed, in the power of signs and wonders, in the power of the Spirit; so that from Jerusalem and round about as far as Illyricum I have fully preached the gospel of Christ. And thus I aspired to preach the gospel, not where Christ was already named, so that I would not build on another man's foundation" (Rom. 15:17–20).

Concerning the principles of his ministry, Paul tells us five things. First, everywhere he went he found himself boasting, or "rejoicing" in a better translation. He says, "I rejoice, I glory in Christ Jesus, in my service to God." Why? Because when this man entered a city, he usually found it in the grip of Roman authority and ruled with an iron hand. He would find the people in widespread despair, empty and longing for something they could not find and fallen into terribly degrading habits that were destroying homes and the fabric of society. He would find them in the grip of superstitious fears.

No church existed where Paul went, but after he had been in a city for a while and had preached these tremendous themes, light began to spring up in the darkness. People were changed; they began to live for the first time. They discovered why they were made, and excitement appeared in their lives. So Paul spent his life rejoicing over what was happening. That is the kind of ministry he had, and he gives us its secret in verse 18: "I will not venture to speak of anything except what Christ has accomplished through me in leading the Gentiles to obey God by what I have said and done." That is the greatest secret God has to teach—that man was designed, not to do something to make God happy, but to let God work through him. God would do the work—that is why Paul said, "Christ has accomplished through me."

Paul's life and ministry were constantly characterized by the display of the power of God to change lives. And look at how widespread his ministry was: "So from Jerusalem all the way around to Illyricum, I have fully proclaimed the gospel of Christ" (v. 19). Jerusalem is way down on the eastern corner of the Mediterranean Sea in Asia. Paul had traveled up and down that coast and into what we call Turkey in Asia Minor, up and across the Dardanelles into Europe, and then into Macedonia and Greece. He had gone into what we call Yugoslavia (Illyricum). And the nature of his ministry was pioneering (v. 20): "It has always been my ambition to preach the gospel where Christ was not known." He never wanted to build on another man's work.

There are two kinds of Christians. Some want to be settlers, to live around the courthouse, and to let the mayor run everything. They have lost all desire to reach out. But then there are the pioneers like Paul. They want to journey into new areas that have never been touched adequately. I believe this is characteristic of the Spirit of God. He loves to thrust out into new areas.

Some of us are praying for a thrust into unreached and needy areas to touch folks who have had little contact with Christians. We should pray to be able to reach into these areas so that something with the touch of God upon it will develop. This is Paul's great hunger. We are to reach out with the good news as he did.

> *I pray that I may not forget that I am still in the battle and that I am still to be your instrument. Help me to partake of the apostle's spirit and to press on until you are ready to call me home.*

Have we settled for apathetic complacency though surrounded by evidence of personal and worldwide spiritual warfare? What steps are urgently needed for us to become God's messengers, empowered by his wisdom and by his indwelling presence?

STRIVING TOGETHER IN PRAYER

A daily devotion for November 26

Read Romans 15:30–33.

> "Now I urge you, brethren, by our Lord Jesus Christ and by the love of the Spirit, to strive together with me in your prayers to God for me, that I may be rescued from those who are disobedient in Judea, and that my service for Jerusalem may prove acceptable to the saints" (Rom. 15:30–31).

What was behind this mighty apostle's ministry? Why has it lasted for two thousand years? What opened the doors and gave him access even to Caesar's household and before the throne of the emperor himself? Paul would say it was the prayers of God's people for him. He was well aware of the ministry of prayer, and here he asks the faithful to pray. Paul also mentions the basis for prayer: "I urge you, brothers, by our Lord Jesus Christ and by the love of the Spirit."

Prayer is born of the Spirit of God within us. The Spirit awakens a desire to help, a sense of love and compassion. We pray to honor the Lord Jesus. This is what will stir people to pray more than anything else—not beating them with a whip. I learned that long ago. When people see that the honor of Christ is involved and that the love of the Spirit is fulfilled when they pray, they will begin to pray in earnest. That truth is what the apostle appeals to here. "Join me in my struggle," he says. Life is a struggle, and Paul sees prayer as a means of combat. This great weapon can batter down doors and open others. It can remove obstacles, withstand tremendous pressure and opposition, and uphold people and sustain them.

If there is one thing the church needs more than anything else, it is this kind of prayer. This is a critical hour in the church's history. We have great opportunities before us. What we need above all else is people who will pray that we can lay hold of these opportunities. Notice what Paul requests: "Pray for protection from the unbelievers, and for acceptance from the saints." He asks for this because these are the two areas that Satan loves to attack. If he can lay a person low with physical illness or spiritual attack, this is what he will do. Prayer is particularly powerful at this point. It can protect someone in danger. When Paul arrived in Jerusalem, he was set upon by a mob in the temple courts. These people were out to kill him. They had rocks in their hands and were going to stone him to death. But at the critical moment, the commander of the Roman legion looked over into the temple court and saw what was going on. He came down with a band of soldiers and rescued the apostle just in time. So that prayer was answered, and Paul was protected from the unbelievers.

> *Father, thank you so much for the many answered prayers that I rejoice in today—the many changed lives, the many homes that have been made right and happy where once they were sad and hostile, and the many lives that have been filled with joy, peace, and thanksgiving.*

Do we consider prayer optional? If we avoid prayer, have we considered the consequences to the glory of God and to the fruitful ministry of his messengers? What is the impact of prayer as a weapon in spiritual warfare?

A FAITHFUL SISTER

A daily devotion for November 27

Read Romans 16:1–16.

> "I commend to you our sister Phoebe, who is a servant of the church which is at Cenchrea; that you receive her in the Lord in a manner worthy of the saints, and that you help her in whatever matter she may have need of you; for she herself has also been a helper of many, and of myself as well" (Rom. 16:1–2).

There is something in all of us that wants to see our names preserved. Years ago I visited the Natural Bridge of Virginia. Thousands of names and initials were scratched on the rocks, but high up on the side of this formation, above almost every other name, was scrawled "George Washington." Even the father of our country felt the urge to gain a kind of immortality by carving his name on the rock.

But in Romans 16 is a list of names of men and women who never knew that they were going to be famous. I am sure that if they had known that mention in one of Paul's letters would give them undying fame, there would have been a long line of people outside his door urging him to include them in the letter. But these people are mentioned only because they were friends of Paul's in Rome to whom he was writing or because they were with him in Corinth from which he wrote.

The first name he mentions is Phoebe. The whole church can be grateful to this woman for her faithfulness. She bore and preserved this letter all along the hazardous route from Corinth to Rome. She is called by the apostle "a servant of the church in Cenchreae." This was the port of Corinth, located about nine miles east of the city. Evidently, a Christian church had grown up there, and Phoebe was a deacon in it. That does not mean that she held some government office in that church; we sometimes read present-day meanings into these words. It means that she had assumed a ministry on behalf of the church. She represented the church in some labor, and whether it was material, physical, or spiritual, she was faithful in it. So Paul commends her to these Christians in Rome and asks them not only to receive her but to help her. "She has been a help to many others," he says, "and to me."

We cannot read chapter 16 of Romans without being impressed by the number of women Paul mentions — many more than in any other literature of that day. In the first twenty-four verses thirty-three names are mentioned. Nine of these people were with Paul—eight men and one woman. Twenty-four names are mentioned in Rome—seventeen men and seven women. Two households are mentioned and two unnamed women—the mother of Rufus and the sister of Nereus—as well as some unnamed brethren. So there is quite a list of people the apostle knew personally in Rome, though he had not yet visited that city. These are people he had known somewhere else in the Roman Empire.

Women occupy a prominent place in these letters of the New Testament. Evidently, they handled important tasks within the church according to the gifts they had. There is strong suggestion here that Phoebe was a teacher or an evangelist—a laborer for the gospel with Paul. We do not know much more about her, but her name has been preserved forever because of this mention.

> *Lord, thank you for women like Phoebe who serve you faithfully. Help me to receive such people in a manner worthy of the saints.*

Do we aspire to serve as helpers? If not, what does that infer about our availability to God's gifts and to his calling? How does our assessment compare with Paul's recognition of Phoebe's contribution as a helper?

THE GOD OF PEACE

A daily devotion for November 28

Read Romans 16:17–20.

> "Now I urge you, brethren, keep your eye on those who cause dissensions and hindrances contrary to the teaching which you learned, and turn away from them. For such men are slaves, not of our Lord Christ but of their own appetites; and by their smooth and flattering speech they deceive the hearts of the unsuspecting. For the report of your obedience has reached to all; therefore I am rejoicing over you, but I want you to be wise in what is good and innocent in what is evil. The God of peace will soon crush Satan under your feet" (Rom. 16:17–20).

There is a helpful passage here on what to do about problems within the church. Here is a group of people who are professing Christians but who, to judge by the apostle's language, are not truly believers. The danger, as Paul outlines it, is that they create factions within a church—little dissident groups that gather and emphasize one point of doctrine or teaching to the exclusion of everything else. There is always a problem within the church when people think one thing is most important. We have people today who emphasize tongues, or prophecy, or some phase of teaching that they think is the mark of a true believer, to the exclusion of everything else. Paul warns about this.

The second thing they do is introduce practices or ceremonies that Paul calls "obstacles to faith," rituals or practices that these groups insist are the marks of true Christianity. They build a sense of superiority. They say, "If you have this mark, then you really are a Christian." Their motives, Paul says, are not to serve Christ, even though they say they do. These factions are really out to advance themselves, to get a following, to gain prestige. What they want is clear from the way they act. Their method is to come on with smooth and plausible talk. They always use scriptural language. They always appear to be the most dedicated and devoted of believers. Have you noticed how many of the cults today are trying to return to the Scriptures, arguing from them a groundwork for their faith? Another method is flattery. They make Christians feel important. They lift them up above the rest and give them a peculiar mark of distinction, boosting their egos by claiming they are members of the true church. These factions always cause division.

When some group like this appears, many of us want to rush in and to excommunicate their members, to read them out from the pulpit, or to violently attack them. Paul does not recommend doing any of those things. His advice is to keep away from them. Ignore them. "You Christians in Rome have a reputation for obedience. You have a spirit of wanting to obey what the Lord says. Now here is what the Lord says: do not follow them; do not get involved with these separatist groups. When you obey this, God will work. The God of peace, who will preserve the peace of the church, will also crush Satan under your feet." Something will happen to open the eyes of people to the unscriptural position of these groups, and they will lose their following. The peace will be preserved without warfare and dissension.

> *Father, thank you for these men and women who long ago preceded me in the pilgrimage of life. Help me to be a peacemaker among your people even when those around me might try to cause dissension.*

Have we discovered the useless folly of endless debates? How can we better fulfill our calling to the ministry of reconciliation? Do we see the wisdom of letting God deal with unruly dissidents?

PAUL'S FRIENDS

A daily devotion for November 29

Read Romans 16:21–24.

> "Timothy, my fellow worker, sends his greetings to you, as do Lucius, Jason and Sosipater, my relatives. I, Tertius, who wrote down this letter, greet you in the Lord. Gaius, whose hospitality I and the whole church here enjoy, sends you his greetings. Erastus, who is the city's director of public works, and our brother Quartus send you his greetings" (Rom. 16:21–24).

Here in the final paragraph Paul takes his pen and writes the last words himself. Up to this point he has been dictating this letter to a man named Tertius. The name indicates that he was a slave. His brother, Quartus, is mentioned in verse 23. They are educated slaves who have become Christians. They can read and write and are part of the group in Corinth.

We can picture them gathered in the home of Gaius, the gracious host in this city, mentioned in Paul's first letter to the Corinthians. Gaius opened his house to the entire Christian community, so here is Paul, sitting there with his friends. Tertius is writing down the letter, and the others are gathered around listening to Paul as he dictates and profiting much from the writing of these great truths. With Paul is Timothy. Paul always spoke of him in the highest terms; he was the apostle's beloved son in the faith, who had stayed with him so long and remained faithful to the end. The last letter Paul wrote from his prison cell in Rome was to Timothy. Paul also mentions Lucius, Jason, and Sosipater, his relatives.

Here in Romans 16 are six members of Paul's family, kinsmen who are now Christians. Some were Christians before he was, but some Paul influenced toward Christ. Lucius appears to be the same one who comes from Cyrene, mentioned in chapter 13 of Acts as one of the teachers in the city of Antioch. Jason was evidently Paul's host when the apostle went to Thessalonica. Paul stayed in Jason's home when a riot broke out in the city. Sosipater may be the man from Beroea, mentioned in Acts 20 as Sopater. Paul met him in Macedonia and may have accompanied him to Jerusalem with the offering to the churches there. The final name is Erastus, director of public works in Corinth. This shows how the gospel penetrated all levels of society, with slaves, public officials, consuls, and leaders of the empire all sharing fellowship in equality in the church of Jesus Christ. All class distinctions disappeared within the church, and that is what happens whenever the church works.

These Christians were noted for four things. First, they were not their own. They no longer had a right to direct their lives. Second, they believed that life is a battle, not a picnic. They were engaged in warfare that never ended until they left this life, so they kept on fighting. Third, they believed in a need for rest and leisure at times but only to restore them to return to the battle. They never envisioned retiring for the remaining years of their lives. They desired only adequate rest so they could come back and fight through to the end. Finally, they understood that the gifts of the Holy Spirit among them opened up a ministry for every believer.

No Christian was without a ministry. Some of these dear people had only the gift of helps, and that is a great gift. They could not teach or preach, but they could help, and they did, right to the end. This passage reminds us that God has called us all to a ministry, and we all must give an account for what we have done with our gifts. We had better find out what they are and get to work, get involved in the battle, because God has not called us to a picnic ground. He has called us to a battleground.

I pray that you will grant to me, Lord, similar faith that I too may share with you in a time of testing, of rebuke, of pressure, and of persecution and stand steadfast to the end for your name's sake.

What four commitments were commonly shared by these early Christians? Do we share with them liberation from class distinctions, honoring all members of the family of Christ?

ESTABLISHED!

A daily devotion for November 30

Read Romans 16:25–27.

> "Now to Him who is able to establish you according to my gospel and the preaching of Jesus Christ, according to the revelation of the mystery which has been kept secret for long ages past, but now is manifested, and by the Scriptures of the prophets, according to the commandment of the eternal God, has been made known to all the nations, leading to obedience of faith; to the only wise God, through Jesus Christ, be the glory forever. Amen" (Rom. 16:25–27).

Those remarkable words constitute a summary of the letter to the Romans—a beautiful finale to this great epistle. You will notice that the goal the apostle has in view in writing this letter is that we who read it may be established.

Have you ever had the desire to be established? Many people think they are established when they are simply stuck in the mud. Most of us think that being established means that all progress ceases. We sit down, set up camp, and that is it. In that sense, many Christians are established. But when Paul speaks of our being established, he means putting us on solid, stable ground. Have you ever erected a picnic table and tried to find a place where all four legs touched the ground at the same time? You tried to establish it so that it would not rock or become shaky or uncertain. That is the idea that Paul has in mind with this word *establish*. God wants to bring us to a place where we are no longer rocking or shaky or unstable but solid and secure. This is basically what all human beings look for—an inner security from which they can handle all the problems of life. They want to become dependable and have a true sense of worth so that nothing gets to them, shakes them up, or throws them off balance.

This is the goal of all Christian teaching in the New Testament (and especially the goal of the letter to the Romans): that we believers might be brought to that place of security where we are not shaken by events so that we do not lose our tempers easily or get frustrated, angry, resentful, or hostile and so that we do not scream at our children, yell at our mates, or get upset at the neighbors.

Notice the resource that the apostle counts on to make that happen: "Now to Him who is able to establish you." It is God himself who is responsible for this. You and I are not given the final responsibility to bring this about. Isn't that encouraging? Now there are things Paul asks us to do. We are to understand what he is saying to us in this letter, and we are to willingly cooperate with it and to give ourselves to it. But even if we do not, Paul is saying, we do not have the ultimate responsibility to bring this about. God will do it.

God did it with Paul. He was a brilliant young Jew with an ambitious heart, a sharp mind, and a strong sense of achievement due to his notable gifts and to his desire to become famous. Yet God broke him, softened him, changed him, and put him through circumstances that Paul did not understand at the time. This finally established him so that no matter what came, he remained strong, steady, trusting, and certain. That is the great good news of this letter. "Now to him who is able to establish you."

Thank you, Lord, for promising to establish me in the faith and to bring me to a place of security and of strength in you.

Are we merely part of the establishment, or are we firmly established in Christ as our true identity? Are we fully and confidently engaged as his fruit-bearing servants?

HEBREWS

All about Faith

An introduction for the month of December

A group of Christians were gathered in a home discussing the state of affairs in the world. They commented on the fears, the tensions, the sense of futility that prevail in so many circles these days. The question arose: "What can we do about this?" As Christians, they knew the answer to the world's woes, but the problem was how to make the world believe the answer. Among them was a young Christian who was troubled by the discussion. With a concerned look on his face, he said, "Why doesn't the world believe what we have to say? I think it's because so many Christians don't act like they believe it themselves." Then he asked the logical, but thorny, question: "How can we make Christians believe what they believe?"

That is the theme of the letter to the Hebrews: how to make Christians believe. This is what the world is waiting to see and what the epistle was written to effect. It is addressed to a group of Jewish Christians who had begun to drift, to lose their faith. They had lost all awareness of the relevance of their faith to the affairs of daily life. They had begun to drift into outward formal religious performance and to lose the inner reality. Doubts were creeping into their hearts because of some of the humanistic philosophies that abounded in the world of their day, as they abound in the world of our day. Some of them were about to abandon their faith in Christ, not because they were attracted again by Jewish ritual and ceremony but because of persecution and pressure. They felt that their faith was not worthwhile, that they were losing too much, and that it was possible that they had been deceived and that the message of Christ was not true after all.

No one knows exactly where these Christians lived. Some feel this letter was written to Hebrew Christians living in Rome. Others believe it was written to believers in Jerusalem. That is my conviction. If anyone wished to influence the world of Jewish Christians, surely that would be the place to start.

No one knows for certain who wrote the letter, either. The King James Version calls it "The Epistle of Paul the Apostle to the Hebrews." It was a favorite jest in seminary to ask, "Who wrote the epistle of Paul to the Hebrews?" No one knows for sure. If you read this letter in English you are almost sure that Paul wrote it, since so many of the thoughts are obviously Pauline. But if you read it in Greek you are equally certain that Paul did not write it, for the language used is different from the other letters of Paul. There have been many guesses throughout the centuries, including Luke, Silas, Peter, Apollos, Barnabas, and even Aquila and Priscilla. Some have felt that Priscilla wrote it; if so, this would be the first letter of the New Testament written by a woman. I believe that Paul wrote it in Hebrew while he was in prison in those two years in Caesarea after his visit to Jerusalem, that it was translated by Luke into Greek, and that this is the copy that has come down to us today.

Whoever the writer was, he sees one thing quite clearly: that Jesus Christ is the answer to every human need. No book of the New Testament focuses upon Christ like the book of the Hebrews. It is the clearest and most systematic presentation of the availability and the adequacy of Jesus Christ in the Bible. It presents Christianity as the perfect and final religion, simply because the incomparable person and work of Jesus Christ permits men free and unrestricted access to God. In every age that is man's desperate need.

GOD'S FINAL WORD

A daily devotion for December 1

Read Hebrews 1:1–4.

> "In the past, God spoke to our people through the prophets. He spoke at many times. He spoke in different ways. But in these last days, he has spoken to us through his Son. He is the one whom God appointed to receive all things. God made everything through him" (Heb. 1:1–2).

When you open the Old Testament you are reading the Word of God spoken to the fathers by the prophets. I hope you understand and value the Old Testament. What a marvelous book! How many different ways God spoke in that book—in dreams, in visions, in sudden appearances, and in that wonderful act of inspiration that nobody fully understands in which somebody speaking the words that come to his mind and his heart is uttering the words of God.

And God's message comes in many forms, as the writer of Hebrews says. Open Genesis and you have first the straightforward but majestic and moving tale of creation, of the fall, and of the flood. This is followed by the simple narrative of the lives of the patriarchs—Abraham, Isaac, and Jacob. Then there is the story of Moses, the exodus, and the thunderings of the law, coming at last to the sweet singing of the psalmist, the homespun wisdom of Proverbs, and the delicate tenderness of the Song of Solomon. The rest of the Old Testament is filled with the exalted visions of the prophets, the mighty men who spoke to times of crisis in the nation and yet lifted their eyes and saw far beyond the horizons of time to great events that God would bring into being when the proper seasons arrived.

Yet when you finish the book and have heard all the matchless oratory of the prophets, you still realize that God's voice has not answered the deep questions of the human heart. It is only when you open the Gospels and begin to read of Jesus—who he was, what he did, where he went, what he said, how he acted, how he lived, and the way he handled situations—that all the utterances of the prophets begin to merge into one great voice and we get God's final word to humankind.

Not far away from where I used to live in Montana is a place called the Three Forks of the Missouri River where three rivers flow together to form the Missouri. They rise up in the mountains in the western part of Montana and form this great river, the Missouri, that flows down through Montana and into North Dakota, South Dakota, through Missouri, and joins the Mississippi along with the Ohio. Altogether this forms the greatest river system and drainage network in the world. All these rivers drain out of hills and valleys and mountain ranges that are widely separated from one another, and I always think of that when I think of the way the Old Testament has flowed together to form the one great voice that speaks in the New. All the themes that God introduces to humankind in the Old Testament are brought together in the voice of Jesus. He is God's final word to man, greater than the prophets, fulfilling everything they have written.

Lord Jesus, you are God's final word. I thank you for allowing me to see how the entire story of the Old Testament finds its fulfillment in you.

Are we missing the grandeur of the world's greatest epic through neglect of either the Old or the New Testament? Is the person at the epicenter of Scripture central in our lives?

HE HOLDS ALL THINGS TOGETHER

A daily devotion for December 2

Read Hebrews 1:1–4.

"The Son is the gleaming brightness of God's glory. He is the exact likeness of God's being. He uses his powerful word to hold all things together" (Heb. 1:3).

That is an amazing statement. The writer puts this in the present tense, saying that Jesus is the One keeping things going right now. Stanford University is the site of a linear accelerator, a mighty two-mile-long atom smasher. It is a great lever with which scientists try to pry the lid off of the secrets of matter and to discover what is in the miniature world of the atom, the neutron, and the proton. Linear accelerator scientists have discovered a complexity they never dreamed of, and they cannot invent enough names for all the particles that they have found. But one thing they are consistently discovering is that there is some strange force that holds everything together. They do not know what to call it, and they do not know how to identify it. They talk about a kind of cosmic glue that holds things together. Isn't it fascinating that here in the Word of God we have that exact kind of terminology used of Jesus? If we want a name for the force that holds the universe together it is simple. His name is Jesus. He sustains the universe by his powerful word.

That is true not only of the physical universe, including our bodies and all that we are, but of all the other forces and powers in the universe—physical, psychological, social, spiritual. Jesus is in charge of them all. After the resurrection, when our Lord appeared to the disciples by the Sea of Galilee, in the most forthright terms, he said to them, "All power is given unto me in heaven and in earth" (Matt. 28:18 KJV). This means he controls not only all the physical forces of the planet and the universe but also all the events that occur everywhere. This is something Christians tend to forget. We get so used to seeing things through the secular eyes of the media and other propaganda forces that we forget that behind the events that fill the pages of our newspapers is a mighty controlling hand that brings them all together, permitting some things to happen, restraining others.

I recall the life of General Douglas MacArthur and those turbulent days of World War II when he was the American commander in the Pacific; then his move to Japan where he became a virtual emperor; then the days of the Korean War when MacArthur was the commander. It is fascinating to remember the headlines and the events that seemed so important at the time. I remember how angry the whole nation became at President Truman when he dismissed MacArthur, and the tremendous, ecstatic response the general received when he returned, first in San Francisco and later in New York. The nation was almost groveling at his feet.

And yet those events seem far away and insignificant now. They do not have much bearing on today. The events that capture our attention today will likewise fade and appear trivial soon enough. Yet they are not without meaning. The Bible tells us a mighty hand is shaping the destiny of nations and of individuals. All of these things have been and will always remain in the power of him who sustains the universe.

Lord Jesus, thank you for being the One who holds all things together. Teach me to trust in you even when things seem to be falling apart.

Do we view the Lord Jesus Christ as the world's central force? Is this merely intellectual, or does the power of his presence translate into confident trust in the everyday events of our lives?

THE POWER TO CLEANSE

A daily devotion for December 3

Read Hebrews 1:3–4.

"He provided the way for people to be made pure from sin. Then he sat down at the right hand of the King, the Majesty in heaven" (Heb. 1:3).

Jesus is the final and complete word of God to man because he has solved the deepest problem in human life—the problem of sinfulness. In the face of the tragic things that are happening today, everybody is asking, "What's wrong with humanity? What's wrong with life? Why is the world in such a mess? Why are our papers filled with murder, violence, hate, and corruption?" The answer of Scripture is, "Man's sin," or to put it even more realistically, "Man's selfishness." That is what lies at the root of all this darkness. Sin is the terrible taint that we can never wash away by our own efforts. Like Lady Macbeth, we all want to cry out and to curse the stain. Yet it is never gone.

The amazing declaration of Scripture is that the reason the Creator of the world became the babe of Bethlehem was that he might offer purification for human selfishness, that he might solve the insoluble problem and wash away the unwashable stain. The good news is that every one of us who has found Christ and who follows him finds again and again that he has the power to cleanse us. He has the power to put away the guilt of the past whether it is the past fifty years of life or the past five minutes. He has the power to cleanse it, to wash it away, and to set us on our feet again with a clean slate and a fresh page to write on every day. We can live life again in the power and the grace of the living God. That is the greatest message of all. When he had made purification for sins (what agony, what terrible hurt is involved in that phrase), "he sat down at the right hand of the King, the Majesty in heaven." Jesus is Lord. This was the early creed of the church, and it is the creed of all who come to know him now. He has solved that desperate problem of human life; he is in control of all human events.

Father, thank you for the Lord of glory. I cannot adequately describe my amazement that he should come in the form of a helpless child, become a man, and die to set me free and to cleanse me from my sins. Thank you for this. I pray that I will never forget that I am a redeemed creature, that I have no value in myself, but that I have eternal value in the One who loved me and gave himself for me.

Have we been scandalized by our selfishness? Are we learning to bring this intolerable burden to Jesus for our cleansing and healing? If not, to whom shall we go? What path shall we take? Is there another?

A SON OR A SERVANT

A daily devotion for December 4

Read Hebrews 1:5–14.

> "For to which of the angels did God ever say, 'You are my Son; today I have become your Father'? Or again, 'I will be his Father, and he will be my Son'?" (Heb. 1:5).

The writer of Hebrews is now comparing Jesus with the angels. The ancient world made a great deal of angels. People worshiped them in many of the ancient religious rites. Angels are the demigods of the Roman and Greek pantheon. Therefore, this letter was written to people who had a particular interest in angels. This subject may not interest us as much today as it did people then, but angels are still a tremendous revelation of the person of Christ.

The Lord Jesus, says the writer, has a greater name than the angels, primarily because of his relationship. The contrast is between a Son and a servant. Angels are servants, but Christ is the Son.

I once visited a ranch as the guest of its hired man. When we arrived at the property we had to drive around the big house and go to the bunkhouse in the rear. I stayed with him there and never once got into the big house with him. There were some beautiful sorrel horses in the pasture, and I suggested we take a ride. He said, "Oh, no, I'm not permitted to ride those horses." So we had to ride some mangy fleabags out to the pasture. A few weeks later I became acquainted with the son of the household, and he invited me out to the ranch. When I went out with him, it was entirely different. We went right into the big house, and he took over the place, as all teenagers do. After a sumptuous meal, we went out and rode the sorrel horses all over the range. What a wonderful time we had.

That is the difference between a son and a servant, and that is the difference between Christ and any angel. He is greater because of his relationship, the fact that he is a Son. Blood is always thicker than water.

As C. S. Lewis points out, what we make with our hands is always something different than we are, but what we beget with our bodies is always the dearest thing in the world to us because it is part of us. Thus the angels were made; the Son was begotten. What we beget has the same nature we have; what we make is always different. The angels, being made, cannot have the same relationship as the Son, who was begotten.

Here is the final answer to the cults. Both Mormonism and Jehovah's Witnesses teach that Jesus Christ was nothing more than an angel, the highest created angel. They identify him with Michael, the archangel. But this passage in Hebrews utterly demolishes that theory, for Christ is a Son and not an angel. To what angel did God ever say, "Thou art my Son"?

Father, the claims of the Lord Jesus are incomparable and can never be surpassed. I pray, therefore, that I may face up to this and realize that there is no way of working out the problems of human life except as I work them out in fellowship with him.

Does the Lord Jesus Christ occupy his rightful and exclusive place as God in our thoughts, words, and deeds? Are we guarding against the worldly pantheon of false gods while delighting in our rich inheritance in Christ?

PAY CAREFUL ATTENTION!

A daily devotion for December 5

Read Hebrews 2:1–4.

> "We must pay the most careful attention, therefore, to what we have heard, so that we do not drift away. For since the message spoken through angels was binding, and every violation and disobedience received its just punishment, how shall we escape if we ignore so great a salvation? This salvation, which was first announced by the Lord, was confirmed to us by those who heard him. God also testified to it by signs, wonders and various miracles, and by gifts of the Holy Spirit distributed according to his will" (Heb. 2:1–4).

The writer says that we need to pay attention! This convinces me that he was a preacher. There is nothing more heartbreaking than preaching to people week after week and seeing them constantly exposed to truth that you know could transform their existence and yet to find they have lost the whole effect of this because they do not pay attention.

This message is particularly valid for two reasons. First, it is valid by comparison with the law. If the word spoken by angels—that is, the law of Moses—had validity and if those to whom it was given found that it was absolutely true in experience, then this message also is true. If angels could give a word like that, how much more the word that comes by the Son?

The second confirmation that this message is valid is the form of its communication to us. It was spoken first by the Lord! Jesus Christ offers the most authoritative word the world has ever heard. This message did not originate with the apostles or come to us by means of prophets. It came through the Lord himself. That is not all. It was confirmed by eyewitnesses and accompanied by signs sent from God himself, by wonders and miracles and gifts of the Holy Spirit. What an compelling argument this is!

All of this leaves us with one question that the writer leaves hanging in the air: how shall we escape if we neglect such great salvation? That is not a threat. It is simply a question. It is addressed both to the Christian and to the non-Christian. To the non-Christian it says, "Where are you going to go? How will you get out of God's universe? How can you escape, and why attempt to do so, especially when his purpose is not to curse but to bless? How can you find deliverance by any other route, since it does not involve the One who is behind all things?"

To the Christian it says that it is not enough to know Jesus Christ. We must use him. We can lose so much, even knowing him, unless we have a day-by-day walk with him. We can lose peace, freedom, joy, and achievement. We are subjected to temptation, frustration, bewilderment, and barrenness without him. And if we do not go on as Christians, if we do not grow, a serious question arises. Have we ever begun the Christian life? Or is this but self-deception, attempted to meet outward standards but without any change in the heart? The writer's question remains haunting and unavoidable: how shall we escape if we neglect such a great salvation?

Lord Jesus, help me to pay careful attention and not to neglect such great salvation.

Are we giving priority to the most significant issue of eternity: our salvation? Do we properly fear God as sovereign and righteous while honoring his holy presence as our eternal Advocate?

RESTORING DOMINION

A daily devotion for December 6

Read Hebrews 2:5–9.

> "In putting everything under them, God left nothing that is not subject to them. Yet at present we do not see everything subject to them. But we do see Jesus, who was made lower than the angels for a little while, now crowned with glory and honor because he suffered death, so that by the grace of God he might taste death for everyone" (Heb. 2:8–9).

This passage describes humanity's present state of futility. Here is human history in a nutshell: God created us to exercise dominion, but we do not yet see everything in subjection to us. We attempt to exercise our dominion, but we no longer can do so adequately. We have never forgotten the position God gave us. Throughout the history of the race, we see a continual restatement of the dreams of humanity for dominion over the earth and the universe. This is why we cannot keep off the highest mountain. We have got to explore the depths of the sea. We have to get out into space. We did this because it is there.

Humans consistently manifest a remarkable racial memory, a vestigial recollection of what God told them to do. The trouble is that when we try to accomplish this now, we create a highly explosive and dangerous situation, for our ability to exercise dominion is no longer there. Even in the individual life this is true. How many have realized the dreams and ideals they began with? Who can say, "I have done all that I wanted to do; I have been all that I wanted to be"? Paul says, "The creation was subjected to futility" (Rom. 8:20 RSV).

"But we do see Jesus," the writer says. This is our one hope. With the eye of faith, we see Jesus already crowned and reigning over the universe, the man Jesus fulfilling humanity's lost destiny. In the last book of the Bible there is a scene in which John beholds the One seated upon the throne of the universe as thousands of angels cry out in unending worship before him. The call goes out to find one who can open the book with seven seals, which is the title deed to earth, the right to run the earth. A search is made throughout human history for someone worthy to open the seals, but no one can be found. John says he wept because no one was found worthy to open the scroll. But the angel says, "Do not weep, for the Lion of the tribe of Judah has conquered and he can open the seals" (Rev. 5:5 RSV). When John turned to see the lion, to his amazement he saw a Lamb, a Lamb that had been slain. As he watched, the Lamb stepped up to the throne and took the book, and all heaven broke into acclaim, for here at last was One worthy to own the title deed of earth.

This is what the writer sees here. Here we see Jesus, who alone has broken through the barrier that keeps us from our heritage. What is that barrier? What is it that keeps us from realizing our dreams of dominion? Death! Death is more than the ending of life. Death means uselessness; it means waste, futility. Death, in that sense, pervades all of life. We can see the signs of it everywhere.

But Jesus fulfilled the qualifications to realize humanity's heritage. He became lower than the angels; he took on flesh and blood; he entered into the human race to become part of it. Here we see Jesus, who alone experienced death. He tasted death for every man, and in doing so he took our place. Those who throw in their lot with him find that he has removed the thing that gives death its sting. In Jesus Christ mankind has that one ray of hope to realize the destiny God has provided. Christ has come to begin a new race of people. That race includes himself and all those who are his, and he promises them that they shall enter into all the fullness God ever intended man to have.

Thank you, Father, for sending your Son to die for me so that I could be restored and joined with you in that dominion that you created me for. Open my eyes that I might see him more clearly.

God's loving, sovereign plan is that we as his subjects should reign in life. How has he provided for this possibility? Are we living by means of the resurrection power of the indwelling Lord Jesus Christ? If not, why not?

PERFECT THROUGH SUFFERING

A daily devotion for December 7

Read Hebrews 2:10–18.

> "In bringing many sons and daughters to glory, it was fitting that God, for whom and through whom everything exists, should make the pioneer of their salvation perfect through what he suffered" (Heb. 2:10).

The earthly life of Jesus is summed up in one phrase, "perfect through what he suffered." Was he not perfect when he came? When Jesus was a babe in Bethlehem's manger, was he not perfect even then? When he was tempted in the desert and Satan tried to turn him from the cross, was he not already perfect? When he was feeding the five thousand, in compassionate ministry to the hungry multitudes, was he not perfect? Why, then, does this passage say he was perfected by suffering?

There are two perfections involved. Jesus was perfect in his person all along, but he was not yet perfect in his work. A person may be perfect in health, in body, in strength, in soundness of humanity, but not yet perfect in the work he is called to do. Suppose Jesus Christ had come full-grown into the world a week before he died. Suppose he had never been born as a baby and grown up into adult life but had stepped into the earth full grown as a man. Suppose he had uttered in one week's time the Sermon on the Mount, the Olivet Discourse, the Upper Room Discourse, and all the other teachings that we have from his lips recorded in Scripture. Imagine that he came on Monday and on Friday the executioners took him out and crucified him, hanging him on the cross, and that he died, bearing the sins of the world. Would he still have been a perfect Savior?

Certainly he would have been perfect as far as bearing our guilt was concerned—that required only a sinless Savior. But he would not have been perfect as far as bearing our infirmities, our weaknesses, was concerned. He would have been able to fit us for heaven but never able to make us ready for earth right now. In such a case, we could always say, "How can God expect me to live a perfect life in my situation? After all, I'm only human! Christ has never been where I am. What does he know of my pressures? What does he know of what I'm up against?" But Jesus was made perfect through his suffering. He does know!

He was a man who experienced fear and uncertainty. If we deny him this, we deny him his identification with us as humans. These were the temptations he faced, the pressures he withstood. Every fear, every sense of uncertainty, is temptation. Of course he never acted out of uncertainty and never spoke out of fear. The moment Jesus felt fear gripping his heart, he leaned back upon the full-flowing life of the indwelling Father and that fear was met by faith. The moment he felt uncertain, he rested back upon the indwelling wisdom of God and was immediately given a word that was the right one for the situation. Yet because he fully entered into our fears and pressures, Jesus is fully one with us and "able to bring many sons and daughters to glory."

> *Lord, grant me depth, honesty, and earnestness that I may believe this marvelous ministry made available to me by the Lord Jesus, who has brought many sons and daughters to glory through his suffering.*

Jesus suffered intense temptation to sin but chose to bear the sins of the world on the cross for our salvation. Do we grasp the depths of his suffering and his total identification with us in our sin and in our suffering?

GOD'S HOUSE

A daily devotion for December 8

Read Hebrews 3:1–6.

> "'Moses was faithful as a servant in all God's house,' bearing witness to what would be spoken by God in the future. But Christ is faithful as the Son over God's house. And we are his house, if indeed we hold firmly to our confidence and the hope in which we glory" (Heb. 3:5–6).

Six times in this short section the word *house* appears, as in "the house of God." Many people, especially Christians, mistakenly believe that this term means a church building. There is nothing more destructive of the greatest message of the New Testament than that belief! A building is never truly called a house of God, either in the New Testament or the Old Testament, in the present or in the past. Certainly no church building, since the beginning of the church, could ever properly be called "the house of God." The early church never referred to any building in that way. In fact, the church had no buildings for two hundred or three hundred years. When early Christians referred to the house of God they meant the people. A church is not a building. It is people!

Even the temple or the tabernacle of old was not God's house. Let someone point out the fact that no building today can properly be called the house of God, and some Bible-instructed Christian nearby wisely nods his head and says, "Yes, you're right. The only building that could properly be called 'the house of God' was the temple." It is true that those buildings were termed that in Scripture, but this was meant only figuratively. They were never intended to be the place where God dwelled.

In his magnificent prophecy, Isaiah records the words of the Lord, saying, "Heaven is my throne and earth is my footstool—where is the house which you would build for me? … All these things my hand has made" (Isa. 66:1–2 KJV). Paul, in preaching to the Athenians, reminded them that "God does not dwell in temples made by hands" (Acts 17:24 KJV). Even as he said those words the temple was still standing in Jerusalem. No, God does not dwell in buildings.

Then what is the house of God that is mentioned here? The answer is clearly stated in verse 6: "We are his house." This is talking about we, his people. God never intended to dwell in any building; he dwells in people, in men and women, in boys and girls. That is the divine intention in making men, that they may be the tabernacle of his indwelling. Paul says, "Know you not that your body is the temple of the Holy Spirit within you which you have of God?" (1 Cor. 6:19). God's purpose is to inhabit our bodies and to make us the manifestation of his life, the dwelling place of all that he is.

In this house of God that is ever people, Moses ministered as a servant but Christ as a Son. Therefore, the Son is much more to be obeyed, much more to be heard, much more to be honored and heeded, than the servant. Moses served faithfully. What is the ministry of a servant? A servant is always preparing things. He must prepare meals; he must prepare rooms; he must prepare the yard. He is always working in anticipation of something yet to come. His work is done in view of the future. "But Christ is faithful as the Son over God's house." The role of a son in a house is to take over everything, to possess it, to use whatever he likes. The house was made for him.

Thank, you, Lord, that you have come to dwell in me. What a privilege it is to be your house!

Incredibly, the Spirit of God has chosen the believer's body as his temple! Who, then, is to be worshiped? For what purpose does the risen Christ honor us with all the resources and the power of his presence?

WARNING! WARNING!

A daily devotion for December 9

Read Hebrews 3:7–15.

> "See to it, brothers and sisters, that none of you has a sinful, unbelieving heart that turns away from the living God. But encourage one another daily, as long as it is called 'Today,' so that none of you may be hardened by sin's deceitfulness. We have come to share in Christ, if indeed we hold our original conviction firmly to the very end" (Heb. 3:12–14).

We share in Christ if that faith that began continues to produce in us what faith alone can produce, the fruit of the Spirit. This is an important warning of this letter against the danger of hardening—of hearing the words and believing them, understanding what they mean, but of taking no action upon them. There is peril in holding truth in the head but never letting it enter the heart. But truth known never does anything; it is truth done that sets us free. Truth known simply puffs us up in pride of knowledge. We can quote Scripture by the yard, can memorize it, can know the message of every book, and know the Bible from cover to cover, but truth known will never do anything for us. It is truth done, truth acted upon, that moves and delivers and changes.

The terrible danger that the writer points out is that truth known but not acted on has an awful effect of hardening the heart so that it is no longer able to act—and we lose the ability to believe. This is what the Lord Jesus meant when he said to his disciples, "If they believe not Moses and the prophets, neither will they believe though one should rise from the dead" (Luke 16:31).

A man said to me, "If only we had the ability to do miracles like the early church did, then we could really make this Christian cause go. If we could perform these things again and had faith enough to do miracles, we could make people believe." But I had to tell him that after thirty years of observing this scene and of studying the Scriptures, I was absolutely convinced that if God granted us this power, as he is perfectly able to do, so that miracles were being demonstrated on every hand, not one Christian would be added to the cause of Christ! At the close of Jesus's ministry, after that remarkable demonstration of the power of God in the midst of people, how many stood with him at the foot of the cross? A tiny band of women and one man, and they had been won not by his miracles but by his words.

This is why God says in verse 11, "I swore in my wrath, 'They shall never enter my rest.'" That is not petulance. That does not mean God is upset because he has offered something and they will not take it. That is simply a revelation of the nature of the case. When truth is known and not acted upon, it always, on every level of life, in any area of human knowledge, has this peculiar quality: it hardens so the heart is not able to believe what it refuses to act on.

Father, may I heed this important warning and act upon this truth that you have shown me.

Are we trivializing the eternal loss to our souls of simply knowing, while deliberately failing to live, biblical truth? What is the short-term as well as long-term loss?

LIVING OUT OF REST

A daily devotion for December 10

Read Hebrews 4:1–13.

> "There remains, then, a Sabbath-rest for the people of God; for anyone who enters God's rest also rests from their works, just as God did from his" (Heb. 4:9–10).

Here is a revolutionary new principle of human behavior on which God intends man to operate. It is from this that man fell, and it is to this in Jesus Christ that he will be restored. Unless this principle is operative in our lives, we can have no assurance that we belong to the body of Christ. This is the clear declaration of this writer throughout Hebrews.

We all have been brainwashed since birth with a false concept of the basis for human activity. We have been sold on the satanic lie that we have in ourselves what it takes to be what we want to be, to achieve whatever we desire. We are sure we have what it takes, and if we do not have it now, we know where we can get it. We can educate ourselves, we can acquire more information, we can develop new skills, and when we get this done we shall have what it takes to reach our goal.

We do not have what it takes, and we never did. The only one who can live the Christian life is Jesus Christ. He proposes to reproduce his life in us. Our part is to expose every situation to his life in us, and by that means, depending upon him and not upon us, we are to meet every situation and to perform every activity. We cease from our own labors.

This is the way you began the Christian life. You came to the place where you stopped trying to save yourself, did you not? You quit trying to be good enough to get into heaven. You said, "I'll never make it." You looked to the Lord Jesus and said, "If he has taken my place, then that is all I need." Thus, receiving him and resting on that fact by faith, you stopped your own efforts, you ceased from your own work, and rested on his.

Paul says, "As therefore you received Christ Jesus the Lord, so live in him" (Col. 2:6 RSV). As you have received him, dependent on his death on the cross, so live in dependence upon his life in you to do all things through you. Step out upon that, and what is the result? Wonderful rest! Relief, release, no longer worrying, straining, for you are resting upon One who is wholly adequate to do through you everything that needs to be done. He does not make automations of us; he does not turn us into robots. He works through our thinking, our feeling, and our reasoning, but our dependence must be upon him.

Lord Jesus, thank you for this wonderful surgery that sets me free. I rejoice that there is a rest remaining into which I can enter. Grant that I will.

What is the operative principle of the Christian life that assures that we are authentically Christian? Are we affirming the complete sufficiency of Christ Jesus our Lord by consistent reliance upon his presence and his power?

THE THRONE OF GRACE

A daily devotion for December 11

Read Hebrews 4:14–16.

> "Therefore, since we have a great high priest who has ascended into heaven, Jesus the Son of God, let us hold firmly to the faith we profess. For we do not have a high priest who is unable to empathize with our weaknesses, but we have one who has been tempted in every way, just as we are—yet he did not sin. Let us then approach God's throne of grace with confidence, so that we may receive mercy and find grace to help us in our time of need" (Heb. 4:14–16).

Four words in this brief passage sum up all it has to say: "the throne of grace." A throne speaks of authority and power, while grace conveys the idea of sympathy and understanding. These two thoughts are combined in Jesus Christ. He is a man of infinite power, yet in complete and utter sympathy with us. He said himself, after his resurrection, "All power is given unto me, in heaven and in earth" (Matt. 28:18 KJV). His title here is "Jesus, the Son of God," possessing the fullness of deity. But more than that, he is the one who has "passed through the heavens." In this space age, this phrase should catch our eye. Jesus not only passed into the heavens but through the heavens.

When we put people into a rocket and hurl them into space, we are throwing them into the heavens. They are still within the space-time continuum. Even if they traveled to the nearest planets or to the outermost reaches of our solar system, which seems utterly impossible now, they would still be in the heavens. But the claim made for Jesus is that he has passed through the heavens, that he has passed outside the limits of time and space. He is no longer contained within or limited by those boundaries that hold us within physical limits. He is outside, above, beyond, over all. Therefore there are no limits to his power.

The writer also makes clear that though the Lord Jesus has passed into the place of supreme power and has absolutely no limits upon his ability to work, he also is tremendously concerned with our problems. The writer says, "We have not a high priest who cannot be touched with the feelings of our infirmities." He has already gone the whole course before us. He has felt every pressure; he has been drawn by every allurement we face. He has been frightened by every fear, beset by every anxiety, depressed by every worry. Yet he faced all this without failure, without sinning. Never once did he fall. "Let us then approach God's throne of grace with confidence, so that we may receive mercy and find grace to help us in our time of need." That is, every help we need every time we need it!

> *Help me, Father, to obey these simple words of admonition: to come with confidence and with boldness to the throne of grace from which all help comes, all light is streaming, all hope is flaming.*

What audacious limitations do we presume to impose upon Jesus Christ, conqueror of time and space? Do we honor his amazing invitation to come boldly to his throne of supreme authority and grace?

STRENGTH AT WIT'S END

A daily devotion for December 12

Read Hebrews 5:1–10.

> "During the days of Jesus' life on earth, he offered up prayers and petitions with fervent cries and tears to the one who could save him from death, and he was heard because of his reverent submission. Son though he was, he learned obedience from what he suffered" (Heb. 5:7–8).

How can Jesus sympathize, how does he understand our pressures, if he has never sinned? The answer to that leads us into the dark shadows of Gethsemane. Few accounts in the Gospels match the power of this passage, which describes how, with prayers and supplications, with loud cries and tears, Jesus pleaded with him who was able to save him from death.

Here we come face to face with mystery. Here is the total unexpectedness of unimagined agony for the Lord. In his anticipation of what he would suffer and in his explanations of this to the disciples, he had never once mentioned Gethsemane, and there is no prediction of this in the Old Testament. There is much that predicts what he would undergo on the cross; there is not one word of what he endured in the garden.

Amid his bafflement and distress of soul, Jesus did an unusual thing. For the first time in his ministry he appealed to his disciples for help. He asked them to bear him up in prayer as he went farther into the shadows, falling first to his knees and then to his face, crying out before the Father. There he prayed three separate times, each time questioning the necessity of this sentence. "Father, if it be possible, let this cup pass from me." He beseeched the Father to make clear to him whether the cross was necessary, so unexpected and deep was his suffering, so suddenly had it come upon him, confusing him, just as sudden catastrophes come bewilderingly to us.

To deepen the mystery of this, the account implies that the Lord Jesus faced the full misery that sin produces in the heart of the sinner while he is yet alive. All the naked filth of human depravity forced itself upon him, and he felt the burning, searing shame of our misdeeds as though they were his. No wonder he cried, "Father, if it be possible let this cup pass from me. Nevertheless, not my will, but thine, be done" (Luke 22:42).

This explains the strange words, "Although he was a Son, he learned obedience through what he suffered." Jesus learned what it means to obey God when every cell in his body wanted to disobey. Yet, knowing this to be the Father's will, he obeyed, trusting God to see him through. He learned what it feels like to hang on when failure makes us want to give up, when we are so defeated, so utterly despairing that we want to forget the whole thing. He knows what this is like. He went the whole way and took the full brunt of our punishment.

How did Jesus win? He refused to question the Father's wisdom. He refused to blame God. He took no refuge in unbelief even though this agony came unexpectedly upon him. Instead, Jesus cast himself upon the Father's loving, tender care and looked to him to sustain him. When he did this, Jesus was brought safely through. So we read, "Let us then with confidence draw near to the throne of grace, that we may receive mercy and find grace to help in time of need." No matter how deep, how serious that need may be, the Lord can fully meet it, though we may be at wit's end.

Father, thank you that the garden of Gethsemane was not a mere play upon a stage. The Lord Jesus did not come into the world to perform a role. He fully entered into life. He went the whole way and bore the full brunt. Help me to trust in him.

Jesus Christ entered fully two of our lives' greatest mysteries: obedience and suffering. Where on the spectrum of obedience do we pray, "Nevertheless, not my will but thine be done"?

ARRESTED DEVELOPMENT

A daily devotion for December 13

Read Hebrews 5:11–14.

> "In fact, though by this time you ought to be teachers, you need someone to teach you the elementary truths of God's word all over again. You need milk, not solid food! Anyone who lives on milk, being still an infant, is not acquainted with the teaching about righteousness. But solid food is for the mature, who by constant use have trained themselves to distinguish good from evil" (Heb. 5:12–14).

This is a case of arrested development. Here are people who have been professing Christians for many years. By this time they ought to have been teachers, but they still need to have someone teach them the ABCs of the gospel. We have in our home a three-year-old daughter. It is the undivided opinion of our family that she is the smartest, cutest little girl who ever lived. But if her body kept growing but her mind stopped, and she went on saying the same clever things she is saying now while her body matured and grew into full womanhood, we would no longer find delight in what she says. Our joy would be turned to sorrow; we would feel great grief at the sight of our dear one suffering from arrested development.

That is what this author feels as he writes to these Hebrews. A cloud of threat hangs over these people due to their immaturity. The writer makes three important and insightful observations about this problem. First, there is the clear suggestion that age alone does not produce maturity. It is amazing how many of us think it does. We love this thought of inevitable growth. How often we say, "Just give us time. We will yet grow out of these hot tempers, catty tongues, and jealous spirits." But time never brings maturity.

The second observation he makes is that immaturity is self-identifying. It has certain clear marks that provide a simple test that anyone can take to determine whether he belongs in this group. There is an inability to instruct others. Though these people have been Christians for years, they have nothing to say to help others who may be struggling with problems. They can only understand the simplest doctrinal treatment. They need milk, the writer says, instead of strong meat. They do not understand the divine program that results in right conduct, because they are children and want only milk. There is also an inability to discern good from evil. Such people are what we may call consecrated blunderers, those who mean right and think they are doing right but are continually doing the wrong thing, creating problem situations and difficulties with others.

The third observation the author makes is that arrested development is a costly thing. "About this," he says, "we have much to say which is hard to explain, since you have become dull of hearing. There is so much I want to tell you which would make your starved humanity burst into bloom like buds in the spring if you could but grasp it, but you would not get it because you are so dull of hearing." The immature lose so much, and they risk even more. Those who continue in this condition of prolonged immaturity face grave danger.

Lord, these words have searched me, have found me out, have made me see myself. Thank you for that. I do not want to be self-deceived. Thank you for telling me the truth even though it may hurt, for I know that this is always to the end that I may be healed.

If we no longer want to be self-deceived, what are three ways we may clearly identify our arrested spiritual development? Have we considered the serious consequences of this immaturity?

CONCEPTION OR BIRTH?

A daily devotion for December 14

Read Hebrews 6:1–12.

> "It is impossible for those who have once been enlightened, who have tasted the heavenly gift, who have shared in the Holy Spirit, who have tasted the goodness of the word of God and the powers of the coming age and who have fallen away, to be brought back to repentance. To their loss they are crucifying the Son of God all over again and subjecting him to public disgrace" (Heb. 6:4–6).

Here is the elaboration of an awful possibility. It is impossible to restore to repentance those who experience certain Spirit-given blessings if they fall away. The problem with the passage is: how can anyone experience all of this and not be Christian? If he is Christian, how can he fall away without any hope of restoration? A hot battle has been waged over these issues throughout the Christian ages.

Can we take these expressions here as describing anything other than Spirit-produced, authentic Christian life? I would like to propose an explanation of this that has long haunted me. The Scripture frequently uses the analogy of human birth and growth to explain spiritual birth and growth. We have that even here. The use of milk by children is an analogy drawn from the physical life. Here is my question: is it not possible that we frequently confuse conception with birth?

Does spiritual life follow the same pattern as physical life? We all know that physical life does not begin with birth but with conception. Have we not perhaps mistaken conception for birth and therefore been confused when certain ones, who seemingly started well, have ended up stillborn? Is there in the spiritual life, as in the natural life, a gestation period before birth when Spirit-imparted life can fail and result in a stillbirth?

Is there not a time when new Christians are more like embryos, forming little by little in the womb, fed by the faith and vitality of others? If this is the case, then the critical moment is not when the Word first meets with faith. That is conception; that is when the possibility of new life arises. The critical moment is when the individual is asked to obey the Lord at cost to himself, contrary to his own will and desire—when the lordship of Christ makes demand upon him and this conflicts with his own plans and program. "If any man will come after me," said Jesus, "let him deny himself, and take up his cross and follow me" (Matt. 16:24). In grace, the Lord may make this appeal over a number of years. But if it is ultimately refused, this is a stillbirth. The months and even years that may be spent in conversion joy simply represented a Christian life in embryo. This is what Jesus's parable describes as seeds sown into unreceptive soil, only to spring up and then die off. The new birth occurs, if at all, when we first cease from our own works and rest in Jesus Christ. That is when the life of faith begins.

If a person refuses this step and rejects the claims of Christ to lordship and control, there follows a hardening, blinding process which, if allowed to continue, may lead such a one to drop out of church and in effect to renounce his Christian faith. Though only God knows the true condition of the heart, the writer says that if this occurs, the case is hopeless.

This brings us to the impossibility of return. "It is impossible to restore such people if they then commit apostasy," the writer argues, "since they crucify the Son of God on their own account and hold him up to contempt." Why won't God permit them to understand more truth? It is simply because they are repudiating the principle of the cross. They become, as Paul terms them, "enemies of the cross of Christ" (Phil. 3:18). From that point on their lives deteriorate, and they shame the profession they once made.

These are challenging words, Father, and I pray that I will be willing to follow you, even to the cross.

Are we committed to a lifelong, life-changing relationship with Jesus Christ, who lives with and in us as our Savior and our Lord? Is our daily experience consistent with the light we have received? Are we being transformed by the renewing of our minds with truth?

BELIEVING IS SEEING

A daily devotion for December 15

Read Hebrews 6:13–20.

> "For when God made the promise to Abraham, since He could swear by no one greater, He swore by Himself, saying, 'I will surely bless you and I will surely multiply you.' And so, having patiently waited, he obtained the promise" (Heb. 6:13–15).

Genesis records that God appeared to Abraham and made him a promise: "Through your seed shall all peoples of the earth be blessed" (Gen. 22:17–18). The immediate seed was Isaac, born of Abraham's old age, but the ultimate seed is Christ. Through faith in Jesus Christ this promise is fulfilled, and all the peoples of the earth are blessed in Abraham. This promise was later confirmed by an oath, God swearing by himself that he would fulfill what he had said. The writer is simply pointing out that Abraham believed God's promise and his oath.

He didn't believe it because he immediately saw it fulfilled! Twenty-five long, weary years passed before Isaac was born, and in the meantime, Abraham and his wife Sarah were growing older and had passed the time of life when it was possible to have children. Still the promise was unfulfilled. So if Abraham did not believe God's promise because he saw immediate results, why did he believe it? Abraham believed that God had told the truth about himself and that God must be true to his own character, which he had expressed through the promise and the oath.

Though he saw no results for twenty-five years, Abraham hung on to the character of God. He never said to himself during that time, *I've tried it and it doesn't work*, or *I've got to convince myself that this is true, even though I secretly believe that it is not.* Instead he said, *The God I know exists is the kind of a God who will do what he says he'll do.* For twenty-five years Abraham clung to that promise. And he won!

I've heard it said about prayer, "I've tried prayer but it doesn't seem to work." It seems to me that is putting things the wrong way. To say that is to repeat a common myth of our day, "Seeing is believing." No greater lie was ever foisted upon the human race by the Father of Lies than this. We are utterly convinced that is the way to come to the knowledge of truth, but the man who sees no longer needs to believe. Faith is not sight, nor sight faith.

Why do I believe in prayer? Well, not because I have tried it and it has worked. I believe in prayer because Jesus Christ says that prayer is the secret of life, and I believe him. Jesus Christ says that man must pray or faint. Because it is Jesus Christ who says this, I believe him, and therefore I pray and find it works. The proof of prayer does not come from my experience; that is simply the demonstration of what I have already believed, and I believe it because of who said it. Believing, therefore, is seeing.

This is true on many levels of life. Albert Einstein did not come to the knowledge of relativity by performing a series of experiments that convinced him that relativity was true. He gradually *saw* the idea of relativity, and convinced in his own mind that this was the secret of the physical universe, he performed experiments that he might demonstrate it to others. This is the way of truth. Believing is seeing.

This, therefore, is the secret of faith: it rests on the character of Jesus Christ. Either he is telling us the truth, and we can trust what this One who is like no one else who ever appeared in human history says to us, or we must reject him and repudiate him as a self-deceived impostor who attempted to foist some crude and foolish ideas upon the human race. That is where faith rests. From that ground everything must follow.

> *I remember, Lord Jesus, how many times you said to your disciples, "Oh you of little faith." I hear these words again in my own heart, Lord. Grant to me that I may have the courage to believe and to step out upon what I believe.*

Are our prayers faith-based? Is our faith based in our prayers rather than in the character of the God to whom we pray? Are we learning to trust the wisdom of our Father in both answered and unanswered prayer?

A BETTER PRIEST

A daily devotion for December 16

Read Hebrews 7:1–25.

> "Now if perfection was through the Levitical priesthood (for on the basis of it the people received the Law), what further need was there for another priest to arise according to the order of Melchizedek, and not be designated according to the order of Aaron? For when the priesthood is changed, of necessity there takes place a change of law also. For the one concerning whom these things are spoken belongs to another tribe, from which no one has officiated at the altar. For it is evident that our Lord was descended from Judah, a tribe with reference to which Moses spoke nothing concerning priests. And this is clearer still, if another priest arises according to the likeness of Melchizedek, who has become such not on the basis of a law of physical requirement, but according to the power of an indestructible life" (Heb. 7:11–16).

One thing clearly marked the fact that the old priesthood was no longer acceptable as help for men. It was the appearance of a new priest with a different address and a different ancestry. If the old priesthood went, the law had to go too. This new priest had a quite different address; he came from the tribe of Judah instead of the tribe of Levi. Judah was not a priestly tribe but a kingly tribe. The new priest was a king. If God recognizes Christ as a priest, then the law that was part of the old priesthood has been set aside.

The new priest also had a different ancestry. It was not necessary for him to trace his genealogy back to Abraham. He had no genealogy, and he ministered in the power of an endless life. He had no beginning and no ending. Therefore the law, which was only temporary, had to go. It had an inherent weakness in that it could not supply what the flesh in its frailty lacked. Every priest, every psychiatrist, every counselor, whether he realizes it or not, is continually working with the law by seeking to relate people to reality. That is what the law is, the revelation of reality. It is the way things are. Any knowledgeable counselor tries to help the people he sees recognize things as they are, but that is sometimes a difficult help to render.

Under the old order, a man would take a sacrifice to the priest, and the priest would offer it, thus for the moment at least, removing the guilt of the act. Though the problem remained, the guilt from it was removed. That is what the modern counselor does. He attempts to dispel guilt by helping his client see his problem in a different light. If he is a Christian counselor, he will help his client to see that God has already forgiven him in Christ and thus removed guilt. But the basic problem remains if resolving guilt is the only result. The psychiatrist may rearrange the problem so it does not grate so strongly upon others, but the problem persists. As C. S. Lewis puts it, "No clever arrangement of bad eggs will ever make a good omelet."

Self-discovery is the end of the line as far as the human counselor can go. But what lies beyond that? If we do not go any further, eventually despair! This is what Paul reflects in Romans 7:24, "Oh, wretched man that I am! Who can set me free from this body of death?" That is where this word from Hebrews comes in. There is a priest who can go further. "What the law could not do in that it was weak through the flesh, God, sending his own Son in the likeness of sinful flesh and for sin, judged sin in the flesh, that the righteousness that the law demanded might be fulfilled in us, who walk not after the flesh but after the Spirit" (Rom. 8:3–4). What is worthless, weak, and useless has been set aside and a new hope introduced that brings us near to God.

> *Thank you, Father, that what I could not do in myself, and what no counselor or priest could do for me, you have accomplished through your Son.*

What inherent weaknesses in the Levitical law are met in the priesthood of Jesus? How can we move beyond the futility of mere self-discovery to inner conflict resolution? Are we led in the triumphal procession of Jesus Christ, both priest and king?

PRIEST AND VICTIM

A daily devotion for December 17

Read Hebrews 7:26–28.

> "[Christ] does not need daily, like those high priests, to offer up sacrifices, first for His own sins and then for the sins of the people, because this He did once for all when He offered up Himself. For the Law appoints men as high priests who are weak, but the word of the oath, which came after the Law, appoints a Son, made perfect forever" (Heb. 7:27–28).

The writer joins two phrases to get the main thought: "he offered up himself" and he "was made perfect." As a priest, there was no unblemished sacrifice Christ could offer except himself, so he offered himself. There was found no other priest worthy of offering such a sacrifice, so Christ became both priest and victim.

In uttering the first three words from the cross, Jesus is a priest: "Father, forgive them, for they know not what they do" (Luke 23:34). He is interceding for the bloody murderers who have nailed him to the tree. Then he turns to the thief at his side and says, "Today shalt thou be with me in paradise" (Luke 23:43 KJV). He is ministering grace to this revolutionary who admitted his need. Then to his mother and to the disciple John who were standing at the foot of the cross, he says, "Woman, behold, your son!" "Behold, your mother!" (John 19:26–27 RSV). He is still a priest, ministering comfort to their hearts, giving one to the other to meet the need of life. But at this moment a change occurs. The sun is hidden and a strange darkness falls across the land.

The first word from the cross out of that darkness is the terrible cry of dereliction—Immanuel's orphaned cry—"My God, my God, why hast thou forsaken me?" (Matt. 27:46). Christ is no longer a priest; he is the victim, offered as a sacrifice on the altar of the cross. Then from the midst of that hot hell of pain, and even more excruciating anguish of spirit, come the words, "I thirst" (John 19:28).

This is followed by the last two cries from the cross when with a loud voice at the end of the three hours, Christ shouts, "It is finished" (John 19:30), and then, "Father, into thy hands I commit my spirit!" (Luke 23:46 RSV). Immediately, he gives up the ghost. In those last words he is still a sacrifice, having completed the work that the Father gave him to do.

If we join two more phrases of this passage, we get the writer's complete thought. Not only did Christ offer up himself as the perfect sacrifice, but he did it "once for all"—forever. The cross is a timeless event. It is not simply a historic occurrence that we may look back upon and study as we would the Battle of Gettysburg. It is an intrusion of eternity into time. It is timeless. It is as though it is going on forever and had been going on since the foundation of the world. It is therefore eternally contemporary experience.

Every age can know for itself the meaning of this cross. It reaches back to cover all history so that it can be said that Jesus is "the Lamb slain from the foundation of the world" (Rev. 13:8 KJV). Thus all those of the Old Testament who had not yet known of the historic presentation of Christ, but who believed God's promise regarding their blood sacrifices, could be saved, just as we are saved today. For the cross reached backward into time as well as forward. The cross of Jesus Christ, from God's point of view, is the central act of history, and everything flows from that. From that great event all hope is flowing, all light is flaming. All events must look to it for meaning.

> *Lord Jesus, thank you for being not only my Great High Priest but also the willing victim of the cruelty of man so that I may know forgiveness and hope.*

God views the cross of Christ as the central act of history. Is it the central focus for us, the ones for whom the Lord Jesus became both priest and victim? In what ways do we compromise the wisdom of the cross with worldly wisdom?

THE NEW CONSTITUTION

A daily devotion for December 18

Read Hebrews 8:1–13.

> "For this is the covenant that I will make with the house of Israel. After those days, says the Lord: I will put My laws into their minds, and I will write them on their hearts. And I will be their God, and they shall be My people. And they shall not teach everyone his fellow citizen, and everyone his brother, saying, 'Know the Lord,' for all will know Me, from the least to the greatest of them. For I will be merciful to their iniquities, and I will remember their sins no more" (Heb. 8:10–12).

In the upper room, Jesus said, "This cup is the new covenant made in my blood." This is the new arrangement, the new constitution, from which the life of all who know Jesus will be lived. This is a covenant made between the Father and the Son. It is not made between us and God. If any man is in Christ, everything in this covenant is available to him. For any individual on the face of the earth who is willing to be "in Christ," to let Christ live in him, this agreement is valid.

The new constitution has four provisions. God says, "I will put my laws into their minds, and write them on their hearts." There is the answer to the problem of human motivation. The problem we face is not uncertainty about what is right; we have known that a long time. It is a problem of motivation. We are overstrained; we are simply undermotivated, but the new arrangement, this new constitution, makes provision for that. We are to look to Christ when we are confronted with the thing we do not want to do. We are to say, "Lord Jesus, you have promised to write your laws in my mind and on my heart that I may do what you want me to do." Then for his dear sake, we do it. There is a new motive, a new power to do what ought to be done. It is Christ himself within us.

Then he says, "I will be their God, and they shall be my people." What an answer to the search for identity, to the hunger to belong to someone! Here is the answer to the aching question of the human heart: who am I? God says, "You are forever mine. I will be your God, and you will be my people."

Then there is the promise, "They shall not teach everyone his fellow or everyone his brother, saying, 'Know the Lord,' for all shall know me, from the least of them to the greatest." Here is the answer to the sigh of humanity for a hero. There is in the human heart a desperate hunger for a hero. We want to look up to someone; we want to know some great one personally. God says, "I will satisfy that in your life. You shall know me!" The one thing that one true Christian can never say to another is, "Know the Lord," for this is the one thing that is always true of even the youngest Christian—he knows the Lord. That is where we start in Christian living. It is the least common denominator.

Then the last thing, "For I will be merciful toward their iniquities, and I will remember their sins no more." This is the answer to the universal sense of condemnation. A man once told me, "I have a difficult boss. I never know where I stand with him." We say, "I never know where I stand with God." But God says if we are looking to the Great High Priest who is ministering to us all the effects of his sacrifice, this is never a problem, for he has said in no uncertain terms, "There is therefore now no condemnation to those who are in Christ Jesus" (Rom. 8:1). None! He is always for us; he is never against us. This does not mean he ignores sin, but he says, "I will be merciful toward it." When we acknowledge it, there is no reproach—and no rehash! God never gets historical, dredging up the past.

> *Father, thank you for this look at the ministry of my Great High Priest, a ministry that so many times I have not taken seriously. Instead I have looked about in all the broken cisterns of earth to try to find something as a substitute. Forgive me, and help me to claim my heritage in him, this new agreement for living.*

What four vital and radical provisions in the new covenant made between the Father and the Son are available to us in Christ Jesus? How does this address our need for motivation and power to live as new creatures in Christ?

A CLEAR CONSCIENCE

A daily devotion for December 19

Read Hebrews 9:1–14.

> "For if the blood of goats and bulls and the ashes of a heifer sprinkling those who have been defiled sanctify for the cleansing of the flesh, how much more will the blood of Christ, who through the eternal Spirit offered Himself without blemish to God, cleanse your conscience from dead works to serve the living God?" (Heb. 9:13–14).

The practical effect of Christ's ministry to us is given in these words, "to cleanse your conscience from dead works." The problem raised in this passage, therefore, is how to handle a nagging conscience.

Each of us has a conscience. We may not be able to analyze it, and we certainly cannot control it, but we know we all possess one. Conscience has been defined as "that still, small voice that makes you feel smaller still," or, as one little boy said, "It is what feels bad when everything else feels good." Conscience is that internal voice that sits in judgment over our will. A common myth abroad says that conscience is the means by which we tell right from wrong. But conscience is never that. It is training that tells us what is right or wrong. But when we know what is right or wrong, it is our conscience that insists that we do what we think is right and avoid what we think is wrong.

Conscience can be terribly mistaken; it is not a safe guide by itself. It accuses us when we violate whatever moral standard we may have, but that moral standard may be quite wrong when viewed in light of God's revelation. Conscience also gives approval whenever we fulfill whatever standard we have, whether that standard is right or wrong. And conscience, we have all discovered, acts both before and after the fact—it can either prod or punish.

In the case of these Hebrews, the problem is not a conscience troubled over evil deeds but "dead works." We must remember that the readers of this letter are Christians who already know how to handle the problem of sins. When they become aware that they have deliberately disobeyed what they knew to be right, they know the only way they can quiet an avenging conscience is to confess the sin before God and to deal with the problem immediately. Christians can easily take care of that aspect of a troubled conscience as they accept the forgiving grace of God. But the problem here may be a conscience plagued with guilt over good left undone—not sins of commission but sins of omission.

They tried to put their consciences to rest by religious activity; they were goaded by uneasy consciences into a high-gear program to please God. Here are people intent on doing what is right and thus pleasing God, and they have therefore launched an intensive program of religious activity. What perceptible difference in motive is there between a poor, blinded pagan who, in his misconception of truth, crawls endlessly down a road to placate God, and an American Christian who busies himself in a continual round of activity to try to win acceptance before God? None!

A woman said to me, "I don't know what is the matter with me. I do all I can to serve the Lord but I still feel guilty, and then I feel guilty about feeling guilty!" Precisely! It is rather discouraging, is it not, to see that all this laudable effort on our part is dismissed here as "dead works." It is disconcerting to see that such labors are not acceptably serving God. He is not impressed by our feverish efforts.

> *I am grateful, Father, that I can have a clear conscience before you, not because of anything I have done but because of what you have done for me through your Son.*

Do our guilty feelings launch us into religious fervor? Why is this never enough to clear our accusing conscience? Are we learning to live and to serve out of gratitude for the amazing grace of God's forgiveness?

THE NEED FOR DEATH

A daily devotion for December 20

Read Hebrews 9:15–22.

> "For this reason He is the mediator of a new covenant, so that, since a death has taken place for the redemption of the transgressions that were committed under the first covenant, those who have been called may receive the promise of the eternal inheritance" (Heb. 9:15).

We cannot avail ourselves of all that Jesus Christ provides for us in terms of release from a guilty conscience unless there is a death. The will is useless without it. In fact, the writer says, death is so important that even the shadow, the picture in the Old Testament, required blood. Not, of course, the blood of Jesus Christ but the blood of bulls and of goats. Blood is inescapable.

But why? We shall never come to the answer until we squarely face the implications of the substitutionary character of the death of Jesus Christ. His death was not for his own sake but for ours. He was our representative. This is what God is so desperately trying to convey to us.

The cross is God's way of saying there is nothing in us worth saving if we remain set apart from Christ. As we were men and women quite apart from Christ, God says, "There is nothing you can do for me, not one thing." But when Christ became what we were, when he was made sin for us, God passed sentence upon him and put him to death. This is God's way of saying to us, "There is not a thing you can do by your own effort that is worth a thing." Without Christ, we can only be totally set aside. Death eliminates us, wipes us out.

That is why our activity does not improve our relationship with God in the least degree. It does not make us any more acceptable. We can see what this does to our human pride. Who has not heard Christians giving the impression in their conversation that the greatest thing that ever happened to God was the day he found them? But we are not indispensable to him; he is indispensable to us. If we become bankrupt to do anything for God, we are then able to receive everything from him.

The point of the whole passage is that if we refuse to reckon this way, to count this as true, then the benefits of the new covenant are not available to us. A covenant is not in effect until the death of the testator, the will maker. Christ the will maker died, and we, through Christ our representative, also died that death. But if we will not accept it, if we will not agree to God's sentence of death upon all that we are, we cannot have the benefits of his covenant. If we fight this sentence of death, for the rest of our Christian lives we shall be troubled with a guilty conscience. We will never rest in any final acceptance before God. We shall always wrestle with the problem of whether we have done enough and have been pleasing enough to God by our activity. But if we accept this reality, we render all our service to him pure delight.

> *Father, open my eyes to this new principle of human behavior. Teach me to grasp this and to accept your sentence of death upon everything in me that is not of Christ.*

Are we learning to be liberated from our futile efforts to please God? Are we experiencing the heritage of God's new arrangement for living, replacing our dead works with the power of Christ's indwelling presence?

A BURNED-OVER PLACE

A daily devotion for December 21

Read Hebrews 9:23–28.

> "For Christ did not enter a holy place made with hands, a mere copy of the true one, but into heaven itself, now to appear in the presence of God for us; nor was it that He would offer Himself often, as the high priest enters the holy place year by year with blood that is not his own" (Heb. 9:24–25).

The writer points out that the old system required endless repetition of sacrifice. The effect of these sacrifices never lasted very long. A man had to bring a fresh sacrifice every time he sinned, and once a year the whole nation had to offer the same sacrifice. The old arrangement required repetition. But the new arrangement is beyond time as well as beyond space. The cross of Christ is a contemporary sacrifice. It was offered at one point in history, but the results and the blessings of it are available at any time, forward or backward from that point of history. What a great advantage this is over the old system!

I was born on the wind-swept plains of North Dakota. As a boy I would sometimes see the flames of a prairie fire lighting the horizon at night and sweeping across the grass. Such fires were terrible threats to the pioneers who crossed the plains in their covered wagons. Often these fires would burn for miles and miles, threatening everything in their paths. When they would see such a fire coming toward them, driven before the wind, settlers had a device they would use to protect themselves. They would simply light another fire, and the wind would catch it up and drive it beyond them. Then they would get in the burned-over place, and when the fire coming toward them reached that spot, it found nothing to burn and went out.

God is saying that the cross of Jesus Christ is such a burned-over place. Those who trust in it, and rest in the judgment that has already been visited upon it, have no other judgment to face. That is why Paul can write with such triumph, "There is therefore now no condemnation to them which are in Christ Jesus" (Rom. 8:1 KJV). In the realm of the spirit we have already been forgiven everything. We need now only acknowledge wrong, confess it, and the moment we do, forgiveness is already ours. We need only say "Thank you" and take it.

> *Father, I pray that I may learn to rest upon this new arrangement and thus be equipped to face any circumstance or any problem with your adequacy that is available to me.*

Are we burdened with continuing self-judgment for sin that is forever covered by Jesus's atoning sacrifice? How does confession of sins free us to experience his forgiveness and to rejoice in the judgment he has borne for us?

WHAT DOES GOD DESIRE?

A daily devotion for December 22

Read Hebrews 10:1–18.

> "After saying above, 'Sacrifices and offerings and whole burnt offerings and sacrifices for sin You have not desired, nor have You taken pleasure in them' (which are offered according to the Law), then He said, 'Behold, I have come to do Your will.' He takes away the first in order to establish the second. By this will we have been sanctified through the offering of the body of Jesus Christ once for all" (Heb. 10:8–10).

Here is what God really wanted. He never cared a snap of his fingers for all the rivers of blood that flowed on Jewish altars. He had no interest in them except as they taught something. What did these sacrifices point to? A human body in which there was a human will that continually chose to depend upon an indwelling God to obey a written Word! That was what God wanted. When Christ came he paused on the threshold of heaven and said, "A body hast thou prepared for me." Within that body was a human soul with the capacity to reason, to feel, and to choose. That will, in that human body, never once acted on its own, never once took any step apart from dependence upon the Father who dwelt within. That is the principle that God has been after all along; that is what he wants.

He has no interest in ritual, in candles, in prayer books, in beads, in chanting, in any ceremony. Ceremonies mean nothing to God. He wants a heart that is his, a life that is his, and a body that is available to him. That is why Paul says, "I beseech you therefore, brethren, by the mercies of God, to present your bodies as a living sacrifice, holy and acceptable to God, which is your reasonable service" (Rom. 12:1 KJV).

When our Lord Jesus acted on that principle, he allowed the direction of his life to come from the Word of God. "Behold, I have come to do Your will." Every temptation he entered into, every problem that came his way, he referred to what God had said, "It is written." That program took him to the cross, calling on him to lay down his life. By means of that sacrifice, we are free now to join him in this program that is God's original intention for man.

In verse 10, this word *sanctified* is widely misunderstood. It usually stirs visions of people passing through some kind of religious sheep-dip and coming out holier and purer on the other side. But it is not that. The word *sanctified* simply means "to put to the proper, intended use." We sanctify the chairs that we sit on; we sanctify the combs we use on our hair. This verse declares that when we adopt the same outlook as Jesus Christ, when, in dependence on him, we are ready to obey the Word of God, we fulfill our humanity. We are used in the way God intended us to be used.

There is one unmistakable mark of this: we are willing to lay down our lives so that God's will may be done! This does not mean we rush out to die. It means giving of ourselves, giving up for the moment something that we might desire to do. It means that we become content to lose standing in the eyes of the world if necessary. We no longer regard that as important. It means we surrender material comfort or gain if this will advance the cause of Christ. We live in a simpler home so that we might invest money in his enterprises. We are willing to be ignored, slighted, or treated unfairly if this advances God's cause.

This is what God wants. He does not care for great cathedrals, beautiful buildings, and ornate ritual and ceremony.. He wants lives, bodies, hearts that are his, available to him to work in the shop, the office, the street, the schools, and everywhere else people are so that his life may be made visible in human terms in those places. That is Christianity.

Father, may I know the joy of ceasing my own efforts and resting quietly upon your ability to work in me.

Fulfillment of our eternal destiny is possible because Jesus Christ our Savior said, "Here I am. I have come to do your will, O God." Do we realize the liberating power that comes to us through him when we say, "Thy will be done"?

SPUR ONE ANOTHER ON

A daily devotion for December 23

Read Hebrews 10:19–25.

> "And let us consider how we may spur one another on toward love and good deeds, not giving up meeting together, as some are in the habit of doing, but encouraging one another—and all the more as you see the Day approaching" (Heb. 10:24–25).

How do you spur someone to love and to good works? These two things are the mark of true Christianity. Christians are never judged by the confessions they make or the creed they recite; it is always by their deeds. How much practical love have you manifested? How far have you responded to the cry for help from someone near you, someone who is destitute or disappointed, who needs an encouraging word, a helping hand, or a generous check? This is the ultimate test.

How do you achieve this? The writer suggests two ways. The first is by meeting together. That is important: "not giving up meeting together, but encouraging one another." That suggests the character of the meetings. They are to be encouraging. They are to be meetings where you can hear again the tremendous, radical principles of Christian faith, where you can see again in human lives the mighty power of the One whom Christians worship and serve, and where you can understand how God works through human society, transforming men everywhere. To thus meet together is to encourage one another in these things. That is what Christian services ought to be like. You should be able to hear the Word of God so that it comes home with power to the heart and to share the results with others.

If our services were more like this, we would not have trouble getting people to come. Too often church services are the kind pictured in the story of the father who was showing his son through a church building. They came to a plaque on the wall, and the little boy asked, "Daddy, what's that for?" His father said, "Oh, that's a memorial to those who died in the service." The little boy said, "Which service, Daddy, the morning service or the evening service?" But meetings of Christians are to be encouraging things, and this is one way we stir up one another to love and to good works.

The second way is a watchful awareness of the time—"all the more as you see the Day approaching." That day is the certain return of Jesus Christ. As evil becomes subtler, as it becomes more and more difficult to tell the difference between truth and error, good and bad, right and wrong, as the clamorous voices of our age pour out deceit, and we find society permeated with false concepts that deny the truth of the Word of God, we need all the more to gather and encourage one another by sharing the secrets of life in Christ Jesus.

> *Father, thank you for the opportunity to spur others on to love and to good deeds. Help me not to neglect meeting with other believers and paying attention to the fact that the last day is drawing near.*

As the media delivers its often bewildering, increasingly threatening news, are we faithfully and fruitfully meeting with others of the family of God? Are we holding one another accountable as living expressions of the Word of Truth and of love?

LIVING BY FAITH

A daily devotion for December 24

Read Hebrews 10:26–39.

> "Remember those earlier days after you had received the light, when you endured in a great conflict full of suffering. Sometimes you were publicly exposed to insult and persecution; at other times you stood side by side with those who were so treated. You suffered along with those in prison and joyfully accepted the confiscation of your property, because you knew that you yourselves had better and lasting possessions. So do not throw away your confidence; it will be richly rewarded" (Heb. 10:32–35).

The author recognizes that most of the people to whom he writes have already given proof of true faith and genuine birth. Their early Christian years were marked by love, joy, and hope despite hardships and persecution. They had followed Christ at cost to themselves. They had submitted themselves to his lordship, even when their own wills would have been different. That is the mark of reality, the proof of faith. They cheerfully and compassionately accepted the persecutions, deprivations, and hardships that came their way. They took Christ's yoke upon them, obeyed his lordship, and manifested it by love and good works. They were living by faith.

You can do these things only when you live by faith. They are possible only when you have accepted God's Word and recognized that Christ is who he says he is, that the history of the world will turn out as he says it will, and that the values of life are what he says they are. You just need to do one more thing—keep on! That is all. You are doing the right thing, so just keep on doing it. The road will end at the dawning of a new day and the coming of the living God.

Does your way sometimes seem difficult? Is it often lonely and are you exposed to the reproach of others? Do not despair; do not give up. That pattern has been predicted. You must continue to live by faith, to accept what the Word says as true, and to count on God's strength to bring about all that he promises. If you thus live by faith, then, though it be through perils and dangers, you will arrive, for "the just shall live by faith" (Rom. 1:17 KJV). This will happen not by circumstances, not by outward appearances, but by faith in what the Word of God says. You need only to endure to reach the goal. You must show toughness.

Hebrews 11 offers illustrations of men and women who have lived by faith. These are the tough people of history. They endured; they toughed it out. They faced all the pressures, all the problems, all the confusing duplicity of life, but because they had their eyes fixed on One who never changes, nothing could divert them. That is what the apostle is calling for, an inner toughness that meets life steadfastly and is never driven from its position of faith. People with this resolve meet every challenge by resting upon the Word of God.

Teach me, Lord, to live by faith, even when all seems to be going wrong in my life.

If or when the integrity of our faith is tested by hardships and persecution, is it up to the challenge? Are we then alert to the need of others for encouragement so that we may stand side by side regardless of the circumstances?

WHAT IS FAITH?

A daily devotion for December 25

Read Hebrews 11:1–7.

> "Now faith is confidence in what we hope for and assurance about what we do not see … And without faith it is impossible to please God, because anyone who comes to him must believe that he exists and that he rewards those who earnestly seek him" (Heb. 11:1, 6).

Hebrews emphasizes an element that is regarded as essential to the Christian life, and that is faith. It is what makes the Christian different from the non-Christian. Henry David Thoreau once said, "If a man does not keep pace with his companions, perhaps it is because he hears a different drummer." That is an exact description of faith: Christians walk as though listening to another drummer.

This chapter centers on what faith means. Faith is greatly misunderstood, and there are many peculiar ideas about what it is. Faith is not positive thinking. Faith is not a hunch that is followed. Faith is not hoping for the best, hoping that everything will turn out all right. Faith is not a feeling of optimism. Faith is none of these things, though all of them have been identified as faith.

What is faith then? Faith begins with "things hoped for"—that is, it starts with a sense of discontent. We can never have much faith unless we are dissatisfied with the way we are now and are longing for something better. That is why, all through the Bible, the great enemy of faith is a complacent spirit, a satisfaction with the status quo. But if we are dissatisfied, if we are looking for something better, then we are in a position to exercise faith.

Then comes "the conviction of things not seen"—not only a desire for something better but an awareness of something else. That is faith. It means we become aware that we are surrounded by an invisible kingdom, that what is seen is not the whole explanation for life, that there are realities that cannot be seen or touched but that are as real and as vital as anything we can see. This is so beautifully seen in the words and the teachings of our Lord Jesus. He speaks of God the Father as though he were standing right there. He does not see the universe as an impersonal machine, grinding and clanking along, as science so frequently does. He sees it as an invisible, but quite real, spiritual kingdom.

Verse 6 says that anyone who comes to God must believe that he exists. Some say, "That's the hard part." No, it is not. The easiest thing in the world to do is to believe that God exists. It requires effort to disbelieve. Everyone starts out believing God exists. It is only when people are carefully trained to disbelieve that they declare that God does not exist. Light from God is streaming in on every side, and all we need to do is open our eyes to see it. That is why children have no problem with this. The concept of God ought to be one of the most difficult ideas for children to grasp, since God cannot be seen. But children have no difficulty at all believing that God exists.

Are you a person of faith? Do you hunger for something better in your life? Do you have a conviction that God is ready to answer your cry? In fact, he has already answered it in Christ. Are you ready then to commit yourself to obey what he says, to accept his verdict, his viewpoint, as the true one despite the cries that will pour into your ears from every side saying this is wrong? That is what faith is, and if you are that kind of person you can join this parade of faith.

> *Father, thank you for this revelation of what faith is today. How I feel the need for it as I live in this confused and bewildered society. Grant me the simple faith of a child. Teach me to live according to this faith, though it be through difficulties, trials, heartache, and tears.*

Are we hopeful for what we hunger for—our not-yet-completed maturity in Christ? Will we rest in the indwelling Christ to work out our salvation, bringing what he has promised to completion? "The one who calls you is faithful, and he will do it" (1 Thess. 5:25 NIV).

FAITH THAT ANTICIPATES AND ACTS

A daily devotion for December 26

Read Hebrews 11:8–39.

> "By faith Abraham, when called to go to a place he would later receive as his inheritance, obeyed and went, even though he did not know where he was going. By faith he made his home in the promised land like a stranger in a foreign country; he lived in tents, as did Isaac and Jacob, who were heirs with him of the same promise. For he was looking forward to the city with foundations, whose architect and builder is God" (Heb. 11:8–10).

Faith believes that God has revealed something about the future—not everything, but something. And what he has revealed is quite enough for us to know. Faith seizes upon a revealed event and begins to live in anticipation of it. Therefore, faith gives our lives a goal, a purpose, and a destination. It is a look into the future.

We see this in Abraham. He is an illustration of the meaninglessness of time in the life of faith. It is amazing how far Abraham saw. He lived about two thousand years before Christ. We live about two thousand years after him. Yet Abraham, looking forward by faith, believing what God had said would take place, looked across forty centuries and beyond to the day when God would bring to pass on earth a city with eternal foundations. Abraham saw what John recorded in the book of Revelation, a city coming down out of heaven onto earth. That is a symbol of what we pray in the Lord's Prayer, "Thy will be done on earth as it is in heaven" (Matt. 6:10). That is what Abraham longed for, an earth run after God's order where people dwell together in peace, harmony, blessing, beauty, and fulfillment. Because of that, he was content to dwell in tents, looking for that coming.

This same anticipation is also evident in Isaac, Jacob, and Joseph. Isaac and Jacob knew that God intended to make nations from their sons, and their final prayers were based upon that fact. They prayed in anticipation of what God had said would come and blessed their children on that basis. When he was dying, Joseph saw four hundred years ahead to the exodus from Egypt, and he arranged by faith for a funeral service in the Promised Land. He did not want to be buried in Egypt. Thus he symbolized his conviction that God would do exactly what he had said. And eventually it happened just that way.

The anticipation of faith is clear in the case of Moses' parents who, when he was born, saw that he was "beautiful in God's sight" (Acts 7:20–21) and acted by faith to save him from the edict of the king that all male children should be slain (Ex. 1:16,22). This was more than the natural desire of parents to preserve their children from death. But these parents knew there was a promise of deliverance from Egypt for their people, and they knew that the time was near. God had foretold how long it would be. They were given assurance that this boy had been singled out by God, they trusted God's word, and acting on that, they defied the king and hid the child for three months (Heb. 11:23).

Related to this quality of faith that accepts as certain a promise of the future is a second quality, that faith always acts. There is today a common misconception that men and women of faith are so occupied with the future that they sit around twiddling their thumbs, doing nothing. We have all heard of those who are "so heavenly minded that they are of no earthly good." That is the common concept of faith. But that is not faith; that is fatalism! Faith works! Faith is doing something now in view of the future. People folding their hands and waiting for the second coming are not living the life of faith. The life of faith entails acting now in view of that coming event.

> *Thank you, Lord, for the opportunities you give to anticipate and to act upon what you have promised. Teach me to see that city from above that one day will come down.*

Is our faith rooted in biblical revelation, which produces our goals for life, our purpose, and our destination? Are our prayers and actions guided consistently by that purposeful faith?

FIX YOUR EYES ON JESUS

A daily devotion for December 27

Read Hebrews 12:1–2.

> "Therefore, since we are surrounded by such a great cloud of witnesses, let us throw off everything that hinders and the sin that so easily entangles. And let us run with perseverance the race marked out for us, fixing our eyes on Jesus, the pioneer and perfecter of faith. For the joy set before him he endured the cross, scorning its shame, and sat down at the right hand of the throne of God" (Heb. 12:1–2).

We are "surrounded by a great cloud of witnesses," the writer says. That does not mean that people who have died and gone to heaven are looking down on us from above. It means that these people are saying something to us, that they are testifying to us and are witnesses in that sense. Their lives are saying that we ought to lay aside every weight, whatever hinders faith. We never say yes to Christ without saying no to something else!

"And the sin that so easily entangles" is unbelief. That is the failure to take revelation seriously. Then what? "Run with perseverance," with persistence, continuing no matter what happens. How? By "fixing our eyes Jesus." That is the answer. The others we read of here can inspire us and challenge us, and some of the men and women of faith who have lived since those days can do the same. I read the lives of Martin Luther and of John Wesley, of D. L. Moody, and of some of the recent martyrs of faith, including Jim Elliot. They have challenged my life and have inspired me to make a fresh start, to resolve anew to walk with God, and to follow their example. They challenge us to mobilize our resources, to clench our fists, to set our jaws, and to determine that we shall be men and women of faith. But if that is our motivation we shall find that we soon run out of gas. Our inspiration will fade, and after a few weeks we will be right back in the same old rut.

The secret of persistence is in the phrase "fixing our eyes on Jesus." Look at these men and women of faith, yes, but then look toward Jesus. He is the author and the finisher of our faith. He can begin it and he can complete it. He is the pioneer; he has gone on ahead. He is also the perfecter of faith. He himself ran the race. He laid aside every weight, every tie of family and friends. Every restraining hand he brushed aside that he might resolutely walk with God. He set his face against the popular sin of unbelief and walked on in patient perseverance, trusting the Father to work everything out for him. He set the example.

But there is more than example in this phrase; there is empowerment. We are to fix our eyes on Jesus because he can do what these others cannot do. They can inspire us, but he empowers us. Moment by moment, day by day, week by week, year by year, if we learn to look to him we find strength imparted to us because he indwells us! That is the secret.

We can find strength to venture out and to start this life of faith in him today. We will also discover strength to continue. Jesus is not "up there" somewhere. As this book has made clear, he is within us by faith. If we have received Jesus Christ, he dwells within. He has entered into the sanctuary, into the inner man, into the place where we need strength, and is available every moment for us. Therefore, in Christ, we can have all that it takes to meet life.

> *Father, thank you for a living Lord Jesus whom I can know and talk to, draw strength from and lean upon. He is my living Lord, ready to make available to me all that I need in every hour.*

Are we grateful for the testimonies of exemplary people of faith, many of them martyrs, now with Christ? Who is the ultimate model of endurance, the only one who can empower us to follow his example?

A NEW KIND OF LIVING

A daily devotion for December 28

Read Hebrews 12:3–17.

> "Therefore, strengthen your feeble arms and weak knees. 'Make level paths for your feet,' so that the lame may not be disabled, but rather healed. Make every effort to live in peace with everyone and to be holy; without holiness no one will see the Lord. See to it that no one falls short of the grace of God and that no bitter root grows up to cause trouble and defile many" (Heb. 12:12–15).

Here the writer summarizes the practical results of trials in our lives: they make possible the demonstration of a new kind of living, which is what the world is seeking. Nonbelievers are not at all impressed with Christians who stop doing something they are doing. But they are tremendously impressed with Christians who have started living the kind of a life they cannot live. That gets their attention! That is the life the writers sets before us here.

This life starts with correction. "Strengthen your feeble arms and weak knees. 'Make level paths for your feet.'" That is, if you keep on going the way you are going things will only get worse—what is lame will be put out of joint. Instead stop and strengthen yourself. Stop being so weak; stop being so anxious, so worried. How will the world get the impression that Christ is victor if people look at you and you are always in defeat? Strengthen yourself and learn how to "live in peace with everyone." And above all, seek to be holy because "without holiness no one will see the Lord."

What does this word *holiness* mean? The Greek word for *holiness* is also translated in this letter as "sanctification." To sanctify means "to put to its proper use." When someone believes that Christ indwells him and gives him everything he needs, he is being "put to the proper use," the use for which God intended man. This is holiness, a sense of dependence on God and availability to him. This is what makes nonbelievers sit up and take notice as they see Christians living the kind of life that is adequate for every circumstance.

The second phrase has to do with our concern for others: "See to it that no one fall short of the grace of God." We are not to live our lives for ourselves. Others are looking to us, and we have a responsibility to them. The writer points out that bitterness will stop the grace of God in any person's life. No matter how justified the cause of bitterness may be, to have a bitter attitude as a Christian is always wrong, for resentment and bitterness are of the flesh. And they are highly contagious diseases. If one person is bitter and continues in an unforgiving spirit, others are infected by this, and it spreads and defiles many. This is the problem in many a church today. So if we know someone who has this problem, we must help him to see that this is a terrible thing that will wreck his life, making it impossible to grow as a Christian.

Here, then, is the ministry to which we are called: to have a life characterized by a display of the holiness, the sanctification, and the proper use of our humanity that makes God visible in us and to manifest this in a deep concern for the welfare of others so that no one else will miss the grace of God.

Father, by your Spirit teach me this new kind of living, which will set me apart for exactly those purposes you have created me for.

Are we intentionally dependent on and available to the power and the presence of the indwelling Lord Jesus Christ? Do we allow bitterness toward others to obstruct God's grace in us and through us to others?

COMING TO MOUNT ZION

A daily devotion for December 29

Read Hebrews 12:18–29.

> "You have not come to a mountain that can be touched and that is burning with fire; to darkness, gloom and storm ... But you have come to Mount Zion, to the city of the living God, the heavenly Jerusalem. You have come to thousands upon thousands of angels in joyful assembly, to the church of the firstborn, whose names are written in heaven. You have come to God, the Judge of all, to the spirits of the righteous made perfect, to Jesus the mediator of a new covenant, and to the sprinkled blood that speaks a better word than the blood of Abel" (Heb. 12:18, 22–24).

The writer is speaking of what motivates us in the Christian life. We are not to be driven by fear—not by the law, which demands of us, "Do this, or else," and not by self-effort, with its gritted teeth, its clenched fist, and its grim determination to serve God. If we serve because we are afraid, as the law frightened Israel in the terrible scene on Mount Sinai, we will lose something from God. Our motive isn't fear but fullness—what God has given us.

We have come not to this Mount Sinai but to Mount Zion, the place of grace, "and to the new Jerusalem, the city of the living God." We have come under a new government "and to angels." Angels are spirits sent forth to minister to those who are to be the heirs of salvation, Christians. "The church of the firstborn whose names are written in heaven" refers to those who are born in Christ and who share his life. God is "the judge of all," whether or not they are Christians. "The spirits of the righteous made perfect" are the Old Testament saints, men and women of God who lived in the days before the cross when the promise was given, who looked forward by faith, and who now await us. Finally we have "Jesus the mediator of a new covenant" and "the sprinkled blood that speaks a better word than the blood of Abel." A mediator is not someone up in heaven in some distant reach of space; he is the indwelling Christ. He is available to us. He is right here to be our strength, our righteousness, our wisdom, whatever we need. Abel's blood cried out for vengeance, as the book of Genesis tells us, but Jesus's blood does not speak of vengeance—it speaks of access, of vindication, of the fact that there is no problem between us and God that is not settled by his blood. There is no longer any question of guilt. We can come completely accepted in the beloved.

Thus, with all this on our side there is no need to fail, is there? That is the point the writer is making. Certainly life gets rough, certainly it gets discouraging, and surely there are times when the pressures are intense, but have we reckoned on our resources? Have we forgotten them?

Gracious Father, I am so grateful that by grace you have led me to Mount Zion. Now help me to stand strong and to be yours in every circumstance of life.

Have we entered Mount Zion, where joy and freedom from fear are our spiritual heritage? Are our worship and our works motivated by God's grace and his love, which casts out fear?

NONCONFORMITY

A daily devotion for December 30

Read Hebrews 13:1–19.

> Marriage should be honored by all, and the marriage bed kept pure, for God will judge the adulterer and all the sexually immoral. Keep your lives free from the love of money and be content with what you have, because God has said, 'Never will I leave you; never will I forsake you'" (Heb. 13:4–5).

Nonconformity to the world must certainly involve these areas. The loose sexual standards of our generation and the intense materialistic spirit of this age are constant perils to our hearts, and we must beware of them. We must realize that God has undertaken to sustain the sacredness of marriage and that he unceasingly judges violations of it. Therefore, we dare not heed the fine-sounding declarations being made today about a "new morality," as though we had passed beyond the ancient standards and they no longer had significance.

As this writer reminds us, God judges the immoral and the adulterous. He does not mean that God looses lightning bolts from heaven against them or that he causes terrible diseases to come upon them; these are not the forms of judgment. But we can see the judgment of God in the anguish and the pain that sweep like a plague across this land. They result from the breakdown of moral standards. The certain deterioration of life is the judgment of God. It is the brutalization of humanity so men become like animals and live on the level of animals. This is so apparent in our day.

Then there is the danger of materialism. We must swim against the strong currents of a luxury-loving age. We must not give in to the pressures to keep up with the Joneses, the mad rush to have all that the world around us has. The weakness of the church is due in large part to the failure of Christians to be content with what God gives them.

This does not mean that all Christians should take a vow of poverty. There is nothing like that in the New Testament. God allows differing levels of prosperity. The point the writer makes is not that there is something wrong in riches but that we must learn to be content with what God has given us. Contentment is not having what we want; it is wanting only what we have.

It is difficult to know where to draw the line between a proper increase in the standard of living and needless luxury, which is really waste, but the latter part of the verse reveals the secret: "God has said, 'Never will I leave you; never will I forsake you.'" That is the promise of God. He is our great and unending resource and will never fail us. Here is the strongest negative in the New Testament. The original carries the thought, "I will never, under any circumstances, ever leave you or forsake you." On the basis of this mighty declaration, the writer says we should declare, "The Lord is my helper. I will not be afraid [of loss or poverty or anything else]. What can man do to me?" If we have God, what can man do to us? The point is that we must be content to have only what God gives us.

Lord, help me not to conform to this world, always grasping for more. Teach me to be content and to believe that you will never leave nor forsake me.

Is either affluence or poverty making us restless and discontented? What effect does our discontent have on our marriage? Whom or what do we trust to determine and to provide our essential needs?

THE GOD OF PEACE

A daily devotion for December 31

Read Hebrews 13:18–25.

> "Now may the God of peace, who through the blood of the eternal covenant brought back from the dead our Lord Jesus, that great Shepherd of the sheep, equip you with everything good for doing his will, and may he work in us what is pleasing to him, through Jesus Christ, to whom be glory for ever and ever. Amen" (Heb. 13:20–21).

Humanity possesses great nuclear submarines that can traverse the oceans without ever coming to the surface. The secret of this tremendous power lies in a nuclear reactor hidden away in the depths of the submarine. That remarkable force does not need any refueling but is constantly giving off energy, so the submarine never needs to go into port for refueling. The same principle is at work in the Christian life. These two verses reveal the nuclear reactor for every believer.

Look at the elements of this, starting with "the God of peace." In this letter we have seen what peace is. The nearest modern equivalent is emotional health. In Christ we are in touch with the God of emotional health, the God who intends life to be lived on a peaceful level. With him is linked the Lord Jesus, the Great Shepherd of the sheep. I came from Montana and know a lot about sheep. If you are from the city you probably think that if you "leave them alone they'll come home, wagging their tails behind them." But I can assure you that is a lie! Sheep have two outstanding characteristics: they have no wisdom, and they have no weapons. They are forever running off and getting lost and are unable to find their way back, and if anything attacks them they are utterly helpless to defend themselves. That is why they need a shepherd. That is why we need a shepherd, and why the Bible likens us to sheep. We have a Great Shepherd. He is our resource, our provision—a God who is concerned about us and a Great Shepherd who is there to watch us—because we have no wisdom and we have no weapons for our defense.

Linked with them is this great process spoken of here, "who brought again from the dead … by the blood of the eternal covenant." Here we have the cross and the resurrection. The cross means the end of the old life of self-reliance, and the resurrection sets forth the power of the new life. That is the power released within the Christian by the indwelling Christ. We tout the conquest of outer space, but the greatest conquest ever made was when the Lord Jesus conquered inner space by moving into the heart of man to plant within us the greatest power by which life can be lived—a power that heals and makes whole.

The result of all this is that God will equip us with everything good that we may do his will. This is the secret of effective service. We do not have to ask God to do this. He will give us everything we need. He has a full supply and full ability. God will work through us, not apart from our wills but right along with them. We choose, we start out, but he is there to carry us through.

We have full acceptance, even before this happens: "working in you that which is pleasing in his sight." We know that we cannot help but please God when we walk in this way and live on this basis. We are fighting a battle already won. But if we try to live in the self-effort of the flesh, we are fighting a battle already lost. This whole set of truths is wrapped in the most life-changing phrase ever uttered by man, "through Jesus Christ; to whom be glory forever and ever. Amen." Through Jesus Christ—that is the secret of life; that is the way God intended man to live. What good news for this present life! God intended it for us that we might live in our present circumstances wherever we are.

> *Father, help me to grasp these truths, but more than that, give me the courage to step out upon them that I might enter into the glorious liberty of the children of God.*

The life-giving, life-changing presence of the indwelling Christ is transcendent power of which nuclear-powered submarines are but a replica! Are we opting to stray as helpless sheep, or are we "beholding the glory of the Lord" and being transformed into his image?